THE PEOPLE, PLACE, AN
SPACE READER

The People, Place, and Space Reader brings together the writings of scholars, designers, and activists from a variety of fields to make sense of the makings and meanings of the world we inhabit. They help us to understand the relationships between people and the environment at all scales, and to consider the active roles individuals, groups, and social structures play in creating the environments in which people live, work, and play. These readings highlight the ways in which space and place are produced through large- and small-scale social, political, and economic practices, and offer new ways to think about how people engage the environment in multiple and diverse ways.

Providing an essential resource for students of urban studies, geography, sociology and many other areas, this book brings together important but, till now, widely dispersed writings across many inter-related disciplines. Introductions from the editors precede each section; introducing the texts, demonstrating their significance, and outlining the key issues surrounding the topic. A companion website, *PeoplePlaceSpace.org*, extends the work even further by providing an on-going series of additional reading lists that cover issues ranging from food security to foreclosure, psychiatric spaces to the environments of predator animals..

Jen Jack Gieseking is a cultural geographer and environmental psychologist and Postdoctoral Fellow in the Digital and Computational Studies Initiative at Bowdoin College.

William Mangold is a partner in a small design firm and Adjunct Professor in Interior Design at Pratt Institute.

Cindi Katz is Professor of Geography, Environmental Psychology, Women's Studies, and American Studies and Executive Officer of the Earth and Environmental Sciences Program at The Graduate Center of The City University of New York.

Setha Low is Professor of Environmental Psychology, Geography, Anthropoly, and Women's Studies, and Director of the Public Space Research Group at The Graduate Center of The City University of New York.

Susan Saegert is Professor of Environmental Psychology, founding director of the Center for the Study of Women and Society, and former director of the Center for Human Environments, all at The Graduate Center of The City University of New York.

The People, Place, and Space Reader

Edited by

Jen Jack Gieseking and

William Mangold

with Cindi Katz,

Setha Low,

and Susan Saegert

Routledge
Taylor & Francis Group

NEW YORK AND LONDON

First published 2014
by Routledge
711 Third Avenue, New York, NY 10017

and by Routledge
2 Park Square, Milton Park, Abingdon, Oxon OX14 4RN

Routledge is an imprint of the Taylor & Francis Group, an informa business

British Library Cataloguing in Publication Data
A catalogue record for this book is available from the British Library

Library of Congress Cataloging-in-Publication Data
The people, place, and space reader / edited by Jen Jack Gieseking,
William Mangold; with Cindi Katz, Setha Low, and Susan Saegert.
pages cm
1. Social ecology. 2. Urban ecology (Sociology) 3. Human ecology.
4. Environmental psychology. 5. Public spaces. I. Gieseking, Jen Jack.
HM861.P46 2014
304.2--dc23
2013037743

ISBN13: 978-0-415-66496-7 (hbk)
ISBN13: 978-0-415-66497-4 (pbk)
ISBN13: 978-1-315-81685-2 (ebk)

Typeset in Goudy and Optima
by Saxon Graphics Ltd, Derby

Printed and bound in Great Britain by
TJ International Ltd, Padstow, Cornwall

For William H. Ittelson, Harold M. Proshansky, and Leanne G. Rivlin:
guiding lights in this journey through space and time

Contents

Editors' biographies

Jen Jack Gieseking is a cultural geographer and environmental psychologist and Postdoctoral Fellow in the Digital and Computational Studies Initiative at Bowdoin College. Her work is engaged in research on co-productions of space and identity in digital, imagined, and material environments, with a focus on sexual and gender identities. She pays special attention to how such productions support or inhibit social, spatial, and economic justice. She is currently working on her first book, *Queer New York: Constellating Lesbians' and Queer Women's Geographies of Justice in New York City, 1983–2008*. She holds a Ph.D. in environmental psychology and has held fellowships with the Alexander von Humboldt Foundation; The Center for Place, Culture, and Politics; The Center for Lesbian and Gay Studies; and the Woodrow Wilson Women's Studies Dissertation Fellows Program.

William Mangold is a partner in a small design firm and Adjunct Professor in Interior Design at Pratt Institute. As a Ph.D. candidate in the Environmental Psychology program at The Graduate Center of The City University of New York, his research looks at social responsibility in design and utopian visions for transforming the social and spatial environment. Trained as an architect at the Rhode Island School of Design (RISD), he has worked on various buildings in New York City for the firm of Ivan Brice Architecture, including a number of restoration and adaptive reuse projects. Most recently he has taken on the design and renovation of an 1872 rowhouse where he lives with his family in Philadelphia.

Cindi Katz is Professor of Geography, Environmental Psychology, Women's Studies, and American Studies, and Executive Officer of the Earth and Environmental Sciences Program at The Graduate Center of The City University of New York. The recipient of fellowships from the National Science Foundation, the Association of University Women, the National Institute of Mental Health, the Center for the Critical Analysis of Contemporary Culture at Rutgers University, and the Radcliffe Institute for Advanced Study at Harvard University, she was the 2011–2012 Diane Middlebrook and Carl Djerassi Visiting Professor of Gender Studies at the University of Cambridge. Her 2004 book *Growing Up Global: Economic Restructuring and Children's Everyday Lives* received the Meridian Award for outstanding scholarly work in geography from the Association of American Geographers. Her other books include *Full Circles: Geographies of Gender over the Life Course* (with Janice Monk), and *Life's Work: Geographies of Social Reproduction* (with Sallie Marston and Katharyne Mitchell).

Setha Low is Professor of Environmental Psychology, Geography, Anthropology, and Women's Studies, and Director of the Public Space Research Group at The Graduate Center of The City University of New York. She received her Ph.D. in Anthropology from the University of California, Berkeley and has been awarded many honors and grants, including fellowships from the Guggenheim Foundation, National Endowment for the Humanities, Hays-Fulbright Commission and Getty Center for ethnographic fieldwork in Latin America and the United

States. Recent books include: *Politics of Public Space* (with Neil Smith), *Rethinking Urban Parks: Public Space and Cultural Diversity* (with Suzanne Scheld and Dana Taplin), *Behind the Gates: Life, Security and the Pursuit of Happiness in Fortress America*, and *On the Plaza: The Politics of Public Space and Culture*. She is currently researching the impact of private governance in New York City and Toronto condominiums with Randy Lippert funded by the Canadian Social Sciences Research Council, and writing a book entitled *Spatializing Culture: An Anthropological Theory of Space and Place*.

Susan Saegert is Professor of Environmental Psychology, founding director of the Center for the Study of Women and Society, and former director of the Center for Human Environments, all at The Graduate Center of The City University of New York. Her research includes studies of crowding; environmental stressors; housing and human development/well-being; and women and environments. She directs the Housing Environments Research Group, which works in partnership with community organizations and coalitions to improve distressed housing and neighborhoods. Her recent research concerns homeowners' experiences of the foreclosure crisis and policy implications; housing and health; and alternative housing policies to promote sustainable, inclusive, democratically governed communities. Her books include *From Abandonment to Hope: Community Households in Harlem* (with Jacqueline Leavitt), *Social Capital and Poor Communities* (with Mark Warren and J. Phillip Thomson), *Urban Health and Society: Interdisciplinary Approaches to Research and Practice* (with Susan Klitzman and Nicholas Freudenberg), and *The Community Development Reader, 1st and 2nd editions* (with James DeFilippis).

Acknowledgments

Preparing this book was a long and elaborate process that drew support and assistance from many different people. Foremost, we would like to thank the students, faculty, and staff at The Graduate Center of the City University of New York (CUNY) for sustaining such a rich interdisciplinary environment that has deeply informed our work. Our work would not be as thorough without the support of Leanne Rivlin, David Chapin, Roger Hart, Michelle Fine, Susan Opotow, John Seley, David Harvey, Neil Smith, Ruthie Gilmore, and the incredible Judith Kubran.

Many colleagues were also instrumental in choices we have made in putting this together, including our friends and co-conspirators who form the environmental psychology program and the CUNY SpaceTime Research Collective. We extend a special thanks to those who gave us input on possible selections for this book, including Naomi Adiv, Christian M. Anderson, Jeff Broxmeyer, Isabel Cuervo, Kate Driscoll Derickson, Gregory T. Donovan, Jason A. Douglas, Martin J. Downing, Desiree Fields, Valerie Francisco, Bradley Gardner, Jesse Goldstein, Lystra Huggins, Amanda Huron, Aida Izadpanah, Elizabeth R. Johnson, Sara Koopman, Fiona Lee, Kimberly Libman, Matthew Mangold, Frank Muscara, Anupama Nallari, Diana Ojeda, Nicole Schaefer-McDaniel, Aga Skorupka, Collette Sosnowy, David Spataro, Lauren Tenney, Rachel Verni, and Marion Werner.

Jack: I am grateful to my colleagues in the SpaceTime Research Collective of the CUNY Graduate Center, and, most especially, those amazing individuals who make up the environmental psychology program. You helped form not only this book but also my own scholarship. I extend special appreciation to Linda Gieseking and Teddy Stephen for promoting this book and ceaselessly supporting me. I thank the Alexander von Humboldt Foundation for the German Chancellor Fellowship that gave me much of the time needed to plan and edit this volume.

William: My thanks to Pratt Institute and Moore College of Art and Design—places where I have been fortunate to teach and that have awarded grants to put this book together. The students and faculty at these schools have challenged me and informed my work, as have my friends and colleagues at the Graduate Center. More than anyone, it is my parents who got me started on the path of thinking deeply about the world in and around me, and it is my wife and children that continue to support and encourage me in this direction.

Jack and William: We would especially recognize Cindi, Setha, and Susan, our mentors, colleagues, and friends. Not only was their teaching the inspiration for this book, but their commitment to this project has helped see it through to the end as the kind of truly interdisciplinary and exciting text we desired to bring to life. We are also thankful to the editorial team at Routledge, Louise Fox, Nicole Solano, Fritz Brantley, and Siobhán Greaney, for their support of this book.

Cindi, Setha, and Susan: We would like to thank the students who have taken our courses, for pushing boundaries, asking astute questions, and consistently challenging our thinking.

Introduction

This book developed from conversations between Jen Jack Gieseking and William Mangold when they began teaching undergraduate courses drawing upon readings and discussions they had with Cindi Katz, Susan Saegert, and Setha Low during their time in the environmental psychology program at The Graduate Center of the City University of New York (CUNY). Jack and William were surprised that no text captured the cross-disciplinary and socially engaged work with which they had become familiar. Further discussion brought the editors of this book together in order to share the resources and scholarship that informs our interdisciplinary field.

There is no volume that draws as widely as the one you are now reading, and, as Susan describes below, it has been decades since the last reader on this material was compiled. In the time since the publication of these previous anthologies in the 1970s, Susan, Cindi, and Setha honed the core courses with the faculty of the environmental psychology program to present a dynamic and critical understanding of space and place. Through this effort certain topics such as home, urban experience, and public space remained significant, while other concepts emerged or challenged previously held ideas about nature or the way in which spaces are socially produced. As an outgrowth of that work, we feel that this book represents a fresh gathering of ideas and the beginning of a renewed conversation on these themes.

The People, Place, and Space Reader brings together the excerpted writings of scholars, designers, and activists from a variety of fields upon which we draw in our teaching and research to make sense of the makings and meanings of the world we inhabit. They help us to understand the relationships between people and the environment at all scales, and to consider the active roles individuals, groups, and social structures play in creating the environments in which people live, work, and play. These readings highlight the ways in which space and place are produced through large- and small-scale social, political, and economic practices, and offer new ways to think about how people engage the environment in multiple and diverse ways. *The People, Place, and Space Reader* provides a road-map for thinking about these concerns, offering guides for some familiar paths while charting new routes to recognizing and heralding differences in perception, experience, and practice that traverse disciplinary boundaries, period, and location. Emphasizing interdisciplinarity, this reader provides multiple entry points to join these conversations about what may seem to be quite disparate works and conceptual worlds.

WORKING DEFINITIONS: PEOPLE, PLACE, AND SPACE

Of the words in the title, *people* may seem least in need of definition. Yet many conceptions of the person sever the individual from the environment without recognizing the extent to which humans come into being and live inextricably connected to places, people, and their material and cultural histories and geographies. This book presents a conception of the person in which people live 'as much in process across and "through" skins as in processes "within skins"' (Dewey 2005 [1934]).

This way of understanding people as connected to each other and their environment allows for a reassessment of the meaning of place and space in planning and policy as well as in everyday life.

Space and place have multiple and sometimes meandering meanings attributed to them. Indeed, these terms are often deployed exactly because of the wide-ranging possibilities and variations they imply metaphorically and conceptually. Most generally, *place* is bounded and specific to a location, and is a materialization of social forms and practices as well as affective experience. *Space* tends to be understood as abstract, unlimited, universalizing, and continuous. The infinite, undefined quality of space makes us think of the cosmos, the ether of flows and travel, or the metaphorical space one needs to think. Places are often more grounded, serve as reference points in our lives, and have distinct qualities that give people a sense of belonging. The ways people, place, and space work together to form one another are complex, varied, and dynamic, and are the focus of this volume.

THE FIELD OF ENVIRONMENTAL SOCIAL SCIENCE AND THE EDITORS OF THIS VOLUME

The field of environmental social science examines how people relate to, create, and define space and place; and how space and place relate to, shape, and define people and their experiences. This field of inquiry has gone by various names, including environmental psychology, psychogeography, environmental sociology, and environmental behavior and design. In the late 1960s, environmental psychology was formalized as an interdisciplinary field drawing primarily upon psychology, sociology, anthropology, geography, architecture, and urban planning (Bell et al. 2005; Pol 2006). As editors of *The People, Place, and Space Reader*, we come from several of these disciplines and were brought together through the environmental psychology program at the CUNY Graduate Center. Subsequently, as the volume and diversity of topics and approaches has steadily grown, the label *environmental psychology* has often seemed too narrow and has been replaced with the term *environmental social science*. In the sections below, each of the co-editors narrates the ways in which our disciplines have come together to inform and learn from environmental social science. Our education, research, and experiences offer a variety of ways to enter and make sense of this interdisciplinary field, while our different points of view allow us to challenge received ideas and build new understandings of people, place, and space.

EARLY DEVELOPMENT OF ENVIRONMENTAL PSYCHOLOGY

Susan Saegert, psychologist

Environmental psychology remains a perpetual work in progress, developing in tension with a psychology that not only bounds people within their skin but also fractures them internally into separable processes like cognition and affect, physiology and phenomenology. The effort to offer an analysis of psychological processes embedded in environmental and social transactions extends back to the American Pragmatists, as well as to continental European Gestalt psychologists. J.J. Gibson is an important figure who connects these traditions throughout his work. We provide an excerpt from Gibson's last book, *Ecological Approaches to Visual Perception* (1979), in which he presents a conception of organisms (including people) as inherently and literally in touch with their surroundings. Keeping with the tradition of John Dewey and William James, organisms are not just registering information but creating it as they go about the activities necessary for life and for the pursuit of goals; Gibson succeeds in removing the psychological construct of a little person in the head who has to interpret perceptions and apprehensions by representing them to the person whose head is occupied. However, as a perception psychologist, Gibson leaves that head unsatisfyingly empty. Harry Heft's (2001) tour de force, *Ecological Psychology in Context*, connects Gibson to the legacy of William James who thought about thought plenty. He places Gibson in relationship to both the ecological psychology of Roger Barker (1968) and the lifespace psychology of Kurt Lewin (Lewin and Gold 1999; Heider 1959). He also attends to the ways in which humans make their environments and are made by the places and objects we create (Lewin 1951). Heft's continuing productive line of inquiry and critique represents one of the most promising offspring of the work of the environmental psychologists of the 1970s. One of the living edges of this work is an attempt to connect the still individualistic psychologies of these authors to a richer understanding of embedded social beings engaged in collective as well as individual, and material as well as psychological and social projects.

Other strands of scholarship in psychology that significantly contribute to the making of a fully situated and robustly social environmental psychology may be found in social and community psychology. The practice of *participatory action research* (PAR) incorporates not only Kurt Lewin's pioneering work to develop that approach to research, knowledge, and social action but also Peirce's concept of *abduction* (Fine 2010), in which inquiry proceeds through simultaneous reasoning about and exploration of a problem. Community psychology has built an area of interdisciplinary research and practice dedicated to two aspects of the aspirations of early environmental psychology: (1) placing the creation of knowledge within real-world contexts; and (2) understanding individuals as transactionally engaged with communities and the broader society. Community psychology has found particularly fertile resonance with environmental psychology on topics such as place attachment (Manzo and Perkins 2006) and an action research approach to environmental sustainability (Schweizer-Ries and Perkins 2012).

Early environmental psychology began a path that continues to lead into engagement with contemporary concerns and continual re-understandings of our place in the world. In fact, *The People, Place, and Space Reader* is the third edited book of readings addressing these issues to be produced by the environmental psychology program of The CUNY Graduate Center. The first two readers, both by Harold M. Proshansky, William H. Ittelson, and Leanne G. Rivlin (1970, 1976), helped define the field, and their contributions still ripple through environmental psychology. Those two *Environmental Psychology* readers, as well as this volume, share the goal of increasing knowledge about the dynamic relationship between people and places while addressing issues of social and spatial inequalities. This work also aims to help develop theories adequate to the everyday experience of environments, as well as to aid in the creation of more just and more sustainable environments. Each of these books has engaged many different disciplinary perspectives on how people and places make each other.

The first reader, *Environmental Psychology: Man and his Physical Settings*, published in 1970, began the decade of institutionalization of the field. The editors brought together extraordinarily diverse collections of papers that situated people in relationship to the built and natural environment as well as specific institutional settings. The collection expressed a deep commitment to the idea that human behavior had to be understood as always situated within a physical milieu. The psychological works represented stemmed from divergent theoretical perspectives from the Lewinian inspiration of Proshansky and Rivlin through Ittelson's transactional approach to visual perception, to several contributions by authors from the behaviorist tradition. The success of these readers and the program in environmental psychology lies in part in bringing these separate pieces together into one area of psychology.

The early readers clearly defined the field as interdisciplinary. The seminal works of anthropologist Edward T. Hall (1966) on an anthropology of space, urban sociologists' contributions on the lives of slum dwellers and suburbanites (cf. Gans 1982a, 1982b), and urban planners such as Kevin Lynch's *The Image of the City* (Section 2) and Jane Jacobs' *Death and Life of Great American Cities* (Section 7) inspired and are represented in the collections. The influences of architecture, urban design, and resource management are evident as well. Many selections also testified to the important cross-fertilization of geography and environmental psychology described by Cindi Katz below. The second edition (1976) of *Environmental Psychology: People and Their Physical Settings* reflected the growth of an actual area of research called environmental psychology, especially around topics of continuing importance such as environmental stress, mental maps, and the role of the environment in child development.

In the time since the initial volumes were published, the program at The CUNY Graduate Center and the field itself moved in increasingly interdisciplinary directions (Saegert and Winkel 1990). The editors of this volume saw a need for a collection that would situate the reader in a much-changed landscape of everyday life, local and global relationalities, and people–environment problematics, including the ever-worsening environmental crises; awareness of the global dimensions and historical, political, and economic power relations that lead to unjust access to and control over environmental resources; and cultural diversity and other differences in the nature of people–place transactions. Research and theorizing have expanded to include a wide range of issues of how people experience, prosper, suffer, and make habitats from urban communities and homes through everything from foodscapes to the physical construction and inhabitation of specific locales, regions, and the globe itself. At the same time, long-standing concerns such as wayfinding, environmental attitudes, environmental aesthetics, place attachment and identity, and the meaning of spaces of everyday life have built significant bodies of research.

The intellectual landscape and cast of characters has changed as well in recent years to shift and multiply our lenses for examining inequality. Identity politics joined with Marxist and critical social theory to influence the growth of feminist, queer, critical race, and disability theories and sensibilities. The hegemony of white and US and European scholars gave way, at least in the discourses that situate this book, to critical race and postcolonial theory. The totalizing narratives of modernism and scientism were challenged by postmodernists, standpoint theorists, and poststructuralists. The work of environmental social science continues to build on past understandings and research into the person-in-the-world, but now engages with a far wider set of concerns. The diverse disciplinary backgrounds of the editors suggest the nature of this broader conception and approach.

EMBODIED SPACE: THE ETHNOGRAPHY OF SPACE AND PLACE

Setha Low, anthropologist

The anthropology of space and place represented in this volume incorporates what I have called *spatializing culture*, the linking of culture and space through material, metaphorical, and social conceptualizations grounded in the field. Regardless of whether it is an ethnographic multi-sited study, a survey of human bone locations, or an archeological dig, in anthropological research there is always an encounter with the inherent materiality and human subjectivity through fieldwork that situates the researcher at their interface. Studies of space and place that emerge from the sediment of anthropological research draw on the strengths of studying people *in situ* producing rich and nuanced sociospatial and critical encounters that are included in the various sections.

I joined the environmental psychology program in 1989 to contribute to this interdisciplinary work, focusing on the social production and social construction of space, and developing the theoretical concept of embodied space to emphasize the importance of the body and bodies in the co-production of the built environment. Methodologically this has meant training students in the craft of ethnography. Ethnography uncovers enabling social structures and political and economic constraints, and their material and symbolic expression through long-term, intimate contact with people in their everyday environments. Participant observation, in-depth interviewing, augmented by activity maps, movement maps, mental maps, photographs, drawings, and many other spatial techniques drawn from environmental psychology and landscape architecture make up a methods toolbox for deciphering the role of culture in the production and construction of space and place.

Historically, anthropologists have contributed "culture" to environmental psychology theory and research. Edward Hall (1966) and his discussion of proxemics, the so-called hidden cultural dimension that guides human-to-human and human-to-environment spatial relations was a first attempt. Architect Amos Rappaport (1969) and social psychologist Irwin Altman (1972) used an essentialized concept of culture to explain why built environments varied in ways that could not be explained by an environmental deterministic point of view. A few anthropologists, including Denise Lawrence Zuniga, Ellen Pader, and myself, took academic positions in design schools that brought us into contact with environmental psychologists who were interested in the cultural aspects of design (see Low and Lawrence 2003).

Today, anthropological discussions of space often start with Pierre Bourdieu (1977) because he moves beyond the constraints of the structural analysis of space by focusing on how meaning and action, or *practice*, interact in interdependent ways to inculcate and reinforce cultural knowledge and behavior. He argues that space can have no meaning apart from practice; the system of generative and structuring dispositions, or *habitus*, constitutes and is constituted by actors' movement through space (1984) (see Section 5). Because social practice activates spatial meanings, they are not fixed, but invoked by actors who bring their own discursive knowledge and strategic intentions to their interpretation.

Anthropologists often use narrative to elicit details of how local populations construct perceptions of and experience place. Much of this kind of ethnography describes "local theories of dwelling" (Feld and Basso 1996) and draws implicitly or explicitly upon phenomenological approaches and *thick description* (Geertz 1973). Narrative and its interpretation are at the center of ethnography, according to Steven Feld and Keith Basso, who suggest that cultural constructions of the environment can only be understood by talking to natives about landscapes.

The inscription of place with meaning is not limited, however, to telling stories, but includes a complex set of sound, smell, touch, and other sense-based perceptions (Feld 1990; Peterson 2010.) But "people do not simply "experience" the world; they are taught—indeed disciplined—to signify their experiences in distinctive ways" (Myers 2002, 103). Alberto Corsín Jiménez goes even further in his insistence on a socially constituted notion of space. For Jiménez, social relationships are inherently spatial, and "space an instrument and dimension of space's sociality" (2003, 140). In his analysis the material landscape recedes as space becomes a dimension and form of agency that configures well with environmental psychology's interest in action and advocacy.

Thus, anthropologists examine the social and environmental forces that produce physical space and place, as well as the lived experience of individuals and their constructions of meaning. This kind of analysis is not a simple task, since there are significant disagreements about the prioritization of space or place and the nature of their relationship, but anthropologists are uniquely anchored in fieldwork in a way that is particularly useful. The goal of the addition of anthropological theory to the mix, therefore, is to demonstrate how anthropological theory, research, and methodology is deployed to understand space and place, and suggests that anthropologists offer an ethnographic and grounded approach to this interdisciplinary endeavor.

One point, however, that needs to be added is that the concepts of place and space—central theoretical constructs in geography, architecture, and planning—pose such a concern for anthropologists that they are often avoided. One reason is that at least for ethnographers it is difficult to discuss *place* or *space* in a way that does not confine the inhabitants. Arjun Appadurai (1988) and Margaret Rodman (1985, 1992) correctly criticize ethnographic conceptions of place and space that provide taken-for-granted settings to locate their descriptions or reduce the ethnographic to a locale that imprisons natives. Instead, anthropologists require a flexible and mobile conception of space, one that speaks to how space is produced historically and physically and came to be in its current material form, but also how it is created by bodies in motion, embodied dreams and desires, and social interaction and environmental interrelations.

The anthropological perspective offers a process-oriented, person-based perspective and allows for agency and new possibilities, even though historically ethnographies relegated space to the description of fixed material culture markers. One solution to this dilemma that continues to develop in the literature during recent years is to consider place and space as always embodied. Their materiality can be metaphoric and discursive, as well as physically located, and thus carried about. Introducing embodiment into sociospatial analysis problematizes these concepts in a way that allows for the exploration of their social construction and production at diverse global and local scales. The body (and bodies), conceptualized as embodied space(s), incorporates metaphors, ideology, and language, as well as behaviors, habits, skills, and spatial orientations derived from global discourses and faraway places, and yet is grounded at any one moment in a specific field context. It is through embodied space that the global is integrated into the inscribed spaces of everyday life where attachment, emotion, and morality come into play. Research that identifies the embodied spaces of individuals and groups as sites of translocal and transnational spatial flows as well as of personal experience and perception solves some of the misplaced rootedness found in anthropological thought. Some topics, however, are not directly discussed in anthropological theories and for these concerns we must turn to the contributions of geography.

CONTRIBUTIONS AND CHALLENGES FROM GEOGRAPHY

Cindi Katz, geographer

Interest in the connections between people and space has followed a number of strands in geography as well. As environmental psychology emerged as a discipline in the 1960s, scholars in geography were thinking through and trying to systematize the role of perception and cognition in practical interactions concerning the environment from policy to everyday practices. One of the key sites of this research was Clark University, where geographers who had done research on environmental perception and behavior had teamed up with psychologists to study the role of perception in individual and social behaviors around hazardous environments, both "natural" and built, resource definition and use, and the management of transformations of the "human environment" (e.g., Kates and Wohlwill 1966; Burton and Kates 1964). Among their influences were economist Kenneth Boulding's (1956) iconoclastic book *The Image*, Kevin Lynch's (Section 2) pivotal *The Image of the City*, and René Dubos' (e.g., 1965) writings, all of which creatively insisted that it was how things, relations, places, or environmental stimuli are seen, symbolized, imagined, known, and understood that matters.

These ideas led planners and other professionals to address environmental problems and hazards such as flood plain management or nuclear facility siting in terms that might resonate more meaningfully with affected populations. Understanding the role of the image—of environmental perception and cognition—in environmental activity and behavior influenced policy and practice in urban design as much as around resource management, the siting of hazardous technologies, the management of environmental risk, and possible responses to large-scale phenomena such as global climate change. These concerns remain vital today as the effects of climate change and the interconnections of global and local practices become everyday more urgent.

At the same time, geographers and developmental psychologists received funding from the US Office of Education for the groundbreaking "place perception project," which examined young children's spatial cognition and the development of their place learning and behavior, including the acquisition of mapping skills in early childhood (Blaut and Stea 1971; cf. Wood 2010). This work eventually expanded to encompass research on children's place experience, knowledge, and home range (Tindal 1971; Hart 1979; Wood 2006), and on the development of children's environmental learning and knowledge (Kates and Katz 1977; Wood and Beck 1994; Katz 2004). These lineages may be seen in the abiding concerns of environmental psychology with cognitive mapping, children's geographies, environmental education, and the development of environmental concern and care (e.g., Chawla and Cushing 2007). There was plenty of important work in behavioral geography that did not address children and the environment. Inspirational here was William Kirk's (1952) original research on the behavioral environment, which engaged psychology theory and emphasized the role of perception—as itself a cultural process filtered through values—in human geography and environmental engagement. Pioneering geographers pursued similar concerns, addressing behavior as an outcome of environmental perception, wherein action is understood as rooted in the images produced at the interface between people and their environments (e.g., Downs and Stea 1973; Golledge 1981, 1998; Gould and White 1986; Downs 1967, cited in Wood 1970; Wood 1992; Kitchin et al. 1997). From its inception, behavioral geography was a counterweight to geographic thought that homogenized "man" as rational decision-makers operating in an objectively knowable world. Drawing insights from the cognitive sciences as much as from phenomenology, the multiple strands of behavioral geography insisted on the place of people—individually and collectively—as social actors; thinking beings with histories, incomplete knowledge, emotions, and agendas, making decisions about, negotiating, and triggering geographic processes and making the worlds they inhabited.

Time-geography was another strand of influence in the late 1960s and grew out of allied concerns with experience and behavior. Associated predominantly with the Swedish geographer Torsten Hägerstrand (e.g., 1970, 1978), time-geography offered a way of looking at the person in space with time as its other dimension to discern patterns in everyday interactions across historical geographies and over the life course. Addressing the various constraints on mobility and activity in time-space, time-geography reckoned with embodiment and understood space as a malleable social form (cf., Pred 1977, 1981, 1984). Although criticized for its masculinism (Rose 1993; but see Friberg 1993; Scholten et al. 2012) and its problematic abstraction from any sort of political economic framing, time-geography offered insights into everyday life and the overlapping structures of the behavioral environment.

These strands of geography, which looked at the role of perception in behavior; the experience of place and environmental cognition; the maps and worlds in people's heads; emotion and environment; and the person in space or the behavioral environment, shared much common ground with—and offered critical insights into—the burgeoning concerns of environmental psychology as they coalesced in response to the social, political economic, and environmental crises of the 1960s/1970s. Among the other important strands of this braid that I can only touch on here was work in humanistic geography, which examined the sensory and affective experience of space and place (see Buttimer 1976; Lowenthal 1961). Among its early and most influential practitioners is Yi-Fu Tuan's pioneering and often beautiful work focused on the relationship between place and space and people's fluid relationships to the two at all scales from the body to the globe. In a series of books, he explored place attachment, love, and reverence as well as fear and insecurity in everyday environmental interactions, in the imagination, through the senses, and in all manner of representations, including mental maps (e.g., Tuan 1974, 1977). As humanists, these scholars looked at relationships between people and place thinking through the role of memory, imagination, identity, emotion, embodiment, and sedimented cultural forms and practices.

Another important strand, scale, is one of the key ideas of geography (see Section 10). Before the contemporary debates on the production of scale (cf., e.g., Smith 1993; Marston 2000; Sheppard and McMaster 2004; Marston et al. 2005), geographers in the late 1960s were considering not just the received descriptive notions of geographic scale such as global, regional, urban, and local, but also the quite intimate such as the body, the home, the city street. They were mindful of the fluid interpenetrations among these scales and the material social practices associated with them. There was a radical impulse to much of this work, a sense that while the environmental impacts of people would be more legible at smaller scales, the global and local infused one another and neither one could be altered—or understood—without attending to the other. James Blaut, for example, examined the geography of a one-acre farm in great detail, and drew on it and other "microgeographies" to interrogate development, agroecology, and diffusion models of knowledge and practice (e.g., Blaut 1953). William Bunge and his collaborators in the Detroit Geographical Expedition and Institute (DGEI) examined one square mile of the city intensively to assess not just the state of the city but also the nation. The DGEI analogized their project to a medical examination wherein a drop of blood can reveal the health of a patient (Bunge 2011). Their work—like that of many of the scholars reviewed here—traverses the porous boundary between the geographical and the psychological, making and remaking the still lively grounds of environmental psychology. The materiality of those grounds is addressed in the next section.

QUESTIONING THE CONVENTIONS OF ARCHITECTURE AND DESIGN

William Mangold, designer

While much of the scholarship in architecture has focused on questions of avant-garde form-making, the interdisciplinary approach of environmental social science offers architecture a critical and dynamic way of thinking about the spaces we design and the places we inhabit. The conventional narrative of 20th-century architecture emphasizes the development of aesthetic styles over the creation of new social situations, but there have always been critics and designers who have used architecture as a medium to discuss and imagine alternative social and spatial situations.

Architecture initially took up questions of space in the late 19th century and has since contributed to understanding the way in which space provides a conceptual and literal territory for social relations (see Forty 2004 for a history of how the term *space* evolved in the architecture discourse). Propelled by material and structural innovations in the use of steel, concrete, and plate glass, the early work of Frank Lloyd Wright, Le Corbusier, and Mies van der Rohe, especially as championed by Sigfried Giedion (1940), provided built examples of this novel concept of architecture as space-making. Excited about the new types of spatial relations, designers were also interested in what this meant for social relations. Transparency, openness, mobility, and interconnection were ideas that permeated design and were intended to challenge the existing spatial and social conventions. However, over time these social ideas were obscured and this early modern architecture became known for the aesthetic style it introduced, rather than for the new social relations these spaces offered.

However, there have always been designers who insisted on understanding and integrating social concerns into their design work. William Morris' pursuit of small-scale craft production in the face of industrialization, and Hannes Meyer's development of the Bauhaus curriculum are early modern examples that contest the emphasis on aesthetic style. Victor Papanek (1971) wrote a scathing critique of design in the context of mass production and advocated for a "high social and moral responsibility from the designer." Felicity Scott (2007) traces a number of critical junctions when designers and critics pursued alternative socio-spatial possibilities, such as those by Buckminster Fuller or Emilio Ambasz, but shows how they were subsumed or rejected by mainstream architectural practice. Other designers and activists have advocated for space to be a terrain of freedom, creativity, and connection. In this volume, Guy Debord and the Situationists, site-specific and socially engaged art practices such as those advocated by Miwon Kwon, and the urban design work of Michael Sorkin each represent attempts to rethink the spatial status quo. These *socially responsible design* practices emerge in response to demands of production and highlight ways in which designers can create spaces that are more democratic, sustainable, and just.

When the aesthetics of modern design were adopted as the style of corporate and bureaucratic architecture in the latter part of the 20th century, social critics also began to voice their objections. In this volume, Henri Lefebvre and David Harvey (1989) feature prominently for their poignant critiques of the ways in which space is used by hegemony to dictate or obfuscate social relations. Using Marxist thought to analyze urban development allows for an understanding of how financial capital shapes spaces and social relations to the benefit of corporate power and capital accumulation. Contemporaneous with these theoretical critiques was the start of research in the social sciences (see Sommer 1969; Hall 1966; for Robert Gutman's writings, see Cuff and Wriedt 2010) concerned with the social and psychological impacts of the spaces that were being mass produced in the boom following World War II. Critics like Jane Jacobs and Kevin Lynch took issue with the way cities were being re-engineered for automobiles instead of people. Others, like J.B. Jackson and Dolores Hayden (1981), all included here examined the impact on the landscape as highways were built and suburbs expanded. These scholars from the edges of architecture were able to look critically at design practices and have contributed significantly to understanding how places shape social life.

During this period, some designers teamed with social science researchers to find more conscientious approaches to design and building. One long-standing concern has been the lack of voice by the people who are living in the places designed for them. David Chapin and his ARC Group colleagues developed ways of studying and making places that involved both children and the elderly (see Bakos et al. 1978, 1980). This alternative is known as the process of inclusive or *participatory planning* (Blundell Jones et al. 2005), and is a user-based process that seeks to gather and integrate ideas from the people who will inhabit the buildings or communities being designed.

Another idea from environmental social science that challenges architecture is a shift in emphasis from space to place. From psychology, we have a better understanding of how and why people like or dislike particular places, and what makes them feel comfortable or uneasy. Sometimes labeled *place attachment*, this research has shown that the formal or aesthetic aspects of design are only part of what creates connection between people and their physical settings (see Section 3). Memories, social interactions, the ability to modify surroundings, and a sense of security are all significant contributors to attachment (see Low and Altman 1992; Bachelard 1994; Cooper Marcus 1992). These qualitative and affective aspects of the relation people have to their environment contribute to what makes a space a place.

Many architects and designers have attempted a more humanist approach to building, emphasizing the qualities of materials and the experience of place over the smooth surfaces, structural logic, and open, empty spaces of modern architecture. Notable figures include Juhani

Pallasmaa (1996; see also Section 10), who argues for a more sensual and multi-sensory experience of place, and Christopher Alexander (Alexander et al. 1977), whose notion of *pattern language* provides a radical template for the built environment based on the scale of human inhabitation. The work of contemporary designers such as Peter Zumthor (2010) and the firm of Diller and Scofidio (1996) also pay close attention to the experiences and interactions of people in the places they create. The field of interior design is likewise concerned with the experiences of inhabitants and tends to emphasize the sensory qualities of materials and spaces. Through attention to the surfaces, details, and objects that people come into direct contact with, interior design remains attentive to the needs and experiences of inhabitants (Weinthal 2011).

While environmental social science has challenged and contributed to design in many ways, well-designed places often remain exclusive, as a privileged class of people often controls the design process. The way in which architecture engages with the power of capitalism continues to be an important issue; many designers and scholars are rethinking this relationship (Awan et al. 2011; Bell et al. 2008; Fisher 2006; Lavin 2011; Thorpe 2012) and how to create meaningful places for people. With increasing pressure for socially and environmentally sustainable responses to our sociospatial conditions, new possibilities are emerging. Developing alternatives depends upon a rich understanding of people, place, and space. Perspectives like those outlined in this volume can enrich the work of designers and architects, and invigorate the discourse in ways that are more socially and environmentally responsible.

EMERGING THEORIES AND METHODS ADDRESSING IDENTITY AND PLACE

Jen Jack Gieseking, geographer and environmental psychologist

Environmental psychology emerged in the context of the civil rights, feminist, lesbian and gay, peace, anti-nuclear, and environmental movements during the 1960s. Each of these movements afforded instances of recognition and ways of multiplying identities and perspectives, and places and experiences. These emerging relationships and spaces have been addressed by revived theoretical approaches, including Marxism and pragmatism, while other critical feminist, racial, and queer perspectives helped develop new theoretical and methodological approaches. Environmental social science has adopted these theories and methodologies because they are able to work across disciplines and support efforts towards social and spatial justice. *Social justice*, based on principles of equality and human dignity, is sought through research and activism to effect structural changes, as well as allow for agency in everyday decisions and practices.

In this vein, Audre Lorde and Adrienne Rich (1981) write, "feminist answers can best be found by movement *toward* all points of stress and difficulty." Feminism, one core theoretical foundation to environmental social science, argues that the personal is political. Bridging critical race and feminist theory, Kimberlé Crenshaw (1996) calls for recognizing the multiple, *intersectional identities* of human beings, including gender, class, race, and so on. In her contributions to theorizing space through a feminist, queer, and critical race lens, Gloria Anzaldúa (1987) presents the concept of the *borderlands* that calls for an intentional crossing and mixing of identities and borders. Queer theory situates pleasure and politics side-by-side to understand practices and processes, and offers ways of being that refuse the common binary distinctions posed in much social theory. The work of queering heralds and makes room for difference, both socially and spatially, by providing recognition and consideration for alternative perspectives that break away from norms (see Sommeila and Wolfe 1997). These frameworks draw upon marginalized perspectives to critique and rework conventional hegemonic narratives, practices, and structures.

Feminist, critical race, queer, and other theories addressing disability and postcolonial perspectives are useful for and embedded in the interdisciplinary work of environmental social science because they engage mutuality, voice, and active listening to different standpoints, all of which are helpful in understanding relations between people and place more fully. Through these theories and methods, the assumed qualities of our environments and our behaviors within them come into question and allow for variation and sustained acceptance of difference. In this volume, the work of scholars such as Melissa Wright, Rob Imrie, Don Mitchell, Susan Ruddick, Ruth Wilson Gilmore, and Alice Friedman highlights how the political is imbricated in the everyday social, economic, and psychological lives of all people ranging from contexts of industrial factory floors to the lives of the homeless in public parks, from state prisons to homes that enact the social and physical feelings of imprisonment upon women and the disabled. Feminist practices ask and encourage us to (re)claim and write our own multiple histories and spaces. In building theory from experience, spatializing feminist thought allows for the recognition of terrain that gets overlooked or is marked as unimportant. For example, thinking critically about home, and the heavy work involved in social reproduction, points to how social productions of space and time may be altered to refuse politics that hide or limit human capacity (Hayden 1980).

Comparatively, the implication of queer theoretical perspectives on environmental social science has just begun. A relatively new theoretical approach, queering destabilizes assumptions and privileges of secure heteronormative models of study and everyday life, and challenges other normative models and conventions such as those associated with gender, race, ownership, hierarchy, and authorship. In this vein, Michel Foucault (1990) politicizes and acknowledges the flux and instability of lives, spaces, cultures, and histories, and recognizes the powerful role of space in shaping what we think of the usual or the norm. A number of scholars in this volume implicitly or explicitly discuss *difference*, such as Judith Jack Halberstam, Iris Marion Young, and George Chauncey, as a mode of recognizing and accepting others. Others point out the binary ways of framing difference that they find impossible to hold as distinct, such as Geraldine Pratt and Victoria Rosner's discussion of the interdependent concepts and experiences of the global and the intimate, thereby queering the purported extremes of everyday life. Troubling the way we label and produce spaces affords the creation of thick, deep understandings of the unrecorded histories and geographies of people's lives and experiences.

These approaches extend beyond the purely theoretical to inform epistemological and methodological frameworks as well. A feminist epistemology recognizes that knowledge is co-constructed from various standpoints and experiences, while critical race and queer methods and methodologies recognize the partiality and incompleteness of knowledge. The participatory, problem-solving, and agentic orientation of environmental psychology likewise acknowledges these limits, having developed from efforts to do research beyond the lab and in the context of everyday lives and places. Environmental psychologists emphasize working *with* research participants rather than studying *about* them, and recent work has advanced the understanding and use of participatory action research (PAR) designs. Even in its model-based studies—which are performed to enhance reasonable and healthy behavior—the field of environmental psychology, like feminist, critical race, and queer perspectives, orients itself in a contextualized approach to solving real-world issues.

Other methods developed at the intersection of different disciplines have also found a home in the cross-disciplinary field of environmental social science. Employed primarily by psychologists and geographers, mental mapping is the representation of an individual or group's cognitive understanding of place captured through drawing or labeling a map (see Section 2). Architects and psychologists have honed methods of environmental behavior mapping (Bakos et al. 1978; Zeisel 2006), which involve systematic observations to trace activity patterns in place over time, whether focused on the physical characteristics of a site, or the activities of an individual or group. Similarly, transect walks involve accompanying an individual or group on a specific path to record their experiences, thoughts, and behaviors moving through space. Post-occupancy evaluation is used to determine if a building's architectural program is successful based on its use (Preiser et al. 1988), and involves interviews and careful examination of building elements and human activity well after construction is complete. The ever-increasing prominence of critical uses of geographic information systems (GIS) by scholars such as Matthew W. Wilson, Sarah Elwood, Rob Kitchin, Martin Dodge, John Seley, Mei-Po Kwan, and Craig Dalton, as well as the digital expansion of geoweb technologies and methodologies, allow for more innovative and participatory analyses. These methods address the material and imagined qualities of space often referenced in this volume, and afford the ability to perform deep and wide-ranging studies of people and places.

The strength of the field of environmental social science comes not only from its interdisciplinary breadth and depth, but also from the wide array of methods it employs to build theories and articulate human–environment relationships. Developing these approaches from feminist, queer, critical race, and other marginalized perspectives increases the potential for radical engagement and social change. Linking the political, personal, and pleasurable, feminist and queer theories and methods use a contextual approach to give voice and depth to people, place, and space.

CONCLUDING THOUGHTS AND SUGGESTIONS

The readings in this volume draw from a variety of fields, including geography, urban studies, sociology, cultural studies, psychology, architecture and design, anthropology, planning, and environmental studies. Drawing on a diverse selection of classic and cutting-edge readings, the editors worked collaboratively to prepare excerpts of approximately 3,000 words that highlight key theoretical contributions and important examples or data from the research. We have tried to bring these fields into conversation and offer readers different ways to enter and make sense of the wide-ranging scholarship on the meaning and experience of place and space. At the same time, this reader frames key issues within and across disciplines through the way in which the sections are organized. It situates theories and studies of space and place in conversation with one another in order to clarify the perspective of particular disciplines while revealing common ground and cross-fertilizations among them. Each of the twelve broad topical sections of the book has an introduction by the editors to orient readers, introduce key ideas, and navigate the concerns raised across—and in the spaces between—the included readings. The organization of the volume flows from an overview of the processes that animate the relationship between people and their environments to an examination of the key material social practices and settings that illuminate this relationship.

A Road-map to the Selections Ahead

The first four sections of the book situate the reader in larger frameworks of the study of people, space, and place. We begin with "Diverse Conceptions of the Relationships between People, Place, and Space" to introduce some of the varying approaches useful for understanding the relationship between people, place, and space. Through the various lenses of the authors we find different entry points, a range of scales, and distinct ways of examining how space and place are created and re-created through the actions and meanings of people. In "Human Perception and Environmental Experience," we refute the false dualism between what is "out there" in the world and what is "in" the human brain or body. Through mental maps, city walks, and personal space, this section explores how perception and experience mutually define human and environment. The section on "Place and Identity" reworks common conceptualizations of how place and identity are formed, and illuminates the myriad ways they co-produce one another. "Power, Subjectivity, and Space" describes how power operates in particular places and through particular bodies and situations. By looking at different situations and forms of power in action, these readings present a complex portrayal of power, subjectivity, agency, and change.

The next four sections focus on particular sites and forms of space and place. "Meanings of Home" dives into how different concepts of home are derived or constructed, as well as ways in which the experience of home is denied or inhibited. This section looks at a range of home environments, including accommodations for disabled people, public housing, and childhood homes. Next, '"Public" and "Private"' takes up how public and private are intertwined, each helping to form the other. As international movements grow to combat inequalities and injustices, public space and private rights are often at the heart of these inquiries and contentious debates. Public space haunts what is at stake in the representation of democracy and community in the social life and economic ownership of public spaces (see Low and Smith 2005). "The Urban Experience" brings to light how cities afford difference and anonymity, leading to justice and injustice, growth or limitation. More than half of the world's population will soon live in cities, suggesting the importance of learning from and enhancing the urban experience for all. In "Landscape: Nature and Culture," the selections address how landscape is produced through the everywhere and ongoing interaction of culture and nature. In this sense, we may understand *landscape* to indicate an environment that has been modified, enhanced, or exploited through human activity, and begin to question how we experience and cultivate our relation to the environment.

In the final four sections, we take up relatively new theoretical-practical approaches to people, space, and place that may be used to rethink our situations and work towards change. In "The Social Production of Space and Time" we highlight not only how people produce and are produced by various understandings and structures of space and time, but also how these productions affect how we live. The selections in "Shifting Perspectives: Optics for Revealing Change and Reworking Space" ask a common question: what are the ways in which we can see our world again and anew? This leads to thinking about how space can be a mechanism to mask or reveal unjust conditions. Studies of space and place can shift our point of view or "optics" in order to unveil hidden ideologies that structure our everyday lives. "The Spatial Imagination" challenges and re-imagines how we understand and represent our place in the world, and exposes how our imagination of the world does not always match up with the world we experience. These ideas help us to take notice of and mind the gaps between how we envision, produce, and experience spaces and places. In our final section of readings, "Democratic Prospects and Possibilities," we bring together selections that envision and look critically at constructions of more democratic, equal, and just environments, in order to offer insights into the ways in which spaces and places can become open to transformation.

Beyond the Book: *peopleplacespace.org*

In addition to the selected excerpts and introductory texts, we have also included a brief list of suggested readings for each section to guide readers to additional resources in their area(s) of concern. Yet this book does not end in the selected or recommended readings because the process of engaging scholarship is ongoing. Like the field of environmental social science, this body of work is always growing, and so this collection will as well. As an open-ended project, we envision that this volume may be read as a whole from beginning to end (and therefore used as an entire course reader), or topics may be explored individually. Each section complements the others in expanding and developing our ways of understanding people, place, and space.

At *peopleplacespace.org*, the editors and a series of expert invited guests whose research develops from an environmental social science perspective are continually updating lists for recommended readings on the twelve sections of this book as well as a series of additional topics. Drawing from experts' work on mapping and resistance to the production of digital place and space, from international perspectives on housing to young people and ecology, a catalog of Further Recommended Reading Lists may be found at the end of this volume with summaries and selected citations on our online site. Other recommendations will continue to be developed and shared via the website, and these lists and citations are easily downloadable. We hope these lists may be of help to the student, instructor, and interested reader as they expand their own understanding of environmental social science. Readers are welcome to add their contributions to these lists as well by commenting on each list and being in dialog with our group of experts.

Our hope is that a new generation of scholarship and activism will recognize the important spatial and temporal aspects of this scholarship, and be able to draw fruitfully upon the contributions of thinkers that have come before. We call special attention to the critical work needed to help confront inequalities and injustices. What in this book can best inform you to help you deal with these issues? What will you read in this book today to help you understand what lies ahead for us and the rest of the world?

New York City and Philadelphia
July 2013

REFERENCES

Alexander, Christopher, Sara Ishikawa, and Murray Silverstein. 1977. *A Pattern Language: Towns, Buildings, Construction*. New York: Oxford University Press.

Altman, Irwin. 1972. *Environment and Culture*. New York and London: Plenum.

Anzaldúa, Gloria. 1987. *Borderlands/La Frontera: The New Mestiza*. San Francisco, CA: Aunt Lute Books.

Appadurai, Arjun. 1988. Introduction: Place and Voice in Anthropological Theory. *Cultural Anthropology*, 3(1), 16–20.

Awan, Nishat, Tatjana Schneider, and Jeremy Till. 2011. *Spatial Agency: Other Ways of Doing Architecture*. New York: Routledge.

Bachelard, Gaston. 1994. *The Poetics of Space*. New York: Beacon Press.

Bakos, Michael, Richard Bozic, David Chapin, and Stephanie Neuman. 1980. Effects of Environmental Change on Elderly Residents' Behavior. *Hospital & Community Psychiatry*, 31(10): 677–682.

Bakos, Michael, Richard Bozic, David Chapin, Judith Gandrus, and Steven Kahn. 1978. Evaluative Tools: Behavioral Mapping, Activity Analysis. *Privacy, Territory, and Participation*, 18–22.

Barker, Roger. 1968. *Ecological Psychology*. Stanford, CA: Stanford University Press.

Bell, Bryan, Katie Wakeford, Steve Badanes, Roberta Feldman, Sergio Palleroni, Katie Swenson, and Thomas Fisher. 2008. *Expanding Architecture: Design as Activism*. New York: Metropolis Books.

Bell, Paul A., Thomas Greene, Jeffrey Fisher, and Andrew S. Baum. 2005. *Environmental Psychology*. New York: Psychology Press.

Blaut, James M. 1953. The Economic Geography of a One-acre Farm in Singapore: A Study in Applied Microgeography, *Journal of Tropical Geography*, 1: 37–48.

Blaut, James M., and David Stea. 1971. Studies of Geographic Learning. *Annals of the Association of American Geographers*, 61(2): 387–393.

Blundell Jones, Peter, Doina Petrescu, and Jeremy Till (eds). 2005. *Architecture and Participation*. London: Routledge.

Boulding, Kenneth E. 1956. *The Image: Knowledge in Life and Society*. Ann Arbor: University of Michigan Press.

Bourdieu, Pierre. 1977. *Outline of a Theory of Practice*. Cambridge: Cambridge University Press.

Bourdieu, Pierre. 1984. *Distinction*. Cambridge, MA: Harvard University Press.

Bunge, William. 2011 [1971]. *Fitzgerald: Geography of a Revolution*. Athens: University of Georgia Press.

Burton, Ian, and Robert W. Kates. 1964. The Perception of Natural Hazards in Resource Management. *Natural Resources Journal*, 3: 412–441.

Buttimer, Anne. 1976. Grasping the Dynamism of Lifeworld. *Annals of the Association of American Geographers*, 66: 277–292.

Chawla, Louise, and Debra F. Cushing. 2007. Education for Strategic Environmental Behavior. *Environmental Education Research*, 13(4): 437–452.

Cooper, Clare. 1974. The House as Symbol of the Self. In J. Lang et al. (eds) *Designing for Human Behavior*. Stroudsberg, PA: Dowden, Hutchinson and Ross, pp. 130–146.

Cooper Marcus, Clare. 1992. Environmental Memories. In Irwin Altman and M. Setha Low (eds) *Place Attachment*. Human Behavior and Environment 12. New York: Springer, pp. 87–112.

Crenshaw, Kimberlé. 1996. Mapping the Margins: Intersectionality, Identity Politics, and Violence Against Women of Color. In Kimberlé Crenshaw, Neil Gotanda, and Garry Peller (eds) *Critical Race Theory: The Key Writings That Formed the Movement* . New York: The New Press, pp. 357–383.

Cuff, Dana, and John Wriedt (eds). 2010. Ar*chitecture From the Outside In: Selected Essays by Robert Gutman*. Princeton, NJ: Princeton Architectural Press.

Dewey, John. 2005. *Art as Experience*. New York: Berkley Publishing.

Diller, Elizabeth, and Ricardo Scofidio. 1996. *Flesh: Architectural Probes*. Princeton, NJ: Princeton Architectural Press.

Downs, Roger M. 1967. "Approaches to, and Problems in the Measurement of Geographical Space Perception," Seminar Paper, Series A, Number 9. Bristol: Department of Geography, University of Bristol.

Downs, Roger M., and David Stea. 1973. *Image and Environment: Cognitive Mapping and Spatial Behavior*. Chicago, IL: Aldine.

Dubos, René. 1965. *Man Adapting*. New Haven, CT: Yale University Press.

Feld, Steven. 1990. *Sound and Sentiment*. Philadelphia: University of Pennsylvania Press.

Feld, Steven, and Keith Basso. 1996. *The Senses of Place*. Santa Fe, New Mexico: School of American Research Press.

Fine, Michelle. 2010. Participatory Evaluation Research and Structural Racism. *Critical Issues Forum: Marking Progress/Movements Toward Racial Justice*. Washington, DC: Philanthropic Initiative for Racial Equity.

Fisher, Thomas R. 2006. *In The Scheme of Things: Alternative Thinking on the Practice of Architecture*. Minneapolis, MN: University Of Minnesota Press.

Forty, Adrian. 2004. *Words and Buildings: A Vocabulary of Modern Architecture*. New York: Thames & Hudson.

Foucault, Michel. 1990. *The History of Sexuality, Vol. 1: An Introduction*. New York: Vintage.

Friberg, Tora. 1993. *Everyday Life: Women's Adaptive Strategies in Time and Space*. Stockholm: Swedish Council for Building Research (trans. Madi Gray).

Gans, Herbert J. 1982a. *Urban Villagers*. New York: Simon and Schuster.

Gans, Herbert J. 1982b. *The Levittowners: Ways of Life and Politics in a New Suburban Community*. New York: Columbia University Press.

Geertz, Clifford. 1973. *The Interpretation of Cultures*. New York: Basic Books.

Gibson, James J. 1979. *Ecological Approaches to Visual Perception*. Boston, MA: Houghton Mifflin.

Giedion, Sigfried. 2009 [1940]. *Space, Time and Architecture: The Growth of a New Tradition*. Cambridge, MA: Harvard University Press.

Golledge, Reginald G. 1981. Misconceptions, Misinterpretations, and Misrepresentations of Behavioral Approaches In Human Geography. *Environment and Planning A*, 13: 1325–1344.

Golledge, Reginald G. (ed.). 1998. *Wayfinding Behavior: Cognitive Mapping and Other Spatial Processes*. Baltimore, MD: The Johns Hopkins University Press.

Gould, Peter, and Rodney White. 1986 [1974]. *Mental Maps* (2nd edn). London: Routledge.

Hägerstrand, Torsten. 1970. What About People in Regional Science? *Papers of the Regional Science Association*, 24: 1–12.

Hägerstrand, Torsten. 1978. Survival and Arena: On the Life History of Individuals in Relation to their Geographical Environment. In T. Carlstein, D. Parkes, and N. Thrift (eds) *Spacing Time and Timing Space, Vol. 2, Human Activity and Time-geography*. London: Edward Arnold, pp. 122–145.

Hall, Edward T. 1966. *The Hidden Dimension*. New York: Doubleday

Hart, Roger A. 1979. *Children's Experience of Place: A Developmental Study*. New York: Irvington Press.

Harvey, David. 1989. *The Condition of Postmodernity: An Enquiry into the Origins of Cultural Change*. Oxford: Wiley-Blackwell.

Hayden, Dolores. 1980. What Would a Non-sexist City Be Like? Speculations on Housing, Urban Design, and Human Work. *Signs: Journal of Women in Culture & Society*, 5(3): S170–S187.

Hayden, Dolores. 1981. *The Grand Domestic Revolution: A History of Feminist Designs for American Homes, Neighborhoods, and Cities*. Cambridge, MA: MIT Press.

Heft, Harry. 2001. *Ecological Psychology in Context. Part II. The Ecological Approach and Radical Empiricism*, pp. 105–193. Mahwah, NJ: Lawrence Erlbaum Associates.

Heider, Fritz. 1959. On Lewin's Methods and Theory. In *On Perception and Event Structure, and the Psychological Environment: Selected Papers*. New York: International Universities Press, Inc., pp. 108–120.

Jiménez, Alberto Corsín. 2003. On Space as a Capacity. *Royal Anthropological Institute*, 9:137–153.

Kates, Robert W., and Cindi Katz. 1977. The Hydrologic Cycle and the Wisdom of the Child. *Geographical Review*, 67: 51–62.

Kates, Robert W., and Joachiam F. Wohlwill (eds). 1966. Man's Response to the Physical Environment. *Journal of Social Issues*, 22(4) (special issue).

Katz, Cindi. 2004.*Growing Up Global: Economic Restructuring and Children's Everyday Lives*. Minneapolis: University of Minnesota Press.

Kirk, William. 1952. Historical Geography and the Concept of the Behavioural Environment. *Indian Geographical Journal*, 25: 152–160.

Kitchin, Roger M., Mark Blades, and Roger G. Golledge. 1997. Relations Between Psychology and Geography. *Environment and Behavior*, 29: 554–573.

Lavin, Sylvia. 2011. *Kissing Architecture*. Princeton, NJ: Princeton University Press.

Lewin, Kurt. 1951. Psychological Ecology. In Kurt Lewin *Field Theory in the Social Sciences*. New York: Harper & Row.

Lewin, Kurt, and Martin Gold (eds). 1999. *The Complete Social Scientist: A Kurt Lewin Reader*, pp. 333–345. Washington, DC: American Psychological Association.

Lorde, Audre, and Adrienne Rich. 1981. An Interview with Audre Lorde. *Signs: Journal of Women in Culture & Society*, 6(4): 713–736.

Low, Setha M., and Irwin Altman. 1992. Place Attachment. In Irwin Altman and Setha M. Low (eds) *Place Attachment*. Human Behavior and Environment, 12. New York: Springer, pp. 1–12.

Low, Setha, and Denise Lawrence-Ziziga. 2003. *The Anthropology of Space and Place: Locating Culture*. London: Blackwell Publishing.

Low, Setha, and Neil Smith (eds). 2005. *The Politics of Public Space*. New York: Routledge.

Lowenthal, David. 1961. Geography, Experience, and Imagination: Towards a Geographical Epistemology. *Annals of the Association of American Geographers*, 51(3): 241–260.

Manzo, Lynne C., and David D. Perkins. 2006. Finding Common Ground: The Importance of Place Attachment to Community Participation and Planning. *Journal of Planning Literature,* 20(4): 335–350.

Marston, Sallie A. 2000. The Social Construction of Scale. *Progress in Human Geography*, 24: 219–242.

Marston, Sallie A., John P. Jones III, and Keith Woodward. 2005. Human Geography without Scale. *Transactions of the Institute of British Geographers*, 30(4): 416–432.

Myers, Fred R. 2002. Ways of Place-Making. *La Ricerca Folklorica*, 45(April 1): 101–119.

Pallasmaa, Juhani. 2012 [1996]. *The Eyes of the Skin: Architecture and the Senses*. New York: Wiley.

Papanek, Victor J. 2012 [1971]. *Design for the Real World: Human Ecology and Social Change*. Chicago, IL: Academy Chicago Publishers.

Peterson, Marina. 2010. *Sound, Space and the City*. Philadelphia: University of Pennsylvania Press.

Pol, Enric. 2006. Blueprints for a History of Environmental Psychology: From First Birth to American Transition. *Medio Ambiente y Comportamiento Humano*, 7(2): 95–113.

Pred, Allan. 1977. The Choreography of Existence: Comments on Hägerstrand's Time-geography and its Usefulness. *Economic Geography*, 53(2): 207–221.

Pred, Allan. 1981. Social Reproduction and the Time-geography of Everyday Life. *Geografiska Annaler, Series B Human Geography*, 63(1): 5–22.

Pred, Allan. 1984. Place as Historically Contingent Process: Structuration and the Time-geography of Becoming Places. *Annals of the Association of American Geographers*, 74(2): 279–297.

Preiser, Wolfgang F., E. Harvey, Z. Rabinowitz, and Edward T. White. 1988. *Post-occupancy Evaluation*. New York: Van Nostrand Reinhold.

Proshansky, Harold M., William H. Ittelson, and Leanne G. Rivlin. (eds). 1970. *Environmental Psychology: Man and his Physical Setting*. New York: Holt, Rinehart and Winston.

Proshansky, Harold M., William H. Ittelson, and Leanne G. Rivlin (eds). 1976. *Environmental Psychology: People and their Physical Settings*. New York: Holt.

Rappaport, Amos. 1969. *House Form and Culture*. Englewood Cliffs, NJ: Prentice-Hall.

Rodman, Margaret. 1985. Moving Houses: Residential Mobility of Residents in Longana, Vanuatu. *American Anthropologist*, 87: 56–72.

Rodman, Margaret. 1992. Empowering Place: Multilocality and Multivocality. *American Anthropologist*, 94(3): 640–656.

Rose, Gillian. 1993. *Feminism and Geography*. Cambridge: Polity Press.

Saegert, Susan, and Gary Winkel. 1990. Environmental Psychology. In M.R. Rosenzweig, and L.W. Porter (eds) *Annual Review of Psychology*. Stanford, CA: Annual Review Press, pp. 441–478.

Scholten, Christina, Tora Friberg, and Annika Sandén. 2012. Re-reading Time-geography from a Gender Perspective: Examples from Gendered Mobility. *Tijdschrift voor Economische en Sociale Geografie*, 103(5): 584–600.

Schweizer-Ries, Petra, and David D. Perkins. 2012. Sustainability Science: Transdisciplinarity, Transepistemology, and Action Research. *Environmental Psychology*, 16: 6–11.

Scott, Felicity Dale Elliston. 2007. *Architecture or Techno-utopia: Politics after Modernism*. Cambridge, MA: MIT Press.

Sheppard, Eric and Robert B. McMaster (eds). 2004. *Scale and Geographic Inquiry*. Oxford: Blackwell.

Smith, Neil. 1993. Homeless/Global: Scaling Places. In J. Bird, B. Curtis, T. Putnam, G. Robertson, and L. Tickner (eds) *Mapping the Futures: Local Cultures, Global Change*. London: Routledge, pp. 87–119.

Sommeila, Laraine, and Maxine Wolfe. 1997. "This Is About People Dying: The Tactics of Early ACT UP and Lesbian Avengers in New York City" (An Interview with Maxine Wolfe by Laraine Sommeila). In Gordon Brent Ingram, Anne-Marie Bouthillette and Yolanda Retter (eds) *Queers in Space: Communities, Public Places, Sites of Resistance*. Seattle, WA: Bay Press, pp. 407–438.

Sommer, Robert. 1969. *Personal Space: The Behavioral Basis of Design*. Lebanon, IN: Prentice Hall Trade.

Thorpe, Ann. 2012. *Architecture & Design Versus Consumerism: How Design Activism Confronts Growth*. New York: Routledge.

Tindal, Margaret. 1971. *The Home Range of Black Elementary School Children: An Exploratory Study in the Measurement and Comparison of Home Range, Place Perception Research Report 8*. Chicago, IL: Environmental Research Group.

Tuan, Yi-Fu. 1974. *Topophilia: A Study of Environmental Perception, Attitudes, and Values*. New York: Prentice-Hall.

Tuan, Yi-Fu. 1977. *Space and Place: The Perspective of Experience*. Minneapolis: University of Minnesota Press.

Weinthal, Lois. 2011. *Toward a New Interior/An Anthology of Interior Design Theory*. New York: Princeton Architectural Press.

Wood, Denis. 1992. *The Power of Maps*. New York: Guilford Press.

Wood, Denis. 2006. Kids and Space in the Puerto Rican Highlands. *The Geographical Review*, 92(2): 229–258.

Wood, Denis. 2010. Lynch Debord: About Two Psychogeographies. *Cartografica*, 45(3): 185–200.

Wood, Denis, and Robert J. Beck. 1994. *Home Rules*. Baltimore, MD: The Johns Hopkins University Press.

Wood, Les J. 1970. Perception Studies in Geography. *Transactions of the Institute of British Geographers*, 50: 129–142.

Zeisel, John. 2006. *Inquiry by Design: Environment/Behavior/Neuroscience in Architecture, Interiors, Landscape, and Planning*. New York: Norton.

Zumthor, Peter. 2010. *Thinking Architecture*. Basel: Birkhäuser Architecture.

SECTION 1

Diverse Conceptions between People, Place, and Space

Photograph of La Marketa (Moore Street Market), Brooklyn, NY.
Source: Amanda Matles, 2012, Brooklyn, NY.
Referenced in: Low, Setha. 2014. "Spatializing Culture," in *The People, Place and Space Reader*. New York: Routledge.

DIVERSE CONCEPTIONS BETWEEN PEOPLE, PLACE, AND SPACE

The essays in this section serve as entry points into the ongoing and interdisciplinary conversation about how people, place, and space are produced, perceived, and experienced. The authors share a common starting point: space and place are not fixed or innate but rather created and re-created through the actions and meanings of people. This critical understanding of space and place confirms our agency and responsibility in producing these spaces, as well as the social relations that are enabled through this approach. Gathering perspectives from sociology, geography, psychology, architecture, history, and anthropology encourages different approaches to uncovering underlying assumptions about people, place, and space. The writings examine these relationships in fresh ways and from radically different vantage points, gaining insights from varied methods and interpretations, and to enact new meanings and purposeful change.

Space and place are co-produced through many dimensions: race and class, urban and suburban, gender and sexuality, public and private, bodies and buildings. Feminist geographer, architect, and philosopher **Susan Ruddick** begins with an examination of the multi-layered relationship of power and place around the highly publicized 1990 shooting at Just Deserts in a Toronto mall. Ruddick unpacks the media attention to this tragic story through dimensions of public space and dynamics of power. She argues how the shooting of a middle-class, white woman by a black, male immigrant is used to create fear about public space, especially for women, and hatred and fear of non-white people and those marked outsiders like immigrants. The author spatializes Kimberlé Crenshaw's (1996) concept of *intersectionality* to show how different identities interconnect with spaces to form different situations. Ruddick shows that the media frenzy around the event was related to what Neil Smith (1992) calls *jumping scale*. The concept of jumping scale explains how an issue at the level of a place can be magnified to commodify and objectify difference, at the same time that society rejects that difference. In this way, places are produced as raced, sexualized, classed, nationalized, ethnicized, and gendered through mechanisms of oppression, and, at the same time, these qualities are projected on to other spaces and places at different scales and these attitudes affect how we see ourselves.

Geographer **David Harvey** articulates three dimensions through which we experience and produce space and time in order to unpack what *space* really means. Rather than a pre-existing container or environment, Harvey finds it most beneficial to work from the idea that space is socially produced (see Lefebvre 1991, Section 9), for which he identifies three simultaneous and mutually produced dimensions. The first dimension is what Harvey refers to as *absolute space and time*, where every person and object occupies a particular point on a universal and mathematically describable grid. The second view of space describes the *relative space-time* of a journey, or flows of information or commodities. While the absolute space between two places may remain fixed, the relative space changes due to changes in technology or access. The third view of space is *relational spacetime*. Harvey suggests that spatial meaning comes through the memories and attachments we forge through relationships.

Social and critical psychologist **Kurt Lewin** is interested in how social, economic, and political experiences overlap with and co-produce the psychological elements of our everyday ecologies. He argues that these structures and processes come together to establish the status quo of different places, and demonstrates this using the example of why we eat what we eat. Writing in 1943, Lewin draws on the lifestyles of low-, medium-, and high-income "housewives," as well as groups of Czech immigrants and African Americans. Bridging the structural social system and everyday environments and experiences of seemingly banal actions, he demonstrates how decision-making processes, structural influences, and power dynamics interdependently effect how food makes its way from outside of the home to the kitchen table through *gatekeepers* (housewives) and *organized institutions* (the flow of social life through specific channels). Changes are produced by the social and cultural rules and economic limits upon and cognitive and motivational tendencies of gatekeepers. Lewin's study is one example of how he understands the *lifespace* as the social-psychological situations of decision-making and the interrelated ways in which identities, health, and power operate. The psychic lifespace resides in a larger ecology of institutions, cultural norms and roles, and interactions among different people. Together the individual lifespace and the broader ecology form a field of transactions, exchanges, and emotional valences.

While social, economic, political, and psychological dynamics shape our environments, the physical spaces are created through processes of design and planning. Architect **Rem Koolhaas** uses the term *junkspace* to describe what is being produced in the constant destruction and construction of our environments. Highlighting the consequences of air-conditioning and other technologies, Koolhaas argues that junkspace is hopelessly casual, a flow without order; it pretends to unite but actually splinters people, places, and experiences. His criticism of contemporary built space—in his writing and his design projects—is articulated through a technique of *over-identification* that exaggerates a situation to its most extreme in order to amplify the issues (see BAVO 2007). This selection looks at an airport, and traces the situations and encounters one may face in simply going from here to there.

Installation artist **Miwon Kwon** likewise questions the layers and meanings of contemporary places. While showing that site-specific art installations have the possibility of being a grounded way of thinking about place, they also may be commodified and manipulated to represent other intentions. Building from the knowledge that all stories are rooted in place, Kwon describes how art that starts with site can tell new narratives and re-imagine possibilities, while also asking questions about originality and authenticity. Investigating the specific qualities of each site, what Kwon calls the *relational specificity* of a piece of art to its site, reveals the processes, structures, and institutions that shape and define the space and art. Kwon's concept helps us to see how art can be a lens to unpack gender, race, and class as well as the social, economic, and political processes that are created and play out within places.

Another way to examine space and place is through its social and cultural dimensions. Anthropologist **Setha Low** suggests that *spatializing culture* is a way of revealing how social relations are grounded by aspects of space and place. By studying the political economy of the production of space as well as the construction of its sociocultural and personal meaning, she demonstrates the social complexity of interactions of people and the built environment and how everyday realities are enacted historically, translocally, and personally. The ethnographic study of Moore Street Market in Brooklyn, New York, a Puerto Rican and Latino city landmark, is at the same time part of an idealized past that is still relevant today (see figure at the beginning of Section 1). Her findings highlight the way in which the urban milieu, moving bodies, and historically produced spaces work together to create a translocal space that is both in New York City but also in Mexico City or San Juan, Puerto Rico. What Low calls *embodied space* extends notions of the social production and construction of space to account for the mobility of people as their own spatial fields and the meanings of those spaces and places.

As may be seen from these readings, the relationships between people and place have many facets—psychological, social, physical, and cultural—and include structural and institutional forces that may originate in distant places or times. Even the way we talk about space has various dimensions in the ways in which it can be understood as simultaneously fixed, relative, and relational. The activities people engage in, the meanings they give spaces, and the opportunities open to them are all informed by the complex dynamics embodied in places and spaces. Basing his concept on over a year's-worth of observations of the entire population of a small town in the Midwestern US in the 1940s, psychologist Roger Barker (1991) posited the theory of *behavior settings* whereby certain settings inform if not enforce certain types of behaviors, such as students entering a classroom being inclined to sit at desks and raise their hands to speak. Some of these theories about how people experience and produce space have shifted over time, often moving increasingly away from frameworks of environmental determinism (Wicker 1991) to argue for the role of human agency in producing spaces and enacting justice. Tony Hiss (1991), writing vividly about Grand Central Terminal, suggests we experience a form of *simultaneous perception*, whereby the combined responses of our senses alter and enrich our perception of the world. Peter Zumthor (2010) identifies similar feelings in environments that have special significance, and asks whether these places have a soul. As we grow with this literature, it is useful to pull these threads apart to examine them more closely to better understand the fascinating dynamics at work in the relationship between people and place. In doing so, we can learn more about the values that shape the environment, and which conversely shape us.

SUGGESTIONS FOR FURTHER READING

Please see *peopleplacespace.org* for extended and additional lists of readings.

Barker, Roger. 1991. "Prospecting in Environmental Psychology: Oskaloosa Revisited." In *Handbook of Environmental Psychology, Volume II*, edited by Daniel Stokols and Irwin Altman, pp. 1413–1432. New York: Krieger Publishing.

Basso, Keith H., and Steven Feld. 2009. *Senses of Place*. Santa Fe, NM: School of American Research Press.

BAVO (eds). 2007. *Cultural Activism Today: The Art of Over-identification*. Rotterdam: Episode Publishers.

Casey, Edward S. 2009. *Getting Back into Place: Toward a Renewed Understanding of the Place-world*. Bloomington: Indiana University Press.

Crenshaw, Kimberlé. 1996. "Mapping the Margins: Intersectionality, Identity Politics, and Violence Against Women of Color." In *Critical Race Theory: The Key Writings That Formed the Movement*, edited by Kimberlé Crenshaw, Neil Gotanda, and Garry Peller, pp. 357–383. New York: The New Press.

Danze, Elizabeth, and Stephen Sonnenberg (eds). 2013. *Space & Psyche*. Center, No. 17. Austin: Center for American Architecture and Design, University of Texas at Austin.

Dean, Tacita, and Jeremy Millar. 2005. *Place*. London: Thames & Hudson.

Forty, Adrian. 2004. *Words and Buildings: A Vocabulary of Modern Architecture*. London: Thames & Hudson.

Hensel, Michael, Achim Menges, and Christopher Hight. 2009. *Space Reader: Heterogeneous Space in Architecture*. Chichester, U.K.: Wiley.

Hiss, Tony. 1991. "Simultaenous Perception." In *The Experience of Place: A New Way of Looking at and Dealing With Our Radically Changing Cities and Countryside*, pp. 3–26. New York: Vintage.

Jackson, John Brinckerhoff. 2000. *Landscape in Sight: Looking at America*, edited by Helen Lefkowitz Horowitz. New Haven, CT: Yale University Press.

Kitchin, Rob, and Martin Dodge. 2011. *Code/Space Software and Everyday Life*. Cambridge, Mass: MIT Press.

Mitchell, Don. 1996. *Lie of the Land: Migrant Workers and the California Landscape*. Minneapolis: University of Minnesota Press.

Proshansky, Harold M., William H. Ittleson, and Leanne G. Rivlin (eds). 1970. *Environmental Psychology: Man and His Physical Setting*. New York: Holt, Rinehart & Winston.

Read, Ian (ed.). 2000. *Architecturally Speaking: Practices of Art, Architecture and the Everyday*. Abingdon: Routledge.

Rivlin, Leanne. 1987. "The Neighborhood, Personal Identity, and Group Affiliations." In *Neighborhood and Community Environments*, edited by Irwin Altman and Abraham Wandersman, pp. 1–34. New York: Plenum Press.

Rose, Gillian. 1993. *Feminism and Geography: The Limits of Geographical Knowledge*. Minneapolis: University of Minnesota Press.

Smith, Neil. 1992. "Contours of a Spatialized Politics: Homeless Vehicles and the Production of Geographical Space." *Social Text*, 33: 54–81.

Soja, Edward W. 2011. *Postmodern Geographies: The Reassertion of Space in Critical Social Theory (2nd edn)*. New York: Verso.

Sparke, Penny. 2008. *The Modern Interior*. London: Reaktion Books.

Tuan, Yi-Fu, and Steven Hoelscher. 2001. *Space and Place: The Perspective of Experience*. Minneapolis: University of Minnesota Press.

Uexküll, Jacob von, Joseph D. O'Neill, Dorion Sagan, and Geoffrey Winthrop-Young. 2010. *A Foray into the Worlds of Animals and Humans with A Theory of Meaning*. Minneapolis: University of Minnesota Press.

Wicker, Allen W. 1991. "Behavior Settings Reconsidered: Temporal Stages, Resources, Internal Dynamics, Context." In *Handbook of Environmental Psychology, Volume I*, edited by Daniel Stokols and Irwin Altman, pp. 613–654. New York: Krieger Publishing.

Zumthor, Peter. 2010. *Thinking Architecture (3rd edn)*. Basel: Birkhäuser Architecture.

1
Constructing Differences in Public Spaces

Race, Class, and Gender as Interlocking Systems (1996)

Susan Ruddick

Nearly two years ago, on April 5, 1994, in downtown Toronto, two patrons of a trendy coffee house called Just Desserts were assaulted in an armed robbery that left one, a young woman, dead and sent the other, an older man, to hospital. The slaying of Vivi Leimonis in the Just Desserts robbery provoked a massive outrage and grief, beginning with the demonstration outside the Café of about 200 citizens who demanded action, and continuing in a public display of grief at the victim's funeral where thousands—some estimate as many as 3,500 people—turned out to mourn her death (Millar, 1994). The reporting of this crime contributed to its construction as a shared public event, with graphic layouts of the restaurant and sketches of the approximate location of perpetrators and victims, and intimate details fixing both the time and space of where the robbers entered and when they left.

Just five months before the Just Desserts shooting, an equally brutal event struck the city of Toronto. Here a man entered a West End after-hours fast-food establishment, known as the Whip Burger Menu, stalking his girlfriend. Frustrated at not finding her there, he began to shoot the patrons as they cowered beneath the tables, killing two and wounding five others (DiMano, 1994). This man, a landed immigrant, had a criminal record of two assaults, both committed after being granted landed status in Canada. The profanity of this crime, however, was met with barely a comment within the larger community of Metro.

The "Just Desserts shooting," as it came to be called, was one of a spate of recent, highly publicized assaults in public spaces in major North American cities. These include the manslaughter of an Asian woman in the wealthy village and shopping enclave of Westwood on the west side of Los Angeles in the mid-1980s (Davis with Ruddick, 1988), and a few years later the assault and rape of an affluent white woman jogging in Central Park in New York by three teenagers (hooks, 1990). Unlike the other two assaults in Toronto cited above, these galvanized public outrage and concern and became the focus of extended debate and report in the media.

Why did these crimes receive so much media attention? Why did they capture the imaginations, and come to represent the collective angst, of their local communities?

First among these is the assumption that public spaces are universally accessible to a civic public. In fact, as recent scholars of urban life have noted, gendered and racialized identities function to constrain participation in the public sphere (Young, 1990; Anderson, 1995). As this paper demonstrates, an examination of the events surrounding the Just Desserts shooting and other spectacular crimes suggests that processes by which gendering and racializing occur are highly interdependent, feeding off of and reinforcing one another in what has been called an *interlocking matrix of power relations* (Collins, 1990). In uncovering these processes, moreover, one must be mindful of the way that gendered and racialized identities vary across time and space.

The second assumption addresses the scale at which public space is commonly understood to function. Public spaces have tended to be equated with the local level, functioning within the neighborhood or urban community, circumscribed within processes that operate at regional, national, and international scales. In fact, the Just Desserts shooting suggests that the scale at which public space is constituted is not foreordained, but is itself a political construction. The "scaling of public spaces" and what Young calls the scaling of bodies, the "structural patterns of group privilege and oppression" (Young, 1990, pp. 166–167), are interdependent, intricately bound up with one another.

RACE, GENDER, AND CLASS AS INTERLOCKING SYSTEMS

Geographers have moved beyond viewing gender, race, and class as distinct categories that operate independently in an additive fashion. These now are recognized as intersecting categories: as several theorists have noted, these categories are mutually *transformative*, and *intersecting*, each altering the experience of the other. Scholars began to investigate, for instance, the ways that race altered the experience of gender, with black women and white women confronted with experiences of gendered relationships that marked systemic similarities and differences in their roles as women (McDowell, 1991).

Scholars in black and cultural studies and black feminist writers have moved this analysis one step further, from an understanding of how gender, race, and class *intersect within* individuals in the structuring of social identities to an analysis of how these positions *interlock between* individuals, as notions of the appropriate roles and behaviors of different social groups have evolved in relation to one another, in what they call *interlocking systems* of oppression. For instance, whereas one can see that the experience of gender differs for white and black women, as McDowell has noted, the identification of interlocking systems analyzes how these differences evolved in relation to one another, each predicated upon the other.

If public space is to become a place where these constructs can be confronted or transformed, as a minimum first step we must become mindful of how these images serve to prefigure unplanned encounters, to reaffirm constructs and images of subject and object, to "catch the imagination" of the public. In this regard, an analysis of the media becomes a critical tool in instructing the public how it should think about such encounters. It is one discursive medium through which such images are generated and maintained, representing interactions to the public at large.

REASSESSING THE JUST DESSERTS SHOOTING

The Just Desserts shooting bears examination in some detail, as it illustrates some of the issues outlined above concerning the structuring of social identities in and through public space. Why did this crime resonate so deeply within the Metro community? Why did it provoke a discussion about the loopholes in the immigration system and debates about the competency of the Immigration Review Board? In both the Just Desserts shooting and the Whip Burger Menu shooting, the perpetrators were landed immigrants. In the Just Desserts case, however, the perpetrator, Victor Augustus Brown, was 25 years old, and had emigrated to Canada in 1976, when he was only 5 or 6. The assailant had lived in Canada nearly three times as long as in his home country, and had entered at just about the time he would begin in the Canadian school system. This fact led critics of the discussion to argue that this was not a problem of *immigration* policy (who should be let in and who should be left out) but rather *immigrant* policy (what programs should be offered to individuals once they arrive here) and should trigger a reexamination of education, job training, and an entire range of programs to ease adaptation to Canadian society. Counter-arguments were launched in the press, citing the first five to eight years of a child's life as being crucial to development of personality—supporting the notion that Victor Augustus Brown was not "Canada's problem," but rather the problem of his country of origin, Jamaica. Moreover, the incident was a catalyst for the formation of a special squad of immigration and police, whose mandate was to track down those immigrants with criminal records who had eluded deportation (Greenwood, 1995). The point here is not that such a squad was not justified, but rather that other murders such as the Whip Burger incident, described above, had failed to elicit the same response.

The Just Desserts incident became a site for contestation of meaning around several images: that of black male, of immigrant, and of nation. Following the incident, debates ensued within the local media and representative groups among the Greek community and black communities, addressing both the incident and how the incident should properly be reported.

When discussing the imagery that underlies relational construction of racialized groups in the Canadian media, one cannot ignore the role the American media plays as an implicit and explicit reference point. Even when the Canadian context is understood to be different, when attempts are made to distinguish social groups and events as they are constituted within Canada, a chain of equivalence often is drawn before it is debunked, and pains are then taken to establish distinction and difference. General discussions about Canadian-ness that arose in the 1960s and early 1970s took pains to distinguish the Canadian mosaic from the American melting pot (Kobayashi, 1993, p. 213). In discussions of more specific events, such as Toronto's reaction to the Rodney King verdict, including protest and smashing and looting of shops along Young Street, the event was portrayed as "like" and "not like" the more massive unrest in Los Angeles. Or, in other reporting, attention to the growing "gang problem" in Canadian cities or rising violence in schools is accompanied by extended debates about the similarities and differences with the American experience.

Here bell hooks offers us some insights into a way to proceed, noting the powerful cultural currency that shaped media response to the Central Park case, specifically the image of black men as a menace to society (hooks, 1990, pp. 61–64). Certainly, like the incident in Central Park, the reporting of the Just Desserts shooting in Toronto's *Sun* resounded with this imagery, playing upon the gendered and racialized nature of the assault—wherein a young, black, unknown male marauder killed a young white woman—and resonated with the gendered and racialized trope of the dangerous black male who threatens the integrity of the white community through sexual or physical violence to its women. The biographies that surfaced in the reporting of that crime featured images of a young, beautiful 23-year-old blonde woman, not yet married, casually murdered without provocation by a disheveled black drifter (Burnett, 1994; Stewart, 1994).

The surfacing and resurfacing of variants of this myth in different historical periods and its inscription in particular geographies is no doubt attributable to several complex causes. However, there are some interesting parallels between the contemporary period, the past 20 years, and the turn of the century; both times were periods of high immigration to North American cities, and both were coincident with the incorporation of "white" women in large numbers into the labor force, then into clerical work (and now the professions), causing them to leave their homes for the "dangers" of the city. In Canadian cities such as Toronto and Winnipeg, as Marianne Valverde points out, a moral panic around the perceived threat to the purity of white women was coincident with their entry into the clerical labor force (Valverde, 1993).

It was in the context of this opposition to attempts to racialize the shooting that arguments around "black crime" and the "black threat to the white community" were deflected into a more covertly racialized discussion about immigration. The latter became the basis of policy initiatives such as the formation of a special squad of immigration police whose mandate was to track down those immigrants with criminal records who had alluded deportation (Greenwood, 1995).

The second myth raised by the Just Desserts shooting is one that we might call the "good immigrant." As an internal colonizer of its native peoples, Canada's nationhood has been founded on the myth of a celebration of "immigrants whose past and future rests on the attraction of new settlers" (Smith, 1993, p. 52). If, as Susan Smith has observed, immigration is the very tool of nation building in Canada, then distinctions that enhance selectivity become a critical tool in that process. This second myth, which might be interpreted as the polite Canadian version of American racism, encodes the distinctions of white and black in references to European and "new immigrant communities," or, more subtly, in an ethnic referent that reflects a repositioning of immigrant communities—the good, traditional immigrants (currently, Pan-European immigrants) versus the potentially dangerous ones (currently, more recent Third World immigrants).

The particular Canadian quality of racialization of this crime was, to borrow from Neil Smith (1993), predicated on a jumping of scales at which the identity of the criminals was constructed: Brown was repositioned as immigrant, neatly sidestepping any allusions to an explicitly racialized discourse. This jumping of scales was accompanied by a repositioning of the public space itself: both as representative of citywide spaces accessed by the middle class, and as a national space under threat by criminalized immigrants.

In this regard, the vehemence of the reaction to the Just Desserts shooting can be attributed in part to the location of the coffee shop in which the crime occurred. As a venue described as a trendy upscale coffee shop, located on the edge of a gentrified neighborhood, the eastern end of the Annex, Just Desserts might be considered a venue frequented by the new middle class: "[a] little neon lit place at the rather genteel corner of Davenport and Bedford Roads … [in] mid-town Toronto, in a posh enclave of nice stores and townhomes and lovely small streets … [advertised as] the meeting place of the nineties" (Blatchford, 1994a).

An attack on Just Desserts was seen to compromise the freedom of middle-class families to move without fear through the city. This commercialized public space was, in this depiction, elevated to the status of every space in the city, a connection that was not drawn in previous or subsequent robberies in the restaurant districts in the city's Chinatown, nor in the Whip Burger shooting. In this case, the location of the Just Desserts coffee shop in an area frequented by the middle class—a "front region" of the city—and bordering a middle-class neighborhood, set in motion a dynamic that depicted the space as belonging to "everyone" and, by extension, making "everyone" a potential victim of the crime that took place there (Blatchford, 1994a, 1994b; Lamberti, 1994; Lem, 1994). This exercise arguably would not have been undertaken had the crime been committed in a poorer community. Scales were jumped a second time in the representation of the crime as "American-style murder" and the repositioning of the criminals (in particular, Brown) as immigrant, i.e., outsider.

RECONCEPTUALIZING PUBLIC SPACE

This examination of the Just Desserts shooting suggests several ways in which we might reconceptualize public space. First, it suggests that the representation of public space is deeply implicated in the process of othering: the way in which certain others are represented in public spaces is not simply a byproduct of other structures of inequity; it is deeply constitutive of our sense of community—who is allowed in, who is excluded, and what roles should be ascribed to "insiders" and "outsiders."

As such, the events surrounding the Just Desserts shooting do more than raise issues about the construction of social identity in and through public space. They raise questions about the nature of public space itself. Yet even a cursory examination of these events suggests several properties that differentiate certain "public" spaces from others—in terms of their ascribed economic and symbolic functions and the meanings that different groups attempt to assign them in the course of a conflict.

Second, and related to the first point, the role that the space plays in class strategies for reproduction also is a critical element: those spaces that function as recreational and leisure areas for the new middle class carry with them different political dynamics than those that serve lower-income groups. Finally, the scale at which public space is constituted is not predetermined, but itself involves a political act. In much of the literature on the subject, public space is assumed to be intrinsically local and particular, situated within a nested hierarchy: public space (i.e., park, street)/neighborhood/city/region/nation. And yet, as these events show, public spaces do far more than inscribe images about local and particular events: they can and do become a medium through which regional, national, and even international identities are constructed or contested.

REFERENCES

Anderson, Elijah, 1995, Street etiquette and street wisdom. In P. Kasinitz (ed.) *Metropolis. Center and Symbol of Our Times.* Washington Square, NY: New York University Press, pp. 331–355.

Blatchford, Christie, 1994a, Good vs. evil. *The Toronto Sun,* April 7, p. 5.

Blatchford, Christie, 1994b, Innocence lost. *The Toronto Sun,* April 7, p. 16.

Burnett, Thane, 1994, Quiet life shattered. *The Toronto Sun,* April 7, p. 5.

Collins, Patricia, 1990, *Black Feminist Thought: Knowledge, Consciousness and the Politics of Empowerment*. New York: Routledge.

Davis, Mike, with Susan Ruddick, 1988, Los Angeles: Civil liberties between the hammer and the rock. *New Left Review*, No. 170: 37–61.

DiMano, Rosie, 1994, The politics of fear. *Toronto Star*, October 1, Section B.

Greenwood, H., 1995, Defense lawyers want say in Just Desserts trial bid. *The Toronto Star*, August 11, p. A5.

hooks, bell, 1990, *Yearning Race, Gender, and Cultural Politics*. Toronto: Between the Lines.

Kobayashi, Audrey, 1993, Multiculturalism: Representing a Canadian institution. In J. Duncan and D. Ley (eds) *Place/Culture/Representation*. London and New York: Routledge, pp. 205–231.

Lamberti, Ron, 1994, Lowest of the low: Chief. *The Toronto Sun*, April 7, p. 18.

Lem, Sharon, 1994, It's just so sick. *The Toronto Sun*, April 7, p. 5.

McDowell, Linda, 1991, The baby and the bath water: Diversity, deconstruction and feminist theory in geography. *Geoforum*, Vol. 22: 123–133.

Millar, Cal, 1994, Suspect is named in Vivi's slaying. *The Toronto Star*, April 12, p. A1.

Smith, Neil, 1993, Homeless/global: Scaling places. In J. Bird et al. (eds) *Mapping the Futures. Local Cultures, Global Change*. London and New York: Routledge, pp. 87–119.

Stewart, M., 1994, Stymied. *The Toronto Sun*, April 14, p. 5.

Valverde, Mariana, 1993, *The Age of Light, Soap, and Water. Moral Reform in English Canada, 1885–1925*. Toronto: McClelland and Stewart, Inc.

Young, Iris Marion., 1990, *Justice and the Politics of Difference*. Princeton, NJ: Princeton University Press.

2
Spacetime and the World
(2005)

David Harvey

The word *space* internalizes multiple meanings. Confusions arise because different meanings get conflated in inadmissible ways. Sorting out these confusions is essential to the clarification of all manner of substantive issues. I would likewise claim that many of the key terms we use to characterize the world around us—such as *city, state, community, neighborhood, ecosystem* and *region*—cannot properly be understood without a prior consideration of the character of both time and space. It is in this sense that I believe Kant was correct to regard a proper knowledge of geography—in this instance, the proper characterization of space and time—as a necessary precondition as well as the ultimate end-point of all forms of human enquiry.

In what follows, I outline a view of space in relation to time that draws in the first instance upon my own practical work on issues of urbanization and uneven geographical development at a variety of scales (from imperialism to social relations in the city). This view has also been shaped by a partial reading of the long history of philosophical debate on the nature of space and time, as well as by scrutinizing the more recent inquiries of many geographers, anthropologists, sociologists, and literary theorists on the subject.

The summary framework to which I appeal operates across two dimensions. On the first, we encounter three distinctive ways of understanding space and time: absolute, relative, and relational. Across the second dimension, we encounter another three definitions (most notably argued for by Lefebvre); space as materially sensed, conceptualized, and lived. I shall go on to argue that space is constituted by the integration of all these definitions. These different ways of understanding space must be kept in dialectical tension with each other if we are to understand how concepts of space and time condition our possibilities, as Kant would put it, to understand the world around us.

THE FIRST DIMENSION

Absolute space is fixed and immovable. This is the space of Newton and Descartes. Space is understood as a preexisting, immovable, continuous, and unchanging framework (most easily visualized as a grid) within which distinctive objects can be clearly identified, and events and processes accurately described. It is initially understood as empty of matter. This is the space to which Euclidian geometry could most easily be adapted. It is amenable to standardized measurement and open to calculation. It is the space of cadastral mapping, Newtonian mechanics, and its derivative engineering practices. It is a primary space of individuation—*res extensa*, as Descartes put it. Individual persons and things, for example, can clearly be identified in terms of the unique location they occupy in absolute space and time. No other person can be exactly in your or my space at a given time. Location in absolute space and time is, therefore, the means to identify the individuality and uniqueness of persons, things, and processes. Distinctive places, for example, can be identified (named) by their unique location on a map. Within this conception, measurement and calculability thrive. When Descartes's engineer looked upon the world with a sense of mastery, it was a world of absolute space (and time) from which all uncertainties and ambiguities could in principle be banished and in which human calculation could uninhibitedly flourish. Socially, absolute space is the exclusionary space of private property in land and other bounded entities (such as states, administrative units, city plans, and urban grids). Bounded spaces can be conceptualized as containers of power. Space of this sort is clearly distinguishable from time. Spatial ordering is one thing. Absolute time unfolding on a linear line stretching to an infinite future is another. History, from this perspective, has to be construed as distinct from geography. This was, as we have seen, Kant's view, so although he departed from Newton in grounding knowledge of space and time in the intuition of the synthetic a priori, he followed the Newtonian separations of space and time in practice.

Relative space is mainly associated with the name of Albert Einstein and the non-Euclidean geometries that began to be constructed most systematically in the nineteenth century. This is preeminently the space of *processes and motion*. Space cannot here be understood separately from time. History and geography cannot be separated. All geography is historical geography, and all history is geographical history. This mandates an important shift of language from absolute space *and* absolute time to the hyphenated concept of relative space-time. The relative space-time of transportation relations and of commodity and monetary circulation looks and is very different from the absolute spaces of private property. The uniqueness of location and individuation defined by bounded territories in absolute space gives way to a multiplicity of locations that are equidistant from, say, some central city location in terms of time it takes to move to and from that location. Relative identity is multiple rather than singular. Many people can be in the same place relative to me, and I can be in exactly the same place as many other people relative to someone else. We can create completely different maps of relative locations by differentiating between distances measured in terms of cost, time, or modal split (car, bicycle, or skateboard), and we can even disrupt spatial continuities by looking at networks and topological relations (the optimal route for the postman delivering mail, or the airline system operating through key hubs). We know, given the differential frictions

of distance encountered on the earth's surface, that the shortest distance (measured in terms of time, cost, energy expended) between two points is not necessarily given by the way the legendary crow flies. Furthermore, the standpoint of the observer plays a critical role in establishing perspectives. The typical New Yorker's view of the world, as the famous Steinberg cartoon suggests, fades very fast as one thinks about the lands to the west of the Hudson River or east of Long Island.

All of this relativization does not necessarily reduce or eliminate the capacity for individuation or control, but it does indicate that special rules and laws are required for the particular phenomena and processes under consideration. Measurability and calculability become more complicated. There are multiple geometries from which to choose. The spatial frame varies according to what is relativized and by whom. When Gauss first established the rules of a non-Euclidean spherical geometry to deal with the problems of surveying accurately upon the curved surface of the earth, he also affirmed Euler's assertion that a perfectly scaled map of any portion of the earth's surface is impossible. If maps accurately represent directions, then they falsify areas (Greenland looks larger than India on the Mercator map). Each map projection tells its relative truth, even though it is mathematically correct and objective. Einstein took the argument further by pointing out that all forms of measurement depended upon the frame of reference of the observer.

Relative space-time frameworks are not necessarily stable, either. New technologies of transport and communications have historically and geographically transformed spatio–temporal relations. Relative distances of social interaction and communication between New York, London, and Paris have changed radically over time. Relative locations have shifted, sometimes rapidly, as a result.

The idea that processes produce their own space and time is fundamental to the relational conception. This idea is most often associated theoretically with the name of Leibniz who, in a famous series of letters to Clarke (effectively a stand-in for Newton), objected vociferously to the absolute view so central to Newton's theories. Leibniz's primary objection was theological. Newton made it seem as if God were inside a preexisting space and time, rather [than] the maker of space-time through the creation of matter. The absolute view diminished God's stature. Our contemporary version of this controversy would ask whether the supposed big bang origin of the universe occurred in space and time or whether it was the creation of space-time.

In the relational view, matter and processes do not exist *in* space-time or even affect it (as in the case of relative space-time). Space and time are internalized within matter and process. It is impossible to disentangle space from time. They fuse into spacetime (the hyphen disappears). Memories and dreams are the stuff of such a fusion. How can we understand things, events, processes in terms of the relational spacetime they produce? Identifications and individuation become problematic, if not seemingly impossible. An event, process, or thing cannot be understood by appeal to what exists only at some point. It (the event, process, or thing) crystallizes out of a field of flows into what Whitehead calls either "an event" or "a permanence." But in so doing "it" internalizes everything going on around it within that field of flows, in past, present, and even future. Many individuals assembled in a room to consider political strategies, for example, bring to their discussion within that absolute space a vast array of past experiences, memories, and dreams accumulated directly or indirectly (through reading, for example) from their engagements with the world, as well as a wide array of anticipations and hopes about the future. Under the relational view disparate influences flow from everywhere to everywhere else. These influences can, at least momentarily, congeal to form "monads" (Leibniz's preferred term), or "events" or "permanences" at identifiable "moments" (in Whitehead's terms). Identity here means something quite different from the sense we have of it from absolute space or even in relative space-time. It becomes open, fluid, multiple, and indeterminate. Identities become, in short, "immaterial but objective." But that is how we live day by day.

What can this possibly mean for everyday understandings and practices? Consider a few examples where the relational conception makes intuitive sense. If we ask, along with Whitehead, what is the time and space of a thought or a memory, then we are hard pressed to find a material answer. But if the thoughts and memories are themselves immaterial, fluid, and unstable, they can and often do have solid material and hence objective consequences when they animate action.

In relational spacetime, direct measurement is problematic, if not impossible. But why should we believe that spacetime only exists if it is quantifiable and measurable? Dreams and memories cannot be dismissed as irrelevant because we cannot quantify and measure their spacetime. Relational conceptions bring us to the point where mathematics, poetry, and music merge, where dreams, daydreams, memories, and fantasies flourish.

But why and how would I, as a working geographer, find the relational mode of approaching spacetime useful? The answer is quite simply that there are certain topics, such as the political role of collective memories in urban processes, that can be approached only in this way. I cannot box collective memories in some absolute space (clearly situate them on a grid or a map), nor can I understand their circulation according to the rules, however sophisticated, of circulation and diffusion of ideas in relative spacetime. I cannot understand much of what Walter Benjamin does in his Arcades project without appealing to relational ideas about the spacetime of memory. I cannot even understand the idea of the city without situating it in relational terms. If, furthermore, I ask the question, of what the Basilica of Sacré Coeur in Paris, Tiananmen Square in Beijing, or "Ground Zero" in Manhattan *means*, then I cannot come to a full answer without invoking relationalities. And that entails coming to terms with the things, events, processes, and socio-ecological relations that have produced those places in spacetime.

So is space (space-time and spacetime) absolute, relative, or relational? I simply don't know whether there is an ontological answer to that question. In my own work I think of it as all three.

THE SECOND (LEFEBVRIAN) DIMENSION

H. Lefebvre constructs a quite different way of understanding spatiality in terms of human practices. He derives (almost certainly drawing upon Cassirer's distinctions among organic, perceptual, and symbolic spaces, though, as is often the case in French intellectual circles, without acknowledgment) a tripartite division of material space (space as experienced through our sense perceptions), the representation of space (space as conceived), and spaces of representation (space as lived). The second set of terms (those placed within parentheses) are not identical to the first, but in what follows I shall largely ignore that problem. I will pay most attention to the bracketed meanings, since these refer concretely to human behavior and social practices.

Material space is, for us humans, the world of our sense perceptions, as these arise out of the material circumstances of our lives: for this reason it can be called the perceptual space of primary experience mediated through human practices. We touch things and processes, feel them, see them, smell them, hear them, and infer the nature of space from those experiences. How we represent this world of experienced sense perceptions is, however, an entirely different matter. We use abstract representations (words, graphs, maps, diagrams, pictures, geometry, and other mathematical formulations) to represent space as we perceive it. In so doing we deploy concepts, codes, and abstractions. The correspondence between the material space of sense perceptions and its representation is always open to question and frequently fraught with dangerous illusions. But Lefebvre, along with other Marxists like W. Benjamin, insists that we also have imaginations, fears, emotions, psychologies, fantasies, and dreams. What Lefebvre calls, rather awkwardly, spaces of representation refers to the way we humans live—physically, affectively, and emotionally—in and through the spaces we encounter. Venturing down a dark street at night we may feel either fearful or adventurous. One person may welcome open space as a terrain of liberty while another, a victim of agoraphobia, may feel so insecure as to experience a panic attack.

The way we live in space cannot be predicted from material stimuli and sense perceptions or even from its manner of representation. But this does not mean that the three dimensions are disconnected. Lefebvre keeps them in a dialectical tension. Mutual and reciprocal influences flow freely between them. The way a space is represented and conceptualized, for example, may affect (though not in easily predictable ways) how the space is lived in and even materially sensed. If I have just read a horror story or Freud, then my feelings about venturing down that dark corridor-like street will surely be affected. Furthermore, my physical experience may be heightened (my senses may be "on edge," as we say) precisely because I am living in that space in a particular state of fear or anticipation. Conversely, the strange spatio-temporality of a dream, a fantasy, a hidden longing, or a lost memory, or even a peculiar thrill or tingle of fear as I walk down a street, may lead me to seek out conceptualizations and representations that can convey something of what I have lived to others.

The spaces and times of representation that envelop and surround us as we go about our daily lives likewise affect both our direct sensory experiences and the way we interpret and understand representations. We may not even notice the material qualities of spatial orderings incorporated into daily life because we adhere to unexamined routines. Yet through those daily material routines of everyday life we absorb a certain sense of how spatial representations work and build up certain spaces of representation for ourselves.

A STRUCTURAL REPRESENTATION

In what space or spacetime is the site known as "Ground Zero" in Manhattan located, and how does this affect our understanding of that site and of what should be built there? It is, plainly, an absolute physical space, and someone holds the property rights to it. It stands to be materially reconstructed as a distinctive thing. There is much discussion about retaining walls and load-bearing capacities. Engineering calculations (informed by Newtonian mechanics) and competing architectural designs (represent-ations) are submitted. Aesthetic judgments on how the space, once turned into a material artifact of some sort, might be lived in by those who visit it or work there are also influential considerations. Only after it is built will we get some sense of how people might live in that space. The problem is to so arrange the physical space as to produce an emotive affect while matching certain expectations (commercial as well as emotive and aesthetic) as to how the space might be experienced. Once constructed, the experience of the space may be mediated by representational forms (such as guide books, museums, and plans) that help us interpret the intended meanings of the reconstructed site. But moving dialectically across the dimension of absolute space alone is much less rewarding than the insights that come from appealing to the other spatio–temporal frames. Capitalist developers are keenly aware of the relative location of the site and judge its prospects for commercial development according to a logic of exchange relations and the flows of people, commodities, and capital that relate to it and give the site its potential commercial and speculative value. Its centrality and proximity to the command and control functions of Wall Street are important attributes, and if transportation access can be improved in the course of reconstruction, then so much the better, since this can only add to future land and property values. For the developers, the site does not merely exist *in* relative space-time: the re-engineering of the site offers the prospect of transforming relative space-time so as to enhance the commercial value of the absolute spaces (by improving access to airports, for example). The temporal horizon is then dominated by considerations of the amortization rate and the interest/discount rate applying to fixed capital investments in the built environment.

But there would almost certainly be popular objections, led by the families of those killed at that site, to thinking and building only in these absolute or relative space-time terms. Whatever is built at this site has to say something about individual and collective memory. Memory is immaterial but objective and hence relational. There will likely also be pressures to say something about the meanings of community and nation, as well as about future possibilities (perhaps even a prospect of eternal truths). Nor could the site ignore the issue of relational spatial connectivity to the rest of the world. Can something experienced as a local and personal tragedy be reconciled with an understanding of the international forces that were so powerfully condensed within those few shattering moments in a particular place? Will we get to feel in that space the widespread resentment in the rest of the world toward the way US hegemony was so selfishly being exercised throughout the 1980s and 1990s? Will we get to know that the Reagan administration played a key role in creating and

supporting the Taliban in Afghanistan in order to undermine the Soviet occupation and that Osama bin-Laden turned from being an ally of the United States into an enemy because of US support for the corrupt regime in Saudi Arabia? Or will we only learn of cowardly, alien, and evil "others" out there who hated the United States and sought to destroy it because of all it stood for in terms of liberty and freedom? The relational spatio-temporality of the event and the site can be exhumed with enough dedicated digging. But the manner of its representation and of its materialization is uncertain. The outcome will clearly depend upon political struggle. And the fiercest battles will have to be fought over what relational spacetime the rebuilding will invoke, what it will project as a symbol to the world. Governor Pataki, for example, in canceling the plans for a Freedom Museum there on the grounds that at some time in the future an exhibit critical of US policies might be mounted, mandated that nothing should be placed at the site that could ever be offensive to the memory of those who died there. His intent was to refuse any and all expression of criticism of US military and financial engagements with the world. Capitalist developers would not be averse to combining their mundane commercial concerns with inspiring symbolic statements (emphasizing the power and indestructibility of the political-economic system of global capitalism that received such a body blow on September 11, 2001) by erecting, say, a towering phallic symbol that spells defiance. They seek their own distinctive expressive power in relational spacetime. But there are all manner of other relationalities to be explored. What will we know about those who attacked, and how far will we connect? The site is and will have a relational presence in the world no matter what is built there, and it is important to reflect on how this "presenting" works: will it be lived as a symbol of US arrogance or as a sign of global compassion, reconciliation, and understanding? Taking up such matters requires that we embrace a relational conception of what the absolute space of Ground Zero is all about. And that, it turns out, is where the most interesting and contested meanings lie.

3
Psychological Ecology

(1943)

Kurt Lewin

The relation between psychological and non-psychological factors is a basic conceptual and methodological problem in all branches of psychology, from the psychology of perception to the psychology of groups. A proper understanding of this relationship must be achieved before we can answer the many questions raised in efforts to produce an integration of the social sciences. A field-theoretical approach to these problems of "psychological ecology" suggests some of the ways in which these questions may be answered.

The following discussion of food habits may suffice as an example of a first step in analyzing a field for the purpose of changing cultural habits. This analysis has the purpose of clarifying exactly where and how psychological and nonpsychological problems overlap. Any type of group life occurs in a setting of certain limitations to what is and what is not possible, what might or might not happen. The nonpsychological factors of climate, of communication, of the law of the country or the organization are a frequent part of these "outside limitations." The first analysis of the field is done from the point of view of "psychological ecology": the psychologist studies "nonpsychological" data to find out what these data mean for determining the boundary conditions of the life of the individual or group. Only after these data are known can the psychological study itself be begun to investigate the factors which determine the actions of the group or individual in those situations which have been shown to be significant.

For planning to adapt the food habits of a group to the requirements of health or of changing social conditions, one obviously should know the *status quo*. But what should one consider in studying this *status quo*? In particular, how should the psychologist proceed to make a contribution toward planned changes?

THE FIELD APPROACH: CULTURE AND GROUP LIFE AS QUASI-STATIONARY PROCESSES

One should view the present situation—the *status quo*—as being maintained by certain conditions or forces. A culture—for instance, the food habits of a given group at a given time—is not a static affair but a live process like a river which moves but still keeps a recognizable form. In other words, we have to deal, in group life as in individual life, with what is known in physics as "quasi-stationary" processes.[1]

Food habits do not occur in empty space. They are part and parcel of the daily rhythm of being awake and asleep; of being alone and in a group; of earning a living and playing; of being a member of a town, a family, a social class, a religious group, a nation; of living in a hot or a cool climate; in a rural area or a city, in a district with good groceries and restaurants or in an area of poor and irregular food supply. Somehow all of these factors affect food habits at any given time. They determine the food habits of a group every day anew just as the amount of water supply and the nature of the river bed determine from day to day the flow of the river, its constancy, or its change.[2]

Food habits of a group, as well as such phenomena as the speed of production in a factory, are the result of a multitude of forces. Some forces support each other, some oppose each other. Some are driving forces, others restraining forces. Like the velocity of a river, the actual conduct of a group depends upon the level (for instance, the speed of production) at which these conflicting forces reach a state of equilibrium. To speak of a certain culture pattern—for instance, the food habits of a group—implies that the constellation of these forces remains the same for a period or at least that they find their state of equilibrium at a constant level during that period.

Neither group "habits" nor individual "habits" can be understood sufficiently by a theory which limits its consideration to the processes themselves and conceives of the "habit" as a kind of frozen linkage, an "association" between these processes. Instead, habits will have to be conceived of as a result of forces in the organism *and* its life space, in the group *and* its setting. The structure of the organism, of the group, of the setting, or whatever name the field might have in the given case, has to be represented and the forces in the various parts of the field have to be analyzed if the processes (which might be either constant "habits" or changes) are to be understood scientifically. The process is but the epiphenomenon, the real object of study is the constellation of forces.

In other words, scientific predictions or advice for methods of change should be based on an analysis of the "field as a whole," including both its psychological and nonpsychological aspects.

AN ILLUSTRATIVE STUDY

The study used here as an illustration of these general principles was conducted by a field staff at the Child Welfare Research Station of the State University of Iowa. Its primary objective was to investigate some of the aspects of *why* people eat what they eat. The method consisted of interviewing housewives. Five groups were studied; three representing economic subdivision (high, medium, and low income levels) of White American stock, and two subcultural groups, Czech and Negro.[3]

A. Channel Theory

The question "why people eat what they eat," is rather complex, involving both cultural and psychological aspects (such as traditional foods and individual preferences caused by childhood experiences), as well as problems of transportation, availability of food in a particular area, and economic considerations. Therefore the first step in a scientific analysis is the treatment of the problem of where and how the psychological and the nonpsychological aspects intersect. This question can be answered, at least in part, by a "channel theory."

Food comes to the table through various channels. One is buying in a store. After the food has been bought, it may be stored in a locker to be taken out later, then to be cooked and brought to the table. Another channel is gardening. There are additional channels such as deliveries, buying food in the country, baking at home, and canning.

To find out what food comes to the table, we have to know how many food channels exist for the particular family or group. To understand the changes after certain channels are blocked, we have to know what new channels open up or in which old channels traffic is increased. For instance, when preparing meals at home becomes difficult, eating in restaurants may increase.

Food does not move by its own impetus. Entering or not entering a channel and moving from one section of a channel to another is effected by a "gatekeeper."

It is very important to realize that the psychological forces which influence the movement of the food may be different for the different channels and for the various sections within the same channel. Each channel offers a certain amount of resistance to movement, and certain forces tend to prevent entrance into the channel.

1. The use of various channels. In our study of a midwestern community we found that in the five groups investigated each of the foods, except desserts, was obtained through the buying channel considerably more frequently than through any other channel.

For all groups together, it was found that about a third of the vegetables and fruits were canned at home. There seemed to be no relation between income levels and the percentage of families who can, although it was found that the *amount* of food canned was greater in the two lower income groups. A pronounced cultural difference was discovered in that all of the Czech families did some canning, and the amount of food they canned was greater than in comparable income groups in other segments of the community.

In general, the data permitted the following conclusions: To some extent financial circumstances and cultural values do influence the extent to which various food channels are used and the uses to which they are put.

2. *Who controls the channel?* It is important to know what members of the family control the various channels, as any changes will have to be effected through those persons. In all our groups the wife definitely controls all the channels except that of gardening where the husband takes an active part. Even there, however, the husband seldom controls this channel alone. Children are never mentioned as controlling any of the channels, although they undoubtedly influence the decisions indirectly through their rejection of food put before them.

B. The Psychology of the Gatekeeper

To understand and influence food habits we have to know in addition to the objective food channels and objective availability, the psychological factors influencing the person who controls the channels.

The psychology of the gatekeeper includes a great variety of factors which we do not intend to cover fully. The factors might be classified under two headings, one pertaining to the cognitive structure, i.e., the terms in which people think and speak about food; and the other pertaining to their motivation, e.g., the system of values behind their choice of food.

1. *The cognitive structure.* The cognitive structure deals with what is considered "food," "food for us," or "food for other members of the family," with meal patterns, and with the significance of the eating situation.

a. Food Outside and Within Consideration. Physical availability is not the only factor which determines availability of food to the individual. One of the determining factors is "cultural availability." There are many edible materials which people never even consider for use because they do not think of them as food for themselves.

If we consider as food all that which some human beings actually eat and like to eat, then live grasshoppers would have to be included in the category of food. If, however, we ask what

people in the United States consider as food, live grasshoppers would be excluded. In other words, the psychological area of food in our culture is only a small part of the objectively edible food, and could be conceived of as a small restricted region within the total region of all objectively edible food.

Even the food that is recognized as that for human beings still may not be accepted as food for one's own family. For example, kidneys or certain viscera are considered by some as food only for poor people, or champagne a drink for the rich. In other words, only a certain part of the area recognized as "food for human beings" is recognized as "food for us." To find out what is considered "food for us" by different groups is one of the first objectives of studying food habits.[...]

c. "Meal Patterns." Other aspects of the cognitive structure of food are the difference between breakfast food, food for lunch, and for dinner; the distinction between main dish and dessert; the concept of balanced meal and of "leftover."

d. The Meaning of the Eating Situation. One important point is the feeling of group belongingness created by eating in the company of others. At a banquet, eating means something very different from eating after a long period of starvation, and may be classified as a social function rather than as a means of survival. On the whole, eating is usually a more complicated function than just taking nourishment.

The psychological meaning of eating is closely related to group situations. Eating with fellow workers in a factory is something different from eating at the family table or eating in a restaurant. The "eating group" influences greatly the eating conduct and the eating ideology of the individual. One can say that every eating group has a specific eating culture.

2. *Motivation.* We will discuss the various factors in motivation under three major headings: (a) values (motives, ideologies) behind food selection, (b) food needs, and (c) obstacles to be overcome.

a. Values Behind Food Selection. There is more than one value which acts as a frame of reference for the individual choosing foods. These values have not always the same weight for the individual; they may change, as during wartime, and in addition may be different in the restaurant and at home.

b. Food Needs. It is important to recognize that the relative weight of the various frames of reference changes from day to day in line with the changing needs. These needs might change because of satiation, of variation in the situation, or because of cultural forces toward diet variations.

c. Obstacles to be Overcome. The interview did not approach the problem of obstacles along the various channels in a specific way, although these problems must be taken into account in planning changes of food habits. Canned foods, for instance, are frequently preferred because of the little time necessary for preparation. The extent to which such obstacles as difficulty in transportation, lack of domestic help, time necessary for preparing and cooking influence the choice of the gatekeeper depends on his particular circumstances.

3. *Conflict.*

a. Buying as a Decision Situation. In general a conflict situation arises when there is, on the one hand, a drive to engage in a certain activity (as buying food) and on the other hand, a force opposing that activity. An increase in prices, acting as a resistance to buying the foods which people have grown accustomed to enhances the conflict in the food area for all groups. Families of low income are likely to experience more conflict in buying food than those of high income since their freedom in buying the foods they want is restricted by their limited finances. Members from the middle income group, however, may experience greater conflict than those from the low income group in so far as they are psychologically a marginal group. They strive to achieve the social status of the financially more able and at the same time fear dropping back to the level of poor people.

GENERALITY OF THE THEORY

The kind of analysis which we have made here with special reference to changing food habits may be applied quite generally. Social and economic channels may be distinguished in any type of formalized institution. Within these channels gate sections can be located. Social changes in large measure are produced by changing the constellation of forces within these particular segments of the channel. The analytic task is approached from the point of view of psychological ecology; nonpsychological data are first investigated to determine the boundary conditions for those who are in control of various segments of the channel.

Gate sections are governed either by impartial rules or by "gatekeepers." In the latter case an individual or group is "in power" to make the decision between "in" or "out." Understanding the functioning of the gate becomes equivalent then to understanding the factors which determine the decisions of the gatekeepers, and changing the social process means influencing or replacing the gatekeeper. The first diagnostic task in such cases is that of finding the actual gatekeepers. This requires essentially a sociological analysis and must be carried out before one knows whose psychology has to be studied or who has to be educated if a social change is to be accomplished.

Similar considerations hold for any social constellation which has the character of a channel, a gate, and gatekeeper. Discrimination against minorities will not be changed as long as forces are not changed which determine the decisions of the gatekeepers. Their decisions depend partly on their ideology—that is, their system of values and beliefs which determine what they consider to be "good" or "bad"—and partly on the way they perceive the particular situation. Thus if we think of trying to reduce discrimination within a factory, a school system, or any other *organized institution*, we should consider the social life there as something which flows through certain channels. We then see that there are executives or boards who decide who is taken into the organization or who is kept out of it, who is promoted, and so on. The techniques of discrimination in these organizations are closely linked with those mechanics which make the life of the members of an organization flow in definite channels. Thus discrimination is basically linked with problems of management, with the actions of gatekeepers who determine what is done and what is not done.

We saw in our analysis of the flow of food through channels that the constellation of forces before and after the gate region is decisively different. Thus, an expensive food encounters a strong force against entering a channel but once it does enter the same force pushes it on through. This situation holds not only for food channels but also for the traveling of a news item through certain communication channels in a group, for movement of goods, and the social locomotion of individuals in many organizations.

The relation between social channels, social perception, and decision is methodologically and practically of considerable significance. The theory of channels and gatekeepers helps to define more precisely how certain "objective" sociological problems of locomotion of goods and persons intersect with "subjective" psychological and cultural problems. It points to sociologically characterized places, like gates and social channels, where attitudes count most for certain social processes and where individual or group decisions have a particularly great social effect.

NOTES

1 For the general characteristics of quasi-stationary processes see Wolfgang Koehler, *Dynamics in Psychology* (New York: Liveright Publishing Co., 1940).
2 The type of forces, of course, is different; there is nothing equivalent to "cognitive structure" or "psychological past" or "psychological future" in the field determining the river.
3 For a full discussion of this study see Kurt Lewin, Forces behind food habits and methods of change. *Bulletin of the National Research Council,* 1943, *108,* 35–65.

4
Junkspace

(2002)

Rem Koolhaas

If space-junk is the human debris that litters the universe, Junk-Space is the residue mankind leaves on the planet. The built (more about that later) product of modernization is not modern architecture but Junkspace. Junkspace is what remains after modernization has run its course, or, more precisely, what coagulates while modernization is in progress, its fallout. Modernization had a rational program: to share the blessings of science, universally. Junkspace is its apotheosis, or meltdown. ... Although its individual parts are the outcome of brilliant inventions, lucidly planned by human intelligence, boosted by infinite computation, their sum spells the end of Enlightenment, its resurrection as farce, a low-grade purgatory. Junkspace is the sum total of our current achievement; we have built more than did all previous generations put together, but somehow we do not register on the same scales. We do not leave pyramids. According to a new gospel of ugliness, there is already more Junkspace under construction in the twenty-first century than has survived from the twentieth. ... It was a mistake to invent modern architecture for the twentieth century. Architecture disappeared in the twentieth century; we have been reading a footnote under a microscope hoping it would turn into a novel; our concern for the masses has blinded us to People's Architecture. Junkspace seems an aberration, but it is the essence, the main thing ... the product of an encounter between escalator and air-conditioning, conceived in an incubator of Sheetrock (all three missing from the history books). Continuity is the essence of Junkspace; it exploits any invention that enables expansion, deploys the infrastructure of seamlessness: escalator, air-conditioning, sprinkler, fire shutter, hot-air curtain. ... It is always interior, so extensive that you rarely perceive limits; it promotes disorientation by any means (mirror, polish, echo). ... Junkspace is sealed, held together not by structure but by skin, like a bubble. Gravity has remained constant, resisted by the same arsenal since the beginning of time; but air-conditioning—invisible medium, therefore unnoticed—has truly revolutionized architecture. Air-conditioning has launched the endless building. If architecture separates buildings, air-conditioning unites them. Air-conditioning has dictated mutant regimes of organization and coexistence that leave architecture behind. A single shopping center is now the work of generations of space planners, repairmen, and fixers, like in the Middle Ages; air-conditioning sustains our cathedrals. (All architects may unwittingly be working on the same building, so far separate, but with hidden receptors that will eventually make it cohere.) Because it costs money, is no longer free, conditioned space inevitably becomes conditional space; sooner or later all conditional space turns into Junkspace. ... When we think about space, we have only looked at its containers. As if space itself is invisible, all theory for the production of space is based on an obsessive preoccupation with its opposite: substance and objects, i.e., architecture. Architects could never explain space; Junkspace is our punishment for their mystifications. O.K., let's talk about space then. The beauty of airports, especially after each upgrade. The luster of renovations. The subtlety of the shopping center. Let's explore public space, discover casinos, spend time in theme parks. ... Junkspace is the body double of space, a territory of impaired vision, limited expectation, reduced earnestness. Junkspace is a Bermuda Triangle of concepts, an abandoned petri dish: it cancels distinctions, undermines resolve, confuses intention with realization. It replaces hierarchy with accumulation, composition with addition. More and more, more is more. Junkspace is overripe and undernourishing at the same time, a colossal security blanket that covers the earth in a stranglehold of seduction. ... Junkspace is like being condemned to a perpetual Jacuzzi with millions of your best friends. ... A fuzzy empire of blur, it fuses high and low, public and private, straight and bent, bloated and starved to offer a seamless patchwork of the permanently disjointed. Seemingly an apotheosis, spatially grandiose, the effect of its richness is a terminal hollowness, a vicious parody of ambition that systematically erodes the credibility of building, possibly forever. ... Space was created by piling matter on top of matter, cemented to form a solid new whole. Junkspace is additive, layered, and lightweight, not articulated in different parts but subdivided, quartered the way a carcass is torn apart—individual chunks severed from a universal condition. There are no walls, only partitions, shimmering membranes frequently covered in mirror or gold. Structure groans invisibly underneath decoration, or worse, has become ornamental; small, shiny, space frames support nominal loads, or huge beams deliver cyclopic burdens to unsuspecting destinations. ... The arch, once the workhorse of structures, has become the depleted emblem of "community," welcoming an infinity of virtual populations to nonexistent theres.

The shiniest surfaces in the history of mankind reflect humanity at its most casual. The more we inhabit the palatial, the more we seem to dress down. A stringent dress code— last spasm of etiquette?—governs access to Junkspace: shorts, sneakers, sandals, shell suit, fleece, jeans, parka, backpack. As if the People suddenly accessed the private quarters of a dictator, Junkspace is best enjoyed in a state of postrevolutionary gawking. Polarities have merged—there is nothing left between desolation and frenzy. Neon signifies both the old and the new; interiors refer to the Stone and Space Age the same time. It exposes what previous generations kept under wraps:

structures emerge like springs from a mattress; exit stairs dangle in a didactic trapeze; probes thrust into space to deliver laboriously what is in fact omnipresent, free air; acres of glass hang from spidery cables, tautly stretched skins enclose flaccid nonevents. Transparency only reveals everything in which you cannot partake.

In previous building, materiality was based on a final state that could only be modified at the expense of partial destruction. At the exact moment that our culture has abandoned repetition and regularity as repressive, building materials have become more and more modular, unitary, and standardized; substance now comes predigitized. ... The joint is no longer a problem, an intellectual issue: transitional moments are defined by stapling and taping, wrinkly brown bands barely maintain the illusion of an unbroken surface; verbs unknown and unthinkable in architectural history—clamp, stick, fold, dump, glue, shoot, double, fuse— have become indispensable. Each element performs its task in negotiated isolation. Whereas detailing once suggested the coming together, possibly forever, of disparate materials, it is now a transient coupling, waiting to be undone, unscrewed, a temporary embrace with a high probability of separation; no longer the orchestrated encounter of difference, but the abrupt end of a system, a stalemate. Only the blind, reading its fault lines with their fingertips, will ever understand Junkspace's histories. ... While whole millennia worked in favor of permanence, axialities, relationships, and proportion, the program of Junkspace is escalation. Instead of development, it offers entropy. ... Junkspace is draining and is drained in return. Everywhere in Junkspace there are seating arrangements, ranges of modular chairs, even couches, as if the experience Junkspace offers its consumers is significantly more exhausting than any previous spatial sensation; in its most abandoned stretches, you find buffets: utilitarian tables draped in white or black sheets, perfunctory assemblies of caffeine and calories— cottage cheese, muffins, unripe grapes— notional representations of plenty, without horn and without plenty. Each Junkspace is connected, sooner or later, to bodily functions: wedged between stainless-steel partitions sit rows of groaning Romans, denim togas bunched around their huge sneakers. ... Because it is so intensely consumed, Junkspace is fanatically maintained, the night shift undoing the damage of the day shift in an endless Sisyphean replay. As you recover from Junkspace, Junkspace recovers from you: between 2 and 5 a.m., yet another population, this one heartlessly casual and appreciably darker, is mopping, hoovering, sweeping, toweling, resupplying. ...

Junkspace is often described as a space of flows, but that is a misnomer; flows depend on disciplined movement, bodies that cohere. Junkspace is a web without a spider; although it is an architecture of the masses, each trajectory is strictly unique. Its anarchy is one of the last tangible ways in which we experience freedom. It is a space of collision, a container of atoms, busy, not dense. ... There is a special way of moving in Junkspace, at the same time aimless and purposeful. It is an acquired culture. Junkspace features the tyranny of the oblivious: sometimes an entire Junkspace comes unstuck through the nonconformity of one of its members; a single citizen of another culture—a refugee, a mother—can destabilize an entire Junkspace, hold it to a rustic's ransom, leaving an invisible swath of obstruction in his/her wake, a deregulation eventually communicated to its furthest extremities. Where movement becomes synchronized, it curdles: on escalators, near exits, parking machines, automated tellers. Sometimes, under duress, individuals are channeled in a flow, pushed through a single door or forced to negotiate the gap between two temporary obstacles (an invalid's bleeping chariot and a Christmas tree): the manifest ill will such narrowing provokes mocks the notion of flows. Flows in Junkspace lead to disaster: department stores at the beginning of sales; the stampedes triggered by warring compartments of soccer fans; dead bodies piling up in front of the locked emergency doors of a disco— evidence of the awkward fit between the portals of Junkspace and the narrow calibrations of the old world.

Judging the built presumed a static condition; now each architecture embodies opposite conditions simultaneously: old and new, permanent and temporary, flourishing and at risk. ... Sections undergo an Alzheimer's-like deterioration as others are upgraded. Because Junkspace is endless, it is never closed. ... Renovation and restoration were procedures that took place in your absence; now you're a witness, a reluctant participant. ... Seeing Junkspace in conversion is like inspecting an unmade bed, someone else's. Say an airport needs more space. In the past, new terminals were added, each more or less characteristic of its own age, leaving the old ones as a readable record, evidence of progress. Since passengers have definitively demonstrated their infinite malleability, the idea of rebuilding on the spot has gained currency. Travelators are thrown into reverse, signs taped, potted palms (or very large corpses) covered in body bags. Screens of taped Sheetrock segregate two populations: one wet, one dry, one hard, one flabby, one cold, one overheated. Half the population produces new space; the more affluent half consumes old space. To accommodate a nether world of manual labor, the concourse suddenly turns into Casbah: improvised locker rooms, coffee breaks, smoking, even real campfires. ...

The formerly straight is coiled into evermore complex configurations. Only a perverse modernist choreography can explain the twists and turns, the ascents and descents, the sudden reversals that comprise the typical path from check-in (misleading name) to the apron of the average contemporary airport. Because we never reconstruct or question the absurdity of these enforced *dérives*, we meekly submit to grotesque journeys past perfume, asylum-seekers, building site, underwear, oysters, pornography, cell phone—incredible adventures for the brain, the eye, the nose, the tongue, the womb, the testicles. ... There was once a polemic about the right angle and the straight line; now the ninetieth degree has become one among many. In fact, remnants of former geometries create ever new havoc, offering forlorn nodes of resistance that create unstable eddies in newly opportunistic flows. ... Who would dare claim responsibility for this sequence? The idea that a profession once dictated, or at least presumed to predict, people's movements now seems laughable, or worse: unthinkable. Instead of design, there is calculation: the more erratic the path, eccentric the loops, hidden the blueprint, efficient the exposure, the more inevitable the transaction. ... Junkspace is postexistential; it makes you uncertain where you are, obscures where you go, undoes where you were. Who do you think you are? Who do you want to be?

Junkspace will be our tomb. Half of mankind pollutes to produce, the other pollutes to consume. The combined pollution of all Third World cars, motorbikes, trucks, buses, sweatshops pales into insignificance compared to the heat generated by Junkspace. Junkspace is political: It depends on the central removal of the critical faculty in the name of comfort and pleasure. Politics has become manifesto by Photoshop, seamless blueprints of the mutually exclusive, arbitrated by opaque NGOs. Comfort is the new Justice. … Junkspace knows all your emotions, all your desires. It is the interior of Big Brother's belly. It preempts people's sensations. It comes with a sound track, smell, captions; it blatantly proclaims how it wants to be read: rich, stunning, cool, huge, abstract, "minimal" historical. Junkspace pretends to unite, but it actually splinters. It creates communities not out of shared interest or free association, but out of identical statistics and unavoidable demographics, an opportunistic weave of vested interests. Each man, woman, and child is individually targeted, tracked, split off from the rest. … Fragments come together at "security" only, where a grid of video screens disappointingly reassembles individual frames into a banalized, utilitarian cubism that reveals Junkspace's overall coherence to the dispassionate glare of barely trained guards: video-ethnography in its brute form. Just as Junkspace is unstable, its actual ownership is forever being passed on in parallel disloyalty. Junkspace happens spontaneously through natural corporate exuberance—the unfettered play of the market—or is generated through the combined actions of temporary "czars" with long records of three-dimensional philanthropy, bureaucrats (often former leftists) that optimistically sell off vast tracts of waterfront, former hippodromes, military bases and abandoned airfields to developers or real-estate moguls who can accommodate any deficit in futuristic balances, or through Default Preservation™ (the maintenance of historical complexes that nobody wants but that the Zeitgeist has declared sacrosanct). As its scale mushrooms—rivals and even exceeds that of the Public—its economy becomes more inscrutable. Its financing is a deliberate haze, clouding opaque deals, dubious tax breaks, unusual incentives, exemptions, tenuous legalities, transferred air rights, joined properties, special zoning districts, public[-] private complicities. Funded by bonds, lottery, subsidy, charity, grant: An erratic flow of yen, Euros, and dollars creates financial envelopes that are as fragile as their contents. Because of a structural shortfall, a fundamental deficit, a contingent bankruptcy, each square inch becomes a grasping, needy surface dependent on covert or overt support, discount, compensation and fund-raising. For culture, "engraved donor bricks"; for everything else: cash, rentals, leases, franchises, the underpinning of brands. Junkspace expands with the economy but its footprint cannot contract—when it is no longer needed, it thins. Because of its tenuous viability, Junkspace has to swallow more and more program to survive; soon, we will be able to do anything anywhere. We will have conquered place. … Instead of public life, Public Space™: what remains of the city once the unpredictable has been removed. … Space for "honoring," "sharing," "caring," "grieving," and "healing" … civility imposed by an overdose of serif. …

Why can't we tolerate stronger sensations? Dissonance? Awkwardness? Genius? Anarchy? … Junkspace heals, or at least that is the assumption of many hospitals. We thought the hospital was unique—a universe that identified by its smell—but now that we are used to universal conditioning we recognize it was merely a prototype; all Junkspace is defined by its smell. Often heroic in size, planned with the last adrenaline of modernism's grand inspiration, we have made them (too) human; life or death decisions are taken in spaces that are relentlessly friendly, littered with fading bouquets, empty coffee cups, and yesterday's papers. You used to face death in appropriate cells; now your nearest are huddled together in atriums. A bold datum line is established on every vertical surface, dividing the infirmary in two: above an endless humanist scroll of "color," loved ones, children's sunsets, signage, and art … below a utilitarian zone for defacement and disinfectant, anticipated collision, scratch, spill, and smudge. … Junkspace is space as vacation; there once was a relationship between leisure and work, a biblical dictate that divided our weeks, organized public life. Now we work harder, marooned in a never-ending casual Friday. … Because we spend our life indoors—like animals in a zoo— we are obsessed with the weather: 40 percent of all TV consists of presenters of lesser attractiveness gesturing helplessly in front of windswept formations, through which you recognize, sometimes, your own destination/ current position. Conceptually, each monitor, each TV screen is a substitute for a window; real life is inside, while cyberspace has become the great outdoors. … Mankind is always going on about architecture. What if space started looking at mankind? Will Junkspace invade the body? Through the vibes of the cell phone? Has it already? Through Botox injections? Collagen? Silicone implants? Liposuction? Penis enlargements? Does gene therapy announce a total reengineering according to Junkspace? Is each of us a mini-construction site? Is mankind the sum of three to five billion individual upgrades? Is it a repertoire of reconfiguration that facilitates the intromission of a new species into its self-made Junksphere? The cosmetic is the new cosmic. ...

5
One Place after Another

Notes on Site Specificity (1997)

Miwon Kwon

Site specificity used to imply something grounded, bound to the laws of physics. Often playing with gravity, site-specific works used to be obstinate about "presence," even if they were materially ephemeral, and adamant about immobility, even in the face of disappearance or destruction. Whether inside the white cube or out in the Nevada desert, whether architectural or landscape-oriented, site-specific art initially took the "site" as an actual location, a tangible reality, its identity composed of a unique combination of constitutive physical elements: length, depth, height, texture, and shape of walls and rooms; scale and proportion of plazas, buildings, or parks; existing conditions of lighting, ventilation, traffic patterns; distinctive topographical features. If modernist sculpture absorbed its pedestal/base to sever its connection to or express its indifference to the site, rendering itself more autonomous and self-referential, and thus transportable, placeless, and nomadic, then site-specific works, as they first emerged in the wake of Minimalism in the late 1960s and early 1970s, forced a dramatic reversal of this modernist paradigm.[1] Antithetical to the claim "If you have to change a sculpture for a site there is something wrong with the sculpture,"[2] site-specific art, whether interruptive or assimilative, gave itself up to its environmental context, being formally determined or directed by it.[3]

In turn, the uncontaminated and pure idealist space of dominant modernisms was radically displaced by the materiality of the natural landscape or the impure and ordinary space of the everyday. The space of art was no longer perceived as a blank slate, a tabula rasa, but a *real* place. The art object or event in this context was to be singularly *experienced* in the here-and-now through the bodily presence of each viewing subject, in a sensorial immediacy of spatial extension and temporal duration, rather than instantaneously "perceived" in a visual epiphany by a disembodied eye. Site-specific work in its earliest formation, then, focused on establishing an inextricable, indivisible relationship between the work and its site, and demanded the physical presence of the viewer for the work's completion. The (neo-avant-garde) aspiration to exceed the limitations of traditional media, like painting and sculpture, as well as their institutional setting; the epistemological challenge to relocate meaning from within the art object to the contingencies of its context; the radical restructuring of the subject from an old Cartesian model to a phenomenological one of lived bodily experience; and the self-conscious desire to resist the forces of the capitalist market economy, which circulates art works as transportable and exchangeable commodity goods—all these imperatives came together in art's new attachment to the actuality of the site.

In this frame of mind, Robert Barry declared in a 1969 interview that each of his wire installations was "made to suit the place in which it was installed. They cannot be moved without being destroyed." Similarly, Richard Serra wrote fifteen years later in a letter to the Director of the Art-in-Architecture Program of the General Services Administration in Washington, D.C., that his 120-feet, Cor-Ten steel sculpture *Tilted Arc* was "commissioned and designed for one particular site: Federal

Plaza. It is a site-specific work and as such not to be relocated. To remove the work is to destroy the work." He further elaborated his position in 1989:

> As I pointed out, *Tilted Arc* was conceived from the start as a site-specific sculpture and was not meant to be "site-adjusted" or … "relocated." Site-specific works deal with the environmental components of given places. The scale, size, and location of site-specific works are determined by the topography of the site, whether it be urban or landscape or architectural enclosure. The works become part of the site and restructure both conceptually and perceptually the organization of the site.[4]

Barry and Serra echo each other here. But whereas Barry's comment announces what was in the late 1960s a new radicality in vanguard sculptural practice, marking an early stage in the aesthetic experimentations that were to follow through the 1970s (i.e., land/earth art, process art, installation art, Conceptual art, performance/body art, and various forms of institutional critique), Serra's statement, spoken twenty years later within the context of public art, is an indignant defense, signaling a crisis point for site specificity—at least for a version that would prioritize the *physical* inseparability between a work and its site of installation.[5]

Informed by the contextual thinking of Minimalism, various forms of institutional critique and Conceptual art developed a different model of site specificity that implicitly challenged the "innocence" of space and the accompanying presumption of a universal viewing subject (albeit one in possession of a corporeal body) as espoused in the phenomenological model. Artists such as Michael Asher, Marcel Broodthaers, Daniel Buren, Hans Haacke, and Robert Smithson, as well as many women artists including Mierle Laderman Ukeles, have variously conceived the site not only in physical and spatial terms but as a *cultural* framework defined by the institutions of art. If Minimalism returned to the viewing subject a physical corporeal body, institutional critique insisted on the social matrix of class, race, gender, and sexuality of the viewing subject.[6] Moreover, while Minimalism challenged the idealist hermeticism of the autonomous art object by deflecting its meaning

to the space of its presentation, institutional critique further complicated this displacement by highlighting the idealist hermeticism of the space of presentation itself. The modern gallery/museum space, for instance, with its stark white walls, artificial lighting (no windows), controlled climate, and pristine architectonics, was perceived not solely in terms of basic dimensions and proportion but as an institutional disguise, a normative exhibition convention serving an ideological function. The seemingly benign architectural features of a gallery/museum, in other words, were deemed to be coded mechanisms that *actively* disassociate the space of art from the outer world, furthering the institution's idealist imperative of rendering itself and its hierarchization of values "objective," "disinterested," and "true."

As early as 1970 Buren proclaimed,

> Whether the place in which the work is shown imprints and marks this work, whatever it may be, or whether the work itself is directly—consciously or not—produced for the Museum, any work presented in that framework, if it does not explicitly examine the influence of the framework upon itself, falls into the illusion of self-sufficiency—or idealism.[7]

But more than just the museum, the site comes to encompass a relay of several interrelated but different spaces and economies, including the studio, gallery, museum, art criticism, art history, the art market, that together constitute a system of practices that is not separate from but open to social, economic, and political pressures. To be "specific" to such a site, in turn, is to decode and/or recode the institutional conventions so as to expose their hidden yet motivated operations—to reveal the ways in which institutions mold art's meaning to modulate its cultural and economic value, and to undercut the fallacy of art and its institutions' "autonomy" by making apparent their imbricated relationship to the broader socioeconomic and political processes of the day.

In these ways, the "site" of art evolves away from its coincidence with the literal space of art, and the physical condition of a specific location recedes as the primary element in the conception of a site. Whether articulated in political and economic terms, or in epistemological terms, it is rather the *techniques* and *effects* of the art institution as they circumscribe the definition, production, presentation, and dissemination of art that become the sites of critical intervention. Concurrent with this move toward the dematerialization of the site is the ongoing de-aestheticization (i.e., withdrawal of visual pleasure) and dematerialization of the art work. Going against the grain of institutional habits and desires, and continuing to resist the commodification of art in/for the market place, site-specific art adopts strategies that are either aggressively antivisual—informational, textual, expositional, didactic—or immaterial altogether—gestures, events, or performances bracketed by temporal boundaries. The "work" no longer seeks to be a noun/object but a verb/process, provoking the viewers' *critical* (not just physical) acuity regarding the ideological conditions of that viewing. In this context, the guarantee of a specific relationship between an art work and its "site" is not based on a physical permanence of that relationship (as demanded by Serra, for example), but rather on the recognition of its unfixed *impermanence*, to be experienced as an unrepeatable and fleeting situation.

But if the critique of the cultural confinement of art (and artists) via its institutions was once the "great issue," a dominant drive of site-oriented practices today is the pursuit of a more intense engagement with the outside world and everyday life—a critique of culture that is inclusive of non-art spaces, non-art institutions, and non-art issues (blurring the division between art and non-art, in fact). Concerned to integrate art more directly into the realm of the social, either in order to redress (in an activist sense) urgent social problems such as the ecological crisis, homelessness, AIDS, homophobia, racism, and sexism, or more generally in order to relativize art as one among many forms of cultural work, current manifestations of site specificity tend to treat aesthetic and art-historical concerns as secondary issues. Deeming the focus on the social nature of *art's* production and reception to be too exclusive, even elitist, this expanded engagement with culture favors "public" sites outside the traditional confines of art in physical and intellectual terms.[8]

Furthering previous (at times literal) attempts to take art out of the museum/gallery space-system (recall Buren's striped canvases marching out the gallery window, or Smithson's adventures in the wastelands of New Jersey or isolated locales in Utah), contemporary site-oriented works occupy hotels, city streets, housing projects, prisons, schools, hospitals, churches, zoos, supermarkets, etc., and infiltrate media spaces such as radio, newspapers, television, and the Internet. In addition to this spatial expansion, site-oriented art is also informed by a broader range of disciplines (i.e., anthropology, sociology, literary criticism, psychology, natural and cultural histories, architecture and urbanism, computer science, political theory) and sharply attuned to popular discourses (i.e., fashion, music, advertising, film, and television). But more than these dual expansions of art into culture, which obviously diversify the site, the distinguishing characteristic of today's site-oriented art is the way in which both the art work's relationship to the actuality of a location (as site) *and* the social conditions of the institutional frame (as site) are *subordinate* to a *discursively* determined site that is delineated as a field of knowledge, intellectual exchange, or cultural debate. Furthermore, unlike previous models, this site is not defined as a *precondition*. Rather, it is *generated* by the work (often as "content"), and then *verified* by its convergence with an existing discursive formation.

A provisional conclusion might be that in advanced art practices of the past thirty years the operative definition of the site has been transformed from a physical location—grounded, fixed, actual—to a discursive vector—ungrounded, fluid, virtual. But even if the dominance of a particular formulation of site specificity emerges at one moment and wanes at another, the shifts are not always punctual or definitive. Thus, the three paradigms of site specificity I have schematized here—phenomenological, social/institutional, and discursive—although presented somewhat chronologically, are not stages in a linear trajectory of historical development. Rather, they are competing definitions, overlapping with one another and operating simultaneously in various cultural practices today (or even within a single artist's single project).

Nonetheless, this move away from a literal interpretation of the site and the multiplicitous expansion of the site in locational and conceptual terms seems more accelerated today than in the past. And the phenomenon is embraced by many artists and critics as an advance offering more effective avenues to resist revised institutional and market forces that now commodify "critical" art practices. In addition, current forms of site-oriented art, which readily take up social issues (often inspired by them), and which routinely engage the collaborative participation of audience groups for the conceptualization and production of the work, are seen as a means to strengthen art's capacity to penetrate the sociopolitical organization of contemporary life with greater impact and meaning. In this sense the possibilities to conceive the site as something more than a place—as repressed ethnic history, a political cause, a disenfranchised social group—is a crucial conceptual leap in redefining the "public" role of art and artists.

But the enthusiastic support for these salutary goals needs to be checked by a serious critical examination of the problems and contradictions that attend all forms of site-specific and site-oriented art today, which are visible now as the art work is becoming more and more "unhinged" from the actuality of the site once again— unhinged both in a literal sense of physical separation of the art work from the location of its initial installation, and in a metaphorical sense as performed in the discursive mobilization of the site in emergent forms of site-oriented art. This "unhinging," however, does not indicate a retroversion to the modernist autonomy of the siteless, nomadic art object, although such an ideology is still predominant. Rather, the current unhinging of site specificity is reflective of new questions that pressure its practices today— questions engendered by both aesthetic imperatives and external historical determinants, which are not exactly comparable to those of thirty years ago. For example, what is the status of traditional aesthetic values such as originality, authenticity, and uniqueness in site-specific art, which always begins with the particular, local, unrepeatable preconditions of a site, however it is defined? Furthermore, what is the commodity status of anti-commodities, that is, immaterial, process-oriented, ephemeral, performative events? While site-specific art once defied commodification by insisting on immobility, it now seems to espouse fluid mobility and nomadism for the same purpose. But curiously, the nomadic principle also defines capital and power in our times. Is the unhinging of site specificity, then, a form of resistance to the ideological establishment of art or a capitulation to the logic of capitalist expansion?

Just as the shifts in the structural reorganization of cultural production alter the form of the art commodity (to services) and the authority of the artist (to "reappeared" protagonist), values like originality, authenticity, and singularity are also reworked in site-oriented art—*evacuated from the art work and attributed to the site*—reinforcing a general cultural valorization of places as the locus of authentic experience and coherent sense of historical and personal identity.[9] An instructive example of this phenomenon is "Places with a Past," a 1991 site-specific exhibition organized by Mary Jane Jacob, which took the city of Charleston, South Carolina, as not only the backdrop but a "bridge between the works of art and the audience."[10] In addition to breaking the rules of the art establishment, the exhibition wanted to further a dialogue between art and the sociohistorical dimension of places. According to Jacob, "Charleston proved to be fertile ground" for the investigation of issues concerning

gender, race, cultural identity, considerations of difference ... subjects much in the vanguard of criticism and art-making. ... The actuality of the situation, the fabric of the time and place of Charleston, offered an incredibly rich and meaningful context for the making and siting of publicly visible and physically prominent installations that rang true in [the artists'] approach to these ideas.[11]

While site-specific art continues to be described as a refutation of originality and authenticity as intrinsic qualities of the art object or the artist, this resistance facilitates the translation and relocation of these qualities from the art work to the place of its presentation, only to have them *return* to the art work now that it has become integral to the site. Admittedly, according to Jacob, "locations ... contribute a specific identity to the shows staged by injecting into the experience the uniqueness of the place."[12] Conversely, if the social, historical, and geographical specificity of Charleston offered artists a unique opportunity to create unrepeatable works (and by extension an unrepeatable exhibition), then the programmatic implementations of site-specific art in exhibitions like "Places with a Past" ultimately utilize art to *promote* Charleston as a unique place. What is prized most of all in site-specific art is still the singularity and authenticity that the presence of the artist seems to guarantee, not only in terms of the presumed unrepeatability of the work but in the ways in which the presence of the artist also *endows* places with a "unique" distinction.

Certainly, site-specific art can lead to the unearthing of repressed histories, provide support for greater visibility of marginalized groups and issues, and initiate the re(dis)covery of "minor" places so far ignored by the dominant culture. But inasmuch as the current socio-economic order thrives on the (artificial) production and (mass) consumption of difference (for difference's sake), the siting of art in "real" places can also be a means to *extract* the social and historical dimensions *out* of places to variously serve the thematic drive of an artist, satisfy institutional demographic profiles, or fulfill the fiscal needs of a city.

Significantly, the appropriation of site-specific art for the valorization of urban identities comes at a time of a fundamental cultural shift in which architecture and urban planning, formerly the primary media for expressing a vision of the city, are displaced by other media more intimate with marketing and advertising. In the words of urban theorist Kevin Robins, "As cities have become ever more equivalent and urban identities increasingly 'thin,' … it has become necessary to employ advertising and marketing agencies to manufacture such distinctions. It is a question of distinction in a world beyond difference."[13] Site specificity in this context finds new importance because it supplies distinction of place and uniqueness of locational identity, highly seductive qualities in the promotion of towns and cities within the competitive restructuring of the global economic hierarchy. Thus, site specificity remains inexorably tied to a process that renders particularity and identity of various cities a matter of product differentiation. Indeed, the exhibition catalogue for "Places with a Past" was a "tasteful" tourist promotion, pitching the city of Charleston as a unique, "artistic," and meaningful place (to visit).[14] Under the pretext of their articulation or resuscitation, site-specific art can be mobilized to expedite the *erasure* of differences via the commodification and serialization of places.

The yoking together of the myth of the artist as a privileged source of originality with the customary belief in places as ready reservoirs of unique identity belies the compensatory nature of such a move. For this collapse of the artist and the site reveals an anxious cultural desire to assuage the sense of loss and vacancy that pervades both sides of this equation.

It seems inevitable that we should leave behind the nostalgic notions of a site as being essentially bound to the physical and empirical realities of a place. Such a conception, if not ideologically suspect, often seems out of synch with the prevalent description of contemporary life as a network of unanchored flows.

Indeed the deterritorialization of the site has produced liberatory effects, displacing the strictures of fixed place-bound identities with the fluidity of a migratory model, introducing the possibilities for the production of multiple identities, allegiances, and meanings, based not on normative conformities but on the nonrational convergences forged by chance encounters and circumstances. The fluidity of subjectivity, identity, and spatiality as described by Gilles Deleuze and Félix Guattari in their rhyzomatic nomadism,[15] for example, is a powerful theoretical tool for the dismantling of traditional orthodoxies that would suppress differences, sometimes violently.

However, despite the proliferation of discursive sites and "fictional" selves, the phantom of a site as an actual place remains, and our psychic, habitual attachments to places regularly return as they continue to inform our sense of identity. And this persistent, perhaps secret, adherence to the actuality of places (in memory, in longing) is not necessarily a lack of theoretical sophistication but a means for survival. The resurgence of violence in defense of essentialized notions of national, racial, religious, and cultural identities in relation to geographical territories is readily characterized as extremist, retrograde, and "uncivilized." Yet the loosening of such relations, that is, the destabilization of subjectivity, identity, and spatiality (following the dictates of desire), can also be described as a compensatory fantasy in response to the intensification of fragmentation and alienation wrought by a mobilized market economy (following the dictates of capital). The advocacy of the continuous mobilization of self- and place-identities as discursive fictions, as polymorphous "critical" plays on fixed generalities and stereotypes, in the end may be a delusional alibi for short attention spans, reinforcing the ideology of the new—a temporary antidote for the anxiety of boredom. It is perhaps too soon and frightening to acknowledge, but the paradigm of nomadic selves and sites may be a glamorization of the trickster ethos that is in fact a reprisal of the ideology of "freedom of choice"—the choice to forget, the choice to reinvent, the choice to fictionalize, the choice to "belong" anywhere, everywhere, and nowhere. This choice, of course, does not belong to everyone equally. The understanding of identity and difference as being culturally constructed should not obscure the fact that the ability to deploy multiple, fluid identities in and of itself is a privilege of mobilization that has a specific relationship to power.

Homi Bhabha has said, "The globe shrinks for those who own it; for the displaced or the dispossessed, the migrant or refugee, no distance is more awesome than the few feet across borders or frontiers."[16] Today's site-oriented practices inherit the task of demarcating the *relational specificity* that can hold in tension the distant poles of spatial experiences described by Bhabha. This means addressing the differences of adjacencies and distances *between* one thing, one person, one place, one thought, one fragment *next* to another, rather than invoking equivalencies via one thing *after* another. Only those cultural practices that have this relational sensibility can turn local encounters into long-term commitments and transform passing intimacies into indelible, unretractable social marks—so that the sequence of sites that we inhabit in our life's traversal does not become genericized into an undifferentiated serialization, one place after another.

NOTES

1   Douglas Crimp has written: "The idealism of modernist art, in which the art object *in and of itself was* seen to have a fixed and transhistorical meaning, determined the object's placelessness, its belonging in no particular place. … Site specificity opposed that idealism—and unveiled the material system it obscured—by its refusal of circulatory mobility, its belongingness to a *specific* site" (*On the Museum's Ruins* [Cambridge: MIT Press, 1993], p. 17).

2   William Turner, as quoted by Mary Miss, in "From Autocracy to Integration: Redefining the Objectives of Public Art," in *Insights/On Sites: Perspectives on Art in Public Places,* ed. Stacy Paleologos Harris (Washington, D.C.: Partners for Livable Places, 1984), p. 62.

3   Rosalyn Deutsche has made an important distinction between an assimilative model of site specificity—in which the art work is geared toward *integration* into the existing environment, producing a unified, "harmonious" space of wholeness and cohesion—and an interruptive model, where the art work functions as a critical *intervention* into the existing order of a site. See her essays *"Tilted Arc* and the Uses of Public Space," *Design Book Review,* no. 23 (Winter 1992), pp. 22–27; and "Uneven Development: Public Art in New York City," *October* 47 (Winter 1988), pp. 3–52.

4   Richard Serra, *"Tilted Arc* Destroyed," *Art in America* 77, no. 5 (May 1989), pp. 34–47.

5   The controversy over *Tilted Arc* obviously involved other issues besides the status of site specificity, but, in the end, site specificity was the term upon which Serra hung his entire defense. Despite Serra's defeat, the legal definition of site specificity remains unresolved and continues to be grounds for many juridical conflicts. For a discussion concerning legal questions in the *Tilted Arc* case, see Barbara Hoffman, "Law for Art's Sake in the Public Realm," in *Art in the Public Sphere,* ed. W.J.T. Mitchell (Chicago, IL: University of Chicago Press, 1991), pp. 113–146.

6   See Hal Foster's seminal essay, "The Crux of Minimalism," in *Individuals: A Selected History of Contemporary Art 1945-1986,* ed. Howard Singerman (Los Angeles, CA: The Museum of Contemporary Art, 1986), pp. 162–183.

7   Daniel Buren, "Function of the Museum," *Artforum* (September 1973).

8   These concerns coincide with developments in public art, which has reprogrammed site-specific art to be synonymous with community-based art. As exemplified in projects such as "Culture in Action" in Chicago (1992–1993) and "Points of Entry" in Pittsburgh (1996), site-specific public art in the 1990s marks a convergence between cultural practices grounded in leftist political activism, community-based aesthetic traditions,

conceptually driven art borne out of institutional critique, and identity politics. Because of this convergence, many of the questions concerning contemporary site-specific practices apply to public art projects as well, and vice versa.

9   This faith in the authenticity of place is evident in a wide range of disciplines. In urban studies, see Dolores Hayden, *The Power of Place: Urban Landscapes as Public History* (Cambridge, MA: MIT Press, 1995). In relation to public art, see Ronald Lee Fleming and Renata von Tscharner, *PlaceMakers: Creating Public Art That Tells You Where You Are* (Boston, San Diego, and New York: Harcourt Brace Jovanovich, 1981). See also Lucy Lippard, *The Lure of the Local: The Sense of Place in a Multicultural Society* (New York: The New Press, 1997).

10 See *Places with a Past: New Site-specific Art at Charleston's Spoleto Festival,* exhibition catalogue (New York: Rizzoli, 1991), p. 19.

11 Ibid., p. 17.

12 Ibid., p. 15.

13 Kevin Robins, "Prisoners of the City: Whatever Can a Postmodern City Be?" in *Space and Place: Theories of Identity and Location,* ed. Erica Carter, James Donald, and Judith Squires (London: Lawrence & Wishart, 1993), p. 306.

14 Cultural critic Sharon Zukin has noted, "it seemed to be official policy [by the 1990s] that making a place for art in the city went along with establishing a marketable identity for the city as a whole" (Zukin, *The Culture of Cities* [Oxford: Blackwell Publishers, 1995], p. 23).

15 Gilles Deleuze and Félix Guattari, *A Thousand Plateaus,* trans. Brian Massumi (Minneapolis: University of Minnesota Press, 1987).

16 Homi K. Bhabha, "Double Visions," *Artforum* (January 1992), p. 88.

6
Spatializing Culture

An Engaged Anthropological Approach to
Space and Place (2014)

Setha Low

INTRODUCTION

Through long-term research and collaborative projects I have found that *spatializing culture*— i.e., studying culture and political economy through the lens of space and place—provides a powerful tool for uncovering material and representational injustice and forms of social exclusion. At the same time, it facilitates an important form of engagement, because such spatial analyses offer people and their communities a way to understand the everyday places where they live, work, shop, and socialize. I define *engaged anthropology* as those activities that grow out of a commitment to the participants and communities anthropologists work with and a values-based stance that anthropological research respect the dignity and rights of all people and have a beneficent effect on the promotion of social justice (Low and Merry 2010). It also provides them with a basis for fighting proposed changes that often destroy the centers of social life, erase cultural meanings, and restrict local participatory practices.

In this chapter I draw upon both my commitment to engaged anthropology and my experience with the effectiveness of spatializing culture for addressing inequality to frame this discussion. These domains are integrated through my contention that theories and methodologies of space and place can uncover systems of exclusion that are hidden or naturalized and thus rendered invisible to other approaches. The systems of sociospatial exclusion I am particularly interested in encompass a range of processes including physical enclosure that limits who can enter or exit, such as fenced and gated spaces; surveillance strategies such as policing, private security and "city ambassadors," and webcam and video cameras that discourage people of color from entering the space because of racial profiling; privatization of property, especially areas that surround public spaces and deny public access; legal and governance instruments that restrict entrance and use such as those found in Business Improvement Districts and condominiums and cooperative housing; and other related issues. All these systems of exclusion reference the underlying structural racism, sexism and classism that permeate contemporary neoliberal society.

In the same way that history sheds light on a cultural change that is incorrectly seen as timeless and therefore not an important object of study, the study of space, too, can direct attention to social and spatial arrangements that are presumed to be given and fixed, and therefore considered "natural" and simply "the way things should be." Space and its arrangement and allocation are assumed to be transparent, but as Henri Lefebvre (1991) asserts, they never are. Instead when critically examined, space and spatial relations yield insights into unacknowledged biases, prejudices and in-equalities that frequently go unexamined.

After reviewing the concept of spatializing culture as it has been developed within anthropology, I draw upon a fieldwork example to illustrate the value of the approach—Moore Street Market, an enclosed Latino food market in Brooklyn, New York—and claim this urban commercial space for a translocal and networked set of social relations rather than a gentrified redevelopment project.

SPATIALIZING CULTURE

Henri Lefebvre's foundational work on the social production of space adds that "space is never empty: it always embodies a meaning" (1991: 154). His well-known argument that space is never transparent, but must be queried through an analysis of spatial representations, spatial practices and spaces of representation is the basis of many anthropological analyses. Nancy Munn (1996) and Stuart Rockerfeller (2010) draw upon Lefebvre to link conceptual space to the tangible by arguing that social space is both a field of action and a basis for action. Margaret Rodman (2001) and Miles Richardson (1982), on the other hand, rely on phenomenology and theories of lived space to focus attention on how different actors construct, contest and ground their personal experience.

In my own ethnographic work, I initially proposed a dialogical process made up of the social production of space and the social construction of space to explain how culture is spatialized (Low 1996, 2000). In this analysis, the social production of space includes all those factors—social, economic, ideological, and technological—that result, or seek to result, in the physical creation of the material setting. Social construction, on the other hand, refers to spatial transformations through peoples' social interactions, conversations, memories, feelings, imaginings and use—or absences—into places, scenes and actions that convey particular meanings. Both processes are social in the sense that both the production and the construction of space are mediated by social processes, especially being contested and fought over for economic and ideological reasons. Understanding them can help us see how local conflicts over space can be used to uncover and illuminate larger issues.

Unfortunately this co-production model was limited by its two-dimensional structure. Adding *embodied space* to the social construction and social production of space solves much of this problem. The person as a mobile spatial field—a spatiotemporal unit with feelings, thoughts, preferences, and intentions as well as out-of-awareness cultural beliefs and practices—

who creates space as a potentiality for social relations, giving it meaning, form, and ultimately through the patterning of everyday movements, produces place and landscape (Low 2009; Munn 1996; Rockerfeller 2010). The social construction of space is accorded material expression as a person/spatiotemporal unit, while social production is understood as both the practices of the person/spatiotemporal unit and global and collective forces. Further, the addition of language and discourse theories expand the conceptualization of spatializing culture by examining how talk and media are deployed to transform the meaning of practices and spaces (Duranti 1992). For example, gated community residents' discourse of fear plays a critical role in sustaining the spatial preference for and cultural acceptance of walled and guarded developments. The concept of spatializing culture employed in this discussion, thus, encompasses these multiple processes—social production, social construction, embodiment, and discursive practices—to develop an anthropological analysis of space and place.

MOORE STREET MARKET, BROOKLYN, NEW YORK

At lunchtime, Moore Street market is bustling, housed in a squat, white cement building that looks more like a bunker than an enclosed food market with its barred windows and painted metal doors. The deserted street in the shadow of the looming housing projects seems oddly quiet for a busy Monday morning. Upon entering, however, carefully stacked displays of fresh fruit, yucca and coriander, passageways lined with cases of water and soda, and high ceilings with vestiges of the original 1940s architecture of wooden stalls, bright panels, and ceiling fans reveal another world. Puerto Rican salsa music emanating from the video store competes with Dominican cumbia blaring from a radio inside the glass-enclosed counter of a narrow restaurant stall where rice, beans, *empanadas*, and *arroz con pollo* glistening with oil and rubbed red spice are arrayed (see Figure at beginning of Section 1). The smell of fried plantains fills the air conditioned space as Puerto Rican pensioners gather at the round red metal tables with red and white striped umbrellas open to offer intimate places to sit and talk. A young boy in a Yankees t-shirt orders lunch for his Columbian mother who is hesitant to pass the security guard perched at the entrance who she thinks might ask for her immigration papers. She remains outside in the already-blazing Brooklyn sun searching for a spot to sell flavored ices on the crowded sidewalk near the subway entrance.

Moore Street Market vendors are made up of Latinos from Puerto Rico, the Dominican Republic, Ecuador, Mexico and Nicaragua. The Puerto Ricans immigrated to New York in the 1940s, while Dominicans, Mexicans, and Nicaraguans immigrated mostly in the 1980s. Their national and cultural identities are spatially inscribed with Puerto Rican vendors located at the market's social and economic heart, a central area near the café that sells Caribbean food and plays *salsa* music, while the relatively new Nicaraguans and Mexican vendors are located in stalls along the periphery. These first generation immigrants keep ties to their homeland alive through music, food, family relationships and visits home. Many travel back and forth from their native countries bringing goods for sale and carrying gifts and merchandise to families living in Latin America.

One of the vendors, Doña Alba, shuts her metal screened stall, locking away her Seven Saints' oil, plastic flowers, and white first communion dresses. She tells me about her most recent trip to Latin America and success at obtaining the special orders and medicinal potions for her regular customers. As a young girl from Mexico she worked her way up from cleaning for white middle-class families who at that time still lived in the neighborhood and selling fruit at a street stand to leasing her own retail space. The recent threat of eviction by the New York City Economic Development Corporation (EDC), however, has slowed what little business there has been during the economic recession, and she worries about her future and the enterprise that she is so proud of and has so painstakingly built.

Moore Street Market, built in 1941 and located in East Williamsburg/Bushwick, Brooklyn, is one of nine enclosed markets constructed to relocate the pushcart vendors and open air markets and supply modernizing New York City with safe and affordable food. During the 1940s and 1950s, it was a thriving Irish, Jewish and Italian immigrant market. Although the neighborhood had a significant Puerto Rican population by 1960, as late as the

early 1970s some of the original residents and market vendors remained. But the market and the neighborhood physically deteriorated with urban disinvestment during the 1970s and 1980s. Despite an architectural renovation in 1995, its tenuous commercial viability due to a decreasing number of vendors and shoppers was exacerbated in March 2007 when the New York City Economic Development Corporation (EDC) announced it would be closed to make way for affordable housing.

With the threat of closure, the Public Space Research Group (PSRG), a team of CUNY faculty and graduate students, joined the remaining vendors and the Project for Public Spaces to help formulate a community-based response to EDC's closure. *The New York Times* reporters also supported the Moore Street market vendors, stating that "the 70-year old Moore Street market was always more than just a place to do business ... [but] part of the fabric of Williamsburg life, with periodic cultural events and tiny shops and stalls that hearken back to the days before glitzy shopping malls and sterile big-box stores" (Gonzalez 2007). New York City officials and private developers who would benefit from building affordable housing argued instead that the market was not supporting itself and was "tired" and "rundown." The media coverage and heated community meetings drew political attention from US Representative Nydia Velazquez and State Assemblyman Vito Lopez who ultimately secured $3.2 million in federal funding to keep Moore Street Market open.

The ethnographic descriptions and vendor life histories collected are being used to reinstate the market as a Latino social center and to offer an alternative to the gentrification project that "saved" Essex Street Market, a boutique food market in Manhattan's Lower East Side. While the revitalization of the market is still in process, one of the members of the PSRG, Babette Audant, continues to attend community meetings and collaborate with stakeholders. This advocacy effort, though, requires a more embodied spatial analysis focused not only on the social production of this historic market, but also on the everyday practices and agency of the vendors, shoppers and neighbors who value it. By embodied spatial analysis I mean the theoretical premise that individuals as mobile spatiotemporal fields realize space, and the importance of bodily movement and mobility in the creation of locality and translocality. While Moore Street Market began as a collaborative advocacy project, it also generated scholarly insights into a translocal and community-based public space through the mobilities, emotions and meanings of the people who work, shop and hang out there.

Analytically the ethnography of Moore Street Market reveals how urban public space links the body in space, the global/local power relations embedded in space, the role of language and discursive transformations of space, and the material and metaphorical importance of architecture and urban design. It is through this embodied space that the global is integrated into the spaces of everyday urban life and becomes a site of translocal, transnational, as well as personal experience. Moore Street Market can be understood as a place where people spend the day listening to music from their homeland, eating lunch and working at stalls where they make their livelihoods. Simultaneously they are enmeshed in networks of relationships, transnational circuits and ways of being that extend from the built environment of the market to the towns from which they migrated, and where, in many cases, the products that they sell as well as other family members remain, supported from the profits of their commercial endeavors.

It is the movement of these vendors, shoppers, pensioners, and visitors—differentiated by gender, age, class, ethnicity, and national identity—and their everyday activities: conversations, purchases, listening to music, eating homemade food, that makes the market space what it is. And it is through the embodied spaces of their social relationships that the market is simultaneously a local and translocal place.

That is not to say that the market as socially produced by the political machinations of New York City institutions and officials does not continue to play a role in its physical condition and architectural form, and pose a challenge to the market's continued existence. Nor that the meanings of the market are not socially constructed differently by the African American residents who live nearby, the tourists who visit, the officials who want to close it, the newspeople who want a story, and the regulars who see it as their place. Even the language and metaphors of state officials and the media, as well as the "talk" of visitors and neighbors contribute to a series of characterizations of the space as "the center of the Latino community" to a place that is "forlorn, decaying and deteriorating." But these contradictory discourses come into dialogue within one another through the space of the market and the people who use it. The market is a form of spatialized culture that encompasses multiple publics and conflicting meanings, contestations, and negotiations. In this case, the engaged practice of community collaboration and activism to preserve the market from gentrification also generated a better understanding of translocality and its role in creating and maintaining a culturally diverse urban public space.

CONCLUSION

Moore Street Market illustrates how engagement and spatialization enhanced the breadth and scope of the research and advocacy project. The market ethnography project was engaged from its inception, incorporating a collaborative place ethnography to assist the local community and vendors in retaining the market for local use. The spatial analysis helped residents to see the social centrality of the market in the neighborhood. It also produced a better way to think about translocality as embodied by users' and residents' circuits of exchange and social networks. Thus, spatial analysis led to engaged practice, and advocacy and application generated spatial and theoretical insights. I believe that one of the strengths of anthropology lies in this close relationship, its theoretical grounding in practice.

My second point is derived from this view of engagement and suggests that anthropologists have an advantage with regard to theorizing space because we begin our conceptualizations in the field. Regardless of whether it is an ethnographic multi-sited study, a survey of human bone locations, or an archeological dig, there is an encounter with the inherent materiality and human subjectivity of fieldwork that situates the anthropologist at their interface. Theories of space that emerge from the sediment of anthropological research draw on the strengths of studying people in situ, producing rich and nuanced sociospatial understandings. Further, when spatial analyses are employed, they offer the engaged anthropologist a powerful tool for uncovering social injustice because so much of contemporary inequality is imposed through the spatial relations of the environment and the discourse that mystifies its material effects. Therefore, anthropological approaches to the study of space, such as the social production and construction of space, embodied translocal spatiality, and discursive elements of Moore Street Market suggest ways to improve the lives of those who live, work, or hang out there. In this sense, spatializing culture can be a first or last step toward engagement, and one that anthropologists can uniquely employ.

REFERENCES

Duranti, Alessandro. 1992. Language and Bodies in Social Space: Samoan Ceremonial Greetings. *American Anthropologist*, 94(3): 657–691.

Foucault, Michel. 1977. *Discipline and Punish: The Birth of the Prison*. New York: Vintage, Random House.

Gonzalez, Juan. 2007. Brooklyn's La Marqueta Buys Time. *New York Daily News*.

Lefebvre, Henri. 1991. *The Production of Space*. Oxford: Blackwell Publishing.

Low, Setha. 1996. Spatializing Culture: The Social Construction and Social Production of Public Space in Costa Rica. *American Ethnologist*, 23(4): 861–879.

Low, Setha. 2000. *On the Plaza: The Politics of Public Space and Culture*. Austin: University of Texas Press.

Low, Setha. 2009. Toward an Anthropological Theory of Space and Place. Special Issue on Signification and Space. *Semiotica*, 175(1–4): 21–37.

Low, Setha, and Sally Merry. 2010. Engaged Anthropology: Diversity and Dilemmas. *Current Anthropology*, 51(2): 203–226.

Munn, Nancy. 1996. Excluded Spaces: The Figure in the Australian Aboriginal Landscape. *Critical Inquiry*, 22(3): 446–465.

Richardson, Miles. 1982. Being-in-the-Plaza versus Being-in-the-Market: Material Culture and the Construction of Social Reality. *American Ethnologist*, 9(2): 421–436.

Rockerfeller, Stuart Alexander. 2010. *Starting from Quirpini: The Travels and Places of a Bolivian People*. Bloomington: Indiana University Press.

Rodman, Margaret. 2001. *Houses Far From Home*. Honolulu: University of Hawaii Press.

SECTION 2

Human Perception and Environmental Experience

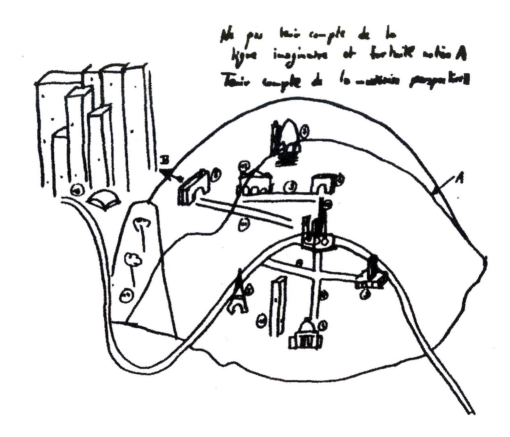

Psychological map of Paris.
Referenced in: Milgram, Stanley and Denise Jodelet. 1970. "Psychological Maps of Paris" in
H.M. Proshansky, et al., eds., *Environmental Psychology: People and their Physical Setting*. New York: Holt,
Rinehart & Winston.

HUMAN PERCEPTION AND
ENVIRONMENTAL EXPERIENCE

Perception describes the multiple ways in which people receive information from their surroundings, allowing them to know their environment. *Cognition*, or the way people understand the environment, occurs through immediate sensory experience coupled with memories and experiences from the past. While psychologists often treat these as different phenomena or faculties, the papers in this section challenge that bifurcation. Psychological studies of perception and cognition look at how we organize, identify, and interpret information through our senses. Other experiments, including projects by artists and designers, have shed light on how we attach meaning to particular places and spaces. Ecological psychology and other interdisciplinary research has demonstrated that human beings and their environments are produced in relation with one another. In this way, knowledge and experience are situated in the interplay between person and environment. Specific places and moments generate particular knowledge and experiences; previous experiences shade understandings and lead people to recognize particular things or respond in specific ways.

Traditionally, the environment was thought of as the *context* for or *container* of human activity, and many areas of psychology have proceeded as if what is "out there" in the environment is perceived by humans "in" our brains. However, John Dewey's (1896) landmark critique of the *reflex arc* denied the separation between external stimulus and internal response by showing the interrelatedness of events, environments, people, and actions. By the mid-20th century, psychologist Kurt Lewin's (1997 [1943]) concept of the *lifespace* described how elements of the environment make up a sort of force field within which people live their lives. Lewin felt that the social and physical environment or *field*—borrowing from the Gestalt psychological framework—is dynamic and changes over time, across spaces, and with experience; as such, people change over time as well. In effect, people and space are connected and co-produce one another rather than exist as distinct, autonomous entities. In this section we have included other classics in this area of research that have further probed the relationship between people and environment through questions of perception and experience.

Where there is space, we make maps to define and navigate it. Beyond books, charts, and global positioning systems (GPS) that people frequently rely upon, human beings possess preconceived cognitive maps of many of the spaces they often traverse and which let us move through the world. The concept of *cognitive mapping* describes the process human beings use to think about space and the ways in which they reflect and act upon those thoughts in their everyday behaviors (Tolman 1948). In their selection, psychologists **Stanley Milgram** and **Denise Jodelet** asked participants to make hand-drawn maps—a technique termed *mental mapping*—in order to glean the cognitive maps Parisians have of Paris (see figure at the beginning of Section 2). This work revealed how these maps steer our actions, and speak to the deeper synchronic processes by which we receive and process knowledge. Their work displaced the idea of fixed mental maps as representations in the minds of individuals with a much more socially and culturally embedded *psychological map* that varies when elicited through different procedures. Milgram and Jodelet found that major elements of the city emerged and project participants linked these elements together through their everyday experiences, as well as through social representations of places that might not even be part of a particular person's daily experience.

The ability to inform design is often limited to architects, engineers, and designers, but who knows the city better than its residents? Urban planner **Kevin Lynch** was the first to employ the method of mental mapping in order to design cities from the perspectives of the citizens who live in them. Rather than focusing on what is inside a person's head, he focused on the elements of the environment that allowed a person to navigate and remember the city. Based on individual interviews and mental maps of residents of three US cities—Boston, Jersey City, and Los Angeles—he outlines five key characteristics of the urban environment: paths, nodes, landmarks, edges, and districts. For Lynch, this research on the mental markers of urban dwellers suggested that the design and planning of urban spaces should be based on people's experience and the ways in which the city could be more legible. In his book *The Image of the City*, he describes *legibility* as the quality of an environment to offer inhabitants clues about where they are and what they can do.

Yet social representations of Paris and mental maps of Boston are different from an individual's immediate visual perception. One of the most seemingly simple yet truly profound theoretical contributions to the work on visual perception is the theory of *affordances* developed by psychologist **James J. Gibson**. Affordances are the qualities of an object or environment that allow or *afford* an individual to perform an action or series of actions. For example, a bowl can afford eating for an adult, but it may also be perceived as a drum or hat by a child, thereby affording other uses. Applications of this theory of affordances today relate not only to analyzing the physical environments of inhabitation, but also in efforts opposing environmental degradation, as the question shifts from the narrow industrial perspective of what the environment can do for us to a more sustainable understanding of environmental affordances.

Both individual perception and social experience inform psychologist **Robert Sommer**'s notion of *personal space*. Personal space is the immediate area surrounding a person that is psychologically regarded as one's own. Often conceived of as a bubble around an individual, it is a form of portable territory that can shift in size and proportion based on situation. Such space is intrinsically tied to what anthropologist Edward Hall (1966) termed *proxemics*, i.e., the study of human relations in layers of proximity based on levels of intimacy. Sommer extends Hall's discursive arguments by looking at where our material comfort zones begin and end to understand our spatial preferences. In his initial studies, described in the included selection, Sommer and his colleagues investigated spatial distances related to psychological comfort through studies of situations where researchers intentionally intruded into other people's spaces. These invasions produced varied responses, and led Sommer to conclude that there are both psychological needs and social conventions at play in human spatial interactions.

Guy Debord, a social theorist and member of a group called the Situationists, wanted to introduce a more radical way of navigating the city and sharing human spaces. His work sought to challenge conventional patterns of activity, through events called *dérives*, which were unplanned tours, or "drifts," through urban environments based on misreading maps or responding to psychological cues. He called this way of navigating the environment through mood and behavior *psychogeography*. By picking up on the feelings evoked by the surroundings and sharing them with one another, a group can embrace a situation or reinterpret it in creative ways. For Debord, the dérive was an experimental method meant to critique or jolt our everyday experience of the environment.

Taken together, these readings suggest that for people the environment exists through interacting with it. As such, the environment is not a passive "out there" condition, but something that everyone participates in creating and defining. Rather than a simple internal–external relationship between people and the environment, there is a complex and dynamic exchange in which the environment informs human knowledge, and human experiences shape the way by which the environment is known. Like Setha Low's description of *embodied space* in Section 1, Máire Eithne O'Neill (2001) describes the role of *corporeal haptic experiences* of space and place that are developed through movement, touch, and other senses and how they can inform design experiences. Furthermore, while scholars agree that spatial knowledge exists, they wrestle with how exactly people are able to maintain cognitive maps and whether these spatial images are analogous to visual maps, or some other type of metaphor or construct. Others argue that cognitive maps are inadequate and that only navigating through a space leads to spatial knowledge (Ingold 2011). There is increasing evidence that builds from both approaches and understands mental maps to be processual *and* representational, i.e., never complete and always becoming (Kitchin and Dodge 2007). This selection of readings examines environmental experience and human perception in the broadest sense to understand the human-environment interplay, and suggests some of the lively ways by which we trace how humans know and creatively interact with their environments.

SUGGESTIONS FOR FURTHER READING

Please see *peopleplacespace.org* for extended and additional lists of readings.

Bachelard, Gaston. 1994. *The Poetics of Space*. Boston, MA: Beacon Press.

Boulding, Kenneth E. 1956. *The Image: Knowledge in Life and Society*. Ann Arbor: University of Michigan Press.

Boydston, Jo Ann (ed.). 2008. *The Collected Works of John Dewey, Index: 1882–1953*. Carbondale, IL: Southern Illinois University Press.

Chown, Eric. 2004. "Cognitive Modeling." In Tucker, A. (ed.) *Computer Science Handbook*. New York: Chapman & Hall.

Cooper Marcus, Clare. 1992. "Environmental Memories." In *Place Attachment*, edited by Irwin Altman and Setha M. Low, pp. 87–112. New York: Springer.

Dewey, John. 1896. "The Reflex Arc Concept in Psychology." *Psychological Review* 3: 357–370.

Downs, Roger, and David Stea. 1977. *Maps in Minds: Reflections on Cognitive Mapping*. New York: Joanna Cotler Books.

Erikson, Erik H. 1964. "Human Strength and the Cycle of Generations" in *Insight and Responsibility*. New York: Norton.

Gieseking, Jack Jen. 2013. "Where We Go from Here: The Mental Sketch Mapping Method and Its Analytic Components." *Qualitative Inquiry* 19(9): 712–724.

Hall, Edward T. 1966. *The Hidden Dimension*. New York: Anchor Press.

Hammond, Kenneth R. 1966. *The Psychology of Egon Brunswik*. New York: Holt, Rinehart and Winston.

Heft, Harry. 2005. *Ecological Psychology in Context: James Gibson, Roger Barker, and the Legacy of William James*. Malwah, NJ: Lawrence Erlbaum Associates.

Heider, Fritz. 1967. *On Perception, Event Structure, and Psychological Environment: Selected Papers*. Madison, CT: International Universities Press.

Holl, Steven, Juhani Pallasmaa, and Alberto Perez-Gomez. 2007. *Questions of Perception: Phenomenology of Architecture*. San Francisco, CA: William K Stout Publishers.

Ingold, Tim. 2011. *Being Alive: Essays on Movement, Knowledge and Description*. New York: Routledge.

Kahn, Louis I., and Robert Twombly. 2003. *Louis Kahn: Essential Texts*. New York: Norton.

Kingwell, Mark. 2004. "Tables, Chairs, and Other Machines for Thinking." In *Practical Judgments: Essays in Culture, Politics, and Interpretation*, pp. 229–247. Toronto: University of Toronto Press, Scholarly Publishing Division.

Kitchin, Rob, and Martin Dodge. 2007. "Rethinking Maps." *Progress in Human Geography* 31(3): 331–344.

Kleinman, Arthur, and Joan Kleinman. 1994. "How Bodies Remember: Social Memory and Bodily Experience of Criticism, Resistance, and Delegitimation Following China's Cultural Revolution." *New Literary History* 25(3): 707–723.

Lewin, Kurt. 1943. "Defining the Field at a Given Time." *Psychological Review* 50: 292–310. Republished in *Resolving Social Conflicts and Field Theory in Social Science*. Washington, DC: American Psychological Association, 1997.

Merleau-Ponty, Maurice. 2008. *The World of Perception*. New York: Routledge.

Milgram, Stanley, and Denise Jodelet. 1970. "Psychological Maps of Paris." In H.M. Proshansky, et al. (eds), *Environmental Psychology: People and their Physical Setting*. New York: Holt, Rinehart & Winston.

O'Neill, Máire Eithne. 2001. "Corporeal Experience: A Haptic Way of Knowing." *Journal of Architectural Education* 55(1): 3–12.

Pallasmaa, Juhani. 2005. *The Eyes of the Skin: Architecture and the Senses*. Chichester: Academy Press.

Tolman, Edward C. 1948. "Cognitive Maps in Rats and Men." *Psychological Review* 55(4): 189–208.

Vygotsky, Lev S., and Michael Cole. 1978. *Mind in Society: The Development of Higher Psychological Processes*. Cambridge: Harvard University Press.

Wood, Denis. 2010. *Rethinking the Power of Maps*. New York: The Guilford Press.

7
Psychological Maps of Paris

(1970)

Stanley Milgram with the collaboration of Denise Jodelet

In this report we shall explore the way in which Parisians mentally represent their city. It is not an examination of Paris as a geographic reality, but rather of the way that reality is mirrored in the minds of its inhabitants. And the first principle is that reality and image are imperfectly linked. The Seine may course a great arc in Paris, almost forming a half circle, but Parisians imagine it a much gentler curve, and some think the river a straight line as it flows through the city.

Paris, the city of stone, is the template from which the mental map draws its structure, but it is not the same as the map. The person harboring a mental model of Paris may die, but the city endures. The city may vanish through flood or nuclear holocaust, but the maps encoded in millions of human brains are not thereby destroyed.

The main problem in investigating a mental entity is to learn how to render it observable. The person's mental image of Paris is not like his driver's license, something he can pull out for inspection. Rather, we shall have to tease the information from the subject, using whatever means psychology can offer to inspect the contents of the mind (Downs and Stea, 1973).

It is not quite as easy as simply asking the person. First, many of the concepts people have about cities are nonverbal, spatial ideas. They are not easily translated into words, particularly on the part of subjects of limited education. Moreover, Parisians are all exposed to stereotypes about their city, readily available clichés, which do not so much tap their personal ideas of the city, as their immersion in a world of prepackaged platitudes. We want to get at something more personal and more closely tied to direct experience.

HANDDRAWN MAPS

To begin, our 218 subjects, drawn from each of the 20 arrondissements (i.e., administrative sectors) of Paris in proportion to their numbers, were asked to draw a map of Paris in which they were to mention all of the elements of the city that came to mind; they could illustrate their maps with monuments, squares, neighborhoods, streets, or whatever elements spontaneously occurred to them. They were told further that their sketch should not resemble a tourist map of Paris, but ought to express their personal view (see Figure 2 at the beginning of this section).

It is clear the subjects did not merely derive their maps from personal, direct experience with the city. They learned them, in part, from other maps. Street maps of Paris, prepared by technically skilled cartographers, are an inherent part of contemporary Parisian culture. Probably not a single subject could have generated a map of the city accurately showing its form and basic structure without reference in his own mind to maps he has already seen. But through processes of selectivity, emphasis, and distortion, the maps become projections of life styles, and express emotional cathexes of the participants.

Second, neither the city, nor the mental maps of the city, are simple agglomerations of elements, they are structures. It is the essence of structure that displacement of one element is not an isolated event, but has consequences for the other elements with which it is linked.

Finally, a map that a person draws of his city is not his mental map, but is only a clue to it. He may not be able to draw very well; he may have images in his mind which he cannot put on paper. He may make errors in his initial strokes that complicate his later completion of the map. But still, the sketch is an opening into his conception of the city.

PARIS AS A COLLECTIVE REPRESENTATION

A city is a social fact. We would all agree to that. But we need to add an important corollary: the perception of a city is also a social fact, and as such needs to be studied in its collective as well as its individual aspect. It is not only what exists but what is *highlighted* by the community that acquires salience in the mind of the person. A city is as much a collective representation as it is an assemblage of streets, squares, and buildings. We discern the major ingredients of that representation by studying not only the mental map in a specific individual, but by seeing what is shared among individuals. Toward this end, we turn from the clinical use of individual maps to an actuarial analysis of the entire group of maps provided by the subjects.

EMERGING ELEMENTS

The sequence that spontaneously emerges as subjects sketch their maps of Paris may tell us what is uppermost in their minds when they think of the city. What is most salient is probably what comes out first. With this point in mind, from the outset we had asked our subjects to number each element as they drew it, emphasizing that the numbering process is to accompany their process of drawing, and not be applied afterward.

Most subjects begin their maps of Paris by drawing a rough ellipse designating the city limits. Unlike many cities in the United States, such as Los Angeles, which do not possess a strong form and whose boundaries bleed off into surrounding areas, Paris possesses a clear boundary and its form impresses itself on the inhabitants. The boundary is sharply etched by the *périphérique*, a highway wrapped around the

city, separating the city from the densely populated suburbs, and providing a contemporary moat-in-motion to replace the historic walls.

Within the city there are almost a thousand different elements included in the maps of our subjects, but only one feature is the first entry of a large number of participants, the Seine. After the city limits are sketched, it is the element that far and away is drawn first. It is not only a basic geographic fact of the city, but its most salient psychological fact as well, and much of the subjects' subsequent mapmaking is organized around it.

But there is a serious distortion in the way the Seine is represented. In reality the path of the Seine resembles a wave that enters Paris at the Quai Bercy, rises sharply northward, tapers slightly as it flows into separate streams around the islands, initiates its flat northernmost segment at the Place de la Concorde, then turns sharply in a great 60° bend at the Place d'Alma to flow out of the south-western tip of the city. But in their drawings, 91.6 percent of the subjects understated the river's degree of curvature. Several subjects pulled it through the city as a straight line, and the typical subject represented the Seine as a gentle arc of slight but uniform curvature.

Why does this systematic distortion occur? Quite clearly it reflects the subjects' experience. Although the Alma bend of the Seine is apparent in high aerial views of the city, it is not experienced as a sharp curve in the ordinary walk or drive through the city. The curve is extended over a sufficient distance so that the pronounced turn of the river is obscured. Such long, slow curves have, in almost all studies of orientation in cities, proved to be the most confusing, and difficult to reconstruct (Lynch, 1960).

We return now to the general question of the sequence with which the elements are set down. After the Seine, Notre Dame and Île de la Cité are set down most often as the first entries. The three elements of the Seine, Île de la Cité, and Notre Dame are at the very heart of the idea of Paris. Lutèce was born on the Île de la Cité; Notre Dame was constructed there 800 years ago. The sequence with which subjects enter their elements in the handdrawn maps recapitulates this history.

Unlike a city such as New York, whose psychological core has shifted continuously northward (and now focuses on the area between 34th and 80th Streets), the psychological center of Paris has remained true to its origins, building outward from the Seine, never shifting its center away from its historic root. The remarkable stability of the "heart of Paris" *confers a* dimension of permanence to the city's psychological structure.

THE MAJOR ELEMENTS

Altogether our subjects entered 4,132 elements in their maps, an average of 19 for each subject. If the city did not impress on its inhabitants a sense of its structure, its highlights and nodes, we would find little agreement among the subjects. But, in fact, time and again we find the same locations, showing up in the handdrawn maps. Indeed, about half of all the 4,132 elements are accounted for by only 26 locations.

Parisians like to say that there is a tourist Paris, but the real Paris is something quite apart. But if we examine the maps produced by the subjects, we see that time and again tourist Paris—the famous monuments and landmarks—reappears as the basic structuring devices in their own productions of the city. Paris is integral, and it is not possible to efface l'Etoile, the Louvre, and others from any intelligent representation of the city.

In scoffing at tourist Paris, Parisians imply they have access to a much deeper treasure, and choose to dissociate themselves from the city's public aspect. But, of course, the very greatness of Paris and its attraction to millions reside in its very availability as a city.

LINKS

No city consists of a set of isolated elements floating in an urban vacuum, but some cities possess a dense set of pathways tying its varied monuments and squares together. A city is either barren or fertile, depending on the degree to which its varied elements are woven into an interconnected web. The sum becomes greater than the parts by virtue of their relationship to each other. To uncover the associational structures of Paris, we posed the following problem to our subjects:

We shall name an element in the Paris scene, then we would like you to wander with the mind's eye to the next specific element in your own mental imagery, which we would then like you to write down. For example, if we say "Tour Eiffel" you might summon up the scene in your mental imagery, probe around mentally, and say "Palais de Chaillot" or "Pont d'Iéna," or you might think of the Clump de Mars. Whatever comes to mind as forming a natural connection is what interests us.

In this way we hoped to see how the varied elements in the subject's mental structure of Paris were held together.

By linking up the separate molecules at points of overlap, one may map the entire network of associations for the city, the reticulate structure of its images.

A related measure of the "embeddedness" is the proportion of subjects who are unable to give any association whatsoever to a stimulus location.

Although we asked our subjects to concentrate on geographic, visual elements, they often included purely social or historical features such as "La Guillotine" or "clochards," as if these elements could simply not be excluded from the meaning of a particular locale.

RECOGNITION OF PARISIAN SCENES

There are numerous representations of things that a person cannot externalize through drawing or verbal recall. He may be able to see a loved one's face in his mind's eye without being able to draw it. But he is likely to recognize it if shown a photograph. And the same is true of cities. A person may have encoded visual aspects of the city that can be most sensitively uncovered through recognition, that is by seeing if the person can match an external stimulus to some memory of it. Accordingly, to supplement the method of "free recall" used in drawing maps of the city, we presented subjects with 40 photographed scenes of Paris, which they were asked to identify. Correct recognition shows that a scene is an active part of the subject's representation of the city, even if he did not spontaneously include it in his map.

We scored recognition by noting the percentage of subjects who correctly identified the scene, and this ranged from 100 percent for Etoile to under 5 percent for Rue de Cambrai and Place d'Israel.

PARIS, KNOWN AND UNKNOWN

The photographic recognition test tells us about the knowledge of specific landmarks, but we wanted a more general picture of the known and unknown parts of the city. Accordingly, we provided each subject with an illustrated map of the city, which we overprinted with the boundaries of the 80 administrative districts (*quartiers*). We asked each subject to study his map and indicate the ten quartiers with which he was most familiar, and those that were least familiar to him. By combining the response for all subjects, we generate a gradient of asserted familiarity across the entire city.

The five most familiar quartiers are contiguous and center on the Quartier Latin and De de la Cité. The next five choices accrete to this cluster, but also extend to the Champs-Elysées and Etoile. When subjects are asked to list the quartier they know least well, we find a striking movement away from the center of Paris to the peripheral arrondissements.

SOCIAL PERCEPTIONS

While ethnic turfs have a salient place in the representation of New York, with exception of the North African districts, and the Jewish quarter around St. Paul, they do not figure greatly in the mental maps of Paris. The city does not have the multiple ethnic concentrations found in New York, and areas are not selectively highlighted and affixed with an ethnic label, a process Suttles (1972) has shown to be important in the definition of ethnic neighborhoods. In pre-World War II Paris, areas of the city were rich in residents from particular provinces, and subjects continue to identify the quartiers around Gare de Montparnasse as *Paris des Bretons*. On the other hand, the Chinese community that once flourished behind the Gare de Lyon receives no prepresentation in the maps of contemporary Parisians.

Subjects locate the very poor in the northeastern district, while the wealthy are overwhelmingly situated in the 16th arrondissement, at the western edge of the city. This is a sharply differentiated perception, with no geographic overlap between the two groups. The criminally dangerous areas of Paris are identified with the 18th and 19th arrondissements, with the greatest threat to personal safety ascribed to the Coutte d'Or quartier, which houses many North African immigrants.

INTUITIONS AND SECRETS

Before drawing the report to a close, we wish to make a few additional observations about Paris and the processes of its mental representation. A person may know many things about a city while not being aware that he possesses such knowledge; and such implicit knowledge may be widely shared. Consider the following hypothetical situation we presented to the subjects:

Suppose you were to meet someone in Paris, a person whom you had never met before, and you knew the exact date and time of the meeting, but not the place. Assume the person you were to meet operated under the similar handicap of not knowing where you would wait for him. Where in Paris would you wait so as to maximize the chances of encountering the person?

Subjects were encouraged to use their intuition in answering the question, but this did not prevent many of them from denouncing the question as illogical, stupid, and unanswerable. But those who responded ($N = 188$) demonstrated that a set of appropriate—even intelligent—responses was possible. (An answer to this question may be considered "appropriate" if it is selected by a large number of other respondents, and thus represents a shared intuition of where others are likely to wait.) Two principles governed the choice of locales (a) some subjects selected a location that was unequivocally representative of the city, (b) other subjects chose locales that by custom and practice had become institutionalized waiting places (much as the clock at Grand Central Station [sic] in New York serves this function).

Six locations accounted for more than 50 percent of all answers. The largest number of Parisians indicated they would wait by the Eiffel

Tower, the preeminent symbol of Paris in modern times. (What would the dominant response have been prior to its construction in 1889? We have no psychological maps to tell us.) The second most popular choice was the Monument des Morts at the Care St. Lazare. The consensus generated by this question shows that the inhabitants share an implicit, intuitive knowledge of the city that can be crystallized given the proper stimulus.

A second observation is that even poorly known areas of a city may exercise a fascination for the inhabitant: thus, three-fourths of the subjects answered affirmatively when asked if there was any part of Paris they did not know well but were attracted to. (The most popular choice was le Marais, a once unfashionable area that has recently experienced a renaissance.) And subjects generated the names of 155 different locales when asked if they had come across any places of particular beauty or interest that were unknown to the general public. Among their responses were: quaint provincial streets off the Parc de Montsouris; Villa Montmorency, a rustic residential enclave of several acres into which the noise of the surrounding streets scarcely penetrates; the courtyards off the Rue de Sèvres, which represent the inner folds of the convoluted brain of Paris, providing a great deal more surface area than a mere skimming of the surface would suggest; Canal St. Martin; Place des Peupliers; Cour du Rohan, and numerous others. Many of the so-called "secret places of beauty" were actually cited by a large number of subjects, yet more important is the subject's attitude that the city yields some secrets to him alone, and that Paris is intricate, variegated, and inexhaustible in its offerings.

But it is false to end this report as a panegyric. For many Parisians assert that the city is declining in quality, succumbing to vehicular pollution, noise, and the flight of artisans from the city; they assert that urban renewal is destroying a good deal of the beauty of Paris, and they locate its worst effects in the 15th, 1st, and 13th arrondissements, where modern apartment buildings and office towers have replaced the greater charm, but also the greater decrepitude, of the older structures.

The problem for modern Paris, then, is to learn something about the transmutation of charm into its contemporary forms, and to learn it quickly, before the old is brutally replaced by the new, and only the street patterns remain.

REFERENCES

Downs, Roger, and David Stea (eds). 1973. *Image and Environment: Cognitive Mapping and Spatial Behaviour.* New York: Hodder & Stoughton Educational.

Lynch, Kevin. 1960. *The Image of the City.* Cambridge, MA: The MIT Press.

Suttles, Gerald D. 1972. *The Social Construction of Communities.* Chicago, IL: University of Chicago Press.

8
The City Image and Its Elements

(1960)

Kevin Lynch

There seems to be a public image of any given city which is the overlap of many individual images. Or perhaps there is a series of public images, each held by some significant number of citizens. Such group images are necessary if an individual is to operate successfully within his environment and to cooperate with his fellows. Each individual picture is unique, with some content that is rarely or never communicated, yet it approximates the public image, which, in different environments, is more or less compelling, more or less embracing.

The contents of the city images so far studied, which are referable to physical forms, can conveniently be classified into five types of elements: paths, edges, districts, nodes, and landmarks. Indeed, these elements may be of more general application, since they seem to reappear in many types of environmental images. These elements may be defined as follows:

1 *Paths*. Paths are the channels along which the observer customarily, occasionally, or potentially moves. They may be streets, walkways, transit lines, canals, railroads. For many people, these are the predominant elements in their image. People observe the city while moving through it, and along these paths the other environmental elements are arranged and related.

2 *Edges*. Edges are the linear elements not used or considered as paths by the observer. They are the boundaries between two phases, linear breaks in continuity: shores, railroad cuts, edges of development, walls. They arc lateral references rather than coordinate axes. Such edges may be barriers, more or less penetrable, which close one region off from another; or they may be seams, lines along which two regions are related and joined together. These edge elements, although probably not as dominant as paths, are for many people important organizing features, particularly in the role of holding together generalized areas, as in the outline of a city by water or wall.

3 *Districts*. Districts are the medium to large sections of the city, conceived of as having two-dimensional extent, which the observer mentally enters 'inside of," and which are recognizable as having some common, identifying character. Always identifiable from the inside, they are also used for exterior reference if visible from the outside. Most people structure their city to some extent in this way, with individual differences as to whether paths or districts are the dominant elements. It seems to depend not only upon the individual but also upon the given city.

4 *Nodes*. Nodes are points, the strategic spots in a city into which an observer can enter, and which are the intensive foci to and from which he is traveling. They may be primarily junctions, places of a break in transportation, a crossing or convergence of paths, moments of shift from one structure to another. Or the nodes may be simply concentrations, which gain their importance from being the condensation of some use or physical character, as a street-corner hangout or an enclosed square. Some of these concentration nodes are the focus and epitome of a district, over which their influence radiates and of which they stand as a symbol. They

may be called cores. Many nodes, of course, partake of the nature of both junctions and concentrations. The concept of node is related to the concept of path, since junctions are typically the convergence of paths, events on the journey. It is similarly related to the concept of district, since cores are typically the intensive foci of districts, their polarizing center. In any event, some nodal points are to be found in almost every image, and in certain cases they may be the dominant feature.

5 *Landmarks*. Landmarks are another type of point-reference, but in this case the observer does not enter within them, they are external. They are usually a rather simply defined physical object: building, sign, store, or mountain. Their use involves the singling out of one element from a host of possibilities. Some landmarks are distant ones, typically seen from many angles and distances, over the tops of smaller elements, and used as radial references. They may be within the city or at such a distance that for all practical purposes they symbolize a constant direction. Such are isolated towers, golden domes, great hills. Even a mobile point, like the sun, whose motion is sufficiently slow and regular, may be employed. Other landmarks are primarily local, being visible only in restricted localities and from certain approaches. These are the innumerable signs, store fronts, trees, doorknobs, and other urban detail, which fill in the image of most observers. They are frequently used clues of identity and even of structure, and seem to be increasingly relied upon as a journey becomes more and more familiar.

The image of a given physical reality may occasionally shift its type with different circumstances of viewing. Thus an expressway may be a path for the driver, an edge for the pedestrian. Or a central area may be a district when a city is organized on a medium scale, and a node when the entire metropolitan area is considered. But the categories seem to have stability for a given observer when he is operating at a given level.

None of the element types isolated above exist in isolation in the real case. Districts are structured with nodes, defined by edges, penetrated by paths, and sprinkled with landmarks. Elements regularly overlap and pierce one another. If this analysis begins with the differentiation of the data into categories, it must end with their reintegration into the whole image.

PATHS

For most people interviewed, paths were the predominant city elements, although their importance varied according to the degree of familiarity with the city. People with least knowledge of Boston tended to think of the city in terms of topography, large regions, generalized characteristics, and broad directional relationships. Subjects who knew the city better had usually mastered part of the path structure, these people thought more in terms of specific paths and their interrelationships. A tendency also appeared for the people who knew the city best of all to rely more upon small landmarks and less upon either regions or paths.

The potential drama and identification in the highway system should not be underestimated. One Jersey City subject, who can find little worth describing in her surroundings, suddenly lit up when she described the Holland Tunnel. Another recounted her pleasure:

> You cross Baldwin Avenue, you see all of New York in front of you, you see the terrific drop of land (the Palisades) … and here's this open panorama of lower Jersey City in front of you and you're going down hill, and there you know: there's the tunnel, there's the Hudson River and everything. … I always look to the right to see if I can see the … Statue of Liberty. … Then I always look up to see the Empire State Building, see how the weather is. … I have a real feeling of happiness because I'm going someplace, and I love to go places.

EDGES

Edges are the linear elements not considered as paths: they are usually, but not quite always, the boundaries between two kinds of areas. They act as lateral references. They are strong in Boston and Jersey City but weaker in Los Angeles. Those edges seem strongest which are not only visually prominent, but also continuous in form and impenetrable to cross movement. The Charles River in Boston is the best example and has all of these qualities.

The importance of the peninsular definition of Boston has already been mentioned. It must have been much more important in the 18th century, when the city was a true and very striking peninsula. Since then the shore lines have been erased or changed, but the picture persists. One change, at least, has strengthened the image: the Charles River edge, once a swampy backwater, is now well defined and developed. It was frequently described, and sometimes drawn in great detail. Everyone remembered the wide open space, the curving line, the bordering highways, the boats, the Esplanade, the Shell.

The Central Artery is inaccessible to pedestrians, at some points impassable, and is spatially prominent. But it is only occasionally exposed to view. It was a case of what might be called a fragmentary edge: in the abstract continuous, but only visualized at discrete points. The railroad lines were another example. The Artery, in particular, was like a snake lying over the city image. Held down at the ends and at one or two internal points, it elsewhere writhed and twisted from one position to the next. The lack of relation felt while driving the Artery was mirrored in its ambiguous location for the pedestrian.

Storrow Drive, on the other hand, while also felt to be "outside" by the driver, was clearly located on the map, because of its alignment to the Charles River. It was the Charles River, despite its role as the basic edge in the Boston image, which was curiously isolated from the detailed structure of the adjoining Back Bay. People were at a loss as to how to move from one to the other. We can speculate that this was not true before Storrow Drive cut off pedestrian access at the foot of each cross street.

Similarly, the interrelation of the Charles River and Beacon Hill was hard to grasp. Although the position of the hill is potentially explanatory of the puzzling bend in the river, and although the hill thereby gains a commanding enfilade view of the river edge, the Charles Street rotary seemed for most people to be the only firm connection between the two. If the hill rose sharply and immediately out of the water, instead of behind a masking foreshore covered by uses which are only doubtfully associated with Beacon Hill, and if it were more closely tied to the path system along the river, then the relation would have been much clearer.

In Jersey City, the waterfront was also a strong edge, but a rather forbidding one. It was a no-man's land, a region beyond the barbed wire. Edges, whether of railroads, topography, throughways, or district boundaries, are a very typical feature of this environment and tend to fragment it. Some of the most unpleasant edges, such as the bank of the Hackensack River with its burning dump areas, seemed to be mentally erased. The disruptive power of an edge must be reckoned with.

DISTRICTS

Districts are the relatively large city areas which the observer can mentally go inside of, and which have some common character. They can be recognized internally, and occasionally can be used as external reference as a person goes by or toward them. Many persons interviewed took care to point out that Boston, while confusing in its path pattern even to the experienced inhabitant, has, in the number and vividness of its differentiated districts, a quality that quite makes up for it. As one person put it:

> Each part of Boston is different from the other. You can tell pretty much what area you're in.

Jersey City has its districts too, but they are primarily ethnic or class districts with little physical distinction. Los Angeles is markedly lacking in strong regions, except for the Civic Center area.

Subjects, when asked which city they felt to be a well-oriented one, mentioned several, but New York (meaning Manhattan) was unanimously cited. And this city was cited not so much for its grid, which Los Angeles has as well, but because it has a number of well-defined characteristic districts, set in an ordered frame of rivers and streets. Two Los Angeles subjects even referred to Manhattan as being "small" in comparison to their central area! Concepts of size may depend in part on how well a structure can be grasped.

NODES

Nodes are the strategic foci into which the observer can enter, typically either junctions of paths, or concentrations of some characteristic. But although conceptually they are small points in the city image, they may in reality be large squares, or somewhat extended linear shapes, or even entire central districts when the city is being considered at a large enough level. Indeed, when conceiving the environment at a national or international level, then the whole city itself may become a node.

The junction, or place of a break in transportation, has compelling importance for the city observer. Because decisions must be made at junctions, people heighten their attention at such places and perceive nearby elements with more than normal clarity. This tendency was confirmed so repeatedly that elements located at junctions may automatically be assumed to derive special prominence from their location. The perceptual importance of such locations shows in another way as well. When subjects were asked where on a habitual trip they first felt a sense of arrival in downtown Boston, a large number of people singled out break-points of transportation as the key places. In a number of cases, the point was at the transition from a highway (Storrow Drive or the Central Artery) to a city street; in another case, the point was at the first railroad stop in Boston (Back Bay Station) even though the subject did not get off there. Inhabitants of Jersey City felt they had left their city when they had passed through the Tonnelle Avenue Circle. The transition from one transportation channel to another seems to mark the transition between major structural units.

LANDMARKS

Landmarks, the point references considered to be external to the observer, are simple physical elements which may vary widely in scale. There seemed to be a tendency for those more familiar with a city to rely increasingly on systems of landmarks for their guides—to enjoy uniqueness and specialization, in place of the continuities used earlier.

Since the use of landmarks involves the singling out of one element from a host of possibilities, the key physical characteristic of this class is singularity, some aspect that is unique or memorable in the context. Landmarks become more easily identifiable, more likely to be chosen as significant, if they have a clear form; if they contrast with their background; and if there is some prominence of spatial location. Figure–background contrast seems to be the principal factor. The background against which an element stands out need not be limited to immediate surroundings: the grass-

hopper weathervane of Faneuil Hall, the gold dome of the State House, or the peak of the Los Angeles City Hall are landmarks that are unique against the background of the entire city.

Spatial prominence can establish elements as landmarks in either of two ways: by making the element visible from many locations (the John Hancock Building in Boston, the Richfield Oil Building in Los Angeles), or by setting up a local contrast with nearby elements, i.e., a variation in setback and height. In Los Angeles, on 7th Street at the corner of Flower Street, is an old, two-storey gray wooden building, set back some ten feet from the building line, containing a few minor shops. This took the attention and fancy of a surprising number of people. One even anthropomorphized it as the "little gray lady." The spatial setback and the intimate scale is a very noticeable and delightful event, in contrast to the great masses that occupy the rest of the frontage.

ELEMENT INTERRELATIONS

These elements are simply the raw material of the environmental image at the city scale. They must be patterned together to provide a satisfying form. The preceding discussions have gone as far as groups of similar elements (nets of paths, clusters of landmarks, mosaics of regions). The next logical step is to consider the interaction of pairs of unlike elements.

Such pairs may reinforce one another, resonate so that they enhance each other's power; or they may conflict and destroy themselves. A great landmark may dwarf and throw out of scale a small region at its base. Properly located, another landmark may fix and strengthen a core; placed off center, it may only mislead, as does the John Hancock Building in relation to Boston's Copley Square. A large street, with its ambiguous character of both edge and path, may penetrate and thus expose a region to view, while at the same time disrupting it. A landmark feature may be so alien to the character of a district as to dissolve the regional continuity, or it may, on the other hand, stand in just the contrast that intensifies that continuity.

Districts in particular, which tend to be of larger size than the other elements, contain within themselves, and are thus related to, various paths, nodes, and landmarks. These other elements not only structure the region internally, they also intensify the identity of the whole by enriching and deepening its character. Beacon Hill in Boston is one example of this effect. In fact, the components of structure and identity (which are the parts of the image in which we are interested) seem to leapfrog as the observer moves up from level to level. The identity of a window may be structured into a pattern of windows, which is the cue for the identification of a building. The buildings themselves are interrelated so as to form an identifiable space, and so on.

Paths, which are dominant in many individual images, and which may be a principal resource in organization at the metropolitan scale, have intimate interrelations with other element types. Junction nodes occur automatically at major intersections and termini, and by their form should reinforce those critical moments in a journey. These nodes, in turn, are not only strengthened by the presence of landmarks (as is Copley Square) but provide a setting which almost guarantees attention for any such mark. The paths, again, are given identity and tempo not only by their own form, or by their nodal junctions, but by the regions they pass through, the edges they move along, and the landmarks distributed along their length.

All these elements operate together, in a context. It would be interesting to study the characteristics of various pairings: landmark–region, node–path, etc. Eventually, one should try to go beyond such pairings to consider total patterns.

Most observers seem to group their elements into intermediate organizations, which might be called complexes. The observer senses the complex as a whole whose parts are interdependent and are relatively fixed in relation to each other. Thus many Bostonians would be able to fit most of the major elements of the Back Bay, the Common, Beacon Hill, and the central shopping, into a single complex. [...] Outside of this complex there are gaps of identity; the observer must run blind to the next whole, even if only momentarily. Although they are close together in physical reality, most people seem to feel only a vague link between Boston's office and financial district and the central shopping district on Washington Street. This peculiar remoteness was also exemplified in the puzzling gap between Scollay Square and Dock Square which are only a block apart. The psychological distance between two localities may be much greater, or more difficult to surmount, than mere physical separation seems to warrant.

Our preoccupation here with parts rather than wholes is a necessary feature of an investigation in a primitive stage. After successful differentiation and understanding of parts, a study can move on to consideration of a total system. There were indications that the image may be a continuous field, the disturbance of one element in some way affecting all others. Even the recognition of an object is as much dependent on context as on the form of the object itself. One major distortion, such as a twisting of the shape of the Common, seemed to be reflected throughout the image of Boston. The disturbance of large-scale construction affected more than its immediate environs. But such field effects have hardly been studied here.

THE SHIFTING IMAGE

Rather than a single comprehensive image for the entire environment, there seemed to be sets of images, which more or less overlapped and interrelated. They were typically arranged in a series of levels, roughly by the scale of area involved, so that the observer moved as necessary from an image at street level to levels of a neighborhood, a city, or a metropolitan region.

This arrangement by levels is a necessity in a large and complex environment. Yet it imposes an extra burden of organization on the observer, especially if there is little relation between levels. If a tall building is unmistakable in the city-wide panorama yet unrecognizable from its base, then a chance has been lost to pin together the images at two different levels of organization. The State House on Beacon Hill, on the other hand, seems to pierce through several image levels. It holds a strategic place in the organization of the center.

Images may differ not only by the scale of area involved, but by viewpoint, time of day, or season. The image of Faneuil Hall as seen from the markers should be related to its image from a car on the Artery. Washington-Street-by-night should have some continuity, some element of invariance, with Washington-Street-by-day. In order to accomplish this continuity in the face of sensuous confusion, many observers drained their images of visual content, using abstractions such as "restaurant" or "second street." These will operate both day and night, driving or walking, rain or shine, albeit with some effort and loss.

The image itself was not a precise, miniaturized model of reality, reduced in scale and consistently abstracted. As a purposive simplification, it was made by reducing, eliminating, or even adding elements to reality, by fusion and distortion, by relating and structuring the parts. It was sufficient, perhaps better, for its purpose if rearranged, distorted, "illogical." It resembled that famous cartoon of the New Yorker's view of the United States.

However distorted, there was a strong element of topological invariance with respect to reality. It was as if the map were drawn on an infinitely flexible rubber sheet; directions were twisted, distances stretched or compressed, large forms so changed from their accurate scale projection as to be at first unrecognizable. But the sequence was usually correct, the map was rarely torn and sewn back together in another order. This continuity is necessary if the image is to be of any value.

We are continuously engaged in the attempt to organize our surroundings, to structure and identify them. Various environments are more or less amenable to such treatment. When reshaping cities it should be possible to give them a form which facilitates these organizing efforts rather than frustrates them.

9
The Theory of Affordances
(1979)

James J. Gibson

The *affordances* of the environment are what it *offers* the animal, what it *provides* or *furnishes*, either for good or ill. The verb to *afford* is found in the dictionary, but the noun *affordance* is not. I have made it up. I mean by it something that refers to both the environment and the animal in a way that no existing term does. It implies the complementarity of the animal and the environment.

MAN'S ALTERATION OF THE NATURAL ENVIRONMENT

In the last few thousand years, as everybody now realizes, the very face of the earth has been modified by man. The layout of surfaces has been changed, by cutting, clearing, leveling, paving, and building. Natural deserts and mountains, swamps and rivers, forests and plains still exist, but they are being encroached upon and reshaped by man-made layouts. Moreover, the *substances* of the environment have been partly converted from the natural materials of the earth into various kinds of artificial materials such as bronze, iron, concrete, and bread. Even the *medium* of the environment—the air for us and the water for fish—is becoming slowly altered despite the restorative cycles that yielded a steady state for millions of years prior to man.

Why has man changed the shapes and substances of his environment? To change what it affords him. He has made more available what benefits him and less pressing what injures him.

In making life easier for himself, of course, he has made life harder for most of the other animals. Over the millennia, he has made it easier for himself to get food, easier to keep warm, easier to see at night, easier to get about, and easier to train his offspring.

This is not a *new* environment—an artificial environment distinct from the natural environment—but the same old environment modified by man. It is a mistake to separate the natural from the artificial as if there were two environments: artifacts have to be manufactured from natural substances. It is also a mistake to separate the cultural environment from the natural environment, as if there were a world of mental products distinct from the world of material products. There is only one world, however diverse, and all animals live in it, although we human animals have altered it to suit ourselves. We have done so wastefully, thoughtlessly, and, if we do not mend our ways, fatally.

The fundamentals of the environment—the substances, the medium, and the surfaces—are the same for all animals. No matter how powerful men become they are not going to alter the fact of earth, air, and water—the lithosphere, the atmosphere, and the hydrosphere, together with the interfaces that separate them. For terrestrial animals like us, the earth and the sky are a basic structure on which all lesser structures depend. We cannot change it. We all fit into the substructures of the environment in our various ways, for we were all, in fact, formed by them. We were created by the world we live in.

THE SURFACES AND THEIR LAYOUTS

I have already said that a horizontal, flat, extended, rigid surface affords support. It permits equilibrium and the maintaining of a posture with respect to gravity, this being a force perpendicular to the surface. The animal does not fall or slide as it would on a steep hillside. Equilibrium and posture are prerequisite to other behaviors, such as locomotion and manipulation. The ground is quite literally the *basis* of the behavior of land animals. And it is also the basis of their visual perception, their so-called space perception. Geometry began with the study of the earth as abstracted by Euclid, not with the study of the axes of empty space as abstracted by Descartes. The affording of support and the geometry of a horizontal plane are therefore not in different realms of discourse; they are not as separate as we have supposed.

The flat earth, of course, lies *beneath* the attached and detached objects on it. The earth has "furniture," or as I have said, it is cluttered. The solid, level, flat surface extends behind the clutter and, in fact, extends all the way out to the horizon. This is not, of course, the earth of Copernicus; it is the earth at the scale of the human animal, and on that scale it is flat, not round. Wherever one goes, the earth is separated from the sky by a horizon that, although it may be hidden by the clutter, is always there. There will be evidence to show that the horizon can always be seen, in the sense that it can be visualized, and that it can always be felt, in the sense that any surface one touches is experienced in relation to the horizontal plane.

Of course, a horizontal, flat, extended surface that is *nonrigid*, a stream or lake, does not afford support for standing, or for walking and running. There is no footing, as we say. It may afford floating or swimming, but you have to be equipped for that, by nature or by learning.

A *vertical*, flat, extended, and rigid surface such as a wall or a cliff face is a barrier to pedestrian locomotion. Slopes between vertical and horizontal afford walking, if easy, but only climbing, if steep, and in the latter case the surface cannot be flat: there must be "holds" for the hand and feet. Similarly, a slope downward affords falling if steep; the brink of a cliff is a falling-off place. It is dangerous and looks dangerous. The affordance of a certain layout is perceived if the layout is perceived.

Civilized people have altered the steep slopes of their habitat by building stairways so as to afford ascent and descent. What we call the steps afford stepping, up or down, relative to the size of the person's legs. We are still capable of getting around in an arboreal layout of surfaces, tree branches, and we have ladders that afford this kind of locomotion, but most of us leave that to our children.

The imminence of collision with a surface during locomotion is specified in a particularly simple way, by an explosive rate of magnification of the optical texture. This has been called looming (e.g., Schiff, 1965). It should not be confused, however, with the magnification of an opening between obstacles, the opening up of a *vista* such as occurs in the approach to a doorway.

THE OBJECTS

The affordances of what we loosely call *objects* are extremely various. It will be recalled that my use of the terms is restricted and that I distinguish between *attached* objects and *detached* objects. We are not dealing with Newtonian objects in space, all of which are detached, but with the furniture of the earth, some items of which are attached to it and cannot be moved without breakage.

Detached objects must be comparable in size to the animal under consideration if they are to afford behavior. But those that are comparable afford an astonishing variety of behaviors, especially to animals with hands. Objects can be manufactured and manipulated. Some are portable in that they afford lifting and carrying, while others are not. Some are graspable and others not. To be graspable, an object must have opposite surfaces separated by a distance less than the span of the hand. A five-inch cube can be grasped, but a ten-inch cube cannot. A large object needs a "handle" to afford grasping. Note that the size of an object that constitutes a graspable size is specified in the optic array. If this is true, it is *not* true that a tactual sensation of size has to become associated with the visual sensation of size in order for the affordance to be perceived.

We have thousands of names for such objects, and we classify them in many ways: pliers and wrenches are tools; pots and pans are utensils; swords and pistols are weapons. They can all be said to have properties or qualities:

color, texture, composition, size, shape and features of shape, mass, elasticity, rigidity, and mobility. Orthodox psychology asserts that *we perceive these objects insofar as we discriminate their properties or qualities*. Psychologists carry out elegant experiments in the laboratory to find out how and how well these qualities are discriminated. The psychologists assume that objects are *composed* of their qualities. But I now suggest that what we perceive when we look at objects are their affordances, not their qualities. We can discriminate the dimensions of difference if required to do so in an experiment, but what the object affords us is what we normally pay attention to. The special combination of qualities into which an object can be analyzed is ordinarily not noticed.

If this is true for the adult, what about the young child? There is much evidence to show that the infant does not begin by first discriminating the qualities of objects and then learning the combinations of qualities that specify them. Phenomenal objects are *not* built up of qualities; it is the other way around. The affordance of an object is what the infant begins by noticing. The meaning is observed before the substance and surface, the color and form, are seen as such. An affordance is an invariant combination of variables, and one might guess that it is easier to perceive such an invariant unit than it is to perceive all the variables separately. It is never necessary to distinguish *all* the features of an object and, in fact, it would be impossible to do so. Perception is economical. "Those features of a thing are noticed which distinguish it from other things that it is not— but not *all* the features that distinguish it from *everything* that it not."

OTHER PERSONS AND ANIMALS

The richest and most elaborate affordances of the environment are provided by other animals and, for us, other people. These are, of course, detached objects with topologically closed surfaces, but they change the shape of their surfaces while yet retaining the same fundamental shape. They move from place to place, changing the postures of their bodies, ingesting and emitting certain substances, and doing all this spontaneously, initiating their own movements, which is to say that their movements are *animate*. These bodies are subject to the laws of mechanics and yet *not* subject to the laws of mechanics, for they are not *governed* by these laws. They are so different from ordinary objects that infants learn almost immediately to distinguish them from plants and nonliving things. When touched they touch back, when struck they strike back; in short, they *interact* with the observer and with one another. Behavior affords behavior, and the whole subject matter of psychology and of the social sciences can be thought of as an elaboration of this basic fact. Sexual behavior, nurturing behavior, fighting behavior, cooperative behavior, economic behavior, political behavior—all depend on the perceiving of what another person or other persons afford, or sometimes on the misperceiving of it.

The other person, the generalized *other*, the *alter* as opposed to the *ego*, is an ecological object with a skin, even if clothed. It is an object, although it is not *merely* an object, and we do right to speak of *he* or *she* instead of *it*. But the other person has a surface that reflects light, and the information to specify what he or she is, invites, promises, threatens, or does can be found in the light.

PLACES AND HIDING PLACES

The habitat of a given animal contains *places*. A place is not an object with definite boundaries but a region. The different places of a habitat may have different affordances. Some are places where food is usually found and others where it is not. There are places of danger, such as the brink of a cliff and the regions where predators lurk. There are places of refuge from predators. Among these is the place where mate and young are, the home, which is usually a partial enclosure. Animals are skilled at what the psychologist calls place-learning. They can find their way to significant places.

An important kind of place, made intelligible by the ecological approach to visual perception, is a place that affords concealment, a *hiding place*. Note that it involves social perception and raises questions of epistemology. The concealing of oneself from other observers and the hiding of a detached object from other observers have different kinds of motivation. As every child discovers, a good hiding place for one's body is not necessarily a good hiding place for a treasure. A detached object can be concealed both from other observers and from the observer himself. The observer's body can be concealed from other observers but *not* from himself. Animals as well as children hide themselves and also hide objects such as food.

One of the laws of the ambient optic array is that at any fixed point of observation some parts of the environment are revealed and the remaining parts are concealed. The reciprocal of this law is that the observer himself, his body considered as part of the environment, is revealed at some fixed points of observation and concealed at the remaining points. An observer can perceive not only that other observers are unhidden or hidden from him but also that he is hidden or unhidden from other observers. Surely, babies playing peek-a-boo and children playing hide-and-seek are practicing this kind of apprehension. To *hide* is to position one's body at a place that is concealed at the points of observation of other observers. A "good" hiding place is one that is concealed at nearly all points of observation. A translucent sheet transmits illumination but not information.

Note also that a glass wall affords seeing through but not walking through, whereas a cloth curtain affords going through but not seeing through. Architects and designers know such facts, but they lack a theory of affordances to encompass them in a system.

SUMMARY: POSITIVE AND NEGATIVE AFFORDANCES

The foregoing examples of the affordances of the environment are enough to show how general and powerful the concept is. Substances have biochemical offerings and afford manufacture. Surfaces afford posture, locomotion, collision, manipulation, and in general behavior. Special forms of layout afford shelter and concealment. Fires afford warming and burning. Detached objects—tools, utensils, weapons—afford special types of behavior to primates and humans. The other animal and the other person provide mutual and reciprocal affordances at extremely high levels of behavioral complexity. At the highest level, when vocalization becomes speech and manufactured displays become images, pictures, and writing, the affordances of human behavior are staggering. No more of that will be considered at this stage except to point

out that speech, pictures, and writing still have to be perceived.

At all these levels, we can now observe that some offerings of the environment are beneficial and some are injurious. These are slippery terms that should only be used with great care, but if their meanings are pinned down to biological and behavioral facts the danger of confusion can be minimized. First, consider substances that afford ingestion. Some afford nutrition for a given animal, some afford poisoning, and some are neutral. As I pointed out before, these facts are quite distinct from the affording of pleasure and displeasure in eating, for the experiences do not necessarily correlate with the biological effects. Second, consider the brink of a cliff. On the one side it affords walking along, locomotion, whereas on the other it affords falling off, injury. Third, consider a detached object with a sharp edge, a knife. It affords cutting if manipulated in one manner, but it affords being cut if manipulated in another manner. Similarly, but at a different level of complexity, a middle-sized metallic object affords grasping, but if charged with current it affords electric shock. And fourth, consider the other person. The animate object can give caresses or blows, contact comfort or contact injury, reward or punishment, and it is not always easy to perceive which will be provided. Note that all these benefits and injuries, these safeties and dangers, these positive and negative affordances are properties of things *taken with reference to an observer* but not properties of the *experiences of the observer*. They are not subjective values; they are not feelings of pleasure or pain added to neutral perceptions.

There has been endless debate among philosophers and psychologists as to whether values are physical or phenomenal, in the world of matter or only in the world of mind. For affordances as distinguished from values, the debate does not apply. Affordances are neither in the one world or the other inasmuch as the theory of two worlds is rejected. There is only one environment, although it contains many observers with limitless opportunities for them to live in it.

THE OPTICAL INFORMATION FOR PERCEIVING AFFORDANCES

The theory of affordances is a radical departure from existing theories of value and meaning. It begins with a new definition of what value and meaning *are*. The perceiving of an affordance is not a process of perceiving a value-free physical object to which meaning is somehow added in a way that no one has been able to agree upon; it is a process of perceiving a value-rich ecological object. Any substance, any surface, any layout has some affordance for benefit or injury to someone. Physics may be value-free, but ecology is not.

The central question for the theory of affordances is not whether they exist and are real but whether information is available in ambient light for perceiving them. The skeptic may now be convinced that there is information in light for some properties of a surface but not for such a property as being good to eat. The taste of a thing, he will say, is not specified in light; you can see its form and color and texture but not its palatability; you have to *taste* it for that.

Nevertheless, however true all this may be, the basic affordances of the environment are perceivable and are usually perceivable directly, without an excessive amount of learning. The basic properties of the environment that make an affordance are specified in the structure of ambient light, and hence the affordance itself is specified in ambient light. Moreover, an invariant variable *that is commensurate with the body of the observer himself* is more easily picked up than one not commensurate with his body.

REFERENCE

Schiff, William. (1965) Perception of impending collision—a study of visually directed avoidant behavior. *Psychol Monograph* 79:1–26.

10
Spatial Invasion

(1969)

Robert Sommer

Dear Abby: I have a pet peeve that sounds so petty and stupid that I'm almost ashamed to mention it. It is people who come and sit down beside me on the piano bench while I'm playing. I don't know why this bothers me so much, but it does. Now you know, Abby, you can't tell someone to get up and go sit somewhere else without hurting their feelings. But it would be a big relief to me if I could get them to move in a nice inoffensive way. ...

Lost Chord

Dear Lost: People want to sit beside you while you're playing because they are fascinated. Change your attitude and regard their presence as a compliment, and it might be easier to bear. P.S. You might also change your piano bench for a piano stool.

(Abigail Van Euren,
San Francisco Chronicle, May 25, 1965)

The best way to learn the location of invisible boundaries is to keep walking until somebody complains. Personal space refers to an area with invisible boundaries surrounding a person's body into which intruders may not come. Like the porcupines in Schopenhauer's fable, people like to be close enough to obtain warmth and comradeship but far enough away to avoid pricking one another. Personal space is not necessarily spherical in shape, nor does it extend equally in all directions. (People are able to tolerate closer presence of a stranger at their sides than directly in front.) It has been likened to a snail shell, a soap bubble, an aura, and "breathing room."

Although some people claim to see a characteristic aura around human bodies and are able to describe its color, luminosity, and dimensions, most observers cannot confirm these reports and must evolve a concept of personal space from interpersonal transactions. There is a considerable similarity between personal space and individual distance, or the characteristic spacing of species members. Individual distance exists only when two or more members of the same species are present and is greatly affected by population density and territorial behavior. Individual distance and personal space interact to affect the distribution of persons. The violation of individual distance is the violation of society's expectations; the invasion of personal space is an intrusion into a person's self-boundaries. Individual distance may be outside the area of personal space—conversation between two chairs across the room exceeds the boundaries of personal space, or individual distance may be less than the boundaries of personal space—sitting next to someone on a piano bench is within the expected distance but also within the bounds of personal space and may cause discomfort to the player. If there is only one individual present, there is infinite individual distance, which is why it is useful to maintain a concept of personal space, which has also been described as a portable territory, since the individual carries it with him wherever he goes although it disappears under certain conditions, such as crowding.

Hospital patients complain not only that their personal space and their very bodies are continually violated by nurses, interns, and physicians who do not bother to introduce themselves or explain their activities, but that their territories are violated by well-meaning visitors who will ignore "No Visitors" signs. Frequently patients are too sick or too sensitive to repel intruders. Once surgery is finished or the medical treatment has been instituted, the patient is left to his own devices to find peace and privacy.

Spatial invasions are not uncommon during police interrogations. One police textbook recommends that the interrogator should sit close to the suspect, with no table or desk between them, since "an obstruction of any sort affords the subject a certain degree of relief and confidence not otherwise obtainable."[1] At the beginning of the session, the officer's chair may be two or three feet away, "but after the interrogation is under way the interrogator should move his chair in closer so that ultimately one of the subject's knees is just about in between the interrogator's two knees."[2]

Lovers pressed together close their eyes when they kiss. On intimate occasions the lights are typically dim to reduce not only the distracting external cues but also to permit two people to remain close together. Personal space is a culturally acquired daylight phenomenon. Strangers are affected differently than friends by a loss of personal space. During rush hour, subway riders lower their eyes and sometimes "freeze" or become rigid as a form of minimizing unwanted social intercourse. Boy-meets-girl on a crowded rush hour train would be a logical plot for an American theater based largely in New York City, but it is rarely used. The idea of meeting someone under conditions where privacy, dignity, and individuality are so reduced is difficult to accept.

A driver can make another exceedingly nervous by tailgating. Highway authorities recommend a "space cushion" of at least one car length for every ten miles per hour of speed. You can buy a bumper sticker or a lapel button with the message "If you can read this, you're too close."

Probably the most feasible method for exploring individual distance and personal space with their invisible boundaries is to approach people and observe their reactions. Individual distance is not an absolute figure but varies with the relationship between the individuals, the distance at which others in the situation are placed, and the bodily orientations of the individuals one to another. The most systematic work along these lines has been undertaken by the anthropologist Ray Birdwhistell who records a person's response with zoom lenses and is able to detect even minute eye movements and hand tremors as the invader approaches the emotionally egotistic zone around the victim.[3]

One of the earliest attempts to invade personal space on a systematic basis was undertaken by Williams, who wanted to learn how different people would react to excessive closeness. Classifying students as introverts or extroverts on the basis of their scores on a personality test, he placed each individual in an experimental room and then walked toward the person, telling him to speak out as soon as he (Williams) came too close. Afterward he used the reverse condition, starting at a point very close and moving away until the person reported that he was too far away for comfortable conversation. His results showed that introverts kept people at a greater conversational distance than extroverts.[4]

The same conclusion was reached by Leipold, who studied the distance at which introverted and extroverted college students placed themselves in relation to an interviewer in either a stress or a non-stress situation. When the student entered the experimental room, he was given either the stress, praise, or neutral instructions. The stress instructions were, "We feel that your course grade is quite poor and that you have not tried your best. Please take a seat in the next room and Mr. Leipold will be in shortly to discuss this with you." The neutral control instructions read, "Mr. Leipold is interested in your feelings about the introductory course. Would you please take a seat in the next room." After the student had entered and seated himself, Mr. Leipold came in, recorded the student's seating position, and conducted the interview. The results showed that students given praise sat closest to Leipold's chair, followed by those in the neutral condition, with students given the stress instructions maintaining the most distance from Leipold's chair behind the desk. It was also found that introverted and anxious individuals sat further away from him than did extroverted students with a lower anxiety level.[5]

In order to explore personal space using the invasion technique, but to avoid the usual connotations surrounding forced close proximity to strangers, my own method was to undertake the invasion in a place where the usual sanctions of the outside world did not apply. Deliberate invasions of personal space seem more feasible and appropriate inside a mental hospital than outside. Afterward, it became apparent that this method could be adapted for use in other settings such as the library in which Nancy Russo spent many hours sitting too close to other girls.

The first study took place at a 1500-bed mental institution situated in parklike surroundings in northern California. Most wards were unlocked, and patients spent considerable time out of doors. In wooded areas it was common to see patients seated under the trees, one to a bench or knoll. The wards within the buildings were relatively empty during the day because of the number of patients outside as well as those who worked in hospital industry. This made it possible for patients to isolate themselves from others by finding a deserted area on the grounds or remaining in an almost empty building. At the outset I spent considerable time observing how patients isolated themselves from one another. One man typically sat at the base of a fire escape so he was protected by the bushes on one side and the railing on the other. Others would lie on benches in remote areas and feign sleep if approached. On the wards a patient might sit in a corner and place magazines or his coat on adjacent seats to protect the space. The use of belongings to indicate possession is very common in bus stations, cafeterias, waiting rooms, but the mental patient is limited in using this method since he lacks possessions. Were he to own a magazine or book, which is unlikely, and left it on an empty chair, it would quickly vanish.

Prospective victims had to meet three criteria—male, sitting alone, and not engaged in any definite activity such as reading or playing cards. When a patient fitting these criteria was located, I walked over and sat beside him without saying a word. If the patient moved his chair or slid further down the bench, I moved a like distance to keep the space between us to about six inches. In all sessions I jiggled my key ring a few times to assert my dominance, the key being a mark of status in a mental hospital. It can be noted that these sessions not only invaded the patient's personal space but also the nurse's territory. It bothered the nurses to see a

high status person (jacket, white shirt, tie, and the title "Doctor") entering their wards and sitting among the patients. The dayroom was the patients' territory vis-à-vis the nurses, but it was the nurses' territory vis-à-vis the medical staff. Control subjects were selected from other patients who were seated some distance away but whose actions could be observed.

Within two minutes, all of the control subjects remained but one-third of the invasion victims had been driven away. Within nine minutes, fully half of the victims had departed compared with only 8 per cent of the controls. Flight was a gross reaction to the intrusion; there were many more subtle indications of the patient's discomfort. The typical sequence was for the victim to face away immediately, pull in his shoulders, and place his elbows at his sides. Facing away was an almost universal reaction among the victims, often coupled with hands placed against the chin as a buffer. Records obtained during the notetaking sessions illustrate this defensive pattern.

We come now to the sessions Nancy Russo conducted in the study hall of a college library, a large high-ceilinged room with book-lined walls. Because this is a study area, students typically try to space themselves as far as possible from one another. Systematic observations over a two-year period disclosed that the first occupants of the room generally sat one to a table at end chairs. Her victims were all females sitting alone with at least one book in front of them and empty chairs on either side and across. In other words, the prospective victim was sitting in an area surrounded by empty chairs, which indicated something about her preference for solitude as well as making an invasion relatively easy. The second female to meet these criteria in each session and who was visible to Mrs. Russo served as a control. Each control subject was observed from a distance and no invasion was attempted. There were five different approaches used in the invasions— sometimes Mrs. Russo would sit alongside the subject, other times directly across from her, and so forth. All of these were violations of the typical seating norms in the library, which required a newcomer to sit at a considerable distance from those already seated unless the room was crowded.

Occupying the adjacent chair and moving it closer to the victim produced the quickest departures, and there was a slight but also significant difference between the other invasion locations and the control condition. There were wide individual differences in the ways the victims reacted—there is no single reaction to someone's sitting too close; there are defensive gestures, shifts in posture, and attempts to move away. If these fail or are ignored by the invader, or he shifts position too, the victim eventually takes to flight. It is noteworthy that the preponderance of flight reactions occurred under these conditions. There was a dearth of direct verbal responses to the invasions. Only two of the 69 mental patients and one of the 80 students asked the invader to move over.

The invasions can also be looked at as nonverbal communication with the victims receiving messages ranging from "This girl considers me a nonperson" to "This girl is making a sexual advance."

The library studies made clear that an important consideration in defining a spatial invasion is whether the parties involved perceive one another as persons. A nonperson cannot invade someone's personal space any more than a tree or chair can. It is common under certain conditions for one person to react to another as an object or part of the background. Examples would be the hospital nurses who discuss a patient's condition at his bedside, seemingly oblivious to his presence, the Negro maid in the white home who serves dinner while the husband and wife discuss the race question, and the janitor who enters an office without knocking to empty the wastebaskets while the occupant is making an important phone call. Many subway riders who have adjusted to crowding through psychological withdrawal prefer to treat other riders as nonpersons and keenly resent situations, such as a stop so abrupt that the person alongside pushes into them and then apologizes, when the other rider becomes a person. There are also riders who dislike the lonely alienated condition of subway travel and look forward to emergency situations in which people become real. When a lost child is looking for his mother, a person has been hurt, or a car is stalled down the tracks, strangers are allowed to talk to one another.

NOTES

1 Fred E. Inbau and John E. Reid, *Criminal Interrogation and Confessions* (Toronto: Burns and MacEachern, 1963).
2 Inbau and Reid, *op. cit.*
3 Ray L. Birdwhistell, *Introduction to Kinesics* (Washington, DC: Foreign Service Institute, 1952).
4 John L. Williams, "Personal Space and its Relation to Extroversion-Introversion" (Master's thesis, University of Alberta, 1963).
5 William E. Leipold, "Psychological Distance in a Dyadic Interview" (Ph.D. thesis, University of North Dakota, 1963).

11
Theory of the Dérive and Definitions

(1958)

Guy Debord

THEORY OF THE DÉRIVE

One of the basic situationist practices is the *dérive* [literally: "drifting"], a technique of rapid passage through varied ambiances. Dérives involve playful-constructive behavior and awareness of psychogeographical effects, and are thus quite different from the classic notions of journey or stroll.

In a dérive one or more persons during a certain period drop their relations, their work and leisure activities, and all their other usual motives for movement and action, and let themselves be drawn by the attractions of the terrain and the encounters they find there. Chance is a less important factor in this activity than one might think: from a dérive point of view cities have psychogeographical contours, with constant currents, fixed points and vortexes that strongly discourage entry into or exit from certain zones.

But the dérive includes both this letting-go and its necessary contradiction: the domination of psychogeographical variations by the knowledge and calculation of their possibilities. In this latter regard, ecological science—despite the narrow social space to which it limits itself—provides psychogeography with abundant data.

The ecological analysis of the absolute or relative character of fissures in the urban network, of the role of microclimates, of distinct neighborhoods with no relation to administrative boundaries, and above all of the dominating action of centers of attraction, must be utilized and completed by psychogeographical methods. The objective passional terrain of the dérive must be defined in accordance both with its own logic and with its relations with social morphology.

In his study *Paris et l'agglomération parisienne* (Bibliothèque de Sociologie Contemporaine, P.U.F., 1952) Chombart de Lauwe notes that "an urban neighborhood is determined not only by geographical and economic factors, but also by the image that its inhabitants and those of other neighborhoods have of it." In the same work, in order to illustrate "the narrowness of the real Paris in which each individual lives ... within a geographical area whose radius is extremely small," he diagrams all the movements made in the space of one year by a student living in the 16th Arrondissement. Her itinerary forms a small triangle with no significant deviations, the three apexes of which are the School of Political Sciences, her residence and that of her piano teacher.

Such data—examples of a modern poetry capable of provoking sharp emotional reactions (in this particular case, outrage at the fact that anyone's life can be so pathetically limited)—or even Burgess's theory of Chicago's social activities as being distributed in distinct concentric zones, will undoubtedly prove useful in developing dérives.

If chance plays an important role in dérives this is because the methodology of psycho-geographical observation is still in its infancy. But the action of chance is naturally conservative and in a new setting tends to reduce everything to habit or to an alternation between a limited number of variants. Progress means breaking through fields where chance holds sway by creating new conditions more favorable to our purposes. We can say, then, that the randomness of a dérive is fundamentally different from that of the stroll, but also that the first psychogeographical attractions discovered by dérivers may tend to fixate them around new habitual axes, to which they will constantly be drawn back.

An insufficient awareness of the limitations of chance, and of its inevitably reactionary effects, condemned to a dismal failure the famous aimless wandering attempted in 1923 by four surrealists, beginning from a town chosen by lot: wandering in open country is naturally depressing, and the interventions of chance are poorer there than anywhere else. But this mindlessness is pushed much further by a certain Pierre Vendryes (in *Médium*, May 1954), who thinks he can relate this anecdote to various probability experiments, on the ground that they all supposedly involve the same sort of antideterminist liberation. He gives as an example the random distribution of tadpoles in a circular aquarium, adding, significantly, "It is necessary, of course, that such a population be subject to no external guiding influence." From that perspective, the tadpoles could be considered more spontaneously liberated than the surrealists, since they have the advantage of being "as stripped as possible of intelligence, sociability and sexuality," and are thus "truly independent from one another."

At the opposite pole from such imbecilities, the primarily urban character of the dérive, in its element in the great industrially transformed cities—those centers of possibilities and meanings—could be expressed in Marx's phrase: "Men can see nothing around them that is not their own image; everything speaks to them of themselves. Their very landscape is alive."

One can dérive alone, but all indications are that the most fruitful numerical arrangement consists of several small groups of two or three people who have reached the same level of awareness, since cross-checking these different groups' impressions makes it possible to arrive at more objective conclusions. It is preferable for the composition of these groups to change from one dérive to another. With more than four or five participants, the specifically dérive character rapidly diminishes, and in any case it is impossible for there to be more than ten or twelve people without the dérive fragmenting into several simultaneous dérives. The practice of such subdivision is in fact of great interest, but the difficulties it

entails have so far prevented it from being organized on a sufficient scale.

The average duration of a dérive is one day, considered as the time between two periods of sleep. The starting and ending times have no necessary relation to the solar day, but it should be noted that the last hours of the night are generally unsuitable for dérives.

But this duration is merely a statistical average. For one thing, a dérive rarely occurs in its pure form: it is difficult for the participants to avoid setting aside an hour or two at the beginning or end of the day for taking care of banal tasks; and toward the end of the day fatigue tends to encourage such an abandonment. But more importantly, a dérive often takes place within a deliberately limited period of a few hours, or even fortuitously during fairly brief moments; or it may last for several days without interruption. In spite of the cessations imposed by the need for sleep, certain dérives of a sufficient intensity have been sustained for three or four days, or even longer. It is true that in the case of a series of dérives over a rather long period of time it is almost impossible to determine precisely when the state of mind peculiar to one dérive gives way to that of another. One sequence of dérives was pursued without notable interruption for around two months. Such an experience gives rise to new objective conditions of behavior that bring about the disappearance of a good number of the old ones.[1]

The influence of weather on dérives, although real, is a significant factor only in the case of prolonged rains, which make them virtually impossible. But storms or other types of precipitation are rather favorable for dérives.

The spatial field of a dérive may be precisely delimited or vague, depending on whether the goal is to study a terrain or to emotionally disorient oneself. It should not be forgotten that these two aspects of dérives overlap in so many ways that it is impossible to isolate one of them in a pure state. But the use of taxis, for example, can provide a clear enough dividing line: if in the course of a dérive one takes a taxi, either to get to a specific destination or simply to move, say, twenty minutes to the west, one is concerned primarily with a personal trip outside one's usual surroundings. If, on the other hand, one sticks to the direct exploration of a particular terrain, one is concentrating primarily on research for a psychogeographical urbanism.

In every case the spatial field depends first of all on the point of departure—the residence of the solo dériver or the meeting place selected by a group. The maximum area of this spatial field does not extend beyond the entirety of a large city and its suburbs. At its minimum it can be limited to a small self-contained ambience: a single neighborhood or even a single block of houses if it's interesting enough (the extreme case being a static dérive of an entire day within the Saint-Lazare train station).

The exploration of a fixed spatial field entails establishing bases and calculating directions of penetration. It is here that the study of maps comes in—ordinary ones as well as ecological and psychogeographical ones—along with their correction and improvement. It should go without saying that we are not at all interested in any mere exoticism that may arise from the fact that one is exploring a neighborhood for the first time. Besides its unimportance, this aspect of the problem is completely subjective and soon fades away.

In the "possible rendezvous," on the other hand, the element of exploration is minimal in comparison with that of behavioral disorientation. The subject is invited to come alone to a certain place at a specified time. He is freed from the bothersome obligations of the ordinary rendezvous since there is no one to wait for. But since this "possible rendezvous" has brought him without warning to a place he may or may not know, he observes the surroundings. It may be that the same spot has been specified for a "possible rendezvous" for someone else whose identity he has no way of knowing. Since he may never even have seen the other person before, he will be encouraged to start up conversations with various passersby. He may meet no one, or he may even by chance meet the person who has arranged the "possible rendezvous." In any case, particularly if the time and place have been well chosen, his use of time will take an unexpected turn. He may even telephone someone else who doesn't know where the first "possible rendezvous" has taken him, in order to ask for another one to be specified. One can see the virtually unlimited resources of this pastime.

Our loose lifestyle and even certain amusements considered dubious that have always been enjoyed among our entourage— slipping by night into houses undergoing demolition, hitchhiking nonstop and without

destination through Paris during a transportation strike in the name of adding to the confusion, wandering in subterranean catacombs forbidden to the public, etc.—are expressions of a more general sensibility which is no different from that of the dérive. Written descriptions can be no more than passwords to this great game.

The lessons drawn from dérives enable us to draw up the first surveys of the psychogeographical articulations of a modern city. Beyond the discovery of unities of ambiance, of their main components and their spatial localization, one comes to perceive their principal axes of passage, their exits and their defenses. One arrives at the central hypothesis of the existence of psychogeographical pivotal points. One measures the distances that actually separate two regions of a city, distances that may have little relation with the physical distance between them. With the aid of old maps, aerial photographs and experimental dérives, one can draw up hitherto lacking maps of influences, maps whose inevitable imprecision at this early stage is no worse than that of the first navigational charts. The only difference is that it is no longer a matter of precisely delineating stable continents, but of changing architecture and urbanism.

Today the different unities of atmosphere and of dwellings are not precisely marked off, but are surrounded by more or less extended and indistinct bordering regions. The most general change that dérive experience leads to proposing is the constant diminution of these border regions, up to the point of their complete suppression.

Within architecture itself, the taste for dériving tends to promote all sorts of new forms of labyrinths made possible by modern techniques of construction. Thus in March 1955 the press reported the construction in New York of a building in which one can see the first signs of an opportunity to dérive inside an apartment:

"The apartments of the helicoidal building will be shaped like slices of cake. One will be able to enlarge or reduce them by shifting movable partitions. The half-floor gradations avoid limiting the number of rooms, since the tenant can request the use of the adjacent section on either upper or lower levels. With this setup three four-room apartments can be transformed into one twelve-room apartment in less than six hours."

DEFINITIONS

constructed situation

A moment of life, concretely and deliberately constructed by the collective organization of unitary environment and the free play of events.

situationist

Relating to the theory or practical activity of constructing situations. One who engages in the construction of situations. A member of the Situationist International.

situationism

A word totally devoid of meaning, improperly derived from the preceding term. There is no situationism, which would mean a theory of interpretation of existing facts. The notion of situationism was obviously conceived by anti-situationists.

psychogeography

The study of the precise effects of geographical setting, consciously managed or not, acting directly on the mood and behavior of the individual.

psychogeographical

Relating to psychogeography. That which manifests the direct effect of geographical setting on mood.

psychogeographer

One who studies and reports on psycho-geographical realities.

dérive

An experimental mode of behavior linked to the conditions of urban society: a technique for hastily passing through varied environments.

Also used, more particularly, to designate the duration of a prolonged exercise of such an experiment.

unitary urbanism

The theory of the combined use of art and technology leading to the integrated construction of an environment dynamically linked to behavioral experiments.

détournement

Used as an abbreviation for the formula: détournement of prefabricated aesthetic elements. The integration of past or present artistic production into a superior environmental construction. In this sense, there cannot be situationist painting, or music, but a situationist use of these media. In a more primitive sense, détournement from within old cultural spheres is a form of propaganda, which lays witness to the depletion and waning importance of these spheres.

culture

The reflection and prefiguration at any given historical moment, of the possible organization of daily life; the complex of mores, aesthetic, and feelings by which a collective reacts to a life which is objectively given to it by its economy. (We define this term only from the perspective of the creation of values, and not of their teaching.)

decomposition

The process by which traditional cultural forms have destroyed themselves, under the effects of the appearance of superior means of dominating nature, permitting and requiring superior cultural constructions. We distinguish between an active phase of decomposition, effective demolition of older superstructures—which ends around 1930—and a phase of repetition, which has dominated since then. The delay in passing from decomposition to new constructions is tied to the delay in the revolutionary liquidation of capitalism.

NOTE

1 "The *dérive* (with its flow of acts, its gestures, its strolls, its encounters) was *to the totality* exactly what psychoanalysis (in the best sense) is to language. Let yourself go with the flow of words, says the psychoanalyst. He listens, until the moment when he rejects or modifies (one could say *detourns*) a word, an expression or a definition. The dérive is certainly a technique, almost a therapeutic one. But just as analysis unaccompanied with anything else is almost always *contraindicated,* so continual dériving is dangerous to the extent that the individual, having gone too far (not without bases, but[...]) without defenses, is threatened with explosion, dissolution, dissociation, disintegration. And thence the relapse into what is termed 'ordinary life,' that is to say, in reality, into 'petrified life.' In this regard I now repudiate the Formulary's propaganda for a *continuous dérive*. It could be continual like the poker game in Las Vegas, but only for a certain period, limited to a weekend for some people, to a week as a good average; a month is really pushing it. In 1953-1954 we dérived for three or four months straight. That's the extreme limit. It's a miracle it didn't kill us." (Ivan Chtcheglov, "Letter from Afar," *Internationale Situationniste* #9, p. 38.)

SECTION 3

Place and Identity

Photograph of Chinese American railroad workers, next to an Anglo American supervisor, near Lang, California, 1876.
Source: Security Pacific Collection, Los Angeles Public Library.
Referenced in: Hayden, Dolores. 1995. "Urban Landscape History: The Sense of Place and the Politics of Space," in *The Power of Place*. Cambridge: MIT Press.

PLACE AND IDENTITY

Thoughts of Brighton, Brisbane, Chicago, Omsk, Lagos, and Hanôi evoke different feelings and conjure different images of place and people. Neighborhood foods, smells, materials, and structures can tell us a lot about who lives, works, and visits there. Why do we feel that we belong in some places and not in others? Place and identity are inextricably bound to one another. The two are co-produced as people come to identify with where they live, shape it, however modestly, and are in turn shaped by their environments, creating distinctive *environmental autobiographies*, the narratives we hold from the memories of those spaces and places that shaped us. Exploring the relationship between place and identity deepens our understandings of identity formation and the role of place in social and psychological development. The bonds between place and identity can influence social formations, cultural practices, and political actions. It may be seen, for instance, in the efforts of groups of emigrants to establish roots in their new homes through the planting of particular tree species or architectural ornamentation (e.g., Mitchell 2004). The readings selected here highlight research from a number of fields in order to show the various and multiple ways in which place and identity intertwine, and the varied stakes in understanding them.

Place identity is a core concept in the field of environmental psychology which proposes that identities form in relation to environments. The term was introduced by environmental and social psychologists **Harold M. Proshansky**, **Abbe K. Fabian**, and **Robert Kaminoff**, who argue that place identity is a sub-structure of a person's self-identity, and consists of knowledge and feelings developed through everyday experiences of physical spaces. A sense of place identity derives from the multiple ways in which place functions to provide a sense of belonging, construct meaning, foster attachments, and mediate change. The place identity of a person can inform their experiences, behaviors, and attitudes about other places. Place identity is a versatile concept upon which many psychological theories of human–environment relations are built. In a related vein, social psychologist Irwin Altman and anthropologist Setha Low's (1992) concept of *place attachment* defines the ways in which people connect to various places, and the effects of such bonds in identity development, place-making, perception, and practice. Both of these concepts help us to understand where and why people feel at home, as well as why displacement—forced or voluntary—can be so traumatic for individuals and groups.

"Place makes memories cohere in complex ways. People's experiences of the urban landscape intertwine the sense of place and the politics of space," writes architectural historian **Dolores Hayden**. Hayden's work is concerned with how some identities are hidden when we represent or talk about place through certain narratives, or fail to talk about the histories of places at all. In this selection from her book *The Power of Place*, she unearths racialized, classed, and gendered accounts of place in order to reveal how those in privileged positions can bury the truth of occupation and inhabitance in historical geographies at various scales. In one example, Hayden describes how Chinese migrants built much of the US railroad system in the 19th century, and yet are frequently absent from the labor narratives of this period celebrating political and economic success framed around American whiteness (see figure at the beginning of Section 3). Her work seeks to find the traces of their laboring presence in place so as to tell a more accurate and inclusive history through geography, space, and built form.

Likewise, geographer **Kay J. Anderson** describes how race and class privilege infused the social production of space in late 19th-century Vancouver, Canada. Anderson's work examines the variety of material and social practices through which both racialized space and constructed notions of racialized difference were produced and naturalized. Her research looks at how "Chinatowns" were fabricated in many cities by white Europeans and Anglo-Americans in the 19th century. She focuses her careful examination on Vancouver to detail how those in power delineated difference and limited people marked as other—in this case the Chinese population—through the spatializations of cultural norms and values. This included labeling their cultural activities such as lodging, eating, gambling, and opium use as unsanitary or immoral, while refusing to extend sanitation services or employment to these communities. Anderson's and Hayden's scholarship help us to see the historical geographies of power in place, and to recognize how these uneven relations of power and privilege continue to inflect and reproduce places today.

Referencing a very different place and time, queer theorist and American Studies scholar **Judith Jack Halberstam** encourages moving beyond the biases associated with space and place, such as those that frame the rural as backward, uneducated, and intolerant. Halberstam asks why a lesbian, gay, bisexual, trans, and/or queer (LGBTQ) person would choose to stay in a rural environment when cities promise more acceptance and freedom. The author examines films, documentaries, news coverage, and documents surrounding the 1993 murder of transman Brandon Teena in rural Nebraska to understand why he chose to remain there, and why Brandon and his friend were killed. In questioning which places are actual threats to LGBTQ people and why, Halberstam inspires us to look at the ways in which class, race, gender, sexuality, and regional attitudes trouble the relationship between LGBTQ people and other marginalized communities, rural and otherwise, and to reckon with the material and imagined ideas we hold of places.

Sometimes identity and place are so tightly bound that it is hard to separate them. This conflation often happens at the scale of the home, perhaps spurred during the 19th century, when it became clear that bourgeois women were judged according to the type of domestic space they maintained (see Sparke 2008). But what if the environment eliminated a person's identity completely? In a fable of design gone awry, architect **Adolf Loos** tells the story of a man whose designer keeps adding to and specifying the layout of his objects and spaces until there is nothing the client can touch or move. In the end, the client is excluded from the space when there is no way left for him to live as he wishes. This story bears a remarkable resemblance to Friedman's analysis in Section 6 of the disturbing design of a glass house for a woman whose dwelling experience is disregarded for the sake of architectural ideals. This cautionary tale is Loos' way of arguing that there must be room for people in built environments, and architects cannot forget about inhabitants in their focus on creating beautiful or efficient designs.

Can the study of a single street capture the place-making and identity formation of the population of an entire city? Anthropologist **Daniel Miller** paints an interesting picture based on his research team's interviews of diverse households on one London street. The project examines the residents' stories of how their material possessions affect and speak to their life trajectories, experiences, and relationships. Miller shares the story of Marcia who, rather than settle into London fully or remain totally attached to her Caribbean family and homeland, creates a home bursting with figurines and objects on every shelf and surface to fill her life from her post-retirement travels. For Marcia and many immigrants like her, the relationships and discipline of the Caribbean are different from and do not apply to London. Her home is a sort of in-between space that reveals and sustains her hybrid identity and varied place attachments, suggesting not only how immigration blurs conventional boundaries of place and people, but also offering an insight into shifting spaces, identities, and cultures the world over. Miller's research builds upon and beautifully advances decades of research on objects and our relations with them, including the influential work of psychologists Mihaly Csikszentmihalyi and Eugene Rochberg-Halton (1981) on the meaning of domestic objects.

The selections in this section encompass the variety of ways in which place has significant meaning for people, and suggest why, in a mobile and hybrid world, place can sometimes become another resource to be exploited or a source of inspiration. In one of our suggestions for further reading, anthropologist Tina Harris (2012) explores questions of authenticity through the lens of tourism and tourist commodities in Tibet. She argues that Tibet has been "exoticized" to such an extent by the tourist market that the traditionally dichotomous meanings between "authentic" and "inauthentic" local cultural practices and objects have become blurred as the core materials of everyday life in Tibet are produced increasingly for visitors' consumption. Other authors explore the relationship between place and identity in a range of milieus. In his work on the Mississippi Delta, geographer Clyde Woods (2000) shows how Blues music sustains efforts toward civil rights for residents of the Mississippi Delta. Gabriela Tôrres Barbosa (2008) uses autobiographical descriptions of the places she experiences growing up in a Brazilian favela to discuss issues of class and access to resources. Looking at the redesign of the Times Square area of New York City, Samuel Delany (2001) lays out the conflicting intentions between gay men cruising pornographic theaters and city plans to create a Disney-like zone for families, suggesting very different identifications with place. All of the work discussed here describes how in making a place, or writing its history, there is often a struggle over what story is privileged and to what ends. Likewise identities and affiliations shift as places gain or lose particular meanings. The ways in which place and identity intertwine both confuse and allow us to make sense of the worlds we inhabit.

SUGGESTIONS FOR FURTHER READING

Please see *peopleplacespace.org* for extended and additional lists of readings.

Agrest, Diana, Patricia Conway, and Leslie Kanes Weisman (eds). 1996. *The Sex of Architecture*. New York: Harry N. Abrams.

Ahrentzen, Sherry. 2003. "The Space between the Studs. Feminism and Architecture." *Signs: Journal of Women in Culture and Society*. 29(1): 179–206.

Altman, Irwin, and Setha M. Low. 1992. *Place Attachment*. New York: Springer.

Anzaldúa, Gloria. 1987. *Borderlands/La Frontera: The New Mestiza*. San Francisco, CA: Aunt Lute Books.

Barbosa, Gabriela Tôrres. 2008. "At the Top of the Hill." *New Internationalist* 386: 4–6.

Bell, David J., and Gill Valentine (eds). 1995. Mapping Desire: Geographies of Sexualities. New York: Routledge.

Csikszentmihalyi, Mihaly, and Eugene Rochberg-Halton. 1981. *The Meaning of Things: Domestic Symbols and the Self*. Cambridge: Cambridge University Press.

Delany, Samuel R. 2001. *Times Square Red, Times Square Blue*. New York: New York University Press.

Dixon, John, and Kevin Durrheim. 2004. "Dislocating Identity: Desegregation and the Transformation of Place." *Journal of Environmental Psychology* 24(4) (December): 455–473.

Doan, Petra L. (ed.). 2011. *Queerying Planning*. London: Ashgate.

Domash, Mona, 1996. *Invented Cities: The Creation of Landscape in Nineteenth-century New York & Boston*. New Haven: Yale University Press.

Erikson, Erik H. 1975. *Life History and the Historical Moment*. New York: Norton.

Fanon, Frantz. 2008. *Black Skin, White Masks*, translated by Richard Philcox. New York: Grove Press.

Fried, Marc, and Peggy Gliecher. 1961. "Some Sources of Residential Satisfaction in an Urban Slum." *Journal of the American Institute of Planners* 27: 305–315.

Gordon, Beverley. 1996. "Woman's Domestic Body: The Conflation of Women and Interiors in the Industrial Age." *Winterthur Portfolio*. 31(4): 281–301.

Gregory, Derek. 2004. *The Colonial Present: Afghanistan, Palestine, Iraq*. Malden, MA: Wiley-Blackwell.

Grewal, Inderpal. 2003. "Transnational America: Race, Gender and Citizenship After 9/11." *Social Identities* 9(4): 535–561.

Grosz, Elizabeth. 1995. *Space, Time and Perversion: Essays on the Politics of Bodies*. New York: Routledge.

Harris, Tina. 2012. "Loom to Machine: Tibetan Aprons and the Configuration of Place." *Environment & Planning D: Society & Space* 30(5): 877–895.

Ingram, Gordon B., Anne-Marie Bouthillette, and Yolanda Retter (eds). 1997. *Queers in Space: Communities, Public Places, Sites of Resistance*. Seattle, WA: Bay Press.

Leach, Neil. 2006. *Camouflage*. Cambridge, MA: The MIT Press.

Manzo, Lynne C. 2003. "Beyond House and Haven: Toward a Revisioning of Emotional Relationships with Places." *Journal of Environmental Psychology* 23(1): 47–61.

Martin, Emily. 1991. "The Egg and the Sperm: How Science has constructed a Romance based on Stereotypical Male–Female Roles." *Signs: Journal of Women in Culture and Society*. 16(3): 485–501.

McKittrick, Katherine, and Clyde Woods (eds). 2007. *Black Geographies and the Politics of Place*. Boston, MA: South End Press.

Mitchell, Katharyne. 2004. *Crossing the Neoliberal Line: Pacific Rim Migration and the Metropolis*. Philadelphia, PA: Temple University Press.

Pain, Rachel, and Susan J. Smith (eds). 2008. *Fear: Critical Geopolitics and Everyday Life*. London: Ashgate.

Pratt, Geraldine, and in collaboration with the Philippine Women Centre, Vancouver, Canada. 1998. "Inscribing Domestic Work on Filipina Bodies." In *Places Through the Body*, edited by Heidi J. Nast and Steve Pile, pp. 283–304. New York: Routledge.

Sibley, David. 1995. *Geographies of Exclusion: Society and Difference in the West*. New York: Routledge.

Sparke, Penny. 2008. *The Modern Interior*. London: Reaktion Books.

Steedman, Carolyn Kay. 1986. *Landscape for a Good Woman: A Story of Two Lives*. Rutgers University Press.

Winddance Twine, Frances, and Bradley Gardner (eds). 2013. *Maps of Privilege: The Local, National, and Global*. New York: Routledge.

Woods, Clyde. 2000. *Development Arrested: The Blues and Plantation Power in the Mississippi Delta*. New York: Verso.

12
Place-Identity
Physical World Socialization of the Self (1983)

Harold M. Proshansky, Abbe K. Fabian, and Robert Kaminoff

At this point what is needed is a brief review of the social and cultural processes involved in the development of self-identity. From this discussion, the theoretical significance of physical settings and their properties in regard to self-identity will clearly emerge. Paradoxically, what will also emerge is the realization of an almost complete neglect of the role of places and spaces in this aspect of human psychological development.

'Place-identity' is a sub-structure of the self-identity of the person consisting of, broadly conceived, cognitions about the physical world in which the individual lives. These cognitions represent memories, ideas, feelings, attitudes, values, preferences, meanings, and conceptions of behavior and experience which relate to the variety and complexity of physical settings that define the day-to-day existence of every human being. At the core of such physical environment-related cognitions is the 'environmental past' of the person; a past consisting of places, spaces and their properties which have served instrumentally in the satisfaction of the person's biological, psychological, social, and cultural needs.

Clearly the theoretical conception of place-identity as an individual's strong emotional attachment to particular places or settings is consistent with the broader conception of place-identity as we have defined it here. Individuals do indeed define who and what they are in terms of such strong affective ties to 'house and home' and/or neighborhood and community. It is however, an important assumption of this paper that physical world definitions of a person's self-identity extend far beyond a conception of this identity in which the home and its surroundings are the necessary and sufficient component referents. It should become evident in the subsequent discussion that place-identity is influenced by a wide range of person/physical setting experiences and relationships based on a variety of physical contexts that from the moment of birth until death define people's day-to-day existence. What emerges as 'place-identity' is a complex cognitive structure which is characterized by a host of attitudes, values, thoughts, beliefs, meanings, and behavior tendencies that go well beyond just emotional attachments and belonging to particular places.

Some properties of place-identity

Place-identity as a cognitive sub-structure of self-identity consists of an endless variety of cognitions related to the past, present, and anticipated physical settings that define and circumscribe the day-to-day existence of the person. These cognitions are evolved through the person's selective engagement with his or her environment on both a conscious and unconscious level. But there is also the process by which the experience of a physical setting moves from the stage of 'now going on' to the stage of 'being remembered'. Through this process, the person's actual experience is modified by the cognitive process of memory and interpretation and such others as fantasy and imagination. We not only experience the physical realities, for example, of the particular neighborhood we grew up in, but also the social meanings and beliefs attached to it by those who live outside of it as well as its residents. All of these 'cognitions' define the person's place-identity.

What we are saying in effect is that place-identity reflects in its clustering of cognitive components the individual's experiences in each of these environments and in the relationships of these environments to each other in defining the day-to-day activities of a person. The cluster of cognitive components for any one physical setting (e.g., memories, ideas, beliefs, etc.) is understandable, but how do components of one setting become related to that of the other? It is more than their successive use in the daily activities of the individual, although long-term and successive use of physical settings also creates cognitive inter-relatedness between and among them.

It follows, therefore, that the individual is generally not aware of the variety of memories, feelings, values, and preferences that subsume and influence his or her responses to the physical world. One is simply comfortable in certain kinds of physical settings, prefers particular spaces, kinds of lighting, furniture arrangements, number of people in a room for a party, number of people in an office, and so on. This 'not in awareness' property of place-identity insofar as its content and influence are concerned is an important and significant feature of its role in shaping the behavior and experience of the person in given physical settings.

The cognitive clusters that comprise place-identity involve far more than the memories, feelings, and interpretations of each of the real world physical settings that the person uses. Interwoven into these clusters are the social definitions of these settings which consist of the norms, behaviors, rules, and regulations that are inherent in the use of these places and spaces. Within any one of these settings are activity-relevant differentiations of the space that are defined by what individuals are expected to do at particular times either alone or with other individuals. However 'physical' or objectively real these settings, they are inextricably tied to the social and cultural existence of a group, as expressed by its valued activities, interpersonal relationships, and individual and group role functions. As we have often said, there is no physical environment that is not also a social environment, and vice-versa (Ittelson *et al.*, 1974).

Attached to the physical settings that substantively define place-identity are not only the general social properties that come from the broad uniformities in a culture, but also those that serve to distinguish different groups in the culture—racial, ethnic, age, sex, social class, religious, etc. This means that place-identities of different ethnic, social, national, and religious groups in a given culture should reveal not only different uses and experiences with space and place, but corresponding variations in the social values, meanings, and ideas which underlie the use of those spaces. The inextricable relationship between a social setting and physical setting is evidenced in place-identity through the merger of the individual's personally held images, feelings, memories, and ideas about a given setting or settings with the relevant attitudes, values, and behavior tendencies that express the sociocultural and demographic characteristics of the individual.

In reviewing the kinds of cognitions which cluster together in the formation and development of place-identity, we have yet to mention an obvious type: those that transcend the varying nature of human societies because of the common biological character of all human beings. What we are referring to is the fact that each human being is also a physically defined object that occupies space, and therefore, no two of them can occupy the same space at the same time. In other words, from both a physical and therefore biological and social point of view, the human organism is at every moment in need of a basic minimum of his or her own exclusive physical space, and it is this need which lies at the root of the fact that all societies evolve norms and values about human *privacy, personal space, crowding,* and *territoriality*. This basic requirement enables the person to meet the essential biological conditions necessary to exist, not to mention the satisfaction of more complex biological and social needs. And to this we must add the view that these norms and values about crowding, one's own space, privacy, and territoriality for a given society or culture are also expressed as place-identity cognitions of the person thereby adding still further to his or her definition of self.

Place-identity shows both stability and change in the nature and organization of its components.

In speaking of change in place-identity, however, we do not mean just the gradual changes that occur in enduring components associated with corresponding changes in social roles over the course of the lifecycle. There are other influences that induce change which are relatively unrelated to social role development and the socialization process generally. Physical settings themselves may change radically over long or relatively short periods of time, and thereby no longer correspond to existing place-related cognitions that serve to define the self-identity of the individual. Every individual must deal with a changing society, with unexpected events, with advances in technology, with social upheavals, and any number of other phenomena that directly or indirectly have an impact on the physical world of the person.

The extent and intensity with which television has invaded American households (and elsewhere as well) means that it is no less an important aspect of the place-identity of the person than say, the automobile. Its significance in defining who the person is goes beyond satisfying his or her entertainment interests. It is a means of escape, a way of having contact with the outside world, a source of learning, and a resource for knowing how to think and feel about many things.

Influences on place-identity resulting from changes in the individual's physical world can be traced to more than simply technological developments. Demographic and ecological changes in a community, themselves the result of economic, political, and social impacts, may have important consequences for the place-identity of the person. As we have already suggested, place-belongingness or strong emotional attachments to one's home and neighborhood can be acquired in adult life because of its role for parents in bringing up their own children. Other factors may also lead to such attachments occurring during the adult stage of the lifecycle. The intrusion of unwanted groups, the evidence of crime in the area, and beginning signs of physical decay, may all precipitate stronger emotional attachments to one's home and neighborhood. Similarly, groups who are dislocated from their residential 'turf' because of urban programs or other governmental or social interventions often feel 'lost' in their new setting and long for the old home and neighborhood. Depending on the stage of the lifecycle that the person is at, and the discrepancy between the old and new locations, a sense of belongingness to the new neighborhood may never be achieved.

FUNCTIONS OF PLACE-IDENTITY

Recognition function

As we have already indicated, an important general function of place-identity is that it provides the *environmental past* against which any immediate physical setting can be judged. Clearly, the first step in this comparative process is the determination of what is familiar or unfamiliar in any given physical setting. This is seldom a conscious process, but whether it is or not, making such a determination undoubtedly occurs each time the individual moves from one physical setting to the next.

One dimension of the person's experience of environmental stability lies in the affirmation of the belief that the properties of his or her day-to-day physical world are unchanging. The individual's recognition of these properties at any given moment in a given situation serves to confirm their continuity from the past, and in turn this perceived continuity portends that they will occur again in the future. The perceived stability of place and space that emerges from such recognitions correspondingly validates the individual's belief in his or her own continuity over time. Since the individual's place-identity mirrors a physical world, the continuing recognition of that world over time gives credence to and support for his or her self-identity.

Meaning function

Physical settings usually have a primary purpose. And it is this purpose that determines their design and sensory characteristics, the objects and facilities they require, and the kinds of individuals and related activities that will be found in them. Place-identity is the source of meaning for a given setting by virtue of relevant cognitive clusters that indicate what should happen in it, what the setting is supposed to be like, and how the individual and others are supposed to behave in it. These groups of cognitions serve as an ever-present background system of meanings of spaces and places which enables the person not only to recognize a setting but to understand its intended purposes and activities in relation to its design and other substantive properties.

Expressive-requirement function

The recognition and meaning functions of place-identity provide a basis for 'diagnosing' the nature, value, and relevancy of a physical setting. But 'diagnosis' is not enough if it turns out that place-identity cognitions are not matched by the properties of a given physical setting. There are those cognitions that express the tastes and preferences of the person; and there are others that represent what spaces and places actually require insofar as their primary purposes are concerned. Tastes and preferences reflect far more what the individual desires because it satisfies some affective or aesthetic choice rather than because the setting actually requires it. 'Requirements' are those characteristics of a setting that are necessary given its primary purpose, the activities underlying this purpose, and the fact that the biological nature of human beings imposes minimal requirements on the use of a space (e.g., light, heat, oxygen, etc.).

Mediating change function

Discrepancies between a person's place-identity and the characteristics of an immediate physical setting arouse relevant and interrelated cognitions in the individual for reducing if not eliminating those discrepancies. They involve knowing what's 'right' and 'wrong' with the physical setting and what has to be done to bring about change in it or reduce the discrepancy between it and the place-identity cognitions of the individual. Change of some kind may be deemed necessary and the individual must therefore also assess what his or her relevant environmental skills and resources are for making this change. It is important to emphasize once again that we are speaking of cognitions and not actions or actual behaviors. Whether the latter will occur depends on a host of other factors besides the availability of appropriate, relevant, and realistic cognitions.

Anxiety and defense function

If, as we have assumed, place-identity represents physical setting cognitions that serve to define, maintain, and protect the self-identity of a person, then it follows that some of these cognitions may function directly as anxiety and defense mechanisms. They may signal threat or danger in physical settings or they may represent response tendencies that defend or protect the person against these dangers.

SOME THEORETICAL CLARIFICATIONS AND IMPLICATIONS

Place-identity is theoretically conceived of in the present paper as clusters of positively and negatively valenced cognitions of physical settings. The substantive and valuative natures of these cognitions help to define who and of what value the person is both to himself and in terms of how he thinks others view him. While there has been more attention paid by psychologists to the impact of social roles on the development of self-identity, we put forward the hypothesis that the places and spaces a child grows up in, those that he or she comes to know, prefer, and seek out or avoid also contribute significantly to self-identity. Negatively valenced cognitions contribute to such a definition of the person by specifying the settings and their properties that are either not him, or even more significantly those settings which actually threaten his or her conceptions of self. Among the latter are first those that serve to identify such settings and thereby signal 'danger', and second, others that cognitively detail behavior mechanisms and strategies for avoiding or minimizing the threats and consequences of such danger. In a very broad sense, it can be said that all place-identity cognitions are positively valenced in that they either define directly who the person is, or they do so indirectly by defending him and protecting him from those settings and properties that threaten who he is and what he wants to be.

Not all physical setting socialization experiences—either positive or negative—end up as cognitions in the place-identity of the person. The human organism is neither capable nor motivated to 'record' all of the properties of a given physical setting (e.g., size of a room, color, location of windows, bed, chairs, etc.). On the other hand, even though physical settings are typically the 'backgrounds' for social interactions and social processes, far, far more of the properties of these settings are assimilated to some degree as aspects of place-identity than one would expect or certainly than the individual is aware of. It is, generally speaking, only when a physical setting becomes dysfunctional that a person becomes aware of his or her expectations for that setting. What was routine and in the background suddenly becomes the 'figure' in the thinking of those using the setting.

It can readily be assumed that some place-identity cognitions are more salient and significant in defining the self-identity of the person than others.

We come now to the end of our paper, and therefore some final summing up and comment is necessary. Social roles and social attributes serve as the conceptual nexus for understanding the development of self-identity via the socialization process that goes on throughout the lifecycle. Place-identity cognitions express and reflect the physical settings and their properties that support and are directly relevant to the social roles and attributes that define who the person is, how he or she is to behave, and what he or she is worth. Whatever the original source of change—the lifecycle itself, changing values of society, or critical changes in the person—at the root of changes in cognitions of place-identity lie changes in the social roles and social attributes of the person and therefore in his self-identity.

What follows from this theoretical point of view is the derivation that the substantive clusters of cognitions that constitute the place-identity of the person will vary as a consequence of the major social roles and social attributes that

distinguish different groups of individuals in our society (e.g., sex, occupation, social class, etc.). Why is this important? Perhaps only because the obvious has been neglected. Little, if any attention has been given to differences between and among these groups insofar as environmental psychologists consider human privacy, territoriality, personal space, crowding behavior, and other person/physical setting interactions. Even in the matter of environmental skills we have given little if any attention to sex differences, class differences, ethnic differences, and still other group differences.

But the fact is that the individual is characterized by not one role or social attribute but a number of them at any point during the entire lifecycle. While each such role or attribute has consequences for the self-identity characteristics of the person, it is the pattern of these roles for various social, ethnic, religious, national, and occupational groups that leaves its unique design on the self-identity of the group member. Correspondingly, the place-identity cognition clusters of this individual will reflect this patterning of roles for individuals of different social groups and categories.

REFERENCE

Proshansky, Harold M., William H. Ittelson, Leanne G. Rivlin, and Gary Winkel. 1974. *An Introduction to Environmental Psychology*. New York: Holt, Rinehart & Winston.

13
Urban Landscape History
The Sense of Place and the Politics of Space (1995)

Dolores Hayden

"Place" is one of the trickiest words in the English language, a suitcase so overfilled one can never shut the lid. In the nineteenth century and earlier, place also carried a sense of the right of a person to own a piece of land, or to be a part of a social world, and in this older sense place contains more political history. Phrases like "knowing one's place" or "a woman's place" still imply both spatial and political meanings.

People make attachments to places that are critical to their well-being or distress. An individual's sense of place is both a biological response to the surrounding physical environment and a cultural creation, as geographer Yi-Fu Tuan has argued.[1] From childhood, humans come to know places through engaging all five senses, sight as well as sound, smell, taste, and touch. Extensive research on perception shows the simultaneous engagement of several senses in orientation and wayfinding. Children show an interest in landmarks at three or earlier and by age five or six can read aerial maps with great accuracy and confidence, illustrating the human ability to perceive and remember the landscape.

As social relationships are intertwined with spatial perception, human attachment to places attracts researchers from many fields. Environmental psychologists Setha Low and Irvin Altman define "place attachment" as a psychological process similar to an infant's attachment to parental figures. They also suggest that place attachment can develop social, material, and ideological dimensions, as individuals develop ties to kin and community, own or rent land, and participate in public life as residents of a particular community.[2]

At the heart of Carl Sauer's definition of the cultural landscape was "the essential character of a place." It has often proved easier to study either the natural or the built components of a cultural landscape than to wrestle with the combination of the two in the concept of place. In recent decades, as geographers John Agnew and James Duncan have shown, social scientists have frequently avoided "place" as a concept, and thus have sidetracked the sensory, aesthetic, and environmental components of the urbanized world in favor of more quantifiable research with fewer epistemological problems. Some have argued for the importance of an increasingly "placeless world," or a "non-place urban realm," but speaking critically of bad places is more effective than dismissing them as places. The process that transforms places demands analysis. As a field of wildflowers becomes a shopping mall at the edge of a freeway, that paved-over meadow, restructured as freeway lanes, parking lots, and mall, must still be considered a place, if only to register the importance of loss and explain it has been damaged by careless development. Places also suffer from clumsy attempts to market them for commercial purposes: when small towns in Iowa that once seemed to embody everyday life in the Midwest developed "themes" to make them more attractive to tourists, the places became caricatures of themselves.

If place does provide an overload of possible meanings for the researcher, it is place's very same assault on all ways of knowing (sight, sound, smell, touch, and taste) that makes it powerful as a source of memory, as a weave where one strand ties in another. Place needs to be at the heart of urban landscape history, not on the margins, because the aesthetic qualities of the built environment, positive or negative, need to be understood as inseparable from those of the natural environment.[3] Together these two provide the basis for considering the history of the American urban landscape.

WORKING LANDSCAPES

The production of space begins as soon as indigenous residents locate themselves in a particular landscape and begin the search for subsistence. The place may grow into a town, inhabited by new waves of settlers. Many cities begin with farming, mining, fishing, or trading rather than manufacturing. The farm laborers, the miners, the fishermen, or the stall holders in the market, and their families, are the earliest builders of the economic enterprise that eventually becomes a city. Space is shaped for both economic production—barns, or mine shafts, or piers, or a factory—as well as for social reproduction—housing for the workers, managers, and owners, a store, a school, a church. As the town grows, configuring streets and lots formalizes the earliest uses of land and path systems. This leads to infrastructure such as paved roads, bridges, water systems, streetcars, and railroads, all of which have substantial environmental effects.

All of these different kinds of private and public planning activities and public works have a social as well as a technological history. People fight for and against them. People also construct and maintain them. The ditchdiggers and piledrivers, the streetcar workers and the railroad mechanics, the canal drivers and crane operators represent class, ethnic, and gender history shaping the landscape in ways that have barely been studied.

The history of the railroad in the nineteenth century offers just one of many possible examples. One can understand the railroad in engineering terms, as the history of trains and tracks, or in architectural terms, as stations and freight yards, or in urban planning terms, as the right and the wrong side of the tracks, without fully capturing its social history as the production of space. Limerick notes that twenty-nine Chinese workers died while building Wrights Tunnel for the South Pacific Coast Railroad through the Santa Cruz Mountains in California

in 1879, and dozens more were injured. Other historians have commented that the Chinese "contributed" to California's economic development. Patricia Nelson Limerick goes farther: the "'price of progress' had registered in the smell of burnt human flesh."[4] She concludes, "In our times the rediscovery of the landscape hinges on just such recognitions as this one." One could add that coming to terms with ethnic history in the landscape requires engaging with such bitter experiences, as well as the indifference and denial surrounding them.

TERRITORIAL HISTORIES OF CITIES BASED ON RACE AND GENDER

Henri Lefebvre emphasized the importance of space for shaping social reproduction. One of the consistent ways to limit the economic and political rights of groups has been to constrain social reproduction by limiting access to space. For women, the body, the home, and the street have all been arenas of conflict. Examining them as political territories—bounded spaces with some form of enforcement of the boundaries—helps us to analyze the spatial dimensions of "woman's sphere" at any given time. And just as gender can be mapped as a struggle over social reproduction that occurs at various scales of space, the same is true of race, class, and many other social issues.

As Michael Dear and Jennifer Wolch have written, the interplay between the social and the spatial is constant: "Social life structures territory … and territory shapes social life."[5] Ghettos and barrios, internment camps and Indian reservations, plantations under slavery and migrant worker camps should also be looked at as political territories, and the customs and laws governing them seen as enforcement of territory. The territories of the gay and lesbian communities can be mapped. So can those of childhood or old age. The spatial dimensions of class can be illuminated by looking at other boundaries and points of access. Since many of these categories interlock, studying how territories defined by gender, class, race, ethnicity, sexual preference, or age affect people's access to the urban cultural landscape can be frustrating.

How can one find evidence about social groups' experiences of these overlapping territories? Frequently observations about urban space are ignored by historians because the comments appear to be spatial description rather than social analysis, but they can form the basis of a territorial history focusing on access to the public spaces of the city. For example, Loren Miller, Jr., an African American lawyer who grew up in a middle-class family in Los Angeles in the 1940s, didn't see a segregated movie house until he went to Kansas in 1948. He could go to the beach any time on the streetcar. But he observed, "As teen-agers, we knew not to drive into Compton, to Inglewood, not to drive into Glendale 'cause you would just be out, with your hands on top of the car, … LAPD did the same thing. You got too far south on Western, they would stop you." This man also remembered, as a child, having Japanese American neighbors interned, going to visit them in temporary quarters at the Santa Anita race track, and finding that "soldiers with guns wouldn't let me go on the other side of the table, and they wouldn't let me play with my friends."[6] This is one individual account of spatial barriers about race. Another writer, Lynell George, comments on this city in the 1940s, "Off-limits for people of color in Los Angeles ran the gamut … not West of Main, not Glendale after dusk, never ever Fontana and its dusty flatlands dotted with burning crosses."[7]

Accounts like these begin to make it possible to map spatial segregation for the larger African American community: not only streets and neighborhoods, but schools, hotels, stores, fire stations, swimming pools, and cemeteries would be some of the places to examine. Photographs often convey territorial history as well, documenting both residential segregation and communities' struggles against territorial exclusion. In images of public space from the 1940s, a small cafe has different entrances for "White" and "Colored" labeled over the doors, while a movie theater has a large arrow painted on the side of the building, pointing "Colored" to an exterior stair leading to a balcony. Documentary photography, newspaper photography, commercial photography, and amateur snapshots all reveal different sides of a city. It can be revealing to consider the gender and ethnic background of the photographer as well as the architectural subject selected for the picture.

A territorial history based on limitations of gender in the public spaces of the city would use similar sources and would put buildings or parts of them off limits, rather than whole neighborhoods. In the twentieth century, spatial segregation includes private men's clubs, university faculty clubs, programs in higher education, and numerous other spaces. The segregation need not be absolute—women might be permitted to attend a class, but sit separately, or they might be allowed to enter a club as men's guests, provided they remained in a special room reserved for ladies, and so on. In the nineteenth century the list would be longer, and forbidden activities might include voting, entering a public saloon, or sitting in the main body of an assembly hall rather than the more restricted balcony. To understand the intersecting segregation of race, class, and gender, the spatial dimensions of traditional "woman's sphere" have to be studied in combination with the spatial limits imposed by race or class. Because white women's clubs, charities, and suffrage organizations were often segregated, African American women sometimes formed their own parallel groups, with their own meeting places, to help working women and girls in their own communities. Or, to take another example, one photograph of a class at a state university open to women in the 1890s shows the men and women sitting separately. It is equally important to ask if there appear to be people of color present, segregated by gender and race, sitting at the very back of each group

Political divisions of territory split the urban world into many enclaves experienced from many different perspectives. Cognitive mapping is a tool for discovering fuller territorial information about contemporary populations. Urban planner Kevin Lynch studied mental images of the city by asking people to draw maps or give directions. At the time, in 1960, Lynch suggested that such images could be combined into a composite portrait of a city, useful to urban designers, but not all Bostonians see Boston the same way. Subsequent studies, including some of Lynch's own, explored class, gender, age, and ethnicity. Most striking was a study done in Los Angeles that showed graphically the differences between the residents of an affluent white suburb, an inner-city African American neighborhood, and a mixed neighborhood close to downtown that had long been home to new immigrants working in downtown factories and using a few downtown bus lines. The space of the city, as understood by these different groups, varied greatly in size as well as in its memorable features. The maps are striking images of inequality of access to the city.

Lynch's work from the 1960s and 1970s suggests not only that the sprawling, spatially segregated city is difficult for citizens to map, but also that architects and planners, as well as specialists in public history, have an important role to play in making the entire city more coherent in the minds of its citizens. Out of Lynch's work comes what Fredric Jameson has called "an aesthetic of cognitive mapping." Acknowledging some of the political limits of Lynch's work, Jameson applauds the potential of his insights about how to give individuals a heightened sense of place, and suggests that mapping can raise political consciousness.[8]

FROM THE URBAN NEIGHBORHOOD TO THE CITY AND THE REGION

A new American urban social history has begun to be written in the last two decades, a history that takes ethnic diversity as a starting point and recognizes disparate experiences of class and gender as well. For many years, urban history was dominated by a kind of "city biography" that projected a single narrative of how city leaders or "city fathers"—almost always white, upper- and middle-class men—forged the city's spatial and economic structure, making fortunes building downtowns and imposing order on chaotic immigrant populations. This narrative tradition in urban history bore many similarities to the "conquest" histories of the American West.

New texts ask, "Who built America?" Not only is the history of different ethnic communities becoming more fully represented, but historians increasingly place women at the center rather than the periphery of economic and social life in the city. In contrast to the older city biographies that focused on city fathers and their conquest of the economic and physical obstacles to economic growth, women's history has brought a new emphasis on city mothers, the half of the city consisting of females of all races and classes, nurturing the rest of the population. Following the lead of scholars who worked on women of color a decade ago, historians studying working women of every ethnic group have led the way to the broadest synthetic accounts of

urban life, exploring textile mills and canneries, tenements and courtyards, where women struggled for sustenance for themselves, their families, and their communities. Work in the home and paid work are complementary parts of women's urban economic activity, suggesting that urban history, ethnic history, women's history, and labor history are not separate categories. All of these studies of urban working women contain the outline of a larger urban narrative uniting women, children, and men in the struggle for survival, both in the market economy and in the home.

This chapter has explored some of the ways that social history is embedded in urban landscapes. Places make memories cohere in complex ways. People's experiences of the urban landscape intertwine the sense of place and the politics of space. If people's attachments to places are material, social, and imaginative, then these are necessary dimensions of new projects to extend public history in the urban landscape, as well as new histories of American cultural landscapes and the buildings within them.

NOTES

1 Yi-Fu Tuan sees both biology and culture forming the human connection to place, in *Space and Place: The Perspective of Experience* (Minneapolis: University of Minnesota Press, 1977), 6. He argues that the experience of place engages all five senses in seeing, smelling, feeling, hearing, and tasting the essence of places.
2 Irwin Altman and Setha M. Low (eds), *Place Attachment* (New York: Plenum Publishing, 1992).
3 But terminology is in flux. Alexander Wilson describes his *The Culture of Nature: North American Landscape from Disney to Exxon Valdez* (Cambridge, MA: Blackwell, 1992) as "a cultural history of nature in North America," 12.
4 Patricia Nelson Limerick, "Disorientation and Reorientation: The American Landscape Discovered from the West," *Journal of American History* 79 (December 1992), 1031–1034.
5 Michael Dear and Jennifer Wolch (eds), *The Power of Geography* (Boston, MA: Hyman Uwin, 1990), 4.

6   Interview with Loren Miller, Jr., in Charles
    Perry, "When We Were Very Young," *Los
    Angeles Times Magazine* (February 4,
    1990), 13–14.
7   Lynell George, *No Crystal Stair: African
    Americans in the City of Angels* (London
    and New York: Verso, 1992), 222–223.
8   Frederic Jameson, *Postmodernism, or, The
    Cultural Logic of Late Capitalism (Post-
    contemporary Interventions)* (Durham,
    NC: Duke University Press Books, 1990),
    54. But how this could operate in terms of
    global capitalism is more difficult to say.

14
The Idea of Chinatown

The Power of Place and Institutional Practice in
the Making of a Racial Category (1987)

Kay J. Anderson

Neighborhoods of Chinese settlement in Western societies have been extensively studied throughout the twentieth century. Subjected to hostile receptions, Chinatowns serve as commentaries on the attitudes and behavior of their host societies. They have also been an entry point to many research questions in sociology and anthropology about cultural transfer overseas and the dynamics of social organization and community stratification in new environments. In social geography, Chinatown has been conceptualized as a launching point in the assimilation of Chinese immigrants, as an urban village pitted against encroaching land uses, as a product of segregation on the basis of race or ethnicity, and as a Chinese architectural form Chinatown has been viewed as either a ghettoized, minority community or as an "ethnic" community. One geographer summarizes the common social science conceptualization in his words: "Chinatown in North America is characterized by a concentration of Chinese people and economic activities in one or more city blocks which forms a unique component of the urban fabric. It is basically an idiosyncratic oriental community amidst an occidental urban environment" (Lai 1973, 101).

It is possible, however, to adopt a different point of departure to the study of Chinatown, one that does not rely upon a discrete "Chineseness" as an implicit explanatory principle. "Chinatown" is not "Chinatown" only because the "Chinese" whether by choice or constraint live there. Rather, one might argue that Chinatown is a social construction with a cultural history and a tradition of imagery and

institutional practice that has given it a cognitive and material reality in and for the West. If we do not assume that the term "Chinese" expresses an unproblematic relationship to biological or cultural constants but is in one sense a classification, it becomes apparent that the study of the Chinese and their turf is also a study of our categories, our practices, and our interests. Only secondarily is the study about host society attitudes; primarily it concerns the ideology that shaped the attitudes contained in the opening quotation. This step beyond "white" attitudes is critical because it is not prejudice that has explanatory value but the racial ideology that informs it. Such an argument is not unimportant for the conceptualization of Chinatown. Indeed it requires a more fundamental epistemological critique of the twin ideas of "Chinese" and "Chinatown," of race and place.

It is not possible to investigate in one brief article the process of the classification of identity and place in the numerous contexts where the race idea has been institutionalized. Rather, my aim here is to argue the case for a new conceptualization of Chinatown as a white European idea with reference to one context, that of Vancouver, British Columbia. There, one of the largest Chinatowns in North America stands to this day, in part as an expression of the cultural abstractions of those who have been in command of "the power of definition," to use Western's (1981, 8) valuable phrase. But the thrust of the paper is not limited to the study of ideas. Indeed the significance of "Chinatown" is not simply that it has been a representation perceived in certain ways, but that it has been, like race, an idea with remarkable social force and material effect—one that for more than a century has shaped and justified the practices of powerful institutions toward it and toward people of Chinese origin.

Such an interpretation of Chinatown might be equally relevant to the making of other racial categories in Vancouver, to "Chinese" and "Chinatowns" in other settings, and to other racially defined people in other settings.

CHINATOWN AS A WESTERN LANDSCAPE TYPE

How was it that the streets of Dupont, Carrall, and Columbia in Vancouver became apprehended as "Chinatown"? Whose term, indeed in one sense whose place was this? No corresponding term—"Anglo town"—existed in local parlance, nor were the residents of the likes of Vancouver's West End known as "Occidentals." Why then was the home of the pioneers known and intelligible as "Chinatown"? Consistent with the prevailing conceptualization of Chinatown as an "ethnic neighborhood," we might anticipate the response that Chinese people—a racially visible and culturally distinct minority—settled and made their lives there through some combination of push and pull forces. One view, then, might be that the East lives on in the West and Chinatown expresses the values and experiences of its residents.

That people of Chinese origin, like other pioneers to North America, brought with them particular traditions that shaped their activities and choices in the new setting can hardly be disputed. Indeed an important tradition of scholarship has outlined the significance of such traditions for North American Chinatowns as overseas Chinese colonies. Needless to say, Chinese residents were active agents in their own "place making" as were the British-origin residents in Vancouver's Shaughnessy. My decision not to give primary attention to the residents' sense of place then is not to deny them an active role in building their neighborhood nor of any consciousness they may have had as Chinese. Some merchants from China might have even been eager to limit contact with non-Chinese, just as China had obviated contact with Western "barbarians" over the centuries. Others, given a choice, might have quickly assimilated.

In itself, the idea of Chinatown would not be so important or enduring but for the fact it has been legitimized by government agents who make cognitive categories stand as the official definition of a people and place. In the Vancouver case, "Chinatown" accrued a certain field of meaning that became the justification for recurring rounds of government practice in the ongoing construction of both the place and the racial category. Indeed the state has played a particularly pivotal role in the making of a symbolic (and material) order around the idiom of race in Western societies. By sanctioning the arbitrary boundaries of insider and outsider and the idea of mainstream society as "white," the levels of the state have both "enforced" and "propagated" a white European hegemony. I pursue the theme of the concept of place and to investigate the manner in which one arm of white European hegemony—the civic authorities of Vancouver—sanctioned the racial and spatial categories of the dominant culture in the late nineteenth and early twentieth centuries.

"CHINATOWN" IN INTELLECTUAL CONTEXT: THE AGE OF THE RACE IDEA

The early nineteenth-century discovery of the vast stretch of geologic time seemed to confirm the European view that human history was a kind of natural progression from barbarism to civilization. Like the transformation of the earth, the evolution of humanity was a formidably slow process in which savages might become "Caucasians," but the latter were thousands of years "ahead" of the other races (Harris 1972, 266). For all contemporary purposes, the races were immutably separate. "John Chinaman," for example, possessed properties that permitted him to achieve only a semicivilized, despotic state. His race was so retarded, claimed Judge J. Gray of the British Columbia Supreme Court, that he could see no reason why "the strong, broad shouldered superior race, superior physically and mentally, sprung from the highest types of the old world and the new world, [should be] expressing a fear of competition with a diminutive, inferior, and comparatively speaking, feminine race" (Canada 1885, 69). More often, however, the evolutionary doctrine was taken as a warning that the higher "races" were vulnerable to contamination from immigration and "hybridization" with those who would pass along their deficiencies.

According to this nineteenth-century world-view, Vancouver's Dupont Street settlement would be a generically "Chinese" or "Oriental" phenomenon. It would be *their* home, *their* evil—evidence, in itself, of a different capacity for achieving civilization. Even before a "Chinatown" had been identified as such in Vancouver, Secretary of State Chapleau conveyed the connotation of the term: "Their custom of living in quarters of their own—in Chinatowns—is attended with evils, such as the depreciation of property, and owing to their habits of lodging crowded quarters and accumulating filth, is offensive if not likely to breed disease" (Canada 1885, 130). Clearly, "Chinatown" would be an evaluative classi-fication. These components of the Chinatown idea in Vancouver converged in a public nuisance definition, which, I shall argue, became both a context and justification for the making of the racial category, "Chinese."

THE "CELESTIAL CESSPOOL": SANITARY DIMENSIONS OF THE CHINATOWN IDEA, 1886–1920

Shortly before the anti-Chinese riot of 1887, a reporter for the *Vancouver News* wrote: "The China Town where the Celestials congregate is an eyesore to civilization" and if the City could be "aroused to the necessity of checking the abuse of sanitary laws which is invariably a concomitant of the Chinese, [it] will help materially in preventing the Mongolian settle-ment from becoming permanent" ("Progress of the agitation" 1887). Four months later, a row of "hateful haunts" on Carrall Street was specifically singled out for the attention of Council. There, warned the *News*, "in the nucleus of the pest-producing Chinese quarter ... strict surveillance by the City will be necessary to prevent the spread of this curse" ("Slave labor" 1887).

It was the "ordinary Chinese washhouse scattered over the city" (CVA, *In Correspon-dence*, Vol. 6, July 4, 1893, 5275) that was an early target of civic concern. For a "race" so dirty, there was certainly plenty of work in the business of cleanliness, and by 1889 as many as

10 of the 13 laundries owned by merchants from China were located outside Dupont Street. One medical health officer found the spread so fearful as to condemn the washhouse "an unmixed evil, an unmitigated nuisance" (CVA, *In Correspondence*, Vol. 17, November 26, 1900, 13301) and from the late nineteenth century, Council sought means of keeping the "Chinese" laundry in its proper place.

Important judicial limits hampered the City of Vancouver, however. For one, Vancouver's municipal charter (and ultimately the British North America Act of 1864) did not grant legal competence to Council to deny business licenses to "particular nationalities or individuals." The city's challenge was to circumvent such legal restrictions on its political will, and in the case of the "Chinese" laundry, numerous indirect strategies were devised. One alderman, for example, arrived at an artful solution. According to his 1893 bylaw, no washhouse or laundry in Vancouver could be erected outside specified spatial limits, "that is to say beyond Dupont Street and 120 feet on Columbia Avenue and Carrall Street, southerly from Hastings" (CVA, *Bylaws* 1893).

During the late nineteenth century, an equally vigorous assault was launched in the name of sanitary reform on the wooden shacks of the Dupont Street settlement. In 1890, fear of cholera gripped the city and the local press demanded the city take action against "the people of Dupont Street" given that "in Chinese style ... they will not fall into line for the purpose of maintaining cleanliness" ("Preserve the public health" 1890). Fear of contamination from "the degraded humanity from the Orient" was widespread in Vancouver society, and it was customary for letters to the editor to argue that although the "white" race was superior, "Oriental" afflictions would eventually subvert it.

The city fully shared this twist of Darwinist logic and in the mid-1890s—in a significant act of neighborhood definition—Council formally designated "Chinatown" an official entity in the medical health officer rounds and health committee reports (see CVA, *Health Committee Minutes*, 1899–1906). Along with water, sewerage, scavenging, infectious disease, slaughter houses, and pig ranches, Chinatown was listed as a separate category and appointed "a special officer to supervise [it] under the bylaws" (CVA, *In Correspondence*, Vol. 17, November 26, 1900, 13292).

The distilled vision that was Vancouver's Chinatown was, for the city, a pressing mandate, and its actions reinforced both the vision and the reality of a neighborhood and a people apart. Almost immediately after the alleged murder of the wife of a well-known West End railway administrator by her "China-boy" in 1914 ("City acts on agitation" 1914), Council led the clamor to have Chinese removed from the schools.

Although Council's request to Victoria for school segregation foundered on legal obstacles, the city continued to wield its own power tirelessly. In the following year, the local press described "Chinatown" as no less than "besieged."

Clearly, the idea of "Chinatown" was being inherited by successive rounds of officials who adopted the conceptual schemes of their predecessors. The health committee of Council described the area as a "propagating ground for disease" in 1919, and, true to old remedies, an inspection team was set up to monitor the area despite the fact that still no concrete evidence confirmed that Chinatown was a threat to public health (CVA, *Council Minutes*, Vol. 22, May 19, 1919, 488). Within ten months, the owners of more than 20 lodgings were threatened with orders to condemn their buildings, including the Chinese Hospital at 106 Pender Street East (*Chinese Times*, January 24, 1920). Indeed, well into the 1920s the city operated assertively in the idiom of race, indiscriminately raiding Chinatown and harassing residents about bylaw compliance (e.g., *Chinese Times*, March 4, 8, April 5, 1921).

In translating racial ideology into official practice, the civic authorities of Vancouver performed an important legitimizing role in the social construction of Chinatown in the late nineteenth and early twentieth centuries. Chinatown was not simply an idea. It had a concrete referent in the form of a concentrated community whose physical presence propped up the vision of identity and place we have been examining. Furthermore, the circumstances of Chinese immigration to Canada probably encouraged objectively poor living conditions in many sectors of the community. In that sense, the material reality of the district justified and fulfilled the prophecy of Chapleau's "China-town." But it was the mutually reinforcing ideas of race and place, and their scope and influence in British Columbian culture, that gave the

district its coherence as a discrete place in the social consciousness of its representers. In the eyes of successive civic officials, "Chinatown" signified no less than the encounter between "West" and "East"; it distinguished and testified to the vast asymmetry between two "races." As such, Chinatown was not a benign cultural abstraction but a political projection, through which a divisive system of racial classification was being structured and institutionalized.

CONCLUSION

I have argued that "Chinatown" was a social construct that belonged to Vancouver's "white" European society, who, like their contemporaries throughout North America, perceived the district of Chinese settlement according to an influential culture of race. From the vantage point of the European, Chinatown signified all those features that seemed to set the Chinese irrevocably apart—their appearance, lack of Christian faith, opium and gambling addiction, their strange eating habits, and odd graveyard practices. That is, it embodied the white Europeans' sense of difference between immigrants from China and themselves, between the East and the West. This is not to argue that Chinatown was a fiction of the European imagination; nor can there be any denying that gambling, opium use, and unsanitary conditions were present in the district where Chinese settled. The point is that "Chinatown" was a shared characterization—one constructed and distributed by and for Europeans, who, in arbitrarily conferring outsider status on these pioneers to British Columbia, were affirming their own identity and privilege. That they directed that purpose in large part through the medium of Chinatown attests to the importance of place in the making of a system of racial classification.

Studies of the social meaning of place in human geography have too rarely taken measure of the role of powerful agents, such as the state, in defining place. Yet those with the "power of definition" can, in a sense, create "place" by arbitrarily regionalizing the external world. In the example here, Chinatown further became the isolated territory and insensitive representation its beholders understood in part through the legitimizing activities of government. Perhaps not all places are as heavily laden with a cultural and political baggage as "Chinatown." But Chinatown is important in pointing up once again the more general principle that a negotiated social and historical process lies behind the apparently neutral-looking taxonomic systems of census districts. More importantly perhaps, the manipulation of racial ideology by institutions is additional testimony to the fact that a set of power relations may underpin and keep alive our social and spatial categories.

In the course of its evolution, Chinatown reflected the race definition process, but it also informed and institutionalized it, providing a context and justification for its reproduction. Pender Street has been the home of the overseas Chinese to be sure, but "Chinatown" is a story, which, in disclosing the categories and consequences of white European cultural hegemony, reveals more the insider than it does the outsider.

REFERENCES

Canada. 1885. *Report of the Royal Commission on Chinese Immigration*. Ottawa: Printed by Order of the Commission.

City acts upon Oriental agitation. 1914. *Province*, Apri 7, p. 3.

City of Vancouver Archives (CVA). City of Vancouver RG2-B1. *Council Minutes*, miscellaneous years, 1886–1920.

City of Vancouver Archives (CVA). City of Vancouver RG2-A1. *City Clerks In Correspondence*, miscellaneous years, 1886–1920.

City of Vancouver Archives (CVA). 1899–1906. *Health Committee Minutes*. Vol. 2. Chairman's report.

City of Vancouver Archives (CVA). Office of the City Clerk. 1893. *Bylaws*. Vol. 1, No. 176. May 15, pp. 1044–45.

Harris, Marvin. 1972. Race. In *International Encyclopedia of the Social Sciences*. New York: Macmillan.

Lai, Chuen-Yon David. 1973. Socioeconomic structures and the viability of Chinatown. In *Residential and Neighborhood Studies*, ed. C. Forward, pp. 101–129. Western Geographical Series, No. 5. Victoria: University of Victoria.

Preserve the public health. 1890. *Vancouver Daily World*, August 30, p. 4.

Progress of the agitation. 1887. *Vancouver News*, January 13, p. 2.

Western, John. 1981. *Outcast Capetown*. Minneapolis: University of Minnesota Press.

15
The Brandon Archive
(2005)

Judith Jack Halberstam

Our relations to place, like our relations to people, are studded with bias, riven with contradictions, and complicated by opaque emotional responses. I am one of those people for whom lonely rural landscapes feel laden with menace, and for many years nonurban areas were simply "out there," strange and distant horizons populated by hostile populations. It is still true that a densely packed urban street or a metallic skyline can release a surge of excitement for me while a vast open landscape fills me with dread. In December 1993, I remember reading a short story in the newspaper about an execution-style killing in rural Nebraska. The story seemed unremarkable except for one small detail buried in the heart of the report: one of the murder victims was a young female-bodied person who had been passing as a man. The murder of this young transgender person sent shock waves through queer communities in the United States, and created fierce identitarian battles between transsexual activists and gay and lesbian activists, with each group trying to claim Brandon Teena as one of their own. The struggles over the legacy of Brandon represented much more than a local skirmish over the naming or classification of fallen brethren; indeed, they testified to the political complexities of an activism sparked by murder and energized by the work of memorializing individuals. The fascination with murder and mayhem that characterizes US popular culture has led some theorists to point to the emergence of a wound culture. It is easy to explain why homophobic violence might generate such fierce activist responses; it is harder to mobilize such responses for purposes that extend beyond demands for protection and recognition from the state. My purpose here is to build on the flashes of insight afforded by violent encounters between "normal" guys and gender-variant people in order to theorize the meaning of gender transitivity in late capitalism. Here I will use the notions of relays of influence between dominant and minority masculinities to consider the place and space of the masculine transgender subject.

The tragic facts in the case of the murder of Brandon Teena and his two friends are as follows: on December 31, 1993, three young people were shot to death, execution style, in Falls City in rural Nebraska. Ordinarily, this story would have evoked only mild interest from mainstream America and a few questions about the specific brutalities of rural America; one of the three victims, however, was a young white person who had been born a woman, but who was living as a man and had been dating local girls. The other two victims, Brandon's friend Lisa Lambert, and her friend Philip DeVine, a disabled African American man, appeared to have been killed because they were in the wrong place at the wrong time, although this too is debatable.

The execution of Brandon, Lisa, and Philip was in fact more like an earthquake or a five-alarm fire than an individualized event: its eruption damaged more than just the three who died and the two who killed; it actually devastated the whole town, and brought a flood of reporters, cameras, and journalists into the area to pick through the debris and size up the import of the disaster. That media rush, in many ways, transformed the Brandon murders from a circumscribed event to an ever evolving narrative.

I use the Brandon material, then, to unpack the meaning of "local homosexualities" or transsexualities in the context of the United States. Like other narratives about nonmetropolitan sexuality, popular versions of this story posit a queer subject who sidesteps so-called modern models of gay identity by conflating gender and sexual variance. Indeed, in the popular versions of the Brandon narrative that currently circulate, like *Boys Don't Cry*, Brandon's promiscuity and liminal identity is depicted as immature and even premodern and as a form of false consciousness. When Brandon explores a mature and adult relationship with one woman who recognizes him as "really female," that film suggests, Brandon accedes to a modern form of homosexuality and is finally "free." Reconstituted now as a liberal subject, Brandon's death at the hands of local men can be read simultaneously as a true tragedy and an indictment of backward, rural communities.

I believe that an extensive analysis of the Brandon murders can serve to frame the many questions about identification, responsibility, class, regionality, and race that trouble queer communities today. Not only does Brandon represent a martyr lost in the struggle for transgender rights to the brutal perpetrators of rural hetero-masculine violences. Brandon also serves as a marker for a particular set of late twentieth-century cultural anxieties about place, space, locality, and metropolitanism. Fittingly, Brandon has become the name for gender variance, for fear of transphobic and homophobic punishment; Brandon also embodies the desire directed at nonnormative masculinities. Brandon represents other rural lives undone by fear and loathing, and his story also symbolizes an urban fantasy of homophobic violence as essentially Midwestern. But violence wherever we may find it marks different conflictual relations in different sites; and homicide, on some level, always depicts the microrealities of other battles displaced from the abstract to the tragically material. While at least one use of any Brandon Teena project must be to connect Brandon's gender presentation to other counternarratives of gender realness, I also hope that Brandon's story can be a vehicle linked to the discussions of globalization, transnational sexualities, geography, and queer migration. On some level Brandon's story, while

cleaving to its own specificity, needs to remain an open narrative—not a stable narrative of female-to-male transsexual identity nor a singular tale of queer bashing, not a cautionary fable about the violence of rural America nor an advertisement for urban organizations of queer community. Brandon's story permits a dream of transformation that must echo in the narratives of queer life in other nonmetropolitan locations.

FALLS CITY, NEBRASKA: A GOOD PLACE TO DIE?

The landscape of Nebraska serves as a contested site on which multiple narratives unfold—narratives, indeed, that refuse to collapse into simply one story, "the Brandon Teena story." Some of these narratives are narratives of hate, or of desire; others tell of ignorance and brutality; still others of isolation and fear; some allow violence and ignorant prejudices to become the essence of poor, white, rural identity; and still others provoke questions about the deployment of whiteness and the regulation of violence. While the video itself encourages viewers to distance themselves from the horror of the heartlands and to even congratulate themselves for living in an urban rather than a rural environment, ultimately we can use Brandon's story as it emerges here to begin the articulation of the stories of white, working-class, rural queers, and to map the immensely complex relations that make rural America a site of horror and degradation in the urban imagination.

For queers who flee the confines of the rural Midwest and take comfort in urban anonymity, this video may serve as a justification of their worst fears about the violent effects of failing to flee; closer readings of Brandon's story, however, reveal the desire shared by many Midwestern queers for a way of staying rather than leaving. While some journalists in the wake of Brandon's murder queried his decision to stay in Falls City, despite having been hounded by the police and raped by the men who went on to murder him, we must consider the condition of "staying put" as part of the production of complex queer subjectivities. Some queers need to leave home in order to become queer, and others need to stay close to home in order to preserve their difference. The danger of small towns as Willa Cather described it, also in reference to rural

Nebraska, emerges out of a suffocating sense of proximity: "lives roll along so close to one another," she wrote in *Lucy Gayheart*, "loves and hates beat about, their wings almost touching." This beautiful, but scary image of rural life as a space all-too-easily violated depends absolutely on an opposite image—the image of rural life as wide open and free ranging, as "big sky" and open plains. Cather captures perfectly the contradiction of rural life as the contrast between wide-open spaces and sparse populations, on the one hand, and small-town claustrophobia and lack of privacy, on the other.

The life and death of Brandon provokes endless speculation about the specificities of the loves and hates that characterized his experiences in Falls City, and any straightforward rendering of his story remains impossible. Some viewers of *The Brandon Teena Story* have accused the filmmakers of an obvious class bias in their depictions of the people of Falls City; others have seen the film as an accurate portrayal of the cultures of hate and meanness produced in small, mostly white towns. Any attempt to come to terms with the resonances of Brandon's murder will ultimately have to grapple with both of these proposals. One way in which *The Brandon Teena Story* deploys and perpetuates a class bias in relation to the depiction of anti-queer violence is by depicting many of its interview subjects in uncritical ways as "white trash." In their introduction to an anthology titled *White Trash: Race and Class in America*, Annalee Newitz and Matt Wray define white trash as both a reference to "actually existing white people living in (often rural) poverty," and a term designating "a set of stereotypes and myths related to the social behaviors, intelligence, prejudices, and gender roles of poor whites" (Newitz and Wray 1996, 7). The editors offer a "local politics of place" to situate, combat, and explain such stereotypes.

In order to understand the kinds of masculinities with which Brandon may have been competing, we can turn to the representations of the murderers themselves. While some accounts of the Brandon case have attempted to empathize with the men who murdered Brandon—Lotter and Nissen—by revealing their traumatic family histories and detailing their encounters with abuse, the video tries to encourage the men to give their own reasons for their brutality. The conversations with Lotter and Nissen are fascinating for the way they allow the men to coolly describe rape and murder scenes, and also because Lotter in particular articulates an astute awareness of the violence of the culture into which he was raised. Nissen, however, shows little power of self-reflection; the video represents him as ultimately far more reprehensible than his partner in crime. For one second in the video, the camera focuses on a small tattoo on Nissen's arm, but does not allow the viewer to identify it. In Aphrodite Jones's book on the Brandon case, *All S/he Wanted*, she provides information that situates this tattoo as a symbol of white supremacy politics. Nissen, we learn, was involved off and on throughout his early life with the White American Group for White America. While Nissen's flirtation with brutally racist white supremacist groups need not surprise us, it does nonetheless flesh out the particular nexus of hate that came to focus on Brandon, Lisa, and Philip.

Nowhere in the documentary, however, nor in media coverage of the case, does anyone link Nissen's racial politics with either the brutalization of Brandon or the execution of the African American, Philip; indeed, the latter is always constructed as a case of "wrong place, wrong time," but Philip's situation needs to be explored in more detail. In *The Brandon Teena Story*, Philip's murder is given little airplay, and none of his relatives or family make an appearance in the video. While every other character in the drama, including Lisa, is carefully located in relation to Brandon and the web of relations among Brandon's friends, Philip alone is given only the most scant attention. No explanation is given for the nonappearance of his family and friends, and no real discussion is presented about his presence in the farmhouse the night of the murders.

It is hard to detach the murder of Philip from the history of Nissen's involvement in white supremacist cults. Many accounts of white power movements in the United States connect them to small, all-white towns in the Midwest and to economically disadvantaged white populations. While one would not want to demonize poor, white, rural Americans as any more bigoted than urban or suburban white yuppie populations in the United States, it is nonetheless important to highlight the particular fears and paranoia that take shape in rural, all-white populations. Fear of the government, fear of the United Nations, and fear of Jews, blacks, and queers mark white rural masculinities in particular ways that can easily produce cultures of hate (Ridgeway 1995). In small towns where few people of color live, difference may be marked and remarked in relation to gender variance rather than racial diversity. As Newitz and Wray point out in their anatomy of white trash, some degree of specificity is necessary when we try to describe and identify different forms of homophobia and transphobia as they are distributed across different geographies.

In "Get Thee to a Big City: Sexual Imaginary and the Great Gay Migration," anthropologist Kath Weston begins a much-needed inquiry into the difference between urban and rural "sexual imaginaries" (Weston 1995). She comments on the rather stereotyped division of rural/urban relations that "locates gay subjects in the city while putting their presence in the countryside under erasure" (262). Weston also traces the inevitable disappointments that await rural queers who escape the country only to arrive in alienating queer urban spaces. As Weston proposes, "The gay imaginary is not just a dream of a freedom to be gay that requires an urban location, but a symbolic space that configures gayness itself by elaborating an opposition between urban and rural life" (274). She wants us to recognize that the distinction between the urban and the rural that props up the gay imaginary is a symbolic one, and as such, it constitutes a dream of an elsewhere that promises a freedom it can never provide. But it is also crucial to be specific about which queer subjects face what kinds of threats, from whom, and in what locations. While in the city, for example, one may find that the gay or transsexual person of color is most at risk for violence from racist cops; in rural locations, one may find that even the white queers who were born and raised there are outlawed when they disrupt the carefully protected homogeneity of white, family-oriented communities. One may also discover that while the brutalization of a transgender sex worker of color raises little outcry in the city from local queer activists, the murder of a white boy in rural North America can stir up an enormous activist response that is itself symbolic of these other imaginary divisions.

Nebraska was not simply "anywhere" in this video, but that the documentary filmmakers had skillfully tried to situate the landscape as a character in this drama.

I decided that one could make use of the Brandon material to study urban attitudes toward queer rural life, and to examine more closely the essential links that have been made between urban life and queerness per se.

The murder of Brandon Teena, like the murder of Matthew Shepard some six years later, did in fact draw public attention to the peculiar vulnerabilities of queer youth (whether transgender or gay/lesbian) living in North America's heartland. In both cases, the victims became martyrs for urban queer activists fighting for LGBT rights, and they were mythologized in a huge and diverse array of media as extraordinary individuals who fell prey to the violent impulses of homophobic and transphobic middle-America masculinities. But while it is tempting to use the materials produced in the aftermath of the killings of both Brandon Teena and Matthew Shepard to flesh out the details of the lives and deaths of the subjects, it makes more sense to my mind to collect the details, the stories, the facts, and the fictions of the cases, and then to create deep archives for future analysis about the many rural lives and desires that were implicated in the lives and deaths of these individuals. Here I do not mean simply a collection of data; rather, I use the word archive in a Foucauldian way to suggest a discursive field and a structure of thinking. The archive is an immaterial repository for the multiple ideas about rural life that construct and undergird urban identity in the twentieth and twenty-first centuries. In the case of Brandon, the archive that has posthumously developed contains vital information about racial and class constructions of identity and desire in rural areas, and it also provides some important details about the elaborate and complex desires of young women coming to maturity in nonurban areas; the young women who were drawn to Brandon's unconventional manhood must have lots to tell us about adolescent feminine fantasy. All too often such girlish desires for boyish men are dismissed within a Freudian model of female sexuality as a form of immaturity and unrealized sexual capacity; the assumption that underpins the dismissal of adolescent female desires is that the young women who fall for a Brandon, a teen idol, or some other icon of youthful manhood, will soon come to full adulthood, and when they do, they will desire better and more authentic manhood. By reckoning only with Brandon's story, as opposed to the stories of his girlfriends, his family, and those other two teenagers who died alongside him, we consent to a liberal narrative of individualized trauma. For Brandon's story to be meaningful, it must be about more than Brandon.

REFERENCES

Muska, Susan, and Gréta Olafsdóttir. 1998. *The Brandon Teena Story*. Documentary, Biography. Zeitgeist Films.

Newitz, Annalee, and Matt Wray (eds). 1996. *White Trash: Race and Class in America*. London: Routledge.

Peirce, Kimberly. 1999. *Boys Don't Cry*. Crime, Drama, Romance. Fox Searchlight.

Ridgeway, J. 1995. *Blood in the Face: The Ku Klux Klan, Aryan Nations, Nazi Skinheads, and the Rise of the New White Culture*. New York: Thunder's Mouth Press.

Weston, Kath. 1995. "Get Thee to a Big City: Sexual Imaginary and the Great Gay Migration." *GLQ: A Journal of Lesbian and Gay Studies* 2(3): 253–277.

16
The Poor Little Rich Man
(1900)

Adolf Loos

I want to tell you about a poor rich man. He had money and possessions, a faithful wife to kiss away the cares of his daily business, and a gaggle of children to make even the poorest of his workers envious. Everything he laid his hands on thrived, and for this he was loved by his friends. But today, everything is very, very different; and this is how it came about.

One day this man talked to himself: "You have money and possessions, a faithful wife, a gaggle of children to make even the poorest of your workers envious, but are you really happy? You see there are people who have none of the things you are envied for. But their worries are utterly wiped away by a great magician; Art! But what is art to you? You don't even know the name of a single artist. Every snob could drop his business card at the door, and your servant would throw it open for him. Nevertheless, you have not once really received art! I know for sure it won't come. But now I will call on it. It shall be received in my home like a Queen who has come to reside with me."

He was a powerful man, and he carried through with great energy whatever he took on. It was his accustomed way of doing business. And so yet on the same day he went to a renowned interior architect and said: "Bring me art, art under my own roof! Money doesn't matter!"

The architect needn't be told twice. He went to the man's house and immediately threw out all of his furniture. Then he let floorers, lackers, painters, masons, tressil-builders, carpenters, installers, potters, wallpaper-hangers, and sculptors move in.

You have never seen the likes of the art that was captured and well cared for inside of the four corners of that rich man's home.

The rich man was overjoyed. Overjoyed he went through the new rooms. Art everywhere he looked. Art in everything and anything. When he turned a door handle he grabbed hold of art, when he sank into a chair he sank into art, when he burrowed his tired bones under the pillows he burrowed into art, his feet sank in art when he walked across the carpet. He indulged himself with outrageous fervour in art. Since his plates were artistically decorated, he cut his bœuf à l'oignon with still more energy.

People praised, and were envious of him. The Art periodicals glorified his name as one of the foremost patrons of the arts. His rooms were used as public examples, studied, described, explained.

But they were worth it. Every room was a complete individual symphony of colour. Walls, furniture, and fabrics were all composed sophisticatedly into perfect harmony with each other. Each appliance had its proper place, and was connected to the others in the most wonderful combinations.

The architect had forgotten nothing, absolutely nothing. Everything from the ashtray and flatware to the candle extinguisher had been combined and matched. It wasn't a common architectural art. In every ornament, in every form, in every nail was the individuality of the owner to be found. (A psychological work of such complication that it would be clear to anyone.)

The architect modestly refused all honours. He only said: "These rooms are not from me.

Over there in the corner stands a statue from Charpentier. Just like anyone else would earn my disgust, if he claimed a room as his design, as soon as he uses one of my door handles, as little as I can claim these rooms as my design." It was nobly, and consequently said. Many carpenters who perhaps used a wallpaper from Walter Crane and nevertheless would want to credit the furniture in the room to themselves because they had created and completed it they were ashamed to the depths of their black souls as they learned about these words.

After flying off at a tangent let us now return to our rich man. I have already told you how overjoyed he was. From now on, he devoted a great deal of his time to studying his dwelling. For everything had to be learned; he saw this soon enough. There was much to be noted. Each appliance had its own definite place. The architect had done his best for him. He had thought of everything in advance. There was a definite place for even the very smallest case, made just especially for it.

The domicile was comfortable, but it was hard mental work. In the first weeks the architect guarded the daily life, so that no mistake could creep in. The rich man put tremendous effort into it. But it still happened, that when he laid down a book without thinking that he shoved it into the pigeonhole for the newspaper. Or he knocked the ashes from his cigar into the groove made for the candleholder. You picked something up and the endless guessing and searching for the right place to return it to began, and sometimes the architect had to look at the blueprints to rediscover the correct place for a box of matches.

Where applied art experiences such a victory, the correlating music can't lag behind. That idea kept the rich man very busy. He made a recommendation to the tramway company to replace the senselessly ringing bells on the trams with the characteristic motif of Parsifal bells. He didn't find any concession there, obviously they weren't ready for such a modern concept. Therefore he was allowed at his own cost, to change the cobblestone in front of his house, so that the carts rolled by in the rhythm of the Radetzky March. Even the electrical bells in his house got new Wagner and Beethoven motifs, and all the competent art critics were full of praise for the man who had opened up the new area of "art as a basic commodity."

One can imagine that all of these improvements would make the man happier.

We can't hide the fact however, that he tried to be home as little as possible. Now and then one needs a break from so much art. Could you live in an art gallery? Or sitting in "Tristan and Isolt" for months at a time? See! Who could blame him for collecting strength in restaurants, cafés, and from friends and acquaintances to face his own home. He had expected something different. But art requires sacrifice. He sacrificed a lot. It brought tears to his eyes. He thought of all the old things that he held so dear, and that he missed. The big armchair! Everyday his father had taken his afternoon nap in it. The old clock, and the old paintings! Art requires it! Don't cave in!

One time it came to pass that he celebrated his birthday, and his wife and children gave him many gifts. He was very pleased with all his birthday presents, and they brought him much happiness and joy. Soon afterwards the architect returned because of his right to check on the placement of objects, and to answer complicated questions. He entered the room. The prosperous man who had many concerns on his mind came to greet him warmly.

The architect didn't recognize the happiness of the prosperous man, but he had discovered something else, and the colour had run out of his cheeks. "Why would you be wearing those slippers?" He blurted out.

The master of the house looked at his embroidered shoes, and sighed in relief. The shoes were made from the original design of the architect himself. This time he felt guiltless. He answered thoughtfully.

"But Mr Architect! Have you forgotten? You designed these slippers yourself!"

"Certainly!" The architect thundered. "But for the bedroom! With these impossible pieces of colour you are destroying the entire atmosphere. Don't you even realize it?"

The prosperous man took the slippers off immediately, and was pleased as punch that the architect didn't find his socks offensive. They went into the bedroom, where the rich man was allowed to put his shoes back on.

"Yesterday", he timidly began "I celebrated my birthday, and my family gave me tons of gifts. I sent for you so that you could give us advice as to where we should put up all of the things I was given."

The architect's face became visibly longer. Then he let loose:

"How dare you presume to receive presents? Didn't I draw everything up for you? Haven't I taken care of everything? You need nothing more. You are complete!" "But" the rich man replied "I should be allowed to buy things."

"No, you are not allowed, never ever! That's just what I was missing, things, that have not been drawn by me. Haven't I done enough, that I put the Charpentier here for you? The statue that steals all the fame out of my work! No, you are not allowed to buy anything else!"

"But what about when my grandchild brings me something from kindergarten as a gift?"

"You are not allowed to take it!"

The prosperous man was decimated, but he still had not lost. An idea! Yes! An idea!

"And when I want to go to Secession to buy a painting?" He asked triumphantly.

"Then try to hang it somewhere. Don't you see that there isn't any room for anything else? For every painting I have hung here there is a frame on the wall. You can not move anything. Try and fit in a new painting!"

Thereupon a transformation took place within the rich man. The happy man felt suddenly deeply, deeply unhappy, and he saw his future life. No one would be allowed to grant him joy.

He had to pass by the shopping stores of the city, perfect, and complete. Nothing would be created for him ever again, none of his loved ones would be allowed to give him a painting. For him there could be no more painters, no artists, no craftsmen again. He was shut out of future life and its strivings, its developments, and its desires. He felt: Now is the time to learn to walk about with one's own corpse. Indeed! He is finished! He is complete!

17
Migration, Material Culture and Tragedy

Four Moments in Caribbean Migration (2008)

Daniel Miller

This paper ends in tragedy. Well, at least in a discussion of tragedy. This may not seem at all unreasonable given that the topic is migration. But the argument made in this paper is that in some cases the primary cause of tragedy is the exact opposite of that which is normally presumed. What creates the condition for tragedy is not disruption, which is generally seen as the negative aspect of migration, but continuity. In particular, the problems that arise from a desire to remain true to one's roots. The reason being that the customs, traditions and expectations that make sense and serve a person well in the context from which they come, may be singularly inappropriate, and betray that individual in the place they have come to. This is important since the concept of roots has generally been celebrated and romanticised as the solution to the issue of disruption in migration. My argument is that there can be loss as well as gain in continuity.

To appreciate this we need to gain a purchase on the concept of tragedy itself which is in some ways implicit in the very form of anthropological analysis and presentation. Since tragedy generally refers to the relationship between the fate of an individual and the extent to which it appears inexorable in the face of much wider forces and generalities which are of the order in which anthropology describes a population. From the perspective of the individual those standard forms of anthropological representation may actually represent the thwarting of the specific ideals and ambitions.

CONTEMPORARY LONDON

I am presently writing up 17 months' worth of fieldwork on a single street in South London, carried out jointly with a PhD student Fiona Parrott. The topic of our project was a concern with how people used their attachments to possessions and material culture as supportive when they have had to deal with episodes of loss such as bereavement, divorce or the ending of relationships. The fieldwork was highly successful as a piece of London ethnography. We worked with 100 households or individuals, almost entirely from this single street, and had only eight clear refusals. Such is the level of ethnic and social diversity both of this street and of contemporary London as a whole (Johnston et al., 2002; Peach, 1996; Simpson, 2007) that we feel there is a sense in which the street can actually be representative of the city.

MY PORTRAIT IS OF MARCIA

My portrait is of Marcia, living on the very same Stuart Street. There must be dozens of ornaments and figures on the central table of Marcia's living-room. In addition the dresser, other side tables and every raised surface has its own share of figures. And while there are a few common souvenir genres such as mini bottles and ashtrays, it is figures that dominate. Black musicians that as Marcia would put it 'bright up' the place jostle the Santas, the religious icons and the toys. In Marcia's room Jesus looks out from the midst of the Last Supper and his eyes fall on Humpty Dumpty, in turn overawed by a three-foot Matador whose arms are now laden with a bunch of pink plastic roses. A litter of six china kittens play at the feet of a Japanese lady. An American Indian joins a beach party of almost naked figures, including one well-endowed sunbather whose modesty is barely saved by a carefully positioned bottle of sun lotion. There must be a dozen saxophonists strategically placed around the room to serenade a picture of Marcia at her wedding, which nestles respectfully below another portrait of Jesus holding his own sacred heart. Fairies nibble on tropical fruit three times their size. Pixies play with peasants. Goats look amazed at basketball champions, while plastic lilies protect Puritans reading epistles to pigeons. Marcia has brought tolerance, though not exactly harmony, to not just one world, but many.

So the room is not just unbelievably crowded, it is indeed populated, and Marcia herself hardly needs to tell us about the overwhelming cause of suffering that afflicts her now and has afflicted her for so many years—her loneliness. One of the more poignant themes in the room is ornamental telephones, china copies of old-fashioned phones that had discs to be dialled. Phones that can never actually ring ... there is not a single object from the Caribbean that I can identify in the entire room. But what is far more surprising is that while Mrs Stone's living-room is covered in signs of her family, either photographs of them or cards such as birthday and Christmas cards sent by them, there is almost nothing similar in Marcia's room. She has a single wedding photo but otherwise you would have no evidence from the room itself that she has a son or several grandchildren. This is almost incomprehensible to anyone familiar with West Indian living-rooms which ... are usually stuffed with mementoes, gifts, photos and other reminders of relatives.

To understand how this situation has come about one has to follow Marcia's own trajectory. Her mother had been a school teacher, probably not very different from the figure of Hortense in Andrea Levy's novel *Small Island*: respectable, working incredibly hard, never taking holidays, and bringing up her children with a strict disciplinarian regime. They were not well off, and Marcia was often hungry since although there were fruit trees sometimes she could not count on the basic staples for meals. This was

the reason she came to London in the first place. She came essentially to 'better herself'. To find a way out of the poverty and limitations of her upbringing.

As so often in Caribbean migration, she may never have been conscious of herself as part of that historical trend, partly because it is of course both historical and a trend only in retrospect. When she first arrived she left behind the child that had already been born to her, in her homeland. She sought qualifications and work, but most likely, as with so many migrants, retained 'a myth of return'. The permanence of settlement may have come gradually. First the desire to have her child with her, but increasingly the orientation of this child to London and his estrangement from the place of her own childhood, as well as the demands on her from people back home to keep earning the money from which they were at least occasional beneficiaries.

So when Marcia comes as a migrant, she would see no initial reason to transform herself in relation to the customs of the English any more than was absolutely required. Especially if at some time, some undefined time, she would be returning home. The problem was that many of the traits, expectations and forms of appropriate behaviour, each of which have derived from a particular position within a Caribbean context, have ended up betraying Marcia within the very different context of London. In London she too worked hard and never took holidays. She cultivated a polite, but never too close, relationship to neighbours or through the church. But London is not the Caribbean, and this respectable distancing actually left her far more cut off and lonely than the same behaviour would have done in the Caribbean setting. Given also the greater autonomy of family, she found that when the few core relationships went badly there was nothing else by way of alternative society. As it happens her relationship with her husband, and in particular his sister, went very badly, and when she tried to treat her grandchildren with the kind of discipline she assumed was appropriate they simply chose distance as a response.

This particular kind of West Indian figure often achieves some sense of fulfilment when they become a sort of family matriarch overseeing the development of grandchildren and others who treat them with consummate respect. Their authority is retained and augmented by age. But in London, without realising it, she found that she had lost the possibility of most close supportive relationships. People in London did not respect her respectability. They did not value her aloofness. They were all too busy to deal with the etiquettes and solicitudes that would have given her an enduring role. They would just see this as playing games with friendship and kinship. They couldn't be bothered. There were other people who were more immediately approachable. In this city you could separate much more easily from family. People didn't need Marcia and she couldn't reveal the degree to which she needed them.

She retains some links with her homeland but now sees these only as people who want to fleece her of the money she has earned and to make her sign away her rights to land, people who never thanked her for the gifts she sent home. In the end, having never taken a holiday, she retired and saw no one whom she now wanted to benefit from her savings, thrift and hard work. So belatedly she started joining her church-organised holidays, and in the past few years has actually visited many parts of the world. It is the souvenirs from these church trips that now populate her living-room and the memories of these trips that keep her company in her loneliness. The irony is that it was the courage that allowed her to remain, as she saw it, true to herself, and to refuse the temptations to relax into lowering the expectations she imposed upon herself, that are the primary cause of her current loneliness and sadness.

DISCUSSION

A presentation given in terms of individuals lends itself to a more literary quality. This is quite reminiscent of the pathos found in Naipaul's novel A House for Mr Biswas (1961), where the primary theme is remarkably similar, in that Biswas is also principally driven by this same life project of building his house, and yet somehow this house is never going to be the substantial structure he envisages in his head. The novel is set in the same town of Chaguanas as my original research and an analysis of Naipaul's themes played a major role in that analysis (Miller, 1994, pp. 164–168). I want, however, to focus more on the extension of this literary analogy to Marcia, because I believe her case highlights something of general relevance

to anthropology and to the anthropology of migrants in particular. Having presented her in a more literary style, she seems to evoke at least our colloquial sense of the term 'tragedy'. I am taking from my own experience what I sense is the implication of the term tragedy generally, rather than specific to this case. I think that when we use the term tragedy, we imply individuals, who are not merely suffering as a result of their own intentionality of actions, though these are involved, but rather larger forces, something closer to what we might call destiny, which seem to be working themselves out through the medium of the individual, a common theme in plays and novels through the ages.

The point here is that I have suggested that Marcia, and I suspect many first generation migrants, are finally oppressed precisely because they strive to be true to the values that they have been brought up to believe in. From the point of view of anthropology this is seen through objectifying analysis. We might say that her distance from her neighbours and her ideals of discipline derive from a specific Caribbean 'habitus' (Bourdieu, 1977) that make them appropriate in that context, but could easily become singularly inappropriate in the radically different setting of London. But from the point of view of the individuals themselves, Marcia talks constantly in terms of more fatalistic experiences. She sits and philosophises about God's will and her fate. Again this expresses something seen in literary criticism that captures this individual perspective. Frye argues that one of the consequences of philosophising about tragedy is that this tends to the construction both of a philosophy of fate and a philosophy of providence (Frye, 1990, p. 64). Fate is unjust. Even if Marcia thinks she got some things wrong or takes some responsibility for what happens to her, it seems we are punished far in excess of our guilt (Steiner, 1961, p. 9).

Furthermore, as A House for Mr Biswas demonstrates, one does not have to be a migrant to be subject to these qualities of pathos or tragedy. Even the original condition of those in Trinidad who did not migrate is forged from their having been brought to that country in slavery and indentured labour. It is entirely possible that it was this initial experience of rupture that gives rise to the subsequent emphasis upon objectifying oneself in settlement.

While land was an integral part of this process within the Caribbean, when we look to subsequent migrations the emphasis is mainly on the house and possessions. We have seen how for Jamaicans the house comes to objectify the whole life process, a process that is never fully completed and ends in a grave that itself speaks to the precise form of the house. Only this degree of integrity between house and life explains why most children are born out of wedlock, taking precedence even over devotion to the church. So these moments of material culture are not an excavation of some minor but previously neglected aspects of people's lives, they are about migration and settlement in the terms which fundamentally determine the sense of success or failure, respectability and tragedy.

This is signified both in the house itself and also through the mundane possessions it contains, which are again highlighted in each of these studies. Marcia's abundant possessions signify most of all what they cannot be. However much she crams her house full of objects, and populates her home, there is that sense of emptiness and the futility of her attempts to stem the tide of loneliness that besets her. These cases are the end point established by the previous moments. They reflect the contradictions of returned migrants to Jamaica who want to be accepted as Jamaican but are devoted to creating English-style gardens. Before that was the original contradictions of the initial settlement in the UK, that took models of respectability from English working-class traditions and now re-construct them as quintessentially West Indian. Initially they are there in the details of ordinary Trinidadian living-rooms that have gradually developed from those fragile conditions of settlement and self so brilliantly evoked in Naipaul's *House for Mr Biswas*. In every case the house and its possessions reflects a wider contradiction of migration that seeks stability and constancy precisely because that is not its inherent condition. It is the centrality of material culture to these projects and their failures that in turn makes them speak to the analytical possibility of uncovering cultural imperatives but also contradictions, failures and discontinuities. The point of this paper is that to appreciate the play of tragedy we need to consider not only the larger forces that appear as destiny, but also the material forces through which destiny appears manifest.

REFERENCES

Bourdieu, P. (1977) *Outline of a Theory of Practice* (Cambridge: Cambridge University Press).

Frye, Northrop (1990) *Anatomy of Criticism* (Harmondsworth: Penguin).

Horst, H. (2004b) A pilgrimage home, *Journal of Material Culture,* 9, pp. 11–26.

Johnston, R., Forrest, J. and Poulsen, M. (2002) Are there ethnic enclaves/ghettos in English cities?, *Urban Studies,* 39, pp. 591–618.

Levy, A. (2004) *Small Island* (London: Headline).

Miller, D. (1994) *Modernity: An Ethnographic Approach* (Oxford: Berg).

Miller, D. (2005) Materiality: an introduction, in: D. Miller (ed.), *Materiality* (Chapel Hill, NC: Duke University Press), pp. 1–50.

Naipaul, V.S. (1961) *A House for Mr Biswas* (London: André Deutsch).

Parrott, F. (2005) It's not forever: the material culture of hope, *Journal of Material Culture,* 10, pp. 245–262.

Peach, C. (1996) Does Britain have ghettos?, *Transactions, Institute of British Geographers,* 21(1), pp. 216–235.

Simpson, L. (2007) Ghettos of the mind: the empirical behaviour of indices of segregation and diversity, *Journal of the Royal Statistical Society: Series A,* 170, pp. 405–424.

Steiner, S. (1961) *The Death of Tragedy* (London: Faber and Faber).

SECTION 4

Power, Subjectivity, and Space

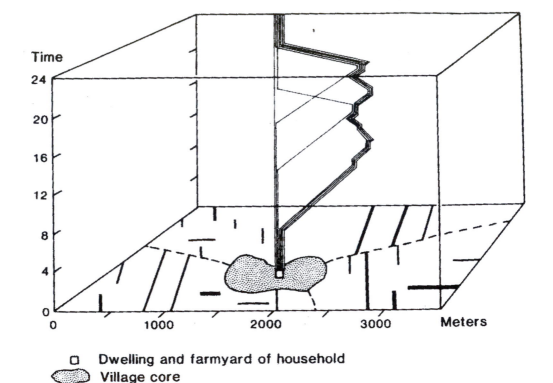

Time

- □ Dwelling and farmyard of household
- 🔵 Village core
- – – – – Field boundaries
- ▤ Field strips worked by household in area nearest village core

Time map showing daily paths of a hypothetical landed-peasant household during spring plowing season in Skåne, Norway, during the 18th century.

Referenced in: Pred, Allan 1985. "The Social Becomes the Spatial, the Spatial Becomes the Social: Enclosures, Social Change and the Becoming of Places in the Swedish Province of Skåne," in *Social Relations and Spatial Structures* edited by Derek Gregory and John Urry, pp. 337-65. NY: Palgrave Macmillan.

POWER, SUBJECTIVITY, AND SPACE

Questions of power and subjectivity underlie the ways in which we understand space and place. Power, in the form of wealth and decision-making, shapes the way in which places are designed and built; through regulations and social conventions power dynamics allow or prevent access to space, and frame our experiences and activities. Thus individual experience and self-identification—what we refer to as subjectivity—is conditioned by social, political, and economic forces. Scholars are particularly interested in how these intertwined dynamics manifest themselves in the built environment and through spatial interactions and relations. In this section, key writers explore how power operates in and through particular places, bodies, and conditions. By looking at different situations and forms of power in action, these readings present a complex portrayal of power, subjectivity, agency, and change.

Power is a multifaceted phenomenon that has the ability to control people, systems, resources, or ideas. It takes many forms and employs a variety of tactics, including soft, interpersonal tactics that rely on social pressure, and hard tactics that employ coercion and force. At times power is manifest, that is, public and observable, while in other situations it operates latently through *ideology*, or prevailing social beliefs and practices (Lukes 2005). It is possible to consider aspects of power at multiple scales from the macro-scale of government to the micro-scale of group or individual interaction. Antonio Gramsci (1971) articulates ways in which *hegemony*, the dominant ideology expressed through social consensus, is used to reinforce the goals of capitalism and the nation-state. Michel Foucault exposes the structures and dynamics of coercive power by tracing the history of institutional practices, monitoring mental illness (2006), sexuality (1978), and discipline (1975).

Subjectivity is a philosophical term that articulates the self in terms of the perceptions, feelings, and experiences from the point of view of an individual person. This concept is useful when attempting to answer this question in a variety of places and situations: "What is it like to be?" A related approach, *standpoint theory*, has also been applied by theorists to understand the experiences and challenges faced by minority and marginalized individuals (see Harding 1987). Standpoint theory, and the idea of subjectivity, recognize that experience is always situated in a social, cultural, and economic context. Individuals, directly and indirectly, are subjects of the conditions of their social milieu. In light of the interwoven and interpolated nature of power and subjectivity, the authors in this section ask: How does power operate in and through space and place?

In the excerpt from his book *Framing Places* (2008), architect **Kim Dovey** describes a variety of settings and ways in which power is manifest in the built environment. While Dovey emphasizes the symbolic and social aspects of power relations, these are underpinned by the power of financial capital. This selection looks at a traditional locus of power: the iconic city skyscraper, and the way tall, urban buildings embody power relations from the mark they make on the skyline to their intimidating lobbies. Dovey shows how owners and developers generate a display of power through the design and marketing of these buildings. He also suggests that the status of a building's inhabitants is represented through the organization of space, like corner offices. Thus, these spaces are used to establish and reinforce social distinction and class through spatial representations.

Geographer and anthropologist **Melissa Wright**'s ethnography delves into the dynamics of power and identity in a Mexican factory. Noting a series of gender assumptions and status distinctions, she looks closely at the interactions between the male management system and the female laborers. Within a clear hierarchy of power, Wright finds that the relations are far more complex than is articulated by management, as the male foremen struggle to exert their power through the physical labor of the women systematically and haphazardly. In this milieu, the identity of the men and their opportunity to show their ability to the factory owners is directly tied to the work of the women. Wright argues that the bodies of the women become prosthetics to the male foremen, who are themselves incomplete. Through this process, women and their work are made invisible, while the men are able to exploit them to remain in power.

Another way that power operates to make people invisible is through the penal system. Research by geographer **Ruth Wilson Gilmore** into the prison population in California clarifies the relationship between power and subjectivity. Prisons adversely affect not only prisoners, but also the mothers of prisoners who persist in engaging the system of incarceration. Gilmore describes the story of Harry Daye who was given at 25-year life sentence after being arrested for shoplifting a package of razor blades from a drug store. His mother found the legal system markedly biased against racial minorities, including Blacks and Latinos. Gilmore argues that the laws' ability to "wobble" under judicial ruling, especially the "three strike rule" by which Daye was convicted, made unequal punishment possible and prevented mothers from fighting this discrimination on stable legal grounds. Bias, racism, and classism are perpetuated through the legal system, shaping the lives of thousands both within and beyond the physical walls of prisons.

Governmental policy also has the power to shape our lives in many ways, from legal rights to land use. Geographer **Allan Pred**'s historical research on village life in Sweden provides a glimpse of how state power influences the day-to-day existence of individual, local subjects through policy. He traces a series of enclosure regulations that eventually reconfigure the spatial and temporal routines of the villagers. Initially, life was clustered in the village with fields surrounding the town, but farmland was eventually broken into more distant tracts no longer accessible during the working day (see figure at the beginning of Section 4). Farmers were compelled to leave the village and settle on their land in order to work it productively. This fragmentation of the social life of the village empowered aristocratic landholders and created a pattern of disintegrated and isolated rural life.

The choices and opportunities of our everyday lives are also shaped by newer policies and technologies, many of which are invisible to us. Urban scholar **Stephen D.N. Graham** analyzes how behavior patterns are shaped through computer code intended to sort "good" consumers and citizens from those that are not compliant with hegemonic ideals. Everyday surveillance operations by corporations and governments record our choices and actions, which are then used to prepare computer algorithms which pre-empt future activity and perpetuate racism, classism, and other forms of inequality. His examples include preferential access in airports and highways, digital maps coded to previously recorded purchases or internet searches, and surveillance cameras programmed to track specific demographic profiles. What he calls *software-sorting* produces unexamined patterns that reproduce social life in a way that all but erases our individual subjectivity into statistical categories.

In addition to corporate and state policies, sociologist **Pierre Bourdieu** demonstrates how culture also has power to structure, condition, and perpetuate everyday subjectivity through what he terms the *habitus*. For Bourdieu, habitus reconciles the subjective experience of the individual with objective social conditions, which, he argues, occurs as the external structures are internalized and embodied to the point that they become pre-reflexive practices. Thus, habitus describes the everyday dispositions and mannerisms—walking, talking, dressing, eating—that reveal our social position. These embodied practices create *distinction*, which is a way power operates to categorize and control people. Bourdieu suggests that social position is an important part of power dynamics that dictates people's degree of freedom and choice.

Subjectivity and the ways in which power constrains and opens up experience enables recognition of the ways in which our lives are structured by forces outside our control. Patterns of racism, sexism, heteronormativity, agism, ableism, and classism have marginalized people and dictated opportunities and experiences. Colonialism and imperialism are processes through which dominant nations have controlled the lives of native populations throughout history. James C. Scott (1987) has examined how these forces have shaped the lives of people in Malaysia. Judith Butler (1993) and Eve Sedgwick (2008) have focused on subjectivity in terms of sex, gender, and the body. Thomas Markus (1993) is a leading scholar on how design and the built environment shapes and is conversely shaped by power relationships, while the theoretical and built work of architects Diller, Scofidio, and Renfro also examines these issues.

The twin issues of power and subjectivity, especially in the context of large-scale corporate, state, or cultural conditions, raise important questions of structure and agency. *Agency*, which we return to in other sections, indicates the capacity we have to make choices and act in the world. Theorists, including those discussed above, have disagreed about the degree to which we have agency in the face of power. Structures of power can preclude agency through many of the tactics highlighted in these selections.

SUGGESTIONS FOR FURTHER READING

Please see *peopleplacespace.org* for extended and additional lists of readings.

Butler, Judith. 1993. *Bodies That Matter: On the Discursive Limits of Sex*. New York: Routledge.

Cresswell, Timothy. 2006. *On the Move: Mobility in the Modern Western World*. New York: Routledge.

Dahl, Robert A. 2005. *Who Governs?: Democracy and Power in an American City, Second Edition*. New Haven, CT: Yale University Press.

Deutsche, Rosalyn. 2002. *Evictions: Art and Spatial Politics*. Cambridge, MA: MIT Press.

Diller, Elizabeth, and Ricardo Scofidio. 1996. *Flesh: Architectural Probes*. Princeton, NJ: Princeton Architectural Press.

Douglas, Mary. 1984. *Purity and Danger: An Analysis of the Concepts of Pollution and Taboo*. New York: Routledge.

Forty, Adrian. 1992. *Objects of Desire: Design and Society Since 1750*. New York: Thames & Hudson.

Foucault, Michel. 1995. "The Means of Correct Training." In *Discipline & Punish: The Birth of the Prison*. New York: Vintage.

Gaventa, John. 1982. *Power and Powerlessness: Quiescence & Rebellion in an Appalachian Valley*. Urbana: University of Illinois Press.

Giddens, Anthony. 1986. *The Constitutions of Society: Outline of the Theory of Structuration*. Berkeley: University of California Press.

Gramsci, Antonio. 1971. *Selections from the Prison Notebooks*, edited by Quintin Hoare and Geoffrey Nowell Smith. New York: International Publishers.

Harding, Sandra. 1987. "Introduction: Is There a Feminist Method?" In Sandra Harding (ed.), *Feminism and Methodology*, pp. 1–14. Bloomington: University of Indiana Press.

Hillier, Jean, and Emma Rooksby (eds). 2005. *Habitus: A Sense of Place*. London: Ashgate.

Jackson, Peter. 1993. *Constructions of Race, Place, and Nation*. Minneapolis: University Of Minnesota Press.

Lukes, Steven. 2005. *Power: A Radical View*. New York: Palgrave Macmillan.

Markus, Thomas A. 1993. *Buildings and Power: Freedom and Control in the Origin of Modern Building Types*. New York: Routledge.

Massey, Doreen B. 2005. *For Space*. Thousand Oaks, CA: Sage Publications.

Newman, Oscar. 1973. *Defensible Space; Crime Prevention Through Urban Design*. New York: Macmillan.

Pred, Allan. 1985. "The Social Becomes the Spatial, the Spatial Becomes the Social: Enclosures, Social Change and the Becoming of Places in the Swedish Province of Skåne." In Derek Gregory and John Urry (eds), *Social Relations and Spatial Structures*, pp. 337–365. New York: Palgrave Macmillan.

Puar, Jasbir. 2007. *Terrorist Assemblages: Homonationalism in Queer Times*. Durham, NC: Duke University Press Books.

Scott, James C. 1987. *Weapons of the Weak: Everyday Forms of Peasant Resistance*. New Haven, CT: Yale University Press.

Sedgwick, Eve Kosofsky. 2008. *Epistemology of the Closet: Updated with a New Preface*. Berkeley: University of California Press.

Sudjic, Deyan. 2006. *The Edifice Complex: How the Rich and Powerful—and Their Architects—Shape the World*. New York: Penguin Books.

Thompson, E.P. 1967. "Time, Work-Discipline, and Industrial Capitalism." *Past & Present* 38(1) (December 1): 56–97.

Zukin, Sharon. 1993. *Landscapes of Power: From Detroit to Disney World*. Berkeley: University of California Press.

18
Tall Storeys

(2008)

Kim Dovey

The corporate office tower dominates the skyline of nearly all major cities—a global building type for the command functions of increasingly global corporations. Expressing the Zeitgeist of the twentieth century, such buildings have long captured a certain element of the public imagination. Early skyscrapers, such as the Woolworth and Chrysler buildings in New York, were full of the romance of reaching for the sky. They were also urbane buildings which sat easily within the city and its vital street life, and not tall by today's standards. We no longer use the term 'skyscraper' so much—the romance of distance has faded. They are now the common buildings of corporate culture, a kind of corporate vernacular, and the allure has faded for a range of reasons.

Tall buildings are a response to market pressure for more rentable space on a given site area, yet there are physical limits to this increase in site efficiency. As a long thin building serviced entirely from one tip, the tower as a type also loses efficiency with height. The necessary service core expands exponentially in relation to the floor area since every additional floor requires an increment of service core to every floor beneath. Banks of elevators progressively consume the building volume until every new floor at the top consumes more service core than it adds in usable space. When this effect is coupled with parking requirements at the base, the tower reaches a point where the cost of increased height exceeds the gains in rental area.

Despite these functional inefficiencies, the corporate tower proliferates. It does so primarily because of its role in the symbolic discourse of corporate culture and it is this culture that I want to explore here. As the towers exceed the limits of functional efficiency, perhaps 10–20 storeys, their market becomes increasingly based in symbolic capital—the capital value attributable to a symbolic, aesthetic or mythological 'aura' (Bourdieu 1977). The building image takes on renewed economic importance as a primary generator of symbolic capital. As capital has become increasingly concerned with the production of signs and images rather than use value (Baudrillard 1981; Ewen 1988) so the tower grows taller based on this new political economy of the sign. To the extent that serviced floor space is a standardized product, symbolic capital and locational advantage (also largely symbolic) are what gives one office building a market advantage over another. In the boom of the late 1980s this quest for symbolic capital reached new heights, transforming our cities in a quest for domination, both symbolic and literal (Barna 1992). This process was multinational, based in a global economy, a new flexibility of capital investment, and a struggle between cities both for this investment and for position in the emerging hierarchy of world cities (King 1990).

My particular window into corporate culture is the advertising of corporate towers in Melbourne during the boom of 1989–91.[1] The advertising portrays an ideal rather than a reality; it distorts as it mythologizes. Distortions are also indications of the ideals and values that may be driving the image-making process. I shall not discuss the intentions of the architects, nor the experiences of the users. This is not because these intentions and experiences are less important, but in order to focus on the source of profit—the decision to lease. I shall also bypass the issue of the extent to which this is a local or global discourse, although clearly I have assumed some powerful global forces.

DISTINCTION

The successful corporate tower offers a distinctive image to which lessees are invited to link their corporate image. This quest is for an image of the building as figure against a background which may be achieved in a variety of ways. One of these is the distinction of the work of art, authentically created by the individual genius building site do not appear. The aesthetic 'aura' masks the facts of social, political and economic process as it constructs an authenticity linked to notions of genius and authority.

Distinction is also achieved through a quest for uniqueness of form whether viewed in the city skyline or in relation to neighbouring buildings. The ideal tower is a landmark in the literal sense of leaving a mark on the land. The buildings are variously described as: 'One of the most significant landmarks in this city' and a 'unique identity when viewed in the city skyline'.

The discourse of distinction is inseparable from that of power; it embodies metaphors of strength, stature and strategy. One building 'towers over the competition', while another is 'designed to dominate'. The tower as a building type is necessary to this symbolism. The terms 'stature', 'status', 'stability', 'establishment' and 'estate' all share the root sta (to stand). Lefebvre theorizes the monumental vertical built form as phallic: 'Metaphorically it symbolizes force, male fertility, masculine violence. ... Phallic erectility bestows a special status on the perpendicular' (Lefebvre 1991: 287).

This discourse reveals a corporate community wherein architectural image is of fundamental importance. Collectively these meanings lead to a city where every building wants to be different, to claim identity, authenticity and power.

PLACE

Location within the city also generates symbolic capital: places embody power.

In every country there is a street which is home to the most powerful and successful businesses. Wall Street in New York, Threadneedle Street in London. And Collins Street in Melbourne. ... That 300 metre corridor of power ... the address has a long history of power and success dating back to the 1890s.

Neighbours are important to the location. Maps proliferate in the brochures showing nearby corporate headquarters, hotels and centres of power. The ideal tower is in 'the very best of company', with spreads of photos showing fragments of the neighbourhood and its amenities. These include street life, restaurants, cafés, shops, historic streetscapes, luxury cars, elegant women and nightlife. The ideal office tower is conceived as in harmony with this context; it contributes to the urban character and preserves the qualities of the past.

PROMENADE

The first impression your clients, business associates and suppliers get of your company occurs when they enter the foyer of your building.

The symbolic importance of the foyer is evident in the ubiquity with which it is illustrated and described. In contrast to the static images of the exterior here the text adopts a narrative form describing the experience of entry:

through a high stone portico into a soaring atrium foyer rising three levels above the floor. In this spacious and airy environment, you'll glance up to dramatic structural ribbing defining the edge of the space.

The foyer is a major site for architectural innovation in spatial grandeur. The aim is quite literally to 'entrance' through impression management. Elsewhere we are offered 'the impression of a grand hall and the ultimate experience of space'.

The prevailing materials in the foyer are marble and smooth stone. As in Speer's Berlin it is the sheer scale and volume of space that constitutes the foyer's contribution to the discourse of power. The vertical dimension lends the building symbolic value as it lays claim to that awe-filled crick in the neck of the grand public and religious buildings of the past. 'One will be immediately uplifted by its size, yet welcomed by the warmth of its colours and textures. A true work of art.' The use of the qualifier 'yet' in this text reveals that the 'uplift' is not entirely commensurate with the 'welcome'. The foyer is both a welcome celebrated with art and architectural display and also a kind of intimidation. The lavish graphics share a shiny coldness and a severe order. There are echoes here of the marble halls and slippery surfaces of Versailles and Berlin. The foyers are populated by people in business dress, walking through or doing business. This is not a place to linger, nor for the casually dressed. The foyers are a showcase in techniques of place celebration, but it is 'place' reduced to image of both behaviour and architecture. In the foyer, the triumph of the surface reaches its peak as a spectacle of art, space and light, and the symbolic choreography of corporate discipline.

PROSPECT/REFUGE

The view available from the corporate tower is a primary selling point and the valued views are of two types. First are the long views of nature and landscape, the parks, gardens, lakes, river, bay, beaches and mountains. Second are the panoramic views of the city and its dominant institutions. The view, as advertised, is never onto a streetscape with people and city life. It is the city in the abstract, from above and at a distance—the surface, not the life. The almost inevitable view directly into nearby office buildings never intrudes on the advertising. The implication is that one is always looking out from the tallest building in the neighbourhood and never at other tall buildings. Thus there is a premium on edge positions with views that cannot be built out: 'the views you lease now will be there forever'. The demand for a long view means that the symbolic capital of a building is linked not only to its site but also to the tower as a building type with a service core surrounded by a rim of rentable space.

The meaning of the view has several components. One is simply aesthetic sustenance, linked to both pleasure and health. One city panorama is captioned 'Consider this as part of your corporate health plan'. The view is an important part of the behaviour setting for corporate decision-making; executives are often shown gazing out while talking or thinking. And the view is a status symbol that is believed to impress visitors, a component in the discourse of corporate negotiation: 'Impress people with your point of view'. To have a view is to be seen to have a vision, and the views are widely described as 'commanding'.

The view, however, is not for everyone. Some of the brochures offer indicative interior layouts and images which may be interpreted for the meanings and social hierarchies they indicate. There are four primary work settings which form these plans: the executive office, the reception area, the board room and the open planned work stations.

Analysis of the indicative plans show that 42 per cent of all work stations receive natural light and views. While there are more egalitarian exceptions, the ideal tower is organized in general terms with an executive (male) rim surrounding a core of production. In the case of many indicative layouts, the private offices and executive areas are shaded on the plan to make the office hierarchy apparent on the image. It must be added to this that the consumption of floor space (and therefore of view) per executive is often several times that of the production worker and that the latter will spend a greater proportion of the working day at the work station. If a view and natural light are healthy, then the male head of the corporate body appears to get a disproportionate benefit.

CREATIVE DESTRUCTION

To immerse oneself in this advertising is to become aware of a range of disturbing contradictions in the production of such a built environment. The ideal and the reality are logically and necessarily at odds with each other. Tall stories are woven around tall storeys. The first contradiction is that of 'dominant contextualism'. The ideal tower achieves symbolic capital through its distinctiveness as a landmark that dominates its surrounds. Yet it also gains symbolically from being seen as in harmony with this context. The references to context cannot proceed beyond rhetoric without massively distorted images. The quest for dominance leads to a fragmentation of the city because, as Clarke (1989: 56) argues, 'symbolic capital must distinguish itself. … It must define its edges to protect itself as a symbol and to protect itself as investment. ... As such it cannot be "infill" within the urban continuum'. The formal result of this contradiction is generally a podium on the street frontage with the tower set back behind. The symbolic spectacle of the foyer often claims the entire street frontage and the first few floors of the building—it separates the inhabitants from the street and inhibits any contribution to street life. At other times the podium becomes a thinly disguised parking garage. The rhetoric of contextualism is a cover for a radical separation between life within the building and the life of the street.

To sell the locational advantages, the advertising shows photographs of human scaled streetscapes, sunshine, trees, street life and traditional buildings. This is the character of the neighbourhood which lends the location symbolic capital. Yet this character will be eventually destroyed by the addition of tall buildings. City districts with an attractive urban character then attract their own destruction at the hands of the corporate tower, a process not dissimilar to what Jacobs (1965) long ago called the self-destruction of urban diversity. Each new tower in a given district contributes to the collective decline in symbolic meaning until such time as the character has been transformed, its symbolic capital consumed.

The quest for locational advantage and the 'powerful address' leads to a clustering of towers. However, as this clustering occurs, the dominant landmark status and the commanding views are lost in the cluster. The quest for dominance and view will lead to both an increase in height and dispersal. The capital value of the building is enhanced by the view, yet every new building blocks everyone else's view and lowers capital value. Corporate culture seeks to inhabit tall buildings in lower rise districts. The towers grow ever upwards and spread outwards. The quest for height, left unchecked, has no limit since every new tower devalues both the view and the dominance of adjacent towers and fuels the quest for both height and dispersal. Symbolic capital is not so much created as it is moved around from one temporary landmark to another.

The contradiction of 'dominant contextualism' is more than a gesture to the forces of urban conservation. It is linked to another contradictory image of 'dynamic stability'—the aggressive corporation with roots in the conservative past. The dynamic thrusting height of the tower juxtaposed on a solid conservative base is the source rather than the limit of its meaning. It is the perceived resolution of this contradiction in the signifier of 'stable dynamism' that maximizes symbolic capital (Harvey 1989: 288). A final contradiction is that of the 'timeless fashion'—the corporate tower is forever chasing an image of timelessness which is paradoxically subject to accelerating cycles of fashion. The appetite for distinction leads to increased turnover of imagery and renders buildings very quickly obsolete. Signifiers of timelessness go in and out of fashion.

I would expect an ongoing development of fluid and crystalline informational imagery which can capture the various mythologies of the natural, high-tech, sustainable and flexible. But corporate imagery will also remain based in older discourses of domination and timelessness. Thus what really persists are the dialectics of dynamism/stability—the timely coupled with the timeless.

So what kind of city are these forces of capital creating? First, I want to acknowledge again the positive side to the character of the high-rise city. This is well expressed by Laszlo Moholy-Nagy's description of New York in the 1930s:

> This is what made it so fantastic—these buildings, the skyscrapers of New York. Obelisks, menhirs, megaliths—every shape, historic and prehistoric. ... There was no detail. Night came and even the sharp edged contours melted. A million lights perforated the huge masses—switching, flickering— a light modulation dissolving the solid form ... I got drunk—from seeing.
> (Moholy-Nagy 1969: 141–143, quoted in Ewen 1988: 166)

This is the evanescent vision of the high-rise city, the play of light on surface with 'no detail'. We can recognize in it the vision of the city that is reproduced in the advertising, in the glossy images and the distant views. This is the place experience of image consumption and even of inebriation. It is a particularly exciting kind of urban place experience which is strongly linked to the experience of the sublime—the encounter with immensity. It is the urban equivalent of being overwhelmed with the immensity of nature and it is reminiscent of Benjamin's celebration of the emancipatory capacity of urban poetics. This intoxicating effect of the high-rise city is one kind of vital urban experience but it is not automatically produced by an unregulated market. The sublime experience of the high-rise city requires the clustering of towers; it is paradoxically created and accentuated by height limits which prevent dispersal.

There is yet a deeper paradox in that this most urban of buildings has not only spread across the suburbs, but also become a profoundly anti-urban building type. The contradictions embodied in the corporate tower can be seen as manifestations of 'creative destruction', the 'perpetual struggle in which capital builds a physical landscape appropriate to its own condition at a particular moment in time, only to have to destroy it ... at a subsequent point in time' (Harvey 1985: 25).

The anti-urban character of the larger towers is also linked to increased parking requirements. Large towers require huge sites where much of the street frontage is dominated by several storeys of parking garage with gaping holes for entry and exit. These back doors and blank walls are highly damaging to urban street life and attempts to ameliorate their effects are generally superficial. The life inside the building becomes severed from the city since there are no windows on the street and many occupants drive in and out without ever setting foot in public space. The paradox is that as we go higher, urban street life becomes less dense and less diverse. Mega-towers are not the next phase of a vital city; they are anti-urban monoliths which kill urban life.

The scale, the grand foyer and the plinth of parking garage have produced a fundamentally different building type from that which captured the imagination earlier in the twentieth century. While the form of such towers may still inspire admiration from a distance and the views may be spectacular from within, their proliferation has become a form of place destruction in which architects and planners are deeply implicated. The advertising discourse above reveals a predatory character—the market preys upon vital and attractive urban places and destroys their value. Corporate towers spread, weed-like, across the landscape. They are not natural,

necessary, or inevitable and they are not produced out of ignorance. Much of their prevalence can be attributed to the rational pursuit of symbolic capital. They are the popular buildings of a patriarchal and predatory corporate culture.

NOTE

1 The analysis involved a total sample of seventy-two brochures and advertisements marketing a total of twenty-three towers ranging from eight to fifty-six levels and from about 3,000 to 82,000 square metres of lettable space. Most were speculative developments with naming rights available. The forms of advertising ranged from a glossy hardback book to once-off newspaper advertisements.

REFERENCES

Barna, Joel. (1992) *The See-Through Years,* Houston, TX: Rice University Press.

Baudrillard, Jean. (1981) *For a Critique of the Political Economy of the Sign,* trans. C. Levin, St Louis, MO: Telos.

Bourdieu, Pierre. (1977) *Outline of a Theory of Practice,* Cambridge: Cambridge University Press.

Clarke, Paul. (1989) 'The Economic Currency of Architectural Aesthetics', in M. Diami and C. Ingraham (eds) *Restructuring Architectural Theory,* Evanston, IL: North-western University Press.

Ewen, Stuart. (1988) *All Consuming Images,* New York: Basic Books.

Harvey, David. (1985) *The Urbanization of Capital,* Baltimore, MD: Johns Hopkins University Press.

Harvey, David. (1989) *The Condition of Postmodernity,* Oxford: Blackwell.

Jacobs, Jane. (1965) *The Death and Life of Great American Cities,* Harmondsworth: Penguin.

King, Anthony D. (1990) *Global Cities,* London: Routledge.

Lefebvre, Henri. (1991) *The Production of Space,* trans. D.Nicholson-Smith, Oxford: Blackwell.

19
Desire and the Prosthetics of Supervision
A Case of Maquiladora Flexibility (2001)

Melissa W. Wright

The instructor told us to act as if we were approving of someone's work performance. "Don't use words," she reminded us, "this is to see if you know how to use your bodies. I want to see your body language." Most nodded their heads, lifted their eyebrows, and smiled. A few gestured quiet applause. One did a "thumbs-up." This was one of several exercises that the participants performed in a training session designed to teach *maquiladora* supervisors some contemporary techniques for monitoring work in a flexible firm.[1] In this class of thirty odd Mexican employees, all but one a man, we practiced communication skills that fostered team spirit without diminishing our social control over the labor process. "Good communication is more important than ever," she emphasized. "You don't have time to tell people how to do things over and over. You use body language. … They need to do things as if *your* ideas were already in their *heads*." In these classes, we were learning about the complex social body of supervision. It is a body formed through the relationship between the supervisor and the supervised, but it exceeds them both in conceptualization and function in the flexible factory of late capitalism. The social body of supervision comes to life around a prosthetic dynamic linking the supervised with the supervisor in a single, functional corporeality.

Critical for seeing the prosthetics of flexible supervision is an understanding of how the supervisor's and supervisee's roles have changed with the transition from Fordist to flexible production in the Mexican maquiladora industry. Workers in a flexible firm are supposed to embody the concept of flexibility. They are expected to self-supervise, learn different tasks, and diagnose problems as they occur. Unlike the fixed-purpose workers of Fordism, who perform a single task in the same way, time and again, the flexible worker is pliable and capable of adjusting to the needs of the system. And, likewise, the emphasis in supervision is now on training as opposed to monitoring.

In the maquilas, however, where flexible production has also taken root, complete flexibility has been largely evasive. Some mixture of Fordist supervision combined with flexible methods is common in a maquiladora industry where the still predominantly female labor force, which holds the vast majority of jobs in electronic assembly, is broadly considered to be not only "unskilled" but also "untrainable." Following this discourse of her untrainability, her supervisor cannot simply coach her. His job is to integrate an inflexibly, untrainable female operator into a flexible production system, which requires skilled work, and to do this he both coaches and monitors a worker who, it is said, is unlikely to retain any skilled training.

My concern here is specifically with how the Mexican male supervisor gains corporeal and social plenitude only by working with the Mexican woman within a framework that renders him incomplete without her. Together, he and she form the single corporeal entity of the supervisory, a subject that does not exist in the material world of bodies but which, nevertheless, operates within that world.

My argument is based on the ethnographic fieldwork I conducted in a maquiladora, which I shall refer to as "COSMO," over a several month period from 1993 to 1994 in Ciudad Juárez, a city located in northern Chihuahua, across the Mexico/United States border from El Paso, Texas. This facility is one of several COSMO factories in Ciudad Juárez. During that time I also attended six weeks of training courses offered to maquila supervisors. Additional material comes from interviews with managers and workers between 1996 and 1997, while I was teaching at a university in Ciudad Juárez.

In the COSMO case, I will demonstrate how the prosthetics of supervision raise a vexing paradox for the flexible male supervisors, who cannot simply state that they, as men, are more capable than women. Rather, it is only through the operators' demonstration of an ability to perform skilled tasks, which she cannot by nature author, do supervisors come to light as the authors of that skill. The women performing the work, even if their jobs require more skill than they once did, are not seen as the skill's point of origination. Therefore, in order to appear skilled in contrast to her skill-lessness, the flexible COSMO supervisor must subordinate himself to a prosthetically arranged body that renders him incomplete without the female components that animate his skilled knowledge. Rather than his extension, she represents the very body through which he materializes.

LIMITED FLEXIBILITY

On my first day at COSMO, the Human Resource Manager, Ed, announced, "We are very proud of this facility because we have shown that flexible production can be done in Mexico." However, as several managers were quick to point out, although COSMO had implemented a significant measure of flexibility, a certain factor limits its full application. As Ed said, "The girls here aren't flexible workers. That's a problem for us, but we have to work with it." The basis for this statement, as he explained it to me, lay in the inherent untrainability of the Mexican female worker, even as her work reveals skilled content. "The televisions coming off our line," Ruben, the Plant Manager, explained, "need more worker know-how than ever before." To understand the nature of COSMO flexibility, we must explore how a product requiring worker know-how emerges from the hands of female workers who are said to know precious little.

Between 1994 and 1997, about 70 percent of the COSMO labor force was female. Most of these women worked in the assembly of the chassis, which covered the first 75 positions on each of the production lines. Women held all of the 1,200 chassis assembly positions for the two shifts. "We put the girls here," Ruben explained, "because they have small hands and can work with the circuitry. The work they do hasn't changed so much, but it's the way we organize it. That's where you see the innovations." An example of an assembly job is described in the "ergonomic outline" for the following position. Position number 29 for one television model is laid out as a series of left and right hand motions calculated to insert seven parts within 22 seconds:

1. Transport time — 3.0 seconds
2. Right hand inserts part A — 1.8 seconds
3. Left hand inserts part B — 1.9 seconds
4. Right hand inserts part C — 1.8 seconds
5. Left hand inserts part D — 1.9 seconds
6. Right hand inserts part E — 1.8 seconds
7. Left hand inserts part F and check the polarity — 2.2 seconds
8. Right hand inserts part G — 0.9 seconds
9. Release the pedal (to move circuit board down the line) — 2.0 seconds

Note: Do not grab more than five components at the same time

Rest time: 4.0 seconds
Efficiency rate: 97 percent

The calculations behind these movements are based on measurements of the amount of time consumed in the movement of a hand at a particular angle and speed from a state of rest and then back to rest. The engineering of this job reveals the time and motion studies, in the fashion traced back to F.W. Taylor, which are based upon a human form that is built of a series of levers and gears. One hand grabs a part, inserts it, and then returns to rest. The other does the same. These motions are controlled for their consumption of time by someone who is watching these motions and not by the individual who is actually moving these body parts and returning them to rest.

COSMO managers described the women who occupied position 29, or one of the other 74 on the chassis assembly line, by references to their brainless bodies. Ed, the Human Resource Manager, put it this way: "The girls here are the same kind of worker that has always worked in the maquilas. They are good with their hands. They don't mind the tedious assembly work. But they aren't here doing brain-work."

"If the women aren't your trained workers," I asked Ernesto, the second shift Production Manager, "then how do you develop a multi-skilled labor force?" He answered, "We look for male workers who will want to learn new things. We need workers who are ambitious and want to improve themselves." About one-quarter of the men who entered the COSMO workforce as operators would eventually be promoted. Their typical promotional trajectory began with an assembly position, such as the fastening of the picture tube or television case to the chassis which is located on the line after the female-dominated circuitry area. From there, they would usually move into inspection or materials handling, both positions in line for a boost to technician. The technicians composed the principal pool that managers used for internally selecting a supervisor.

Ed said, "Most of our, O.K., almost all of our supervisors are men. That's the gender break down here. Women in assembly and men in supervision. It's how it is in Mexico." Miguel spelled out the masculinization of training this way, "We have two different kinds of workers here. The ones we can train and the ones we can't. The female workers are the ones we cannot train. So they do assembly. That's the women's work here because they are good with small work."

In COSMO, references to female workers as dexterous and attentive employees dovetail with discourses of their intrinsic inability to acquire skill. As Ed put it, "You can't teach these girls to be more ambitious. I have tried. But what can I do? Change the Mexican culture?" He continued, "We are flexible here, but I would not say that our female workers are flexible workers. You find that in our other workers," he later told me.

This branding of female and male workers as inflexible and flexible, respectively, occurs in the visual as well as in the aural field of explanation. Gendered smocks delineate sex difference and job position on the line such that the social context of limited flexibility is vibrantly displayed as an issue of gender throughout the workspace. Women on the line

wear different colored smocks depending upon their position. Yellow smocks indicate new operators, blue smocks indicate a line worker, red smocks signify quality control, and orange smocks mean "special operator." The color of the cloth broadcasts her position and where she should be sitting. Blue smocks work within the line. Red smocks sit in the inspection stations. Orange smocks move among positions in assembly, and yellow smocks should never be on the floor unaccompanied. However, men have the option of wearing a single blue lab coat (some wear a yellow smock at first). Men wearing this lab coat include men in assembly, men in quality control, men who are special operators, men who are supervisors, men who are assistant engineers, and men in materials handling. These positions are located throughout the floor and are situated at different positions within the social hierarchy. Unlike the women's uniforms that indicate where the worker belongs in both the social hierarchy and on the factory floor, the men's uniforms provide no such information. In accordance with the flexible philosophy of minimized hierarchies and team spirit, the anonymous lab coats display the potential mobility of the male workers. They also display their antithetical condition to the fixed-purpose woman, who wears her status and position on her sleeve.

Flexible production, however, does not emerge at COSMO simply through the training and marking of male employees. Flexibility must, in the end, be apparent in the process for creating televisions, and more than seventy percent of the workers who build COSMO television sets are women. COSMO flexibility does not emerge through the exclusion of women from the project but rather from their inclusion. And the supervisor receives training precisely for this purpose, but, unlike the Fordist supervisor who monitored the worker's movements as an external brain, the flexible supervisor is expected to transfer his own training into her body. Her motions are to proceed as if receiving signals directly from his head.

Supervisors have several tools, we learned in this class, for accomplishing this feat of inserting one's own knowledge into another person's mind. "Use the group concept. Have a team captain. Then the workers can talk, and you can hear what they think of their jobs. What they know. And you can talk with them," she advised. Other tactics included physically moving workers' bodies to perform the jobs as scripted in the ergonomic manuals. "Don't be afraid of physical contact. Be confident with your body." The Fordist supervisor who stood apart as the external brain is a figment of the past at COSMO. "Things have changed," Miguel told me. "Our supervisors don't give orders and then sit back. ... What they [supervisors] do is think. They do the thinking and the girls do the assembly." The "total people" of flexible COSMO—the hands and arms and legs with minds—are crafted from the joining of the women's hands with the men's heads in a prosthetic arrangement of supervision. They are not found in the individual bodies that enter and leave the workplace.

This social body of supervision represents a prosthetic dynamic since as it completes a whole subject—the total people of flexible production—it renders incomplete the individuals who provide its components. In its configuration, we find a strategy for continually refusing to recognize Mexican women as the authors of the skill their bodies demonstrate. The male supervisor provides proof of her limitations—her missing brain and untrained memory. Despite the fact that she completes many different tasks, including supervision and on-the-spot diagnosis, she is not the source of the knowledge necessary for these operations. She remains skill-less in a labor process requiring skill as her mind and memory are replaced by those of her supervisor. She, however, is not the only partial body that results from this corporeal logic of supervision. Her supervisor is also an incomplete being, a truncated figure whose own abilities work through this unskilled woman. The male supervisors become heads in need of a body because their own corporeal forms are not only useless to them but also dangerous to their social position in the firm. The last thing a COSMO supervisor wants is to be caught performing the assembly work on the line. "They [management] are always watching us," an afternoon supervisor, Ramon, said. "If they see us work on the line then they think, 'He is not a good supervisor, he can't train his workers.'" Ruben said, "Why would I allow my supervisors to do assembly work when I pay them many times more to do many other things? That doesn't make any sense. Their job is to train operators to do that work." Miguel said, "If you see a supervisor putting in the circuitry, that

means he isn't communicating with his workers."

Since his own body disappears under the prohibition against its use that is assumed in the prosthetic relationship he has with the operators, evidence of the supervisor's work emerges from the body who is allowed to interact with the material. The supervisor's skill materializes when the female operator performs her job. All eyes are on her and the product she puts together and, depending upon what is seen, the supervisor appears either to be competent or not. In other words, evaluations of a supervisor's job performance occur through an evaluation of the operator's actions. As Ed told me, "The only way we know if our supervisors are up to par is by looking at the workers. If their workers are messing up, then we know. But if they have workers who are doing a good job, then we know we have a good supervisor. It's as simple as that."

The supervisory assemblage of supervised and supervisor body parts reveals the partiality of all Mexican subjects in the COSMO production schema. Managerial discourses of "immature" and "undeveloped" Mexican personnel offer a glimpse into the national character of this prosthetic supervisory subject. For it's not only that Mexican women lack certain qualities for representing total people, the Mexican men are wanting as well.

Managerial renditions of the partially developed Mexican male further support the logic behind COSMO's brand of flexibility. The third body of supervision is necessary for forming complete subjects where only partial ones exist. Neither the Mexican female nor the Mexican male is up to the tasks of a new flexible firm. She is inflexible and untrainable. He is immature and lacking in social development. The prosthetic supervisory overcomes their respective shortcomings. It brings the best of the Mexican female (her dexterity and patience) together with that of the Mexican man (his ambition and training) and forms the link between boss and laborer required of every capitalist workplace. A contradiction, however, lies deep in the heart of this prosthetically arranged figure. For although expected to function as a single corporeality, it is held together across the tensions of binary oppositions. And some of the men who find themselves dependent upon women for their own existence desire to be recognized as subjects in their own right.

VEXED DESIRE AND TURNOVER

Supervisors I interviewed expressed their frustration and resentment over their dependence upon the women, whom they saw as inferior to them. "If I were the plant manager," Ramon told me, "then I would help out the supervisors. We've got our hands tied down here. Everything that the girls do, even if we tell them not to do it, they [the managers] say it's our fault. There's a difference between us and the operators, but they don't always see it." "If I could change something here," Isaac said, "I would give the supervisors more power to run off the lazy workers. Now, we get blamed if we run off a worker who doesn't do anything all day." "If I tell my boss," Sergio explained, "that this operator won't do the job, he says I'm doing something wrong."

In these statements, I hear a vexation of desire among supervisors who want to be seen as the boss on their production lines but who also want to change the conditions under which they are allowed to exist at COSMO. They want an independence from the Mexican woman that would disentangle their job performances from hers. This, to use Butler's words, represents a "vexation of desire" (1997: 9) since the supervisor, who desires independence from the operator and, correspondingly, his own totality as a subject, logically desires the dissolution of the supervisory prosthetic that renders him incomplete. This desire is therefore dangerous to the supervisory position as it challenges its arrangement within the COSMO organizational strategy. On the other hand, when the supervisor performs his job well—or, put another way, when the supervised workers do a good job— and receives laudatory evaluations from his managers, he reinforces his own incompleteness. His choice is to perform his job and accept his dependence on female operators in order to do so, or to assert his independence of this inferior female and, thereby, risk his job.

The COSMO supervisor sees himself caught in a paradox. While he feels that he is superior to the female operator in every respect, a feeling reinforced throughout his working day, he runs into the fact that she is not so worthless that her labor is unnecessary. That turnover represents a problem in COSMO, as in other maquilas, reveals the contradiction that, as Marx (1990) indicated in a different context, wage laborers embody a great deal of value precisely because they are said to embody so little. The value of the undereducated, unskilled, and inflexible female Mexican operators lies in their representation as beings of such little value that, despite years of solid production experience as a group and the technological advances that their labor has supported, their real wages have continually declined over the last decade. Moreover, these women are broadly viewed by the maquiladora elite and the Mexican state that supports the industry as not deserving any higher pay. The less value these women are seen to merit, the more value they represent for capital.

The male supervisor's very constitution as a subject is inextricable from the contrary value of the invaluably cheap Mexican woman. When he comes to life as the COSMO supervisor—a partial figure bound in a dependent relationship with his antipathetic, female other—he contributes to the recreation of the contradiction that he also temporarily resolves. For in participating in COSMO skilling programs, which exclude Mexican women, he demonstrates a potential for acquiring the skill that she lacks. His presence on the shopfloor reveals that he is the mental force behind her actions. The value of the skilled labor emanating from her hands and eyes resides in him. He is, therefore, living proof of her steadfast and unskilled nature. Yet, the value of her labor, paradoxically, lies in the power of the discourse of her valuelessness. And the supervisor must never forget this paradox. If he treats the Mexican female as if she were really not worth keeping around, he makes a terrible error. He must nurture the value of her lack of value. As Marx demonstrated, it is one thing to insist on the cheapness of human laborers, but it is another not to recognize the value of their labor. Consequently, a supervisor who declares his own worth in contrast to that of a laborer has to mind the regulations for ensuring that his desired superiority does not materialize at the expense of the invaluably cheap laborer. And in COSMO his superiority can be seen only when the Mexican woman goes to work in a system where he can never be complete without her.

NOTE

1   *Maquiladora* refers to the export-processing facilities located in Mexico.

REFERENCES

Butler, Judith (1997) *The Psychic Life of Power: Theories of Subjection*. Stanford, CA: Stanford University Press.

Marx, Karl (1990 [1867]) *Capital, Volume I*. London: Penguin Books.

20
Mothers Reclaiming Our Children

(2007)

Ruth Wilson Gilmore

Now that you have touched the women, you have struck a rock, you have dislodged a boulder, and you will be crushed.

> Women's political chant, Anti-Pass
> Law Movement, South Africa, 1956,
> quoted in Angela Y. Davis,
> *Women, Culture & Politics* (1989)

Mothers Reclaiming Our Children (Mothers ROC) began to organize in November 1992 in response to a growing crisis: the intensity with which the state was locking their children, of all ages, into the criminal justice system. At the outset, the ROC consisted of only a few mothers and others, women and men, led by its founder and president, Barbara Meredith, and the life-long activist Francie Árbol. The initial project was to mobilize in defense of Meredith's son, an ex-gangster, who had been instrumental in the historic 1992 Los Angeles gang truce. The ROC lost his case but gained the makings of a movement. By the spring of 1993, when the LA Four went to trial, Mothers ROC had developed a network throughout greater Los Angeles and achieved recognition as an organization devoted to action rather than to commentary.

Mothers ROC's mission was "to be seen, heard, and felt in the interest of justice." To achieve this goal, Mothers ROC convened its activism on the dispersed stages of the criminal justice system. The group extended an unconditional invitation to all mothers and others struggling on behalf of their children, and it reached its audience in various ways. The primary method was leafleting public spaces around jails, prisons, police stations, and courthouses to announce the group's existence and purpose. When distributing flyers and business cards, members engaged people in conversation to explain the purpose of Mothers ROC (whose members are known as ROCers). ROCers gave talks and workshops at elementary and secondary schools, colleges and universities, churches, clubs, and (at the outset, but with decreasing frequency) prisons and jails. They also appeared on regional and local radio and television programs. Using these means, Mothers ROC established a presence at many locations throughout the political geography of the penal system.

ROCers attracted hundreds of mothers to fight on behalf of their own children in the system. Many were already solitarily performing the arduous labor of being on the outside for someone—trying adequately to switch among the many and sometimes conflicting roles required of caregivers, wageworkers, and justice advocates. Some would attend one meeting and never return; others have persisted, whether their loved one's case lost or won. Often newcomers brought someone to the meeting for moral support—a marriage or other partner, relative, child, or friend from church or neighborhood, and that person also became active. Each weekly gathering averaged twenty-five women and men. Most of them learned about the ROC from one of the outreach practices noted above, or from an acquaintance who had direct contact with a member. The rest, however, were guided to the organization by their loved ones in custody. Among the tens of thousands awaiting trial or doing time in the juvenile detention camps and centers, and in the county adult jails throughout the Southland, knowledge of Mothers ROC circulated by word of mouth, and a standard part of the message was that the women were willing to help with even apparently hopeless cases.

Every flyer proclaimed the ROC's principle: "We say there's no justice. What are we going to do about it? ... EDUCATE, ORGANIZE, EMPOWER." Mothers ROC made no judgment about the innocence of those whose families turned to the group for help. Not a service organization, the group helped mothers learn how each part of the system works, and, as we shall see, to grasp the ways in which crisis can be viewed as an opportunity rather than a constraint. In the process of cooperative self-help, the mothers transformed their caregiving or reproductive labor into activism, which then expanded into the greater project to reclaim all children, regardless of race, age, residence, or alleged crime. Experienced ROCers teamed up with newcomers to call on investigators and attorneys. They researched similar cases, and became familiar with the policies and personalities of prosecutors and judges. In addition, ROCers attended one another's hearings or trials. They also observed courtroom practices in general, monitoring individual officers of the court or state's witnesses believed to be promoting injustice. The group's periodic demonstrations outside courthouses and police stations brought public attention to unfair practices. Finally, ROCers sponsored monthly legal workshops with attorneys and requested research reports from scholar-activist members to help mothers become familiar with the bewildering details of the system in action.

Although never an exclusively Black organization, Mothers ROC presumed at first that it would appeal most strongly to African American women, because the state seemed to focus on taking their children. However, the sweeping character of the state's new laws, coupled with the organization's spatially extensive informational campaigns, brought Chicanas, other Latinas, and white women to Mothers ROC for help. A few years into its existence, the group had Black, Brown, Asian American, and white women, and some men. Most participants had loved ones in custody. People came to meetings from all over Los Angeles County, western San Bernardino and Riverside Counties, and northern Orange County, while their loved ones were locked up throughout California.

Mothers ROC consciously identified with Third World activist mothers, the name deliberately invoking South African, Palestinian, and Central and South American women's struggles. As we shall see, the organization was neither spontaneous and naive nor vanguard and dogmatic, but rather, mixing methods and concepts, it exemplified the type of grassroots organization that "renovates and makes critical already-existing activities" of both action and analysis to build a movement (Gramsci 1971: 330–331).

ONE STATE + TWO LAWS = THREE STRIKES

When Pearl Daye's thirty-one-year-old son called from the police station to say he had been arrested for allegedly shoplifting a package of razor blades from a discount drugstore, she was confused—he had a steady job—and distressed—he had not been in any kind of trouble for more than eight years. Going to the station to post bail, Pearl found it set at an absolutely unattainable $650,000, because the Los Angeles County District Attorney's office had charged Harry Daye with a third-strike felony rather than a petty theft misdemeanor. Suddenly, the African American man faced a mandatory minimum sentence of twenty-five years to life without possibility of parole.

As Pearl related the compounding events of Harry's arrest and accusation at her first Mothers ROC meeting, she often had to pause because of the breathtaking anxiety of revealing seemingly unbelievable adverse family circumstances to strangers. However, the roomful of women recognized the Dayes' drama as neither bureaucratic error nor bad dream, but rather as an increasingly ordinary conflict between families like theirs and the law. The plot had already become so familiar, one year into implementation of California's three strikes act, that at certain moments, a number of women, as though they were a chorus, recited with Pearl what the public defender and others had told her—especially the guaranteed sentence of twenty-five years to life without the possibility of parole, known on the street more briefly as "twenty-five to ... without."

Harry Daye faced the death of freedom because at that time the Los Angeles County district attorney's written policy was to enforce the three strikes law vigorously. Such vigor included charging defendants to ensure the longest possible prison sentences, regardless of the current character of the defendant's life. Harry's alleged petty theft constituted what California law designates a "wobbler"—a charge that can be treated as either a misdemeanor or a felony. Three strikes and other minimum-mandatory-sentence laws, conventionally portrayed to work with a machinelike disregard for individual circumstance, actually explicitly allow prosecutors and judges to use discretion "in the furtherance of justice." However, throughout California—especially in the southern counties that produce most prisoners—the practice of prosecutorial or judicial discretion in favor of second or third strike defendants was throughout the 1990s so rare as to be newsworthy.

Pearl ended her introductory testimony to Mothers ROC with an observation about the entire system: "The way I see it there are two laws, one for the Black, and one for the white." Leticia Gonzales, a Chicana whose husband had started a "twenty-five to … without" sentence some months earlier, disagreed. "No. I think there is one law for the people of color, and another law for the white." By this time, everyone was talking. Francie Árbol proposed another structure: "Poor people and rich people." But poor versus rich failed to explain the state versus O.J. Simpson. Why was the Los Angeles County District Attorney's Office spending so much time and money to convict one Black defendant? Therefore, the distinction could not be rich versus poor. At the same time, because virtually all the prisoners anyone in the room knew or could imagine were people of modest means from working-class families, the money question could not simply be dropped. Anti-Black racism seemed to explain a great deal, but could not account for all poverty, powerlessness, and vulnerability before the law.

In the year or so before Pearl Daye brought her case to ROC, Latino (mostly Chicano and Mexicano) prisoners surpassed African Americans as the largest group in absolute numbers in CDC custody. The unevenness in outcome for people of color lies in both patterns of policing and the offense with which defendants are charged. For example, in Los Angeles County, white defendants would be far more likely to have charges reduced from felonies to misdemeanors or dropped completely,

while people of color are more likely to have the harshest possible charge leveled against them. Both federal and California laws allow radically different treatment of people who have done essentially the same thing. Such police, prosecutorial, and judicial capacity—which, since its introduction in the early 1980s, has remained fundamentally impervious to challenges based on "equal protection" and other constitutional principles—provides both the means and the encouragement for application of substantively different rules and punishments to various kinds of defendants.

It is not surprising, then, that the ROCers had a hard time developing a summary of how the law discriminates against and among those who are most vulnerable to the system. The law's ability to wobble made routinely unequal punishments possible. At the same time, the wobble made developing a commonsense definition of how such inequality is achieved and reproduced on a case-by-case basis very difficult indeed. Everyone who spoke—nearly everyone in the room—had no doubt that the system operated on a dual track. But how is each defendant routed?

Finally, one of the women proposed a solution. There are, as Pearl had said, two laws—one for Black people and one for white people. Given how the prosecutors had started charging more and more Brown and other poor defendants under the new laws, especially the three strikes act, then perhaps the explanation could be put this way: You have to be white to be prosecuted under white law, but you do not have to be Black to be prosecuted under Black law. The resolution satisfied that evening's debaters, because it provided a way for the women to recognize one another through the extension of prosecutorial practices without ignoring African Americans' indisputable experience of the new laws' most intensive application.

Not long after discovery of the Black/White law solution, a local power broker came calling on the ROC. The African American man, who had made a small fortune running secured (locked-down) drug rehabilitation units for the state, wanted the ROC's blessing to build a private prison (owned by him) in the neighborhood where the CDC would send selected prisoners to serve the final year of their sentences. He assured the women that the prison would be run in accordance with community wishes, since the city would not grant a conditional use permit for the location without community approval. For many ROCers, this visit crystallized the dynamic contradiction in the system they had taken on. If the ROC was right, then the prison was unnecessary. If the prison came in, accompanied by "jobs," then part of the ROC's critique—poverty—would seem to have been addressed by expanding the specific object of the ROC's opposition—cages.

As the carceral entrepreneur—himself an ex-prisoner—explained how much good the prison would bring to South Central, the ROCers listened closely. Then, in an orderly show of political passion, each one told him why, from her perspective, the ROC would never endorse the facility. His claim that somehow the community could control the inner workings of a prison because of its location struck them as ludicrous; they had learned that distance is not simply measured in miles, and that the prison would not be a neighborhood or community facility, but rather a state incapacitation facility run according to state rules. His promise that perhaps their own children might be in the prison elicited, at first, an emotional moment of hope on the part of some women, who drove fifteen-year-old cars four hundred miles round-trip on Saturdays to see their sons. But the record of failures in many of the campaigns to have children moved closer to their families indicated that the people in the proposed South Central prison would not likely come from the area. The ROC told the entrepreneur, over and over, that they would not remedy the disappearance of jobs at GM, Firestone, and Kaiser by putting half the population into prisons so the other half could make money watching them. They sent him on his way, somewhat bruised by their blunt words.

The visit provoked the members to ask themselves what else they should be doing to stop the prison from going up in South Central. They knew that the prison would go up somewhere—the power broker had assured them of that—and so protesting at the local level would not solve the problem. Clearly, the ROC had to expand its activities to an adequate scale. At the next meeting, they decided to take on the brutal three strikes law in order to build a statewide coalition of people who would be likely to help fight the expansion of prisons as California's all-purpose solution to social

problems involving the poor. That project, inaugurated in January 1996, built slowly over a year, eventually culminating in a "Three Strikes Awareness Month" during which teach-ins, radio and television appearances, and leafleting outside courthouses raised consciousness of the legislation's effect.

FROM THE CRISIS OF PLACE TO THE POLITICS OF SPACE

For millions of people in the United States each year, the individual nature of arrest produces fragmentation rather than connection, because each person and household, dealing with each arrest, must figure out how to undo the detention—which appears to be nothing more than a highly specific confrontation between the individual and law enforcement. The larger disorder is then distorted to reflect only a portion of social fragilities, and measured, like unemployment, as though its changing rate in a society were a force of nature. ROCers gradually but decisively refused to be isolated and began to develop oppositional political arts centered on creating an order different from the one built by the state out of more and bigger prisons. They arrived at their art through critical action. Action, crucially, includes the difficult work of identification—which entails production, not discovery, of a "suture or positioning" (Hall 1990).

By enlivening African American practices of social mothering, the ROCers engaged a broadening community in their concern for the circumstances and fate of prisoners. That social opening provided avenues for all kinds of mothers (and others) to join in the work, because the enormous labor confronting each mother tended to encourage all of them both to accept and extend help. I make no claim for "social mothering" as an exclusively or universally African American cultural practice; it is neither. However, Barbara Meredith's commonsense invocation of mothering as collective action made possible the group's integration of mothers with similar or quite different maternalist assumptions. In other words, techniques developed over generation on behalf of Black children and families within terror-demarcated, racially defined enclaves provided contemporary means to choreograph interracial political solidarity among all kinds of caregivers losing their loved ones into the prison system. These mothers and others identified one another in the tight public spaces between their socially segregated residential living places and the unitized carceral quarters in which their loved ones are caged. Some were shy about jumping into the process, while others came to the ROC for help on their individual cases only; but all who persisted practiced the "each one teach one" approach.

The process of integrating different kinds of mothers and others into the ROC involved extensive outreach designed to permeate the social organization of space. These projects also caught people in the "betweens" of segregated lives: at work, for example, or on the bus. Like the Justice for Janitors Los Angeles crusade, however, this approach raised a more general problem of identification. The ROCers easily recognized one another in the spaces of the criminal justice system. Outside those areas, how do people resemble each other? If we are not all Black, and if all activists are not mothers, and if all prisoners are not (minor) children, then who are we? Poor people who work. As a community of purpose, Mothers ROC acted on the basis of a simple inversion: we are not poor because our loved ones are in prison; rather, our loved ones are in prison because we are poor. It followed that outreach should target working poor people and their youth. Class, then, while the context for this analysis and action, cannot displace or subsume the changing role and definitions of race: poor people of color have the most loved ones in prison.

As a matter of fact, the primacy of class is thoroughly gendered: women who work to support their families and to free their loved ones encounter one another as laborers with similar triple workdays—job, home, justice. Moreover, mothers who reject the disposal of their children and ask why they themselves should not be compensated for struggling against the state raise a challenge to both their children's and their own devaluations from the vantage of the declining welfare state and the perils of labor. The communist organizational and analytical influences in the ROC kept these complicated interrelated issues in the foreground of activism. In the context of shared opposition, the activists "discovered"—which is to say, created—shared values; in turn, that collective work produced community solidarity, or

political integration, enabling further action. Solidarity increased with increased knowledge about the complexity of how power blocs have built the new state by building prisons. Thus an individual police precinct house no longer loomed as the total presence of the state, shrinking back toward its real position—the neighborhood outpost of what both the ROCers and FACTS characterized as a military occupation. If it takes a village to raise a child, it certainly takes a movement to undo an occupation. As Mothers ROC went deep and FACTS went broad, both sought to immerse themselves in other communities of activism, reaching out nationally and internationally to similar organizations. Such motion then and now heightens the potential for connections between women struggling against prison expansion and women throughout the global workforce who struggle daily against the actual processes and effects of worldwide structural adjustments.

Mothers ROC critically used the ideological power of motherhood to challenge the legitimacy of the changing state. All prisoners are somebody's children, and children are not alienable. The racial and gendered social division of labor required mothers of prisoners to live lives of high visibility; ROCers turned that visibility to a politically charged presence, voice, and movement against injustice, such that their activism became the centerpiece of their reproductive—and socially productive—labor. As with mothers' movements in Latin America, South Africa, and Palestine, Mothers ROC's frontline relation to the state was not as a petitioner for a share in the social wage but rather as an opponent of the state's changing form and purpose with respect to the life chances of their family members and those like them. The insistence on the rights of mothers to children and children to mothers was not a defense of traditional domesticity as a separate sphere; rather, it represented political activation around rising awareness of the specific ways that the contemporary working-class household is a site saturated by the neoliberal racial state.

Mothers Reclaiming Our Children evolved from a self-help group that formed in response to a crisis of place—a police murder in South Central Los Angeles—into a pair of political organizations trying to build a powerful movement across the spaces of domestic militarism.

A small, poor, multiracial group of working-class people, mostly prisoners' mothers, mobilized in the interstices of the officially abandoned, heavily policed, declining welfare state. They came forward in the first instance because they could not let their children go. They remained at the fore, in the spaces created by intensified imprisonment of their loved ones, because they encountered many mothers and others in the same locations eager to join in the reclamation project. And they pushed further, because from those breaches they saw and tried to occupy positions from which collectively to challenge their political, economic, and cultural de-development brought about by the individualized involuntary migration of urban "surplus population," and the potential values that go with that population, into rural prisons. For the ROC and FACTS successfully to oppose the disposal of their loved ones, they organized to challenge the fullest possible reach of state (and civilian) powers arrayed against them. Working through cases, they built alliances of and as multiracial groups that create and sustain solid centers of activism throughout and across

the "nested scales" (Smith 1992) of the rising prison state. Thus both groups demonstrate the possibilities and the urgent difficulties of organizing across the many boundaries that rationalize and reinforce apartheid America. Indeed, their work might well exemplify what utopia is these days—social perfectibility recognizable in something as modest as people getting on a bus.

REFERENCES

Gramsci, Antonio. 1971. *Selections from the Prison Notebooks*. New York: International Publishers.

Hall, Stuart. 1990. "Cultural Studies and its Theoretical Legacies." In *Cultural Studies Now and in the Future*. Urbana-Champaign: University of Illinois Press.

Smith, Neil. 1992. "Contours of a Spatial Politics: Homeless Vehicles and the Production of Geographical Scale." *Social Text*, 33, pp. 54–81. Raleigh, NC: Duke University Press.

21
The Social Becomes the Spatial, the Spatial Becomes the Social

Enclosures, Social Change and the Becoming of Places in the Swedish Province of Skåne (1985)

Allan Pred

Place always represents a human product; it always involves an appropriation and transformation of space and nature that is inseparable from the reproduction and transformation of society in time and space. As such, place is characterised by the uninterrupted flux of human practice—and experience thereof—in time and space.

Since place is conceptualised partly in terms of the unbroken flow of what takes place locally, the proposed theory attempts to take into account both the material continuity of the people who participate in that process and the material continuity of any natural and social objects employed in time–space specific practices. Thus, the participating individuals, without whom there is no place as process, are not treated in the reified, fragmented, and atomised manner characteristic of conventional human geography and social science—regarded in one instance solely as producers, in another solely as residents, in another solely as consumers, and so on. Instead, process-participants are regarded as integrated human beings who are at once objects and subjects and whose thoughts, actions, experiences, and ascriptions of meaning are constantly *becoming*, through their involvement in the workings of society and its structural components as they express themselves in the becoming of places.

As a place becomes under any given set of historical circumstances, power relations are at the heart of its social structure. No matter how they are conceptualised, power relations are usually institutionally embedded and always involve one or more acting individuals, groups, or classes together with actually-performed or potentially-executable behaviours. Hence, at all levels, power relationships ultimately cannot be separated from the realm of action and everyday practices, from the direct or indirect control of who does what, when and where. Put otherwise, as a social relation power may be conceptualised not only as the capacity to define, require, permit, govern or somehow control the time–space specific *path* couplings of others for the purpose of bringing off some particular project, but also as the capacity to forbid, inhibit or restrict such path couplings.

Individual biography formation—including language acquisition, personality development, the evolution of a not-always articulated or self-understood ideology, and the development of consciousness—is one with the becoming of place. *Biographies are formed through the becoming of places, and places become through the formation of biographies.*

Any place or region expresses a process whereby the reproduction of social and cultural forms, the formation of biographies, and the transformation of nature and space ceaselessly become one another at the same time that power relations and time–space specific path-project intersections continuously become one another in ways that are not subject to universal laws, but vary with historical circumstances.

ENCLOSURES IN SKÅNE

While annotating his famed trip through Skåne in 1749, Linnaeus marvelled at the richness of the grain fields which extended as far as the eye could see around the villages situated on the plains of the south-western and south-eastern parts of the province. Except for Malmö, Ystad, Landskrona, a few other small ports and fishing communities, and the university town of Lund, the mid- and late eighteenth-century settlement pattern of this virtually treeless 'Land of Canaan' was characterised by a fairly dense pattern of nucleated vinagre. These villages, which numbered twenty or more per 100 square kilometres, commonly had several hundred residents.

As a group these villages had much in common in terms of the agricultural, household, religious and festive projects through which socialisation occurred and social relations between groups and the sexes were reproduced. However, each of the villages was a *distinctly becoming place* where the details of biography-formation and everyday life varied somewhat, and where macro-structural features made their inroads and were reacted upon in almost similar but unique ways.

During the turn of the eighteenth and nineteenth centuries the villages of Skåne's fertile plains underwent dramatic spatial and social changes, which were associated with three interrelated phenomena. First, there was an intensified commercialisation of village agricultural production. Marked by an increased involvement in national and international markets, this shift away from subsistence cultivation was paralleled by a general rise in domestic grain prices until 1812, a slowly mounting demand for grains in Göteborg, Stockholm and other Swedish cities, and a modest but significant growth in English demand for Swedish oats during the 1830s and 1840s. Second, there was unprecedented population growth which, in combination with traditional inheritance practices and the finiteness of local land resources, led to a rapid upsurge in the number of people belonging to the landless proletariat of each village. Third, there were the series of enclosures that thoroughly revamped the spatial structure of most villages and facilitated the production of an agricultural surplus big enough both to meet growing market demands and to feed locally burgeoning populations.

Legislated enclosures in Sweden took three different forms. The first of these was the so-called *storskifte* which was designed to overcome the obvious production inefficiencies which arose from each peasant household working many widely dispersed and quite narrow strips.

But the impact of *storskifte* enclosures upon the villages of Skåne's south-western plains was rather limited. Because every peasant was to have approximately the same quantity of land in each of the village's three fields—and because there were variations in soil quality, title rights and distance to the village centre—the surveyors responsible for reapportioning land seldom found solutions that left peasants with less than twelve to fifteen scattered strips.

It was the next round of enclosures, referred to as *enskifte*, that most radically transformed the spatial structure of almost all the villages under discussion. Although no *enskifte* regulations were formally enacted for Skåne until 1803, a single large landlord, Rutger Maclean, innovated this type of enclosure in 1783 when he began replanning the four villages which comprised his estate on the south-western plains. Maclean rearranged the holdings of individual peasants so that they no longer included from sixty to one hundred land parcels, but instead were confined to a single rectangular farm where fallowing was prohibited and a rotation of fodder roots, barley, and clover or vetches was mandatory. This replanning not only facilitated an increase in the number of peasant farmsteads, but it also required the construction of new buildings and roads *and was synonymous with the breaking-up of the settlement cluster at the core of village*.

The village core was quickly thinned out, for only a few peasant homes persisted; many landless inhabitants remained but others had their small houses torn down and were completely displaced; and the great majority of landed peasant households now conducted most of their activities in relative isolation from one another.

INFORMED QUESTIONS

What were some of the basic components of the daily paths followed by landed-peasant household members during the decades immediately preceding *enskifte* enclosures on the plains of Skåne? What, in other words, were some of the general characteristics of the path-project intersections that were part of biography formation and the village-level unfolding of the structuration process? What were the power relations underlying daily paths? What characteristics of practice-based consciousness predisposed some landed peasants to initiate enclosure proceedings? How were daily paths and power relations altered as a consequence of *enskifte* enclosures? Or, to combine all these questions: how did the social become the spatial and the spatial become the social in the becoming villages of Österlen and south-western Skåne?

DAILY PATHS AND AGRICULTURAL PROJECTS OF THE LANDED-PEASANT HOUSEHOLD PRIOR TO *ENSKIFTE* ENCLOSURES

In the mid- and late eighteenth century, the daily round of activities of peasant households was not normally confined to the landholder, his wife and any unmarried children who were not serving as hired help in another household. It typically also involved a teenage male farmhand, a somewhat older male farmhand and two young female servants. While the activities incorporated into the daily paths of household members varied seasonally, through-out most of the year work-projects were interrupted frequently for eating, drinking alcohol and resting. During spring, summer and autumn, when the household was in motion from 3 or 4 a.m. until about 9 p.m., the day usually began with a sandwich and a shot of aqua vitae before all the males and some of the females left the house. Subsequent snacks and meals, each accompanied by a swig or two, occurred at 6 a.m., 7.30 a.m., 10 a.m., 12 noon to 1 p.m. (followed by a rest), 3 p.m., 5 p.m. and sometime during early evening. When ploughing, sowing, harrowing, fertilising, harvesting or other field-centred dominant agricultural projects were undertaken, all but the last of these additional repasts were eaten at or near the work-site. Since most field-strips were highly elongated and at some distance from the homestead, it follows that a large amount of time was taken up by women and young boys bringing out food to the fields and, perhaps, by periodic down-field movement toward the village centre.

At one level, major agricultural projects required considerable daily path synchronisation and 'synchorisation' (or spatial co-ordination) among peasant household members as well as livestock and implements. Spring and autumn ploughing, for example, required the use of anything from three to seven pairs of horses and oxen, depending on soil characteristics and the crop to be planted. The large number of creatures needed to pull a plough in turn called for the presence of three or more adult males and any younger boys or girls in the household who might be available to help out or shout encouragement (see figure at beginning of Section 4). Harvesting projects represented the extreme case of daily path synchronisation and synchorisation, normally involving all a household's men and women (who were responsible for most of the raking, binding and stacking) as well as draught animals, wagons and various hand-held implements.

Seen in isolation, the household execution and co-ordination of ploughing, fertilising and harvesting projects, and attendant eating and drinking activities, was inseparable from the reproduction of certain household power relations. The male peasant more or less casually oversaw major agricultural projects, influencing the tempo and intensity of labour and the duration of rests and eating- or drinking-breaks.

From another perspective, the spinning-out of specific daily paths in connection with dominant agricultural projects was inextricably bound up with the reproduction of long-standing village-wide power relations. All landed peasants were automatically members of the village council and bound both to the decisions of that body and the traditional rules that it enforced. The spatial pattern of strip-holdings splintered in three fields necessitated co-operation so as to guarantee everyone access to his own parcels. Co-operation was also required to prevent damage to neighbouring holdings during ploughing and harvesting and in connection with livestock grazing. Thus, the timing and content of major agricultural projects carried out by landed peasant house-holds presupposed village council decisions on such matters as when ploughing, sowing and harvesting were to commence; the usage of common outfields; when and how many livestock could be put out to fallow-field pasture; and the date by which field-separating fences or walls were to be fully repaired in order to hinder livestock from wandering onto cultivated land.

DAILY PATHS AND AGRICULTURAL PROJECTS SUBSEQUENT TO *ENSKIFTE* ENCLOSURES

As the land redistribution and new house, fence, and road construction required by *enskifte* enclosures was completed in any village, the daily paths of landed peasant households and the population as a whole were quickly altered— now stamped by new and modified agricultural projects.

Many of the path changes were connected with the more intensive cultivation of land that became necessary and feasible with the implementation of *enskifte*. The moving and construction costs incurred as holdings were consolidated forced some landholders to sell off a portion of their new property units. In more exceptional instances new landed peasant households were also formed because family property could now be split between two or more brothers or sons, whereas the pre-existing narrow parcels did not lend themselves to further division. Those who were confronted with a smaller total area of land to work and who desired to live at least as well as previously had no choice but to cultivate more intensively. Those whose holdings had either not diminished, or had expanded slightly because of the allocation of limited common lands, found it feasible to cultivate more intensively and enhance their incomes through taking on more long- and short-term hands from among the burgeoning landless class, who were now without pasturing rights and often displaced. In addition, all landed peasants, regardless of the size of their holdings, could cultivate more intensively through the substitution of labour time for travel time and the more flexible co-ordination of individual paths which was now possible. After all, movement between widely separated parcels of land was no longer necessary and the average house-to-field distance was noticeably reduced.

Whether or not more hands were employed, the household's daily execution of agricultural projects required at least as much path co-ordination as ever. This was so because usage of the heavy wheel plough persisted as late as the 1850s, eating and drinking frequency was little changed, and livestock were now more commonly fed at home throughout the year, rather than being sent to the commons or fallow field with the village shepherd. Under these circumstances, and in the absence of any need for the village council either to determine land-uses and project starting-dates, or to implement its grazing and parcel-protection rules, the importance of individual decision-making and household-centred power relations was magnified.

The increased project-definition and role-assignment power of the landed peasant within the realm of agricultural activities was gradually translated into new household interaction patterns and further social differentiation. Over a period varying from years to decades, and especially where holdings were relatively large, daily path-segments in and about the home began to reflect a new or strengthened sense of social superiority on the part of the landed peasant and his wife. In many instances she began to relinquish heavier tasks out in the fields and to spend more time around the house. It became increasingly common for the peasant and his family to stop eating together with their hired help and to establish their own sleeping quarters. The 'all-purpose' room also began to function less frequently as a meeting-ground for the family and their employed hands. As a corollary, clearer distinctions were made between child and servant. In addition, landed peasants who had moved from the village core presumably found it especially easy to establish a social distance between themselves and those small-plot holders and landless people who were not associated with their households on a long- or short-term basis.

If post-*enskifte* agricultural projects were characterised by the exercise of individual discretion, initiative, and authority, they were also affected, at least indirectly, by the reproduction of another set of power-relations— those between urban grain and aqua vitae merchants and landed peasants who, in their concern for profits and reinvestment, were being transformed into professional farmers. Insofar as self-determined operations enabled landed peasants to be newly or further enveloped in market-oriented production, and insofar as developing needs for prestige and self-esteem led them to include coffee, fine biscuits, pocket-watches, and other non-essential consumption items among their urban purchases, their agricultural strategies were apt to become more influenced by the demands and conditions set by urban middlemen. In particular, since it was a common practice for grain wholesalers to extend credits and cash advances, the rural residents with whom they dealt were not likely either to neglect repayment schedules or completely ignore any inside market advice when choosing between the planting of rye, oats, and barley. To the extent that he was himself influenced by price fluctuations and market circumstances in setting credit and cash-advance terms, the urban merchant functioned as an intermediary through whom new customs policies and other macro-structural changes filtered down to the everyday practices and consciousness of the landed peasant.

The spatial rearrangement of village settlements in Österlen and south-western Skåne further affected path-project intersections and biography-formation by leading to the elimination or dislocation of certain agricultural and non-agricultural projects. With common lands no longer in existence, village women could no longer co-operatively deliver geese to that location in the spring and co-operatively retrieve them in the fall. (Nor could some of the village's older women use those geese-tending days as an occasion for ritually checking the breasts of unmarried girls for milk in order to discover forbidden pregnancies.) Without common meadows communal hay harvests also disappeared along with the traditional festivities that occurred immediately afterwards. Moreover, the spatial structure of the now dispersed village, coupled with the synchro-nisation and synchorisation demands of domi-

nant agricultural projects, made it impossible or extremely difficult for children to participate in games on the village 'street', women from different households to card wool or work flax together, or adults of both sexes to exchange advice and engage in unplanned social interaction with their neighbours.

The elimination or dislocation of these and other projects, together with the spatially transformed village scene, must have greatly influenced the sense of place, structure of feeling and other elements of consciousness held by residents by breaking down the grammar of taken-for-granted codes.

VARIATIONS IN THE BECOMING OF PLACE

Any place is an ongoing process whereby the reproduction of social and cultural forms, the formation of biographies, and the transformation of nature and space become one another at the same time that time–space specific path-project intersections and power relations continuously become one another in ways that are not subject to universal laws, but vary with historical circumstances.

The post-*enskifte* spatial configuration of villages in Österlen and south-western Skåne arose out of pre-*enskifte* practices and their underlying micro- and macro-level power relations. Spatial rearrangement—the replace-ment of scattered strips by consolidated holdings—led to new and modified daily paths and power relations.

22
Software-sorted Geographies
(2005)

Stephen D.N. Graham

INTRODUCTION: CODE AND THE REMEDIATION OF INEQUALITY

> The modern city exists as a haze of software instructions.
>
> (Amin and Thrift, 2002: 125)

> Values, opinions and rhetoric are frozen into code.
>
> (Bowker and Leigh-Star, 1999: 35)

Computer software mediates, saturates and sustains contemporary capitalist societies. Enrolled into complex technoscientific and machinic systems, stretched across time-space, a vast universe of code provides the hidden background to the functioning and ordering of such societies. The flows, mobilities and transactions; the folded geographies of inclusion and exclusion; the construction, consumption and experience of place; the very operation of distanciated webs of production, distribution and consumption, all, very literally, are now *performed*, at least in part, through the continuous agency of vast realms of computer software.

With computerized systems now actually becoming the 'ordinary' sociotechnical world in many contemporary societies, code orchestrates a widening array of public, private and public-private spheres and mobility, logistics and service systems and spaces. This new 'calculative background that is currently coming into existence', as Nigel Thrift describes it, is based on ubiquitous, pervasive and interlinked arrays of computerized spaces, systems and equipment which increasingly blend seamlessly into the wider urban environment, code-based technologized environments continuously and invisibly classify, standardize, and demarcate rights, privileges, inclusions, exclusions, and mobilities and normative social judgements across vast, distanciated domains.

Given all this, it is curious that remarkably little attention had been paid to 'the millions of lines of code that have come to run cities, as computing power has increased and as many former bodily practices have been written into code' (Amin and Thrift, 2002: 125). What Nigel Thrift and Shaun French (2002: 309) term the *automatic production of space*, through the simultaneous enaction of multiple, interacting worlds of computer software, remains largely ignored in human geography and social science more generally. Sunk in the taken for granted background of everyday life, these worlds of code exert their power over the geographies and lifeworlds of capitalism continuously and powerfully, but with scarcely any analytical or day-to-day scrutiny. Thus, it seems, 'code is in some sense invisible compared with its computer carapace' (Amin and Thrift, 2002: 125).

Encouragingly, a range of recent work has turned away from discussions suggesting that such technologies offer access to some 'virtual' domain which is somehow distinct and separable, in some binary way, from the 'real' spaces and places of cities and material urban life. Far from being separated domains, then, such perspectives underline that the coded worlds of the 'virtual' actually work to continually constitute, structure and facilitate the place-based practices of the material world.

The specific focus here is on the ways in which software code actively shapes and structures social and geographical inequalities within and between places in a wide variety of ways. In what follows, I review emerging research which addresses particularly important domains where social and economic inequalities within and between places are directly mediated, and shaped, by hidden worlds of code.

'ONE PERSON'S INFRASTRUCTURE IS ANOTHER'S DIFFICULTY': SOFTWARE-SORTING AND POLITICAL ECONOMIES OF 'UNBUNDLING'

To capture the ways in which software code mediates contemporary social worlds automatically (i.e., with little immediate human supervision), with very little delay (i.e., in real time) and continuously, I coin the term 'software-sorting' (Graham, 2004). Software-sorting is a critical landscape of power within what Jeremy Rifkin (2001) has termed the 'age of access'. Rifkin uses this term to describe the way in which individual and collective life chances are shaped increasingly by their treatment within computer-controlled, custom-ized, service domains. These, Rifkin argues, are increasingly orchestrated through technological networks which are structured to operate automatically using consumerist criteria. Such systems enrol selected, privileged users while precisely controlling access for those deemed unprofitable, risky or deviant.

Software-sorting is the means through which such selective access is organized. Such processes operate through a vast universe of 'obligatory passage points'. These are particular topological spaces within sociotechnical systems through which actors have to 'pass' in order that the system actually functions in the way that dominant actors desire. The obligatory passage points within software-sorting systems involve a burgeoning array of subscriptions, passwords, service entitlements, physical and virtual access control points, electronically surveilled passage points and transaction systems, automated, biometric judgements, and normative data-bases—all of which are continuously enacted and sustained through code and computerized systems based on machine-readable inputs.

The term software-sorting captures the crucial and often ignored role of code in directly, automatically and continuously allocating social or geographical access to all sorts of critical goods, services, life chances or mobility opportunities to certain social groups or geographical areas, often at the direct expense of others. It is crucial to stress, then, that the 'mobile publics' inhabiting the extending neoliberal geographies of flow and access are publics that are often prioritized, enacted and kept apart by hidden worlds of software-sorting.

Often intensely individualized and com-modified, the immense transactional flexibility and surveillance power of software-sorting means that the essential infrastructures, spaces and services of everyday can thus undergo a process of 'mass-customization' (Andrejevic, 2003) or widescale 'unbundling' (Graham and Marvin, 2001).

Very often, then, software-sorting techniques are being used to undermine some of the classic characteristics of urban public goods, allowing at least some of these limits to recommodification to be reconfigured or even swept away. Packaged, delivered through consumerist markets, sorted through the endless distinctions of geodemographic profiles, and linked closely to the surveillance of actual consumer behaviours, market potentials or desires, fully unbundled service and access packages thus become possible. Under pressure to maintain or increase profits, within the context of widespread privatization and liberalization, service packages geared towards more lucrative market niches can thus be customized and 'splintered' from the wider societal fabric through software-sorting techniques. At the same time, less lucrative users of streets, mobility systems, services, electronic communications grids, and places can be electronically (and/or physically) pushed away and marginalized, either absolutely or relatively, through software-sorting and machin-ations of code.

Such processes of unbundling can thus allow targeted users to enjoy enhanced mobility, reliability, service quality, quality of life, or (real or perceived) freedom from risk, crime, congestion, or contact with (sometimes demonized or humiliated) Others. Crucially, however, because most processes of software-sorting are actually invisible from the point of the users, these prioritizations are often not evident either to the favoured groups or places or to the marginalized ones.

CODE SPACE: SOFTWARE-SORTED MOBILITIES

It is clear that physical mobility systems increasingly utilize powerful software-sorting techniques to address imperatives of profit maximization, social control, or perceived risk minimization. Emerging research has successfully revealed the ways in which key physical mobility spaces such as airports can only sustain the astonishing transactional complexity now expected of them because they are saturated with, and, indeed, constituted through, complex sets of software-sorting and coding systems.

Taking airports as paradigmatic sites of ubiquitous tracking, it is now clear that 'the control of international mobilities that cross *through* airports and border zones are effectively managed, filtered and screened *within* these sites' (Aday, 2004: 1365, original emphasis). This work demonstrates that, traditionally, the use of machine-readable tags and tickets allowed all human, cargo, baggage and worker flows in and around airport spaces, and, indeed, airline systems, to be surveilled, tracked, and socially controlled with a high degree of precision.

Such systems are being augmented by software-sorting systems where the identifier of a person is actually biometric—that is, a supposedly unique signifier scanned directly from part of the human body (usually a finger, face or iris scan). Initially, biometrics have been used to allow 'premium', business travellers to bypass conventional border controls. Aday argues that through the practices and framings of biometric approaches to software-sorted mobilities a politics of differential speed is established.

Highway and urban transport systems are facing similar transformations; in some premium highways in California—for example, 1–15 highway in San Diego—software-sorting can actually display variable pricing in real time. This is based on algorithms which estimate exactly the level of price per journey that is likely to deter enough drivers to guarantee free-flowing traffic—no matter how bad the congestion is on the surrounding public highway system.

Here we confront software-sorting to guarantee speed, and time saving, to those able and willing to pay for technoscientific, urban bypass, using a 'premium' roadspace, on a per-journey basis. Such techniques herald new inter- and intra-urban geographies of differential mobility.

Remarkably similar techniques are also being mobilized, much more discreetly, to sort people's access to a whole suite of electronic mobility, communications, and service systems. The Internet, for example, was originally developed to accord all the 'packets' of information that flowed within it equal status. This was the so-called 'best effort' model of packet switching where equal efforts were made to allow all packets to flow to desired destinations at all times. Now, however, the Internet is being re-engineered into a corporately controlled system of systems dominated by a vast range of commercial services.

In the process, complex software-sorting techniques are now being enrolled, by the transnational media firms who run the Internet, to actually sift and prioritize each of the billions of data packets that flow over the net at any one time. While this will allow a guaranteed quality of service to 'premium' users and prioritized services, even at times of major Internet congestion, those packets deemed unprofitable will actually be deliberately 'dropped', leading to a dramatic deterioration in the electronic mobilities of marginalized users or non-prioritized services.

Such potent 'netscapes of power,' as Winseck (2003) terms them, are completely at odds with the widespread surviving perception that the Internet somehow intrinsically embodies deeply egalitarian exchange. Internet networks 'are technologies of discrimination that regulate information flows according to fine-grained criteria set by network owners. In essence gatekeeping functions have been hardwired into network architectures as part of the communication industries' strategies to cultivate and control markets.'

Moreover, as mobile phones emerge as peripatetic appliances mediating users' relationships with geographic and city spaces and services, so they, too, are opening up whole new realms of software-sorting (Andrejevic, 2003). Here, such techniques promise to customize 'mobile commerce' services to detailed records of an individual's own consumption and mobility habits, targeting advertising spam for goods and services that are geographically and geodemographically appropriate, as the user moves around the city. Individually tailored city maps will be directly customized to software records of users' consumption habits. Andrejevic points out that 'time-space paths will be used as a strategy for customization. Advertising and marketing appeals will be directed to consumers based on where they are in time and space.'

CODE PLACE: SOFTWARE-SORTED CITIES

A substantial body of research has revealed the importance of geographical information and geodemographic systems (GIS and GDIS) in shaping the production and consumption of contemporary urban spaces. With their tendency to exaggerate and reify homogeneously constructed 'ideal type' neighbourhood profiles, and so to ossify spatial and social classifications, such techniques have been widely shown to underpin redlining and socially regressive location decision-making and service planning.

GIS and GDIS do indeed provide powerful urban software-sorting devices. Here code is used both to surveil the social geographies of cities and provide the means to construct powerful, and often highly biased, simulations and visualizations of those geographies. Linked to locational referencing, postcode databases, mobile and electronic commerce systems, and geopositioning networks, this palimpsest of code is increasingly determinate in support of self-reinforcing spatial categorizations. In the process, 'databases become increasingly determinate: you become where you live' (Amin and Thrift, 2002: 45).

Thus the city itself becomes a software-based simulation, a fine-grained dynamic map of consumption and spending potential, as the large geodemographic bureaux now attempt to capture more and more direct consumption information into GIS-based 'data warehouses' from store credit cards, credit bureaux, direct marketing campaigns, Internet responses and the like. The reach and power of GDIS is now extending to directly shape the consumption of neighbourhoods, the processes of individual and collective identity formation, and the dynamics of housing markets and educational systems.

Burrows and Ellison (2004) argue that 'the informatization of neighbourhood consumption that online GIS websites of various sorts make available provides the informational resources by which strategically inclined social groups are able to find "their" place within complex and dynamic urban spaces'.

Thus, as online GIS support a consumerization of the consumption and production of urban social geographies, the real concern is that such processes will further support an unbundling of notions of universal urban citizenship that elsewhere, in my book with Simon Marvin, I have termed a process of 'splintering' urbanism (Graham and Marvin, 2001). Individualized, online-GIS-based decisions and behaviour, based on self-identities and reflective, lifestyle choices, are likely to allow socially powerful groups to further their secession from the wider space-times of the city, as they seek to locate in, and consume, the privileged, best serviced and highest amenity neighbourhoods. The algorithms that support such choices, simulations, orderings, and classifications—the very guts of online GIS systems—meanwhile remain completely opaque and utterly unscrutinized.

CODE FACE: SOFTWARE-SORTED STREETS

Our final exploration of the extension of software-sorting techniques addresses the proliferation of 'algorithmic' closed circuit television systems, covering city streets and public places, which attempt to automatically recognize people's faces using inputted image databases.

In digital, facial recognition CCTV, the software-sorting process involves the inputting of the facial, biometric imagery of a 'target' population which computer algorithms then actively seek out. Crucially, this inputting tends to go on without the subject's consent. The code within the facial recognition system becomes a key political site because its operation automatically stipulates the subjects, locations or behaviours that are deemed by the operators to be 'abnormal', 'threatening' and worthy of further scrutiny or tracking.

As well as stipulating the digitized signatures of 'target' faces, software-based CCTV can also be programmed to search for the signature walking styles that are deemed to be most often used by those committing criminal acts, for the number plates of suspect cars, even—when linked with microphones or smelling sensors—for stipulated, suspect, sounds or smells. One report on the growth of such automated, 'intelligent', detection systems, from a leading CCTV industry representative, bluntly explains the process through which software is designed to 'target' apparently 'abnormal' behaviours, presences, and people. 'Recognizing aberrant behaviour', it writes, 'is for a scientist a matter of grouping expected behaviour and writing an algorithm that recognizes any deviation from the "normal".'

Importantly, the potential for effective recognition also varies heavily between different social or ethnic groups. An analysis by Lucas Introna of various trials of facial recognition CCTV systems concludes, for example, that 'for the top systems … identification rates for males were 6% to 9% points higher than for females. … Recognition rates for older people were higher than for younger people.' Moreover, Introna quotes the official report evaluating the trial which confirms that 'Asians are easier [to recognize] than whites, African-Americans are easier than whites, [and] other race members are easier than whites'. Incorporated into complex, ongoing software-sorting CCTV systems, the potential for such discrepancies to be translated into major geographical and social inequalities is clearly immense.

Finally, there are grave dangers that algorithmically controlled CCTV systems might work to deepen already established ecologies of normalization, and demonization, within neoliberal urban landscapes of power. Exaggerating logics of exclusion against 'failed consumers', the young, refugees/asylum seekers, or other demonized minorities, within the increasingly polarized landscapes of many contemporary cities, these very logics could, conceivably, be embedded in biases within the very code that makes facial recognition CCTV systems work. Indeed, it is conceivable that such biometric and individualized systems could destroy the anonymized interactions that have long been central characteristics of city spaces. A new ontology of the body could be ushered in which uses software-sorting techniques to continuously police and stipulate notions of the purported value, fitness, riskiness, worth and legality of subjects, based on the continuous

scanning of a whole suite of biometric signatures, as people move within and between city spaces.

CONCLUSIONS: TOWARDS A SPATIAL POLITICS OF CODE

This paper has begun to demonstrate how, through the application of software-sorting techniques, whole swathes of the social and public realms of cities, and the essential private and pubic service domains of advanced industrial nations, are rapidly being 'mass customized', unbundled, commodified, individualized, and coordinated through networked technologies linking scales from the globe to the body. Very often, this is being accomplished based on combinations of neoliberal, consumeristic principles and ideologies of governance, new technological assemblages, and intensifying surveillance capabilities. In post-Keynesian, neoliberal contexts, it is clear that software-sorting techniques provide critical political sites. This is especially so as, currently, they are being overwhelmingly implemented to address perceived imperatives among service providers of offering favoured groups and places enhanced services, rights and mobilities, and improved real or perceived security, while, very often, working directly to undermine the prospects of marginalized groups and communities.

In addressing this wide research, policy and activist agenda, the challenge is to maintain a critical and informed position without falling foul of dystopian and absolutist scenarios suggesting that software-sorting techniques are somehow limitless, completely integrated, and all-powerful. As Koskela (2003) suggests, 'urban space will always remain less knowable and, thus, less controllable than the restricted panoptic space'. Spaces which escape the reach of regressive software-sorting systems do and will remain. A politics of transgressing, resisting, and even dismantling such increasingly inequitable systems is possible.

REFERENCES

Aday, Peter. 2004: Surveillance at the airport: Surveilling mobility/mobilising surveillance. *Environment and Planning A* 26, 1365–1380.

Amin, Ash and Thrift, Nigel. 2002: *Cities: reimagining the urban*. Cambridge: Polity Press.

Andrejevic, Mark. 2003: Monitored mobility in the era of mass customization. *Space and Culture* 6, 132–150.

Bowker, Geoffrey and Leigh-Star, Susan. 1999: *Sorting things out*. Cambridge, MA: MIT Press.

Burrows, Roger and Ellison, Nick. 2004: Sorting places out? Towards a social politics of neighbourhood informatization. *Information, Communication and Society* 7, 321–326.

Graham, Stephen. 2004: Beyond the 'dazzling light': from dreams of transcendence to the 'remediation' of urban life. *New Media and Society* 6, 33–42.

Graham, Stephen and Marvin, Simon. 2001: *Splintering urbanism: networked infra-structures, technological mobilities and the urban condition*. London: Routledge.

Koskela, Hille. 2003: 'Camera'—the contemporary urban panopticon. *Surveillance and Society* 1, 292–313.

Rifkin, Jeremy. 2001: *The age of access: the new culture of hypercapitalism where all of life is a paid-for experience*. New York: Penguin.

Thrift, Nigel and French, Shaun. 2002: The automatic production of space. *Transactions of the Institute of British Geographers* NS 27, 309–335.

Winseck, Dwayne. 2003: Netscapes of power: convergence, network design, walled gardens, and other strategies of control in the information age. In Lyon, D., editor, *Surveillance as social sorting: privacy, risk and digital discrimination*. London: Routledge, pp. 176–198.

23
The Habitus and the Space of Life-Styles

(1984)

Pierre Bourdieu

As if carried away by their quest for greater objectivity, sociologists almost always forget that the 'objects' they classify produce not only objectively classifiable practices but also classifying operations that are no less objective and are themselves classifiable. The division into classes performed by sociology leads to the common root of the classifiable practices which agents produce and of the classificatory judgements they make of other agents' practices and their own. The habitus is both the generative principle of objectively classifiable judgements and the system of classification (*principium divisionis*) of these practices. It is in the relationship between two capacities which define the habitus, the capacity to produce classifiable practices and works, and the capacity to differentiate and appreciate these practices and products (taste), that the represented social world, i.e., the space of life-styles, is constituted.

The relationship that is actually established between the pertinent characteristics of economic and social condition (capital volume and composition, in both synchronic and diachronic aspects) and the distinctive features associated with the corresponding position in the universe of life-styles only becomes intelligible when the habitus is constucted as the generative formula which makes it possible to account both for the classifiable practices and products and for the judgements, themselves classified, which make these practices and works into a system of distinctive signs. When one speaks of the aristocratic asceticism of teachers or the pretension of the petit bourgeoisie, one is not only describing these groups by one, or even the most important, of their properties, but also endeavouring to name the principle which generates all their properties and all their judgements of their, or other people's, properties. The habitus is necessity internalized and converted into a disposition that generates meaningful practices and meaning-giving perceptions; it is a general, transposable disposition which carries out a systematic, universal application—beyond the limits of what has been directly learnt—of the necessity inherent in the learning conditions. That is why an agent's whole set of practices (or those of a whole set of agents produced by similar conditions) are both systematic, inasmuch as they are the product of the application of identical (or interchangeable) schemes, and systematically distinct from the practices constituting another life-style.

Because different conditions of existence produce different habitus—systems of generative schemes applicable, by simple transfer, to the most varied areas of practice—the practices engendered by the different habitus appear as systematic configurations of properties expressing the differences objectively inscribed in conditions of existence in the form of systems of differential deviations which, when perceived by agents endowed with the schemes of perception and appreciation necessary in order to identify, interpret and evaluate their pertinent features, function as life-styles.

The habitus is not only a structuring structure, which organizes practices and the perception of practices, but also a structured structure: the principle of division into logical classes which organizes the perception of the social world is itself the product of internalization of the division into social classes. Each class condition is defined, simultaneously, by its intrinsic properties and by the relational properties which it derives from its position in the system of class conditions, which is also a system of differences, differential positions, i.e., by everything which distinguishes it from what it is not and especially from everything it is opposed to; social identity is defined and asserted through difference. This means that inevitably inscribed within the dispositions of the habitus is the whole structure of the system of conditions, as it presents itself in the experience of a life-condition occupying a particular position within that structure. The most fundamental oppositions in the structure (high/low/rich/poor etc.) tend to establish themselves as the fundamental structuring principles of practices and the perception of practices. As a system of practice-generating schemes which expresses systematically the necessity and freedom inherent in its class condition and the difference constituting that position, the habitus apprehends differences between conditions, which it grasps in the form of differences between classified, classifying practices (products of other habitus), in accordance with principles of differentiation which, being themselves the product of these differences, are objectively attuned to them and therefore tend to perceive them as natural.

Life-styles are thus the systematic products of habitus, which, perceived in their mutual relations through the schemes of the habitus, become sign systems that are socially qualified (as 'distinguished', 'vulgar' etc.). The dialectic of conditions and habitus is the basis of an alchemy which transforms the distribution of capital, the balance-sheet of a power relation, into a system of perceived differences, distinctive properties, that is, a distribution of symbolic capital, legitimate capital, whose objective truth is misrecognized.

As structured products (*opus operatum*) which a structuring structure (*modus operandi*) produces through retranslations according to the specific logic of the different *fields*, all the practices and products of a given agent are objectively harmonized among themselves, without any deliberate pursuit of coherence, and objectively orchestrated, without any conscious concertation, with those of all members of the same class. The habitus continuously generates practical metaphors,

that is to say, transfers (of which the transfer of motor habits is only one example) or, more precisely, systematic transpositions required by the particular conditions in which the habitus is 'put into practice' (so that, for example, the ascetic ethos which might be expected always to express itself in saving may, in a given context, express itself in a particular way of using credit). The practices of the same agent, and, more generally, the practices of all agents of the same class, owe the stylistic affinity which makes each of them a metaphor of any of the others to the fact that they are the product of transfers of the same schemes of action from one field to another. An obvious paradigm would be the disposition called 'handwriting', a singular way of tracing letters which always produces the same writing, i.e., graphic forms which, in spite of all the differences of size, material or colour due to the surface (paper or blackboard) or the instrument (pen or chalk)—in spite, therefore, of the different use of muscles—present an immediately perceptible family resemblance, like all the features of style or manner whereby a painter or writer can be recognized as infallibly as a man by his walk.

Systematicity is found in the opus operatum because it is in the modus operandi. It is found in all the properties—and property—with which individuals and groups surround themselves, houses, furniture, paintings, books, cars, spirits, cigarettes, perfume, clothes, and in the practices in which they manifest their distinction, sports, games, entertainments, only because it is in the synthetic unity of the habitus, the unifying, generative principle of all practices. Taste, the propensity and capacity to appropriate (materially or symbolically) a given class of classified, classifying objects or practices, is the generative formula of life-style, a unitary set of distinctive preferences which express the same expressive intention in the specific logic of each of the symbolic sub-spaces, furniture, clothing, language or body hexis. Each dimension of life-style 'symbolizes with' the others, in Leibniz's phrase, and symbolizes them. An old cabinetmaker's world view, the way he manages his budget, his time or his body, his use of language and choice of clothing are fully present in his ethic of scrupulous, impeccable craftsmanship and in the aesthetic of work for work's sake which leads him to measure the beauty of his products by the care and patience that have gone into them.

Taste is thus the source of the system of distinctive features which cannot fail to be perceived as a systematic expression of a particular class of conditions of existence, i.e., as a distinctive life-style, by anyone who possesses practical knowledge of the relationships between distinctive signs and positions in the distributions—between the universe of objective properties, which is brought to light by scientific construction, and the no less objective universe of life-styles, which exists as such for and through ordinary experience.

This classificatory system, which is the product of the internalization of the structure of social space, in the form in which it impinges through the experience of a particular position in that space, is, within the limits of economic possibilities and impossibilities (which it tends to reproduce in its own logic), the generator of practices adjusted to the regularities inherent in a condition. It continuously transforms necessities into strategies, constraints into preferences, and, without any mechanical determination, it generates the set of 'choices' constituting life-styles, which derive their meaning, i.e., their value, from their position in a system of oppositions and correlations. It is a virtue made of necessity which continuously transforms necessity into virtue by inducing 'choices' which correspond to the condition of which it is the product. As can be seen whenever a change in social position puts the habitus into new conditions, so that its specific efficacy can be isolated, it is taste—the taste of necessity or the taste of luxury—and not high or low income which commands the practices objectively adjusted to these resources. Through taste, an agent has what he likes because he likes what he has, that is, the properties actually given to him in the distributions and legitimately assigned to him in the classifications.

I shall merely indicate, very schematically, how the two major organizing principles of the social space govern the structure and modification of the space of cultural consumption, and, more generally, the whole universe of life-styles.

In cultural consumption, the main opposition, by overall capital value, is between the practices designated by their rarity as distinguished, those of the fractions richest in both economic and cultural capital, and the practices socially identified as vulgar because they are both easy and common, those of the fractions poorest in both these respects. In the intermediate position are the practices which are perceived as pretentious, because of the manifest discrepancy between ambition and possibilities.

The fact that in the realm of food the main opposition broadly corresponds to differences in income has masked the secondary opposition which exists, both within the middle classes and within the dominant class, between the fractions richer in cultural capital and less rich in economic capital and those whose assets are structured in the opposite way. Observers tend to see a simple effect of income in the fact that, as one rises in the social hierarchy, the proportion of income spent on food diminishes, or that, within the food budget, the proportion spent on heavy, fatty, fattening foods, which are also cheap—pasta, potatoes, beans, bacon, pork—declines, as does that spent on wine, whereas an increasing proportion is spent on leaner, lighter (more digestible), non-fattening foods (beef, veal, mutton, lamb, and especially fresh fruit and vegetables). Because the real principle of preferences is taste, a virtue made of necessity, the theory which makes consumption a simple function of income has all the appearances to support it, since income plays an important part in determining distance from necessity. However, it cannot account for cases in which the same income is associated with totally different consumption patterns. Thus, foremen remain attached to 'popular' taste although they earn more than clerical and commercial employees, whose taste differs radically from that of manual workers and is closer to that of teachers.

The true basis of the differences found in the area of consumption, and far beyond it, is the opposition between the tastes of luxury (or freedom) and the tastes of necessity. The former are the tastes of individuals who are the product of material conditions of existence defined by distance from necessity, by the freedoms or facilities stemming from possession of capital; the latter express, precisely in their adjustment, the necessities of which they are the product. Thus it is possible to deduce popular tastes for the foods that are simultaneously most 'filling' and most economical from the necessity of reproducing labour power at the lowest cost which is forced on the proletariat as its very definition. The idea of taste, typically bourgeois, since it presupposes absolute freedom of choice, is so closely associated with the idea of freedom that many people find it hard to grasp the paradoxes of the taste of necessity. Some simply sweep it aside, making practice a direct product of economic necessity (workers eat beans because they cannot afford anything else), failing to realize that necessity can only be fulfilled, most of the time, because the agents are inclined to fulfil it, because they have a taste for what they are anyway condemned to. Others turn it into a taste of freedom, forgetting the conditionings of which it is the product, and so reduce it to pathological or morbid preference for (basic) essentials, a sort of congenital coarseness, the pretext for a class racism which associates the populace with everything heavy, thick and fat. Taste is *amor fati,* the choice of destiny, but a forced choice, produced by conditions of existence which rule out all alternatives as mere daydreams and leave no choice but the taste for the necessary.

Not content with lacking virtually all the knowledge or manners which are valued in the markets of academic examination or polite conversation nor with only possessing skills which have no value there, they are the people 'who don't know how to live', who sacrifice most to material foods, and to the heaviest, grossest and most fattening of them, bread, potatoes, fats, and the most vulgar, such as wine; who spend least on clothing and cosmetics, appearance and beauty; those who 'don't know how to relax', 'who always have to be doing something', who set off in their Renault 5 or Simca 1000 to join the great traffic jams of the holiday exodus, who picnic beside major roads, cram their tents into overcrowded campsites, fling themselves into the prefabricated leisure activities designed for them by the engineers of cultural mass production; those who by all these uninspired 'choices' confirm class racism, if it needed to be confirmed, in its conviction that they only get what they deserve.

THREE STYLES OF DISTINCTION

The basic opposition between the tastes of luxury and the tastes of necessity is specified in as many oppositions as there are different ways of asserting one's distinction vis-à-vis the working class and its primary needs, or—which amounts to the same thing—different powers whereby necessity can be kept at a distance. Thus, within the dominant class, one can, for the sake of simplicity, distinguish three structures of the consumption distributed under three items: food, culture and presentation (clothing, beauty care, toiletries, domestic servants).

Tastes in food also depend on the idea each class has of the body and of the effects of food on the body, that is, on its strength, health and beauty; and on the categories it uses to evaluate these effects, some of which may be important for one class and ignored by another, and which the different classes may rank in very different ways. Thus, whereas the working classes are more attentive to the strength of the (male) body than its shape, and tend to go for products that are both cheap and nutritious, the professions prefer products that are tasty, health-giving, light and not fattening. Taste, a class culture turned into nature, that is, *embodied,* helps to shape the class body. It is an incorporated principle of classification which governs all forms of incorporation, choosing and modifying everything that the body ingests and digests and assimilates, physiologically and psychologically. It follows that the body is the most indisputable materialization of class taste, which it manifests in several ways. It does this first in the seemingly most natural features of the body, the dimensions (volume, height, weight) and shapes (round or square, stiff or supple, straight or curved) of its visible forms, which express in countless ways a whole relation to the body, i.e., a way of treating it, caring for it, feeding it, maintaining it, which reveals the deepest dispositions of the habitus.

THE VISIBLE AND THE INVISIBLE

But food—which the working classes place on the side of being and substance, whereas the bourgeoisie, refusing the distinction between inside and outside or 'at home' and 'for others', the quotidian and the extra-quotidian, introduces into it the categories of form and appearance—is itself related to clothing as inside to outside, the domestic to the public, being to seeming. And the inversion of the places of food and clothing in the contrast between the spending patterns of the working classes, who give priority to being, and the middle classes, where the concern for 'seeming' arises, is the sign of a reversal of the whole world view. The working classes make a realistic or, one might say, functionalist use of clothing. Looking for substance and function rather than form, they seek 'value for money' and choose what will 'last'.

Thus, despite the limits of the data available, one finds in men's clothing (which is much more socially marked, at the level of what can be grasped by statistics on purchases, than women's clothing) the equivalent of the major oppositions found in food consumption. In the first dimension of the space, the division again runs between the office workers and the manual workers and is marked particularly by the opposition between grey or white overalls and blue dungarees or boiler-suits, between town shoes and the more relaxed moccasins, kickers or sneakers (not to mention dressing-gowns, which clerical workers buy 3.5 times more often than manual workers). The increased quantity and quality of all purchases of men's clothing is summed up in the opposition between the suit, the prerogative of the senior executive, and the blue overall, the distinctive mark of the farmer and industrial worker (it is virtually unknown in other groups, except craftsmen); or between the overcoat, always much rarer among men than women, but much more frequent among senior executives than the other classes, and the fur-lined jacket or lumber jacket, mainly worn by agricultural and industrial workers. In between are the junior executives, who now scarcely ever wear working clothes but fairly often buy suits.

Among women, who, in all categories (except farmers and farm labourers), spend more than men (especially in the junior and senior executive, professional and other high-income categories), the number of purchases increases as one moves up the social hierarchy; the difference is greatest for suits and costumes—expensive garments—and smaller for dresses and especially skirts and jackets. The top-coat, which is increasingly frequent among women at higher social levels, is opposed to the 'all-purpose' raincoat, in the same way as overcoat and lumber jacket are opposed for men. The use of the smock and the apron, which in the working classes is virtually the housewife's uniform, increases as one moves down the hierarchy (in contrast to the dressing-gown, which is virtually unknown among peasants and industrial workers).

The interest the different classes have in self-presentation, the attention they devote to

it, their awareness of the profits it gives and the investment of time, effort, sacrifice and care which they actually put into it are proportionate to the chances of material or symbolic profit they can reasonably expect from it.

The self-assurance given by the certain knowledge of one's own value, especially that of one's body or speech, is in fact very closely linked to the position occupied in social space (and also, of course, to trajectory).

Although it is not a petit-bourgeois monopoly, the petit-bourgeois experience of the world starts out from timidity, the embarrassment of someone who is uneasy in his body and his language and who, instead of being 'as one body with them', observes them from outside, through other people's eyes, watching, checking, correcting himself, and who, by his desperate attempts to reappropriate an alienated being-for-others, exposes himself to appropriation, giving himself away as much by hypercorrection as by clumsiness. The timidity which, despite itself, realizes the objectified body, which lets itself be trapped in the destiny proposed by collective perception and statement (nicknames etc.), is betrayed by a body that is subject to the representation of others even in its passive, unconscious reactions (one feels oneself blushing). By contrast, ease, a sort of indifference to the objectifying gaze of others which neutralizes its powers, presupposes the self-assurance which comes from the certainty of being able to objectify that objectification, appropriate that appropriation, of being capable of imposing the norms of apperception of one's own body, in short, of commanding all the powers which, even when they reside in the body and apparently borrow its most specific weapons, such as 'presence' or charm, are essentially irreducible to it.

Thus, the spaces defined by preferences in food, clothing or cosmetics are organized according to the same fundamental structure, that of the social space determined by volume and composition of capital. Fully to construct the space of life-styles within which cultural practices are defined, one would first have to establish, for each class and class fraction, that is, for each of the configurations of capital, the generative formula of the habitus which retranslates the necessities and facilities characteristic of that class of (relatively) homogeneous conditions of existence into a particular life-style. One would then have to determine how the dispositions of the habitus are specified, for each of the major areas of practice, by implementing one of the stylistic possibles offered by each field (the field of sport, or music, or food, decoration, politics, language etc.). By superimposing these homologous spaces one would obtain a rigorous representation of the space of life-styles, making it possible to characterize each of the distinctive features (e.g., wearing a cap or playing the piano) in the two respects in which it is objectively defined, that is, on the one hand by reference to the set of features constituting the area in question (e.g., the system of hairstyles), and on the other hand by reference to the set of features constituting a particular life-style (e.g., the working-class life-style), within which its social significance is determined.

SECTION 5

Meanings of Home

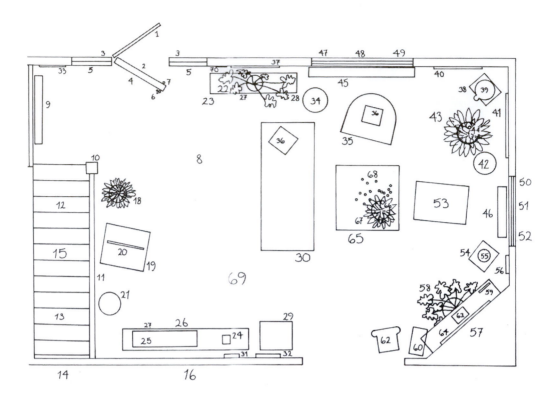

1. The Screen Door
2. The Door
3. The Doorframe
4. The Window in the Door
5. The Glass in the Sidelights
6. The Bells on the Door
7. The Lock
8. The Floor
9. The Radiator by the Stair
10. The Newel Post
11. The Banister
12. The Stair Treads
13. The Risers in the Stairs
14. The Landing
15. The Stair
16. The Walls
17. The Little Window by the Stair
18. The Plant on the Floor in Front of the Easel
19. The Easel
20. The Max Ernst Lithograph
21. The Speaker in the Sewer Pipe
22. The Plant on the Record Cabinets Just Inside the Door
23. The Small Record Cabinets
24. The Cherokee Basket
25. The Mexican Ferris Wheel
26. The Large Record Cabinets
27. The Records
28. The Tintins
29. The David Rowland Chair
30. The White Couch
31. Peter's Box
32. Denis's Collage
33. Denis's Collage at the Foot of the Stairs
34. The Couch Lamp
35. The Wicker Rocker
36. The Throw Pillows
37. Ron's Drawing
38. The Left Speaker
39. The Lacandon Drum
40. Adja's Lithograph
41. Peter's Malatesta
42. The Round Lamp
43. The Plant by the Speakers
44. The Koala Bear in the Plant
45. The Front Radiator
46. The Side Radiator
47. The Front Windows
48. The Front Screens
49. The Front Storm Windows
50. The Side Window
51. The Side Screen
52. The Side Storm Windows
53. Mies van der Rohe's Lounge Chair
54. The Right Speaker
55. The King
56. The Paul Strand Photograph
57. The Fireplace
58. The Plant in the Fireplace
59. The Plaited Fan
60. The Wooden Chair
61. The Electric Fan
62. The Mantleshelf
63. The Piece of Wire on the Mantleshelf
64. Peter's Genovevo de la O
65. Mies van der Rohe's Coffee Table
66. Chandler's Turtle on the Table
67. The Plant on the Table
68. The Baseball Game
69. The Ceiling
70. The Light Switches

Plan drawing of Wood family living room.
Referenced in: Wood, Dennis, and Robert J. Beck. 1994. *Home Rules*. Baltimore: Johns Hopkins U.

MEANINGS OF HOME

Home, both a place and an idea, is complex and multifaceted. It resonates as a spatial metaphor in everyday conversations—"home is where the heart is" or "there's no place like home"—and is the subject of scholarly debate across many disciplines. While some research suggests that home has such potent meaning because it is the locus of everyday family life and a repository of objects and memories, other accounts question whether this experience is true for everyone. Home operates at a variety of overlapping scales indicating how and where people feel a sense of belonging. At the same time, issues of homelessness and migration contribute to how we understand the impact of deracination and alternate ways of feeling attachment. In this section, we consider how home is lived and experienced by people as a place, sometimes with conflicted or variable meanings. Included are readings that pay special attention to how values of home are derived or constructed, as well as the ways in which experiences of home are denied or inhibited. These readings show that while home possesses a deep significance as a space where habitual and thoughtfully created life goes on, there are many ways in which these meanings emerge and are experienced.

Dwelling is a key term related to questions of home that German philosopher Martin Heidegger probes in an essay entitled "Building Dwelling Thinking" (1971 [1951]). He argues that people, through both language and action, regularly conflate building and dwelling. He gives an example through the word *bauen*:

> The Old English and High German word for building, *buan,* means to dwell. This signifies: to remain, to stay in a place. … Where the word *bauen* still speaks in its original sense it also says *how far* the nature of dwelling reaches. That is, *bauen, buan, bhu, beo* are our word *bin* in the versions: *ich bin,* I am, *du bist,* you are, the imperative form *bis,* be. What then does *ich bin* mean? The old word *bauen,* to which the *bin* belongs, answers: *ich bin, du bist* mean: I dwell, you dwell. The way in which you are and I am, the manner in which we humans *are* on the earth, is *buan,* dwelling. To be a human being means to be on the earth as a mortal. It means to dwell.

Heidegger's argument in this quote is that all places we inhabit offer us the possibility of home through the way in which we dwell. The reverse holds as well: dwelling depends on a rootedness that comes through building. For Heidegger, dwelling and building form the basic character of *being* on the earth, though more recent work brings into question the degree to which we are bound to specific places. Tim Ingold, a British social anthropologist, picks up the question of dwelling in his book *The Perception of the Environment* (2011), where he discusses how people make a home in the world, especially in relation to the landscape.

Domesticity, like dwelling, is a word which suggests a pattern of activity and the role people play in those activities as much as a particular type of environment. **Witold Rybczynski** is an architect and historian who looks at how the conventional understanding of home as a single-family dwelling has been transmitted through time and space. His chapter, "Domesticity," locates the start of this convention in 16th-century Netherlands. Rybczynski attributes its development to a number of factors, including the physical geography and resources of the Dutch lowlands, a growing middle class, and social standards that valued family, thrift, and neatness. Within this milieu, home came to signify the domestic abode of the conventional family—father, mother, and children—overseen and distinguished as a female realm.

Home does not mean the same thing to all people, especially when it is inaccessible. Social geographer **Rob Imrie** elucidates the experiences of disabled people in their home environments, and shows that conventional attitudes and design of homes are not sufficient for all people. The people he interviews point out ways in which traditionally designed homes do not offer adequate privacy or security, and often neglect other basic needs. These examples indicate how residences perpetuate disability and fail to provide a sense of belonging when houses do not fit people's physical abilities. In elaborating this friction between home and user, Imrie brings the normative idea of home as a place of comfort and satisfaction into question.

Talja Blokland is an urban sociologist who, like Imrie, complicates the conventional interpretations of what home means. By studying people living in public housing, she suggests how power dynamics and socio-economic conditions inform the ways in which people view their homes. For the residents she worked with, public housing was not and could never be their home, as it was seen as a temporary situation. Blokland demonstrates that for these residents there is a disconnect between their idealized view of home (e.g., a single-family residence surrounded by a picket fence) and the place in which they actually live. In fact, her work highlights how home—a sense of connection to a place of dwelling—is often denied to different groups, namely the poor and people of color in Western cultures, and relates to larger issues of injustice and social structure.

While physical access and domestic inhabitation are important ways in which we connect to our homes, our psychological connections and ideas of home are equally profound. **Clare Cooper**, an architect and psychologist who draws on the work of psychoanalyst Carl Jung, suggests that home may be understood as a shared archetypal experience in which people express themselves through a language of symbols. For Jung, home was a combination of a strong tower and a sheltering cavern. Cooper uses Jung's symbolic interpretation to understand what people desire in their homes, and how those things affect people at a psychic level. Addressing the idea of home as an expression of the "separate, unique, private, and protected" family unit, she cites statistics that 85 percent of Americans hold the single-family residence as ideal. Cooper argues that these psychic desires play out at a social level in the cultural patterns of suburban housing and how we speak about our homes, and questions whether these attitudes are sustainable in the forms they have taken.

Geographers **Denis Wood** and **Robert J. Beck** take a structural approach to the question of home, but at a very intimate scale. Their detailed analysis of the physical features and social codes that organize our experience of home reveals the cultural meanings of our living spaces. Like Rybczynski and Cooper, they indicate that our understanding and sense of home has been deeply engrained through cultural patterns. The authors offer evidence by closely examining every object and surface in a typical family living room and articulating the set of rules and restrictions that go along with each artifact. The plan drawing at the beginning of Section 5 shows the types of details from which these rules are constructed in Wood's home. By looking at the rules, they show how family members across generations learn how one should behave in a living room, which through action (and expected inaction) constitute the meaning of the place.

Drawing on the work of Gilles Deleuze and Félix Guattari, communications theorist **J. Macgregor Wise** argues that the way in which we define home can be much looser and less regulated. Wise suggests that we can understand home as a territory—one that we take with us—defined by something as simple as a song that makes someone feel safe in the dark. Home, while deeply cultural, is also something that escapes the bounds of culture because it is continually made and remade through our actions. As such it is something that moves with us and always opens onto other spaces. This understanding of home offers ways to grapple with contemporary questions of mobility and belonging, and suggests how technology may impact how and where we feel at home.

While this set of readings on home opens many ways to think about the places in which we live, it remains a partial look. Those interested in further reading might start with the work of Barbara Miller Lane (2006), which expands and adds to the perspectives offered here. Another edited volume is *The Domestic Space Reader* (Briganti and Mezei 2012), which looks more closely at how home is gendered and contested. In thinking about home, it is important to understand the dynamics of power and status that shape the space and experience. People who are poor, disabled, or otherwise marginalized may experience home in very different ways from how it is conventionally portrayed. Likewise, women and men tend to have different ideas and experiences of home. Dolores Hayden (1982, 2002) and Karen Franck (1991) have made excellent contributions that help us to think about alternative forms of housing and home based on nuanced understandings of class and gender. A number of interesting texts combine experiential description with social analysis of home, such as those by Winifred Gallagher (2006), Michael Ruhlman (2006), and Tracy Kidder (1985). Maureen Ogle (2000), and Ellen Lupton and J. Abbott Miller (1996) have looked specifically at how kitchens and bathrooms have impacted the spaces and meanings of home. A superb resource on the historical development of dwelling is *6,000 Years of Housing* by Norbert Schoenauer (2000), while Thomas Hubka (2004) and Pierre Bourdieu (1970) offer close analysis of the cultural and social implications of particular dwellings. There are many more projects and readings that further our understanding of home, but in all of them it is important to keep in mind that there is no single, fixed way of dwelling. Home is a place and an idea that is contingent upon and always intertwined with issues of power and subjectivity, gender and class, culture and individuality.

SUGGESTIONS FOR FURTHER READING

Please see *peopleplacespace.org* for extended and additional lists of readings.

Arnold, Jeanne E. 2013. *Life at Home in the Twenty-first Century: 32 Families Open Their Doors*. Los Angeles, CA: Cotsen Institute of Archaeology Press.

Bourdieu, Pierre. 1970. "The Berber House or the World Reversed." *Social Science Information* 9(2): 151–170.

Briganti, Chiara, and Kathy Mezei, eds. 2012. *The Domestic Space Reader*. Toronto: University of Toronto Press, Scholarly Publishing Division.

Franck, Karen A. 1991. *New Households, New Housing*, edited by Sherry Ahrentzen. New York: Van Nostrand Reinhold.

Gallagher, Winifred. 2006. *House Thinking: A Room-by-room Look at How We Live*. New York: Harper Perennial.

Grier, Katherine C. 2010. *Culture and Comfort: Parlor Making and Middle-class Identity, 1850–1930*. Washington, DC: Smithsonian Books.

Hayden, Dolores. 1982. *The Grand Domestic Revolution: A History of Feminist Designs for American Homes, Neighborhoods and Cities*. Cambridge, MA: The MIT Press.

Hayden, Dolores. 2002. *Redesigning the American Dream: Gender, Housing, and Family Life*. New York: W.W. Norton.

Heidegger, Martin. 1971. "Building Dwelling Thinking," From *Poetry, Language, Thought*, trans. Alfred Hofstadter. New York: Harper and Row.

Hubka, Thomas C. 2004. *Big House, Little House, Back House, Barn: The Connected Farm Buildings of New England*. Lebanon, NH: University Press of New Hampshire.

Ingold, Tim. 2011. *The Perception of the Environment: Essays on Livelihood, Dwelling and Skill*. London; New York: Routledge.

Jung, Carl G. 1989. "The Tower." In *Memories, Dreams, Reflections*. New York: Vintage.

Kidder, Tracy. 1985. *House*. New York: Houghton Mifflin.

Lane, Barbara Miller. 2006. *Housing and Dwelling: Perspectives on Modern Domestic Architecture*. New York: Routledge.

Lupton, Ellen, and J. Abbott Miller. 1996. *The Bathroom, the Kitchen, and the Aesthetics of Waste*. Princeton, NJ: Princeton Architectural Press.

McDowell, Linda. 2007. "Spaces of the Home: Absence, Presence, New Connections and New Anxieties." *Home Cultures* 4(2): 129–146.

Ogle, Maureen. 2000. *All the Modern Conveniences: American Household Plumbing, 1840–1890*. Baltimore, MD: The Johns Hopkins University Press.

Ruhlman, Michael. 2006. *House: A Memoir*. New York: Penguin Books.

Saegert, Susan, Desiree Fields, and Kimberly Libman. 2009. "Deflating the Dream: Radical Risk and the Neoliberalization of Homeownership." *Journal of Urban Affairs*. 31(3): 297–317.

Schoenauer, Norbert. 2000. *6,000 Years of Housing*. New York: W. W. Norton & Company.

Somerville, Peter. 1992. "Homelessness and the Meaning of Home: Rooflessness or Rootlessness?" *International Journal of Urban and Regional Research* 16(4): 529–539.

Verschaffel, Bart. 2002. "The Meanings of Domesticity." *The Journal of Architecture* 7(3): 287–296.

Wood, Denis, and Robert J. Beck. 1994. *Home Rules*. Baltimore, MD: The Johns Hopkins University Press.

Wright, Gwendolyn. 1983. *Building the Dream: A Social History of Housing in America*. Cambridge, MA: The MIT Press.

24
Domesticity
(1986)

Witold Rybczynski

> Domesticity, privacy, comfort, the concept of the home and of the family: these are, literally, principal achievements of the Bourgeois Age.
>
> John Lukacs
> *The Bourgeois Interior*

The appearance of intimacy and privacy in homes in Paris and London, and soon after even in such out-of-the-way places as Oslo, was an unwitting, almost unconscious, reaction to the changing conditions of urban life, and it appeared to be more a question of popular attitudes than of anything else. It is difficult to trace the evolution of something so amorphous, and it would be dangerous to claim that there was a single place where the modern idea of the family home first entered the human consciousness. There was, after all, no identifiable moment of discovery, no individual inventor who can be credited with the intuition, no theory or treatise on the subject. There was one place, however, where the seventeenth-century domestic interior evolved in a way that was arguably unique, and that can be described as having been, at the very least, exemplary.

The United Provinces of the Netherlands was a brand-new state, formed in 1609 after thirty years of rebellion against Spain. It was among the smallest countries in Europe, with a population one-quarter that of Spain, one-eighth that of France, and with a landmass smaller than Switzerland's. It had few natural resources—no mines, no forests—and what little land there was needed constant protection from the sea. But this "low" country surprisingly quickly established itself as a major power. In a short time it became the most advanced shipbuilding nation in the world and developed large naval, fishing, and merchant fleets. Its explorers founded colonies in Africa and Asia, as well as in America. The Netherlands introduced many financial innovations that made it a major economic force—and Amsterdam became the world center for international finance. Its manufacturing towns grew so quickly that by the middle of the century the Netherlands had supplanted France as the leading industrial nation of the world. Its universities were among the best in Europe; its tolerant political and religious climate offered a home for émigré thinkers such as Spinoza, Descartes, and John Locke. This fecund country produced not just venture capitalists and the speculative tulip trade, but also Rembrandt and Vermeer; it devised not only the first recorded war game, but also the first microscope; it invested not only in heavily armed East India men but also in beautiful towns. All this occurred during a brief historical moment—barely a human lifetime—which lasted from 1609 until roughly the 1660s, and which the Dutch call their "golden age."

These unlikely achievements were the result of several different factors, such as the Netherlands' advantageous location in European maritime trade, as well as the defensibility of its national borders, but it was in great measure a result of the peculiar character of the Dutch social fabric, which was different from that of the rest of Europe. The Dutch were primarily merchants and landowners. Unlike England, the Netherlands lacked a landless peasantry (most Dutch farmers owned their land); unlike France, it had no powerful aristocracy (the nobility, decimated by the wars for independence, was small and no longer wealthy); unlike Spain, it had no king (the head of state, or *stadhouder*, was a national symbol, but with limited real power). This republic—the first in Europe—was a loose confederation ruled by a States General, which consisted of representatives of the seven sovereign provinces, chosen from the patrician upper middle class.

The bourgeois nature of Dutch society in the seventeenth century needs some explanation. To say that it was "bourgeois" does not mean that it consisted exclusively of a middle class. There were farmers (*boers*), seamen, and, in manufacturing towns such as Leiden, factory workers. The last-named, especially, did not share in the prosperity of that time, and their living conditions were as miserable as in other countries. There was also, as in all European cities, an urban rabble (*grauw*), composed of paupers and criminals, the unemployed and the unemployable, itinerant beggars and tramps. However, the middle class predominated, and was broad enough to encompass the international financier as well as the shopkeeper.

By European standards, this was a greatly expanded democracy, and this "social dictatorship of the merchant class," as one historian called it, created the first bourgeois state.

These circumstances produced a people who admired saving, frowned on conspicuous spending, and naturally evolved conservative manners. The simplicity of the Dutch bourgeois expressed itself in many ways.

Simplicity and thrift were apparent in Dutch houses, which lacked the architectural pretension of town-houses in London or Paris, and which were built of brick and wood instead of stone. These materials were used for their light weight, since the boggy soil of the Low Countries frequently required pile foundations, the cost of which could be reduced if the foundations carried less weight. Brick does not lend itself to elaborate decoration—unlike stone, it cannot be carved, and unlike cement plaster, it cannot be formed into moldings and reliefs. Consequently, Dutch buildings were plain, only occasionally relieved by stonework at the corners and around the doors and windows. The material was appreciated mainly for its pleasant texture; undoubtedly its economy also appealed to the practical-minded Dutch, who used it even for their public buildings.

The expense of building canals and pilings dictated that street frontages be reduced as much as possible; as a result, the building plots in Dutch towns were extremely narrow, sometimes only one room wide. The houses were built adjacent to each other in a row, usually sharing common walls. The roofs were covered in red clay tiles. Their gable ends, which were often stepped, faced the street and produced the characteristic silhouettes for which Dutch towns became famous.

These houses were "small houses," literally as well as figuratively. They did not need to be large, because they contained few people; the average number of people per house in most Dutch towns was not more than four or five, compared to as many as twenty-five in a city such as Paris. Why was this? For one thing, there were no tenants, for the Dutch preferred, and were prosperous enough, to afford the luxury of owning their own homes, however small. The house had ceased to be a place of work, and as many artisans became well-to-do merchants or *rentiers*, they built separate establishments for their businesses, and employees and apprentices had to provide their own lodgings. Nor were there as many servants as in other countries, for Dutch society discouraged the hiring of servants and imposed special taxes on those who employed domestic help. Individual independence was more highly prized than elsewhere, and, equally importantly, it could be afforded. As a result, most homes in the Netherlands housed a single couple and their children. This brought about another change. The publicness that had characterized the "big house" was replaced by a more sedate—and more private—home life.

The emergence of the family home reflected the growing importance of the family in Dutch society. The glue that cemented this unit was the presence of children. The mother raised her own children—there were no nurses. Young children attended infant school at the age of three, and then primary school for four years. The Netherlands had, it is generally agreed, the highest level of literacy in Europe, and even secondary education was not uncommon. Most children lived at home until they were married, and the relations between Dutch parents and their children were characterized by affection, rather than by discipline. Foreign visitors considered this permissiveness to be a dangerous habit. Given the excessive indulgence with which parents treated their children, one observed, "it is surprising that there is not more disorder than there is." For the Frenchman who wrote this, children were small and unruly, but nevertheless adults; the idea of childhood did not yet exist for him. The historian Philippe Ariès has described how the substitution of school for apprenticeship throughout Europe reflected a rapprochement between parents and family, and between the concept of family and the concept of childhood. This is precisely what happened in the Netherlands, where the family centered itself on the child and family life centered itself on the home, only in the Dutch home it occurred about a hundred years earlier than elsewhere.

The Dutch loved their homes. They shared this old Anglo-Saxon word—ham, hejm in Dutch—with the other peoples of northern Europe.[1] "Home" brought together the meanings of house and of household, of dwelling and of refuge, of ownership and of affection. "Home" meant the house, but also everything that was in it and around it, as well as the people, and the sense of satisfaction and contentment that all these conveyed. You could walk out of the house, but you always returned home.

The furniture and adornment of a seventeenth-century Dutch home were meant, although in a typically restrained way, to convey the wealth of its owner. There were still benches and stools, especially in the homes of the less prosperous, but, as in England and France, the chair had become the most common sitting device. It was almost always without arms, padded, and upholstered in velvet and other rich materials, usually attached to the frame with copper nails. Tables, like chairs, were of oak or walnut and had elegantly turned legs. Curtained four-poster beds were similarly constructed, but less common than in England or France; instead, the Dutch slept in beds that were built into the wall. Such beds, of medieval origin, were set into an alcove, completely enclosed on three sides, and the opening was screened with a curtain or solid shutters. The most important piece of bourgeois furniture was the cupboard, which the Dutch borrowed from Germany, and which replaced the horizontal chest as the means of storage. There were usually two such cupboards, often ornamented with inlays of precious wood, one for the linens and another for tableware. For storing and displaying the latter there were also glass-fronted credenzas,

descendants of the medieval plate cupboards, which held silver and crystal, Delft porcelain and oriental china.

The type of furniture in a Dutch house was similar to that found in a Parisian bourgeois home; the difference was in the effect. The French interior was crowded and frenetic, the many pieces of furniture jostling each other in rooms whose papered walls were illustrated with scenic landscapes and where all surfaces were embroidered, gilded, or decorated. Dutch decor, by comparison, was sparse. Furniture was to be admired, but it was also meant to be used, and it was never so crowded as to detract from the sense of space that was produced by the room and by the light within it. The walls were rarely papered or covered, although they were adorned with paintings, mirrors, and maps—the last-named a uniquely Dutch practice. The effect was far from severe, and was not intended to be. These rooms, with one or two chairs under a window, or a bench beside the door, were intensely human, and were directed to private use, rather than to entertaining and socializing. They exhibited an intimacy that is inadequately described by words such as "serene" or "peaceful."

As every homemaker knows, the less furniture there is, the easier it is to keep a room clean, and this too may have had something to do with the relative sparseness of the Dutch interior, for these houses were spotlessly, immaculately, unbelievably clean. The well-scrubbed Dutch stoop is famous and has come to serve as an example of public exhibition and bourgeois pretentiousness. Public it certainly was—not only the stoop but the entire road pavement in front of the house was washed and sanded by the householder—but it was no pretense; the interiors of Dutch houses were equally scrubbed and scoured. Sand was scattered on the floor, recalling the medieval practice of covering floors in rushes. Pots were shined, woodwork varnished, brickwork tarred. This was all taken seriously by the Dutch, and produced some curious customs which never failed to elicit comment from foreigners. A German visitor to Delft in 1665 wrote that "in many houses, as in the holy places of the heathens, it is not permissible to ascend the stairs or set foot in a room without first removing one's shoes." Jean-Nicolas de Parival, a French traveler, observed the same thing, adding that frequently straw slippers were put on over one's shoes.

The cleanliness of the Dutch interior was not simply a part of the national character, nor a response determined by external causes, but evidence of something much more important. When visitors were required to take off their shoes or put on slippers, it was not immediately on entering the house—the lower floor was still considered to be a part of the public street—but on going upstairs. That was where the public realm stopped and the home began. This boundary was a new idea, and the order and tidiness of the household were evidence neither of fastidiousness nor of a particular cleanliness, but instead of a desire to define the home as a separate, special place.

That we are able to know so much about the appearance of Dutch homes is thanks to two happy accidents: the predominance of painting in seventeenth-century Holland, and the popularity of domestic scenes as a subject of these paintings.

Pieter de Hooch painted wonderful scenes of domestic life, as also did Jan Steen and Gabriel Metsu. Less than forty paintings remain by the great Jan Vermeer, and almost all of them are set within the home. But it was Emanuel de Witte, who specialized in views of church interiors, another popular genre, who painted a domestic scene that has come to epitomize the seventeenth-century Dutch interior. This little masterpiece, painted around 1660, shows a series of rooms opening off each other, bathed in sunlight that falls through the large leaded windows.

The furniture is not complicated; the padded chairs look comfortable but lack the fringes and embroidered material that were then popular in France. The rooms are *enfilade*, but the effect is not intimidating. The walls are plain, although they are typically adorned with a mirror, as well as with a map visible through the doorway. The stone floor is a simple pattern of black and white squares of marble. This is a well-to-do household—the musical instrument, the oriental carpet and the gilded mirror attest to that—but the atmosphere is not one of luxury. Objects are not on display; instead, we have the impression of a simple practicality from the way that the furnishings are arranged. The bed is located in a corner, behind the door; the rug is thoughtfully placed beside the bed, to take the morning chill off the cold stone floor. The mirror hangs over the virginals. The table and chairs sit next to the window, near the light.

And what light! The rooms are illuminated to emphasize their depth and distance, as well as their physical, material reality. It is above all this sense of interior space, and hence of insideness, that distinguishes this painting. Instead of being a picture of a room, it is a picture of a home.

The feminization of the home in seventeenth-century Holland was one of the most important events in the evolution of the domestic interior. It had several causes, chief among them the limited use made of servants. Even the wealthiest household rarely employed more than three servants, while a typical prosperous bourgeois family included, at most, a single maidservant.

Dutch law was explicit on contractual arrangements and on the civil rights of servants, so that the relationship between employer and employee was less exploitive and closer than elsewhere in Europe; servants ate with their masters at the same table, for instance, and housework was shared instead of delegated. All this produced, for the seventeenth century, a remarkable situation: Dutch married women, irrespective of their wealth or social position, did most of their own household chores.

This included taking charge of the cooking, and this small change had far-reaching consequences. When servants were doing the cooking, the room containing the kitchen was hardly differentiated from the other rooms, and was in any case accorded a secondary position. In Parisian bourgeois houses, for example, the kitchen occupied a room off the courtyard but without direct access to the main rooms. In English terrace houses the kitchen, adjacent to the servant quarters, continued to be located in the basement until the nineteenth century. In most *appartements* the "kitchen" was no more than a pot hanging in the fireplace.

In the Dutch home the kitchen was the most important room; according to one historian, "the kitchen was promoted to a position of fantastic dignity and became something between a temple and a museum." Here were located the cupboards that held the prized table linens, china, and silver. Copper and brass utensils, brightly polished, hung on the walls. The chimney piece was enormous and elaborately decorated—overly so to modern tastes—and contained not only the hearth with the traditional hanging pot, but also a simple kind of stove. The sink was copper, sometimes marble. Some kitchens had interior hand pumps (one is visible in de Witte's painting) and even reservoirs with a continuous supply of hot water. The presence of such amenities signified the growing importance of domestic work and the premium that was beginning to be placed on convenience. This was natural. For the first time, the person who was in intimate contact with housework was also in a position to influence the arrangement and disposition of the home. Servants had to put up with inconvenient and ill-thought-out arrangements because they had no say in the matter. The mistress of the house, particularly when she was as independent-minded as the Dutch woman, did not.

The importance accorded the kitchen reflected the central position of the woman in the Dutch household. The husband may have been the head of the family and led the mealtime prayers, but in household matters he was no longer "master in his own house." It was the wife, not her husband, who insisted on cleanliness and tidiness, not the least because it was she who had to do the cleaning.

Stories of the strictness, if not tyranny, of the Dutch mistress abounded; undoubtedly many were apocryphal. But they all pointed to a change in domestic arrangements. Not only was the house becoming more intimate, it was also, in the process, acquiring a special atmosphere. It was becoming a feminine place, or at least a place under feminine control. This control was tangible and real. It resulted in cleanliness, and in enforced rules, but it also introduced something to the house which had not existed before: domesticity.

To speak of domesticity is to describe a set of felt emotions, not a single attribute. Domesticity has to do with family, intimacy, and a devotion to the home, as well as with a sense of the house as embodying—not only harboring—these sentiments. It was the atmosphere of domesticity that permeated de Witte's and Vermeer's paintings. Not only was the interior a setting for domestic activity—as it had always been—but the rooms, and the objects that they contained, now acquired a life of their own. This life was not, of course, autonomous, but existed in the imagination of their owners, and so, paradoxically, homely domesticity depended on the development of a rich interior awareness, an awareness that was the result of the woman's role in the home. If domesticity was, as John Lukacs suggested, one of the principal achievements of the Bourgeois Age, it was, above all, a feminine achievement.

NOTE

1 This wonderful word, "home," which connotes a physical "place" but also has the more abstract sense of a "state of being," has no equivalent in the Latin or Slavic European languages. German, Danish, Swedish, Icelandic, Dutch, and English all have similar sounding words for "home," all derived from the Old Norse "heima."

25
Disability, Embodiment and the Meaning of the Home
(2004)

Rob Imrie

It has been well established in housing studies that the home is one of the fundamental places that gives shape and meaning to people's everyday lives. A burgeoning literature has, in various ways, explored the social, health and psychological effects of the home. For example, Sixsmith and Sixsmith (1991) note that the home is a symbol of oneself or a powerful extension of the psyche. It is a context for social and mental well-being or, as Lewin (2001) suggests, a place to engender social psychological and cultural security. For others, the home is the focus for personal control and a place that permits people to fashion in their own image. In this sense, the domestic setting is, for Lewin (2001), a mirror of personal views and values (also, see Cooper, 1995).

Gilman's (1903; reprinted 2002, p.3) seminal text suggests that the home, ideally, should offer a combination of rest, peace, quiet, comfort, health and be a place for personal expression. Indeed, throughout the 20th century, the home has been counterposed to work, as a place of retreat, social stability and domestic bliss far from the travails of everyday life. From builders' marketing brochures that seek to sell the dream of the ideal home, to television programmes about selling a place in the sun, the home is popularly portrayed as the focus of convivial social relationships and a source of human contentment. It is, first and foremost, a place for family interaction and the setting for personal seclusion and intimate behaviour free from public comment or restraint. The home is also the setting for the development of personal values, and patterns of socialisation and social reproduction more generally.

These characterisations of the home, however, do little to reveal the complexity of the cross-cutting variables that imbue domestic space with meaning. For Saunders and Williams (1988), the meaning of the home is not fixed but varies, potentially, between different household members, especially in terms of gender and age, and between households, especially in relation to differences in social class. They also suggest that people's experiences of, and meanings attributed to, the home may differ according to geographical context or setting.

Such studies indicate that the meaning of the home is unstable and transitory. For Gilman (2002, p. 8), despite the prevailing wisdom that homes were "perfect and quite above suspicion", the home was a potential source of repression. In particular, she referred to women's exclusive confinement to the home as leading to 'mental myopia' in which the individual was made into 'less of a person'. Likewise, a range of feminist writers have sought to deconstruct ideal images of the home by suggesting that the home, for some women, is a place of captivity and isolation (Allan, 1985; McDowell, 1983). Others note that the home is as much about the focus for the drudgery of domestic work as for personal pleasure, and a place of fear where, potentially, domestic violence takes place.

While these, and related, studies have done much to destabilise popular representations of the home, they tend to refer to abstract categories (e.g. gender, ethnicity, etc.) that rarely relate to, or reveal, how specific bodily or physiological phenomena interact with dwellings to produce personal experiences of, and generate particular meanings about, the home. Indeed, as Gurney (1990) notes, it is problematical to explain the meaning of the home with reference only to generalised categories, such as class, income or tenure. Rather, for Gurney, the significance of the home is influenced by different personal experiences. Foremost, it is contended, it relates to the body in that, as Twigg (2002, p. 436) comments, the body is a necessary condition of life in as much that "social life cannot proceed without this physiological substratum".

Others concur in noting that the body is the most significant referent of a person or, as Merleau-Ponty (1962, p. 150) notes, "I am not in front of my body, I am in it, or rather I am it". For Merleau-Ponty (1963, p. 5), the "body is not in space like things; it inhabits or haunts space … through it we have access to space". Here, the body, as a sensory and physiological entity, is constitutive of space or, as Lefebvre (1991, p. 174) comments, "the most basic places and spatial indicators are first of all qualified by the body". Physiological substratum is also core to domestic life in that the home is the focus for the care of the body, including washing, dressing, grooming and preparation for entry to the world beyond the front door. The physical design of dwellings is 'thoroughly embodied' in that each part of the domestic environment can be thought of as a 'body zone', or where particular bodily functions, both physical and mental, are attended to. Thus, the bathroom is the place for washing the body, while the bedroom is the place for physical and mental recuperation.

While such functional demarcations are neither inevitable nor unchangeable, they are part of a broader and powerful, social and cultural encoding of what constitutes appropriate domestic space and their legitimate (bodily) uses. Such encoding, however, rarely relates to impairment, or to bodies that may require an integration of rooms and/or functions, or more flexible forms of domestic design. In particular, disabled people often experience the home as a series of 'disembodied spaces', or places that are designed in ways that are rarely attentive to their physiological and bodily needs and functions. Thus, interactions between features of bodily physiology, such as muscle wasting, and domestic design, such as heavy doors, can combine to demarcate domestic spaces that are off limits to (particular types of) impaired bodies. For Hockey (1999, p. 108), such embodied experiences, in which people are excluded from participation "in the performance of home as idealised, is to undermine a view of home as a sanctuary or 'place of secure retreat'".

Insights into disabled people's experiences of, and meanings associated with, the home, ought to proceed, however, by rejecting reductive conceptions of disability and impairment. Thus, the body is neither a naturalistic organic entity, unaffected by socialisation, nor a socialised entity, unaffected by physiology. Rather, the body, and its interactions with domestic space, reflects a complex conjoining of physiological and social and cultural relations to produce specific, person-centred, meanings of the home. For instance, doorsteps have long been part of the aesthetic decor of dwellings, and reflect values about what constitutes appropriate design. However, for wheelchair users, steps prevent ease of entry to homes. In such instances, the experience, and potential meaning, of the home as a form of embodied encounter, is influenced by the interplay between physiological matter (i.e. the absence of use of limbs) and those social and cultural relations that give rise to, and legitimate, particular design features (i.e. steps).

DISABILITY, DOMESTIC DESIGN AND THE HOME ENVIRONMENT

In investigating disabled people's feelings about disability and domestic design, two research methods were adopted. First, two focus groups were held in October 2002 with members of a disabled persons user group located in a south coast conurbation. This was followed, over the course of the next five months, by interviews with 20 individuals living in three different towns.

The subjects are all individuals with various mobility impairments, ranging from those with problems of balance due to the early onset of Parkinson's disease, to individuals with advanced stages of multiple sclerosis that render them dependent, for some of the time, on a wheelchair.

The respondents live in a mixture of different types of dwellings including flats (5 respondents), detached homes (4), institutional care settings (3), and terraced and semi-detached dwellings (8).

Corporeal Dys-appearance and Privation in the Home

The physical design of housing tends to reflect a particular conception of corporeality based around a body that is not characterised by impairment, disease and illness. For instance, most kitchen units in homes are provided as a standardised package in which tabletop and cupboard heights are reachable only by an upright person. People who are dependent on a wheelchair, or whose mobility is such that they have to hold onto a support structure to stabilise themselves, often find it impossible to use their kitchen unless it is adapted to meet their needs. Thus, as Ann recounted, about her kitchen before it was adapted:

> It was too high, I couldn't have used the wheelchair, the cupboards were too high, the cooker was completely unusable, I would leave the thing on and oh, it just went on and on and on. … As a mum it totally demoralised me.

The design of most dwellings is also underpinned by values that rarely relate to, or incorporate, the needs of wheelchair users. Some respondents were angry that their homes were short of space to permit them ease of movement from one room to another, or even within rooms. For John, his bedroom is an apt example of where design values have been applied without relating to impairment. As he recalled:

> There are some basic assumptions. I'm just talking about a very simple basic thing like there is no way on this earth that my wheelchair can go to the other side of my bed. It doesn't matter what you do you can't configure the bedroom any other way, so the assumption must be that I'm not going to make my bed, that I don't need to get to the other side of the room.

Others commented on the lack of space as the most important factor in preventing them from getting access to rooms and living as they please in their homes. As Carol said:

> The kitchen is really very small and when you're manoeuvring a wheelchair you do need a bit of space. You can hardly get your furniture in the lounge and you have to eat

in it. It's things like this, and I'm thinking to myself, you've got a life and you want to lead your life and this isn't really helping you.

Similarly, Janet was unhappy with the shortage of space in her WC which, she felt, compromised the quality of her life:

> If my loo had been built eighteen inches longer it would've meant I could've got my whole wheelchair in, but as it is I can't use it with the wheelchair … I have to leave the door open, and it just brings it home to you about what you can't do in your own home.

Such examples serve to illustrate what Leder (1990, p. 84) refers to as the "dys-appearing" body or where, as he suggests, "the body appears as a thematic focus of attention but precisely in a dys-state" (also, see Paterson and Hughes, 1999). What Leder (1990) is inferring is that, in everyday life, consciousness of the body, either by oneself or by others, is minimal or non-existent. That is, the body has, more or less, disappeared from consciousness. It only reappears, explicitly, in a context of pain, disease or bodily dysfunction. Its reappearance is characterised by encounters with the embodied norms of everyday life, or those that are reflective of, primarily, non-impaired forms of carnality. Such norms serve to reproduce a world in the image of non-impaired bodies, with the consequence that, in Paterson and Hughes' (1999, p. 603) terms, the impaired body is experienced "as-alien-being-in-the-world".

The body is simultaneously there but not there, characterised by material practices (i.e. moving from room to room, bathing, etc.) which draw attention to 'out-of-place' bodies, or bodies unable to operate wholly in environments characterised by the embodied norms of society.

For most respondents, living in the home is achieved by accepting, and adapting to, the standards of design that reflect the primacy of non-impaired bodies. While respondents often expressed anger about this, they felt that there were few options open to them. For instance, Joe commented on the unfairness of imposing on him domestic design that tended to amplify, and draw attention to, his impairment: "If I try and use that room then it only shows up that my body isn't up to it … it's not me though, it's the lack of space in there." However, he felt he had no option but to compromise, although he felt it was all one-sided in that disabled people are the ones who have to take what is on offer. As he said: "You compromise all the time. I hear people all the time saying 'It's good, I can get by, I make do, I'm quite happy'. I don't hear that from temporarily able-bodied people. They're not saying that about their homes."

The feelings of a state of body-out-of-place in the home were, more often than not, related to design details, or the micro-architecture, of the dwelling. Thus, it was often the subtle aspects of the design of the home environment that caused most problems. For instance, John referred to the fitting of an electric window to permit ease of opening of windows by the use of remote control. However, as he said:

I mean, my electric window is beautiful, wonderful, but the switch is on the pelmet [laughter] and out of reach. It's like when they fitted it they didn't look at me or ask me if it was OK. They just did it.

Impairment and De-stabilising the Meaning of the Home

Binns and Mars (1984, p. 664) suggest that the ideal of the home as sanctuary is undermined in circumstances where the home environment becomes "the product of withdrawal from wider social networks". Indeed, for some respondents, broader social, attitudinal and environmental circumstances, beyond the immediate confines of their home, had led them to 'stay-at-home', rarely venturing beyond the front door. For instance, Harry recounted demeaning reactions from 'friends' concerning his inability to access, unaided, stepped thresholds into their homes: "they think I'm being awkward … it's not as friendly an atmosphere as what it used to be, when I was up and walking … people say I'm seeking attention or whatever. They're wrong about that [laughs]." For Harry, it has become easier not to visit friends or to expose himself to possible ridicule or suggestions that 'he's putting it on'. Rather, as Harry said, "I spend most time indoors, and it feels like I'm confined to quarters."

In other instances, social interactions have been curtailed or have stopped altogether. As Harry noted, "I don't get invited to some of the parties any more, as they've got to lift me into the house."

Likewise, Elaine said that because of her weakening muscles, and physical impediments on the pavement and the lack of access into the local shops, she had stopped going out. For her, 'it all stops at the garden gate'.

Others recalled the loss of independence and personal control in their home due to interactions between impairment and physical design.

For Trish, the home became associated with a complete loss of independence and the performance of personal acts in degrading situations. As she said:

My husband used to carry me upstairs and there were so many practical issues. He had to get my dresses from upstairs and I had to use a bucket for a toilet and I had to be bathed on towels downstairs in the living room. The experience made me realise that the correlation between psychological and physical states should not be under-estimated.

For others too, the home was less a place of independence and more a context in which things had to be done for them. Thus, everyday household activities became, with the onset of impairment, more or less impossible to do without some assistance. Moreover, the idea that the home might provide for personal privacy is not always the case.

Such experiences were destabilising for these respondents and left them feeling that they had little control over circumstances. This, then, suggests that the nature of privacy in the home is never stable or guaranteed and, as Allan and Crow (1989, p. 3) suggest, "an individual's ability to secure some degree of privacy is conditional". Likewise, the idea of the home as a retreat, haven, or place of sanctuary and security is not always borne out, particularly in a context where a deteriorating body requires third party care and attention.

Insecurity was also felt by those who said that they had attracted negative comment when outside, and did not want to draw attention to the fact that an impaired person lived in the house. For Harry: "you want to blend in and not reveal that you can't walk. It makes you a target." Others concurred and some respondents were wary about fitting a ramp up to their front door for fear of it labelling them as 'defective' and 'different'. As Carol said:

I mean, I want to be able to live in my home but I don't want it to be screaming at anybody that walks in, to be inhibited because a disabled person lives here. That's the other thing, you know. I'm very, very conscious of this because one of my sons particularly found it very, very difficult to come to terms with it, and I don't want it screaming 'Oh dear, this poor woman lives on her own, she's in a wheelchair'.

This, then, illustrates, the point, that the external physical features of the house convey subtle shades of meaning and act as signifiers to the outside world.

Resisting Domestic Design and Generating Usable Spaces

In concurring with Allen (2000), I suggest that disabled people are not passive victims of insensitive design, nor necessarily resigned to dependence on others to facilitate aspects of their home lives. Far from it, the experiences of disabled people in this study, and elsewhere, illustrate the capacity to generate usable spaces out of the social and physical impediments that are placed in their way. For instance, Allen *et al.* (2002, p. 65) note that parents of vision-impaired children do not necessarily see them as victims of the built environment. This is because most are able to construct what Allen *et al.* (2002) refer to as 'memory maps' or guides of their home and neighbourhood environment that permit them to navigate, with relative ease, from one space to another.

The strategies deployed by respondents were, in part, dependent on income and social class. For respondents on low incomes, and living in council or housing association property, it was often a struggle to get things changed. As Jenny observed:

If you've got no income and Social Services are making the alterations for you, you will have had a fight that's probably gone on three or four years to get it, and the chances of you succeeding again getting it if you move to another house is not very high, so you never want to move, you stay where you are.

Others concurred in expressing their frustration with delays in getting adaptations done. As

Stan noted, "this is one of the arguments I've had with Social Services for years and years and years. If you need handrails and a ramp, or a toilet adapted, you need it quickly … you know, when you're disabled you need help quickly."

In contrast, those with higher incomes, and who owned their home, had more choice about how and when to adapt the domestic environment. Jenny expressed a common view: "If you're middle class and you can afford to do it in the manner that I have, and you've got an income, you're earning money … then you do it."

Regardless of income or tenure, respondents were able to rearrange layout by, primarily, 'clearing up the clutter' and making space to facilitate ease of movement and use of rooms. Jenny moved into her house when she could walk and furnished it throughout. As she said: "the house was designed for no more than a walking disabled person … and now it's inconvenient for me." However, her more or less constant use of a wheelchair now means that "if I wanted to get into a room I have to push chairs out of the way to get to the far wall … there was furniture everywhere". For Jenny, the solution was to sell the furniture, or, as she said: "I've just chucked everything out and we're now in a situation where there's not even any chairs for anybody to sit on." Others have done similar things and Heather, living in housing association property, "got rid of the big furniture and put up grab rails everywhere".

Like Heather, other respondents have changed aspects of the micro-architecture of their homes that had previously made a big difference to their mobility around the home. For Carol, the floor surface had to be changed when she became dependent on a wheelchair. Likewise, Jim persuaded the local authority to provide a grant to adapt the downstairs toilet door, so that it now slides open and permits easier access than was hitherto the case.

For most respondents the need to think ahead is paramount because of the knowledge that bodily deterioration will necessitate different ways of using the home. Jenny bought her present house when she was able to walk without the use of a wheelchair, but knew that, in time, she would be dependent on a wheelchair to get around. As she explained:

I bought the house because it was very flat. I was actually going round saying to my relatives 'Oh, this will do for a wheelchair'. And they were going 'Don't be stupid, you'll never go in a wheelchair'. And I always sort of knew my limitations; I knew it was on the cards.

However, such behaviour and/or actions appear to be no more than 'little victories' in a context whereby the design of most homes remains resistant to the needs of impaired bodies. Indeed, respondents were of the view that the only way to (re)claim domestic space for impairment is if professional experts, such as builders, architects and occupational therapists, respond to experiential information and guidance provided by disabled people themselves. Others concurred, with Jane expressing her frustration at the attitudes of the builders who had adapted her house: "that's the interesting assumption about disabled people, isn't it, we obviously have got nothing to contribute back."

CONCLUSIONS

The testimonials in this paper suggest that there are tensions between ideal conceptions of the home and the material, lived, domestic realities of disabled people. While aspects of the home may well provide for privacy, sanctuary, security and other aspects of 'ideal' domestic habitation, such provisions are always conditional, contingent, never secure, and likely to be challenged by, amongst other things, the onset and development of bodily impairment. However, explorations of the meaning of the home, and housing studies more generally, rarely consider the body and impairment and its interactions with domestic space. This is curious because impairment is a significant, and intrinsic, condition of human existence and can affect anyone at any time. In this sense, a person's feelings about, and experiences of, the home cannot be dissociated from their corporeality or the organic matter and material of the body.

Indeed, dominant representations of the meaning of the home, propagated by builders, architects and others, are underpinned by specific conceptions of embodied domestic spaces that do little to acknowledge the possibilities of bodily impairment as part of domestic habitation. Such representations revolve around the home as part of the ideal of family life, in which non-impaired bodies with relative independence of movement and mobility are paramount. The dominance of non-impaired carnality is reflected in physical design that, as the testimonials suggested, rarely includes the fixtures, fittings or spaces to enable the ease of use of domestic spaces by disabled people. Rather, such spaces, for many disabled people, are potentially disembodying in the sense that they deny the presence or possibility of bodily impairment and, as a consequence, are likely to reduce the quality of their home life.

Bodily impairment is neither fixed nor static, or something that acquires meaning or function independent from social context or setting. Rather, as respondents noted, their home lives revolved around resolving issues relating to functioning in restrictive spaces, in contexts whereby bodily changes, particularly organic deterioration, were manifest realities. Housing quality, then, cannot be understood or defined separately from an understanding of the interactions between organic matter and the domestic setting, of which physical design is a component part. This should be one focus for seeking to develop an approach to housing studies that recognises the importance of embodiment in influencing people's experiences of, and meanings attributed to, the home.

REFERENCES

Allan, Graham. 1985. *Family Life: Domestic Roles and Social Organisation* (Oxford, Blackwell).

Allan, Graham and Crow, Graham. (eds) 1989. *Home and Family: Creating the Domestic Sphere* (London, Allen and Unwin).

Allen, Chris. 2000. On the 'physiological dope' problematic in housing and illness research: towards a critical realism of home and health, *Housing, Theory and Society*, 17, pp. 49–67.

Allen, Chris. 2003. On the socio-spatial worlds of visual impaired children, *or, Merleau-Ponty + Bourdieu = the socio-spatiality of the habitus*, *Urban Studies*, 41(3), pp. 487–506.

Allen, Chris, Milner, Joe and Price, Dawn. 2002. *Home is Where the Start is: The Housing and Urban Experiences of Visually Impaired Children* (York, Joseph Rowntree Foundation).

Binns, David and Mars, Gerald. 1984. Family, community and unemployment: a study in change, *Sociological Review,* 32, pp. 662–695.

Cooper, Marcus Clare. (1995. *House as a Mirror of Self* (Berkeley, CA, Conan Press).

Gilman, Charlotte Perkins. (2002) *The Home: Its Work and Influence* (London, Alta Mira Press).

Gleeson, Brendan. (1998. *Geographies of Disability* (London, Routledge).

Goldsack, Laura. (1999. A haven in a heartless world? Women and domestic violence, in: T. Chapman and J. Hockey (eds) *Ideal Homes? Social Change and Domestic Life,* pp. 121–132 (London, Routledge).

Gurney, Craigh. (1990. *The meaning of the home in the decade of owner occupation.* Working Paper 88 (Bristol, School for Advanced Urban Studies, University of Bristol, SAUS Publications).

Gurney, Craigh. 2000. Transgressing private–public boundaries in the home: a sociological analysis of the coital noise taboo, *Venereology,* 13, pp. 39–46.

Gurney, Craigh. undated. 'The neighbours didn't dare complain': some taboo thoughts on the regulation of noisy bodies and the disembodied housing imagination. Available at <www.cf.ac.uk/uwcc/cplan/enhr/ files/Gurney-C2.html>.

Hockey, Jenny. 1999. The ideal of home, in: T. Chapman and J. Hockey (eds) *Ideal Homes? Social Change and Domestic Life,* pp. 108–118 (London, Routledge).

Imrie, Rob. 2003. Housing quality and the provision of accessible homes, *Housing Studies,* 18, pp. 395–416.

Imrie, Rob and Hall, Peter. 2001. *Inclusive Design: Developing and Designing Accessible Environments* (London, Spon Press).

Leder, Drew. 1990. *The Absent Body* (Chicago, IL, Chicago University Press).

Lefebvre, Henri. 1991. *The Production of Space* (Oxford, Blackwell).

Lewin, Fereshtah. 2001. The meaning of home amongst elderly immigrants: directions for future research and theoretical development, *Housing Studies,* 16, pp. 353–370.

McDowell, Linda. 1983. Towards an understanding of the gender divisions of urban space, *Society and Space,* 1, pp. 59–72.

Merleau-Ponty, Maurice. 1962. *The Phenomenology of Perception* (London, Routledge and Kegan Paul).

Merleau-Ponty, Maurice. 1963. *The Primacy of Perception* (Evanston, IL, Northwestern University Press).

Millen, Dianne. 1997. Some methodological and epistemological issues raised by doing feminist research on non-feminist women, *Sociological Research Online, 2.* Available at <www.socresonline.org.uk>.

Oldman, Christine and Beresford, Bryony. 2000. Home sick home: using the housing experience of disabled children to suggest a new theoretical framework, *Housing Studies,* 15, pp. 429–442.

Oliver, Michael. 1990. *The Politics of Disablement* (Basingstoke, Macmillan).

Paterson, Kevin and Hughes, Bill. 1999. Disability studies and phenomenology: the carnal politics of everyday life, *Disability and Society,* 14, pp. 597–611.

Saunders, Peter. 1989. The meaning of 'home' in contemporary English culture, *Housing Studies,* 4, pp. 177–192.

Saunders, Peter. 1990. *A Nation of Home Owners* (London, Unwin Hyman).

Saunders, Peter. and Williams, Peter. 1988. The constitution of the home: towards a research agenda, *Housing Studies,* 3, pp. 81–93.

Sixsmith, Andrew and Sixsmith, Judith. 1991. Transitions in home experience in later life, *The Journal of Architectural and Planning Research,* 8, pp. 181–191.

Twigg, Julia. 2002. The body in social policy: mapping a territory, *Journal of Social Policy,* 31, pp. 421–439.

26
You Got to Remember You Live in Public Housing

Place-making in an American Housing Project (2008)

Talja Blokland

We navigate through our everyday lives with mental geographies of places we like, dislike, fear or call home. These simplified images:

> serve us well by reducing the complexity of the urban landscape. … They help us decide where to live, where to walk at night, and when to start worrying about our children's absence; they help us make a welter of day-to-day decisions in which what we do depends heavily on where we think we are.
> (Suttles 1972: 4)

Since the early Chicago School, urban sociologists have argued that people's definitions of situations often include spatial referents. Geographers have also proclaimed that they, too, should investigate symbolic, cultural or even mental understandings of space. We have since learnt to see places as socially constructed. How, then, do we *socially* make places?

This paper, drawing on Tilly's work (Tilly 1998), argues that mental geographies come about *relationally*. People not only make places as articulations of social relationships, but through place-making processes also create, renew and restructure such relationships. As stigmatization is a special form of these general processes, a stigmatized neighbourhood can empirically shed light on such processes, and help explore the potential of relational sociology for analysing place. I turn to a low-income African American housing development in a New England college town for an ethnographic description.

THE GHETTO: CASE AND METHODS

"The Ghetto", as residents named their public housing development in a New England college town, consisted of two dead-end streets of 240 units of 2–4 bedrooms. The apartments had replaced the crowded tenements in a predominantly Italian 19th-century working-class area in 1942. According to Housing Authority statistics, most residents lived below the poverty line. More than 85% of the households were headed by a single female with child(ren). Most were African American, a handful Hispanic or mixed race. The area was known for high crime rates. Businesses deemed it unsafe for deliveries (a designated "two-person area" for the telephone repairmen, for example, and Chinese food was delivered only to a corner) or loans (the postcode bars residents from a rent-to-buy furniture shop).

Between 2000 and 2004, I conducted ethnography here in three long stretches over a period of two years, consisting of participant observation, unstructured interviewing and taped conversations. Structured interviews were conducted with a sample of 36 residents who I was not close to. I focus on a community meeting that took place after a number of drug-related murders.

Ms. Magnolia, chair of the tenants' organization of the Ghetto, had called a meeting with public officials a few days after another local boy was shot dead.

Ms. Magnolia opened the meeting by saying that they had called it because "the police has been chasing us out here until it got to the point of a boy being killed out here" and "we are not secure". She connected the shootings, safety, and intensive police control. The police captain leaned over the table and said that "no-one was chasing anyone", but that he first wanted to point out something about trespassing—the dead boy had had a trespassing notice:

> It doesn't matter if you have a relative here, or even if your own mother lives here, if you have been involved in a problem here, or anywhere else on housing authority property in the city, then you get a notice you're not allowed on the property, that is Trespassing of the 1st degree. That is how we try to help people keeping people out, and it is your responsibility too to keep them out.

After all, residents were responsible for their guests. He thus ignored the ambivalent meaning of "safety" and excluded those who were stopped by the police from the residents, easily dividing decent residents and unwelcome others. Nobody asked the residents what they thought of this, nor did they take the floor. The Housing Authority managers added that residents should only stick to their lease: "In the lease it says it all, in the lease it says that you are responsible for your guests … this is nothing new." Such trespassing regulations were meant to work "alongside residents" on "improving their living conditions", and residents themselves could "play a part in increasing awareness about the regulations". *They* had to make sure that people in *their* community obeyed the rules (that the Housing Authority had set).

The deputy director illustrated how in an elderly housing complex elsewhere in town residents talked to newcomers to explain the rules. She suggested that here, too, they could meet with new residents or those they didn't know. The social services manager called this a good idea "but it needed to have people on the committee that were going to do this that were not abusing the system themselves, that were not breaking the law themselves". She looked straight at Ms. Magnolia, who had several sons in and out of jail. Rumours had it that dealers paid Ms. Magnolia "to give back to the community", and financed some of the tenants' organization's activities. The manager carried on: "You got to remember you're living in public housing. You are being subsidized, you have to accept that when you live in a subsidized apartment you have to be able to live by the rules."

Ms. Magnolia had visibly had enough of listening, and said she thought there "must be a way of securing the people here", maybe by putting up a fence to have a "gated community". This again was ambivalent: people felt they were living "in a prison camp" as the control exercised was humiliating and experienced as a privacy violation. They also felt, however, that a lot of the drug dealing attracted "suburban" customers. These in turn attracted outside dealers who engaged in deadly competition. A gated community would reduce the clientele, and thus economic vitality of the neighbourhood.

Nobody reacted to her technical suggestion, which contrasted with the community-solutions of the officials, so another ambivalence was not addressed. Instead, the police captain moved back to a focus on residents, who he said were too passive: "You can help policing this community. They [pointing to the officials present] all go home. They don't live here. You have to be the eyes and ears of a community." People should report what they saw to the police, and should call when "someone was there who shouldn't be there". Ms. Magnolia muttered "I agree, I agree" but "even so", it was impossible because "how to do it?" Kyara, a well-dressed young woman, who worked as a catering worker at a college, and mother of a toddler, spoke up that "there is nothing we can do about it". It was impossible to report: "Who is me to say who belongs here? This guy, he is standing outside of my house, hanging right in front of my window. I telling him to go someplace else? No sir. I must be realistic…. They know I called the cops. They know."

Joe tried to change the subject: "The guy that got killed, he was my cousin. He came to here to bring his baby's mother some breakfast. And he got killed. What I am talking about is trying to improve it here." Again, the responsibility of the residents was core of the reply, when the deputy director said there was "a lot the residents themselves can do", because there "were lots of housing projects where they had had similar problems", and where things improved after "residents got together to work on safety issues". She again demarcated easily between residents and outsiders, and the singular understanding of an ownership of place, and ignored the relationship of the victim to the community.

When the example of the elderly complex was brought up again, Keesha, a full-time nurse assistant and single mother of three children under the age of 10 years, commented that elderly people "stick together" and young people "are not like that and have their own lives and things to take care of", so that it was not as easy as was suggested. However, the people behind the table collectively argued against her, speaking at the same time, that "it is all based on the people" and that "right now they were scared", but that they now had "to set their rules" in the streets. The social services manager said that with "the attitude that is presented here, you're feeding into it, you're encouraging it". So: "Don't just stand there, hold out your hand!"

The atmosphere became a little tense; people all talked at the same time. Before the discussion evolved into a full-blown argument and after some further belittling remarks about residents having boyfriends staying who were not on their lease, the police captain interrupted, calmly:

> Let me give you an analysis from our side…. When an area starts to look dilapidated, things get worse and worse. And that's what you need to do here. I drive through here every day on my way to work. And I see people throwing their trash out. We have scheduled pick-ups…. But there is a lot of junk out here.

He stressed "this is not a good living environment", because in this way people were giving the message: "these people don't care about their properties, so we might as well sell drugs out here".[1] He urged people to get together and clean up: "your kids are out there, my kids are not". A resident responded that the Housing Authority cleaners "don't do their jobs around here". A lively discussion about rubbish followed. Someone behind the table suggested that residents here could collect cans and hand them in at the shop across the road. When Kyara yelled angrily "they don't take them in large numbers!" one at the table said "well bring them one by one then" and someone else said "hand them in somewhere else!" The distance between those on either side grew: "Oh sure," Keesha said softly, "if we all had cars we could all go to Stop & Shop." Then someone said a homeless man from the shelter nearby searched the rubbish and threw things out. The property

manager asked the police captain "can he be issued a non-trespassing notice?" The police captain laughed: "sure". The social services manager then announced they should bring this meeting to an end. Ms Magnolia thanked everyone for attending and they all left.

ANALYSIS: MAKING A STIGMATIZED PLACE

The image of the participants in the meeting was thus one of a passive, if not hostile, group of residents who were uncommitted to improving their neighbourhood. It was a stigmatizing image, as it included references to dimensions of stigmatizing the poor, such as blame, social rejection, perceived danger and visible unattractiveness or disorder.

Mental geographies seen relationally carry through earlier understandings that then shape further performances. The ghetto is "a uniquely racial formation that spawns a society-wide web of material and symbolic associations between colour, place and a host of negatively valued social properties" (Wacquant 1999). The history of American public housing affected its image from its start under the New Deal, in combination with historically rooted disapproval of the poor and racism. The New Deal programs attempted to reform the economy "more to bring stability to financial institutions than to fight poverty and destitution" (Judd and Swanstrom 1994: 118). Its relief programs, however, were seen as an "embarrassing necessity" and were believed to "undercut the cherished principles of work and independence", expressing a "culture that extolled individualism, competition and hard work" in which people "were ill at ease with the idea of relief" (Judd and Swanstrom 1994: 119). The *Housing Act* (1937) and *Title III* (1949) provided housing to the very poor, but from the start this was "regarded as a welfare program for people who had failed". It passed Congress amidst intense criticism. Many local communities build it only as the price to pay for urban renewal grants. The legacy of public housing was too negative to "allow it ever to be a successful program" (Judd and Swanstrom 1994: 149). Several factors made it worse: restricted eligibility concentrated the poorest families—social mobility meant eviction;[2] as it was connected with clearance, it was built mostly in or near slum areas, not suburbs; segregation practices in the housing market were common, closing alternatives for blacks displaced by slum clearance; and cost and design restrictions, intended to avoid unfair competition, guaranteed that the units were uncomfortable: "Public housing served as a constant reminder to its tenants and everyone else that this was a grudging welfare program."

Wider historical meanings of housing projects as undesirable, temporary shelter for unsuccessful, aid-dependent people, and symbols of violence, crime and promiscuity were stored in relationships between Housing Authority officials and residents. With female-headed households, very young mothers pushing prams (seen by outsiders as "dysfunctional families"), crack-houses, a vivid underground economy, and three homicides in four years, the Ghetto may live up to this image.

Stigmatization was not based on whether or not the neighbourhood concentrated problems, but on how people attached historically embedded moral dimensions to these, or *de facto* confirmed these. This occurred in three ways.

First, the officials conveyed that the Ghetto was a place where people did not care about "their community", but should. This carried through the general historical view of projects as populated by lethargic people living in dependency, uncommitted to anything. The thought that welfare dependency encouraged the erosion of values of self-reliance has sunken in so deeply and widely in dominant discourse and fitted so well with the pre-existing ideology that such assumed idleness informed the professionals' arguments. They were not alone. Residents did so too, as we will see.

Secondly, they affirmed the historical understanding of the housing projects as temporary accommodation until one had a "normal" place to live. As a social worker of the housing authority said: "it's temporary, you're not supposed to live there forever, it's just a place to live until you get back on your feet". Public housing was not a right that came with entitlements, but a favour that came with duties, such as obeying rules.

Thirdly, Housing Authority officials distinguished between deserving residents suffering from crime and undeserving "guys" causing trouble – as did service providers, the police and volunteers from charities. The violence then was a matter of a lack of residents' participation in their neighbourhood, allowing worthless "guys" to take over the public space, intimidating residents.

In these ways, then, history informed current understandings; such understandings affected interactions that then informed new storytelling. The officials, occupying positions of authority, dominated the labelling process, but the residents also engaged in such labelling: tensions were resolved when the homeless man who roamed the rubbish bins became the culprit. The answer to the concerns of residents about safety in their neighbourhood where a child was killed thus became the issuing of a trespassing notice to a homeless man.

The sharp line that officials and others drew between residents echoed the distinction between respectable poor and deviants. The women at the meeting could not afford to lose their position as "respectable", which was constructed by their very presence there, so they kept quiet. And by not addressing the ambivalences, or, as did Ms. Magnolia, only implicitly so, they helped reproduce the either/or opposition as well as the imagery of residents as passive victims, depending on others to take care of their issues, conforming with the historic imagery of the welfare-dependent poor in public housing.

Residents brought their relational positions to each other and to "other" others from other settings into the place-making process at the meeting. It would be a mistake to regard "the residents" as a coherent group with a single set of shared experiences. There was a lot of variety in relations, adaptations, resilience and exploitations of the stigma attached to place, race, class and gender. The pattern of emulation that occurred at the meeting, where residents showed disengagement and withdrawal rather than activism for change, reflected more widely shared positions, visibly in other settings.

They acted on a positioning of themselves as "not really belonging" in the housing projects, attaching value to dis-identifying oneself from "the community". Sometimes, they "managed" the stigma in actual interactions showing only one's "better" self and holding on to that image of being respectable.

More importantly, dis-identifying also resulted because of cultural axioms that residents included in place-making. They did not need to be told they had to remember they lived in subsidized housing—they knew, and shared the value that this was "for failures".

Thus, if the projects are meant to shelter failures temporarily, and failure is a personal shortcoming, it is not surprising that everybody whom I asked about moving plans said they were going to move out.

Only "failures" would, in short, consider the Ghetto "home". Effectively, then, one *could* not care about the community and one *could* not call it "home".

CONCLUSION

Three conclusions may be drawn from this. First, mental geographies are not given by dominant discourse. Although not all define the frame within which such images are formed, they are not simply produced by one party and taken in by others. Secondly, the creative interactions of people with unequal relational positions, such as the residents and officials at the meeting described here, may produce outcomes that alter their future relations or reinforce their understanding of each other. Thus, when the social services manager said to the residents that "you're feeding into it" she may not have been correct about the direct link between crime and collective efficacy, but *everyone* was certainly feeding into a further relational setting of passive, defiant residents and public officials holding them responsible for "their" community. And they take unexpected turns, as in the case of the trespassing notice for a homeless person, affecting the positioning of actors towards others outside the interaction.

NOTES

1 He thus presented a "broken window theses" that has "acquired iconic status in public discourse" (Innes 2004: 337), which is remarkable "because of the lack of empirical research evidence that supports the thesis".

2 This is not the case under current regulations, but as the rent is means-tested, any increase in income results in a higher rent, making it unattractive for residents to stay once they find stable employment and a decent wage.

REFERENCES

Innes, Martin. 2004. Signal crimes and signal disorders: notes on deviance as communicative action, *British Journal of Sociology*, 55(3), pp. 335–355.

Judd, Dennis R. and Swanstrom, Todd. 1994. *City Politics. Private Power and Public Policy* (New York: Harper Collins).

Suttles, Gerald D. 1972. *The Social Construction of Communities* (Chicago, IL: University of Chicago Press).

Tilly, Charles. 1998. *Durable Inequality* (Berkeley: University of California Press).

Wacquant, Loic J.D. 1999. Urban marginality in the coming millennium, *Urban Studies*, 36(10), pp. 1639–1647.

27
The House as Symbol of the Self

(1974)

Clare Cooper

My work of the last few years has comprised sociological surveys of people's responses to the designs of their houses and communication of the resultant guidelines to architects. But I have experienced a nagging doubt that I was merely scratching the surface of the true meaning of "the house." There seemed to be something far deeper and more subliminal that I was not admitting, or that my surveys and investigations were not revealing. The exciting personal discovery of the work of the psychologist Carl Jung has opened a door into another level of my own consciousness which has prompted me to consider the house from a wholly different viewpoint. This paper is a tentative initial exploration into the subject.

JUNG'S CONCEPTS OF THE COLLECTIVE UNCONSCIOUS, THE ARCHETYPE, AND THE SYMBOL

Three of the most significant contributions of Carl Jung to understanding the human psyche are the concepts of the *collective* unconscious, the archetype, and the symbol. ...

Initially embracing Freud's theories, Jung became increasingly dissatisfied as his studies of persistent motifs in his patients' dreams and fantasies, and in primitive mythology and folk tales, revealed what seemed to be *universal* patterns which could not be accounted for solely by the theory of an *individual* unconscious. He began to postulate the theory of an individual unconscious plus a universal or collective

unconscious linking man to his primitive past, and in which are deposited certain basic and timeless nodes of psychic energy, which he termed *archetypes*.

... The archetype can only provide a potential or possibility of representation in the conscious mind, for as soon as we encounter it through dreams, fantasies, or rational thought, the archetype becomes clothed in images of the concrete world and is no longer an archetype: it is an *archetypal image or symbol*. ... If we can think of the archetype as a node of psychic energy within the unconscious, then the symbol is the medium by which it becomes manifest in the here and now of space and time. Thus a symbol, although it has objective visible reality, always has behind it a hidden, profound, and only partly intelligible meaning which represents its roots in the archetype.

Although impossible for most of us to define or describe, we are all aware of the existence of something we call "self": the inner heart of our being, our soul, our uniqueness—however we want to describe it. It is in the nature of man that he constantly seeks a rational explanation of the inexplicable, and so he struggles with the questions: What is self? Why here? Why now? In trying to comprehend this most basic of archetypes—self—to give it concrete substance, man grasps at physical forms or symbols which are close and meaningful to him, and which are visible and definable. The first and most consciously selected form to represent self is the body, for it appears to be both the outward manifestation, and the encloser, of self. On a less conscious level, I believe, man also frequently selects the house, that basic protector of his internal environment (beyond skin and clothing) to represent or symbolize what is tantalizingly unrepresentable.

The French philosopher Gaston Bachelard has suggested that just as the house and the nonhouse are the basic divisions of geographic space, so the self and the nonself represent the basic divisions of psychic space (Bachelard, 1969). The house both encloses space (the house interior) and excludes space (everything outside it). Thus it has two very important and different components; its interior and its façade. The house therefore nicely reflects how man sees himself, with both an intimate interior, or self as viewed from within and revealed only to those intimates who are invited inside, and a public exterior (the *persona* or *mask*, in Jungian terms) or the self that we choose to display to others.

Most of us have had the experience of moving from one house to another, and of finding the new abode initially strange, unwelcoming, perhaps even hostile. But with time, we get used to the new house and its quirks, and it seems almost as though it gets used to us; we can relax when we return to it, put our feet up, become ourselves. But why in this particular box should we be ourselves more than in any other? It seems as though the personal space bubble which we carry with us and which is an almost tangible extension of our self expands to embrace the house we have designated as ours. As we become accustomed to, and lay claim to, this little niche in the world, we project something of ourselves onto its physical fabric. The furniture we install, the way we arrange it, the pictures we hang, the plants we buy and tend, all are expressions of our image of ourselves, all are messages about ourselves that we want to convey back to ourselves, and to the few intimates that we invite into this, our house. Thus, the house might be viewed as both an avowal of the self— that is, the psychic messages are moving from self to the objective symbol of self—and as a revelation of the nature of self; that is, the messages are moving from objective symbol back to the self. It is almost as if the house–self continuum could be thought of as both the negative and positive of a film, simultaneously.

THE HOUSE AS SYMBOL-OF-SELF: EXAMPLES FROM CONTEMPORARY ARCHITECTURE

For so-called civilized man, the conscious recognition of the symbolism of what we do, how we live, and the houses we live in, has been all but lost. But if we start to delve beneath the surface, the symbolism is still there.

In a recent study of how contemporary California suburbanites chose their homes, Berkeley sociologist Carl Werthman (1968) concluded that many people bought houses to bolster their image of self—both as an individual and as a person in a certain status position in society. In one large suburban development near San Francisco, for example, he noted that extroverted self-made businessmen tended to choose somewhat ostentatious, mock-colonial display homes, while people in the helping professions, whose goals revolved around personal satisfaction rather than financial success, tended to opt for the quieter, inward-looking architect-designed styles conforming to current standards of "good design."

In the contemporary English-speaking world, a premium is put on originality, on having a house that is unique and somewhat different from the others on the street, for the inhabitants who identify with these houses are themselves struggling to maintain some sense of personal uniqueness in an increasingly conformist world. On the other hand, one's house must not be too way-out, for that would label the inhabitant as a nonconformist, and that, for many Americans, is a label to be avoided.

The house as symbol-of-self is deeply engrained in the American ethos (albeit unconsciously for many), and this may partly explain the inability of society to come to grips with the housing problem—a problem which is quite within its technological and financial capabilities to solve and which it persistently delegates to a low level in the hierarchy of budgetary values. America is the home of the self-made man, and if the house is seen (even unconsciously) as the symbol of self, then it is small wonder that there is a resistance to subsidized housing or to the State's providing houses *for* people. The frontier image of the man clearing the land and building a cabin for himself and his family is not far behind us. To a culture inbred with this image, the house–self-identity is particularly strong. In some barely conscious way, society has decided to penalize those who, through no fault of their own cannot build, buy, or rent their own housing. They are not self-made men.

Numbers of studies in England, Australia, and the United States have indicated that when asked to describe their ideal house, people of all incomes and backgrounds will tend to describe a free-standing, square, detached, single-family house and yard. For example, in a recent survey of 748 men and women in thirty-two metropolitan areas in the US 85 percent said they preferred living in a single-family house rather than in an apartment (Michelson, 1968). It is difficult to say whether the attachment to this form is the form itself, or the fact that it subsumes territorial rights over a small portion of the earth, or the fact that apartments can rarely be owned. But we do know that almost universally the image of the high-rise building for family living is rejected. An apartment is rarely seen as home, for a house can only be seen as a free-standing house-on-the-ground.

One could argue that people have been conditioned to want this through advertising, model homes salesmanship, and the image of the good life portrayed on television. To a certain extent this must be true, but these media are in turn only reflecting what seems to be a universal need for a house form in which the self and family unit can be seen as separate, unique, private, and protected.

The contrasting views which people of different socioeconomic classes in the US have of their houses reflect again the house as a symbol-of-self in a self–world relationship. The greater are people's feelings of living in a dangerous and hostile world with constant threats to the self, the greater is the likelihood that they will regard their house as a shell, a fortress into which to retreat.

With increasing economic and psychic stability (and in some cases, these are linked), a person may no longer regard his house as a fortress-to-be-defended, but as an attractive, individual expression of self-and-family with picture windows so that neighbors can admire the inside. Thus, for many in the middle-income bracket, the house is an expression of self, rather than a defender of self. The self-and-environment are seen in a state of mutual regard instead of in a state of combat.

The fact that the decoration of the house interior often symbolizes the inhabitants' feelings about self is one that has long been recognized. It has even been suggested that the rise in popularity of the profession of interior decorating is in some way related to people's inability to make these decisions for themselves since they're not sure what their self really is. The phenomenon of people, particularly women, rearranging the furniture in their house at times of psychic turmoil or changes-in-self is a further suggestion that the house is very intimately entwined with the psyche.

In a recently published study of living rooms, Edward Laumann and James House (1972) have found that the presence or absence of certain objects are good if not perfect clues to status and attitudes. It is the living room rather than any other room in the house which provides these clues because the living room is the area where "performances" for guests are most often given, and hence the "setting" of it must be appropriate to the performance. Thus we expect that more than any other part of the home, the living room reflects the individual's conscious and unconscious attempts to express a social identity.

These are just a few examples of how the house-as-self linkage becomes manifest in individual and societal behavior and attitudes; no doubt the reader can add many more instances from his personal experience. The thesis is not a new one: but it seems that the Jungian notions of the collective unconscious, the archetype and the symbol, may offer a useful conceptual structure to tie these examples together. Since the house–self symbolism seems to arise again and again, in many disparate settings, and since there appears to be little conscious sharing of this phenomenon, it seems reasonable to suggest that it is through the medium of the collective unconscious that people are in touch with an archaic and basically similar archetype (the self) and with a symbol for that archetype that has changed little through space and time (the house).

If we start to consider the messages from the unconscious made manifest through dreams, we have even more striking evidence of the house-as-self symbol. Carl Jung (1969, pp. 182–183) in his autobiography describes quite vividly a dream of himself as house, and his explorations within it.

His own interpretation of the dream was as follows:

It was plain to me that the house represented a kind of image of the psyche—that is to say, of my then state of consciousness, with hitherto unconscious additions. Consciousness was represented by the salon. It had an inhabited atmosphere, in spite of its antiquated style.

The ground floor for the first level of the unconscious. The deeper I went, the more alien and the darker the scene became. In the cave, I discovered remains of a primitive culture, that is the world of the primitive man within myself—a world which can scarcely be reached or illuminated by consciousness. The primitive psyche of man borders on the life of the animal soul, just as the caves of prehistoric times were usually inhabited by animals before man laid claim to them.

(p. 184)

Jung describes here the house with many levels seen as the symbol-of-self with its many levels of consciousness; the descent downward into lesser known realms of the unconscious is represented by the ground floor, cellar, and vault beneath it. A final descent leads to a cave cut into bedrock, a part of the house rooted in the very earth itself. This seems very clearly to be a symbol of the collective unconscious, part of the self–house and yet, too, part of the universal bedrock of humanity.

Returning to Jung's autobiography, he describes how, later in his life, he made manifest in stone the symbol which had at times stood for self in his dreams. He describes how he yearned to put his knowledge of the contents of the unconscious into solid form, rather than just describe them in words. In the building of his house—the tower at Bollinger on Lake Zurich—he was to make "a confession of faith in stone":

At first I did not plan a proper house, but merely a kind of primitive one-storey dwelling. It was to be a round structure with a hearth in the center and bunks along the walls. I more or less had in mind an African hut where the fire, ringed with stone, burns in the middle, and the whole life of the family revolves around this center. Primitive huts concretize an idea of wholeness, a familial wholeness in which all sorts of domestic animals likewise participate. But I altered the plans even during the first stages

of building, for I felt it was too primitive. I realized it would have to be a regular two-storey house, not a mere hut crouched on the ground. So in 1923 the first round house was built, and when it was over I saw that it had become a suitable dwelling tower.

The feeling of repose and renewal that I had in this tower was intense from the start. It represented for me the maternal hearth.

(p. 250)

Feeling that something more needed to be said, four years later Jung added another building with a tower-like annex. Again, after an interval of four years, he felt the need to add more and built onto the tower a retiring room for meditation and seclusion where no one else could enter; it became his retreat for spiritual concentration. After another interval of four years he felt the need for another area, open to nature and the sky, and so added a courtyard and an adjoining loggia. The resultant quantemity pleased him, no doubt because his own studies in mythology and symbolism had provided much evidence of the completeness and wholeness represented by the figure four. Finally, after his wife's death, he felt an inner obligation to "become what I myself am," and recognized that the small central section of the house

which crouched so low and hidden was myself! I could no longer hide myself behind the "maternal" and "spiritual" towers. So in the same year, I added an upper storey to this section, which represents myself or my ego-personality. Earlier, I would not have been able to do this; I would have regarded it as presumptuous self-emphasis. Now it signified an extension of consciousness achieved in old age. With that the building was complete.

(p. 252)

Jung had thus built his house over time as a representation in stone of his own evolving and maturing psyche; it was the place, he said, where "I am in the midst of my true life, I am most deeply myself."

CONCLUSION

If there is some validity to the notion of house-as-self it goes part of the way to explain why for most people their house is so sacred and why they so strongly resist a change in the basic form which they and their fathers and their fathers' fathers have lived in since the dawn of time. Jung recognized that the more archaic and universal the archetype made manifest in the symbol, the more universal and unchanging the symbol itself. Since self must be an archetype as universal and almost as archaic as man himself, this may explain the universality of its symbolic form, the house, and the extreme resistance of most people to any change in its basic form.

This long statement on house-as-symbol-of-the-self brings me back to my original problem: how to advise architects on the design of houses for clients who are often poor, whom they will never know, let alone delve into their psychic lives or concepts of self. I have no pat answer, but if there is some validity to the concept of house-as-self, we must learn ways—through group encounters, resident-meetings, partici-pant observation, interviews—of empathizing with the users' concepts of self, and we must devise means of complementing and enhancing that image through dwelling design.

REFERENCES

Bachelard, Gaston, 1969, *The Poetics of Space*. Boston: Beacon Press.

Jung, Carl. 1969. *Man and His Symbols*. Garden City, NY: Doubleday.

Laumann, Edward and House, James. 1970. "Living room styles and social attributes: the patterning of material artifacts in a modern urban community." *Sociology and Social Research*. 54(3): 321–42.

Michelson, Stephan. 1968. *Income of Racial Minorities*. Stanford: Michelson.

Werthman, Carl. 1968. *The Social Meanings of the Physical Environment*. Berkeley: Werthman.

28
Home Rules

(1994)

Denis Wood and Robert J. Beck

What is home for a child but a field of rules? From the moment he rouses into consciousness each morning, it is a consciousness of what he must and must not do. If during the night his pillows have fallen to the floor, he must pick these up, for *pillows do not belong on the floor, they belong on the bed*. If he thinks of turning on the radio, he must keep it low, for *we do not play the radio loud before everyone is up*. If he needs to urinate, he must go to the bathroom, for we *put our wee-wee in the toilet*. If he is old enough to stand, he must lift the seat, for otherwise he might splash and spatter, and *we do not that in this house*. When he has finished he must flush the toilet—for *we always flush the toilet when we're done*—and lower the seat—*because that's how we do things around here*. He is not to sing gloriously in welcome of the day, nor dance a fandango back to his bed, nor wake his brother by eagerly whispering in his startled ear, "Quick, Watson! The game is afoot!" because *we don't wake people up until they're ready*—unless they're kids and they've got to go to school. Then the rule is, *you've got to get up in plenty of time for school!*

So many rules! No matter how you count them, the number is enormous. Is it one rule that the spoon must go to the right of the knife, and another that the knife must go to the right of the plate? Or is the way we set the table one rule altogether? Either way, the number of rules about no more than the way we eat, where we eat, when we eat, what we eat, and who eats with us is alarmingly large. Around these, like electrons about the nucleus, swarm still others, rules about how we come together to eat (for instance, *with clean hands*)

and rules about how we dissolve the meal (*may I please be excused?*) and still others about washing the dishes and putting them away and who cleans up the dining room and when and how thoroughly, though it is difficult to say which rules swarm around which others—hierarchies are hard to see through the haze of rules, and those that at first blush seem superordinate often turn out to be no more than vague (*you know better than that*).

Hundreds of rules? If the meaning of rule is taken narrowly (*those spoons go in the drawer to the right of the stove*), there are more likely thousands. Yet without them the spoons might end up anywhere, *would* end up anywhere, out in the sandbox when it's time to eat, or down at the bottom of the creek, though why would anyone care, dinner would be ... dinner *wouldn't* be, there wouldn't be any dinner, no sitting down together, no shared breaking of bread, no shared gulping of milk (*if you're going to gulp your milk like that, you can just go out to the kitchen*). Without the rules the home is not a home, it is a house, it is a sculpture of wood and nails, of plumbing and wiring, of wallpaper and carpet.

The question that the teacher asked the student, "You wouldn't do that at home, would you?" takes as granted the universality of the rules, which, we pretend, either make sense or are natural, or both, and so, like sunlight, are always and everywhere the same. Rules are justified as rational—it is demonstrated that failure to comply leads to catastrophe (*if everybody talked at the same time, no one would be able to understand them*)—or as no more than simple codifications of human behavior, the way everyone has always acted (*a man never wears a hat inside a building*). That the very necessity of saying the rule denies the foundations on which these justifications are erected is ignored or denied: but how else to expect obedience without coercion? Or else there *is* recourse to coercion (*if you're not going to do what I say, you can just go up to your room*), the issue of justification is never broached, and rules are emitted as edicts ex cathedra, often precisely because they make no sense (*I know you don't like what they gave you, but you have to thank them for it anyway*) or because the natural way is condemned (*I know it's difficult, but you must control yourself*). Nevertheless, whether rational, natural, or arbitrary, the expectation always is that they will provide guides for the conduct of actions everywhere (*we expect you to be as well behaved at Greg's house as you are at home*).

But at the same time it is widely acknowledged that when in Rome one does as the Romans do—or at least that when having dinner at the Schaffners' one does as the Schaffners do (*if they insist on saying grace, the least you can do is wait until they're done before you start eating*). But it's not just the Schaffners; other homes are legion, there are many Romes, and any number of places, times, and conditions under which the rules are expected to be adapted, bent, or canceled (*yes, but you're supposed to use your head*). Nor is it only that everyone agrees that the behavior appropriate to the beach might be inappropriate at a ball. It is that there are rules observed at school which are not observed on the street, rules observed in the playground which are not observed at home, and rules observed in the living room which are not observed in the bathroom. The pretense to universality crumbles under the demands of every specific site (culture is concrete: it is not manifested in general, but necessarily in situ), and although people *say* the rules, the rules are embodied in specific actions and things. To enter a room is to find oneself immediately amid objects whose character and arrangement admit only of certain possibilities, it is always to enter a unique system of rules. But what is the room?

To say. "To enter a room is to find oneself immediately amid objects whose character and arrangement admit of certain possibilities" is not to lie, but only to unfold sequentially (that is, in time) an experience of simultaneity (that is, of space) for one does not first enter a room, second, perceive objects in it, and third, attach significance to them (language makes us do that), but one enters all at once this room/objects/significance-thing.

The walls and floor do not speak before, or after, the rest of the room. They are not apart, not other, from the rest of the room. The room without objects and the meanings they shed is another room, it is not this one, it is not the one we entered. In our human living, the petty kingdoms ruled quite independently by architect and decorator and sociologist have no independence: it is not the painted plaster alone that sings to us, but whether something hangs upon it. And if it is a mirror, the song is other than if it is a painting or a print or a calendar whose nudes cradle in their creamy arms replacement parts for pumps and fans.

Which is not to deny the walls, not to deny the volume of air, not to deny the doors or the windows or that quality of sunlight which at any rate at night ceases pouring through them. We have no wish to deny the room in the experience; but to reduce the experience to the room is to leave life for architecture, as it is to leave life for the social sciences when the experience is boiled down to its meaning, or to move into a furniture store when all that is regarded are the furnishings. Even to refer to them as furnishings is to miss the point, for few rooms are furnished; they are not stages set by a designer on which some actors will recite their lines, they are not settings: they are the resultant—in the sense of a sum of vectors—of a living.

THE ROOM IS AN EXPRESSION OF VALUES

This is not to say that there exists between the room and the values it incarnates an isomorphism, or that the room may not constitute itself an attempted deception, fraud, or illusion. The expression of values in a room is neither certain nor univocal. It is constrained by the available resources (the room is an economy), or the values are self-contradictory and the room must represent one position at the expense of the other (the room is an interpretation), or the room variously embodies the values (the room is a performance), or it embodies yesterday's values (the room is an archeological site) or the values of one's parents (the room is an echo, a memory, a shrine). Moreover, the room may be constrained to express the values of more than a single person, and one expression may be garbled by that of another, or unnaturally reinforced, or completely canceled. Or a novel expression may be observed, the resultant purely of the simultaneous expression of unrelated values: a room may embody the values of both husband and wife, for instance, each imperfectly, and the resultant expression may be of a certain sociability or sense of compromise. Or a rented room may express the values of both owner and occupant, and thus lend substance to no more than an empty and conceivably unintended sense of subordination (as when the bare walls of the occupant substantiate nothing but the owner's proscription of putting holes in them).

Because it is not presumed that children will be capable of reading these values, the presence of children in a room precipitates a veritable orgy of rule enunciations: *don't touch, be careful, that's fragile, stay away from that table, don't sit in that chair, that clock's not something to play with, NO RUNNING IN THE LIVING ROOM!* It is like lowering the cathode into an old-fashioned battery: immediately a stream of electrons is stripped from the anode. So too the introduction of kids into a room strips rules from every space or object the kids approach, rules dissociate themselves from walls and floor (*I don't want to see any dirty hand marks on these walls; don't just leave your stuff all over the floor*), from glass surfaces and wooden ones (*please keep your fingerprints off the windows; you know putting your wet glass down there is going to leave a ring, why do you do that?*), from individual objects and the room as a whole (*you are not to touch those speakers; when people are talking in the living room, you don't just barge in and interrupt*). No part or aspect of the room escapes being implicated in this reaction whereby values are transformed into rules. To put it slightly differently, kids excite adults to express the values manifested in the room as—in the form of—prescriptive rules. This enables the adults to *maintain* their values (by protecting the room from the barbarians,

from the kids) at the same time that it enables them to *reproduce* them (that is, to instill the values in the barbarians, to inject them into the kids through the hypodermic of the rules).

"Don't leave *Tintins* on the table."

"Don't play with anything that will scratch it up."

"Try to keep your fingers off the table."

"Don't lift the glass part off."

"Don't put your feet on the table."

"Don't leave your stuff on the table."

Why not? the kid asks and whatever the answer it is clear that the voices heard dimly through these rules are anything but those of Comfort and Convenience. Civilized folk can play the civil game of subtle deceptions in which none are taken in but all pretend to be, but the imperatives educed by kids cut through even honest ambiguity, slice through to the parent rock from which all the rest is made. It is this property that has determined our dependence on the rules, not merely our study of them: in their utterance, preserved against our forgetting in the perfect memories of kids, the mask is dropped: the world otherwise so transparent (*it is only a coffee table*) and natural (*what else could you put there?*) is suddenly opaque (*but what is a coffee table?*) and cultural (*how about a fire pit?*). Linking the rules through their codes to the voices which speak through them points to a network of consistencies that is no more than another way of saying *culture*, no more than another way of recognizing and reaching the boundaries of a freedom which is essentially illusory and in any event entirely contingent. Or is it real, but unused? It makes a difference, this distinction, but only at the level of the parent rock. One's culture may be constructed, not inherited, but given the culture, the rooms we live are granted too, these rooms which for children first and last are fields of rules, fields of rules established by the things whose nature (as we say, but really whose culture) is renounced by the voices whose timbre is most clearly caught … in the rules.

29
Home

Territory and Identity (2000)

J. Macgregor Wise

Gilles Deleuze and Félix Guattari relate a story of a child in the dark. The child, 'gripped with fear, comforts himself by singing under his breath' (1987: 311). The song is calming, a stability amidst the chaos, the beginning of order. The song marks a space, the repetition of the simple phrases structures that space and creates a milieu. The milieu is 'a block of space-time constituted by the periodic repetition of the component' (1987: 313). The song begins a home, the establishment of a space of comfort. Home is not an originary place from which identity arises. It is not the place we 'come from'; it is a place we are. Home and territory: territory and identity. This essay is about home and identity, though home and identity are not the same. They are of course inextricably linked, and they are both the product of territorializing forces.

We begin with the tunes that we hum to accompany ourselves, to fill a void, to reassure ourselves. Doing so, we create a milieu. Whistle while you work; whenever I feel afraid I whistle a happy tune. Songbirds mark space, an area of influence, by sound. The bass-heavy rhythm pounding from a car driving by shapes the space of the street, changes the character of that space. Heads turn (toward, away), feelings (repulsion, identification, recognition) arise. The resonant space thus created is a milieu. Milieus cross, 'pass into one another; they are essentially communicating' (Deleuze and Guattari, 1987: 313); rhythms blend and clash. The car and its occupants cross from one milieu to the next as they venture down the street; a figure on the sidewalk is enveloped in the bubble of sound, by the milieu, and is then released

again as the car turns the corner down by the light. The street had its milieus before the car arrived (quiet suburban, congested downtown) which are altered by the arrival of the car and its rhythm, but reassert themselves after it leaves.

But space is marked, and shaped, in other ways as well. It is marked physically, with objects forming borders, walls and fences. Staking a claim, organizing, ordering. The marker (wall, road, line, border, post, sign) is static, dull, and cold. But when lived (encountered, manipulated, touched, voiced, glanced at, practised) it radiates a milieu, a field of force, a shape of space. Space is in continual motion, composed of vectors, speeds. It is 'the simultaneous co-existence of social interrelations at all geographical scales, from the intimacy of the household to the wide space of transglobal connections' (Massey, 1994: 168).

Beyond the walls and streets of built place and the song of the milieu, we mark out places in many ways to establish places of comfort. A brief list of ways of marking: we may mark space more subtly by placing objects (a coat saves the seat), or by arranging our stuff (to make sure no one sits beside us on the bus or the bench) or even our bodies (posture opens and closes spaces; legs stretched out, newspaper up). Smoke from a cigarette marks space (different types of cigarettes, like clove, inflect the shape of the space, and then there are pipes, cigars, reefers) as do spices and scents. Symbols also mark space from clothing style (preppie, biker, grunge) to words on a t-shirt, but also graffiti, posters, and so on. The very words we use, the language we speak, the accent we speak it in, the ideas we expound on, have an effect on the space about us (attracts or repels others, drawing some together around the same theme, or tune). In and of themselves markers are traces of movement that has passed. 'To live means to leave traces', as Benjamin once wrote. And as Ivan Illich put it: 'all living is dwelling, the shape of a dwelling. To dwell means to live the traces that past living has left. The traces of dwellings survive, as do the bones of people.'

As practised, our life-world is flooded by the variant radiance of the milieus. Each milieu opens up onto others; indeed, it is these connections with other milieu beyond the immediate place that give the markers their resonance—'the identity of place is in part constructed out of positive interrelations with elsewhere' (Massey, 1994: 169). An encountered photograph glows with memories (though not necessarily nostalgia) of experience, of history, of family, friends. What creates that glow is the articulation of subject (homemaker) to object (home-marker), caught up in a mutual becoming-home. But that becoming opens up onto other milieus, other markers, other spaces (distant in space and/or time). One's apartment opens up onto a distant living room in a house far away, or onto a beach with those waves. But it not only articulates with a then (memory-space), but nows (that building has been pulled down, he's now living in Phoenix, she's in law school). The milieu opened up to is not just memory, not just the 'real', but also imagined places (where one has never been, photographs of objects that never existed, at least *in that way*). And it is not just photographs that open up in this way (see Barthes' *Camera Lucida*), but all markers. A small figurine—a Ganesha, the elephant-headed Hindu god—sits on the shelf above my desk. Its milieu-radiance comes from associated meanings (Ganesha helps one overcome obstacles, an empowering reminder while at work), a childhood in New Delhi, my father who purchased the idol, and so on. No space is enclosed, but is always multidimensional, resonant and open to other spaces.

What creates the *territory* is an accretion of milieu effects. Each milieu affects the space, bends it, inflects it, shapes it. Compound these effects, but then make these effects expressive rather than functional (Deleuze and Guattari, 1987: 315). The resultant space is the territory. Territories are not milieus. 'A territory borrows from all the milieus; it bites into them, seizes them bodily (although it remains vulnerable to

intrusions). It is built from aspects or portions of milieus' (Deleuze and Guattari, 1987: 314). A territory is an *act*, territorialization, the expression of a territory. The car with its rhythm, discussed earlier, creates a territory when the space it moves through does not just react to it, but when the car and its music expresses something. Though some objects are unique in the resonance they provide (the only photograph of a great-grandparent, a cherished childhood toy), what is most important for the milieu is the effect of the object rather than the object itself, the effects on the space. In terms of territory, what is important is how the object expresses (e.g. a home). So one might rid oneself of all one's possessions each time one moves, but might recreate a similar space, a similar home, with a similar feel (a sense of light, of leisure, of tension) in the next place, drawing around oneself an expressive space from a variety of markers and milieus. One makes oneself at home (and, indeed, is often asked to do just that).

My office in early morning reflected sunlight: most wall-space is covered in over-laden bookshelves, what's free is papered with calendars and posters from old conferences. The surface of my desk is well-hidden under rather random-seeming stacks of papers. I settle into my chair and turn on the computer, log on to email—a link from this space to a broader world (often to spaces of colleagues in offices much like mine). The shelf above my desk is cluttered with photographs, two Hindu idols, a Darth Vader action figure (facing off against figures of Scully and Mulder), a Batman PEZ dispenser, a dried rose.

Home, likewise, is a collection of milieus, and as such is the organization of markers (objects) and the formation of space. But home, more than this, is a territory, an expression. Home can be a collection of objects, furniture, and so on that one carries with one from move to move. Home is the feeling that comes when the final objects are unpacked and arranged and the space seems complete (or even when one stares at unpacked boxes imagining). The markers of home, however, are not simply inanimate objects (a place with stuff), but the presence, habits, and effects of spouses, children, parents, and companions. One can be at home simply in the presence of a significant other. What makes home-territories different from other territories is on the one hand the living of the territory (a temporalization of the space), and on the other their connection with identity, or rather a process of identification, of articulation of affect. Homes, we feel, are ours:

> It was not the space itself, not the house, but the way of inhabiting it that made it a home…
>
> (Boym, 1994: 166)

THE PROCESS OF HOMEMAKING IS A CULTURAL ONE

To label a space 'home' in and of itself territorializes that space depending on cultural and social norms (though never absolutely). For instance, to use the term 'home' as I have throughout may strike one as odd in the regions of the world that this essay is most likely to circulate, because of strong articulations of the term to gender, passivity, leisure (gendered, again), both household and sexual labour, and so on. Home, as I am using it, is the creation of a space of comfort (a never-ending process), often in opposition to those very forces (Deleuze and Guattari cite a housewife whistling while she labours at home; it is the whistling and comfort-effect that is home, not the house necessarily). Indeed, much in the same way as it is essential to differentiate between nation and state and not conflate the two, it is crucial that we separate the ideas of *home* and *the home*, home and house, home and *domus*. The latter terms in these pairs of contrasts are proper, normative, and may have little to do with comfort. Indeed, the home may be a space of violence and pain; home then becomes the process of coping, comforting, stabilizing oneself, in other words: resistance. But home can also mean a process of rationalization or submission, a break with the reality of the situation, self-delusion, or falling under the delusions of others. Home is not authentic or inauthentic, it does not exist a priori, naturally or inevitably. It is not individualistic. The relation between home and the home is always being negotiated, similar to what Foucault once called 'the little tactics of the habitat'.

It is crucial because only then can we begin to disarticulate the idea of home from ideas of stasis, nostalgia, privacy, and authenticity (which, as Doreen Massey has argued, are then coded as female), and present a more open and dynamic concept that does not tie identity to static place or reproduce gender inequality by articulating women to enclosed prison-homes while the men wander free, wistfully nostalgic for the gal they left behind. This is not to argue that homes are not gendered, they are. As Ivan Illich has put it:

> Gender shapes bodies as they shape space and are in turn shaped by its arrangements. And the body in action, with its movements and rhythms, its gestures and cadences, shapes the home, the home as something more than a shelter, a tent, or a house.
>
> (1982: 118–119)

One cannot deny that the car-space and office-space described at the opening of this essay are gendered male; the important point is not to universalize that experience—I mean to do just the opposite, to ground it in the specificity of forces. This is why it is so important to differentiate between home as I have been describing it and the home or house; home is a becoming within an always already territorialized space (the home, the house, the domestic). Witold Rybczynski, for example, in his book *Home: A Short History of an Idea* (1986), focuses much more on the changing nature of The Home (or at least, the Western European home) than on the territorializing process itself. His chapter titles clearly set out the normative (and gendered) dimensions of the home: nostalgia, intimacy and privacy, domesticity, commodity and delight, ease, light and air, efficiency, style and substance, austerity, and comfort and wellbeing. Home can be a site of resistance, a leverage point against normative structurations of space, especially as the home becomes a domestic network terminal and the idea of homework further expands beyond unpaid gendered labour and the extension of education after school hours.

At the centre of the home, the territory, is not a singular rational subject, picking and choosing milieu, arranging one's space like flowers in a vase. The space called home is not an expression of the subject. Indeed, the subject is an expression of the territory, or rather of the process of territorialization. Territories, homes, have subject-effects. Identity is territory, not subjectivity. In that milieu-effects are always the result of connections to elsewhere, home and identities are always permeable and social. This is not to deny the existence of individuals, but rather to deny the illusion of individualism. As Henri Lefebvre (1991) once argued, the idea of private life is a key source of alienation in everyday life in the modern world, denying the social nature of identity.

The subject is the expression of repeated (or repeating) milieus and territories. The repetition that constitutes the subject we may call *habit*. Habit is a repetition of behaviour that is no longer conscious and reflects a process of learning. A series of actions become automatic and seemingly divorced from conscious thought. Habit is a contraction, a synthesis of a series of actions, a grasping. Playing the piano, for example, once learned bypasses conscious thought and appears to be 'in the hands.'

The term habit derives from the Latin *habere*, to have. It initially indicated 'the external appearance, manner, or bearing by which one would recognize an individual or class of individuals.' We are who we are, not through an essence that underlies all our motions and thoughts, but through the habitual repetition of those motions and thoughts.

Our identity, in other words, is comprised of habits. We are nothing but habits, Deleuze was fond of saying.

It is through habits that we are brought into culture in a very fundamental way. We cultivate habits, they are encultured. Culture is a way of behaving, of territorializing. We live our cultures not only through discourse, signs and meaning, but through the movements of our bodies. Ways of behaving, of moving, of gesturing, of interacting with objects, environments, technologies, are all cultural. Our habits are not necessarily our own. Most are created through continuous interaction with the external world (Gaston Bachelard wrote that habits are the 'passionate liaison of our bodies' with a space, a house, a home; 1969: 15). We are the result of our own reactions to the world, and are as such an enfolding of the external; indeed there is no internal to oppose the external (no noumena to oppose phenomena), just as there is no place that does not open up onto other places. We are spoken by our spaces, by the effects of territorializations, which pre-exist us, but never absolutely. We are disciplined through habit (Foucault, 1977).

The fact that habits participate and respond to our spaces is illustrated in an example from William James of absent-minded individuals who go to their bedrooms to dress for dinner,

but instead remove their clothes and get into bed because those are the triggers of being in that place at that time of day. We may wander into a room to get something but then forget what it was that we went there to get. That second room, the ways it shapes our space and movement, triggers other habits of thought and behaviour, which override our original vector.

Home is not a static place. We begin to get a sense of this in the previous discussion of difference, the introduction of inevitable change (chaos) into an otherwise static structure. 'One can never step into the same river twice', as they say. Home is always movement (even if we never move, if we spend our whole lives in the same room):

A large component of the identity of that place called home derived precisely from the fact that it had always in one way or another been open; constructed out of movement, communication, social relations which always stretched beyond it.

(Massey, 1994: 170–171)

'One ventures from home on the thread of a tune', Deleuze and Guattari write (1987: 311), but home is the thread, a line and not a point. At the same time it is non-linear. It is neither an originary point to which we may return, nor an end point (a telos) at which we will eventually arrive. We are always in-between. The nomad is not the tourist the exile, or the rebel son always longing for home; the nomad is the continual struggle between spatial forces and identity, the struggle to make a home, to create a space that opens onto other spaces.

REFERENCES

Bachelard, Gaston (1969) *The Poetics of Space,* trans. Maria Jolas, Boston, MA: Beacon Press.

Boym, Svetlana (1994) *Common Places: Mythologies of Everyday Life in Russia,* Cambridge, MA: Harvard University Press.

Deleuze, Gilles and Guattari, Félix (1987) *A Thousand Plateaus: Capitalism and Schizophrenia,* trans. B. Massumi, Minneapolis: University of Minnesota Press.

Foucault, Michel (1977) *Discipline and Punish: The Birth of the Prison,* trans. A. Sheridan, Harmondsworth: Penguin.

Illich, Ivan (1982) *Gender,* New York: Pantheon.

Lefebvre, Henri (1991) *Critique of Everyday Life: Vol. one,* trans. John Moore, New York: Verso.

Massey, Doreen (1994) *Space, Place, and Gender,* Minneapolis: University of Minnesota Press.

SECTION 6

"Public" and "Private"

Gay men at the beach, circa 1930. East Coast, US.
Source: 2012 Lesbian & Gay Community Services Center, Inc. New York City.
Reference to: Chauncey, George. 1995. "Privacy Could Only Be Had in Public: Gay Uses of the Streets" from
Stud: Architectures of Masculinity. Princeton, NJ: Princeton Architectural Press, pp. 224–267.

"PUBLIC" AND "PRIVATE"

Public and private are social constructs that conceptualize different domains of everyday life—from the interiority and privacy of our bodies and homes to the publicness of city streets and public space. In common usage it refers to the degree of access granted to "outsiders," however outsiders are defined. But despite digital privacy agreements and no-trespassing signs, the boundaries between public and private are often ill-defined and contested. Rather than existing in a binary opposition, public and private spaces operate at a variety of scales that overlap and intersect, creating a mosaic of spaces and degrees of access. Rarely is a space either public or private, but is instead multi-layered and often disputed physically and politically.

Public and private are contested realms, open to debate and intervention. In one sense, public may be addressed primarily as an issue of politics, as Jürgen Habermas (1991) and Hannah Arendt (1998) consider it in their work on the *public sphere*, debating who the public is and how the public expresses itself and makes its will known. Tangential to this is the question of ownership and property: who owns and determines how resources are used, and what then is truly private? Another way of thinking about public and private is through individual rights and activities. In this case, public is often used to define the spaces of approved social interaction, while private refers to personal space and intimate encounter. These understandings of public and private as psychological, social, and political processes are addressed in the following readings.

Looking at the multiple ways that the term public describes spaces and gatherings of people, geographer **Kurt Iveson** outlines the ways in which public space is configured and the types of interactions each model of public space supports. What he calls the *ceremonial model* of public space, based on traditional European plazas, is provided by the state as a place of public gathering, structured according to the rules and regulations of that state. The *community model* of public space fosters social relations from the ground up. The *liberal model* of public space advocated by Habermas (1991) guarantees equal access for all; however, the reality of such a space often results in the exclusion of those different from the group that holds power. To bring these frameworks together, Iveson argues for a multi-public model of public space, which he develops from the work of Iris Marion Young (see Section 7). A *multi-public model* does not establish a singular notion of public, but accommodates a variety of subcultures and groups in spaces that embrace difference.

Geographer **Don Mitchell** makes a compelling argument that access and the ability to inhabit public space must be understood as a "right." Drawing upon the work of Henri Lefebvre (1968), Mitchell argues that the *right to the city* is one way in which the idea of the public can be tested. By examining how ideas of public and private are politicized and operate spatially, especially through his work on the regulation of homeless populations and use of public parks, Mitchell refutes the many processes of capital and rhetorics of fear that call for the privatization of public space. By centering his argument on what he calls the *right to inhabit*, he suggests that our ability to occupy public space—in much more diverse ways than typically imagined—is a fundamental human right, rather than a right to property.

Issues of public and private transect class, racial, and gender lines, and the forms of contestation vary from place to place. Anthropologist **Li Zhang** looks at Beijing, China, and the experiences of rural-to-urban migrants, their labor, and the way it is criminalized. She describes how these practices place this group outside the bounds of public space and authorized activity because of governmental interest in control. These migrants, after constructing large-scale residential complexes and economic infrastructures, find that they have no rights or ability to stave off the destruction of their homes, despite playing an important role in the local economy. Their contingent existence is regulated through what is deemed appropriate by the government, yet they continue to self-organize in their effort to be recognized.

Historian **George Chauncey** describes how oppression and privilege are intertwined in the way that gay men were not able to meet or create private space at the turn of the 20th century in New York City. At the same time, gay men drew upon society's encouragement of working-class men to occupy public and semi-public spaces such as parks, docks, beaches, bath houses, and movie theaters (see figure at the beginning of Section 6). Through encounters in these spaces, gay men were able to create modes of access and to develop a culture, supporting Chauncey's argument that, for this group, "privacy could only be had in public." His work sparks thinking about marginalization, not only of specific groups in public space, but also of their rights to private spaces and privacy. Public and private are not equally accessible, but depend upon sexuality, gender, economic status, age, and other markers of identity and behavior.

Art historian **Alice T. Friedman**'s essay helps us understand how privacy is qualified and contested even in the space of the private home. Her case study is the architecturally renowned Farnsworth House which architect Mies van der Rohe designed for owner Edith Farnsworth in the 1950s. Expecting a private getaway in the country, the female owner instead found herself with glass walls and no adequate space for dressing. Friedman shows how Farnsworth was stripped of her privacy first through van der Rohe's designs, and subsequently by the many people who came to view this famous glass house in which she sought solitude but found herself on display. Drawing on popular portrayals of women from this time through archival research, Friedman argues that because Farnsworth was an older, single woman, she was viewed by society as someone who had forfeited the full right to private space. Despite the house's appearance of openness, Friedman shows how the design intentionally repressed this woman's sexuality and failed to afford her space to regulate or find privacy for her body.

Hegemony often obscures or monopolizes our rights and resources, including access and use of public space. However, if people were to suppose that our spaces and actions are shared—or at least should serve the public good—it could challenge the status quo of assuming things are private and solely for our individual benefit. **Mark Kingwell**'s philosophical essay suggests just that: to destabilize the dominant ideology of private rights, human beings reverse our understanding of public and private. To make this case, Kingwell shows how Herman Melville's character of Bartelby refuses to concede to the norms of capitalism dictating discrete places of work and leisure (office and home). He argues that this is a way of reclaiming territory for the public. Kingwell prompts us to ask: "Why can't we work, play, eat, and sleep in ways that are less fixed and regulated?" In arguing against our spaces, institutions, and actions as beholden to private interests rather than public good, Kingwell suggests that if people were to turn our understanding of public and private inside out, public space would no longer be interstitial or marginal, but could occupy the center of democratic processes.

The public or private character of space is contested politically, economically, socially, psychologically, and spatially as evidenced from these readings. Since the emergence of the notion of public in ancient Greece, access and use of public space has always been limited and disputed, and there has never been a perfect model for how it should work (Brill 1989). Space is always layered in the way it is perceived and regulated, as well as in the way it is physically constructed. Literary critic Michael Warner (2002) asserts that the idea of public also accounts for *publicity* and *publicness*, arguing that multiple *publics* (groups and agendas) may be operating in any given place or time. For example, Erving Goffman (1959) contends with the way our personalities shift throughout our everyday spaces through the lens of class. Further, in line with the thinking of Mitchell and Kingwell, it is important to note that public means everyone has a shared interest in spaces. In this way, public relates to the concept of the *commons*—resources that are available to all members of a society—a framework that is contested in ancient land disputes and newer digital divides (see Blackmar 2006). Examples such as the public uprising of Occupy Wall Street in Zucotti Park in New York City and the "revolution" in Tahrir Square in Cairo highlight recent events in which there was a struggle for public spaces and political rights. It is also useful to consider how the body is an especially important site in debates about public and private, whether in terms described by Chauncey or Friedman, or other ways in which women and minorities are objectified, commodified, sexualized, and spatially segregated by people in power. Lastly, and most important, the idea of rights is fundamental to discussions of public and private, and these scholars demonstrate the continued need and responsibility of every person in working to establish and maintain rights and spaces that are equitable.

SUGGESTIONS FOR FURTHER READING

Please see *peopleplacespace.org* for extended and additional lists of readings.

Arendt, Hannah. 1998. "The Public and the Private Realm." In *The Human Condition*, pp. 182–230. Chicago, IL: University Of Chicago Press.
Blackmar, Elizabeth. 2006. "Appropriating 'the Commons': The Tragedy of Property Rights Discourse." In *The Politics of Public Space*, edited by Setha Low and Neil Smith, pp. 49–80. New York: Routledge.
Brill, Michael. 1989. "Transformation, Nostalgia, and Illusion in Public Life and Public Space." In *Public Places and Spaces*, edited by Irwin Altman and Erwin H. Zube, pp. 7–29. New York: Springer.
Carr, Stephen, Mark Francis, Leanne G. Rivlin, and Andrew M. Stone. 1993. *Public Space*. Cambridge: Cambridge University Press.
Colomina, Beatriz. 1996. *Privacy and Publicity: Modern Architecture as Mass Media*. Cambridge, MA: The MIT Press.
Duneier, Mitchell. 2000. *Sidewalk*. New York: Farrar, Strauss and Giroux.
Engels, Friedrich. 2010. *The Origin of the Family, Private Property, and the State*. London; New York: Penguin Classics.
Goffman, Erving. 1959. *The Presentation of Self in Everyday Life*. New York: Anchor Press.
Habermas, Jürgen. 1991. *The Structural Transformation of the Public Sphere: An Inquiry into a Category of Bourgeois Society*. Cambridge, MA: The MIT Press.
Iveson, Kurt. 2007. *Publics and the City*. Malden, MA: Wiley-Blackwell.
Kingwell, Mark, and Patrick Turmel (eds). 2009. *Rites of Way: The Politics and Poetics of Public Space*. Ontario: Wilfrid Laurier University Press.
Lefebvre, Henri. 1968. "The Right to the City." In *Writings on Cities*, edited by E. Kofman and E. Lebas. Cambridge, MA: Blackwell.
Locke, John. 1980. *Second Treatise of Government*. Indianapolis, IN: Hackett Publishing Company.
Low, Setha M. 2000. *On the Plaza: The Politics of Public Space and Culture*. Austin: University of Texas Press.
Madanipour, Ali. 2003. *Public and Private Spaces of the City*. New York: Routledge.
Marcuse, Peter (ed.). 2011. *Searching for the Just City*. New York: Routledge.
Mernissi, Fatima. 1987. *Beyond the Veil: Male–Female Dynamics in Modern Muslim Society*. Indianapolis: Indiana University Press.
Miller, Kristine F. 2007. *Designs on the Public: The Private Lives of New York's Public Spaces*. Minneapolis: University Of Minnesota Press.

Orum, Anthony M., and Zachary P. Neal. 2009. *Common Ground?: Readings and Reflections on Public Space*. New York: Routledge.

Parry, Bronwyn, and Cathy Gere. 2006. "Contested Bodies: Property Models and the Commodification of Human Biological Artefacts." *Science as Culture* 15(2): 139–158.

Smithsimon, Greg, and Benjamin Shepard. 2011. *The Beach Beneath the Streets: Contesting New York City's Public Spaces*. New York: State University of New York Press.

Warner, Michael. 2002. *Publics and Counterpublics*. New York: Zone Books.

30
Putting the Public Back into Public Space

(1998)

Kurt Iveson

Answering the question 'what is public space?' is immediately complicated by the multiple meanings of 'public' that exist in English-speaking countries.[1] 'Public' can refer specifically to the state, in distinction to the 'private' market. It can refer to all things beyond the 'privacy' of the home. People might be spoken of collectively as 'the public'. Getting 'publicity' describes the process of bringing an event or person to the notice of this 'public'. To conflate or confuse these different meanings of 'public' has analytical, as well as political, consequences (Fraser 1992). Using any of these definitions of 'public' would yield very different understandings of the nature of contemporary public space. For this reason, it is important to be more explicit about the model of public space that informs contemporary urban analysis.

CEREMONIAL MODEL OF PUBLIC SPACE

The ceremonial model considers genuine public space to be space that represents the triumph of the public over the market, usually through state ownership and large-scale civic design. These are the grand spaces where significant events in the life of the nation, state or city can be celebrated. Often, those using the ceremonial model invoke the grand public squares of ancient European cities as examples of good public space. For example, Sennett's (1978) critique of contemporary public space is in large part informed by his appreciation for the public culture of ancient European cities. Most of the writers who praise such public spaces are not

blind to their limits. But at least, they argue, the grand city squares of the past allowed for a notion of public and civic good to be inscribed in space over and above private market interests, in what Habermas (1989) describes as "representative publicness".

The nature of ceremonial public spaces can make them potent sites for protest as well as celebration (Davison 1994). Media images of protest in China's Tiananmen Square, or the 1996 protest at Parliament House in Canberra,[2] attest to the extra significance of action which takes place in ceremonial public spaces. Largely because of the representative function of these spaces, people have gathered in them to claim that *they* should be included in the public represented through the space. Further, the physical size of these grand public spaces facilitates the presence of a large number of people in a way that smaller public spaces do not. Davison and others have noted that the significance of mass protest in the large civic spaces of the 1960s has resulted in less of them being built today (Carr *et al.* 1992; Davison 1994). Of course, some grand public spaces of the kind celebrated in the ceremonial model were themselves constructed to facilitate increased levels of social control. For example, Haussman's reconstruction of Paris, with grand boulevards replacing the narrow streets which had been barricaded by revolutionaries, was in part an attempt to gain more control over city (see Harvey 1985, ch. 3).

The ceremonial model of public space makes an important contribution by considering the issue of the state *provision* of public space, and its impact on how people occupy public spaces. It is argued that the state should be more open to claims for access to public space than private owners, whose concerns are more market driven. But advocates of this model often fail to consider some of its consequences for the *quality* of public space. The state or 'public' provision of public space does not by itself ensure openness or accessibility for 'members of the public'. By defining genuine public space as state-owned, the ceremonial model fails to "appreciate the full force of the distinction between apparatuses of the state, on the one hand, and public arenas of citizen discourse and association, on the other" (Fraser 1992, pp. 109–110).[3] We must be careful not to idealise the representative publicness that guided the design of large civic spaces in ancient European cities, and we must be careful to distinguish this meaning of 'public' from others.

THE COMMUNITY MODEL OF PUBLIC SPACE

For others writing about public space, the quality of 'public life' that is facilitated by different kinds of public space is of central importance. Many urban designers have explored the link between public space and community, and consider that the 'publicness' of a space is contingent not on state ownership, but rather on its ability to foster or house community.

One group of writers, advocating what they call 'new urbanism', believe that well-designed public space, centrally located within an urban village, will foster or create community by bringing people closer together (see e.g. Katz 1994). The urban village concept explicitly draws its inspiration from older, pre-capitalist and early twentieth-century villages. Pockets of development are designed around central public places such as pedestrian plazas, which contain shops, services and recreational space. Housing of reasonably high density is located within walking distance of this central public place and major public transport nodes. The new urbanism is usually contrasted to suburban post-war urban development, which is accused of fostering car dependence, isolation from neighbours, and alienation from others in public space.

The arguments of the new urbanists are beset with physical determinism, where design becomes the primary influence on 'community life'.

Other town planners focusing on the issue of public space are less deterministic, and have attempted to develop a more sophisticated community model which takes into account the wide range of influences on the public life of public spaces. In *Public Space* (1992), Carr et al. are attuned to the real impact of design and management on the kinds of interaction that can take place in a given space, but temper such insights with a recognition of other issues impacting on public space.

So rather than fixing purely on these physical attributes, these planners would have us focus on establishing public spaces that meet people's *needs*, protect their *rights*, and offer people a range of *meanings* to attach to public spaces.

While Carr et al. do not believe that good public space will create community, they argue successful public spaces are most easily achieved in cities where community already exists.

Carr et al. therefore long for the kind of "multicultural" public space which contributes to "the American dream of cultural integration, or at the very least cultural understanding" (Carr et al. 1992, p. 8).

How is the planner or urban designer to develop successful public spaces where community does not exist? Ideally, it is hoped by progressive planners like Carr et al. that a community of users can be established in a non-exclusionary way, and that the dilemma posed by diversity can be alleviated through good design, which can establish a balance of users and activities in public space (Carr et al. 1992, p. 158). But even in their best case scenarios of successful public space, this level of community is achieved via the coincidence or construction of homogeneity at someone's expense.

THE LIBERAL MODEL OF PUBLIC SPACE

The parks and inner city street spaces of pre-World War II liberal capitalist cities provide the inspiration for a liberal model of public space. In this model, good public space is considered as space which is open and accessible to all, with social difference ignored. It is the venue of citizen participation in everyday life and public affairs. This model focuses more explicitly on issues of inclusion and exclusion than the ceremonial or community models. For writers advocating this model, liberal public spaces provide a template because they were more disposed to multifunctional use by a diverse range of citizens than contemporary uni-functional spaces, which are designed as thoroughfares and spaces of consumption.

Davis (1992) argues instead that the liberal 'public philosophy' of pre-war city planning made streets and parks more open to a wide range of people, not just their density. He attributes this limited accessibility to the liberal ideals of civic planners such as Olmsted who argued for a mixing of classes to encourage the civility of the lower classes.

The liberal public space described here by Davis sounds very much like a spatial equivalent of the liberal 'public sphere' that has been the subject of work by Habermas and other critical theorists (Habermas 1989; Calhoun 1992). The public sphere is the metaphorical 'space' where public opinion is formed through rational discourse between private individuals. Habermas argues that the liberal public sphere did not live up to its own ideals, and that in fact openness and accessibility for everyone was not the reality. However, he concludes that the ideal of an openly accessible public sphere constructed on rational discourse and the bracketing of difference has significant normative power and emancipatory potential. Similarly, writers such as Davis argue that while liberal public spaces may not have lived up to their claim to be accessible to all, at least such an ideal made accessibility possible and perhaps even desirable.

Some historians such as Fraser and Eley have criticised aspects of Habermas' understanding of the public sphere, and their criticisms apply to liberal models of public space. They argue that the liberal public sphere did not simply fail to live up to its ideals of inclusion, but that the ideals themselves were exclusionary (Eley 1992; Fraser 1992). They agree with Habermas that the liberal public sphere was built in the process of challenging the authority imposed by an unrepresentative state from above. But they argue it was also built by a bourgeoisie attempting to represent its own interests as universal interests, in opposition to others in society, particularly women and the working class, from *below*. The ideal of bracketing or ignoring differences in status was not only never achieved, but the ideal itself actually *contributes* to exclusion—'open to everyone' effectively meant 'open to everyone *like us*' as liberal norms regarding participation were universalised.

The liberal model of public space risks reproducing the form of exclusion upon which the liberal public sphere was built. The inclusion of a range of citizens via a liberal model of a universal public sphere is certainly preferable to one in which these groups are physically prevented from occupying public space at all. However, this access is premised on the exclusion of different norms of behaviour and cultures.

MULTI-PUBLIC MODEL OF PUBLIC SPACE

The multi-public model of public space replaces the liberal model's attachment to the ideal of a universal public sphere with an ideal of the public sphere as the structured setting for the interaction of a number of publics. This model draws explicitly on the criticisms of Habermas' account of the liberal public sphere discussed in the previous section.

According to some revisionist historians, subaltern or counter-publics, whose interests are not represented by the dominant public, take shape in order to promote their own interests in the wider public sphere. For those marginalised from the dominant public, the formation of 'counter-publics' allows a zone where they can establish their own cultural norms and define their interests collectively (see Fraser 1992).

In *Justice and the Politics of Difference* (1990), Young attempts to develop the model of public space implied by this alternative conception of the public sphere. She aims to demonstrate the implications of a politics of difference, by "envisioning an ideal of city life as a being together of strangers in openness to group difference" (1990, p. 256). Her model of city life is explicitly developed as an alternative to models based on communitarian politics and the universal public sphere. Rather than privileging public spaces where difference is ignored, or where there is 'community', Young builds a model of good public space as one which contains multiple publics. The model is a celebration of difference, generated from the unrealised possibilities that Young identifies in contemporary cities.

Envisioning public space as a space of difference proposes a space that disrupts the connection between diversity and exclusion that characterises other models of public space. These models hope to assimilate difference into community or ignore it in the universal public sphere. Young, on the other hand, theoretically achieves the uncoupling of social difference and exclusion from public space by acknowledging and embracing the continued existence of social difference.

DIFFERENT KINDS OF DIFFERENCE

Young recognises that contemporary cities are characterised by all sorts of inequalities. However, her normative vision of public space only generates suggestions to address inequalities resulting from lack of *recognition* and acceptance of cultural difference. However, Young's planning suggestions do little to address problems in public space that arise due to the inequitable *distribution* of material and economic resources that characterises capitalist cities.

As a result there are "some unresolved tensions between the cultural and the political-economic dimensions of [Young's] framework" (Fraser 1997a, p. 192). Young often fails to acknowledge that there are different kinds of difference. In some cases, redistribution may in fact "obviate the need for recognition" by removing sources of social difference (Fraser 1997a, p. 194). So, managing the impact of social differences such as homelessness in public space presents a more complex set of problems for planners than Young acknowledges. Fraser's point here is not that we have an either/or choice between redistribution and recognition, but rather that progressive politics must strive to address *both*, not just one or the other (Fraser 1997b, p. 126).

Group formation and multi-public public space

In most considerations of the public *sphere*, when public *space* is considered at all it is treated simply as the container or field of public life. It is inert rather than constitutive—the surface upon which the interaction of publics is played out. Recall Young's statement that "by definition, public space is a place accessible to everyone, where anyone can participate" (1990, p. 240). While Young has rejected the universalist notion of the public *sphere*, she risks reproducing a universalist notion of public *space* in her model. The social groups that are the bearers of the

difference that Young wishes to embrace are not formed *prior* to their occupation of public space, but *through* this occupation. The role of space in group formation has significant consequences for a multi-public model of public space.

This understanding of the relationship between the formation of publics and public space has a number of implications for the multi-public model.

First, if the organisation of various publics differs this will have consequences for how each public conceives of public space.

Second, membership of various publics is often fluid and overlapping (Young 1990; Fraser 1992).

Third, if some counter-publics form in order to contest the very meaning of what is legitimately considered as 'public' or 'private', might they also contest the definition of particular spaces as 'public' or 'private'?

Fourth, if counter-publics are not just formed in space but *through* their use of public spaces, then we must understand the range of global processes that shape these spaces beyond local agency.

Finally, the relationship between publics and the state will have implications for our understanding of public spaces.

Local community empowerment over space is often idealised, but it could just as easily result in a denial of access to 'others' (Young 1990).

The multi-public model of public space developed by Young is the most promising of the models discussed in this paper. The application of an alternative vision of the public sphere, conceived of as the structured setting where a range of publics interact, is powerful in helping to conceptualise a model of public space that addresses exclusion and inequality. However, this discussion suggests that the model needs further refinement in a number of areas. In particular, a more fundamentally spatial approach to the nature of interaction between publics is called for.

NOTES

1   Habermas describes a similar problem with the word meaning 'public' in the German language, although I confess to having only been made aware of this via an English translation of his work! See Habermas (1989).

2   A national rally organised by a coalition of trade union and welfare organisations held at Parliament House in Canberra on 19 August, one day before the 1996 Federal Budget, was attended by around 30,000 people concerned about conservative budget cuts and labour market reforms. The rally was promptly renamed a 'riot' by the government and media, following attempts by some protesters to enter Parliament House, resulting in scuffles between themselves and police, and some property damage.

3   Fraser's comment is referring to a failure in socialist models of the public sphere, but her analysis is also relevant in discussing the ceremonial model of public space that has been discussed here.

REFERENCES

Calhoun, Craug. (1992) 'Introduction: Habermas and the Public Sphere', in C. Calhoun (ed.) *Habermas and the Public Sphere,* Cambridge, MIT Press.

Carr, Stephen, Francis, Mark, Rivlin, Leahme G., and Stone, Andrew M. (1992) *Public Space,* Cambridge, Cambridge University Press.

Davis, Mike. (1992) 'Fortress Los Angeles: The Militarization of Urban Space', in M. Sorkin (ed.) *Variations on a Theme Park— The New American City and the End of Public Space,* New York, Hill and Wang.

Davison, Graeme. (1994) 'Public Life and Public Space: A Lament for Melbourne's City Square', in *Historic Environment* 11(1): 4–9.

Eley, Geoff. (1992) 'Nations, Publics and Political Cultures: Placing Habermas in the Nineteenth Century', in C. Calhoun (ed.) *Habermas and the Public Sphere,* Cambridge, MA, MIT Press.

Fraser, Nancy. (1992) 'Rethinking the Public Sphere: A Contribution to the Critique of Actually Existing Democracy', in C Calhoun (ed.) *Habermas and the Public Sphere,* Cambridge, MA,MIT Press.

Fraser, Nancy. (1997a) *Justice Interruptus: Critical Reflections on the 'Postsocialist' Condition,* New York, Routledge.

Fraser, Nancy. (1997b) 'A Rejoinder to Iris Young', in *New Left Review* 223: 126–130.

Habermas, Jürgen. (1989) *The Structural Transformation of the Public Sphere,* Cambridge, MA, Massachusetts Institute of Technology Press.

Harvey, David. 1985. *Consciousness and the Urban Experience,* Baltimore, MD, Johns Hopkins University Press.

Katz, Peter. (1994) *The New Urbanism: Towards an Architecture of Community,* New York, McGraw-Hill.

Sennett, Richard (1978) *The Fall of Public Man: On the Social Psychology of Capitalism,* New York, Vintage Books.

Young, Iris Marion. (1990) *Justice and the Politics of Difference,* Princeton, NJ, Princeton University Press.

31
To Go Again to Hyde Park
Public Space, Rights, and Social Justice (2003)

Don Mitchell

Public space engenders fears, fears that derive from the sense of public space as uncontrolled space, as a space in which civilization is exceptionally fragile. The panic over "wilding" in New York City's Central Park in the late 1980s (rampaging young men violently terrorizing joggers and other park users for the sheer joy of it), the fright made palpable by the explosions in Atlanta's Olympic Park in 1996, and the newfound fear of public space spurred by the sense of vulnerability attendant upon the September 11, 2001, terrorist attacks, no less than the everyday gnawing uneasiness we feel when we step around a passed-out homeless person on a sidewalk, often convince us that public space is the space of anarchy. Such an association of public space with anarchy is, of course, not new; it is not just a feature of the contemporary city, of the current media-encouraged, overweening concern about crime, homelessness, and random terrorism that makes public space seem such an undesirable attribute of the contemporary American city.

Raymond Williams (1997 [1980], 3–5) reminds us, for example, that Matthew Arnold's (1993) famous declaration in *Culture and Anarchy*—that culture represents (or ought to represent) "the *best* knowledge and thought of the time" (1993, 79)—was made in response to working people forcing their way into Hyde Park in 1866 to hold an assembly in support of the right to vote. For Arnold, the Hyde Park demonstrators were "a symptom of the general anarchy" (Williams 1997 [1980], 6) rather than people struggling for their rights—their right to assemble, their right to speak, their right to

vote. A Hyde Park "rioter," according to Arnold, "is just asserting his personal liberty a little, going where he likes, assembling where he likes, bawling where he likes, hustling as he likes" (Arnold 1993, 88, quoted in Williams 1997 [1980], 6).

The proper response, according to Arnold, was repression, the reigning in of "rights," and the asserting of firmer control over public space, for "without order there can be no society; and without society there can be no human perfection" (Arnold 1993, 181, quoted in Williams 1997 [1980], 6). Only with order can culture flourish, can cities be centers of civilization. Williams's point in resurrecting the context of Arnold's arguments about culture is important: those rights we take as "immemorial," such as the right to assemble in and use public space, are not only relatively new, they are always hotly contested and only grudgingly given by those in power. *Always* hotly contested: rights over and to public space are never guaranteed once and for all. New struggles emerge, if not only over the right to vote then over the right to live a sane and peaceful life in the nuclear age, the right to control over government in totalitarian states, or, especially in the "postmodern" cities of the Western world, the right, in the absence of decent, affordable housing, simply to live.[1] As Williams (1997 [1980], 8) rightly proclaims: "it will always be necessary to go again to Hyde Park."

Without order, the argument goes, liberty is simply impossible. And that order must be explicitly geographic: it centers on the control of the streets and the question of just *who* has *the right to the city*.

PUBLIC SPACE AND THE RIGHT TO THE CITY

"The right to the city" is a slogan closely associated with the French Marxist philosopher Henri Lefebvre.

There are several issues here that are critical to the development of the argument about public space and social justice that I will make. The first is Lefebvre's insistence on a right to the city. Lefebvre was deeply attached to the rural countryside, especially the village of his birth (Merrifield 2002; Shields 1998), but he shared with Marx a disdain for the *idiocy* of rural life. Idiocy in this sense does not refer to the intelligence of the inhabitants, or even the nature of their customs, but to the essential *privacy*—and therefore isolation and homogeneity—of rural life. In contrast, cities were necessarily *public*—and therefore places of social interaction and exchange with people who were necessarily different. Publicity demands heterogeneity and the space of the city—with its density and its constant attraction of new immigrants—assured a thick fabric of heterogeneity, one in which encounters with difference were guaranteed. But for the encounter with difference to really succeed, then, as we will see in a moment, the right to *inhabit* the city—by different people and different groups—had always to be struggled for. This is the second issue. The city is the place where difference lives. And finally, in the city, different people with different projects must necessarily struggle with one another over the shape of the city, the terms of access to the public realm, and even the rights of citizenship. Out of this struggle the city as a work—as an ouvre, as a collective if not singular project—emerges, and new modes of living, new modes of inhabiting, are invented.[2]

Moreover, this right is related to objective needs, needs that any city should be structured toward meeting: "the need for creative activity, for the ouvre (not only of products and consumable material goods), the need for information, symbolism, the imaginary and play" (Lefebvre 1996 [1968], 147). More sharply: "The right to the city manifests itself as a superior form of rights: right to freedom, to individualization in socialization, to habitat and to inhabit. The right to the *ouvre*, to participation and *appropriation* (clearly distinct

from the right to property), are implied in the right to the city" (Lefebvre 1996 [1968], 174).

And for Lefebvre, this implied the development (finally) of a fully urban society. The right to the city was the right "to urban life, to renewed centrality, to places of encounter and exchange, to life rhythms and time uses, enabling the full and complete *usage* of ... moments and places" (Lefebvre 1996 [1968], 179). That is to say, the *use-value* that is the necessary bedrock of urban life would finally be wrenched free from its domination by exchange-value. The right to the city implies the right to the uses of city spaces, the right to *inhabit*.

That is to say, the right to housing is one form of *appropriation* of the city, and that is why Lefebvre was at pains to set this off from the right to property. For property, of course, is the embodiment of alienation, an embodied alienation backed up by violence (Blomley 1998, 2000a, in press; Rose 1994). More accurately, property *rights* are necessarily exclusive: the possession of a property right allows its possessor to exclude unwanted people from access (Blomley 2000b, 651; MacPherson 1978). And this act of expulsion, this right of property, Blomley (2000a, 88) notes, frequently involves invoking the power of the state: "Police can be called to physically remove a trespasser; injunctions prepared, criminal sanctions sought. As such, expulsion is a violent act. Violence can be explicitly deployed or (more usually) implied. But such violence has state sanction and is thus legitimate." This issue is particularly important in a world where some members of society are not covered by *any* property right (Waldron 1991) and so must find a way to inhabit the city *despite* the exclusivity of property—either that, or they must find ways, as with squatting, and with the collective movements of the landless, to undermine the power of property and its state sanction, to otherwise appropriate and inhabit the city. In the contemporary city of homelessness the right to inhabit the city must always be asserted not within, but against, the rights of property. The right to housing needs to be dissociated from the right to property and returned to the right to inhabit.

The cry and the demand for the *right* to the city is the best means there is to begin to assure what William Bunge has called "the geography of survival."

"RIGHTS TALK"

"Rights"—to the degree that they are institutionalized and protected within specific social situations, to the degree that they are and are not backed by the violence and the power of the state, and to the degree that they protect the interests of *some* at the expense of others (despite and because of the universalizing qualities)—are social relations and hence a means of organizing the actual social content of justice.[3]

That is precisely what "rights" do: they provide a set of instructions about the use of power. But they do so by becoming *institutionalized*—that is, by becoming practices backed up by force (as Marx recognized).

The struggle for rights—for example, the right to sleep unmolested in a city park if you are homeless—becomes an important, if still limited, tool in the production of space against powerful abstracting forces. But rights talk is more than a tool; if successful (and thus inscribed in law and policy), it provides institutional support for produced differentiated space to be maintained against the forces of abstraction that seek to destroy it. Rights themselves, therefore, are part of the process of producing space.

The "cry and demand" for rights is a means for *producing* the right to the city—it *is* "that critique of human geography" Guy Debord called for.

REPRESENTATION AND PUBLIC SPACE

While occupying some place or space is vitally necessary to life, it is not necessarily guaranteed as a right. Rather, private property rights hedge in space, bound it off, and restrict its usage. As David Smith (1994b, 42) argues, "the right to own land differs from other commonly enunciated rights, in that it concerns the appropriation of the scarce material world, and can impinge on the rights of others to meet such vital needs as food and shelter." Moreover, private property rights also potentially trump what Smith (1994b, 43) calls membership rights but which in the American context might be more commonly understood as the right to assembly—that is, those rights that make possible the formation of political communities, that make possible political *representation*.

In a world defined by private property, then, *public space* (as the space for representation) takes on exceptional importance. At the level of basic needs, as Jeremy Waldron (1991) argues, in a society where *all* property is private, those who own none (or whose interests aren't otherwise protected by a right to access to private property) simply cannot *be*, because they would have no place to *be*. At a less immediate but still vital level, in a world defined by private property, the formation of a *public sphere* that is at all robust and inclusive of a variety of different publics is exceedingly difficult.

Implicit in much theorizing about the public sphere is the assumption that the provision of an adequate space (or in some renderings, an adequate technology) will perforce create a vibrant public sphere.[4] The proliferation of and perhaps democratic control over places to meet, gather, and interact (whether these places be town squares, electronic communities, television chat shows, or "the media") are often seen as sufficient to the creation of a public sphere. The erosion of such places (and their replacement by privately controlled spaces and means of communication) is likewise often argued to be crucial to the closing down of the public sphere. The images—or ideals—of the public sphere and its relationship to space are important and in their normative force often drive much political organizing and action. And yet these arguments are limited to the degree that they assume that the construction of either singular or multiple public spheres is an issue of planning, and that such planning is—or could be—sufficient to the promotion of political discourse. The planning and provision of public spaces will lead, the argument often goes, to the ability of various groups to represent themselves.

And yet, as careful analyses of the community network movement in the United States show, even the most well-designed spaces for interaction (in this case the electronic space of the internet) often lead to a remarkably limited and ineffectual public discourse. Indeed, Michael Longan (2000) found that the most effective arenas of public discourse arose around specific issues and specific needs. That is to say, political debate developed not because it *could*, but because *it had to*—and in the process often the least likely sites for political representations became the most important.

That is to say, for all the importance and power of recent "end of public space" arguments, what makes a space *public*—a space in which the cry and demand for the right to the city can be seen and heard—is often not its preordained "publicness." Rather, it is when, to fulfill a pressing need, some group or another *takes* space and through its actions *makes* it public. The very act of representing one's group (or to some extent one's self) to a larger public creates a space for representation. Representation both demands space and creates space.

But it rarely does so under conditions of its own choosing. And so here the desires of other groups, other individuals, other classes, together with the violent power of the state, laws about property, and the current jurisprudence on rights all have a role to play in stymieing, channeling, or promoting the "taking" and "making" of public space and the claim to representation.

The production of public space—the means through which the cry and demand of the right to the city is made possible—is thus always a dialectic between the "end of public space" and its beginning. This dialectic is both fundamental to and a product of the struggle for rights in and to the city. It is both fundamental to and a product of social justice (which thus cannot be universal except to the degree it relates to the particular and the spatial—particular struggles for rights and particular struggles over and for public space).

NOTES

1   In late 1999, responding to a highly publicized assault that was wrongly linked to a homeless street person, Mayor Rudy Giuliani of New York reiterated his (and many others') staunch belief that there simply is "no right to live on the streets." Giuliani put it starkly: "Streets do not exist in civilized societies for the purpose of sleeping there. Bedrooms are for sleeping in" (Bumiller 1999, A1)—which, of course, is fine if you have one. For those who do not, Giuliani announced a new program to arrest those sleeping on the streets if they did not "move on" when ordered to do so by the police. Simultaneously, Giuliani announced that shelter beds would be conditional on employment. Most of the homeless, under this policy, were caught in a quite sharp "Catch-22." As the *New York Times* put it

in an analysis, "many New Yorkers seemed puzzled by a policy that would throw homeless people out of shelters and into the streets, and yet arrest them for being there if they would not go to a shelter" (Bernstein, 1999, 1). Indeed.

2   There are, of course, more basic arguments as to why the city must be at the heart (but not at all the exclusive focus) of any struggle for a progressive, socially just world. Among these are the simple fact that most of the world's population is now urban, that cities have become the command and control centers of the global economy and of the practices and policies that are transforming the global environment, and that, in fact, increased rather than decreased urbanization will have to be at the heart of any move toward sustainability under continued population growth: cities are every bit as much a solution as they are a problem.

3   All this is to say (to put it bluntly), "rights" must be at the heart of any Marxist and socialist project of urban transformation, even while the limits of rights, and the need to continually struggle over them, must constantly be acknowledged.

4   "Public sphere" is a complicated term in that it indicates public interaction at a range of scales and across several levels of abstraction. Both people gathering at a town meeting and the sum total of discourse in the media are often referred to as aspects of the public sphere. My argument is not that these are not constituents of public spheres but rather that much academic debate about the public sphere occurs amidst a high level of analytical imprecision.

REFERENCES

Arnold, Matthew. 1993. *Culture and Anarchy and Other Writings*. Cambridge: Cambridge University Press, edited by S. Collini.

Bernstein, Nina. 1999. "Labeling the Homeless, in Compassion and Contempt," *The New York Times* December 5, 1:53.

Blomley, Nicholas. 1998. "Landscapes of Property," *Law and Society Review* 32, 567–612.

Blomley, Nicholas. 2000a. " 'Acts,' 'Deeds,' and the Violences of Property," *Historical Geography* 28, 86–107.

Blomley, Nicholas. 2000b. "Property Rights," in R. Johnston et al., *The Dictionary of Human Geography*. Oxford: Blackwell (4th edition), 651.

Bunge, William. 1971. *Fitzgerald: Geography of a Revolution*. Cambridge MA: Schenkman.

Debord, G. 1994 (1967). *The Society of the Spectacle*. New York: Zone Books (translated by D. Nicholson-Smith).

Lefebvre, Henri. 1996 (1968). "The Right to the City," in *Writing on Cities*. Oxford: Blackwell (edited and translated by E. Kofman and E. Lebas), 63–181, originally published as *Le Droit à la Ville*. Paris: Anthropos.

Longan, Michael. 2000. *Community and Place in Cyberspace: The Community Networking Movement in the United States,* Unpublished PhD Dissertation, Department of Geography, University of Colorado.

MacPherson, Crawford B. 1978. *Property: Mainstream and Critical Positions*. Toronto: University of Toronto Press.

Merrifield, Andrew. 2002. *Metromarxism*. New York: Routledge.

Rose, C. 1994. *Property and Persuasion: Essays on the History, Theory and Rhetoric of Ownership*. Boulder: Westview Press.

Shields, Rob. 1998. *Lefebvre, Love and Struggle*. New York: Routledge.

Smith, Neil. 1992b. "New City, New Frontier: The Lower East Side as Wild, Wild, West," in M. Sorkin (ed.), *Variations on a Theme Park: The New American City and the End of Public Space*. New York: Hill and Wang, 61–93.

Waldron, Jeremy. 1991. "Homelessness and the Issue of Freedom," *UCLA Law Review* 39, 295–324.

Williams, Raymond. 1997. (1980) *Problems of Materialism and Culture*. London: Verso.

32
Contesting Crime, Order, and Migrant Spaces in Beijing

(2001)

Li Zhang

In November 1995, an order signed by Premier Li Peng was issued by the Beijing municipal government to "clean up and bring order back to" Zhejiangcun, the largest migrant settlement in Beijing.

This campaign to remove migrant housing was part of a fierce battle over power, space, and urban citizenship that ensued as millions of rural transients, known as the "floating population" (*liudong renkou*), streamed into Chinese cities.[1]

The contestation over migrant spaces in China is closely intertwined with the issue of crime and the power of representation. The "floating population" is often represented by the media and official discourse as an aimless, intractable, and menacing peril unleashed by the invisible hand of the free market. In the social imagination of the majority of urbanites, this floating population stands as a metaphor for uncertainty, insecurity, and instability brought by the post-Mao reforms. Urban settlements created by rural migrants are imagined and represented as hotbeds of crime and disorder, eroding the existing urban social order and public security.

Yet what constitutes order, what kind of space comes to be marked as safe or unsafe, and what leads to increased crime in cities are highly contentious issues.

ZHEJIANGCUN AND THE EMERGENCE OF "BIG YARDS"

The so-called Zhejiangcun (meaning "Zhejiang village") is neither an administratively defined village nor a squatter settlement exclusively occupied by migrants. It is a large migrant congregating zone embedded in a number of preexisting suburban communities in Nanyuan Township in the southern part of Beijing. Because the majority of migrants in this area came from rural Wenzhou, Zhejiang Province, this settlement was named by Beijing residents after these migrants' provincial origin to demarcate a perceived "alien" social body from the established Beijing community.

Historically, Wenzhou merchants had traveled to many parts of China and to Europe for small family businesses and trade. Wenzhou migrants began to come to Beijing in the early 1980s as China's economic reforms began. As the nation's capital, Beijing was viewed by the migrant pioneers as a vast potential consumer market for emerging private businesses. By 1995, there were roughly one hundred thousand migrants working and living in this settlement. Using their settlement as the economic base, Wenzhou migrants' garment businesses soon came to dominate Beijing's informal clothing market. Their booming entrepreneurial activities have significantly transformed the physical and social landscape of the local community (Nanyuan) from a poor, bleak, and marginal suburban area into a wealthy and dynamic commercial zone. Most farmland was replaced with migrants' commercial buildings, marketplaces, and numerous private shops.[2] Such economic success, however, was overshadowed by the municipal government's concern with the subversive potential of migrant settlements with regard to political stability and social order in the city. Particularly, the controversial development of Wenzhou migrants' walled housing compounds intensified such political anxieties.

It was in this context that the migrant residential compounds known as "big yards" (*dayuan*) came into being. Big yards were developed mainly by Wenzhou migrants who possessed money and social prestige. Due to their non-permanent-resident status in Beijing, migrants were prohibited from using land for housing construction. But migrant housing bosses were able to cut private deals with the local village authority for short-term land leases without reporting them to the district-level government. In the context of waning agricultural production, members of these suburban villages were interested in seeking alternative economic profits by cooperating with Wenzhou migrants even if this was officially considered illegal. Further, officials in local government agencies, who were bought off by big yard bosses with cash, banquets, and expensive goods, purposely overlooked the presence of these new compounds. They also offered migrants highly demanded resources such as water, gas, electricity, and sewage at a higher market price than what was charged to locals. Such commodified personal networks (*guanxi*) opened up new channels through which migrants without urban hukou could make use of the urban space and services monopolized by the state (cf. Pieke 1995; Yang 1989). The first Wenzhou migrants' big yard was constructed in 1992. In the following three years, over forty large and small private housing compounds were created in this area. Nearly half of the migrant households in the area moved into these walled residential compounds.

REPRESENTING MIGRANT SPACES

The formation of migrant settlements in general and Wenzhou migrants' big yards in particular has both fascinated and daunted the social imagination of the Beijing public. Such new migrant spatial formations provoked heated debates about their social and political effect on the quality of life and the social order of the city.

In Beijing, official and urban public discourses share a great deal of commonality despite some subtle differences. They tend to regard "migrant congregating zones" and big yards as a crystallization of the "urban cancer" or

"filth and mire" (Hao 1992) brought by free market forces. The popular perception that links migrants to crime and instability both draws from and is reflected in the press and media. Here are two typical examples that magnify one aspect of migrant settlements as their overall reality. A report by city officials delineates Zhejiangcun as a place that is dirty (*zang*), chaotic (*luan*), and miserable (*cha*):

> Although they [migrants] have some positive influences on enlivening markets and making local people's lives more convenient, they have created a series of problems, including overpopulation, traffic jams, poor hygiene, disorder, crime, and other lawbreaking activities. All of these problems have seriously damaged the orderly regulation of the local government.
> (*Beijing Evening Daily*, November 28, 1995)

The ultimate concern of officials is not just disorder within migrant settlements but more importantly their potential for jeopardizing state control and political stability.

In contrast, popular newspapers and magazines are more interested in spicy, exaggerated anecdotes about the crime, drugs, and prostitution associated with the floating population in order to attract more readers and make greater profits under increasing market competition. For instance, the *Beijing Evening Daily*, the most widely read newspaper in the city, recently created a special column entitled "People and Law" (*ren yu fa*) to cover the crimes and illegal activities of "outsiders" (*waidiren*), presumably migrants. Urban residents who retreat into their small, fortified homes tend to regard these social reports as a popular "window on society" (*shehui zhi chuang*) through which they can discern the social climate and problems of Beijing in order to ensure their personal safety. These images and the information produced by the popular press become the raw materials with which the urban public shapes its knowledge of, imagination of, and action toward the migrant population.

THE CULTURAL LOGIC OF MIGRANT CRIMINALITY

The criminalization of the floating population is by no means a phenomenon unique to Chinese society. People who do not fit in the existing categorical order of things tend to be viewed by most societies as "out of place" and thus a source of danger and pollution (Douglas 1966). In other cultural contexts, scholars have analyzed similar processes in which displaced and marginalized groups—refugees, immigrants, blacks, gays, and the homeless poor—have become the subjects of criminalization and pathologization (see Gilroy 1991; Malkki 1992; Chavez 1992; Foucault 1980; Santiago-Irizarry 1996). In China, peasants who have left the farm and "float" in the cities are regarded as perilous and threatening because they do not occupy a proper structural position in the existing national order, which denounces spatial mobility.[3]

The demoralization of spatial mobility extends even further into the projection of political stability and order. The notion of *dongluan* in the Chinese political semantics readily links spatial mobility or movement to "chaos" and "disorder."

Second, displaced rurality is viewed as a form of social pollution and another source of illegality. In the discourse on Chinese modernization, peasantry and the countryside are regarded as lagging behind in the nation's march to modernity.

Third, the dominant discourse construes crime as a result of migrants' greed for wealth, presumably unleashed by the market-oriented city experiences that promise too many unfulfilled dreams. Migrant workers are frequently depicted as ignorant, poverty driven, and jealous about the urban affluence they lack.

ALTERNATIVE DISCOURSE: RELOCATING THE ORIGIN OF CRIME

While migrant communities are viewed as dirty and chaotic places that need to be eliminated or tightly controlled, these are precisely the places where migrants can find shelter and a sense of order and security. Outside the settlements, migrants are constantly driven by police and scorned by urbanites.

The most critical alternative discourse was developed in the arena of contesting the origin of crime. Rather than limiting our gaze simply to the symptoms of crime, Wenzhou migrants insist that one must question under what social conditions criminal activities are able to

reproduce. They argue that the problem of crime should be sought in the existing social structure, which perpetuates a particular form of criminal culture, instead of in migrant dispositions and spatial mobility. Notice how Chen, a Wenzhou migrant businessman, articulated this point:

> Beijing people only know that Zhejiangcun is disorderly, but they do not ask why. And they do not know what the real origin of such disorder is…. I can assure you that the majority of us are good, law-abiding people. The emergence of crime is closely related to recent societal changes. The problem is more serious here because no one can do anything to stop it. With guanxi and bribery money, criminals can easily get out of the police station. This way, lawbreakers are not afraid of anybody and can assault people again and again. In my view, the real origin of crime is rooted in the corruption of the police as well as the entire legal system.

This narrative represents a widely shared view among migrants. First, they argue that one must differentiate criminals from victims and ask who commits crimes against whom rather than criminalizing the entire migrant group. Second, Wenzhou migrants subvert the dominant discourse by relocating the origin of crime in the disorder of the state bureaucracy itself. In the eyes of many migrants, the post-Mao party-state, operating on the basis of the idiosyncratic power of officials (*quan*) rather than the rule of law (*fa*), is deeply corrupt. In the new era of marketization, local officials' formal incomes have declined relatively, which makes them more vulnerable to the temptations of bribes and payoffs from gangsters and criminals. The corrupt nature of the government allows crime and disorder to proliferate and perpetuate.

The failure of governmental control over order in Zhejiangcun also reveals serious problems within the socialist system of regulation, which does not fit the new reality of a market-oriented society. In postrevolutionary China, state regulation in cities has been primarily based on vertical chains of hierarchical work units in the same system (*tiao*) and local government control of localities (*kuai*). Urban residents are simultaneously located and controlled by these two systems, namely, one's work unit and the local government of one's place of residence. Migrants in the cities, however, are not subject to either of these regulation systems because they do not belong to a work unit nor are they counted as full members of any urban community. Local officials are interested in charging migrants regulation fees, but they do not provide promised services or keep order. Meanwhile, because of frequent unfair treatment by the police, many migrants do not believe that justice can be served by them and have therefore formed an antagonistic attitude toward state intervention in policing. An alternative way to manage migrant spaces is through their own popular leadership (such as housing and market bosses), which mediates the relationship between the migrant group and the local government. Such an emerging leadership in the migrant community, however, is deemed by the government to be alien and dangerous.

DEMOLITION AS A REMEDY FOR DISORDER?

The campaign to "clean up and reorder" (*qingli zhengdun*) Zhejiangcun began in early December of 1995. A special governmental work team, consisting of two thousand local officials and cadres, was formed under the order of the Beijing municipal government and directly led by the Fengtai District government. Members of the work team went to Zhejiangcun daily to pressure migrants to give up their housing compounds and leave Beijing. Although many local officials were unwilling to carry out this task, since their own economic interests were tied to the informal migrant economy (e.g., through land leases, housing rentals, and taxes on migrants), refusal to participate in the campaign would jeopardize their political careers. Well aware of multiple-level hidden conflicts, the campaign headquarters constantly called for internal solidarity and urged local officials to give up factionalism and self-interest for the higher call of the central party-state. Meanwhile, five thousand armed policemen were called in, waiting for immediate deployment in case a migrant protest erupted.

Big yard bosses played a crucial role in mediating the relationship between ordinary migrants and the work team. They also mobilized their own regional governments in Zhejiang Province to negotiate with the city government of Beijing. Migrants confronted the work team by delaying their departure to support the negotiation. They criticized the city government's antimigrant sentiment as a typical expression of parochialism that opposed the fundamental principles of reform promised by former Chinese leader Deng Xiaoping. They also invoked the notion of equal citizenship to contest the unequal treatment they had received from the state.

Despite pervasive popular resistance from migrants, local farmers, and local officials, the central and city governments decided to remove all the big yards by the end of 1995. The fact that Wenzhou migrants were able to mobilize support from their provincial and city governments and defy the order of the central state also upset some top officials and made them more determined than ever to destroy this growing nonstate power. Before the official destruction began, big yard owners were ordered to dismantle their compounds to avoid fines and other punishments. With tears and broken hearts, most of them removed parts of their roofs and walls in symbolic compliance. "It is no different than burning your own wealth or killing your own baby," many migrants told me. During the next several days, most compounds were dismantled, creating more than two thousand tons of debris. Thousands of migrants lost their homes and were driven out of Beijing.

Did the demolition campaign really improve social order and public security in the area? Throughout the campaign, it was the law-abiding, propertied, migrant households that were hurt most because they were least mobile and their production hinged upon direct access to Beijing's market. In contrast, those engaged in illegal activities were not seriously affected because they did not live in the big yards, the major targets of demolition. Instead, they took advantage of the disorderly situation created by the demolition to rob and loot even more. The policing of social order in Zhejiangcun was actually set back by this political cyclone. But in a few limited official reports, the narrative of the campaign presented an innocent story of the triumph of justice over evil, order over disorder.[4] These reports highlight the government's achievements in cleaning up the "dead corners" occupied by migrants and widening local streets by demolishing illegal housing. Not a single word was said about where the tens of thousands of displaced migrants went and how they coped with their shattered lives. An abstract notion of social order was claimed.

NOTES

1 Elsewhere I argue that the floating population is a socially constructed category that has helped transform migrants with diverse experiences into a new kind of subject of the state during the very recent history of reform (Zhang 2002).

2 In China, almost all land is officially owned by the state. Yet, use rights to land are often distributed to work units and villages, which now enjoy some freedom to lease certain kinds of land to private entrepreneurs.

3 This mode of national order is not unique to the socialist state but has deep roots in the Confucian political ideology that attempted to adhere people to the moral order by tying them to the spatial order.

4 The media were prohibited from reporting this event. Only four short articles in slightly different versions, drafted and sanctioned by the Beijing government, appeared in local newspapers such as the *Beijing Evening Daily* and *Beijing Youth Daily*.

REFERENCES

Chavez, Leo R. 1992. *Shadowed Lives*. Fort Worth, TX: Harcourt Brace Jovanovich.

Douglas, Mary. 1966. *Purity and Danger: An Analysis of the Concepts of Pollution and Taboo*. London: Routledge.

Foucault, Michel. 1980. *The History of Sexuality*. Vol. 1: *An Introduction*, trans. Robert Hurley. New York: Vintage.

Gilroy, Paul. 1991. *There Ain't No Black in the Union Jack: The Cultural Politics of Race and Nation*. Chicago, IL: University of Chicago Press.

Hao Zaijin. 1992. "Zhongguo Liudong Renkou Baogao" (Reports on China's floating population). *Liberation Daily*.

Malkki, Liisa. 1992. "National Geographic: The Rooting of People and the Territorialization of National Identity among Scholars and Refugees." *Cultural Anthropology* 7, no. 1: 24–44.

Pieke, Frank. 1995. "Bureaucracy, Friends, and Money: The Growth of Capital Socialism in China." *Comparative Study of Society and History* 37, no. 3: 494–518.

Santiago-Irizarry, Vilma. 1996. "Culture as Cure." *Cultural Anthropology* 11, no. 1: 3–24.

Yang, Mayfair Mei-hui. 1989. "The Gift Economy and State Power in China." *Comparative Studies in Society and History* 31, no. 1: 25–54.

Zhang, Li. 2002. *Strangers in the City: Reconfigurations of Space, Power, and Social Networks Within China's Floating Population*. Stanford, CA: Stanford University Press.

33
Privacy Could Only Be Had in Public

Gay Uses of the Streets (1995)

George Chauncey

There is no queer space; there are only spaces used by queers or put to queer use. Space has no natural character, no inherent meaning, no intrinsic status as public or private. As Michel de Certeau has argued, it is always invested with meaning by its users as well as its creators, and even when its creators have the power to define its official and dominant meaning, its users are usually able to develop tactics that allow them to use the space in alternative, even oppositional ways that confound the designs of its creators.[1]

Nothing illustrates this general principle more clearly than the tactics developed by generations of gay men and lesbians to put the spaces of the dominant culture to queer purposes. Struggles over the control of space have been central to gay culture and politics throughout the twentieth century. In the 1930s, after the upheavals and urban cultural experimentation sparked by Prohibition (1920–33) had allowed gay life to become remarkably integrated into the broader cultural life of New York (and other cities) and visible in its "public" spaces, a series of measures were enacted to exclude homosexuality from the public sphere—the city's cafés, bars, streets, and theaters—where authorities feared it threatened to disrupt public order and the reproduction of normative gender and sexual arrangements. For the next thirty years, many of the most important sites of public sociability, including bars, restaurants, and cabarets, were threatened with closure if they allowed lesbians or gay men to gather openly on their premises; and men and women risked arrest if they carried themselves openly as homosexuals on the streets of the city or even at gay parties held in "private" apartments. Even before formal anti-gay regulations were enacted in the 1920s and 1930s, the social marginalization of homosexuals had given the police and popular vigilantes even broader informal authority to harass them. The formal and informal prohibition of gay visibility in the spaces of the city had a fundamental influence on the development of gay cultural practices.[2]

This essay examines the tactics used by gay men in early twentieth-century New York City to claim space for themselves in the face of the battery of laws and informal practices designed to exclude them from urban space altogether. One of my purposes is to challenge the myths that govern most thinking about gay life before Stonewall, particularly the myths that gay people before the 1960s inevitably remained isolated from one another, invisible to straight people and to other gay people alike, or confined to the most marginalized and hidden of urban spaces. But analyzing the queer uses of urban space also highlights the degree to which struggles over the production and control of space played a central role in shaping gay cultural practices more generally—and the degree to which the struggles over queer uses of the city were shaped by and influenced broader class, gender, and racial/ethnic struggles over urban space. Analyzing the role of the production and contestation of queer space in the everyday life of gay men with a high degree of historical specificity also has implications for the theorization of urban space in general. Most importantly, it demonstrates the degree to which the boundaries between spaces defined as "public" and "private" are socially constructed, contingent, and contested; and it illuminates the range of forces—informal as well as official, oppositional as well as dominant—seeking to exert definitional and regulatory power over the production of urban space.

Part of the gay world taking shape in the streets was highly visible to outsiders, but even more of it was invisible. Gay men had to contend with the threat of vigilante anti-gay violence as well as with the police. In response to this challenge, gay men devised a variety of tactics that allowed them to move freely about the city, to appropriate for themselves spaces that were not marked as gay, and to construct a gay city in the midst of, yet invisible to, the dominant city. They were aided in this effort, as always, by the disinclination of most people to believe that any "normal"-looking man could be anything other than "normal," and by their access, as men, to public space.

Although gay street culture was in certain respects an unusual and distinctive pheno-menon, it was also part of and shaped by a larger street culture that was primarily working class in character and origin. Given the crowded conditions in which most working people lived, much of their social life took place in streets and parks. The gay presence in the streets was thus masked, in part, by the bustle of street life in working-class neighborhoods. Gay uses of the streets, like other working-class uses, also came under attack, however, because they challenged bourgeois conceptions of public order, the proper boundaries between public and private space, and the social practices appropriate to each.

THE SOCIAL ORGANIZATION OF THE STREETS

Along with the parks and beaches, the streets themselves served as a social center, cruising area, and assignation spot. Gay men interacted on streets throughout the city, but just as various immigrant groups predominated in certain neighborhoods and on certain streets, so, too, gay men had their own streets and corners, often where gay-oriented saloons and restaurants could be found and along which men strolled, looking for other men to pick up.

The streets could be dangerous, though, for men faced there the threat of arrest or harassment from the police and from anti-gay vigilantes. The police regularly dispatched

plainclothes officers to the most popular cruising areas, and the results of their surveillance could be devastating. An arrest made in 1910 illustrates both the police's familiarity with gay haunts and the hazards the police could pose. At midnight on December 15 a forty-four-year-old clerk from Long Island had gone to Union Square, one of the city's best-known cruising areas at the time, and met a seventeen-year-old German baker who had walked over from his Park Row lodging house. They agreed to spend the night together and walked to a hotel on East 22nd Street at Third Avenue where they could rent a room. Both men had evidently known that the Square was a place where they could meet other men. So, too, had the police. Two detectives, apparently on the look-out for such things, saw them meet, followed them to the hotel, spied on them from the adjoining room through a transom, and arrested them after watching them have sex. The older man was convicted of sodomy and sentenced to a year in prison.[3]

The police action at Union Square was not an isolated event. Around 1910 the police department added the surveillance of homo-sexuals (whom they often labeled "male prosti-tutes") to the responsibilities of the vice squad, which already handled the investigations of female prostitutes. Around 1915, the squad assigned one of its plainclothes officers, Terence Harvey, to "specialize in perversion cases." He patrolled the parks, theaters, and subway rest-rooms known as centers of homosexual and heterosexual rendezvous alike; he arrested some men after seeing them meet in gay cruising areas and following them home, and he entrapped others. He appears to have been quite effective, for he won the praise of the anti-vice societies and was responsible for almost a third of the arrests of men charged with homosexual activity in the first half of 1921.

Most of the men he and the other members of the vice squad arrested were charged not with sodomy, a felony, but with disorderly conduct, a misdemeanor that was much easier to prove and did not require a trial by jury. By the early 1910s the police had begun to specify in their own records which of the men arrested for disorderly conduct had been arrested for "degeneracy." The state legislature formalized this categori-zation in 1923 as part of its general revision of the disorderly conduct statute. The statute, like the use of the vice squad to pursue homosexual cases, reflected the manner in which the authorities associated homosexual behavior with female prostitution, for it used wording strikingly similar to that used to prosecute female prostitutes in its definition of the crime as the "frequenting or loitering about any public place soliciting men for the purpose of committing a crime against nature or other lewdness." As a practical matter, the authorities generally interpreted this statute to apply only to the "degenerates" who solicited "normal men" for sex and not to the men who responded to such solicitations, just as prostitutes were charged while their customers' behavior remained uncensured. In most cases this was because the "normal" man was a plainclothes policeman (who, presumably, had responded only to the degree necessary to confirm the "degenerate's" intentions), but it also applied to some cases in which the police had observed "fairies" solicit men they regarded as "normal." In other cases, the police labeled and arrested both of the men involved as "degenerates."

Although the law was used primarily to prosecute men for trying to pick up another man (cruising), the police and sympathetic judges sometimes interpreted it loosely enough to encompass the prosecution of men who simply behaved in a campy, openly gay way, as in the case of men arrested when the police raided a cafeteria or bar homosexuals frequented. An exceptionally high percentage of the arrests on such charges resulted in convictions—roughly 89 percent in one 1921 study. Although different judges were likely to impose different sentences, the same study found that in general they were unusually harsh in such cases. Less than a quarter of the men convicted had their sentences suspended, while more than a third of them were sentenced for a period of days or even months to the workhouse, and a similar number were fined. An average of 650 men were convicted for degeneracy each year in Manhattan in the 1920s and 1930s.

The police and the social purity groups were not the only forces to threaten gay men's use of the streets. A variety of other groups also sought to ensure the maintenance of moral order in the city's streets on a more informal—but nonetheless more pervasive, and, often, more effective—basis. The men who gathered at the corner saloon or poolroom often kept an eye on the street and discussed the events unfolding there, shopkeepers took an interest in the activities outside their stores, and mothers watched the movements of their children and neighbors from their stoops and windows. On most blocks in the tenement neighborhoods, gangs of youths kept "their" street under near-constant surveillance from their street corner outposts. Although the first concern of such gangs was to protect their territory from the incursions of rival gangs, they also kept a close watch over other strangers who threatened the moral order of the block. These groups often disagreed among themselves about what that moral order properly was, but gay men had to contend with the threat of the popular sanctions any of them might impose against "inverts" and homosexuals, from gossip to catcalls to violence.

Gay men responded to the threat of both formal and informal sanctions by developing a variety of strategies for negotiating their presence on the streets. Perhaps nowhere were more men willing to venture out in public in drag than in Harlem. Drag queens regularly appeared in the neighborhood's streets and clubs, where they tended to be more casually tolerated than in most of the city's other neighborhoods.

Still, it took considerable courage for men to appear in drag even in Harlem, since they risked harassment by other youths and arrest by the Irish policemen who patrolled their neighborhood. Over the course of two weeks in February 1928 the police arrested thirty men for wearing drag at a single club, Lulu Belle at 341 Lenox Avenue near 127th Street. Five men dressed in "silk stockings, sleeveless evening gowns of soft-tinted crepe de chine and light fur wraps" were arrested on a single night.[4]

THE CONTESTED BOUNDARIES BETWEEN PUBLIC AND PRIVATE SPACE

The streets and parks had particular significance for gay men as meeting places for gay men because of the special constraints they faced as homosexuals, but they were hardly the only people to use these culturally contested spaces. That culture sustained a set of sexual values and a way of conceptualizing the boundaries between public and private space that paralleled those governing many aspects of gay men's behavior—and that middle-class ideology found almost as shocking in the case of heterosexual couples as in homosexual. The purposes and tactics of gay men out cruising resembled those of young men and women out looking for a date in many respects. The casual pickups men made on the streets were hardly unique to male couples in this era, for many young women depended on being picked up by men to finance their excursions to music halls and amusement parks, as the historians Kathy Peiss and Joanne Meyerowitz have shown. It was common on the streets for men to approach women with whom they were unacquainted to make a date. This distressed middle-class moral reformers, who considered casual pickups almost as undesirable as professional prostitution, if they distinguished the two at all.[5] The fact that these couples met in unsupervised public places and even had sex there was even more shocking to middle-class reformers, in part because it challenged the careful delineation between public and private space that was so central to bourgeois conceptions of public order.

The efforts of the police to control gay men's use of "public" space, then, were part of a much broader effort by the state to (quite literally) police the boundaries between public and private space, and, in particular, to impose a bourgeois definition of such distinctions on working-class communities. Gay men's strategies for using urban space came under attack not just because they challenged the heteronormativity that normally governed men and women's use of public space, but also because they were part of a more general challenge to dominant cultural conceptions of those boundaries and of the social practices appropriate to each sphere. The inability of the police and reformers to stop such activity reflects their failure to impose a single, hegemonic map of the city's public and private spaces on its diverse communities.

Gay men developed a gay map of the city and named its landmarks: the Fruited Plain, Vaseline Alley, Bitches' Walk. Even outsiders were familiar with sections of that map, for the "shoals of painted, perfumed, … mincing youths that at night swarm on Broadway in the Tenderloin section, … the parks and 5th avenue" made the gay territorialization of the city inescapable to Bernarr Macfadden and many others. But even more of that map was unknown to the dominant culture. Gay men met throughout the city, their meetings invisible to all but the initiated and carefully orchestrated to remain so. Certain subway stations and public

comfort stations, as well as more open locales such as parks and streets, were the sites of almost constant social and even sexual interactions between men, but most men carefully structured their interactions so that no outsiders would recognize them as such.

The boundaries of the gay world were thus highly permeable, and different men participated in it to different degrees and in different ways. Some passed in and out of it quickly, making no more than occasional stops at a subway tearoom for a quick sexual encounter that had little significance for their self-identity or the other parts of their life. Even those men who were most isolated from the organized gay world got a glimpse of its size and diversity through their anonymous encounters in washrooms and recessed doorways, however, and those encounters provided other men with an entree into a world much larger and more highly organized than they could have imagined. The streets and parks served them as social centers as well as sites of sexual rendezvous, places where they could meet others like themselves and find collective support for their rejection of the sexual and gender roles prescribed them. The "mysterious bond" between gay men that allowed them to locate and communicate with one another even in the settings potentially most hostile to them attests to the resiliency of their world and to the resources their subculture had made available to them.

NOTES

1 Michel de Certeau, *The Practice of Everyday Life,* trans. Steven F. Rendall (Berkeley: University of California Press, 1984), esp. pp. xviii–xx, pp. 29–42.
2 For a more fully developed analysis of the changing regulation of gay life in the early twentieth century, see my *Gay New York: Gender, Urban Culture, and the Making of the Gay Male World 1890–1940* (New York: Basic Books, 1994), from which this essay is drawn.
3 *People v. Williams.* DAP 80,706 (CGS 1910). The fate of the younger man is uncertain.
4 *Amsterdam News* (15 February 1928), p. 1.
5 Kathy Peiss, *Cheep Amusements,* pp. 54–55; 106; idem. "'Charity Girls' and City

Pleasures: Historical Notes on Working-Class Sexuality, 1880–1920," in *Passion and Power; Sexuality in History*. ed. Kathy Peiss and Christina Simmons (Philadelphia, PA: Temple University Press, 1989), pp. 57–69; Joanne J. Meyerowitz, *Women Adrift: Independent Wage Earners in Chicago, 1880–1930* (Chicago, IL: University of Chicago Press, 1988), pp. 101–106.

34
People Who Live in Glass Houses

Edith Farnsworth, Ludwig Mies van der Rohe,
and Phillip Johnson (1998)

Alice T. Friedman

The Farnsworth House (1945–1951), in Plano, Illinois, by Ludwig Mies van der Rohe (1886–1969) is one of a handful of modern buildings that always seem extraordinary: it is among the most frequently illustrated of all twentieth-century houses, yet like Le Corbusier's Villa Savoye (1929–1930) and Wright's Fallingwater (1936), the sight of the Farnsworth House still takes one's breath away. Countless architecture students have memorized its canonic image, its plan, the name of its architect, and the date and place of construction, but the house remains surprising, elusive, ungraspable. Once seen, it lingers in the mind's eye, but somehow it never becomes completely familiar.

Perched in the middle of a grassy meadow on the bank of the Fox River, some fifty miles west of Chicago, the Farnsworth House appears to be the perfect embodiment of Mies's dictum "Less is more." Even from a distance one is struck by the elegance and simplicity of its form. Eight slender columns of white-painted steel support a transparent glass box; two horizontal planes—crisp, parallel bands of steel hovering above the ground—represent the floor and the roof. Though barely making physical contact with its site, the house seems securely anchored in the green sea that surrounds it; there is a toughness and immutability to the structure, which contrast with the thinness and apparent insubstantiality of the forms. With its low terrace and ladderlike suspended staircases, the house appears to be a life raft or a tent platform, a place of refuge from the turbulence of nature. This image (and experience) of insularity is reinforced by the fact that the interior of the house is almost totally sealed off from the outside world: the only openings in the glass "skin" are a door on one short side of the rectangle, which serves as the entrance, and two small windows set low on the opposite wall.

A thin but seemingly impermeable membrane of glass thus forms the boundary between inside and outside on all four sides of the box; grass, trees, and river are visible through the "walls," yet they seem distant and abstracted, like elements in a landscape painting. This is not simply because the views from the house are framed by the rectilinear structure, but because objects and landscape beyond the glass appear recessed and diminished, as though the surface of the wall were a picture plane and the objects behind it were imaginary, not real. When one looks at things inside the house, however, this equation is reversed: there is an immediacy that is inescapable—one's awareness of the material world is heightened. In part this is due to the fact that the interior is simply one large room (the entire platform measures 77 x 28 feet), subdivided by a freestanding wooden core, which encloses two bathrooms, a fireplace, and a galley kitchen. This block at the center and a lower bank of cupboards at the far end of the house screen and subdivide the space to some degree, but the living areas remain essentially open and unbounded. Within this interior environment, sights and sounds are magnified, people and objects move closer and seem more tangible and tactile.

Mies's architecture thus calls attention not only to itself but also to the physical and aesthetic experience of the occupant. It is important to note that the experience is not always positive.

The "occupant" in this case was Edith Farnsworth (1903–1977), an unmarried doctor who lived and worked in Chicago. In her mid-forties and financially secure, Farnsworth had begun to think about the advantages of owning a small weekend house in the country some months, or even years, before she met the German architect Ludwig Mies van der Rohe, in 1945. At the outset her concerns were those of a typical client: what she was looking for was "a really fine [design] solution for an inexpensive weekend retreat for a single person of my tastes and pre-occupations," as she later recalled in her memoirs.[1] She assumed that whatever else happened in the process of working with an architect, her new house would be a place in which she could relax and find some relief from the strain of her life as a doctor. There is no evidence to suggest that she sought to have her behavior challenged by the "inner logic" of Mies's unyielding architectural vision; on the contrary, she seems to have had a clear idea about how she wanted to live and she expected the architect to respect her views.

Farnsworth's assumptions about her role and rights in the architect–client relationship proved to be unfounded; she soon discovered that what Mies wanted, and what he thought he had found in her, was a patron who would put her budget and her needs aside in favor of his own goals and dreams as an architect. By 1945 Mies and his followers were acutely aware of the fact that what he needed most was a wealthy patron and a job. The lack of opportunities for building in wartime Germany, combined with the strict minimalism of his formal language, had ensured that Mies had few clients and even fewer realized buildings over the last fifteen years. He had built a handful of well-known works in Europe, including the German Pavilion at the Barcelona World's Fair in 1929 and the Tugendhat House in Brno, Czechoslovakia, in 1930, but the majority of his designs remained on paper. This was especially true of his houses: although he had come up with some radically new ideas for living spaces and produced some extraordinary drawings, nothing much had come of them in either Germany or the US[2] Mies's reputation was impressive and his work was admired in elite and academic circles, but he needed exposure— he needed to build. Dr. Edith Farnsworth seemed to be the answer to his prayers.

THE FARNSWORTH HOUSE

The experience of being a single, professional woman in the Midwest in the late 1940s played a critical role in Farnsworth's decision to build a custom-designed weekend house, and it colors the entire history of the project. A wide range of sources, from women's magazines to popular novels and private diaries, celebrated marriage and home ownership in 1940s America, establishing them as virtually unchallenged prerequisites for success and social acceptance. From 1944 on, for example, mortgage programs administered by the Federal Housing Administration favored returning veterans in making loans, thus promoting the ideal of suburban family life.[3] Women were encouraged to embrace motherhood and homemaking in newly built single-family homes: books like Benjamin Spock's *Common Sense Book of Baby and Child Care* (1946) suggested that good mothers would be attentive to the "natural" rhythms of a child's experience, rejecting rigid rules and feeding schedules—which effectively made motherhood a full-time occupation. Suburban houses, with their playrooms, TVs, backyards, and picture windows, were intended not simply as retreats from the city and its "old-fashioned" ways (including jobs for women) but as havens for children and the young families whose activities increasingly focused on their needs.

According to one survey, conducted in 1957 and published under the title *Americans View Their Mental Health*, childless people, particularly women, were viewed with compassionate condescension "as people who have missed the full richness of adult experiences." Moreover, in the popular imagination, single men and women were regarded with suspicion and could be subject to accusations of mental instability or homosexuality. The unmarried woman was seen as a "frustrated old maid" who had "failed so seriously in her understanding of a woman's role that she hadn't even established the marriage prerequisite of having a home." As such, she forfeited her place, both physical and symbolic, within American society, despite her not infrequent role as doting aunt or beloved eccentric, the latter being the role Edith Farnsworth played in her own family.[4]

Two key themes circulate throughout Farnsworth's narrative: uncertainty about the contradiction between family life and singleness, and concern with cultural values, particularly the choice between taste and "mediocrity." These issues would resurface throughout the project, structuring Farnsworth's experience as she was to represent it in interviews and in her writings, and shaping critical reaction in the professional and the popular press. Because they also loomed large on the broader American scene, fueled by the growth of suburban consumer culture and contact with European art and architecture, the Farnsworth House would become an emotional *cause célèbre* invested with meaning that went far beyond matters of architectural design. Although the principal players in this drama—Ludwig Mies van der Rohe, Edith Farnsworth, and the weekend house in Plano, Illinois—were in every respect atypical of the categories they were supposed to represent, they became the focus of an intense debate, hashed out in newspapers and magazines, about American domesticity, sexuality, and the politics of modern architecture.

The house as built, with its open plan, glass walls, and freestanding partitions, was as pure an exercise in architectural minimalism as Mies could have hoped for; he would later cite the fact that it was intended for a single person as a significant opportunity because programmatic demands intruded so little on his thinking. As Fritz Neumeyer has shown, Mies's work was shaped by philosophical principles, in particular a search for architectural order and truth based on a rational approach to design. His goal was to develop a language of form that reflected universal, rather than particular, aspects of human activity and concern.[5] Principles of design and form, rather than programmatic or even typological concerns, always came first. Thus, while Farnsworth may have been, for Mies, an entertaining companion and a committed partisan, as a client she represented a means to an architectural end.

Relations between Mies and Farnsworth had begun to cool by the time construction was started in the summer of 1949: the two socialized together less, and Edith spent less time at the office. The reasons for this change remain unclear, but the situation deteriorated further as problems with the building became evident. When Farnsworth moved in, in December 1950, the roof leaked badly and the heating produced a film that collected on the inside of the windows. A local plumber, seeing that the systems were all gathered together in one inaccessible stack, suggested the house be named "My Mies-conception." The electrician

advised that the wiring be completely redone. Nevertheless, according to Mies's office notes, the two were "still on good terms in February 1951."

The final rupture was precipitated by disagreements over money. With costs mounting to almost twice the original estimate of $40,000 (already a high figure considering that a house in a suburban development such as Levittown could be bought in 1950 for less than one quarter of that price) and under pressure from family and friends, Farnsworth began to voice some of her concerns about the unconventional design and construction methods used in her house. To add insult to injury, he also seems to have decided at this point to charge a fee for his services, something that Farnsworth claimed had never been discussed; this demand was especially galling as Farnsworth had acted as his physician without fee.

The most important battle, however, was not fought in the courtroom, but in the press. Once the case was brought to the attention of the public, the architect and his costly building were treated with incredulity and derision. Farnsworth too was ridiculed. To her horror, crowds of people came on weekends to look at the house "reputed to be the only one of its kind" but in reality "a one-room, one-story structure with flat roof and glass and steel outer walls." She wrote that she found it "hard to bear the insolence and boorishness of those who invaded the solitude of [her] shore and [her] home ... flowers brought in to heal the scars of the building were crushed by those boots beneath the noses pressed against the glass."

While it is unlikely that these concerns were as grievous as Farnsworth made them sound in the thick of combat with Mies—she did, after all, remain in the house for twenty years—they nonetheless contain critical indices for the meaning of the building in its time and place. Concerns over family, gender, and the control of appearances, particularly in the domestic environment, loom large. Much of what was said against the house and modern architecture generally focuses on its departure from the traditions of the American home, and the vulnerability of its occupant to the prying eyes of others. Farnsworth complained more than once, in her memoirs and to the press, about the problem of being looked at by people both inside and outside her home. In an interview published by *Newsweek* she complained that

Mies had wanted to build the interior partitions 5 feet high "for reasons of art and proportion" but that she had objected: "I'm six feet tall," she said, "and I wanted to be able to change my clothes without my head looking like it was wandering over the top of the partition without a body."[6]

The way the house foregrounded Farnsworth's single life and her middle-aged woman's body struck at the heart of American anxiety. As Lynn Spigel has shown, the popularity of television in the US in the 1950s stemmed in part from American preoccupations with privacy, consumerism, and family life. Through its ability to provide a close-up look at other people's lives and homes, television filled a need to know and compare that was fueled by the ever-present lure of the marketplace through advertising. Moreover, television, like the picture window itself, blurred the distinction between public and private realms and problematized the very act of looking, parti-cularly at women.[7]

Gendered language pervades Farnsworth's own expression of her doubts about the workability of the house. She complained that it had two bathrooms, including one for guests, but no enclosed bedroom. In addition, guests were expected to sleep on the sofa or on a mattress on the floor. While Mies may have seen this arrangement as liberating, for Farnsworth, the real-life occupant of the house, it was embarrassing. She complained that she and her guests would "inhabit a sort of three-dimensional sketch, I in my 'sleeping space' and he in his—unless sheer discomfort and depression should drive us together." In a house for a single woman, such an arrangement in fact represents a repressed (or negated) rather than a freed sexuality, just as the doubling of the bathrooms suggests a desire to modestly hide the female body and its functions. Despite pronouncements about freedom, Mies let it be known that the provision of a "guest bathroom" at the Farnsworth House was meant to keep visitors from "seeing Edith's nightgown on the back of the bathroom door." Ultimately, this piece of women's clothing, this emblem of femaleness, sexuality, and the body, had to be hidden away precisely because it served as a reminder of the very things that Mies (and mainstream culture generally) wanted to deny.

In Mies's view, it seems, Farnsworth had very little of a "private life" to conceal: as a single woman, the only thing that could possibly be worth hiding was her nightgown, the sign for her body.

It is well worth asking, by way of conclusion, how Farnsworth could possibly have been as offended and shocked by her house as she professed to be, given her frequent visits to Mies's studio and close association with the project over the five or six years of design development. Having seen the model and the plans, Farnsworth ought to have known better. She could see that the house was going to have glass walls, so why was she so surprised when they finally appeared? The obviousness of the question pushes us to look further for answers, for, of course, the essence of Mies's design, and of Farnsworth's objections to it, ultimately lie less with the exterior walls than with the severity of the interior. The latter is something Farnsworth could have known little about from the model, and even if she knew the drawings well, she would hardly have recognized—as, indeed, very few critics have—how the subtleties of interior planning and furnishing profoundly alter the experience of the house. Mies's rigid axial planning, evident in the rectilinear arrangement of the freestanding core and minimalist furniture, is what gives the house its discipline and creates the effect of a domestic theater—in which Farnsworth became an isolated object of scrutiny, a moving figure in a landscape of immovable forms. Unlike Johnson's Glass House, which features clusters of large and small objects throughout the interior and doorways on all four walls, the interior of the Farnsworth House is unrelenting in its ordered geometry—and this was something Farnsworth discovered only through living in the house over time.

In the end Farnsworth gave up the struggle, but she fought a good fight. She spent twenty years in her glass house, furnishing it with her family heirlooms, working to make it a home; in spite of her complaints, she was no doubt aware of the fact that the house was widely recognized as one of the masterpieces of modern architecture, not only in the United States but in the world. She battled Mies in court and in the press, and she managed to win support for her position. Yet having sold the house (to a Mies enthusiast who filled it with furniture designed by the architect) and moved to Italy in the early 1970s, she looked back on the whole experience with bitterness. She had been for too long the focus of other people's curiosity, too long a nonconformist. Now she wanted nothing more than to become invisible.

NOTES

1 Edith Farnsworth, "Memoirs," unpublished ms. in three notebooks, Farnsworth Collection, Newberry Library, Chicago, ch. 11, unpag.

2 For an overview of Mies's career, see Franz Schulze, *Mies van der Rohe: A Critical Biography* (Chicago, IL: University of Chicago Press, 1985), esp. chs 4–6.

3 Gwendolyn Wright, *Building the Dream: A Social History of Housing in America* (Cambridge, MA: MIT Press, 1981), ch. 13.

4 Gerald Gurin et al., *Americans View Their Mental Health* (New York: Basic Books, 1960), esp. 117. The survey also found that single women were happier but worried more than single men, and that they "experienced an approaching nervous breakdown less often than other women"; 233–235.

5 Fritz Neumeyer, *The Artless Word: Mies van der Rohe on the Building Art*, trans. Mark Jarzombek (Cambridge, MA: MIT Press, 1991), esp. part 5.

6 "Glass House Stones," *Newsweek*, June 8, 1953, 90.

7 Lynn Spigel, *Make Room for TV: Television and the Family Ideal in Postwar America* (Chicago, IL: University of Chicago Press, 1992), esp. chs 3, 4.

35
The Prison of "Public Space"
(2008)

Mark Kingwell

Public space is the age's master signifier, a loose and elastic notion variously deployed to defend (or attack) architecture, to decry (or celebrate) civic squares, to promote (or denounce) graffiti artists, skateboarders, jaywalkers, parkour aficionados, pie-in-the-face guerrillas, underground capture-the-flag enthusiasts, flash-mob surveillance busters and other grid-resistant everyday anarchists. It is the unit of choice when it comes to understanding pollution predicting political futures, thinking about citizenship, lauding creativity and worrying about food, water or the environment. It is either rife with corporate creep and visual pollution, or made bleak by intrusive surveillance technology, or both. It is a site of suspicion, stimulation and transaction all at once. For some, it is the basis of public discourse itself, the hardware on which we run reason's software. Simultaneously everywhere and nowhere, it is political air.

Given the seeming inexhaustibility of the political demand to reclaim public space, what is strange is that nobody admits they have no idea what it is. Most of us assume we know, but more often the assumption is a matter of piety rather than argument—and confused piety at that. Consider the text of a recent open letter to the mayor of Toronto from the Toronto Public Space Committee, an activist group concerned about surveillance cameras:

> The proposed police cameras will be surveying public spaces throughout the city. We feel that it is reasonable to assume that law-abiding citizens should be free to walk the streets and enjoy the public spaces

without being monitored by the police. The very act of continuous monitoring reduces the freedoms we all value within our public spaces. It puts into jeopardy our rights to privacy, and anonymity, on the streets of our city.

Even opponents of the surveillance society can see that something has gone wrong in this form of thinking. What, exactly? To find out, I want to raise two rude, basic questions that nobody seems to ask: Is public space actually a public good? And if so, what kind?

First of all, let us understand public goods as a subcategory of goods in general. In classical economics, a good is public when access to it is not gated by ownership, so that its benefits— what make it a good—are available to everyone, and one person's use of the good does not diminish another's ability to use it. In the jargon, such goods are non-rival and non-excludable. Public goods come in different forms: they may concern "tangible" things (grazing land, fish in the sea, the air we breathe) or intangible ones (education, cultural identity, political participation). Since they are non-rival, public goods are theoretically unlimited by definition; in fact they often become scarce as a result of use.

How? Well, imagine the public good is a natural resource, such as potable water, whose supply is limited even as its value to everyone is obvious. Access to such goods is supposed to be of common interest. Unfortunately, when unmanaged, even abundant public goods are frequently subject to what the economist Garrett Hardin called "the tragedy of the commons." It is rational for each one of us to take advantage of a public good, but, to the extent that we all do, and we increase our advantage as interest dictates, the ultimate effect is the destruction of the resource. Hardin's common grazing land example makes the point vivid: each one of us has an interest in feeding as many of our livestock as we can, but as more and more people do so, the common land is soon brought up to its limit, and then, as quickly, passes that limit. Result: everybody loses for winning.

The typical responses to this threat are regulation or privatization. Neither is without cost. Privatization of some goods—air, for example—is economically untenable as well as offensive to the common need (although privately supplied water, sold in bottles for profit, is now widely accepted: a red flag). Regulation, like all law, is difficult to enforce at the margins. It also risks what economists call the ratchet effect: the more law you have, the more you will need, and you can't go back once you've begun. (To be sure, depletion of the resource is also subject to ratchet effects: use begets more and greater use, to the point of failure.)

Other problems afflict non-material public goods. Take education, which most people like to consider—and all politicians claim to be— a public good. In theory, there is no reason why it should not be: my enjoyment of the benefits of education should not hamper yours, after all; there is more than enough to go around. But in practice, education is structured in the form of institutional access, and the competition for that access generates a zero-sum game—my having the good means you cannot have it. We find education quickly sliding into the paradoxical category of a positional public good: something that in principle is universally available but that nevertheless falls prey to rivalry and exclusion.

In the ideal theory, positional public goods are a contradiction in terms because anything zero-sum is not public; in reality, the hybrid of publicness and exclusive competition is unfortunately common. And that is much harder to regulate than ordinary goods. Environmental quality or beauty in a landscape are other positional public goods: in theory open to all and non-rival, in practice they are frequently gated by access and opportunity costs. The given landscape view may be

obtained only from a private house, for example, or the university place may be preferentially available to the child of a graduate. Theoretical general access is almost always unevenly distributed in fact. Here we have only to think of the alleged public goods known as equality before the law and the rightful pursuit of happiness. The latter tends to generate the competitive equivalent of a commons tragedy, a race to the bottom. Ever struggling to establish position against their neighbours, individuals compete so hard that everyone ends up spending more than they have. Once more working in ratchet, they progressively price themselves out of their own happiness market, but on a wide social scale.

Since happiness is not itself subject to political regulation, at least in liberal states, and because the public good of status lies beyond their ambit, governments tend to manipulate the competition instead, using regulation, taxation or reparation to express a common interest in the distribution of public goods. In an ideal world, the income produced by regulation can end up managing the first kind of public goods, such as scarce land or fresh water, so that they survive commons tragedies, or maintaining a vigorous public interest in goods that tend toward competition, such as education, to avoid unequal use or races to the bottom.

Is public space one of these goods? Framing an answer to that question is difficult in part because space falls somewhere between the tangible and the intangible. It can mean material facts such as right-of-way easements on private fields, or the sidewalks and parks of a city. These are there for everyone's use and enjoyment and, absent vandalism or overuse, they remain non-rival and non-excludable.

But public space can also mean something larger and looser: the right to gather and discuss, to interact with and debate one's fellow citizens. Indeed, the first definition is too narrow for most activists because, even if material facts and built forms are crucial to public space, the merely interstitial notion of public space is too limited. This larger notion of public space brings it closer to the very idea of the public sphere, that place where, in the minds of philosophers at least, citizens hammer out the common interests that underlie—and maybe under-write—their private differences and desires. Here we seek to articulate, according to an ideal theory, *the* common good, not just a bundle of specific ones. Public space enables a political conversation that favours the unforced force of the better argument, the basis of just social order.

A different sort of tragedy of the commons obtains when the order of priority runs from private to public, from individual to social. Instead of the destruction of a public resource from overuse by individuals, we observe the conceptual negation of publicness itself because of presuppositions of propertarian individualism. A shopping arcade or street is a public space only in the sense that in it each one of us pursues our own version of the production of consumption. Note the two crucial ironies of this clash.

First, private individuals enter into the so-called public space as floating bubbles of private space, suspicious of intrusion by strangers and jealous of their interests. On this model, "public" space is not public at all; it is merely an open marketplace of potential transactions, monetary or otherwise, between isolated individuals.

Second, and as a direct result, any porousness of public and private, say from technological change, generates a confusion that is invariably resolved in favour of the private, as in the protest letter from the Public Space Committee, which confuses public space with individual extension of private space. Social networking websites, to take another example, are sometimes praised as a form of public space; but they are invariably defended by users as, in the breach, private. Narcissistic, competitive and isolating, these systems leach interest and energy away from the real world even as, user by user, they work social interaction free of actual spaces.

Thus the strange case of unpublic public space. Even when nobody in particular owns a given area of a city, concrete or virtual, it doesn't matter. That space is, conceptually speaking, owned by the dominant rules of the game, which are hinged to the norm of private interest—notwithstanding that they may destroy privacy at the very same time. Conceiving ourselves as individuals, the great gift of modern political thought reveals itself as a kind of booby prize, because the presumption of clashing private interests everywhere suffuses the spaces, all spaces, of life. Typical arguments for safeguarding public space, inevitably phrased against this background and so in its terms, are always already lost. For illustration of this point,

consider one haunting narrative of that dominance, from a century and a half ago.

Herman Melville's "Bartleby the Scrivener" —significantly subtitled "A Story of Wall Street"—has for generations offered readers the unsettling spectacle of a man who appears to refuse to live. Bartleby, the mysterious copyist who appears one day in the "snug" chambers of a smug, well-to-do Manhattan lawyer, at first takes hungrily to the objectively dispiriting job of hand-copying legal documents:

The narrator is a master of chancery, an office that provides him a comfortable and untroubled livelihood. Readers will not need to be reminded that chancery is the court of law concerned with wills and estates. The lawyer is a man who makes his living at the transactional margin between life and death—especially in dispute.

Bartleby, that paragon of biddable labour, soon reveals new depths. First he refuses to check over his work. Then to fetch a document for the lawyer. Then to join an office conference with the other copyists, Nippers and Turkey. Then to speak, move or eat. And yet, *refuse* is not quite right, because Bartleby's notorious expression of non-cooperation, the phrase that irks the narrator even as his other underlings begin subconsciously to echo it, is "I would prefer not to." This is not refusal in the sense of active objection, but neither is it the expression of an active desire, the way we might speak of a voting preference or a preference among offered goods. Bartleby's progression is one of staged nullification, as he moves from not-working to not-answering to not-moving to, finally, not-living. He dies in prison, removed there from the lawyer's former offices when, in a panic of frustration, the lawyer has uprooted his practice rather than continue to confront immovable Bartleby and his "dead-wall reveries," so different from daydreaming or wool gathering. Cajoling him with promises of comfort and food even in prison, the lawyer receives the story's most affecting line: "I know where I am," Bartleby says to him, and turns his face to the final wall.

Bartleby's is a story of walled streets and walls, as well as of Wall Street, the "cistern" of the lawyer's office and the blank wall of emergent skyscrapers blotting the sky from Bartleby's window view. But it is also the story of a wall of peculiar resistance to the logic of capitalist presupposition, expressed in the norms of work and pleasure, office and home.

Bartleby will not play the game of capital by the rules of general economy—rules that demand, first, the production of consumption and then, as a consequence, the production of excess, paroxysms of luxury. Bartleby's course is itself excessive, however, a luxury of not-doing. He prefers not to work. He prefers not to eat. He prefers not to leave work for the sake of either an unprivate private or an unpublic public. And although his preference ultimately means death, he lives on as a challenge to the accepted order of things.

This is not an overtly political act—there is no call to arms—but it is one with political significance. Just note how the otherwise comfortable lawyer cannot shake off his sense of responsibility and confusion in the encounter. The lawyer is beholden because Bartleby is infinitely withdrawing from care and sense, without actively resisting anything and certainly without being infinitely demanding. His is not a utopian gesture; rather, it is a gesture of refusal to engage. His withdrawal is not an objection, which might be taken over and nullified by power's dominant play; it is, rather, a refusal to play the game at all as currently ruled—thus creating the possibility of a new game altogether, albeit one with a grim end.

"At present I would prefer not to be a little reasonable," Bartleby tells the lawyer in response to one especially desperate charitable offer. With this, he gently rejects—note that oddly formal mitigation of "at present"—the basic tenet of all private-to-private exchange, the very foundation of a liberal public sphere and public goods: the norm of reasonableness. Once situated, Bartleby will not submit to the ironies of public space structured by consumption. He will not be reasonable. Result: prison, starvation, death. But Bartleby is not Kafka's hunger artist, baffled by his own refusals; he knows, to the end, exactly where he is—and how he got there.

Can we say the same?

In addition to the realm of wills and estates, chancery law was historically concerned with matters of bankruptcy and confession. Let us confess, as Melville does in his story, the bankruptcy of our current notions of public space. We are all masters of chancery in the sense that we profit to varying degrees from the current arrangement, but in the end, as for

Melville's lawyer, the inequalities and contradictions of that arrangement will not be resolved by more pious gestures in the direction of revitalized or reclaimed public space. What is needed is a more radical reorientation.

On the prevailing view, public space is a public good at worst of the positional sort, where enjoyment is a competition, and at best of the simple sort, available for everyone's selfish use. Nowhere does it manage to evade or transcend the presuppositions of the property model. In the collective unconscious public space is leftover space, the margins that remain between private holdings and commercial premises, the laneways and parks in which we negotiate not our collective meanings but our outstanding transactional interests, the ones not covered by production and consumption. Even nominally public institutions, such as the large cultural temples of museum or art gallery—artifact-holding artifacts of a democratization of aesthetic experience—do not outpace this unconscious diminution of meaning. They are beholden to private donors, their architecture decided by opaque competition, the curation a matter of esoteric intimidation.

There can be no useful recourse to public space unless and until we reverse the polarity of our conception of publicness itself. It is sometimes said that the threshold between public and private must be a public decision. True, but go farther: the public is not a summing of private preferences or interests, nor even a wide non-rival availability of resources to those preferences or interests. It is, instead, their precondition: for meaning, for work, for identity itself. We imagine that we enter public space with our identities intact, jealous of interest and suspicious of challenge, looking for stimulus and response. But in fact the reverse is true. We cannot enter the public because we have never left the public; it pervades everything, and our identities are never fixed or prefigured because they are themselves achievements of the public dimension in human life.

So conceived, public space is not interstitial, marginal or left over. It is contested, always and everywhere, because identity is ever a matter of finding out who we are. Not a public good so much as an existential one: one without which democratic politics is impossible.

SECTION 7

The Urban Experience

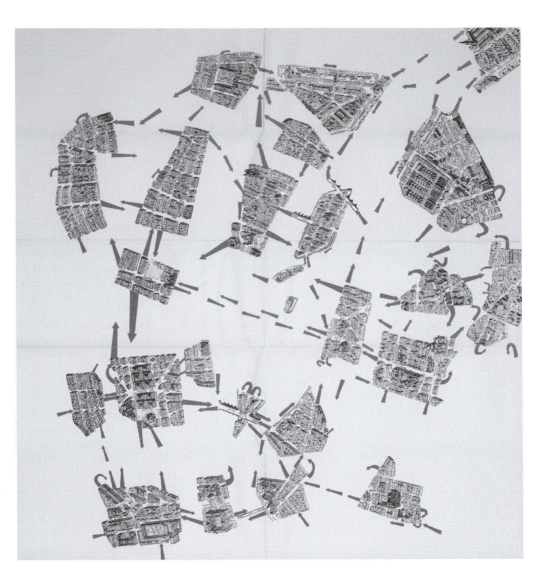

Psychogeographic map of Paris, 1956 by Situationists Guy Debord and Asger Jorn.
Source: Beinecke Rare Book and Manuscript Library, Yale University.
Reference to: Debord, Guy. 1959. "Preliminary Problems in Constructing a Situation" and "Theory of the
Derive" in Situationist International Anthology. Ed. and trans. Ken Knabb. (2006) Oakland, CA: Bureau of

THE URBAN EXPERIENCE

Public Secrets/AK Press.

Urban experiences are diverse and dynamic, changing often with advances in technology, shifts in capital investment, and migrations of people. They are shaped by power and wealth, as well as ingenuity and labor. Urbanity is layered with cultural and social histories, and the demands of day-to-day living. Getting from place to place puts a city dweller in contact with a stimulating variety of people and material conditions. At the same time, these experiences can be exhausting and tend to render the urbanite anonymous within the crowd. Curious about the changing social norms attributed to city living, sociologists of the Chicago School led by Louis Wirth, Ernest Burgess, Robert Park, and Roderic McKenzie used ethnographic fieldwork in the 1920s and 1930s to demonstrate connections between social life and urban planning and policies, arguing that the urban environment shapes human behavior. While sometimes viewed as overly deterministic and too reliant on biological metaphors, the Chicago School deserves credit for grounding their theories in rigorous fieldwork and initiating debate on the effects of urban life. Other scholars, artists, and activists have taken diverse approaches to conveying or contesting experiences of the city, finding examples of both injustice and delight. It is unsurprising then that the urban environment, and the many social and material circumstances people encounter, continues to intrigue authors who seek to learn from the urban experience.

Sociologist **Georg Simmel** is one of the earliest scholars to look specifically at the social and psychological experiences of urban living. Writing in 1903 about rapidly growing cities in Germany, he describes a fascination with what he believed was a new phenomenon in the way people interacted in response to increased density. He identifies the *blasé* attitude as one of the postures that city dwellers adopt to survive the intense stimuli of the urban environment. He also speculates on ways in which industrial production and the demands of time and money influence the human psyche, suggesting that individuals embrace the anonymity offered in cities at the same time that they strive to assert their individuality. Simmel introduced the urban environment as a new realm for research, and suggested that there are both positive and negative social and psychological aspects of city life.

Looking back at Paris of the nineteenth century from a more critical vantage point, literary critic **Walter Benjamin** traces what he refers to as the *phantasmagoria* of modernity. Writing in vignettes, he suggests that the spaces and commodities produced through industrial capitalism alter everyday urban life in fantastic ways. He cites four particular manifestations of phantasmagoria: the arcaded shopping areas; an urban character he calls the *flâneur*; private bourgeois residential interiors; and the wide boulevards created by Baron Haussmann intended to prevent social uprisings. Benjamin argued that these places and activities expressed new attitudes and possibilities for urban experience, but also carried the seeds for the collapse of the French Second Empire. Expansive interior environments enclosed by steel and glass, luxury goods and collectibles, and large capital investment in urban infrastructure characterize the dynamism of this period in Benjamin's account, which ends in class struggle with the burning of Paris during the Commune of 1871. For Benjamin, modernity is a fantastic intersection of technological innovation and shifting cultural norms, fed by capitalist investment. Urban experiences are dizzying and electric, but they are also underlined by distinctions of class and status.

While urban life may be examined at a variety of scales and through many different lenses, the everyday experience of walking in the city has been especially fruitful for contemporary thinkers. French social theorist **Michel de Certeau** outlines connections between language and walking to argue that there are two modes of operating in the urban environment. The mode of *strategy* treats the city as a planned, readable, and stable totality that is visible from above and subject to intentional operations of power. A counter mode of *tactics* is embodied by the person on the ground, walking across the grid, transgressing and leaping across boundaries. Moving in the city, de Certeau argues, complicates the history and meaning of the urban fabric and the agency available in shifting one's ways of operating, allowing room for places that are as yet only imagined. Guy Debord and the Situationists were similarly interested in complicating and reimagining the experience of moving in the city (see Section 2 and figure at the beginning of Section 7).

Jane Jacobs elucidates the notion of tactics in her fight against the power of Robert Moses. Renowned for her efforts in the 1950s and 1960s to oppose the New York City urban renewal projects, she argues that the insertion of large-scale modern buildings and infrastructure would destroy neighborhoods that supported the lives of local inhabitants. Her pivotal book, *The Death and Life of American Cities*, based on her own observations and experiences of living in Manhattan's Greenwich Village, was instrumental in convincing people of the benefits of neighborhood life and the problems with top-down urban planning. The selection included here focuses on the day-to-day interactions of the neighborhood that take place in the most unassuming and public of places: the sidewalk. She describes interactions among residents and shopkeepers as a *sidewalk ballet*, and suggests how urban neighborhoods allow for both personal interaction and a degree of privacy and anonymity.

While Western cities have developed relatively fixed patterns and rigid infrastructures, other places are more fluid and demand flexible interactions. Anthropologist **AbdouMaliq Simone**'s interest is in the encounters and networks that allow people to operate in the unpredictable and heterogeneous environments found in African cities. These spaces, like those of many cities in the global South, are often sprawling, chaotic, or leftover after the flight of the upper and middle classes. In studying post-apartheid Johannesburg, Simone finds areas in which immigrants from rural areas temporarily come together in ways that provide for and reproduce life in the city. He frames these assemblages of people and activities as the *infrastructure* that enables everything from drug dealing to automobile repair. At the same time Simone acknowledges that this infrastructure is unreliable and describes how people must be deft in reading situations and able to switch modes quickly in order to survive in this makeshift and impermanent world.

Underlying many experiences and studies of urban life are questions of justice and injustice. Who experiences what and how are different perspectives accounted for? Feminist philosopher **Iris Marion Young** asks these questions by dissecting our typical understanding of urban relations from a more macro perspective to unpack how cities support equality through *difference*. Young is concerned that in the critique of capitalist society the main alternative posited is *community*. Her fear is that community idealizes unity and common values, and does not adequately allow for differences in identity, activity, or belief. Young suggests that city life, which she insightfully characterizes as the "being together of strangers," is a better sociospatial alternative because it allows people to cluster according to a variety of affinities as well as come in contact with people of differing approaches and attitudes. In this way Young offers us a means of thinking and imagining cities as environments of expression and diversity that depend upon the political engagement of people speaking and listening to one another.

As is apparent from these accounts, the urban experience is fragmented and uneven, stimulating and liberating; there are vast differences in the experiences people have depending on their status, race, gender, sexuality, and other aspects of identity and belief. Elijah Anderson

(2011), John Jackson (2003), and Steven Gregory (1999) have done excellent work exploring questions of race in places like Philadelphia and New York City. Jen Jack Gieseking (2013) has looked at the ways in which lesbian and queer experience changes over time in the city, while Janice Perlman (2011) and Ida Susser (1982) have studied issues of class and poverty in different urban situations, from the favelas of Brazil to the neighborhoods of New York. Andrew Merrifield's *Metromarxism* (2002) is a synthesis of the ways in which authors like Benjamin, Lefebvre, Harvey, and Marshall Berman understand and interpret urban spaces and experiences through a Marxist framework of capital investment and class struggle. Contemporary scholars like Mike Davis (2006), Don Mitchell (2003), Susan Fainstein (2011), and Setha Low (2005, 2014) focus on contemporary injustices and argue that there should be greater equality in city planning and urban experience. Davis digs into the formation of contemporary Los Angeles through the power exerted on its planning by different groups with varying agendas (Caltech scientists, the Catholic Church, etc.). As discussed in Section 6, Mitchell builds upon Lefebvre's idea of the *right to the city*, Low is concerned with broader formulations of social justice, while Fainstein uses the work of Young to advocate for planning and policies that account for more diverse experiences.

Like the boundary between public and private spaces, urban experience is not fixed. The intensity of urban encounter may magnify our sense of these spaces, or cause us to miss them altogether. Cities are malleable, pliable, and constantly changing, and as such the experience we have of urban spaces is always a negotiation between various powers and influences.

SUGGESTIONS FOR FURTHER READING

Please see *peopleplacespace.org* for extended and additional lists of readings.

Anderson, Elijah. 2011. *The Cosmopolitan Canopy: Race and Civility in Everyday Life*. New York: W.W. Norton & Company.

Berman, Marshall. 1988. *All That is Sold Melts Into Air: The Experience of Modernity*. New York: Penguin.

Borden, Iain, Joe Kerr, and Jane Rendell (eds). 2000. *The Unknown City: Contesting Architecture and Social Space*. Cambridge, MA: The MIT Press.

Brenner, Neil, Peter Marcuse, and Margit Mayer (eds). 2011. *Cities for People, Not for Profit: Critical Urban Theory and the Right to the City*. New York: Routledge.

Burgess, Ernest, Robert E. Park, and Roderic Mckenzie. 1925. *The City: Suggestions of Investigation of Human Behaviour in the Urban Environment*. Chicago: University of Chicago Press.

Caro, Robert A. 1975. *The Power Broker: Robert Moses and the Fall of New York*, 1st edn. New York: Vintage.

Davis, Mike. 2006. *City of Quartz: Excavating the Future in Los Angeles*. London: Verso.

Edensor, Tim, and Mark Jayne. 2011. *Urban Theory Beyond the West: A World of Cities*. New York: Routledge.

Fainstein, Susan S. 2011. *The Just City*. Ithaca, NY: Cornell University Press.

Gehl, Jan. 1989. "A Changing Street Life in a Changing Society." *Places* 6(1): 8–17.

Gieseking, Jen Jack. 2013. "Queering the Meaning of 'Neighbourhood': Reinterpreting the Lesbian-Queer Experience of Park Slope, Brooklyn, 1983-2008." In *Queer Presences and Absences*, edited by Yvette Taylor and Michelle Addison, pp.178–200. London: Palgrave Macmillan.

Gregory, Steven. 1999. *Black Corona: Race and the Politics of Place in an Urban Community*. Princeton, NJ: Princeton University Press.

Harvey, David. 2005. *Paris, Capital of Modernity*, new edn. New York: Routledge.

Jackson, John L. 2003. *Harlemworld: Doing Race and Class in Contemporary Black America*, 1st edn. Chicago, IL: University Of Chicago Press.

LeGates, Richard T., and Frederic Stout (eds). 2011. *The City Reader*, 5th edn. London: Routledge.

Low, Setha. 2014. "Spatializing Culture." In *The People, Place, and Space Reader*. New York: Routledge.

Low, Setha, Dana Taplin, and Suzanne Scheld. 2005. *Rethinking Urban Parks: Public Space and Cultural Diversity*. Austin: University of Texas Press.

Marcuse, Peter. 1997. "The Enclave, the Citadel, and the Ghetto: What Has Changed in the Post-Fordist U.S. City." *Urban Affairs Review* 33 (2): 228–264.

Merrifield, Andrew. 2002. *Metromarxism: A Marxist Tale of the City*. New York: Routledge.

Milgram, Stanley. 1970. "The Experience of Living in Cities." *Science* 167(3924): 1461–1468.

Mitchell, Don. 2003. *The Right to the City: Social Justice and the Fight for Public Space*, 1st edn. New York: The Guilford Press.

Myers, Garth A. 2011. *African Cities: Alternative Visions of Urban Theory and Practice*. London: Zed Books.

Perlman, Janice. 2011. *Favela: Four Decades of Living on the Edge in Rio De Janeiro*. Reprint. New York: Oxford University Press.

Pinder, David. 2006. *Visions of the City: Utopianism, Power and Politics in Twentieth Century Urbanism*, new edn. New York: Routledge.

Robinson, Jennifer. 2006. *Ordinary Cities between Modernity and Development*. New York: Routledge.

Rybczynski, Witold. 2010. *Makeshift Metropolis: Ideas about Cities*. New York: Scribner.

Smith, P.D. 2012. *City: A Guidebook for the Urban Age*, 1st edn. London: Bloomsbury Press.

Susser, Ida. 2012 [1982]. *Norman Street: Poverty and Politics in an Urban Neighborhood*, updated edn. New York: Oxford University Press.

Wirth, Louis. 1938. "Urbanism as a Way of Life: The City and Contemporary Civilization." *American Journal of Sociology* 44: 1–24

Whyte, William H. 2001. *The Social Life of Small Urban Spaces*. Project for Public Spaces Inc.

Zukin, Sharon. 1996. *The Cultures of Cities*. Oxford: Blackwell Publishers.

36
The Metropolis and Mental Life

(1903)

Georg Simmel

The deepest problems of modern life flow from the attempt of the individual to maintain the independence and individuality of his existence against the sovereign powers of society, against the weight of the historical heritage and the external culture and life.

The psychological foundation, upon which the metropolitan individuality is erected, is the intensification of emotional life due to the swift and continuous shift of external and internal stimuli. Man is a creature whose existence is dependent on differences, i.e. his mind is stimulated by the difference between present impressions and those which have preceded. Lasting impressions, the slightness in their differences, the habituated regularity of their course and contrasts between them, consume, so to speak, less mental energy than the rapid telescoping of changing images, pronounced differences within what is grasped at a single glance, and the unexpectedness of violent stimuli. To the extent that the metropolis creates these psychological conditions—with every crossing of the street, with the tempo and multiplicity of economic, occupational and social life—it creates in the sensory foundations of mental life, and in the degree of awareness necessitated by our organization as creatures dependent on differences, a deep contrast with the slower, more habitual, more smoothly flowing rhythm of the sensory-mental phase of small town and rural existence.

Thus the metropolitan type—which naturally takes on a thousand individual modifications—creates a protective organ for itself against the profound disruption with which the fluctuations and discontinuities of the external milieu threaten it. Instead of reacting emotionally, the metropolitan type reacts primarily in a rational manner, thus creating a mental predominance through the intensification of consciousness, which in turn is caused by it. Thus the reaction of the metropolitan person to those events is moved to a sphere of mental activity which is least sensitive and which is furthest removed from the depths of the personality.

This intellectualistic quality which is thus recognized as a protection of the inner life against the domination of the metropolis, becomes ramified into numerous specific phenomena. The metropolis has always been the seat of money economy because the many-sidedness and concentration of commercial activity have given the medium of exchange an importance which it could not have acquired in the commercial aspects of rural life. But money economy and the domination of the intellect stand in the closest relationship to one another. They have in common a purely matter-of-fact attitude in the treatment of persons and things in which a formal justice is often combined with an unrelenting hardness. The purely intellectualistic person is indifferent to all things personal because, out of them, relationships and reactions develop which are not to be completely understood by purely rational methods—just as the unique element in events never enters into the principle of money. Money is concerned only with what is common to all, i.e. with the exchange value which reduces all quality and individuality to a purely quantitative level. All emotional relationships between persons rest on their individuality, whereas intellectual relationships deal with persons as with numbers, that is, as with elements which, in themselves, are indifferent, but which are of interest only insofar as they offer something objectively perceivable. It is in this very manner that the inhabitant of the metropolis reckons with his merchant, his customer and with his servant, and frequently with the persons with whom he is thrown into obligatory association. These relationships stand in distinct contrast with the nature of the smaller circle in which the inevitable knowledge of individual characteristics produces, with an equal inevitability, an emotional tone in conduct, a sphere which is beyond the mere objective weighting of tasks performed and payments made. What is essential here as regards the economic-psychological aspect of the problem is that in less advanced cultures production was for the customer who ordered the product so that the producer and the purchaser knew one another. The modern city, however, is supplied almost exclusively by production for the market, that is, for entirely unknown purchasers who never appear in the actual field of vision of the producers themselves. Thereby, the interests of each party acquire a relentless matter-of-factness, and its rationally calculated economic egoism need not fear any divergence from its set path because of the imponderability of personal relationships. This is all the more the case in the money economy which dominates the metropolis in which the last remnants of domestic production and direct barter of goods have been eradicated and in which the amount of production on direct personal order is reduced daily. Furthermore, this psychological intellectualistic attitude and the money economy are in such close integration that no one is able to say whether it was the former that effected the latter or vice versa. What is certain is only that the form of life in the metropolis is the soil which nourishes this interaction most fruitfully,

The relationship and concerns of the typical metropolitan resident are so manifold and complex that, especially as a result of the agglomeration of so many persons with such differentiated interests, their relationships and activities intertwine with one another into a many-membered organism. In view of this fact, the lack of the most exact punctuality in promises and performances would cause the whole to break down into an inextricable chaos. If all the watches in Berlin suddenly went wrong in different ways even only as much as an hour, its entire economic and commercial life would be derailed for some time. Even though this may seem more superficial in its significance, it transpires that the magnitude of distances results in making all waiting and the breaking of appointments an ill-afforded waste of time. For this reason the technique of metropolitan life in general is not conceivable without all of its activities and reciprocal relationships being organized and coordinated in the most punctual way into a firmly fixed framework of time which transcends all subjective elements. But here too there emerge those conclusions which are in general the whole task of this discussion, namely, that every event, however restricted to this superficial level it may appear, comes immediately into contact with the depths of the soul, and that the most banal externalities are, in the last analysis, bound up with the final decisions concerning the meaning and the style of life. Punctuality, calculability and exactness, which are required by the complications and extensiveness of metropolitan life, are not only most intimately connected with its capitalistic and intellectualistic character but also colour the content of life and are conductive to the exclusion of those irrational, instinctive, sovereign human traits and impulses which originally seek to determine the form of life from within instead of receiving it from the outside in a general, schematically precise form.

The same factors which, in the exactness and the minute precision of the form of life, have coalesced into a structure of the highest impersonality, have on the other hand, an influence in a highly personal direction. There is perhaps no psychic phenomenon which is so unconditionally reserved to the city as the blasé outlook. Just as an immoderately sensuous life makes one blasé because it stimulates the nerves to their utmost reactivity until they finally can no longer produce any reaction at all, so, less harmful stimuli, through the rapidity and the contradictoriness of their shifts, force the nerves to make such violent responses, tear them about so brutally that they exhaust their last reserves of strength and, remaining in the same milieu, do not have time for new reserves to form. This incapacity to react to new stimulations with the required amount of energy constitutes in fact that blasé attitude which every child of a large city evinces when compared with the products of the more peaceful and more stable milieu.

Combined with this physiological source of the blasé metropolitan attitude there is another, which derives from a money economy. The essence of the blasé attitude is an indifference toward the distinctions between things. Not in the sense that they are not perceived, as is the case of mental dullness, but rather that the meaning and the value of the distinctions between things, and therewith of the things themselves, are experienced as meaningless. They appear to the blasé person in a homogeneous, flat and grey colour with no one of them worthy of being preferred to another. This psychic mood is the correct subjective reflection of a complete money economy to the extent that money takes the place of all the manifoldness of things and expresses all qualitative distinctions between them in the distinction of how much. To the extent that money, with its colourlessness and its indifferent quality, can become a common denominator of all values, it becomes the frightful leveller—it hollows out the core of things, their peculiarities, their specific values and their uniqueness and incomparability in a way which is beyond repair. They all float with the same specific gravity in the constantly moving stream of money. They all rest on the same level and are distinguished only by their amounts. In individual cases this colouring, or rather this de-colouring of things, through their equation with money, may be imperceptibly small. In the relationship, however, which the wealthy person has to objects which can be bought for money, perhaps indeed in the total character which, for this reason, public opinion now recognizes in these objects, it takes on very considerable proportions. This is why the metropolis is the seat of commerce and it is in it that the purchasability of things appears in quite a different aspect than in simpler economies. It is also the peculiar seat of the blasé attitude.

Whereas the subject of this form of existence must come to terms with it for himself, his self-preservation in the face of the great city requires of him a no less negative type of social conduct. The mental attitude of the people of the metropolis to one another may be designated formally as one of reserve. If the unceasing external contact of numbers of persons in the city should be met by the same number of inner reactions as in the small town, in which one knows almost every person he meets and to each of whom he has a positive relationship, one

would be completely atomized internally and would fall into an unthinkable mental condition. Partly this psychological circumstance and partly the privilege of suspicion which we have in the face of the elements of metropolitan life (which are constantly touching one another in fleeting contact) necessitates in us that reserve, in consequence of which we do not know by sight neighbours of years standing and which permits us to appear to small-town folk so often as cold and uncongenial.

The mutual reserve and indifference, and the intellectual conditions of life in large social units are never more sharply appreciated in their significance for the independence of the individual than in the dense crowds of the metropolis, because the bodily closeness and lack of space make intellectual distance really perceivable for the first time. It is obviously only the obverse of this freedom that, under certain circumstances, one never feels as lonely and as deserted as in this metropolitan crush of persons. For here, as elsewhere, it is by no means necessary that the freedom of man reflect itself in his emotional life only as a pleasant experience.

It is not only the immediate size of the area and population which, on the basis of world-historical correlation between the increase in the size of the social unit and the degree of personal inner and outer freedom, makes the metropolis the locus of this condition. It is rather in transcending this purely tangible extensiveness that the metropolis also becomes the seat of cosmopolitanism. Comparable with the form of the development of wealth—beyond a certain point property increases in ever more rapid progression as out of its own inner being—the individual's horizon is enlarged. In the same way, economic, personal and intellectual relations in the city (which are its ideal reflection) grow in a geometrical progression as soon as, for the first time, a certain limit has been passed. Every dynamic extension becomes a preparation not only for a similar extension but rather for a larger one, and from every thread which is spun out of it there continue, growing as out of themselves, an endless number of others. At this point the quantitative aspects of life are transformed qualitatively. The most significant aspect of the metropolis lies in this functional magnitude beyond its actual physical boundaries and this effectiveness reacts upon the latter and gives to it life, weight, importance and responsibility. A person does not end with the limits of his physical body or with the area to which his physical activity is immediately confined but embraces, rather, the totality of meaningful effects which emanates from him temporally and spatially. In the same way the city exists only in the totality of the effects which transcend their immediate sphere.

Exactly in the measure of its extension, the city offers to an increasing degree the determining conditions for the division of labour. It is a unit which, because of its large size, is receptive to a highly diversified plurality of achievements while at the same time the agglomeration of individuals and their struggle for the customer forces the individual to a type of specialized accomplishment in which he cannot be so easily exterminated by the other. The decisive fact here is that in the life of a city, struggle with nature for the means of life is transformed into a conflict with human beings, and the gain which is fought for is granted, not by nature, but by man. For here we find not only the previously mentioned source of specialization but rather the deeper one in which the seller must seek to produce in the person to whom he wishes to sell ever new and unique needs. The necessity to specialize one's product in order to find a source of income which is not yet exhausted and also to specialize a function which cannot be easily supplanted is conducive to differentiation, refinement and enrichment of the needs of the public which obviously must lead to increasing personal variation within this public.

All this leads to the narrower type of intellectual individuation of mental qualities to which the city gives rise in proportion to its size. There is a whole series of causes for this. First of all there is the difficulty of giving one's own personality a certain status within the framework of metropolitan life. Where quantitative increase of value and energy has reached its limits, one seizes on qualitative distinctions, so that, through taking advantage of the existing sensitivity to differences, the attention of the social world can, in some way, be won for oneself. This leads ultimately to the strangest eccentricities, to specifically metropolitan extravagances of self-distantiation, of caprice, of fastidiousness, the meaning of which is no longer to be found in the content of such activity itself but rather in its being a form of 'being different'—of making oneself noticeable.

For it is this which requires from the individual an ever more one-sided type of achievement which, at its highest point, often permits his personality as a whole to fall into neglect. In any case this over-growth of objective culture has been less and less satisfactory for the individual. Perhaps less conscious than in practical activity and in the obscure complex of feelings which flow from him, he is reduced to a negligible quantity. He becomes a single cog as over against the vast overwhelming organization of things and forces which gradually take out of his hands everything connected with progress, spirituality and value. The operation of these forces results in the transformation of the latter from a subjective form into one of purely objective existence. It need only be pointed out that the metropolis is the proper arena for this type of culture which has outgrown every personal element. Here in buildings and in educational institutions, in the wonders and comforts of space-conquering technique, in the formations of social life and in the concrete institutions of the State is to be found such a tremendous richness of crystalizing, de-personalized cultural accomplishments that the personality can, so to speak, scarcely maintain itself in the fact of it. From one angle life is made infinitely more easy in the sense that stimulations, interests, and the taking up of time and attention, present themselves from all sides and carry it in a stream which scarcely requires any individual efforts for its ongoing. But from another angle, life is composed more and more of these impersonal cultural elements and existing goods and values which seek to suppress peculiar personal interests and incomparabilities.

It is the function of the metropolis to make a place for the conflict and for the attempts at unification of both of these in the sense that its own peculiar conditions have been revealed to us as the occasion and the stimulus for the development of both. Thereby they attain a quite unique place, fruitful with an inexhaustible richness of meaning in the development of the mental life.

37
Paris, Capital of the Nineteenth Century
Exposé of 1939 (1939)

Walter Benjamin

INTRODUCTION

Our investigation proposes to show how the new forms of behavior and the new economically and technologically based creations that we owe to the nineteenth century enter the universe of a phantasmagoria. These creations undergo this "illumination" not only in a theoretical manner, by an ideological transposition, but also in the immediacy of their perceptible presence. They are manifest as phantasmagorias. Thus appear the arcades—first entry in the field of iron construction; thus appear the world exhibitions, whose link to the entertainment industry is significant. Also included in this order of phenomena is the experience of the flâneur, who abandons himself to the phantasmagorias of the marketplace. Corresponding to these phantasmagorias of the market, where people appear only as types, are the phantasmagorias of the interior, which are constituted by man's imperious need to leave the imprint of his private individual existence on the rooms he inhabits. As for the phantasmagoria of civilization itself, it found its champion in Haussmann and its manifest expression in his transformations of Paris.—Nevertheless, the pomp and the splendor with which commodity-producing society surrounds itself, as well as its illusory sense of security, are not immune to dangers; the collapse of the Second Empire and the Commune of Paris remind it of that.

A. FOURIER, OR THE ARCADES

Most of the Paris arcades are built in the fifteen years following 1822. The first condition for their development is the boom in the textile trade. *Magasins de nouveautés,* the first establishments to keep large stocks of merchandise on the premises, make their appearance. They are the forerunners of department stores. This is the period of which Balzac writes: "The great poem of display chants its stanzas of color from the Church of the Madeleine to the Porte Saint-Denis." The arcades are centers of commerce in luxury items. In fitting them out, art enters the service of the merchant. Contemporaries never tire of admiring them. For a long time they remain an attraction for tourists. An *Illustrated Guide to Paris* says: "These arcades, a recent invention of industrial luxury, are glass-roofed, marble-paneled corridors extending through whole blocks of buildings, whose owners have joined together for such enterprises. Lining both sides of the arcade, which gets its light from above, are the most elegant shops, so that the *passage* is a city, a world in miniature." The arcades are the scene of the first attempts at gas lighting.

The second condition for the emergence of the arcades is the beginning of iron construction. Under the Empire, this technology was seen as a contribution to the revival of architecture in the classical Greek sense. The architectural theorist Boetticher expresses the general view of the matter when he says that, "with regard to the art forms of the new system, the Hellenic mode" must come to prevail. The Empire style is the style of revolutionary terrorism, for which the state is an end in itself. Just as Napoleon failed to understand the functional nature of the state as an instrument of domination by the bourgeoisie, so the architects of his time failed to understand the functional nature of iron, with which the constructive principle begins its domination of architecture. These architects design supports resembling Pompeian columns, and factories that imitate residential houses, just as later the first railroad stations will assume the look of chalets. Construction plays the role of the subconscious. Nevertheless, the concept of engineer, which dates from the revolutionary wars, starts to gain ground, and the rivalry begins between builder and decorator, Ecole Polytechnique and Ecole des Beaux-Arts.—For the first time since the Romans, a new artificial building material appears: iron. It will undergo an evolution whose pace will accelerate in the course of the century. This development enters a decisive new phase when it becomes clear that the locomotive—object of the most diverse experiments since the years 1828–1829—usefully functions only on iron rails. The rail becomes the first prefabricated iron component, the precursor of the girder. Iron is avoided in home construction but used in arcades, exhibition halls, train stations—buildings that serve transitory purposes.

B. GRANDVILLE, OR THE WORLD EXHIBITIONS

I

World exhibitions are places of pilgrimage to the commodity fetish. "Europe is off to view the merchandise," says Taine in 1855. The world exhibitions were preceded by national exhibitions of industry, the first of which took place on the Champ de Mars in 1798. It arose from the wish "to entertain the working classes, and it becomes for them a festival of emancipation." The workers would constitute their first clientele. The framework of the entertainment industry has not yet taken shape; the popular festival provides this.

World exhibitions glorify the exchange value of the commodity. They create a framework in which its use value becomes secondary. They are a school in which the masses, forcibly excluded from consumption, are imbued with the exchange value of commodities to the point of identifying with it: "Do not touch the items on display." World exhibitions thus provide access to a phantasmagoria which a person enters in order to be distracted. Within these *divertissements*, to which the individual abandons himself in the framework of the entertainment industry, he remains always an element of a compact mass. This mass delights in amusement parks—with their roller coasters, their "twisters," their "caterpillars"—in an attitude that is pure reaction. It is thus led to that state of subjection which propaganda, industrial as well as political, relies on.—The enthronement of the commodity, with its glitter of distractions, is the secret theme of Grandville's art. Hence the split between its utopian and cynical elements in his work. The subtle artifices with which it represents inanimate objects correspond to what Marx calls the "theological niceties" of the commodity. The concrete expression of this is clearly found in the *spécialité*—a category of goods which appears at this time in the luxuries industry. World exhibitions construct a universe of *spécialités*. The fantasies of Grandville achieve the same thing. They modernize the universe.

II

Fashion prescribes the ritual according to which the commodity fetish demands to be worshipped. Grandville extends the authority of fashion to objects of everyday use, as well as to the cosmos. In taking it to an extreme, he reveals its nature. It couples the living body to the inorganic world. To the living, it defends the rights of the corpse. The fetishism which thus succumbs to the sex appeal of the inorganic is its vital nerve. The fantasies of Grandville correspond to the spirit of fashion that Apollinaire later described with this image:

Any material from nature's domain can now be introduced into the composition of women's clothes. I saw a charming dress made of corks. ... Steel, wool, sandstone, and files have suddenly entered the vestmentary arts. … They're doing shoes in Venetian glass and hats in Baccarat crystal.

C. LOUIS PHILIPPE, OR THE INTERIOR

I

Under the reign of Louis Philippe, the private individual makes his entry into history. For the private individual, places of dwelling are for the first time opposed to places of work. The former come to constitute the interior. Its complement is the office. (For its part, the office is distinguished clearly from the shop counter, which, with its globes, wall maps, and railings, looks like a relic of the baroque forms that preceded the rooms in today's residences.) The private individual, who in the office has to deal with realities, needs the domestic interior to sustain him in his illusions. This necessity is all the more pressing since he has no intention of grafting onto his business interests a clear perception of his social function. In the arrangement of his private surroundings, he suppresses both of these concerns. From this derive the phantasmagorias of the interior—which, for the private individual, represents the universe. In the interior, he brings together remote locales and memories of the past. His living room is a box in the theater of the world.

The interior is the asylum where art takes refuge. The collector proves to be the true resident of the interior. He makes his concern the idealization of objects. To him falls the Sisyphean task of divesting things of their commodity character by taking possession of them. But he can bestow on them only connoisseur value, rather than use value. The collector delights in evoking a world that is not just distant and long gone but also better—a world in which, to be sure, human beings are no better provided with what they need than in the real world, but in which things are freed from the drudgery of being useful.

II

The interior is not just the universe of the private individual; it is also his étui. Ever since the time of Louis Philippe, the bourgeois has shown a tendency to compensate for the absence of any trace of private life in the big city. He tries to do this within the four walls of his apartment. It is as if he had made it a point of honor not to allow the traces of his everyday objects and accessories to get lost. Indefatigably, he takes the impression of a host of objects; for his slippers and his watches, his blankets and his umbrellas, he devises coverlets and cases. He has a marked preference for velour and plush, which preserve the imprint of all contact. In the style characteristic of the Second Empire, the apartment becomes a sort of cockpit. The traces of its inhabitant are molded into the interior. Here is the origin of the detective story, which inquires into these traces and follows these tracks. Poe—with his "Philosophy of Furniture" and with his "new detectives"—becomes the first physiognomist of the domestic interior. The criminals in early detective fiction are neither gentlemen nor apaches, but simple private citizens of the middle class ("The Black Cat," "The Tell-Tale Heart," "William Wilson").

D. BAUDELAIRE, OR THE STREETS OF PARIS

I

Baudelaire's genius, which feeds on melancholy, is an allegorical genius. With Baudelaire, Paris becomes for the first time the subject of lyric poetry. This poetry of place is the opposite of all poetry of the soil. The gaze which the allegorical genius turns on the city betrays, instead, a profound alienation. It is the gaze of the flâneur, whose way of life conceals behind a beneficent mirage the anxiety of the future inhabitants of our metropolises. The flâneur seeks refuge in the crowd. The crowd is the veil through which the familiar city is transformed for the flâneur into phantasmagoria. This phantasmagoria, in which the city appears now as a landscape, now as a room, seems later to have inspired the décor of department stores, which thus put flânerie to work for profit. In any case, department stores are the last precincts of flânerie.

In the person of the flâneur, the intelligentsia becomes acquainted with the marketplace. It surrenders itself to the market, thinking merely to look around; but in fact it is already seeking a buyer. In this intermediate stage, in which it still has patrons but is starting to bend to the demands of the market (in the guise of the feuilleton), it constitutes the *bohème*. The uncertainty of its economic position corresponds to the ambiguity of its political function. The latter is manifest especially clearly in the figures of the professional conspirators, who are recruited from the *bohème*. Blanqui is the most remarkable representative of this class. No one else in the nineteenth century had a revolutionary authority comparable to his. The image of Blanqui passes like a flash of lightning through Baudelaire's "Litanies de Satan." Nevertheless, Baudelaire's rebellion is always that of the asocial man: it is at an impasse. The only sexual communion of his life was with a prostitute.

II

The flâneur plays the role of scout in the marketplace. As such, he is also the explorer of the crowd. Within the man who abandons himself to it, the crowd inspires a sort of drunkenness, one accompanied by very specific illusions: the man flatters himself that, on seeing a passerby swept along by the crowd, he has accurately classified him, seen straight through to the innermost recesses of his soul—all on the basis of his external appearance. Physiologies of the time abound in evidence of this singular conception. Balzac's work provides excellent examples. The typical characters seen in passersby make such an impression on the senses that one cannot be surprised at the resultant curiosity to go beyond them and capture the special singularity of each person. But the nightmare that corresponds to the illusory perspicacity of the aforementioned physiognomist consists in seeing those distinctive traits—traits peculiar to the person—revealed to be nothing more than the elements of a new type; so that in the final analysis a person of the greatest individuality would turn out to be the exemplar of a type. This points to an agonizing phantasmagoria at the heart of flânerie. Baudelaire develops it with great vigor in "Les Sept Vieillards," a poem that deals with the seven-fold apparition of a repulsive-looking old man. This individual, presented as always the same in his multiplicity, testifies to the anguish of the city dweller who is unable to break the magic circle of the type even though he cultivates the most eccentric peculiarities. Baudelaire describes this procession as "infernal"

in appearance. But the newness for which he was on the lookout all his life consists in nothing other than this phantasmagoria of what is "always the same."

III

The key to the allegorical form in Baudelaire is bound up with the specific signification which the commodity acquires by virtue of its price. The singular debasement of things through their signification, something characteristic of seventeenth-century allegory, corresponds to the singular debasement of things through their price as commodities. This degradation, to which things are subject because they can be taxed as commodities, is counterbalanced in Baudelaire by the inestimable value of novelty. *La nouveauté* represents that absolute which is no longer accessible to any interpretation or comparison. It becomes the ultimate entrenchment of art. The final poem of *Les Fleurs du mal*: "Le Voyage." "Death, old admiral, up anchor now." The final voyage of the flâneur: death. Its destination: the new. Newness is a quality independent of the use value of the commodity. It is the source of that illusion of which fashion is the tireless purveyor. The fact that art's last line of resistance should coincide with the commodity's most advanced line of attack—this had to remain hidden from Baudelaire.

E. HAUSSMANN, OR THE BARRICADES

I

Haussmann's activity is incorporated into Napoleonic imperialism, which favors investment capital. In Paris, speculation is at its height. Haussmann's expropriations give rise to speculation that borders on fraud. The rulings of the Court of Cassation, which are inspired by the bourgeois and Orleanist opposition, increase the financial risks of Haussmannization. Haussmann tries to shore up his dictatorship by placing Paris under an emergency regime. In 1864, in a speech before the National Assembly, he vents his hatred of the rootless urban population. This population grows ever larger as a result of his projects. Rising rents drive the proletariat into the suburbs. The *quartiers* of

Paris in this way lose their distinctive physiognomy. The "red belt" forms. Haussmann gave himself the title of "demolition artist." He believed he had a vocation for his work, and emphasizes this in his memoirs. The central marketplace passes for Haussmann's most successful construction—and this is an interesting symptom. It has been said of the De de la Cité, the cradle of the city, that in the wake of Haussmann only one church, one public building, and one barracks remained. Hugo and Mérimée suggest how much the transformations made by Haussmann appear to Parisians as a monument of Napoleonic despotism. The inhabitants of the city no longer feel at home there; they start to become conscious of the inhuman character of the metropolis.

The true goal of Haussmann's projects was to secure the city against civil war. He wanted to make the erection of barricades in the streets of Paris impossible for all time. With the same end in mind, Louis Philippe had already introduced wooden paving. Nevertheless, barricades had played a considerable role in the February Revolution. Engels studied the tactics of barricade fighting. Haussmann seeks to forestall such combat in two ways. Widening the streets will make the erection of barricades impossible, and new streets will connect the barracks in straight lines with the workers' districts. Contemporaries christened the operation "strategic embellishment."

II

Haussmann's ideal in city planning consisted of long straight streets opening onto broad perspectives. This ideal corresponds to the tendency—common in the nineteenth century —to ennoble technological necessities through spurious artistic ends. The temples of the bourgeoisie's spiritual and secular power were to find their apotheosis within the framework of these long streets. The perspectives, prior to their inauguration, were screened with canvas draperies and unveiled like monuments; the view would then disclose a church, a train station, an equestrian statue, or some other symbol of civilization. With the Haussmann-ization of Paris, the phantasmagoria was rendered in stone. Though intended to endure in quasi-perpetuity, it also reveals its brittleness.

III

The barricade is resurrected during the Commune. It is stronger and better designed than ever. It stretches across the great boulevards, often reaching a height of two stories, and shields the trenches behind it. Just as the *Communist Manifesto* ends the age of professional conspirators, so the Commune puts an end to the phantasmagoria that dominates the earliest aspirations of the proletariat. It dispels the illusion that the task of the proletarian revolution is to complete the work of '89 in close collaboration with the bourgeoisie.

Side by side with the overt position of philanthropy, the bourgeoisie has always maintained the covert position of class struggle. As early as 1831, in the *Journal des débats*, it acknowledged that "every manufacturer lives in his factory like a plantation owner among his slaves." If it was fatal for the workers' rebellions of old that no theory of revolution had directed their course, it was this absence of theory that, from another perspective, made possible their spontaneous energy and the enthusiasm with which they set about establishing a new society. This enthusiasm, which reaches its peak in the Commune, at times won over to the workers' cause the best elements of the bourgeoisie, but in the end led the workers to succumb to its worst elements. Rimbaud and Courbet took sides with the Commune. The burning of Paris is the worthy conclusion to Baron Haussmann's work of destruction.

38
Spatial Practices
Walking in the city (1984)

Michel de Certeau

Seeing Manhattan from the 110th floor of the World Trade Center. Beneath the haze stirred up by the winds, the urban island, a sea in the middle of the sea, lifts up the skyscrapers over Wall Street, sinks down at Greenwich, then rises again to the crests of Midtown, quietly passes over Central Park and finally undulates off into the distance beyond Harlem. A wave of verticals. Its agitation is momentarily arrested by vision. The gigantic mass is immobilized before the eyes. It is transformed into a texturology in which extremes coincide—extremes of ambition and degradation, brutal oppositions of races and styles, contrasts between yesterday's buildings, already transformed into trash cans, and today's urban irruptions that block out its space. Unlike Rome, New York has never learned the art of growing old by playing on all its pasts. Its present invents itself, from hour to hour, in the act of throwing away its previous accomplishments and challenging the future. A city composed of paroxysmal places in monumental reliefs. The spectator can read in it a universe that is constantly exploding. In it are inscribed the architectural figures of the *coincidatio oppositorum* formerly drawn in miniatures and mystical textures. On this stage of concrete, steel and glass, cut out between two oceans (the Atlantic and the American) by a frigid body of water, the tallest letters in the world compose a gigantic rhetoric of excess in both expenditure and production.

VOYEURS OR WALKERS

To what erotics of knowledge does the ecstasy of reading such a cosmos belong? Having taken a voluptuous pleasure in it, I wonder what is the source of this pleasure of "seeing the whole," of looking down on, totalizing the most immoderate of human texts.

To be lifted to the summit of the World Trade Center is to be lifted out of the city's grasp. One's body is no longer clasped by the streets that turn and return it according to an anonymous law; nor is it possessed, whether as player or played, by the rumble of so many differences and by the nervousness of New York traffic. When one goes up there, he leaves behind the mass that carries off and mixes up in itself any identity of authors or spectators. An Icarus flying above these waters, he can ignore the devices of Daedalus in mobile and endless labyrinths far below. His elevation transfigures him into a voyeur. It puts him at a distance. It transforms the bewitching world by which one was "possessed" into a text that lies before one's eyes. It allows one to read it, to be a solar Eye, looking down like a god. The exaltation of a scopic and gnostic drive: the fiction of knowledge is related to this lust to be a viewpoint and nothing more.

Must one finally fall back into the dark space where crowds move back and forth, crowds that, though visible from on high, are themselves unable to see down below? An Icarian fall. On the 110th floor, a poster, sphinx-like, addresses an enigmatic message to the pedestrian who is for an instant transformed into a visionary: *It's hard to be down when you're up.*

The desire to see the city preceded the means of satisfying it. Medieval or Renaissance painters represented the city as seen in a perspective that no eye had yet enjoyed. This fiction already made the medieval spectator into a celestial eye. It created gods. Have things changed since technical procedures have organized an "all-seeing power"? The totalizing eye imagined by the painters of earlier times lives on in our achievements. The same scopic drive haunts users of architectural productions by materializing today the utopia that yesterday was only painted. The 1370 foot high tower that serves as a prow for Manhattan continues to construct the fiction that creates readers, makes the complexity of the city readable, and immobilizes its opaque mobility in a transparent text.

Is the immense texturology spread out before one's eyes anything more than a representation, an optical artifact? It is the analogue of the facsimile produced, through a projection that is a way of keeping aloof, by the space planner urbanist, city planner or cartographer. The panorama-city is a "theoretical" (that is, visual) simulacrum, in short a picture, whose condition of possibility is an oblivion and a misunderstanding of practices. The voyeur-god created by this fiction, who, like Schreber's God, knows only cadavers, must disentangle himself from the murky intertwining daily behaviors and make himself alien to them.

The ordinary practitioners of the city live "down below," below the thresholds at which visibility begins. They walk—an elementary form of this experience of the city; they are walkers, *Wandersmänner,* whose bodies follow the thicks and thins of an urban "text" they write without being able to read it. These practitioners make use of spaces that cannot be seen; their knowledge of them is as blind as that of lovers in each other's arms. The paths that correspond in this intertwining, un-recognized poems in which each body is an element signed by many others, elude legibility. It is as though the practices organizing a bustling city were characterized by their blindness. The networks of these moving, intersecting writings compose a manifold story that has neither author nor spectator, shaped out of fragments of trajectories and alterations of spaces: in relation to representations, it remains daily and indefinitely other.

Escaping the imaginary totalizations produced by the eye, the everyday has a certain strangeness that does not surface, or whose surface is only its upper limit, outlining itself against the visible. Within this ensemble, I shall try to locate the practices that are foreign to the "geometrical" or "geographical" space of visual, panoptic, or theoretical constructions. These practices of space refer to a specific form of *operations* ("ways of operating"), to "another spatiality" (an "anthropological," poetic and mythic experience of space), and to an *opaque and blind* mobility characteristic of the bustling city. A *migrational,* or metaphorical, city thus slips into the clear text of the planned and readable city.

FROM THE CONCEPT OF THE CITY TO URBAN PRACTICES

The World Trade Center is only the most monumental figure of Western urban development. The atopia-utopia of optical knowledge has long had the ambition of surmounting and articulating the contradictions arising from urban agglomeration. It is a question of managing a growth of human agglomeration or accumulation. "The city is a huge monastery," said Erasmus. Perspective vision and prospective vision constitute the twofold projection of an opaque past and an uncertain future onto a surface that can be dealt with. They inaugurate (in the sixteenth century?) the transformation of the urban *fact* into the *concept* of a city. Long before the concept itself gives rise to a particular figure of history, it assumes that this fact can be dealt with as a unity determined by an urbanistic *ratio.* Linking the city to the concept never makes them identical, but it plays on their progressive symbiosis: to plan a city is both to *think the very plurality* of the real and to make that way of thinking the plural *effective*; it is to know how to articulate it and be able to do it.

AN OPERATIONAL CONCEPT?

The "city" founded by utopian and urbanistic discourse is defined by the possibility of a threefold operation:

1. The production of its *own* space (*un espace propre*): rational organization must thus repress all the physical, mental and political pollutions that would compromise it;

2. the substitution of a nowhen, or of a synchronic system, for the indeterminable and stubborn resistances offered by traditions; univocal scientific strategies, made possible by the flattening out of all the data in a plane projection, must replace the tactics of users who take advantage of "opportunities" and who, through these trap-events, these lapses in visibility, reproduce the opacities of history everywhere;

3. finally, the creation of a *universal* and anonymous *subject* which is the city itself: it gradually becomes possible to attribute to it, as to its political model, Hobbes' State, all the functions and predicates that were previously scattered and assigned to many different real subjects—groups, associations, or individuals. "The city," like a proper name, thus provides a way of conceiving and constructing space on the basis of a finite number of stable, isolatable, and inter-connected properties.

Administration is combined with a process of elimination in this place organized by "speculative" and classificatory operations. On the one hand, there is a differentiation and redistribution of the parts and functions of the city, as a result of inversions, displacements, accumulations, etc.; on the other there is a rejection of everything that is not capable of being dealt with in this way and so constitutes the "waste products" of a functionalist administration (abnormality, deviance, illness, death, etc.). To be sure, progress allows an increasing number of these waste products to be reintroduced into administrative circuits and transforms even deficiencies (in health, security, etc.) into ways of making the networks of order denser. But in reality, it repeatedly produces effects contrary to those at which it aims: the profit system generates a loss which, in the multiple forms of wretchedness and poverty outside the system and of waste inside it, constantly turns production into "expenditure." Moreover, the rationalization of the city leads to its mythification in strategic discourses, which are calculations based on the hypothesis or the necessity of its destruction in order to arrive at a

final decision. Finally, the functionalist organization, by privileging progress (i.e., time), causes the condition of its own possibility—space itself—to be forgotten; space thus becomes the blind spot in a scientific and political technology. This is the way in which the Concept-city functions; a place of transformations and appropriations, the object of various kinds of interference but also a subject that is constantly enriched by new attributes, it is simultaneously the machinery and the hero of modernity.

Today, whatever the avatars of this concept may have been, we have to acknowledge that if in discourse the city serves as a totalizing and almost mythical landmark for socioeconomic and political strategies, urban life increasingly permits the re-emergence of the element that the urbanistic project excluded. The language of power is in itself "urbanizing," but the city is left prey to contradictory movements that counterbalance and combine themselves outside the reach of panoptic power. The city becomes the dominant theme in political legends, but it is no longer a field of programmed and regulated operations. Beneath the discourses that ideologize the city, the ruses and combinations of powers that have no readable identity proliferate; without points where one can take hold of them, without rational transparency, they are impossible to administer.

"These often miniscule ruses of discipline," these "minor but flawless" mechanisms, draw their efficacy from a relationship between procedures and the space that they redistribute in order to make an "operator" out of it. But what *spatial practices* correspond, in the area where discipline is manipulated, to these apparatuses that produce a disciplinary space? In the present conjuncture, which is marked by a contradiction between the collective mode of administration and an individual mode of reappropriation, this question is no less impor-tant, if one admits that spatial practices in fact secretly structure the determining conditions of social life. I would like to follow out a few of these multiform, resistance, tricky and stubborn procedures that elude discipline without being outside the field in which it is exercised, and which should lead us to a theory of everyday practices, of lived space, of the disquieting familiarity of the city.

THE CHORUS OF IDLE FOOTSTEPS

Their story begins on ground level, with footsteps. They are myriad, but do not compose a series. They cannot be counted because each unit has a qualitative character: a style of tactile apprehension and kinesthetic appropriation. Their swarming mass is an innumerable collection of singularities. Their intertwined paths give their shape to spaces. They weave places together. In that respect, pedestrian movements form one of these "real systems whose existence in fact makes up the city." They are not localized; it is rather they that spatialize. They are no more inserted within a container than those Chinese characters speakers sketch out on their hands with their fingertips.

It is true that the operations of walking on can be traced on city maps in such a way as to transcribe their paths (here well-trodden, there very faint) and their trajectories (going this way and not that). But these thick or thin curves only refer, like words, to the absence of what has passed by. Surveys of routes miss what was: the act itself of passing by. The operation of walking, wandering, or "window shopping," that is, the activity of passers-by, is transformed into points that draw a totalizing and reversible line on the map. They allow us to grasp only a relic set in the nowhen of a surface of projection. Itself visible, it has the effect of making invisible the operation that made it possible. These fixations constitute procedures for forgetting. The trace left behind is substituted for the practice. It exhibits the (voracious) property that the geographical system has of being able to transform action into legibility, but in doing so it causes a way of being in the world to be forgotten.

PEDESTRIAN SPEECH ACTS

A comparison with the speech act will allow us to go further and not limit ourselves to the critique of graphic representations alone, looking from the shores of legibility toward an inaccessible beyond. The act of walking is to the urban system what the speech act is to language or to the statements uttered.

Walking affirms, suspects, tries out, transgresses, respects, etc., the trajectories it "speaks." All the modalities sing a part in this chorus, changing from step to step, stepping in through

proportions, sequences, and intensities which vary according to the time, the path taken and the walker. These enunciatory operations are of an unlimited diversity. They therefore cannot be reduced to their graphic trail.

The long poem of walking manipulates spatial organizations, no matter how panoptic they may be: it is neither foreign to them (it can take place only within them) nor in conformity with them (it does not receive its identity from them). It creates shadows and ambiguities within them. It inserts its multitudinous references and citations into them (social models, cultural mores, personal factors). Within them it is itself the effect of successive encounters and occasions that constantly alter it and make it the other's blazon: in other words, it is like a peddler, carrying something surprising, transverse or attractive compared with the usual choice. These diverse aspects provide the basis of a rhetoric. They can even be said to define it.

By analyzing this "modern art of everyday expression" as it appears in accounts of spatial practices, J.-F. Augoyard discerns in it two especially fundamental stylistic figures: synecdoche and asyndeton. The predominance of these two figures seems to me to indicate, in relation to two complementary poles, a formal structure of these practices. *Synecdoche* consists in "using a word in a sense which is part of another meaning of the same word." In essence, it names a part instead of the whole which includes it. Thus "sail" is taken for "ship" in the expression "a fleet of fifty sails"; in the same way, a brick shelter or a hill is taken for the park in the narration of a trajectory. *Asyndeton* is the suppression of linking words such as conjunctions and adverbs, either within a sentence or between sentences. In the same way, in walking it selects and fragments the space traversed; it skips over links and whole parts that it omits. From this point of view, every walk constantly leaps, or skips like a child, hopping on one foot. It practices the ellipsis of conjunctive *loci*.

In reality, these two pedestrian figures are related. Synecdoche expands a spatial element in order to make it play the role of a "more" (a totality) and take its place (the bicycle or the piece of furniture in a store window stands for a whole street or neighborhood). Asyndeton, by elision, creates a "less," opens gaps in the spatial continuum, and retains only selected parts of it that amount almost to relics. Synecdoche replaces totalities by fragments (a *less* in the place of a *more*); asyndeton disconnects them by eliminating the conjunctive or the consecutive (nothing in place of something). Synecdoche makes more dense: it amplifies the detail and miniaturizes the whole. Asyndeton cuts out: it undoes continuity and undercuts its plausibility. A space treated in this way and shaped by practices is transformed into enlarged singularities and separate islands. Through these swellings, shrinkings, and fragmentations, that is, through these rhetorical operations a spatial phrasing of an analogical (composed of juxtaposed citations) and elliptical (made of gaps, lapses, and allusions) type is created. For the technological system of a coherent and totalizing space that is "linked" and simultaneous, the figures of pedestrian rhetoric substitute trajectories that have a mythical structure, at least if one understands by "myth" a discourse relative to the place/nowhere (or origin) of concrete existence, a story jerry-built out of elements taken from common sayings, an allusive and fragmentary story whose gaps mesh with the social practices it symbolizes.

From this point of view, after having compared pedestrian processes to linguistic formations, we can bring them back down in the direction of oneiric figuration, or at least discover on that other side what, in a spatial practice, is inseparable from the dreamed place. To walk is to lack a place. It is the indefinite process of being absent and in search of a proper. The moving about that the city multiplies and concentrates makes the city itself an immense social experience of lacking a place—an experience that is, to be sure, broken up into countless tiny deportations (displacements and walks), compensated for by the relationships and intersections of these exoduses that intertwine and create an urban fabric, and placed under the sign of what ought to be, ultimately, the place but is only a name, the City. The identity furnished by this place is all the more symbolic (named) because, in spite of the inequality of its citizens' positions and profits, there is only a pullulation of passer-by, a network of residences temporarily appropriated by pedestrian traffic, a shuffling among pretenses of the proper, a universe of rented spaces haunted by a nowhere or by dreamed-of places.

Places are fragmentary and inward-turning histories, pasts that others are not allowed to read, accumulated times that can be unfolded but like stories held in reserve, remaining in an enigmatic state, symbolizations encysted in the pain or pleasure of the body. "I feel good here": the well-being under-expressed in the language it appears in like a fleeting glimmer is a spatial practice.

39
The Uses of Sidewalks
Contact (1961)

Jane Jacobs

Reformers have long observed city people loitering on busy corners, hanging around in candy stores and bars and drinking soda pop on stoops, and have passed a judgment, the gist of which is: "This is deplorable! If these people had decent homes and a more private or bosky outdoor place, they wouldn't be on the street!"

This judgment represents a profound misunderstanding of cities. It makes no more sense than to drop in at a testimonial banquet in a hotel and conclude that if these people had wives who could cook, they would give their parties at home.

The point of both the testimonial banquet and the social life of city sidewalks is precisely that they are public. They bring together people who do not know each other in an intimate, private social fashion and in most cases do not care to know each other in that fashion.

Nobody can keep open house in a great city. Nobody wants to. And yet if interesting, useful and significant contacts among the people of cities are confined to acquaintanceships suitable for private life, the city becomes stultified. Cities are full of people with whom, from your viewpoint, or mine, or any other individual's, a certain degree of contact is useful or enjoyable; but you do not want them in your hair. And they do not want you in theirs either.

In speaking about city sidewalk safety, I mentioned how necessary it is that there should be, in the brains behind the eyes on the street, an almost unconscious assumption of general street support when the chips are down—when a citizen has to choose, for instance, whether he will take responsibility, or abdicate it, in combating barbarism or protecting strangers.

There is a short word for this assumption of support: Trust. It grows out of people stopping by at the bar for a beer, getting advice from the grocer and giving advice to the newsstand man, comparing opinions with other customers at the bakery and nodding hello to the two boys drinking pop on the stoop, eyeing the girls while waiting to be called for dinner, admonishing the children, hearing about a job from the hardware man and borrowing a dollar from the druggist, admiring the new babies and sympathizing over the way a coat faded. Customs vary: in some neighborhoods people compare notes on their dogs; in others they compare notes on their landlords.

Most of it is ostensibly utterly trivial but the sum is not trivial at all. The absence of this trust is a disaster to a city street. Its cultivation cannot be institutionalized. And above all, *it implies no private commitments*.

Formal public organizations in cities require an informal public life underlying them, mediating between them and the privacy of the people of the city. We catch a hint of what happens by contrasting, again, a city area possessing a public sidewalk life with a city area lacking it, as told about in the report of a settlement-house social researcher who was studying problems relating to public schools in a section of New York City:

> Mr. W—— [principal of an elementary school] was questioned on the effect of J—— Houses on the school, and the uprooting of the community around the school. He felt that there had been many effects and of these most were negative. He mentioned that the

project had torn out numerous institutions for socializing. The present atmosphere of the project was in no way similar to the gaiety of the streets before the project was built. He noted that in general there seemed fewer people on the streets because there were fewer places for people to gather. He also contended that before the projects were built the Parents Association had been very strong, and now there were only very few active members.

Mr. W—— was wrong in one respect. There were not fewer places (or at any rate there was not less space) for people to gather in the project, if we count places deliberately planned for constructive socializing. Of course there were no bars, no candy stores, no hole-in-the-wall *bodegas*, no restaurants in the project. But the project under discussion was equipped with a model complement of meeting rooms, craft, art and game rooms, outdoor benches, malls, etc., enough to gladden the heart of even the Garden City advocates.

Why are such places dead and useless without the most determined efforts and expense to inveigle users—and then to maintain control over the users? What services do the public sidewalk and its enterprises fulfill that these planned gathering places do not? And why? How does an informal public sidewalk life bolster a more formal, organizational public life?

To understand such problems—to understand why drinking pop on the stoop differs from drinking pop in the game room, and why getting advice from the grocer or the bartender differs from getting advice from either your next-door neighbor or from an institutional lady who may be hand-in-glove with an institutional landlord—we must look into the matter of city privacy.

Privacy is precious in cities. It is indispensable. Perhaps it is precious and indispensable everywhere, but most places you cannot get it. In small settlements everyone knows your affairs. In the city everyone does not—only those you choose to tell will know much about you. This is one of the attributes of cities that is precious to most city people, whether their incomes are high or their incomes are low, whether they are white or colored, whether they are old inhabitants or new, and it is a gift of great-city life deeply cherished and jealously guarded.

Architectural and planning literature deals with privacy in terms of windows, overlooks, sight lines. The idea is that if no one from outside can peek into where you live—behold, privacy. This is simple-minded. Window privacy is the easiest commodity in the world to get. You just pull down the shades or adjust the blinds. The privacy of keeping one's personal affairs to those selected to know them, and the privacy of having reasonable control over who shall make inroads on your time and when, are rare commodities in most of this world, however, and they have nothing to do with the orientation of windows.

A good city street neighborhood achieves a marvel of balance between its people's determination to have essential privacy and their simultaneous wishes for differing degrees of contact, enjoyment or help from the people around. This balance is largely made up of small, sensitively managed details, practiced and accepted so casually that they are normally taken for granted.

Perhaps I can best explain this subtle but all-important balance in terms of the stores where people leave keys for their friends, a common custom in New York. In our family, for example, when a friend wants to use our place while we are away for a week end or everyone happens to be out during the day, or a visitor for whom we do not wish to wait up is spending the night, we tell such a friend that he can pick up the key at the delicatessen across the street. Joe Cornacchia, who keeps the delicatessen, usually has a dozen or so keys at a time for handing out like this. He has a special drawer for them.

Now why do I, and many others, select Joe as a logical custodian for keys? Because we trust him, first, to be a responsible custodian, but equally important because we know that he combines a feeling of good will with a feeling of no personal responsibility about our private affairs. Joe considers it no concern of his whom we choose to permit in our places and why.

A service like this cannot be formalized. Identifications … questions … insurance against mishaps. The all-essential line between public service and privacy would be transgressed by institutionalization. Nobody in his right mind would leave his key in such a place. The service must be given as a favor by someone with an unshakable understanding of the difference between a person's key and a person's private life, or it cannot be given at all.

Or consider the line drawn by Mr. Jaffe at the candy store around our corner—a line so well understood by his customers and by other storekeepers too that they can spend their whole lives in its presence and never think about it consciously. One ordinary morning last winter, Mr. Jaffe, whose formal business name is Bernie, and his wife, whose formal business name is Ann, supervised the small children crossing at the corner on the way to P.S. 41, as Bernie always does because he sees the need; lent an umbrella to one customer and a dollar to another; took custody of two keys; took in some packages for people in the next building who were away; lectured two youngsters who asked for cigarettes; gave street directions; took custody of a watch to give the repair man across the street when he opened later; gave out information on the range of rents in the neighborhood to an apartment seeker; listened to a tale of domestic difficulty and offered reassurance; told some rowdies they could not come in unless they behaved and then defined (and got) good behavior; provided an incidental forum for half a dozen conversations among customers who dropped in for oddments; set aside certain newly arrived papers and magazines for regular customers who would depend on getting them; advised a mother who came for a birthday present not to get the ship-model kit because another child going to the same birthday party was giving that; and got a back copy (this was for me) of the previous day's newspaper out of the deliverer's surplus returns when he came by.

After considering this multiplicity of extra-merchandising services I asked Bernie, "Do you ever introduce your customers to each other?"

He looked startled at the idea, even dismayed. "No," he said thoughtfully. "That would just not be advisable. Sometimes, if I know two customers who are in at the same time have an interest in common, I bring up the subject in conversation and let them carry it on from there if they want to. But oh no, I wouldn't introduce them."

When I told this to an acquaintance in a suburb, she promptly assumed that Mr. Jaffe felt that to make an introduction would be to step above his social class, Not at all. In our neighborhood, storekeepers like the Jaffes enjoy an excellent social status, that of businessmen. In income they are apt to be the peers of the general run of customers and in independence they are the superiors. Their advice, as men or women of common sense and experience, is sought and respected. They are well known as individuals, rather than unknown as class symbols. No; this is that almost unconsciously enforced, well-balanced line showing, the line between the city public world and the world of privacy.

This line can be maintained, without awkwardness to anyone, because of the great plenty of opportunities for public contact in the enterprises along the sidewalks, or on the sidewalks themselves as people move to and fro or deliberately loiter when they feel like it, and also because of the presence of many public hosts, so to speak, proprietors of meeting places like Bernie's where one is free either to hang around or dash in and out, no strings attached.

Under this system, it is possible in a city street neighborhood to know all kinds of people without unwelcome entanglements, without boredom, necessity for excuses, explanations, fears of giving offense, embarrassments respecting impositions or commitments, and all such paraphernalia of obligations which can accompany less limited relationships. It is possible to be on excellent sidewalk terms with people who are very different from oneself, and even, as time passes, on familiar public terms with them. Such relationships can, and do, endure for many years, for decades; they could never have formed without that line, much less endured. They form precisely because they are by-the-way to people's normal public sorties.

In city areas that lack a natural and casual public life, it is common for residents to isolate themselves from each other to a fantastic degree. If mere contact with your neighbors threatens to entangle you in their private lives, or entangle them in yours, and if you cannot be so careful who your neighbors are as self-selected upper-middle-class people can be, the logical solution is absolutely to avoid friendliness or casual offers of help. Better to stay thoroughly distant. As a practical result, the ordinary public jobs—like keeping children in hand—for which people must take a little personal initiative, or those for which they must band together in limited common purposes, go undone.

A thorough and detailed report by Ellen Luric, a social worker in East Harlem, on life in a low-income project there, has this to say:

It is … extremely important to recognize that for considerably complicated reasons, many adults either don't want to become involved in any friendship-relationship at all with their neighbors, or, if they do succumb to the need for some form of society, they strictly limit themselves to one or two friends, and no more.

Suspicion and fear of trouble often outweigh any need for neighborly advice and help. For these families the sense of privacy has already been extensively violated. The deepest secrets, all the family skeletons, are well known not only to management but often to other public agencies, such as the Welfare Department. To preserve any last remnants of privacy, they choose to avoid close relationships with others.

The social structure of sidewalk life hangs partly on what can be called self-appointed public characters. A public character is anyone who is in frequent contact with a wide circle of people and who is sufficiently interested to make himself a public character. A public character need have no special talents or wisdom to fulfill his function—although he often does. He just needs to be present, and there need to be enough of his counterparts. His main qualification is that he *is* public, that he talks to lots of different people. In this way, news travels that is of sidewalk interest.

Most public sidewalk characters are steadily stationed in public places. They are storekeepers or barkeepers or the like. These are the basic public characters. All other public characters of city sidewalks depend on them— if only indirectly because of the presence of sidewalk routes to such enterprises and their proprietors.

One need not have either the artistry or the personality of such a man to become a specialized sidewalk character—but only a pertinent specialty of some sort. It is easy. I am a specialized public character of sorts along our street, owing of course to the fundamental presence of the basic, anchored public characters. The way I became one started with the fact that Greenwich Village, where I live, was waging an interminable and horrendous battle to save its main park from being bisected by a highway. During the course

of battle I undertook, at the behest of a committee organizer away over on the other side of Greenwich Village, to deposit in stores on a few blocks of our street supplies of petition cards protesting the proposed roadway. Customers would sign the cards while in the stores, and from time to time I would make my pickups. As a result of engaging in this messenger work, I have since become automatically the sidewalk public character on petition strategy. Before long, for instance, Mr. Fox at the liquor store was consulting me, as he wrapped up my bottle, on how we could get the city to remove a long abandoned and dangerous eyesore, a closed-up comfort station near his corner. If I would undertake to compose the petitions and find the effective way of presenting them to City Hall, he proposed, he and his partners would undertake to have them printed, circulated and picked up. Soon the stores round about had comfort station removal petitions. Our street by now has many public experts on petition tactics, including the children.

Not only do public characters spread the news and learn the news at retail, so to speak. They connect with each other and thus spread word wholesale, in effect.

A sidewalk life, so far as I can observe, arises out of no mysterious qualities or talents for it in this or that type of population. It arises only when the concrete, tangible facilities it requires are present. These happen to be the same facilities, in the same abundance and ubiquity, that are required for cultivating sidewalk safety. If they are absent, public sidewalk contacts are absent too.

The tolerance, the room for great differences among neighbors—differences that often go far deeper than differences in color—which are possible and normal in intensely urban life, but which are so foreign to suburbs and pseudosuburbs, are possible and normal only when streets of great cities have built-in equipment allowing strangers to dwell in peace together on civilized but essentially dignified and reserved terms.

Lowly, unpurposeful and random as they may appear, sidewalk contacts are the small change from which a city's wealth of public life may grow.

40
People as Infrastructure
Intersecting Fragments in Johannesburg (2004)

AbdouMaliq Simone

The inner city of Johannesburg is about as far away as one can get from the popular image of the African village. Though one of Africa's most urbanized settings, it is also seen as a place of ruins—of ruined urbanization, the ruining of Africa by urbanization. But in these ruins, something else besides decay might be happening. This essay explores the possibility that these ruins not only mask but also constitute a highly urbanized social infrastructure. This infrastructure is capable of facilitating the intersection of socialities so that expanded spaces of economic and cultural operation become available to residents of limited means.

This essay is framed around the notion of *people as infrastructure*, which emphasizes economic collaboration among residents seemingly marginalized from and immiserated by urban life. Infrastructure is commonly understood in physical terms, as reticulated systems of highways, pipes, wires, or cables. These modes of provisioning and articulation are viewed as making the city productive, reproducing it, and positioning its residents, territories, and resources in specific ensembles where the energies of individuals can be most efficiently deployed and accounted for.

By contrast, I wish to extend the notion of infrastructure directly to people's activities in the city. African cities are characterized by incessantly flexible, mobile, and provisional intersections of residents that operate without clearly delineated notions of how the city is to be inhabited and used. These intersections, particularly in the last two decades, have depended on the ability of residents to engage complex combinations of objects, spaces, persons, and practices. These conjunctions become an infrastructure—a platform providing for and reproducing life in the city. Indeed, as I illustrate through a range of ethnographic materials on inner-city Johannesburg, an experience of regularity capable of anchoring the livelihoods of residents and their trans- actions with one another is consolidated precisely because the outcomes of residents' reciprocal efforts are radically open, flexible, and provisional. In other words, a specific economy of perception and collaborative practice is constituted through the capacity of individual actors to circulate across and become familiar with a broad range of spatial, residential, economic, and transactional positions. Even when actors do different things with one another in different places, each carries traces of past collaboration and an implicit willingness to interact with one another in ways that draw on multiple social positions.

Urbanization conventionally denotes a thickening of fields, an assemblage of increasingly heterogeneous elements into more complicated collectives. The accelerated, extended, and intensified intersections of bodies, landscapes, objects, and technologies defer calcification of institutional ensembles or fixed territories of belonging.

According to conventional imaginaries of urbanization, which locate urban productivity in the social division of labor and the consolidation of individuation, African cities are incomplete. In contrast to these imaginaries, African cities survive largely through a conjunction of heterogeneous activities brought to bear on and elaborated through flexibly configured landscapes. But it is important to emphasize that these flexible configurations are pursued not in some essential contrast to non-African urban priorities or values but as specific routes to a kind of stability and regularity that non-African cities have historically attempted to realize. Consider the incomplete, truncated, or deteriorated forms and temporalities of various, seemingly incompatible institutional rationalities and modes of production—from the bureaucracies of civil administration to the workshop, the industrial unit, subsistence agriculture, private enterprise, and customary usufruct arrangements governing land use. All are deployed as a means of stabilizing a social field of interaction. In part, this is a way to continuously readapt residents' actions to engage the open-ended destinations that their very collaborations have produced.

For example, the transport depot in Abidjan is full of hundreds of young men who function as steerers, baggage loaders, ticket salespersons, hawkers, drivers, petrol pumpers, and mechanics. There are constantly shifting connections among them. Each boy who steers passengers to a particular company makes a rapid assessment of their wealth, personal characteristics, and the reason for their journey. This reading determines where the steerer will guide prospective passengers, who will sell their tickets, who will load their baggage, who will seat them, and so forth. It is as if this collaboration were assembled to maximize the efficiency of each passage, even though there are no explicit rules or formal means of payment to the steerers. Although each boy gives up control of the passenger to the next player down the line, their collaboration is based not on the boys adhering to specific rules but on their capacity to improvise.

Such a conjunction of heterogeneous activities, modes of production, and institutional forms constitutes highly mobile and provisional possibilities for how people live and make things, how they use the urban environment and collaborate with one another. The specific operations and scopes of these conjunctions are constantly negotiated and depend on the particular histories, understandings, networks, styles, and inclinations of the actors involved. Highly specialized needs arise, requiring the application of specialized skills and sensitivities that can adapt to the unpredictable range of scenarios these needs bring to life. Regularities

thus ensue from a process of incessant convertibility—turning commodities, found objects, resources, and bodies into uses previously unimaginable or constrained. Producer-residents become more adept at operating within these conjunctions as they deploy a greater diversity of abilities and efforts. Again it is important to emphasize that these conjunctions become a coherent platform for social transaction and livelihood. This process of conjunction, which is capable of generating social compositions across a range of singular capacities and needs (both enacted and virtual) and which attempts to derive maximal outcomes from a minimal set of elements, is what I call *people as infrastructure*.[1]

This concept is not meant to account for inner-city Johannesburg in its entirety. Many residents, battered by the demands of maintaining the semblance of a safe domestic environment, find few incentives to exceed the bounds of personal survival. But *people as infrastructure* describes a tentative and often precarious process of remaking the inner city, especially now that the policies and economies that once moored it to the surrounding city have mostly worn away. In many respects, the inner city has been "let go" and forced to reweave its connections with the larger world by making the most of its limited means. Still, the inner city is embedded in a larger urban region characterized by relative economic strength, an emerging pan-African service economy, political transformations that have sought to attenuate the more stringent trappings of population control, and a highly fragmented urban system whose regulatory regime was never geared toward high-density residential areas. This ensemble, in turn, has given rise to a markedly heterogeneous domain of people.

SPACES OF THE INNER CITY

Under apartheid, Johannesburg was designed as a cosmopolitan, European city in Africa, but only for a small segment of its population. When this truncated cosmopolitanism could no longer be enforced by a white minority regime, whites fled to distant northern suburbs and gated communities where cosmopolitanism was precluded, thus leaving the inner city open to habitation of all kinds. Roughly 90 percent of

Johannesburg's inner-city residents were not living there ten years ago.

A drive around the circumference of the inner-city neighborhoods of Hillbrow, Berea, Joubert Park, Yeoville, and Bertams takes less than twenty minutes. Yet navigation of their interior requires familiarity with many different and, on the surface, conflicting temporal trajectories through which Johannesburg has changed, with its sudden switches across ruin, repair, and redevelopment. For example, a five-minute walk along Quartz Street starting at Smit Street takes you from Death Valley, a strip of seedy prostitution hotels and clubs, to a concerted effort to resecure the tenancy of working families in a series of tightly controlled renovated buildings.

The immediate area emptied out yet remains a kind of no-go zone, with the traces of the wild recent past still keeping other prospects at bay. Still, just one block away is the New Yorker, a relatively well-appointed block of studio apartments recently fixed up and with a long waiting list restricted to South Africans who can show five pay stubs.

Further north there is a single block along Quartz Street where hundreds of Ibo Nigerians gather on the street, usually between 2 and 7 p.m. They are here not so much to deal narcotics, for which they are renowned, but to display impunity and solidarity while buying daily meals from the curbside street vendors.

A few bide their time selling cigarettes and candy; almost all engage in shifting conversations. Many wait to take their turn at the Internet cafe just around the corner (where one can buy five hours of computer time and get the sixth free) to engage in credit card fraud, check shipping orders, or write e-mails to mom or 419 letters.[2]

On the other side of Pretoria Street is a block representing an early effort by the Metropolitan Council to draw street traders into an organized market with rented stalls and shedding. A variety of fruits and vegetables are sold here, as well as clothing, shoes, and kitchen goods. But the traders must pay rent for their stalls. Although the money is used to provide a clean and safe environment, its goods are consequently more expensive than those of the hawkers who still line much of Pretoria Street and whose trade this formal market was supposed to dispel. As we continue north along Quartz Street, the formal market dissipates in a contiguous block

of unregulated street hawkers and alleys where stolen goods are sold. But in the surrounding arteries there are large apartment blocks, and it is clearly an area where the South African township has moved in. The pool halls and game rooms are crowded, and the block pulses with hip-hop and *kwaito* music.

The next block is inhabited by homeless squatters, whose cardboard edifices and stolen shopping carts line mounds of burnt ash from fires they use to cook and keep warm. There is an acrid smell and the incessant sounds of whistles and catcalls. Young street toughs, Congolese mechanics who use a nearby petrol station to repair and store cars, and Malawians who have long dominated the residential buildings all engage in a territorial dance for control of the block.

Finally the street ends at a major lateral artery, Louis Botha Avenue, and the Mimosa Hotel. The Mimosa is one of about ten hotels operated, if not owned, by Nigerian syndicates, where rooms are shared to keep accommodations for an army of "foot soldiers" under R10 (roughly $1.50) per night. Here, recent doctorates in designer frames mingle across street-side card tables with ex–Area boys from Lagos on the run from being framed. Some keep an eye out for everything. Others wait to unload the small quota of narcotics that will allow them to eat that night. There are those who direct old and new clients to choice rooms in the hotel in order to meet their needs; and still others are there to tell stories, often about deals both real and made up. These are imported tricksters, whose job is to celebrate the ruthless economy that most of these young Ibo guys pursue, provide occasional cautionary tales, but in the end get others to reveal what they are after, what their capacities are, where they have been, and how well they might fit certain jobs. The police and the city council have declared victory over Nigerians several times by shutting down the hotel. On the ground level, a passing observer might be fooled into thinking that the place is finished, but if you look up you might notice that the windows are full of freshly laundered clothes.

REWORKED INTERSECTIONS

This is an inner city whose density and highly circumscribed spatial parameters compel uncertain interactions and cooperation among both long-term Johannesburg residents and new arrivals, South Africans and Africans from elsewhere. There are interactions among various national and ethnic groups, between aspiring professionals and seasoned criminals, and between AIDS orphans living on the streets and wealthy Senegalese merchants living in luxurious penthouses. At the same time, life in the inner city fosters intense cooperation among fellow nationals and ethnics. The coupling of these trajectories produces an intricate territorialization and a patchwork of zones of relative security.

For example, common national identity can provide a concrete framework for support among individuals who may have very different kinds of jobs, ranging from repairing automobiles to teaching French at the Alliance Française. These articulations are used by larger corporate groupings—cutting across several national identities—that facilitate various business efforts through subcontracting arrangements. One such enterprise might draw on the professional legitimacy of teachers, use their students as potential customers or corporate informants, and incorporate the trading circuits developed by petty traders and the repair skills of mechanics.

While residents of different backgrounds try to keep out of one another's way, they do form emergent interdependencies ranging from crude patron–client relations to formally constituted pan-African entrepreneurial collaborations. The sheer proximity of Africans from diverse ethnic and national backgrounds leads many residents to explore tentative cooperation based on trust. Such relationships are risky in a climate of insecurity and incessant trickery, but also enable participants to exploit, in highly profitable ways, the common assumption that trust is not really possible. Given the various skills and networks that different immigrant groups bring to the table, the potential profits in combining trades, markets, and networks far exceed those from commercial activities compartmentalized within narrow ethnic and national groupings. Examples include the buying, selling, and repairing of cars or the domestic or international consigning of goods by individual traders using informal credit systems and flexible collateral. Other activities, usually managed by women, include the cultivation of informal restaurants and bars as safehouses for

potentially volatile negotiations among those conducting illegal business. Young women of various nationalities are increasingly enrolled and partnered as foot soldiers in barter schemes— for example, gems for luxury accessories—that may take place in Brazil or Venezuela.

It is difficult to infer the existence of a collective system from even scores of individual interviews or multisite field observations. Yet it may be possible that this texture of highly fragmented social space and these emerging interdependencies complement each other in forming an infrastructure for innovative economic transactions in the inner city.

INFRACITY: JOHANNESBURG AND URBAN AFRICA

On the surface, inner-city Johannesburg has many features in common with inner cities in the United States. Many of the economic and political mechanisms that produced American inner-city ghettos have been at work in Johannesburg, and these are only reinforced by the strong influence of US urban policy on South Africa. But large swathes of Johannesburg reflect the failures of strong regulatory systems and the economic and social informalities commonly associated with urban Africa. To this extent, inner-city Johannesburg is a kind of hybrid: part American, part African.

The potential significance of reflections on Johannesburg, in contrast to other global cities, rests in how the city embodies, speeds up, and sometimes brutalizes aspects of urban life common to many African cities.

One such aspect is its urban residents' constant state of preparedness. Driven by discourses of war, contestation, and experimentation, many African cities seem to force their inhabitants to constantly change gears, focus, and location. Of course, there are some quarters whose residents have grown up, raised families, and devoted themselves to the same occupation or way of life without moving. Yet even this stability is situated within a larger, more fluid arena where people must be prepared to exert themselves. There is the need to ensure oneself against a lifetime without work or the means to establish a family or household of one's own. There is the need to prepare for the possibility that even hard work will produce nothing.

This sense of preparedness, a readiness to switch gears, has significant implications for what residents think it is possible to do in the city.

The inner city is a domain that few want to belong to or establish roots in. But it keeps alive residents' hopes for stability somewhere else, even as it cultivates within them a seemingly permanent restlessness and capacity to make something out of the city.

Increasing numbers of Africans are situated in what could be called half-built environments: underdeveloped, overused, fragmented, and often makeshift urban infrastructures where essential services are erratic or costly and whose inefficiencies spread and urbanize disease.

The international community has made a substantial effort over the last decade to help African municipalities direct urban growth and restructuring. Here, capacity building centers on developing proficient forms of codification.

In other words, it is to be an arena where spaces, activities, populations, flows, and structures are made visible, or more precisely, recognizable and familiar.

Once this enhanced visibility is accomplished, urban spaces and activities are more capable of being retrieved and compared for analysis and planning.

But it is clear that much of what takes place in African cities is fairly invisible: the number of people who reside in a given compound; how household incomes that can support only one week's survival out of every month are supplemented; or how electricity is provided for ten times as many households as there are official connections.

In Johannesburg's inner city, the heightened emphasis on visible identities and the converse need of actors to hide what they are actually doing generates a highly volatile mix. But it is in this play of the visible and invisible that limited resources can be put to work in many possible ways. Throughout urban Africa, residents experience new forms of solidarity through their participation in makeshift, ephemeral ways of being social. At the same time, these makeshift formations amplify the complexity of local terrain and social relationships by engaging the dynamics of a larger world within a coherent, if temporary, sense of place. Sometimes this sense of place coincides with a specific locality; other times,

and with increasing frequency, it is dispersed across or in between discernible territories. In this economy of interpenetration, notions about what is possible and impossible are upended, and urban residents are ready to take up a variety of attitudes and positions.

Take, for example, African urban markets. They are renowned for being well run and for their multitude of goods and services overflowing whatever order is imposed upon them. In these markets, cooking, reciting, selling, loading and unloading, fighting, praying, relaxing, pounding, and buying happen side by side, on stages too cramped, too deteriorated, too clogged with waste, history, energy, and sweat to sustain all of them. Entering the market, what do potential customers make of all that is going on? Whom do they deal with and buy from? People have their networks, their channels, and their rules. But there are also wide spaces for most people to insert themselves as middlemen who might provide a fortuitous, even magical, reading of the market "between the lines," between stall after stall of onions or used clothes, between the fifty-cent profit of the woman selling Marlboros and five thousand freshly minted twenty-dollar bills stuffed into sisal bags with cassava and hair grease, tossed on top of a converted school-bus heading somewhere into the interior.

These linkages are sometimes the constructions of individuals who desire to master self-limitations as opposed to merely straddling divides. At other times, urban residents invent a range of practices—religious, sexual, institutional—capable of relocating individual actors within different frames of identity or recognition. This relocation enables them to understand their relationships with other actors and events in new, broader ways. Actors speak and deal with one another in ways that would otherwise be impossible. Such unanticipated interactions can be used to rehearse new ways of navigating complex urban relationships and to construct a sense of commonality that goes beyond parochial identities.

For example, throughout urban Africa, the proliferating neighborhood night markets do not simply provide an opportunity for localized trade or for extending trading hours, but serve primarily as occasions to be public, to watch others and whom they deal with, and to listen to their conversations. The task is to find ways to situate oneself so one can assess what is happening—who talks to whom, who is visiting whose house, who is riding in the same car, who is trading or doing business together.

What the inner city provides is an intersection where different styles, schemes, sectors, and practices can make something out of and from one another. In these respects, inner-city Johannesburg is the quintessential African city. Johannesburg becomes a launching pad not only for better livelihoods within the inner city but also for excursions into a broader world, whether Dubai and Mumbai or the pool halls of Hillbrow and the white suburb of Cresta only a few kilometers away. On the other hand, the density of skills, needs, aspirations, and willingness brought to work in the inner city makes it a sometimes brutal place, where everything seems to be on the line.

NOTES

1   This notion attempts to extend what Lefebvre meant by social space as a practice of works—modes of organization at various and interlocking scales that link expressions, attraction and repulsion, sympathies and antipathies, changes and amalgamations that affect urban residents and their social interactions. They participate in a diversifying series of reciprocal exchanges, so that positions and identities are not fixed or even, at most times, determinable.

2   *419* refers to a type of scheme in which mass mailings are sent out, seemingly from a prominent, usually Nigerian, figure or company that needs to get large amounts of money out of the country.

41
City Life and Difference

(1990)

Iris Marion Young

Many philosophers and political theorists criticize welfare capitalist society for being atomistic, depoliticized, fostering self-regarding interest-group pluralism and bureaucratic domination. The most common alternative vision offered by such critics is an ideal of community. Spurred by appeals to community as an alternative to liberal individualism made by Michael Sandel, Alasdair MacIntyre, and others, in recent years political theorists have debated the virtues and vices of communitarianism as opposed to liberalism. Many socialists, anarchists, feminists, and others critical of welfare capitalist society formulate their vision of a society free from domination and oppression in terms of an ideal of community. Much of this discussion would lead us to think that liberal individualism and communitarianism exhaust the possibilities for conceiving social relations.

I share many of the communitarian criticisms of welfare capitalist liberal democratic theory and society. I shall argue however that the ideal of community fails to offer an appropriate alternative vision of a democratic polity. This ideal expresses a desire for the fusion of subjects with one another which in practice operates to exclude those with whom the group does not identify. The ideal of community denies and represses social difference, the fact that the polity cannot be thought of as a unity in which all participants share a common experience and common values. In its privileging of face-to-face relations, moreover, the ideal of community denies difference in the form of the temporal and spatial distancing that characterizes social process.

As an alternative to the ideal of community, I propose an ideal of city life as a vision of social relations affirming group difference. As a normative ideal, city life instantiates social relations of difference without exclusion. Different groups dwell in the city alongside one another, of necessity interacting in city spaces. If city politics is to be democratic and not dominated by the point of view of one group, it must be a politics that takes account of and provides voice for the different groups that dwell together in the city without forming a community.

THE ROUSSEAUIST DREAM

The ideal of community expresses a longing for harmony among persons, for consensus and mutual understanding, for what Foucault calls the Rousseauist dream of

> a transparent society, visible and legible in each of its parts, the dream of there no longer existing any zones of darkness, zones established by the privileges of royal power or the prerogative of some corporation, zones of disorder. It was the dream that each individual, whatever position he occupied, might be able to see the whole of society, that men's hearts should communicate, their vision be unobstructed by obstacles, and that the opinion of all reign over each.[1]

Whether expressed as shared subjectivity or common consciousness, or as relations of mutuality and reciprocity, the ideal of community denies, devalues, or represses the ontological difference of subjects, and seeks to dissolve social inexhaustibility into the comfort of a self-enclosed whole.

Whether expressed as common consciousness or as mutual understanding, the ideal is one of the transparency of subjects to one another. In this ideal each understands the others and recognizes the others in the same way that they understand themselves, and all recognize that the others understand them as they understand themselves. This ideal thus submits to what Derrida calls the metaphysics of presence, which seeks to collapse the temporal difference inherent in language and experience into a totality that can be comprehended in one view. This ideal of community denies the ontological difference within and between subjects.

In community persons cease to be other, opaque, not understood, and instead become mutually sympathetic, understanding one another as they understand themselves, fused. Such an ideal of the transparency of subjects to one another denies the difference, or basic asymmetry, of subjects.

UNDESIRABLE POLITICAL CONSEQUENCES OF THE IDEAL OF COMMUNITY

I have argued that the ideal of community denies the difference between subjects and the social differentiation of temporal and spatial distancing. The most serious political consequence of the desire for community, or for copresence and mutual identification with others, is that it often operates to exclude or oppress those experienced as different. Commitment to an ideal of community tends to value and enforce homogeneity.

In ordinary speech in the United States, the term community refers to the people with whom one identifies in a specific locale. It refers to neighborhood, church, schools. It also carries connotations of ethnicity, race, and other group identifications. For most people, insofar as they consider themselves members of communities at all, a community is a group that shares specific heritage—a common self-identification, a common culture and set of norms.

In many towns, suburbs, and neighborhoods people do have an image of their locale as one in which people all know one another, have the

same values and life-style, and relate with feelings of mutuality and love. In modern American society such an image is almost always false; while there may be a dominant group with a distinct set of values and life-style, within any locale one can usually find deviant individuals and groups. Yet the myth of community operates strongly to produce defensive exclusionary behavior: pressuring the Black family that buys a house on the block to leave, beating up the Black youths who come into "our" neighborhood, zoning against the construction of multiunit dwellings.

CITY LIFE AS A NORMATIVE IDEAL

Appeals to community are usually antiurban. Much sociological literature diagnoses modern history as a movement to the dangerous bureaucratized *Gesellschaft* from the manageable and safe *Gemeinschaft*, nostalgically reconstructed as a world of lost origins. Many others follow Rousseau in romanticizing the ancient *polis* and the medieval Swiss *Bürger*, deploring the commerce, disorder, and unmanageable mass character of the modern city. Throughout the modern period, the city has often been decried as embodying immorality, artificiality, disorder, and danger—as the site of treasonous conspiracies, illicit sex, crime, deviance, and disease. The typical image of the modern city finds it expressing all the disvalues that a reinstantiation of community would eliminate.

Yet urbanity is the horizon of the modern, not to mention the postmodern, condition. Contemporary political theory must accept urbanity as a material given for those who live in advanced industrial societies. Urban relations define the lives not only of those who live in the huge metropolises, but also of those who live in suburbs and large towns. Our social life is structured by vast networks of temporal and spatial mediation among persons, so that nearly everyone depends on the activities of seen and unseen strangers who mediate between oneself and one's associates, between oneself and one's objects of desire. Urbanites find themselves relating geographically to increasingly large regions, thinking little of traveling seventy miles to work or an hour's drive for an evening's entertainment. Most people frequently and casually encounter strangers in their daily activities. The material surroundings and structures available to us define and presuppose urban relationships. The very size of populations in our society and most other nations of the world, coupled with a continuing sense of national or ethnic identity with millions of other people, supports the conclusion that a vision of dismantling the city is hopelessly utopian.

Starting from the given of modern urban life is not simply necessary, moreover; it is desirable. Even for many of those who decry the alienation, bureaucratization, and mass character of capitalist patriarchal society, city life exerts a powerful attraction. Modern literature, art, and film have celebrated city life, its energy, and cultural diversity, technological complexity, and the multiplicity of its activities. Even many of the most staunch proponents of decentralized community love to show visiting friends around the Boston or San Francisco or New York in or near which they live, climbing up towers to see the glitter of lights and sampling the fare at the best ethnic restaurants.

I propose to construct a normative ideal of city life as an alternative to both the ideal of community and the liberal individualism it criticizes as asocial. By "city life" I mean a form of social relations which I define as the being together of strangers. In the city persons and groups interact within spaces and institutions they all experience themselves as belonging to, but without those interactions dissolving into unity or commonness. City life is composed of clusters of people with affinities—families, social group networks, voluntary associations, neighborhood networks, a vast array of small "communities." City dwellers frequently venture beyond such familiar enclaves, however, to the more open public of politics, commerce, and festival, where strangers meet and interact. City dwelling situates one's own identity and activity in relation to a horizon of a vast variety of other activities, and the awareness of these unknown, unfamiliar activities affects the conditions of one's own.

City life is a vast, even infinite, economic network of production, distribution, transportation, exchange, communication, service provision, and amusement. City dwellers depend on the mediation of thousands of other people and vast organizational resources in order to accomplish their individual ends. City dwellers are thus together, bound to one another, in what should be and sometimes is a single polity. Their being together entails some common problems and common interests, but they do not create a community of shared final ends, of mutual identification and reciprocity.

A normative ideal of city life must begin with our given experience of cities, and look there for the virtues of this form of social relations. Defining an ideal as unrealized possibilities of the actual, I extrapolate from that experience four such virtues.

SOCIAL DIFFERENTIATION WITHOUT EXCLUSION

City life in urban mass society is not inconsistent with supportive social networks and subcultural communities. Indeed, for many it is their necessary condition. In the city social group differences flourish. Modernization theory predicted a decline in local, ethnic, and other group affiliations as universalist state institutions touch people's lives more directly and as people encounter many others with identifications and life-styles different from their own. There is considerable evidence, however, that group differences are often reinforced by city life, and that the city even encourages the formation of new social group affinities. Deviant or minority groups find in the city both a cover of anonymity and a critical mass unavailable in the smaller town. It is hard to imagine the formation of gay or lesbian group affinities, for example, without the conditions of the modern city. While city dwelling as opposed to rural life has changed the lives and self-concepts of Chicanos, to take another example, city life encourages group identification and a desire for cultural nationalism at the same time that it may dissolve some traditional practices or promote assimilation to Anglo language and values. In actual cities many people express violent aversions to members of groups with which they do not identify. More than those who live in small towns, however, they tend to recognize social group difference as a given, something they must live with.

In the ideal of city life freedom leads to group differentiation, to the formation of affinity groups, but this social and spatial differentiation of groups is without exclusion. The urban ideal expresses difference as a side-by-side particularity neither reducible to identity nor completely other. In this ideal groups do not stand in relations of inclusions and exclusion, but overlap and intermingle without becoming homogeneous. Though city life as we now experience it has many borders and exclusions, even our actual experience of the city also gives hints of what differentiation without exclusion can be. Many city neighborhoods have a distinct ethnic identity, but members of other groups also dwell in them. In the good city one crosses from one distinct neighborhood to another without knowing precisely where one ended and the other began. In the normative ideal of city life, borders are open and undecidable.

VARIETY

The interfusion of groups in the city occurs partly because of the multiuse differentiation of social space. What makes urban spaces interesting, draws people out in public to them, gives people pleasure and excitement, is the diversity of activities they support. When stores, restaurants, bars, clubs, parks, and offices are sprinkled among residences, people have a neighborly feeling about their neighborhood, they go out and encounter one another on the streets and chat. They have a sense of their neighborhood as a "spot" or "place," because of that bar's distinctive clientele, or the citywide reputation of the pizzas at that restaurant. Both business people and residents tend to have more commitment to and care for such neighborhoods than they do for single-use neighborhoods. Multifunctional streets, parks, and neighborhoods are also much safer than single-use functionalized spaces because people are out on the streets during most hours, and have a commitment to the place.

EROTICISM

City life also instantiates difference as the erotic, in the wide sense of an attraction to the other, the pleasure and excitement of being drawn out of one's secure routine to encounter the novel, strange, and surprising. The erotic dimension of the city has always been an aspect of its fearfulness, for it holds out the possibility that one will lose one's identity, will fall. But we also take pleasure in being open to and interested in people we experience as different. We spend a Sunday afternoon walking through Chinatown, or checking out this week's eccentric

players in the park. We look for restaurants, stores, and clubs with something new for us, a new ethnic food, a different atmosphere, a different crowd of people. We walk through sections of the city that we experience as having unique characters which are not ours, where people from diverse places mingle and then go home.

The erotic attraction here is precisely the obverse of community. In the ideal of community people feel affirmed because those with whom they share experiences, perceptions, and goals recognize and are recognized by them; one sees oneself reflected in the others. There is another kind of pleasure, however, in coming to encounter a subjectivity, a set of meanings, that is different, unfamiliar. One takes pleasure in being drawn out of oneself to understand that there are other meanings, practices, perspectives on the city, and that one could learn or experience something more and different by interacting with them.

The city's eroticism also derives from the aesthetics of its material being: the bright and colored lights, the grandeur of its buildings, the juxtaposition of architecture of different times, styles, and purposes. City space offers delights and surprises. Walk around the corner, or over a few blocks, and you encounter a different spatial mood, a new play of sight and sound, and new interactive movement. The erotic meaning of the city arises from its social and spatial inexhaustibility. A place of many places, the city folds over on itself in so many layers and relationships that it is incomprehensible. One cannot "take it in," one never feels as though there is nothing new and interesting to explore, no new and interesting people to meet.

PUBLICITY

Political theorists who extol the value of community often construe the public as a realm of unity and mutual understanding, but this does not cohere with our actual experience of public spaces. Because by definition a public space is a place accessible to anyone, where anyone can participate and witness, in entering the public one always risks encountering those who are different, those who identify with different groups and have different opinions or different forms of life. The group diversity of the city is most often apparent in public spaces.

This helps account for their vitality and excitement. Cities provide important public spaces—streets, parks, and plazas—where people stand and sit together, interact and mingle, or simply witness one another, without becoming unified in a community of "shared final ends."

Politics, the critical activity of raising issues and deciding how institutional and social relations should be organized, crucially depends on the existence of spaces and forums to which everyone has access. In such public spaces people encounter other people, meanings, expressions, issues, which they may not understand or with which they do not identify. The force of public demonstrations, for example, often consists in bringing to people who pass through public spaces those issues, demands, and people they might otherwise avoid. As a normative ideal, city life provides public places and forums where anyone can speak and anyone can listen.

Because city life is a being together of strangers, diverse and overlapping neighbors, social justice cannot issue from the institution of an Enlightenment universal public. On the contrary, social justice in the city requires the realization of a politics of difference. This politics lays down institutional and ideological means for recognizing and affirming diverse social groups by giving political representation to these groups, and celebrating their distinctive characteristics and cultures. In the unoppressive city people open to unassimilated otherness. We all have our familiar relations and affinities, the people to whom we feel close and with whom we share daily life. These familial and social groups open onto a public in which all participate, and that public must be open and accessible to all. Contrary to the communitarian tradition, however, that public cannot be conceived as a unity transcending group differences, nor as entailing complete mutual understanding. In public life the differences remain unassimilated, but each participating group acknowledges and is open to listening to the others. The public is heterogeneous, plural, and playful, a place where people witness and appreciate diverse cultural expressions that they do not share and do not fully understand.

NOTE

1 Michel Foucault, *Power/Knowledge* (New York: Pantheon, 1980).

SECTION 8

Landscape: Nature and Culture

PLANTING THE RICE.

A group of female slaves hoeing rice on a plantation in South Carolina.
Source: *Harper's Monthly Magazine.* 1859. vol. 19, p. 726; accompanies article by T. Addison Richards,
"The Rice Lands of the South" (pp. 721–38).
Reference to: Carney, Judith. 2000. "The African Origins of Carolina Rice Culture" *Cultural Geographies,*
7(125). pp. 125–149.

LANDSCAPE: NATURE AND CULTURE

Many questions and concerns arise when we discuss the relationship between people and the material world of rocks, trees, earth, plants, animals, and oceans. For most, this non-human environment is the "natural" world, and "nature" is largely imagined as something prior to and separate from human activity. Yet there really is no *natural* environment in the sense of being untouched, and we are increasingly recognizing the impact people have upon the earth and well beyond. All places that people experience have, to some degree, been shaped by human activity. William Cronon (1983) demonstrates that all of human history has an ecological dimension, and Neil Smith (1984) makes this more explicit in his argument that nature is produced. This way of thinking about how the environment has been shaped by human activity invokes the title above, which suggests that landscape is produced through the everywhere and ongoing interaction of nature and culture (Cosgrove 1984; Cosgrove and Daniels 1988; Kaplan and Kaplan 1989).

In this sense, the term *landscape* denotes an environment that has been modified, cultivated, enhanced, or exploited through human activity. While this notion captures the dynamic process of shaping the earth, even landscape is not a perfect term: historically it has privileged the visual aspect of the environment and failed to fully address the other senses. Further, this concept tends to ignore areas that are not "land," like oceans or icecaps, and has been oblivious to the nano-scale microbes and organisms that can have widespread environmental consequences (Braun 2007). Although landscape has been a term used traditionally to describe the geographic form and representation of the land, more recent scholarship has placed emphasis on the dynamic processes that occur through human manipulation and flows of information and materials across all kinds of spaces (Swyngedouw 2004). As such, landscape remains a useful term and tool for thinking about the interface between humans ("culture") and the non-human world ("nature") at a range of scales and across a variety of terrains. This understanding crosses disciplines and reaches into areas of political ecology, sustainability studies, landscape architecture, and cultural studies.

Landscape is employed in a variety of ways, sometimes to analyze macro-scale movements and global mobilities (Appadurai 1996) and other times in a more humanistic vein to understand the cultural meanings of particular places (Lippard 1998; Cosgrove and Daniels 1988). In fields such as landscape architecture, landscape describes a physical place that is designed and constructed to be inhabited and appreciated aesthetically (e.g., Wilson 1991). Landscape is an idea that artists and scholars have grappled with, and remains a term that is useful for the way it begins to show how places are connected across time and space because of the ground they share (e.g., Corner 1996). Some writers look closely at small, local places, while others have tried to make connections across the globe. What they have in common is an understanding that people act on and even produce the natural world, and in so doing cultivate a new relationship with the environment, one aspect of which is landscape.

As the pre-eminent scholar of the *vernacular landscape*, **James Brinkerhoff (J.B.) Jackson** was one of the first writers to articulate the important connection between landscape and culture in the US. His selection here provides an overview of landscape as an idea, and suggests how territory is defined physically and culturally. Jackson discusses two landscapes: one is political and defined by socially recognized markers and boundaries, the other is inhabited and understood through layers of meaning produced by people's engagements with their environments and the spaces of their everyday lives. He suggests that the political landscape represented through symbols such as monuments, fences, and steeples is a manifestation of the social order. The inhabited landscape—often without formal markings— is where people feel an emotional connection to nature and a sense of belonging in the world. For Jackson, these landscapes are not separable; in fact, they come together in the way people have lived and learned to work the land.

Geographer **Judith Carney** sheds further light on the historical meaning of landscape and the intersections of culture and nature. Looking at rice cultivation in the US south, Carney traces the social relations and geographical implications of agricultural knowledge and practices, showing how these patterns are inscribed in the landscape. She argues convincingly that it was the environmental knowledge of African slaves that brought rice cultivation to the US. Carney looks at the origins of rice cultivation in West Africa and discusses how success depends upon growing rice in anaerobic wetland conditions. Knowledge of this system was foreign to most of those colonizing the Americas, but rather was introduced and advanced by involuntary black migrants to what became the southeastern US. She demonstrates how women were especially instrumental in rice cultivation, as the milling process required special care to export the product for international markets (see figure at the beginning of Section 8). For Carney, the landscape may be read as a text that connects and makes visible agricultural and social processes that span oceans and decades and discrete knowledge formations. Carney's work compellingly demonstrates that transforming the American landscape, which made the US a world power, depended completely upon the work and knowledge of slaves and other historically marginalized people.

These power dynamics make clear that all landscapes are shaped through labor processes that are often changing and conflicted. Geographer **Wendy Wolford** examines landscapes that are defined by situations and issues that originate at the state level, but which are negotiated more locally through the decisions and practices of individuals and groups. Wolford's work examines the Movement of Rural Landless Workers in Brazil from a political ecology perspective, and addresses the ways in which mobilization is shaped by the specific relationships people have with the land. She compares two groups, family farmers in the south and rural plantation workers in the northeast, and their reasons for and interests in joining the movement. She concludes that the degree to which people participated—and whether people saw space as open or closed—was shaped by how they had traditionally related to the land through their labor.

Journalist and sustainability activist **Michael Pollan** argues that the United States has made two important contributions to understanding landscape: the *wilderness* and the *lawn*. Pollan suggests that in order to develop our understanding of and relation to the landscape, we need to move beyond this dichotomy. For Pollan, these two types of landscape represent contradictory understandings of the natural environment. On the one hand, there is an insistence on the preservation of an ideal wilderness untouched by civilization, while on the other is the lawn—nature utterly dominated by civilization, an industrial product in many ways. In telling the history of these opposing relations to nature, Pollan argues that dispensing with both lawn and wilderness and replacing them with a notion of the *garden*, as a place of careful cultivation, might offer a better alternative and a more appropriate model for the human relation to nature.

In addition to considering the making of social and cultural landscapes, researchers are also attentive to how the landscape is perceived and experienced. Environmental psychologist **Louise Chawla** argues that experiencing landscape as place is valuable because it is sensory-rich, restorative, and character-forming. She examines autobiographic accounts to discover what types of places stay in our memory and inform who we are as adults. Chawla suggests that these places create *ecstatic memories* which sustain and delight us, and, as places remembered, are the landscapes that have been most intensely felt. Her work explores how these experiences are connected to people's creative abilities, inspired by the strong correlation she found among artists, poets, and authors who wrote about ecstatic landscape experiences.

The selections we have included are intended both to help us understand our relationship to the environment and suggest more sustainable directions for our interaction with the natural world in which we may more thoughtfully and carefully work with the landscape. At the same time, these selections only begin to explore the research and scholarship that looks at the place of people in the world. Bruno Latour's (2007) *actor-network theory* offers a novel approach to understanding our relationship to things around us, arguing that "objects too have agency." Paul Cloke and Owain Jones (2002) use this idea to look at role which trees play in our lives. Bruce Braun's (2002) work also draws upon these ideas, but takes us closer to *political ecology*, a field that studies how our environment is produced through political, economic, and social processes at a variety of scales (see also Escobar 1999; Robbins 2007). Recent studies have mapped the origins and transportation of food to construction materials, as a reminder that everything comes from somewhere (McDonough and Braungart 2002). Lucy Lippard (1998) and Dolores Hayden (Section 3) expanded on the cultural landscape work of J.B. Jackson by looking more closely at layers of history and politics ingrained in the landscape. The list goes on, but we encourage you to use this view of landscape to inform your experience of place and understand that our interaction with the environment is dynamic, sensory-rich, and intimately tied to our futures together on this planet.

SUGGESTIONS FOR FURTHER READING

Please see *peopleplacespace.org* for extended and additional lists of readings.

Appadurai, Arjun. 1996. *Modernity At Large: Cultural Dimensions of Globalization*. Minneapolis: University Of Minnesota Press.

Appleton, Jay. 1975. *Experience of Landscape*. New York: John Wiley & Sons Inc.

Betsky, Aaron. 2006. *Landscrapers: Building with the Land*. London: Thames & Hudson.

Braun, Bruce. 2002. *The Intemperate Rainforest: Nature, Culture, and Power on Canada's West Coast*, 1st edn. Minneapolis: University of Minnesota Press.

Braun, Bruce. 2007. "Biopolitics and the Molecularization of Life." *Cultural Geographies* 14: 6–28.

Carney, Judith A. 2002. *Black Rice: The African Origins of Rice Cultivation in the Americas*. Cambridge, MA: Harvard University Press.

Carson, Rachel. 2002. *Silent Spring*. Anniversary. New York: Houghton Mifflin Company.

Castree, Noel. 2013. *Making Sense of Nature*. New York: Routledge.

Cloke, Paul, and Owain Jones. 2002. *Tree Cultures: The Place of Trees and Trees in Their Place*. New York: Berg Publishers.

Corner, James. 1996. *Taking Measures Across the American Landscape*. New Haven, CT: Yale University Press.

Cosgrove, Denis E. 1984. *Social Formation and Symbolic Landscape*. London: Croom Helm.

Cosgrove, Denis E., and Stephen Daniels. 1988. *The Iconography of Landscape: Essays on the Symbolic Representation, Design, and Use of Past Environments*. Cambridge; New York: Cambridge University Press.

Cronon, William. 1992. *Nature's Metropolis: Chicago and the Great West*, 1st edn. New York: W.W. Norton & Company.

Cronon, William. 2003 [1983]. *Changes in the Land: Indians, Colonists, and the Ecology of New England*, revised edn. New York: Hill and Wang.

Escobar, Arturo. 1999. "After Nature: Steps to an Antiessentialist Political Ecology." *Current Anthropology* 40(1)(February): 1–30.

Kaika, Maria. 2004. *City of Flows: Modernity, Nature, and the City*. New York: Routledge.

Kaplan, Rachel, and Stephen Kaplan. 1989. *The Experience of Nature: A Psychological Perspective*. Cambridge: Cambridge University Press.

Latour, Bruno. 2007. "Objects Too Have Agency." In *Reassembling the Social: An Introduction to Actor-Network-Theory*, pp. 63–86. New York: Oxford University Press.

Lippard, Lucy R. 1998. *The Lure of the Local: Senses of Place in a Multicentered Society*. New York: New Press.

McDonough, William, and Michael Braungart. 2002. *Cradle to Cradle: Remaking the Way We Make Things*. New York: North Point Press.

Olmstead, Fredrick Law. 1870. "Public Parks and the Enlargement of Towns." Presented at the Lowell Institute, Lowell, Massacheusetts. Reprinted in *Civilizing America's Cities. A selection of Fredrick Law Olmstead's Writings on City Landscape*. Edited by S.B. Sutton. Cambridge, MA: MIT Press. 1975.

Robbins, Paul. 2007. *Lawn People: How Grasses, Weeds, and Chemicals Make Us Who We Are*. Philadelphia, PA: Temple University Press.

Saunders, William S. (ed.). 2008. *Nature, Landscape, and Building for Sustainability: A Harvard Design Magazine Reader*. Minneapolis: University of Minnesota Press.

Smith, Neil. 1984. *Uneven Development: Nature, Capital, and the Production of Space*. Savannah: University of Georgia Press.

Swyngedouw, Erik. 2004. *Social Power and the Urbanization of Water: Flows of Power*. New York: Oxford University Press.

Thoreau, Henry David. 1966. *Walden*. Peter Pauper Press.

Williams, Raymond. 1975. *The Country and the City*. New York: Oxford University Press.

Wilson, Alexander. 1991. *The Culture of Nature: North American Landscape from Disney to the Exxon Valdez*. London: Between the Lines.

42
A Pair of Ideal Landscapes

(1984)

John Brinkerhoff (J.B.) Jackson

Those of us who undertake to study landscapes in a serious way soon come up against a sobering truth: even the simplest, least interesting landscape often contains elements which we are quite unable to explain, mysteries that fit into no known pattern. But we also eventually learn that every landscape, no matter how exotic, also contains elements which we at once recognize and understand. We may be baffled by the layout of the towns and the crops the people raise, and the architecture may be unlike anything we have encountered, but the fields and fences and houses, for instance, are easy to understand; we have only to look at them once to see the role they play.

No group sets out to create a landscape, of course. What it sets out to do is to create a community, and the landscape as its visible manifestation is simply the by-product of people working and living, sometimes coming together, sometimes staying apart, but always recognizing their interdependence.

This process is well illustrated in our own American landscape history, and it is in order to understand that history that I am enumerating some of the simplest and most visible elements in what can be called the political landscape: the landscape which evolved partly out of experience, partly from design, to meet some of the needs of men and women in their political guise. The political elements I have in mind are such things as walls and boundaries and highways and monuments and public places; these have a definite role to play in the landscape. They exist to insure order and security and continuity and to give citizens a visible status. They serve to remind us of our rights and obligations and of our history.

The most basic political element in any landscape is the boundary. Politically speaking what matters first is the formation of a community of responsible citizens, a well-defined territory composed of small holdings and a number of public spaces; so the first step toward organizing space is the defining of that territory, after which we divide it for the individual members. Boundaries, therefore, unmistakable, permanent, inviolate boundaries, are essential.

We would all agree that insofar as every landscape is a composition of spaces it is also a composition or web of boundaries. But here we must be cautious, for boundaries can serve a variety of functions. In the contemporary Western world we assume that a boundary is the point (or line) of contact between two defined spaces, a way of regulating contact and communication with neighbors, even while it protects us against invasion or unwanted entry. We assume—and rightly from our point of view—that the boundary is like a skin: a thin surface which is in fact part of the body, part of space which it protects. We therefore assume that the boundary corresponds as closely as possible to the area of the content.

In geographical terms we try to discover a forest or a range of hills which will divide one area or region from another, or to locate the line marking a difference in language or religion or ethnic stock. Planners and sociologists are no less concerned with establishing the boundaries of economic or social territories, and so we have boundaries based on the circulation of newspapers or the drawing capacity of a shopping center. In every case we try to establish a boundary closely adjusted to its social or natural content, and back of this effort is the notion that the space (or the way the space is used) is an essential characteristic of the contents. A nation, we say, is not simply a collection of people, it is also the territory they occupy, and the boundary in consequence should be drawn so that the two entities correspond as closely as possible.

This may seem obvious, but there is reason to believe that the traditional political landscape had a very different concept of a boundary: it was intended less to define a region and establish an effective relationship with the outside world than to isolate and protect something within it. It was not so much a skin as it was a packaging, an envelope.

A typical man-made space in a political landscape, whether farm or village or nation, is likely to contain near its center an isolated, independent structure surrounded by a buffer zone and a very visible boundary, and communication between this structure (or collection of structures) and the outside world is formalized in some manner: by a portal or gate or architectural entrance way.

In a greatly modified form, our early American landscape displayed much the same attitude toward boundaries: they were designed to isolate and protect the objects or people within them. The device persisted longest, I think, in the siting of important buildings: the freestanding church, the freestanding courthouse, the freestanding school or college building—all of them edifices of some sanctity—relied on an enclosing-and-excluding-fence or wall and a surrounding buffer zone of empty space to give them dignity and aloofness. We are grateful that they did, for the result was almost always a composition of great effectiveness. But it is *we* who have learned to perceive that composition; the classical building of white clapboard or brick in the midst of smooth, green lawn and towering trees, fenced off from the secular world is in our eyes a single harmonious unit. Yet I cannot help feel that when those structures were built they were in no way seen as related to the open space encompassing them. That space was merely the protective envelope or packaging, and the fence or wall was merely the ultimate legal symbol of autonomy.

When we hear mention of political spaces and their value, what comes to mind is the familiar space—plaza or market or town square or forum—where we gather to enjoy the company of others and pass the time of day. It would be hard to find a community without such a space: alive and full of action, with people buying and selling, talking and listening, walking and looking about, or merely resting. Sometimes the space is the civic center, ornate and immense, sometimes it is nothing more than an empty lot or a wide space in the street. It is always enjoyable, and instinct tells us that a public space of one kind or another is essential to any community.

Here is a characteristically modern definition of the public square: a place of passive enjoyment, a kind of playground for adults, and it says a good deal about how slack our current definition of community can be. Zucker and many others are content to describe the public square strictly in terms of gregariousness: how it offers a spatial experience shared by a heterogeneous public which will sooner or later go its separate ways; an urban form which acts to draw people together and give them a momentary pleasure and sense of well-being. No one should underestimate those benefits, but in the political landscape the public square serves an entirely different purpose. It is assumed that those who come there are *already* aware that they are members of the community, responsible citizens, and that on occasion they will participate in public discussions and take action on behalf of the community.

True, every traditional public square has served several ends: marketplace, a place of business and a place of informal sociability and amusement, a place for pageantry. The agora in Athens, far from being architecturally impressive, was a jumble of crowded downtown streets and irregular open spaces where shrines and altars, public buildings and monuments stood in the midst of workshops, market stalls, and taverns.

It was, and in many places still is, a manifestation of the local social order, of the relationship between citizens and between citizens and the authority of the state. The plaza is where the role of the individual in the community is made visible, where we reveal our identity as part of an ethnic or religious or political or consumer-oriented society, and it exists and functions to reinforce that identity.

Every traditional public space, whether religious or political or ethnic in character, displays a variety of symbols, inscriptions, images, monuments, not as works of art but to remind people of their civic privileges and duties—and tacitly to exclude the outsider. The Roman Forum was cluttered with such reminders, and though the colonial New England town was hostile to public art it nevertheless contained a number of powerful symbols, impossible to misinterpret: the church with its steeple and bell, its front door covered with public notices and decrees; the whipping post, the stocks, the graveyard, and sometimes the tree ceremoniously planted by the first settlers. All of these served to tell those who came to the church services or town meeting or to the militia drill that they were part of a tight-knit religious community and had obligations. The public space was not for relaxation or environmental awareness; it was for *civic* awareness.

As we might expect, the ideal public square in the political landscape has a strong architectural quality. It occupies the most prestigious location in the principal town and is surrounded by politically significant buildings: law court, archives, treasury, legislative hall, and often military headquarters and jail as well. The space itself is adorned with statues of local heroes and divinities, monuments to important historic events. All important ceremonies are enacted here. Typical of the political emphasis on boundaries, the area is well defined by markers and has its own laws and its own officers. Finally, it is here in the agora or forum, that history is made visible and where speech becomes a political instrument, eloquence a form of political action.

The political landscape, the landscape designed to produce law-abiding citizens, honest officials, eloquent orators, and patriotic soldiers, let us have a final glimpse of it. Here is a description or survey of Italy in the last years of the Roman Empire, written in the third century A.D. by Tertullian:

All places are now accessible, all are well known, all open to commerce; most pleasant farms have obliterated all traces of what were once dreary and dangerous wastes; cultivated fields have subdued forests; flocks and herds have expelled wild beasts; sandy deserts are sown; rocks are planted; marshes are drained; and where once were hardly solitary cottages, there are now large cities. No longer are

[savage] islands dreaded, nor their rocky shores feared; everywhere are houses, and inhabitants, and settled government, and civilized life.

It must have been impressive; for it made visible two qualities very uncommon in those remote times and by no means universal even now: order and prosperity. It was a *livable* landscape, it was an achievement, socially speaking.

Only when we think about the private, the more emotional side of existence do we find something missing in the political landscape. It is time therefore to explore that alternative landscape, the one in which we feel at home as inhabitants of the earth. The contrast between the two is clear: man, the political animal, thinks of the landscape as his own creation, as belonging to him; thinks of it as a well-defined territory or domain which confers on him a status totally distinct from that of all other creatures; whereas man the inhabitant sees the landscape as a habitat which was there long before he appeared. He sees himself as belonging to the landscape in the sense that he is its product. Yet the two points of view have this in common: they see the landscape as something shared; they assume that human beings cannot survive and fulfill themselves unless there is a landscape to hold them together in a group.

These two landscapes—the political and the one which for brevity's sake I call the inhabited landscape—in real life are always found together. As a usual thing the political landscape is on a larger, more impressive scale, more permanent and easier to spot, whereas the inhabited landscape is likely to be poor and small and hard to find. But both of them, in one degree or another, are always there, and it is only when we discuss them in the abstract that we are able to separate them.

Yet they *do* differ, and not only in appearance or what for the lack of a better term I refer to as spatial organization, but in their underlying purpose, and I would tentatively say that while the political landscape is deliberately *created* in order to make it possible for men to live in a just society, the inhabited landscape merely *evolves* in the course of our trying to live on harmonious terms with the natural world surrounding us.

Almost by definition an inhabited landscape is the product of incessant adaptation and conflict: adaptation to what is often a new and bewildering natural environment, conflict between groups of people with very dissimilar views as to how to make that adaptation. The political landscape, artificial though it may be, is the realization of an archetype, of a coherent design inspired by philosophy or religion, and it has a distinct purpose in view. But the inhabited landscape is, to use a much distorted word, an existential landscape: it achieves its identity only in the course of existence.

The political landscape is indifferent to the topography and culture of the territories it takes over, but the inhabited landscape sees itself as the center of the world, an oasis of order in the surrounding chaos, inhabited by the People. Insularity is what gives it character; size, wealth, beauty have nothing to do with it; it is a law unto itself.

Actually not a law, but a set of habits and customs accumulated over the centuries, each the outcome of a slow adaptation to place—to the local topography and weather and soil, and to the people, the superfamily which lived there: a special accent, a special way of dressing, a special form of greeting; special dances and holidays—all the picturesque idiosyncrasies that are the stuff of tourist folklore, and then some: passwords and gestures, taboos and secrets—secret places and secret events that exclude the outsider more effectively than any boundary. Strange how many of these customs, these ways of identifying an inhabited landscape and its inhabitants are sensory: the unmistakable taste of a local dish or a local wine, the smell of certain seasons, the sound of a local song! There was a time when the territory of many villages was the countryside where the church bell could be heard—like the old-fashioned definition of a Cockney: someone born within sound of Bowbells. Sensations such as these are never entirely forgotten; not that they are much thought about, but they remind us that we are where we belong—and equally important, I think: they are not shared with outsiders.

Is that what we mean by a sense of place? Is this total adjustment to and immersion in the inhabited landscape what we aspire to? I hope not, for at their most beautiful and rewarding, our European–American landscapes stand for a very different relationship. Explain it how we will—religious insight, psychological shift, growing awareness of the wider world outside the village, or whatever—there came a time some five centuries ago when we began to see the landscape from a new and more detached perspective. The villager in the old inhabited landscape was never an efficient farmer nor interested in changing his ways. He had not presumed to inquire into the hidden aspects of nature: the composition of the soil, the development of plants, the vagaries of the weather; all that he knew was what his senses told him. But then he discovered that he had a distinct, human role to play. "The farmer," says an ancient handbook of agriculture, "should study the nature of the land from which he expects to make a living, and diligently learn whether the soil is cold or warm, moist or dry, sandy or clayey. ... For just as every man and every animal has his own peculiarities, every field has its own nature." He was further urged to treat the land as a teacher treats a child whom he wants to develop into a responsible individual, or think of himself as a midwife, helping bring something into the world. He was to see himself as a trainer who patiently encourages the best and most useful traits in a colt or a young dog. In short, he was no longer to be a drudge, blindly following routines from the past, he was to be a guardian, a teacher, a helper. In the old sense of the word, the farmer undertook to *improve* his land, to bring it to its natural perfection, and this required of him that he learn to recognize the *invisible* potential of soils and animals and plants, the landscape of universal law instead of the landscape of local custom.

43
The African Origins of Carolina Rice Culture

(2000)

Judith Carney

Twenty-five years ago historian Peter Wood broke with prevailing accounts of Carolina rice beginnings by attributing the crop's successful adaptation to slaves. Building upon earlier ideas of Converse Clowse, who showed rice slaves as anything but unskilled laborers, *Black majority* argued that the candidates for rice origins were the 'unlikely innovators' from West Africa's extensive rice-growing region.[1] Archival evidence led Wood to challenge numerous accounts written by apologists of slavery, planters and their descendants, celebrating the 'ingenious' achievements of their ancestors in finding a crop so eminently suitable to the low country of South Carolina.

One enduring achievement of Wood's scholarship was to direct research interest beyond the Carolina shores and eastwards across the Atlantic Ocean to West Africa. His thesis in effect would demand an intellectual journey, one that reversed the direction followed by slaves across the Middle Passage. The early history of Carolina rice cultivation asked new questions about African contributions to the agricultural history of the Americas. But this journey demanded a different type of research optic, one similar in spirit to that pioneered by French historians of the *Annales* school with its attention to space and time, or geography and history, for understanding long-term historical processes. Fernand Braudel in particular illuminated the possibilities of such an approach in his focus on the Mediterranean as the appropriate geohistorical unit for analysing the history of capitalism. Wood's attribution of rice beginnings to West African slaves similarly required an innovative framework, one that

would emphasize the Atlantic basin. It is within this holistic approach, focused on the Atlantic world, that this article is written.

Three themes related to rice history and the role of slaves in its diffusion to the Americas are considered in this article. One builds upon the research of historian Daniel Littlefield and geographer Carville Earle. In examining the cultural origins of rice cultivation in South Carolina, Littlefield illuminated its African antecedents. Earle's parallel interest in the intersection of geography with history draws attention to agriculture as the connective tissue between nature and culture, and thus to its potential for investigating questions of culture, technology and the environment. This article emphasizes the identification of distinctive farming systems and their location in specific regions of the world as the result of indigenous knowledge formed *in situ* over time. The second theme, which reviews scholarship on rice origins in West Africa, addresses the manner in which scholars learned that a separate rice species evolved there, and the question why scientific knowledge of this fact remained unexplored until this century. The significance of gendered practices in the cultivation and processing of rice, especially the role of female knowledge systems in the crop's diffusion across the Atlantic from West Africa to South Carolina, forms the third theme.

AN AFRICAN AGRICULTURAL SYSTEM IN SOUTH CAROLINA

Until Wood's 1974 pathbreaking book, *Black majority*, accounts of rice beginnings in South

Carolina routinely attributed the crop's introduction and adaptation to Europeans rather than Africans. Rice was promoted by English pamphleteers as a potential commodity for their American colonies as early as 1609 and, as historian Daniel Littlefield observes, rice figured among the promising crops mentioned in 1648 by one Virginia pamphleteer in a letter sent to England:

> The Governor Sir William [Berkeley], caused half a bushel of Rice (which he had procured) to be sowen, and it prospered gallantly and he had fifteen bushels of it, excellent good Rice, so that all those fifteen bushels will be sowen again this year; and we doubt not in a short time to have Rice so plentiful as to afford it at 2d a pound if not cheaper, for we perceive the ground and Climate is very proper for it as our Negroes affirme, which in their Country is most of their food, and very healthful for our bodies.[2]

While the development of the tobacco economy over the next decades would overshadow further consideration of rice cultivation in Virginia, the quotation reveals several key points. From an early period of settlement planters were aware of rice cultivation in Africa even though the consolidation of slavery during the ante-bellum period effaced the common knowledge of an earlier era. Secondly, Virginia colonists actually grew rice, although no direct statement indicates how the crop was cultivated. However, if rice was to become a successful plantation crop, it depended upon developing wetland cultivation, not the lower-yielding upland or rain-fed system.

The English settled Virginia as they did South Carolina, with the first colonists initially arriving from Barbados in search of land to extend the plantation system. Colonists from England, as well as Protestant Huguenots displaced from France, soon joined them. Slaves figured prominently among the first settlers of South Carolina, arriving on the mainland via Caribbean plantations or directly from West Africa. An examination of the cropping systems known to Europeans and Africans in the initial decades of settlement of South Carolina from the 1670s illuminates which ethnic tradition should be credited with the development of Carolina rice cultivation. There exists a lingering doubt as to African agency in colonial rice history, because

English settlers in Virginia heeded the advice of pamphleteers to experiment with rice during the seventeenth century. But the key to rice history in colonial America lies in understanding the types of farming system known to both black and white settlers of the southern colonies. This evidence suggests that the rice briefly planted in Virginia was of the upland type, reliant solely upon rainfall. It formed part of a rain-fed farming system known to both European and African. But only West African slaves knew the wet rice farming system.

At the time of their emigration, the English and French practised an agricultural system based on the cultivation of crops by rainfall. With settlement of the southern colonies, they adjusted this farming system to subtropical conditions and began planting crops new to them, such as rice and tobacco. When early experiments in Virginia during the mid-seventeenth century showed that rice would produce a 'gallant' harvest with adequate rainfall, colonists thus added another plant to their existing farming system, even though its potential as an export crop would be later abandoned in favour of tobacco. However, just a few decades later, at the end of the seventeenth century, an entirely new way of growing rice had developed in South Carolina. This form of cultivation involved planting the crop under submersion in low-lying swamps.

But cultivation of wetland rice depended upon knowing how to grow the crop under anaerobic conditions. The European settlers of South Carolina, as those of Virginia, did not practise a cultivation system that involved planting crops in standing water. Instead, theirs was a rain-fed farming system, with rice cultivated by rainfall in the same manner as oats, wheat and barley. Wetland rice farming, on the other hand, demands a sophisticated understanding of lowland landscapes and their skilled manipulation for irrigation, drainage and tidal farming. West Africa is the likely source of origin for the wetland rice system that emerged in South Carolina during the early colonial period.

At the time of settlement of the South Carolina colony, the tidal rice system existed in only two areas of the world, Asia and West Africa. Contact with Asia during the period of Carolina settlement, however, was indirect and brokered by English mariners and merchants, whose interest was trade goods, not agricultural systems. No evidence from the crucial period of rice development in South Carolina, from the 1690s to 1750s, indicates that Europeans possessed a comprehensive understanding of the Asian rice system, which relied on the techniques of transplanting, irrigation and drainage. However, the type of rice cultivation that developed along Carolina floodplains differed in one crucial respect from that of Asia. It did not involve transplanting, and in this sense reveals the linkage of the Carolina rice system to West Africa.

In fully evolved wetland farming systems such as those that developed in Asia and West Africa, human beings act as geomorphological agents on a grand scale, transforming swamp into rice paddy through a sophisticated understanding of lowland gradient and water flow. The Asian rice system responded to land scarcity with the development of techniques like transplanting to increase yields. The rice systems of West Africa unfolded along a different trajectory, of labour rather than land scarcity. Under such circumstances the labour-intensive practice of transplanting developed only in response to specific environmental constraints, as a way to improve seed survival along floodplains swept by high tides, in areas menaced by seasonal saltwater intrusion or by the irregular onset of rainfall. In these circumstances rice seeds are first established on higher ground and then the hardier seedlings transplanted. Otherwise rice is direct-seeded on floodplains in the same manner that characterized Carolina tidal cultivation.

While *sativa* varieties from Asia transferred to the emergent rice economy of South Carolina during the seventeenth century, long in advance of any migration of Asians to North America, the seeds became established because human beings already familiar with wet rice farming would grow them. These were slaves, among whom were many already familiar with rice cultivation in West Africa.

THE ORIGINS OF RICE CULTIVATION IN WEST AFRICA

Until the twentieth century the cultivation of rice in Africa was viewed as the result of the diffusion of systems from Asia. But this view proved problematic, since the earliest observations of rice cultivation were from West and not the geographically more proximate East Africa. The crop's cultivation along the upper Guinea coast captured the interest of Portuguese mariners from their earliest voyages. In 1453, decades before ships would reach India and Asian rice systems, the Portuguese chronicler Gomes Eanes de Azurara visited the mouth of the Gambia River and recorded the first European mention of West African rice cultivation:

> They arrived sixty leagues beyond Cape Verde [Senegal], where they met with a river which was of good width, and into which they entered with their caravels ... they found much of the land sown, and many ... fields sown with rice. ... And ... all that land seemed ... like marshes.

Over the following decades, Portuguese commentaries observe the importance of rice as a dietary staple and its widespread cultivation along the West African coast south from Senegal to Liberia. Portuguese ships came to depend upon the availability of rice for provisions, as did mariners of other European nations who began competing with Portugal for the West African trade from the second half of the sixteenth century.

As a crucial dietary staple for millions in West Africa, rice sustained the dense populations of numerous societies subsequently swept into the Atlantic slave trade. While rice was cultivated principally as a subsistence crop, the deepening of Atlantic slavery resulted in its being planted as a commodity near the Atlantic Coast and slave markets. African captives were often forced to cultivate food staples for armies or for sale to slave ships.

As the Atlantic slave trade augmented, so did the demand for rice, with slave ships purchasing the cereal to provision its human cargo across the Middle Passage.

The global transfer of seeds with European voyages, often referred to as the Columbian Exchange, has received a great deal of attention, but it privileges European and male agency in their diffusion. At times, entire cultivation and processing systems were transferred as well. And, as with rice in the Americas, when this occurred it was because the bearers of the indigenous knowledge system were also mobile.

The history of rice cultivation surrounding the Atlantic basin, however, suggests that the crop's appearance in South Carolina was not the outcome of European agency and ingenuity but the result of a sophisticated knowledge system of wetland cultivation brought by involuntary black migrants.

Rice crossed the Middle Passage of slavery to the Americas as food in ship cargoes, as an indigenous knowledge system known to many of the Atlantic slave trade's victims, and in the processing and culinary traditions of African women. The gendered aspects of African rice systems and their import for South Carolina are discussed below.

GENDERED PRACTICES IN AFRICAN RICE CULTURE AND LINKAGES TO SOUTH CAROLINA

Evidence from archival and historical sources as well as illustrations yield clues on the labour system, which indicates that female slaves constituted the majority of 'prime hands' on Carolina and Georgia rice plantations. Women were especially involved in the tasks of sowing the seeds, weeding and hoeing, their group labour with long-handled hoes described by one observer of an ante-bellum rice plantation as a 'human hoeing machine'. The association of females with field labour in rice cultivation, which planter descendant Duncan Heyward termed 'woman's wuck', is represented in an engraving from the era. A field labour force that was disproportionately female characterized rice cultivation, with the less arduous 'skilled' work assigned to male bondsmen. An examination of the division of labour on Carolina rice plantations consequently reveals the importance of gender for the allocation of work, but the resulting feminization of rice culture probably resulted from men's greater involvement in non-agricultural tasks, which left fieldwork disproportionately to women. However, as the principal rice growers in West Africa and in the preparation of rice for consumption, African women would have played an important role in the transfer of rice culture to South Carolina.

Rice is either a female crop or one cultivated with a sharply demarcated gender division of labour, men preparing the land for cultivation and women in charge of sowing, weeding and hoeing. From the earliest European observations of rice culture in West Africa, the crop is associated with female labour (see figure at the beginning of Section 8).

During the time of the Atlantic slave trade, therefore, wherever rice was grown it was a crop that involved women. Their knowledge would have proved critical in developing the cultivation of rice in the Americas, even if the gendered practices informing the cropping system became transformed under slavery. The significance of female knowledge for cultural practices becomes especially evident when examining rice processing and cooking.

While the successful transfer of rice culture to South Carolina depended on learning how to raise the crop in wetland environments, of equal importance to its development as an export crop was knowledge of how to process or mill rice for international markets.

Research on agriculture too often focuses solely on cultivation, ignoring the significance for seed or crop adoption of the related processes of milling and cooking. Across the world this is traditionally women's work. As with all food preparation in Africa, rice was hand-milled by women, in the manner of cereals throughout most rural areas of the continent. Even during the period of Atlantic slavery, the crews on slave ships recognized that the processing of rice was female work, with references to ship captains requiring female captives to mill the unhulled rice for consumption.

Knowing how to mill rice without breakage proved crucial for the adoption of rice culture in South Carolina, thus illustrating a transfer from Africa of a gendered knowledge system. Perhaps indirect recognition of the importance of women's skills in growing and processing rice is behind Thomas Nairne's observation in 1710 that female slaves in the colony fetched the same market price as males. And perhaps the value of female knowledge of rice culture may explain the unusual feature of the Carolina slave trade in its tendency to import more females than other plantation systems.

Unlike the cereals planted by Europeans, where grain is pulverized to produce flour, the processing of rice aims to minimize grain breakage as the heavy wooden pestle bears down upon the hulls. This represents a skilled operation and one that is not easily mastered.[3] Until the 1780s, when machines finally managed to perform the operation without breaking the grain, the entire export crop, some hundreds of millions of pounds of rice, required milling by hand in the African manner, with a mortar and pestle.

Two other aspects of Carolina rice culture represent the transfer of a female knowledge system across the Atlantic: the device used for winnowing, and the manner of cooking rice. On Carolina plantations, rice hulls were winnowed in a straw basket, known as a fanner basket. Dale Rosengarten's careful study of the origins of these baskets establishes their affinity with West Africa. She shows that the weaving style is not Native American, since those of the southeast Indians employed a twilled or plaited design. Fanner baskets are coiled, as can be seen in the ones marketed by African American female vendors in the Charleston area today. Woven in the identical manner as those used for winnowing during the period of rice plantations, these baskets derive from a prototype used by African women in the secondary centre of rice domestication located in the Senegambia area.

An examination of rice cooking provides additional evidence for the transmission of a female knowledge system from Africa to South Carolina. Despite the familiar logo of Uncle Ben on the converted rice marketed by that name in the United States, it was African women who perfected rice cooking in a distinctive manner that characterizes both African and Carolinian culinary traditions. The objective was to prepare dishes to prevent rice from clumping together, as in the Asian style, a plate where every grain remained separate. The method involved steaming and absorption, boiling rice first for 10–15 minutes, draining off excess water, removing the pan from direct heat for the grains to absorb the moisture, and leaving the pot covered for at least an hour before eating. This is the same manner in which rice is traditionally prepared throughout the West African rice region, where wood is scarce for cooking and the task for its procurement often the additional responsibility of women.

CONCLUSION

For at least 2000 years rice culture in Africa has been practised over a broad area of the upper Guinea coast and its hinterland. Rice is either planted solely by women or organized in a system where males and females assume gender-specific tasks. The transfer of rice cultivation by slaves from this region of Africa, whence derived more than half those brought to South Carolina in bondage during the eighteenth century, involved the diffusion of cultural practices from one part of the Atlantic basin to another. A crucial component of the successful establishment of rice cultivation in South Carolina was the transfer of a farming and crop processing system deeply associated with female knowledge.

In reversing the direction of the Atlantic slave trade back to West Africa, this research reveals the role of Africans and African women in introducing an important agricultural system that forever changed the food culture of the Americas. Rice formed the crucial component of the gumbo, bouillabaisse and Hoppin' John that distinguish southern regional cooking. Through the cultivation and preparation of rice in slavery and freedom black men and women reaffirmed their cultural identity in the Americas. The fact that their role is only becoming fully understood at the close of the twentieth century speaks volumes concerning the pernicious legacy of human bondage.

NOTES

1 Wood, Peter. 1974. *Black majority*. New York, Norton.
2 Littlefield, Daniel, C. 1981. *Rice and slaves: ethnicity and the slave trade in colonial South Carolina*. Baton Rouge: Louisana State University Press.
3 Slavery broke down this gender division of labour as women taught young boys as well as girls rice mortar and pestle processing: see Carney, Judith. 1996 "Rice Milling, Gender and Slave Labour in Colonial South Carolina." *Past & Present* (153): 108–34.

44
This Land is Ours Now

Spatial Imaginaries and the Struggle for Land
in Brazil (2004)

Wendy Wolford

On April 17, 1997, more than 50,000 people marched through the streets of Brasília in a historic demonstration of support for what had become the largest grassroots social movement in Brazilian history—O *Movimento Dos Trabalhadores Rurais Sem Terra* (the Movement of Rural Landless Workers, or the MST). Created officially in 1984, in the wake of a repressive military dictatorship, MST members aggressively occupied "unproductive" land as a way of pressuring the newly elected government for rights to the property. Over the next 19 years, the Brazilian government responded to the MST's actions with an erratic combination of violence and diplomacy that generated a frightening list of rural victims, but also led to the redistribution of over 1,000 rural properties. Today, the MST represents approximately 1 million people on land reform settlements and in temporary squatter camps throughout Brazil.

In their discussion of the movement's origins, academics and movement leaders have consistently stressed the importance of agricultural restructuring, political opportunity, and religious mobilization. The MST's formation is so uniformly attributed to these three factors that they now constitute what I call the Official Genesis Story: the MST was formed because agricultural restructuring in the countryside created a "landless class" at the same time as the return to democracy provided the opportunity for large-scale mobilization, and progressive religious activists served as natural incubators, or "institutional hosts" for the fledgling movement.

In this paper, I suggest that we will only have a complete picture of movement formation if we go beyond the sort of structural factors outlined in the Official Genesis Story to show how mobilization is shaped by—and shapes—the way people internalize and engage with their specific material and symbolic spatial environments.

A geography of resistance needs to examine the ways in which the physical environment is internalized, embodied, imagined, and remembered. In Foucault's (1979) conceptualization of modern society, the importance of Bentham's panopticon was not simply that physical space was reordered in ways that allowed for isolation and effective supervision; rather, the panopticon was powerful because the threat of supervision was internalized by those within. The spaces of incarceration shaped the prisoners' consciousness and, in so doing, shaped their perception of, and relationship to, the outside world.

In relation to the struggle for land in Brazil, the spatial construction of social relations shaped people's decision to join the MST. The formation of resistance was embedded in particular understandings of space, or what I call "spatial imaginaries"—cognitive frameworks, both collective and individual, constituted through the lived experiences, perceptions, and conceptions of space itself (Lefebvre 1991). Analyzing these spatial imaginaries will help to explain more precisely how people in rural Brazil experienced agricultural modernization, political opening, and religious mobilization in ways that made them choose to leave everything behind and join a radical landless movement.

In order to illustrate the importance of spatial imaginaries, I compare settlers who were originally small family farmers in the southern state of Santa Catarina to settlers who were originally rural plantation workers in the northeastern state of Pernambuco. These two groups possessed very different spatial imaginaries that shaped their perception of the MST and their decision to join the movement. Ultimately, people from both groups joined the movement even though the small farmers' spatial imaginaries were much more compatible with the movement's methods and ideology than the rural workers'. In the southern case study, small farmers used their experiences of production and reproduction on the land to question the large landholders' claim to property. They joined the movement because they had the social, cultural, and material resources to fund their struggle, and they believed that doing so was worthwhile. In the northeastern case study, the poorest and most mobile rural workers were the first to join the MST—not because they had the resources or because they necessarily believed in the movement's methods or ideology, but because the local sugarcane economy had collapsed, and they felt the movement was their best alternative.

HISTORICAL BACKGROUND: A MOVEMENT IN THE MAKING

Brazil is one of the most developed, industrialized, and urban economies in Latin America. And yet it is in Brazil that rural unrest is making headlines. The reasons for this seeming contradiction have everything to do with the legacies of inequitable land tenure. From the year 1500 (when Brazil was "discovered" by the Portuguese) until the present, power and prestige in Brazil have derived in large part from access to land.

Because of the enormous inequalities in access to land, the agrarian elite was able to manipulate the allocation of labor in such a way as to maintain both status and production. The various labor allocation strategies employed by the elite—slavery, subsidized immigration, and family labor—created high levels of poverty and uneven access to social infrastructure (schools, health services, etc.) throughout the countryside.

Changing labor requirements due to mechanization spawned a massive exodus from the rural areas into the cities. The concentration

of landownership grew, and in 1985, just over 10 percent of the landowners in the country controlled almost 80 percent of the land.

This was the year that the Movement of Rural Landless Workers (MST) held its first National Congress.

As early as 1978, several hundred families in the southernmost states of Rio Grande do Sul and Santa Catarina had organized land occupations. These occupations met with immediate state censure, but they were ultimately successful and provided the impetus for the formation of an official movement. In 1985, MST members established a short-term goal of securing "land for those who work it" and a long-term goal of creating a just, socialist society.

The movement's aggressive tactics of occupying land exploited contradictions at the heart of the Brazilian state. On paper, the Brazilian Constitution was extremely progressive. Article 186 of the most recent (1988) constitution states that if land is not fulfilling its "social responsibility to be productive" then the federal government is empowered to expropriate the area from the owner. But in practice, the law is rarely upheld without aggressive actions undertaken by groups of squatters. The Brazilian state acknowledges and reinforces the contradictions between formal law and practice by sometimes legalizing the occupations and sometimes criminalizing them and depicting the squatters as illegal invaders.

MST activists worked in poor rural and urban communities, spreading news of the movement and informing people of their right to land. Church leaders and union workers often helped the activists by using their connections within local communities to spread word of the movement. When a group of interested people were organized, the immediate goal was to occupy land, setting up temporary *barracos* (barracks) made out of heavy black plastic and wood. The squatters often had to reoccupy a given area several times as the government and/or private landlord usually responded with violence before negotiations.

These methods have been extremely effective. In the past nineteen years, the MST has carried out approximately 230,000 occupations, secured over 1,000 settlements and expanded its base from 3 states to 22 (of 26).

Many different groups of people joined the movement, and the best way to explain why is not simply to research the development of capitalism, or the rise in political opportunity, or the actions of radical priests. The best way to explain who joined the MST is to investigate the relationship between members and the movement's methods and ideology—a relationship shaped by spatial imaginaries. I have chosen two groups for this paper, a group of small family farmers in southern Brazil and a group of rural workers in northeastern Brazil. People from both groups joined the movement, and their unofficial genesis stories point to the importance of imagination as a lens for turning context into action. In each case, the decision to join the MST was shaped by culturally specific relationships formed between individuals and their spatial environments.

WHO JOINED THE MST AND WHY?

The MST community in Santa Catarina being presented as a case study for the purposes of this paper will be referred to as Vento. A land reform settlement with 97 families, Vento is located in the center of the state. Most of the 97 families were previously small farmers who owned or rented land in western Santa Catarina. They came to the settlement in 1989 after living in MST squatter camps for several years. On the settlement, the families were given 18 hectares of land and funds to build a simple house. By 1998, most of the settlers were planting corn and beans, along with a few vegetables, and raising chickens, pigs, and the occasional cow.

These families came from a tradition of farming that was inherently expansive, and migrating along the edge of the spatial frontier was a traditional survival strategy in the face of that expansion.

The families on Vento had migrated an average of two times each before joining the MST. They decided to join the movement because the spatial frontier in Santa Catarina (and in southern Brazil more generally) had come to an end and they were at the point in their demographic cycle where some members of the family needed new land.

Farmers who had sufficient land to farm often joined the movement as a way to escape the position of sharecropping.

Many of the settlers described paying their landlord as an unfair imposition and said that

they joined the MST in search of land of their own.

The search for new land was also a legacy of the environmental degradation experienced by small family farmers in western Santa Catarina.

Years of planting corn and beans on hillside slopes led to deteriorating soil conditions and lower yields. When the land in one area became exhausted, families were forced to move on and look for new land.

While the historical search for new land was motivated, in large part, by productive and reproductive concerns, the settlers shared a desire to continue farming that was embedded in culturally informed notions of an honest life. The settlers expressed a real love for the land; land was a tradition in and of itself and a means for continuation of a life many found extremely valuable. As one young MST settler who was preparing to become an activist "on the front lines" (*frente da massa*) of the movement said, having land meant having "citizenship, and the dignity of being able to produce. Land is life."

The settlers on Vento had formed their spatial imaginaries on the moving frontier, and they used these imaginaries to justify participation in the MST. Their lived spaces were altered by the increasing penetration of agro-industrial capitals into the countryside, but the way they experienced that change was shaped by their historical understanding of the land, family, and community. In the face of the decreasing availability of land, the small farmers who ended up on Vento created a political frontier, using the moral and material support of family and friends to help them colonize new land.

The situation on the settlement in the sugarcane region of northeast Brazil was in many ways the opposite of the South. The MST community in Pernambuco being presented as a case study for the purposes of this paper will be referred to as Flora. Forty-seven families lived on Flora, 13 of whom received land because they occupied the area with the MST. The other 33 families had been given land because of their previous association with the property, which had been a large-scale sugarcane plantation before its expropriation in 1997.

In this region, it was difficult for people to imagine joining the MST because the spatial imaginaries produced through plantation labor clashed with the MST's methods and ideology. Local traditions of work, family, and community in the sugarcane region of Pernambuco created a perception of the plantation as "not-frontier," and this perception was not compatible with the idea of occupying "someone else's land" for distribution. A not-frontier is the opposite of the spatial frontier; it is a space that may be technically or legally "empty," but is represented, perceived, and experienced as not available for occupation or exchange. It is not always clear who "owns" not-frontiers, but possession is usually backed up by significant political and economic strength.

In the context of limited land availability, the majority of the plantation workers in Pernambuco had little experience with family farming, and there was no widespread belief that having land was necessary for beginning a new family. The workers had occasionally been allowed to plant subsistence crops by their houses inside the plantation, but they were always at the whim of the plantation owner. Landlords who did provide their workers with land for planting did so as a *dom* (gift), and many plantation owners simply refused ever to allow their workers access to land.

Without access to land, the workers were dependent on employment in the plantations.

The monopolistic production of sugarcane had created a tradition of mobility in search of work that actually weakened family ties across generations. As a result, families on the settlement tended to be small, and there were very few extended families on the settlements. There was no strong tradition of investment in either land or jobs for the future generations.

In spite of the many factors discouraging rural workers from joining the MST, the movement began to build its membership in the region when agricultural restructuring in the 1980s generated a massive crisis in the sugarcane industry.

In this new political environment, the MST offered the best representation vis-à-vis both the local mayor and the state government. According to a settler, "The movement helps us. They put pressure on the government to make the projects happen for us; it's always the strength of the movement." Because of the elitist character of politics in the Northeast, a political voice is synonymous with an economic voice. For a community that often feels as powerless as the plantation workers do, the political visibility that the movement provides is extremely significant. Not everybody is happy

about the change, however. Some settlers argued that they joined the movement unwillingly, but felt they had to. One older man who had been a team leader before receiving land on Flora said, "Whether I want to or not I have to be part [of the movement] because we arrange things within the movement."

In spite of the clear clashes between the MST's peasant-based ideology and the rural workers' spatial imaginaries, so many people have joined the movement in this area that the MST considers it a focal point of their organization in the Northeast.

WHAT DIFFERENCE DOES IT MAKE? ONGOING PARTICIPATION IN THE MST

In the southern settlement of Vento, the small farmers who joined the movement did so because they wanted land. This land was central to their plans for the future, and most of them worked it with the idea that it would eventually be passed on to their children. One settler, an energetic man with three children, was constantly engaged in agricultural experiments (he planted small patches with watermelon and strawberries one season to see how they would do on his land) that he hoped would pay off so that he could leave an inheritance for his children.

As small farmers who had had difficulty making a living on their land before joining the movement, the settlers on Vento were acutely aware of how hard life could be on the settlement. Most thought that if they worked hard enough, they would have enough to eat, but to prosper on the land, they needed the MST's help. As one settler said, "Even though we have a lot of things now, we cannot stop yet because the situation is not easy." The movement was seen as an extremely effective vehicle for pressuring the state to distribute the resources it had promised the settlers. These resources included investment credit as well as basic infrastructure on the settlement, including good roads and potable water. As one settler said, "Today the movement is respected because we have won some of the things that we wanted. Our credit is subsidized, for example, and not even the union got that!" Access to credit provides a fundamental justification for participation in the movement because working the land requires investment capital. As one settler said, "Without the movement, there would be no money to work on the land and without that, we wouldn't be able to stay."

In the northeastern settlement of Flora, things were very different because most of the MST settlers in the sugarcane region had joined the movement out of desperation, rather than out of a deep desire for land, and so they tended to participate much less in movement activities than their counterparts on Vento. Many did not even think of themselves as being integral to the movement; rather, they saw the movement as an assistance organization they signed up for much like a trade union or a political party. One man said, "I think it's good. They are always doing marches and things, and it's to help us, isn't it? They confront INCRA, they pressure the government, they even make the projects happen for us." As members of an association, the settlers expected the MST to provide certain services and were sometimes reluctant to pay their dues if they did not see the material manifestation of those services.

CONCLUSION

After examining the stories of people who joined the MST, I would restate the movement's genesis stories in these terms: in the context of agricultural restructuring, political opening, and religious mobilization, a small group of landless farmers in southern Brazil used—and reformulated—their spatial imaginaries to embrace the act of occupying land and to create new frontiers for colonization, while a small group of unemployed rural workers in north-eastern Brazil overcame the spatial imaginaries put in place by the local sugarcane economy and joined the movement because they had few other options available to them.

These different genesis stories are the product of very different representations and perceptions of space. Whether people saw space as open or closed was shaped by their historical experiences on the land and in various labor arrangements. The way social life was embedded in particular spaces—or the way those spaces were "lived"—informed both the decision to join or not to join the MST. As participation in the movement moved past the initial act of gaining land, those same spatial experiences engaged with new spatial arrangements to produce very different political actors within the movement.

Bringing geography into the study of social movements through the careful study of how political actors are constituted in meaning and in practice can shed light on the critically important relationships between context and imagination, or perception. It is never enough to know what factors might facilitate the formation of a movement; the critical study of resistance requires an analysis of the ways different historical-cultural frameworks shape the decision to mobilize in particular people and places.

REFERENCES

Foucault, Michael. 1979. *Discipline and punish: the birth of the prison*. Hamondsworth: Penguin.

Lefebvre, Henri. 1991. *The production of space*. Oxford: Blackwell.

45
Beyond Wilderness and Lawn
(1998)

Michael Pollan

My subject is the future of the garden in America. My conviction is that gardening, as a cultural activity, matters deeply, not only to the look of our landscape but also to the wisdom of our thinking about the environment.

When I speak of the future of gardens, I have two things in mind: literal dirt-and-plant gardens, of course, but also the garden as a metaphor or paradigm, as a way of thinking about nature that might help us move beyond the either/or thinking that has historically governed the American approach to the landscape: civilization versus wilderness, culture versus nature, the city versus the country. These oppositions have been particularly fierce and counterproductive in this country and deserve much of the blame for the bankruptcy of our current approach to the environment.

One fact about our culture can frame my argument: the two most important contributions America has made to the world history of landscape are the front lawn and the wilderness preserve. What can one say about such a culture? One conclusion would be that its thinking on the subject of nature is schizophrenic, that this is a culture that cannot decide whether to dominate nature in the name of civilization, or to worship it, untouched, as a means of escape from civilization. More than a century has passed since America invented the front lawn and the wilderness park, yet these two very different and equally original institutions continue to shape and reflect American thinking about both nature and the garden. I would argue that we cannot address the future of gardening in America—and the future of the larger American landscape—until we have come to terms with (and gotten over) the lawn, on the one side, and the wilderness, on the other.

As the unlikely coexistence of these two contradictory ideas suggests, we tend reflexively to assume that nature and culture are intrinsically opposed, engaged in a kind of zero-sum game in which the gain of one entails the loss of the other. Certainly the American landscape that we have created reflects such dichotomous thinking: some 8 percent of the nation's land has been designated as wilderness, while the remaining 92 percent has been deeded unconditionally to civilization—to the highway, the commercial strip, the suburban development, the parking lot, and, of course, the lawn. The idea of a "middle landscape"—of a place partaking equally of nature and culture, striking a compromise or balance between the two—has received too little attention, with the result that the garden in America has yet to come into its own.

Whether the wilderness ideal or the convention of the front lawn is more to blame for this situation is debatable. But one indisputable fact strikes me as particularly significant: the lawn and the wilderness were "invented" during the same historical moment, in the decade after the Civil War around 1870. This suggests that these two very different concepts of landscape cannot only coexist but may even be interdependent. In fact, the wilderness lover and the lawn lover probably have more in common with one another than with the American gardener. But before addressing the prospects for the American gardener, I want to address briefly the history of his two adversaries.

WILDERNESS

On March 1, 1872, President Ulysses S. Grant signed the act that designated more than two million acres in northwestern Wyoming as Yellowstone National Park; thus was created the world's first great wilderness preserve. Grant was responding to a brilliant campaign on behalf of wilderness preservation waged by (among many others) Henry David Thoreau and Frederick Law Olmsted. Why should the peculiar idea of preserving wilderness arise at this time? Clearly, it owed to the fact that the wilderness was disappearing; as early as 1850 visionary Americans began to realize that the frontier was not limitless and that, unless action were taken, no wilderness would be left to protect. America grew rapidly in the period following the Civil War—and so too did the movement to preserve at least a portion of the fast-receding western wilderness. It is remarkable how quickly the movement developed, given that half a century earlier the wilderness had been demonized as worthless, heathen, unregenerate—the haunt of Satan. Of course, the appreciation of wild nature was an invention of the late eighteenth century, of the Romantics—and more specifically, an invention of people who lived in cities. The urbanization of America in the second half of the nineteenth century formed the essential, indispensable context for the creation of the wilderness park—a good example of the mutual interdependence of civilization and wilderness.

From a philosophical perspective, the romance of "undisturbed" land has done much to keep American gardens from attaining the distinction and status of the other arts in this country. Our appreciation of wild land was not, as in the case of the English, primarily aesthetic—it was imbued with moral and spiritual values. The New England transcendentalists regarded the untouched American landscape as sacred. Nature, to Ralph Waldo Emerson and his followers, was the outward symbol of spirit. To alter so spiritual a place, even to garden it, is problematic, verges, in fact, on sacrilege. For how could one presume to improve on what God had made?

LAWN

The romance of wilderness is a quintessential American sentiment, but it is one indulged primarily in books or on vacation. The rest of the time we tend to act in accordance with a very different idea of nature: the idea that the land is ours to dominate, whether in the name of God, during the nation's early days, or later, in the name of Progress. It is astonishing that one culture could give birth to two such antagonistic strains—to both the worship of wilderness and the worship of progress, which usually entails the domination of wilderness. This latter notion, more manifest in the actual landscape than in our writings about it, has been as deleterious to the making of good gardens as has been the wilderness idea. It is far more likely to give us parking lots and shopping centers … and lawns.

Anyone who has ever mowed a lawn can appreciate the undeniable pleasure of bringing a heedless landscape under control, however temporarily. But this is not, except perhaps in America, the same thing as gardening. For when we read that gardening is "the number one leisure activity" in this country, we need to remember that the statistics accommodate all those people for whom "gardening" consists exclusively of the pushing, or often driving, of an internal combustion engine over a monoculture of imported grass species.

The ideology of lawns cannot be reduced to the drive to dominate nature, though certainly that is one element of it. The love of closely cropped grass may well be universal, as Thorstein Veblen speculated in *The Theory of the Leisure Class*; it is a reminder of our pastoral roots and perhaps also of our evolutionary origins on the grassy savannas of East Africa.[1] America's *unique* contribution to humankind's ancient love of grass has been, specifically, the large, unfenced patches of lawn in front of our houses—the decidedly odd custom, to quote one authority, "of uniting the front lawns of however many houses there may be on both sides of a street to present an untroubled aspect of expansive green to the passerby."[2] This definition was set forth by the historian Ann Leighton, who concluded after a career spent studying the history of American gardens that the front lawn was our principal contribution to world garden design. How depressing.

The same rapid post-Civil War growth that made wilderness preservation seem imperative also gave us the institution of the front lawn, the birth of which, as near as I can determine, should be dated on or about 1870. At that time several developments—some social and economic, others technological—combined to make the spread of front lawns possible.

First was the movement to the suburbs, then called "borderlands." Before 1870, anyone who lived beyond the city was a farmer, and the yards of farmers were strictly utilitarian.

All that began to change with the migration to the borderlands. For the first time urban, cosmopolitan people were choosing to live outside of town and to commute, by way of the commuter railroad system then being built. Their homes, also for the first time, were homes in the modern sense: centers of family life from which commerce—and agriculture—have been excluded. These homes were refuges from urban life, which by the late nineteenth century was acquiring a reputation for danger and immorality. The rapidly expanding middle class was coming to believe that a freestanding house surrounded by a patch of land, allowing you to keep one foot in the city and the other in the countryside, was the best way to live.

But how should this new class of suburbanites organize their yards? No useful precedents were at hand. So, as often happens when a new class of affluent consumers in need of guidance arises, a class of confident experts arose as well, proffering timely advice. A generation of talented landscape designers and reformers came forward, from midcentury on, to advise the middle class in its formative landscaping decisions. Most prominent were Frederick Law Olmsted, his partner Calvert Vaux (a transplanted Englishman), Andrew Jackson Downing, and Frank J. Scott, a disciple of Downing's who would prove to be the American lawn's most brilliant propagandist.

These men were seeking the proper model for the new American suburban landscape. Although they were eventually to develop a distinctly American approach, they began, typically, by looking to England, specifically to the English picturesque garden, which, of course, featured gorgeous lawns, the kind that only the English seem able to grow.

Clearly, Americans did not invent lawns per se; they had been popular in England for centuries. But in England lawns were found mainly on estates. The Americans set out to democratize them, cutting the vast, manorial greenswards into quarter-acre slices everyone could afford.

The rise of the classic American front lawn awaited three developments, all of which were in place by the early 1870s: the availability of an affordable lawn mower, the invention of barbed wire (to keep animals out of the front yard), and the persuasiveness of an effective propagandist. In 1832 a carpet manufacturer in England named Edwin Budding invented the lawn mower; by 1860 American inventors had perfected it, devising a lightweight mower an individual could manage; and by 1880 this machine was relatively inexpensive. Before the invention in Peoria, Illinois, of barbed wire in 1872, the fencing of livestock was a dubious proposition, and the likelihood was great that one's beautiful front lawn would be trampled by a herd of livestock on the lam. But soon after the mass-marketing of barbed wire, municipal ordinances were being passed penalizing anyone who let livestock wander freely through town.

As for the effective propagandist, the man who did most to advance the cause of the American front lawn—and thus to retard the development of the American garden—was Frank J. Scott, who wrote a best-selling book called *The Art of Beautifying Suburban Home Grounds*. Published in 1870, the book is an ecstatic paean to the beauty and indispensability of the front lawn. "A smooth, closely shaven surface of grass is by far the most essential element of beauty on the grounds of a suburban house," Scott wrote.[3] Unlike the English, who viewed lawns not as ends in themselves but as backdrops for trees and flower beds, and as settings for lawn games, Scott subordinated all other elements of the landscape to the lawn. Shrubs should be planted right up against the house so as not to distract from, or obstruct the view of, the lawn (it was Scott who thereby ignited the very peculiar American passion for foundation planting); flowers were permissible, but they must be restricted to the periphery of the grass. "Let your lawn be your home's velvet robe," he wrote, "and your flowers its not-too-promiscuous decoration."[4] It is clear that his ideas about lawns owe much to puritan attitudes that regarded pure decoration, and ornamental gardening, as morally suspect. Lawns fit well with the old American preference for a plain style.

Scott's most radical departure from old-world practice was to insist upon the individual property owner's responsibility to his neighbors. "It is unchristian," he declared, "to hedge from the sight of others the beauties of nature which it has been our good fortune to create or secure."[5]

He railed against fences, which he regarded as selfish and undemocratic—one's lawn should contribute to the collective landscape. Scott elevated an unassuming patch of turf grass into an institution of democracy. The American lawn becomes an egalitarian conceit, implying that there is no need, in Scott's words, "to hedge a lovely garden against the longing eyes of the outside world" because we all occupy the same (middle) class.[6]

The problem here, in my view, is not with the aspirations behind the front lawn. In theory at least, the front lawn is an admirable institution, a noble expression of our sense of community and equality. With our open-faced front lawns, we declare our like-mindedness to our neighbors. And, in fact, lawns are one of the minor institutions of our democracy, symbolizing as they do the common landscape that forms the nation. Since there can be no fences breaking up this common landscape, maintenance of the lawn becomes nothing less than a civic obligation. (Indeed, the failure to maintain one's portion of the national lawn—for that is what it is—is in many communities punishable by fine.) Our lawns exist to unite us. It makes sense, too, that in a country whose people are unified by no single race or ethnic background or religion, the land itself—our one great common denominator—should emerge as a crucial vehicle of consensus. And so across a continent of almost unimaginable geographic variety, from the glacial terrain of Maine to the desert of Southern California, we have rolled out a single emerald carpet of lawn.

A noble project, perhaps, but one ultimately at cross purposes with the idea of a garden. Indeed, the custom of the front lawn has done even more than the wilderness ideal to retard the development of gardening in America. For one thing, we have little trouble ignoring the wilderness ideal whenever it suits us; ignoring the convention of the front lawn is much harder, as anyone who has ever neglected mowing for a few weeks well knows. In fact it is doubtful that the promise of the American garden will be realized as long as the lawn continues to rule our yards and minds.

The front lawn and the wilderness ideal still divide and rule the American landscape and will not be easily overthrown. But American attitudes toward nature are changing, and viewed from one perspective at least, this leaves room for hope. One of the few things we can say

with certainty about the next five hundred years of American landscape history is that they will be shaped by a much more acute environmental consciousness—by a pressing awareness that the natural world is in serious trouble and that serious actions are needed to save it. So how will the American garden fare in an age dominated by such an awareness? What about the wilderness ideal? And the front lawn?

It might seem axiomatic that the greater the concern for the environment, the greater the regard for wilderness. But it is becoming clear that attention to wilderness no longer constitutes a sufficient response to the crisis of the environment.

We must continue to defend wilderness, but adding *more* land to the wilderness will not solve our most important environmental problems. But even more important, nor will an environmental ethic based on the ideal of wilderness—which is, in fact, the only one we have ever had in this country. About any particular piece of land, the wilderness ethic says: leave it alone. Do nothing. Nature knows best. But this ethic says nothing about all those places we cannot help but alter, all those places that cannot simply be "given back to nature," which today are most places. It is too late in the day to follow Thoreau back into the woods. There are too many of us and not nearly enough woods.

But if salvation does not lie in wilderness, nor is it offered by the aesthetic of the lawn; in fact, the lawn, as both landscape practice and a metaphor for a whole approach to nature, may be insupportable in a time of environmental crisis. Remarkably, the lawn has emerged as an environmental issue in the past few years. More and more Americans are asking whether the price of a perfect lawn—in terms of pesticides, water, and energy—can any longer be justified. The American lawn may well not survive a long period of environmental activism—and no other single development would be more beneficial for the American garden. For as soon as an American decides to rip out a lawn, he or she becomes, perforce, a gardener, someone who must ask the gardener's questions: What is right for this place? What do *I* want here? How might I go about creating a pleasing outdoor space on this site? How can I make use of nature here without abusing it?

The answers to these questions will be as different as the people posing them and the places where they are posed. For as soon as people start to think like gardeners, they begin to devise individual and local answers.

That would be very good news for the quality of our gardens and also, in turn, for the quality of our thinking about the environment. For if environmentalism is likely to be a boon to the American garden, gardening could be a boon to environmentalism, a movement which, as I have suggested, stands in need of some new ways of thinking about nature. The garden is as good a place to look as any. Gardens by themselves obviously cannot right our relationship to nature, but the habits of thought they foster can take us a long way in that direction—can even suggest the lineaments of a new environmental ethic that might help us in situations where the wilderness ethic is silent or unhelpful. Gardening tutors us in nature's ways, fostering an ethic of respect for the land. Gardens instruct us in the particularities of place. Gardens also reach the necessary, if still rather un-American, lesson that nature and culture can be reconciled, that it is possible to find some middle ground between the wilderness and the lawn—a third way into the landscape. This, finally, is the best reason we have to be optimistic about the garden's prospects in America: we need the garden, and the garden's ethic, too much today for it not to flourish.

NOTES

1 Thorstein Veblen, *The Theory of the Leisure Class* (New York: Viking Press, 1967 [1899]), 134.

2 Ann Leighton, *American Gardens of the Nineteenth Century* (Amherst: University of Massachusetts Press, 1987), 249.

3 Frank J. Scott, excerpted in *The American Gardener: A Sampler,* ed. Allen Lacy (New York: Farrar Straus & Giroux, 1988), 317.

4 Ibid., 321.

5 Ibid., 322.

6 Ibid., 323.

46
Ecstatic Places

(1990)

Louise Chawla

This article reports a study of ecstatic memories of childhood places. If we are fortunate enough to have a fund of them, by itself the phrase *ecstatic memories* should release a cascade of associations. We do not need to consciously preserve these memories; we know that we can never lose them. They are like radioactive jewels buried within us, emitting energy across the years of our life. On each occasion when we dig them up, repolishing them as we reclaim them, they reendow us. An eloquent writer, composing an autobiography, may impart these memories with such force that they radiate across a reader's lifetime also.

Memories of this kind may be properly termed *ecstatic* in keeping with the word's derivation and primary definition: "a state of intense, overpowering emotion," so that we can speak of "an ecstasy of fear" and "an ecstasy of delight." In contemporary usage, the word is usually treated as a synonym for *delight*, but its ancient Greek roots justify the more general, flexible meaning—*ek stasis* ("out standing" or "standing outside ourselves").

When we stand outside ourselves, we stand in the place that surrounds us. In some ecstatic memories, the place is taken up by the presence of another person. In many memories of this kind, however, what we are enthrallingly attuned to is not another person, but every particular of the place itself.

This article examines the landscape qualities and social and psychological contexts in which memories of this kind have been recorded. Recognizing that ecstasy may involve shivers of fear as well as delight, the article reviews memories distinguished by the general charac-

teristic that the narrator is taken up entirely by the experience of a place. It is not loved or feared for its associations with other inhabitants. It is intensely felt in response to what it contains in itself—so that, for this moment at least, his or her childhood was this place.

This article takes as its point of departure an often quoted statement by the person first to bring attention to environmental autobiographies, Edith Cobb.

An avid reader of autobiographies throughout a long lifetime, Cobb collected her observations in an essay (1959) and book, *The Ecology of Imagination in Childhood* (1977). Emphasizing the importance of remembered encounters with the landscape in middle childhood, she summarized her findings in the following suggestive claim:

> In my collection of some three hundred volumes of autobiographical recollections of their own childhood by creative thinkers from many cultures and eras, ranging from the sixteenth century to the present, it is principally to this middle-age range in their early life that these writers say they return in memory in order to renew the power and impulse to create at its very source, a source which they describe as the experience of emerging not only into the light of consciousness but into a living sense of a dynamic relationship with the outer world. In these memories the child appears to experience both a sense of discontinuity, an awareness of his own unique separateness and identity, and also a continuity, a renewal of relationship with nature as process.
>
> (Cobb, 1959, p. 539)

This conclusion has intriguing implications. If it is true, it traces a line of influence in which the nature of the outer world that creative thinkers encounter as children and the nature of their encounter profoundly affect their thought as adults. Their thought, in turn, affects the course of our culture. At the root of creative advance, it suggests, are the conservative effects of remembered landscapes. For, if memories of an emerging sense of relationship with the outer world serve as a touchstone for creative renewal, it is reasonable to expect that part of the effort they inspire are attempts to perpetuate the essential conditions of this relationship.

The present article systematically reviews Cobb's claim in the context of 20th-century autobiography. Cobb's collection, which she deeded to Columbia University Teacher's College, predominantly records 19th-century British childhoods. Does her claim hold true of 20th-century autobiographies, representing more diverse backgrounds? It does, this study found, but only sometimes, within a specific cluster of conditions.

METHOD

To reconsider Cobb's conclusions, 38 autobiographies by men and women born since 1900 were gathered to represent three broad categories of professions: the arts and humanities; the sciences; and law, journalism, and politics. Within these categories, books were selected at random from university and public library lists. The method of analysis and the different forms of environmental memory that emerged were described in detail in Chawla (1986). The present article focuses on memories that express ecstatic communion with the environment.

Based on a close reading of the autobiographies, definitions of seven types of memory were derived. Three independent judges and I then matched definitions to a sample of passages, with close agreement (coefficient of reliability = .92).

The most common form of memory (18 authors) was simple affection for a place where one had felt comfortable, secure, and well loved, where place affiliations and social affiliations happily overlapped. Ecstatic memories of heightened attention to a place were second in frequency (15 authors). Other forms of memory

were ambivalence (3 authors) when childhood ties were complicated by family weaknesses or social stigma; outright rejection when a place failed to meet needs (11 authors, all recalling adolescence in this case); the idealization of an imagined rather than concretely lived-in place (3 authors, also recalling adolescence); detachment (7 authors); and the omission of all but brief allusions to where events occurred (11 authors).

In identifying passages that revealed "the experience of emerging not only into the light of consciousness but into a living sense of a dynamic relationship with the outer world," the distinguishing characteristic that judges applied was that descriptions showed intense responsiveness to an individual place, which itself appeared imbued with life. More than recording simple comfort or affection, these passages documented an experience that was an event.

Using this collection of ecstatic memories by 15 authors, the following questions were addressed: Were there any characteristics that distinguished people who recorded such memories? What types of places inspired them? What were the conditions under which authors encountered these places as children? According to these writers, what effect did these memories have on them?

RESULTS

In response to these questions, this small but randomly chosen set of autobiographies presented the following regularities.

Characteristics of People Who Recorded Ecstatic Memories

Evidence that certain characteristics distinguished people who recorded ecstatic places was decisive. Eight of the 15 authors who revealed memories of this kind won their way in the world as artists, and, although the remaining 7 made their name in other professions, they all also showed serious involvement in the arts, either by pursuit of an artistic career early in life or by a lifetime of committed amateur engagement.

It was not the case that all artists recorded ecstatic memories. Descriptions of this kind and artistic interests did not invariably coincide. An artistic turn of mind, however, was always associated with ecstatic memories.

Inspiring Places and Conditions

Ecstatic memory was reported under conditions so constant that they appeared inflexible. In my interpretation, these conditions combine to constitute multiple dimensions of environmental freedom. Freedom was evident as a physical fact and as a slate of mind.

The environment itself offered freedom in the sense of potentiality—an openness to exploration and discovery in a place that beckoned enthrallingly. In most cases, this quality belonged to the natural environment: gardens, the seashore, a lake, prairie land, forests, and fields. Usually it was open space that the child could move through untiringly. For example, North Carolina beaches and woods fostered Howard Thurman (1979), a fatherless Black boy who became a minister:

> The woods befriended me. In the long summer days, most of my ti... was divided between fishing in the Halifax River and exploring the woods, where I picked huckleberries and gathered orange blossoms from abandoned orange groves. ... I was usually with a group of boys as we explored the woods, but I tended to wander away to be alone for a time for in that way I could sense the strength of the quiet and the aliveness of the woods.
>
> (p. 7)

Three cities were accessible urban versions of such a setting—the Santiago and San Francisco that Pablo Neruda (1978) and Maya Angelou (1970) haunted as adolescents and the London of C. Day Lewis (1960), which he learned lamppost by flower box as he bicycled through the city:

> With this bicycle, at weekends and during holidays, I extended my demesne. It was never a large one, being bounded at its most extensive by the south side of Kensington Gardens and Hyde Park, Shepherd's Bush to the west, the Edgware Road to the east, and the northern purlieus of Bayswater: but in this part of London I knew every road, street, and

square; and when I went to live on Campden Hill thirty-five years later, it was like returning to the heart of a country diminished, altered, yet deeply familiar, so that walking among the blind, dank, stuccoed terraces, melancholy and seedy now after a second war, I seemed to see them opening out before me in vistas of what they were to my boyhood—flowering shrubs, geraniums in window-boxes, barrel-organs, white paint, sunshine and spaciousness—and the Portobello Road market was lit again with the naphtha flares of those far-off winter evenings.

(p. 78)

Ecstatic places were usually outdoors; in this respect, they did not differ significantly from other forms of memory, which as a whole showed a ratio of outdoor to indoor places of 4 to 1. Even those authors who recalled ecstatic indoor experiences said that they had had ecstatic outdoor experiences first; further, in their indoor memories, the room was always washed by an influx of light, air, and exterior noises.

In addition to being associated with the physical freedom of multisensory discovery, ecstatic memories were always marked by the psychological freedom of undisturbed encounter. In contrast to memories of nostalgic affection, which were often filtered through a sociable "we," ecstatic places were always recorded by a solitary "I." It was not always clear whether the child was alone because no one else happened to be near, because he or she had made a point of going off alone, or because absorption in the environment left the child oblivious to others. Whatever the case, the child was free from intrusion, distraction, surveillance, and prohibition—free to encounter the place spontaneously.

A sense of appropriation was another psychological freedom. The child belonged to a place because the place, in some way, belonged to the child. This mutual sense of belonging always had a socioeconomic basis: The land was family property or public property; it was wild or unclaimed; or it was part of a summer resort or a boarding school where the child's family had a secure social standing that ensured "belonging." Ecstatic places were never the territory of a vigilant other, where the child felt like an interloper. They were places the child could claim.

Familiarity with the autobiographies revealed a final unvarying psychological freedom: The child enjoyed the basic emotional security of his or her family's love. Regardless of family troubles, some relative provided a fund of unconditional love, freeing the child from self-preoccupation so that he or she could give full attention to the place itself.

Effects of Memories

When Cobb first directed attention to ecstatic environmental memories in autobiographies, she introduced them as the special gift of middle childhood to creative maturity and the primary source of lifelong inspiration. On the whole, in this contemporary collection these claims did not hold. Treasured memories originated during early childhood and adolescence as well as during middle childhood, and different effects were attributed to them. Only two authors argued, as Cobb did, that there was any necessary connection between ecstatic memories and adult creativity. Instead, authors repeatedly named two other benefits: a fund of strength and stability and a sense of the integration of nature and human life.

Seven authors identified ecstatic memories as a fund of strength within themselves.

In the words of Spender (1951), the exceptional harmony of his childhood setting "enabled me to retain throughout life a central calm and happiness, amid violent divisions of my own nature" (p. 311). In the words of Lewis (1960), to that harmony he owed "a certain fund of calm within myself ... which I am able to draw upon in an emergency" (p. 36).

Perhaps more eloquently than any other author, Thurman (1979) expressed his sense of the integration of nature and human life and indicated that this sense of integration was his foundation for a firm footing in life. As a child, he walked the mid-Atlantic seacoast by day and by night, during murmuring stillness and during wild storms:

I had the sense that all things, the sand, the sea, the stars, the night, and I were one lung through which all of life breathed. Not only was I aware of a vast rhythm enveloping all, but I was a part of it and it was a part of me.

(p. 226)

These experiences

gave me a certain overriding immunity against much of the pain with which I would have to deal in the years ahead when the ocean was only a memory. The sense held: I felt rooted in life, in nature, in existence.

(p. 8)

Stability, integration with nature, core images— ecstatic memory leaves these residues, but what happened to its serving as a point of return "to renew the power and impulse to create at its very source," as Cobb (1959, p. 539) predicted it would do? Only two authors explicitly connected memories of this kind to their adult creativity. Eiseley believed that these memories predisposed him to an openness to the potentiality of the unknown. Lewis (1960) believed that they were evidence that he had the quality essential to poets, "the gift of passively accepting and conceiving, with the will in abeyance, which allows them to absorb whatever they may need in the world around them" (p. 57).

In both statements, these memories contribute to creativity in two ways. In themselves, they may serve as raw material for poetry or reflection. In addition, they represent a practiced way of perceiving the world—a habit of being. As these two authors understood this habit to be vital to their work, it can be said of them at least that their memories of their childhood relationship with the world preserved "the power and impulse to create at its very source."

DISCUSSION

In reevaluating Cobb's claims regarding environmental memory, this study has come to differing conclusions regarding its form and its significance. Cobb attributed universal values to remembered childhood experience of the world; the present analysis of randomly selected 20th-century autobiographies revealed various forms of memory and various attributions by authors themselves regarding the influence of memory. Whatever the source of the power and impulse to create may be, it appears more complex than Cobb proposed. It appears to vary with the type of creativity demonstrated and with childhood opportunities. Even when this report focuses on the type of memories that Cobb herself emphasized, this variability remains.

From a conclusion that the connection between childhood memory and adult creativity is more complex than Cobb suggested, it does not follow that environmental memories are less important. The legacies of ecstatic memories alone are impressive: meaningful images; an internalized core of calm; a sense of integration with nature; and, for some, a creative disposition. Most of these benefits are general human advantages, whether or not we make our way in the world as creative thinkers.

In reviewing the conditions of these memories, I was struck by the fragility of their setting. They did not originate anywhere, under any circumstances. They required space, freedom for appropriation and discovery, an extravagant display for all five senses. Through them, even in cities, the presence of nature was felt. Behind them hovered that difficult-to-define yet effusive quality of loveliness. As the absence of these memories in most of the sampled autobiographies suggests, this combi-nation of conditions cannot be taken for granted.

REFERENCES

Chawla, Louise. 1986. The ecology of environ-mental memory. *Children's Environments Quarterly, 3*(4), 34–42.

Cobb, Edith. 1959. The ecology of imagi-nation in childhood. *Daedalus, 88,* 537–548.

Cobb, Edith. 1977. *The ecology of imagi-nation in childhood.* New York; Columbia University Press.

Lewis, C. Day. 1960. *The buried day.* New York: Harper.

Spender, Stephen. 1951. *World within world.* London: Hamish Hamilton.

Thurman, Howard. 1979. *With head and heart.* New York: Harcourt Brace Jovanovich.

SECTION 9

The Social Production of Space and Time

THE
ARMORY CELEBRATES
THE TAMING OF

THE WILD | WILD WEST

WITH 10% DOWN PAYMENT, 10% MORTGAGE AND
12 MONTHS FREE MAINTENANCE.

The trailblazers have done their work. West 42nd Street has been tamed, domesticated, and polished into the most exciting, freshest, most energetic new neighborhood in all of New York.

And you can savor it all, in a state of the art co-op at The Armory, where over sixty people have already found that living well in the heart of Manhattan doesn't have to break your budget. In fact, if you're paying an inflated Manhattan rent, its probably costing you more in after tax dollars than living intimely better at The Armory.

And what's more you get equity, which means your apartment is a meaningful investment, both now and in the future.

Consider the success of Manhattan Plaza, just half a block away. Once its apartments went begging, now the waiting list is several years long, because 1500 tenants, including some of the greatest names in theater, music and dance, have discovered its convenient location, terrific shopping and restaurants, and one of New York's finest health, swimming and racquet clubs on the premises.

There's also Theater Row, across the street, once the home of the down-and-out, now two blocks of innovative off-Broadway theaters, great restaurants, and the city's newest important video facility.

Then there's the Convention Center, due to open in 1984, and the complete upgrading of the block between Broadway and 8th Avenue into renovated theaters, major office buildings and luxury hotels.

But most of all, for really savvy buyers, there's the rapid escalation of prices along the western corridor of 42nd Street. (After all, if the real estate people don't know when a neighborhood's about to just loose, who does?)

As for The Armory itself, you can be a part of this great neighborhood in a magnificent light, airy, roomy apartment. Your choices range from a unique terraced penthouse studio to living lofts finished like none you've ever seen, to spectacular one and two bedroom duplexes, to cathedral-like maisonettes.

With features that'll stagger the eye and delight the senses. Solid oak kitchens with terra cotta tiled floors, huge windows, 24 hour concierge, sophisticated electronic security, ceilings up to 18 feet high, oversized bathrooms, room-sized closets, laundry rooms on every floor, many apartments have woodburning fireplaces, terraces up to 500 square feet, roof gardens, greenhouse windows, and much, much, more.

The best time to buy is right now. With our apartments, our deal, and our neighborhood, The Armory makes all the sense in the world—the real world, where you can own a home in Manhattan even if you're not super-rich.

But where you can live as though you are.

Maisonettes, from $307,000 min. from $441. Open plan lofts, from $292,000 min. from $431. One and two bedroom duplexes, from $126,000 min. from $509. Penthouse studios, from $209,000 min. from $405.

Come see us 12-7, Mon.-Sat. and 11-7, Sun. Our fabulously decorated model apartments are worth the visit themselves. Call: 212 868-3800. A development of The Next City Corporation. Offering by prospectus only.

THE ARMORY
529 WEST FORTY-SECOND STREET

"Real estate capital rides the new urban frontier."
Source: *NY Times* advertisement, circa 1995.
Referenced in: Smith, Neil. 1996. *The New Urban Frontier: Gentrification and the Revanchist City*. New York: Routledge.

THE SOCIAL PRODUCTION OF
SPACE AND TIME

While space and time may seem ubiquitous, human experiences of space and time are remarkably specific to certain groups and cultures in particular places and times. The production of space occurs through both social practices and material conditions, meaning that space and time are contingent upon and shaped by macro-scale policies and innovations, such as calendars and maps, as well as by everyday routines like finding a parking space. Not only does the structuring of space and time produce specific social patterns and relationships, but it also affects cultural values and economic prospects. As discussed in previous sections, specific experiences (like privacy) and places (such as landscapes) are highly contested because of conflicting social attitudes, though there are also many patterns that go relatively unexamined. The selections in this section represent scholars who have looked at hegemonic and quotidian forces that shape space and time, lives and opportunities.

Sociologist **Henri Lefebvre** is credited with introducing the idea that space is socially produced. His analysis includes a historical reading of how spatial experience has changed over time depending upon social circumstances. Up until the medieval period, space and time were largely experienced through local, lived conditions; times and distances were established by the capacity of the body. In the Renaissance, mathematical systems were developed that allowed space to be broken into fixed units which could be mapped over the land, establishing a system of abstraction allowing for exact measurement and location. Lefebvre contends that *abstract space*, produced and perpetuated through grids, plans, and schedules, is utilized and dominated by the capitalist system of production. So why do we continue to live our lives structured in this way? Lefebvre suggests that socially produced space and time is held in place through administrative policies, social conventions, and technological systems for living so that each day as people wake up to an alarm, commute to work, watch television, or pay bills, this system of space and time is perpetuated and reproduced.

In addition to the contributions Lefebvre has made in recounting the historical changes to the way we experience space and time, he offers a useful scheme to understand how space is socially produced. Lefebvre theorized a tripartite production of space that exists in dialectical tension: spatial practice, representations of space, and representational space. *Spatial practice* describes the cohesive patterns and places of social activity. It can be perceived in the everyday acts of buying, playing, traveling, and laboring, as much as in the everyday spaces of the home, office, school, and streets. *Representations of space* are how space is conceived by engineers, cartographers, architects, and bankers through plans, designs, drawings, and maps. It is a system of signs and codes that are used to organize and direct spatial relations. *Representational spaces* are those spaces that the imagination seeks to change and appropriate. Usually dominated by the other modes of spatial production, these are clandestine and underground spaces lived by artists and others who seek to describe alternative spaces. This triad helps clarify the social patterns that produce the abstract space of contemporary capitalism, which Lefebvre is seeking to move beyond. He outlines an idea of *differential space* that would dissolve the social relations of abstract space and generate new, heterogeneous relations that accentuate difference and "shatter the integrity of the individual body, the social body … and the corpus of knowledge."

Lefebvre's work has influenced scholars in multiple directions. Some, like Schivelbusch and King below, have looked closely to understand historical shifts in the way space is produced and experienced, analyzing the technological developments or changes in social attitudes and conventions. Other scholarship is more aligned with Lefebvre's critique of contemporary spatial representation and practice, and looks for modes of resistance and examples of differential spaces. The selections below by Woolf and McKittrick offer insights into how intentional and unintentional insurgent spatial practices clash with and resist the representations and practices employed by those in power.

As suggested by Lefebvre, as well as David Harvey (1991), transportation systems have played a major role in the shaping of space and time. Cultural studies scholar **Wolfgang Schivelbusch** traces how space and time contracted through the development and expansion of the railroad. He argues that up until the 1850s, space and time were experienced locally because people were limited in the distances they could travel. After the advent of the railroads, the space of one's life was stretched to bring far-off places—the seaside or the country, for example—within easy reach. Time likewise shifted, changing from being organized through the chimes of the nearest clock tower, to being universally calibrated to the railroads' Greenwich Standard Time, which subsequently led to the establishment of the time zones that today serve as the global standard for determining time. While the sense of time was altered, Schivelbusch also describes how people's imagination of place shifted to adjust to the new spatial and temporal experience brought about by the railroads.

Sociologist **Anthony King** also discusses how the sense of time and place changed during this period of rapidly developing industrial production. In writing about the spatiotemporality of vacation, he argues that prior to the Industrial Revolution, time, especially time for work, was based in the rhythms of the day and the season. Yet these paces, spaces, and times quickly became regulated to the demands of factory production. This system of industrial capitalism produced surplus time for the middle and upper classes, as the work-week was defined and the weekend emerged. King looks at how vacation houses, as space-times away from work, developed as a spatial response to this change in time. The vacation house, made accessible by the railroad, was a place that could be occupied during the new leisure times opened up to the wealthy through capitalist production. King also demonstrates how architecture responded to the space-time of leisure: vacation houses themselves took particular forms— open plans and more common spaces for the family—due to the way in which they were inhabited and their orientation to the landscape. King's research emphasizes how space and time is socially produced through patterns of production and consumption that still continue today.

While Lefebvre suggests that the body is one useful way to locate and understand how space is socially produced, other scholars are a great deal better at elucidating the ways in which people are subject to spatial production (see also Section 4). It is important to recognize that space structures and is structured by a great array of social relations, including gender, sexuality, race, age, language, and disability. Inspired and frustrated by the spaces to which she was not allowed access, essayist **Virginia Woolf** was critical of the gendered nature of space and effectively exposes how space has been and continues to be male dominated. Her essay charts her experience of London in the early 20th century, including being barred from the Oxbridge library because of her gender. Woolf argues that what is needed for a woman to write successfully is a "room of one's own," guaranteeing an amount of privacy and seclusion historically unavailable to women.

Like Woolf, geographer **Katherine McKittrick** argues that for some people the freedom to be/become oneself occurs through the struggle to have space. McKittrick looks at the way spaces are organized and produced along racial and sexual lines in her examination of the narrative of a 19th-century US slave, Linda Brent, the pseudonym used by Harriet A. Jacobs. Brent was compelled to live for seven years in an attic space too small to stand up in, in order to eventually free her children and escape herself from the conditions of slavery. McKittrick shows how Brent is able to achieve a degree of freedom from the spatial conditions of slavery—confinement under the gaze of the white, patriarchal society—by hiding in the garret from which she can see and hear, but is herself unseen and immobile. McKittrick connects the spaces and displaces of Brent to larger questions of bodily confinement and territorialization, arguing that the legacies of racism and sexism are perpetuated through spatial constructions.

Geographer **Neil Smith** concludes this section by showing us ways in which contemporary urban spaces are produced through processes of *gentrification*. Smith demonstrates how gentrification works: neighborhood property values shift through financial manipulation, real estate development, and myths of the frontier (see figure at the beginning of Section 9). Due to large-scale social and economic crises as well as specific *redlining* practices by banks refusing loans to racial minorities (see Squires 1992), certain areas of cities go into decline because of neglect by property owners. Real estate prices fall and conditions further decline until these areas can be re-conquered by "pioneering" artists and marginalized LGBTQ people looking for affordable spaces to work and live. For property owners and developers, this re-entrance of means and "chic" signals an opportunity to reinvest, improving the quality of the neighborhood and opening it up to more mainstream residents. This process, underpinned by the practices of financial institutions, as well as the policies and operations of city governments, is how Smith explains gentrification and shows that urban areas are produced through specific actions and policies.

Covering a variety of scales and historical periods, the readings in this section show how space and time are produced through attitudes, actions, inventions, and policies. These spaces and social relations also shape and are shaped by multiple layers of identity. As Lefebvre and others have argued, space and time make up the fabric of modern life, but it is helpful to realize that they are not static or universal but socially produced and subject to manipulation and change. There are a number of publications that have looked more closely at how space and time are structured and restructured through the development of clocks, shipping logistics, communication tools, and other technologies (see Aveni 1989; Kern 2003; Najafi 2013). Other writers have focused on specific places or phenomena: Jason Hackworth (2006) looks at how financial policies mold municipal development, Abigail Van Slyck (2010) has studied summer camps and the ways in which they have shaped culture through particular youthful experiences of wilderness. Architectural critic Sigfried Giedion's *Building in France, Building in Iron, Building in Ferroconcrete* (1995 [1929]) both analyzed trends in building in the first part of the 20th century and played a pivotal role in shaping the conventions of modern architecture. There are many more stories to be told about the simultaneous multiplicity of spaces and the ways in which social relations are continually produced and constantly changing.

SUGGESTIONS FOR FURTHER READING

Please see *peopleplacespace.org* for extended and additional lists of readings.

Aveni, Anthony F. 1989. *Empires of Time: Calendars, Clocks, and Cultures*, 1st edn. New York: Basic Books.
Bakhtin, Mikhail. 1982. "Forms of Time and of The Chronotope in the Novel." In *The Dialogic Imagination: Four Essays*, edited by Michael Holquist and Vadim Liapunov, trans. Vadim Liapunov and Kenneth Brostrom. Austin: University of Texas Press.
Brenner, Neil, Bob Jessop, Martin Jones, and Gordon Macleod (eds). 2003. *State/Space: A Reader*. New York: Wiley-Blackwell.
Buck-Morss, Susan. 2002. *Dreamworld and Catastrophe: The Passing of Mass Utopia in East and West*, reprint. Cambridge, MA: The MIT Press.
Doron, Assa, and Robin Jeffrey. 2013. *The Great Indian Phone Book: How the Cheap Cell Phone Changes Business, Politics, and Daily Life*. Cambridge, MA: Harvard University Press.

Fabian, Johannes. 1983. *Time and the Other: How Anthropology Makes Its Object*. New York: Columbia University Press.

Flowers, Benjamin. 2009. *Skyscraper: The Politics and Power of Building New York City in the Twentieth Century*. Philadelphia: University of Pennsylvania Press.

Friedland, Roger, and Deirdre Boden. 1995. *NowHere: Space, Time, and Modernity*. Berkeley: University of California Press.

Giedion, Sigfried. 1995 [1929]. *Building in France, Building in Iron, Building in Ferroconcrete*, trans. J. Duncan Berry. New York: Oxford University Press.

Hackworth, Jason. 2006. *The Neoliberal City: Governance, Ideology, and Development in American Urbanism*. Ithaca, NY: Cornell University Press.

Hall, Stuart. 1997. "Subjects in History: Making Diasporic Identities." In *The House That Race Built: Original Essays by Toni Morrison, Angela Y. Davis, Cornel West, and Others on Black Americans and Politics in America Today*, edited by Wahneema Lubiano, pp. 289–299. New York: Vintage.

Harvey, David. 1991. *The Condition of Postmodernity: An Enquiry into the Origins of Cultural Change*. Maiden, MA: Wiley-Blackwell.

Interrante, Joseph. 1979. "You Can't Go to Town in a Bathtub: Automobile Movement and the Reorganization of Rural American Space, 1900–1930." *Radical History Review* 21(October 1): 151–168.

Katz, Cindi. 2001. "Vagabond Capitalism and the Necessity of Social Reproduction." *Antipode* 33(4): 709–728.

Kern, Stephen. 2003. *The Culture of Time and Space, 1880–1918: With a New Preface*, 2nd edn. Cambridge, MA: Harvard University Press.

Lefebvre, Henri, Gerald Moore, and Stuart Elden. 2004. *Rhythmanalysis: Space, Time and Everyday Life*. London: Bloomsbury Academic.

Najafi, Sina (ed.). 2013. *Cabinet 47: Logistics*. Cabinet.

Ross, Kristin. 2008. *The Emergence of Social Space: Rimbaud and the Paris Commune*. New York: Verso.

Sassen, Saskia. 2008. *Territory, Authority, Rights: From Medieval to Global Assemblages*. Princeton: Princeton University Press.

Slyck, Abigail A. Van. 2010. *A Manufactured Wilderness: Summer Camps and the Shaping of American Youth, 1890–1960*. Minneapolis: University of Minnesota Press.

Smith, Neil. 1996. *The New Urban Frontier: Gentrification and the Revanchist City*. New York: Routledge.

Sterne, Jonathan. 2012. *MP3: The Meaning of a Format*. Durham, NC: Duke University Press.

Squires, Gregory D. 1992. *From Redlining to Reinvestment: Community Responses to Urban Disinvestment*. Philadelphia, PA: Temple University Press.

Vidler, Anthony. 2002. *Warped Space: Art, Architecture, and Anxiety in Modern Culture*, reprint. Cambridge, MA: The MIT Press.

47
The Production of Space
(1991)

Henri Lefebvre

XII

(Social) space is a (social) product. This proposition might appear to border on the tautologous, and hence on the obvious. There is good reason, however, to examine it carefully, to consider its implications and consequences before accepting it. Many people will find it hard to endorse the notion that space has taken on, within the present mode of production, within society as it actually is, a sort of reality of its own, a reality clearly distinct from, yet much like, those assumed in the same global process by commodities, money and capital. Many people, finding this claim paradoxical, will want proof. The more so in view of the further claim that the space thus produced also serves as a tool of thought and of action; that in addition to being a means of production it is also a means of control, and hence of domination, of power; yet that, as such, it escapes in part from those who would make use of it. The social and political (state) forces which engendered this space now seek, but fail, to master it completely; the very agency that has forced spatial reality towards a sort of uncontrollable autonomy now strives to run it into the ground, then shackle and enslave it. Is this space an abstract one? Yes, but it is also 'real' in the sense in which concrete abstractions such as commodities and money are real. Is it then concrete? Yes, though not in the sense that an object or product is concrete. Is it instrumental? Undoubtedly, but, like knowledge, it extends beyond Instrumentality. Can it be reduced to a projection—to an 'objectification' of knowledge? Yes and no: knowledge objectified in a product is no longer coextensive with knowledge in its theoretical state. If space embodies social relationships, how and why does it do so? And what relationships are they?

It is because of all these questions that a thoroughgoing analysis and a full overall exposition are called for. This must involve the introduction of new ideas—in the first place the idea of a diversity or multiplicity of spaces quite distinct from that multiplicity which results from segmenting and cross-sectioning space *ad infinitum*. Such new ideas must then be inserted into the context of what is generally known as 'history', which will consequently itself emerge in a new light. Social space will be revealed in its particularity to the extent that it ceases to be indistinguishable from mental space (as defined by the philosophers and mathematicians) on the one hand, and physical space (as defined by practico-sensory activity and the perception of 'nature') on the other. What I shall be seeking to demonstrate is that such a social space is constituted neither by a collection of things or an aggregate of (sensory) data, nor by a void packed like a parcel with various contents, and that it is irreducible to a 'form' imposed upon phenomena, upon things, upon physical materiality.

XV

More generally, the very notion of social space resists analysis because of its novelty and because of the real and formal complexity that it connotes. Social space contains—and assigns (more or less) appropriate places to—(1) the *social relations of reproduction,* i.e. the bio-physiological relations between the sexes and between age groups, along with the specific organization of the family; and (2) the *relations of production*, i.e. the division of labour and its organization in the form of hierarchical social functions. These two sets of relations, production and reproduction, are inextricably bound up with one another: the division of labour has repercussions upon the family and is of a piece with it; conversely, the organization of the family interferes with the division of labour. Yet social space must discriminate between the two—not always successfully, be it said—in order to 'localize' them.

To refine this scheme somewhat, it should be pointed out that in precapitalist societies the two interlocking levels of biological reproduction and socio-economic production together constituted social reproduction—that is to say, the reproduction of society as it perpetuated itself generation after generation, conflict, feud, strife, crisis and war notwithstanding. That a decisive part is played by space in this continuity is something I shall be attempting to demonstrate below.

The advent of capitalism, and more particularly 'modern' neocapitalism, has rendered this state of affairs considerably more complex. Here *three* interrelated levels must be taken into account: (1) *biological reproduction* (the family); (2) the *reproduction of labour power* (the working class *per se*); and (3) the *reproduction of the social relations of production*— that is, of those relations which are constitutive of capitalism and which are increasingly (and increasingly effectively) sought and imposed as such. The role of space in this tripartite ordering of things will need to be examined in its specificity.

To make things even more complicated, social space also contains specific representations of this double or triple interaction between the social relations of production and reproduction. Symbolic representation serves to maintain these social relations in a state of coexistence and cohesion. It displays them while displacing them—and thus concealing them in symbolic fashion—with the help of, and onto the backdrop of, nature. Representations of the relations of reproduction are sexual symbols, symbols of male and female, sometimes accompanied, sometimes not, by symbols of age—of youth and of old age. This is a symbolism which conceals more than it reveals, the more so since the relations of reproduction are divided into frontal, public, overt—and hence coded— relations on the one hand, and, on the other, covert, clandestine and repressed relations which, precisely because they are repressed, characterize transgressions related not so much to sex *per se* as to sexual pleasure, its preconditions and consequences.

Thus space may be said to embrace a multitude of intersections, each with its assigned location. As for representations of the relations of production, which subsume power relations, these too occur in space: space contains them in the form of buildings, monuments and works of art. Such frontal (and hence brutal) expressions of these relations do not completely crowd out their more clandestine or underground aspects; all power must have its accomplices—and its police.

A conceptual triad has now emerged from our discussion, a triad to which we shall be returning over and over again.

1. *Spatial practice*, which embraces production and reproduction, and the particular locations and spatial sets characteristic of each social formation. Spatial practice ensures continuity and some degree of cohesion. In terms of social space, and of each member of a given society's relationship to that space, this cohesion implies a guaranteed level of *competence* and a specific level of *performance*.
2. *Representations of space*, which are tied to the relations of production and to the 'order' which those relations impose, and hence to knowledge, to signs, to codes, and to 'frontal' relations.
3. *Representational spaces*, embodying complex symbolisms, sometimes coded, sometimes not, linked to the clandestine or underground side of social life, as also to art (which may come eventually to be defined less as a code of space than as a code of representational spaces).

XVII

If space is a product, our knowledge of it must be expected to reproduce and expound the process of production. The object of interest must be expected to shift from *things in space* to the actual *production of space*.

It might be objected that at such and such a period, in such and such a society (ancient/

slave, medieval/feudal, etc.), the active groups did not 'produce' space in the sense in which a vase, a piece of furniture, a house, or a fruit tree is 'produced'. So how exactly did those groups contrive to produce their space? The question is a highly pertinent one and covers all 'fields' under consideration.

Specialists in a number of 'disciplines' might answer or try to answer the question. Ideologists, for example, would very likely take natural ecosystems as a point of departure. They would show how the actions of human groups upset the balance of these systems, and how in most cases, where 'pre-technological' or 'archaeo-technological' societies are concerned, the balance is subsequently restored. They would then examine the development of the relationship between town and country, the perturbing effects of the town, and the possibility or impossibility of a new balance being established. Then, from their point of view, they would adequately have clarified and even explained the genesis of modern social space. Historians, for their part, would doubtless take a different approach, or rather a number of different approaches according to the individual's method or orientation. Those who concern themselves chiefly with events might be inclined to establish a chronology of decisions affecting the relations between cities and their territorial dependencies, or to study the construction of monumental buildings. Others might seek to reconstitute the rise and fall of the institutions which underwrote those monuments. Still others would lean toward an economic study of exchange between city and territory, town and town, state and town, and so on.

To follow this up further, let us return to the three concepts introduced earlier.

1 *Spatial practice:* The spatial practice of a society secretes that society's space; it propounds and presupposes it, in a dialectical interaction; it produces it slowly and surely as it masters and appropriates it. From the analytic standpoint, the spatial practice of a society is revealed through the deciphering of its space.

What is spatial practice under neocapitalism? It embodies a close association, within perceived space, between daily reality (daily routine) and urban reality (the routes and networks which link up the places set aside for work, 'private' life and leisure). This association is a paradoxical one, because it includes the most extreme separation between the places it links together. The specific spatial competence and performance of every society member can only be evaluated empirically. 'Modern' spatial practice might thus be defined—to take an extreme but significant case—by the daily life of a tenant in a government-subsidized high-rise housing project. Which should not be taken to mean that motorways or the politics of air transport can be left out of the picture. A spatial practice must have a certain cohesiveness, but this does not imply that it is coherent (in the sense of intellectually worked out or logically conceived).

2 *Representations of space:* conceptualized space, the space of scientists, planners, urbanists, technocratic subdividers and social engineers, as of a certain type of artist with a scientific bent—all of whom identify what is lived and what is perceived with what is conceived. (Arcane speculation about Numbers, with its talk of the golden number, moduli and 'canons', tends to perpetuate this view of matters.) This is the dominant space in any society (or mode of production). Conceptions of space tend, with certain exceptions to which I shall return, towards a system of verbal (and therefore intellectually worked out) signs.

3 *Representational spaces:* space as directly *lived* through its associated images and symbols, and hence the space of 'inhabitants' and 'users', but also of some artists and perhaps of those, such as a few writers and philosophers, who *describe* and aspire to do no more than describe. This is the dominated—and hence passively experienced—space which the imagination seeks to change and appropriate. It overlays physical space, making symbolic use of its objects. Thus representational spaces may be said, though again with certain exceptions, to tend towards more or less coherent systems of nonverbal symbols and signs.

In seeking to understand the three moments of social space, it may help to consider the *body*. All the more so inasmuch as the relationship to space of a 'subject' who is a member of a group or society implies his relationship to his own body and vice versa. Considered overall, social practice presupposes the use of the body: the use of the hands, members and sensory organs, and the gestures of work as of activity unrelated to work. This is the realm of the *perceived* (the practical basis of the perception of the outside world, to put it in psychology's terms). As for *representations of the body*, they derive from accumulated scientific knowledge, disseminated with an admixture of ideology: from knowledge of anatomy, of physiology, of sickness and its cure, and of the body's relations with nature and with its surroundings or 'milieu'. Bodily *lived* experience, for its part, may be both highly complex and quite peculiar, because 'culture' intervenes here, with its illusory immediacy, via symbolisms and via the long Judaeo-Christian tradition, certain aspects of which are uncovered by psychoanalysis. The 'heart' as *lived* is strangely different from the heart as *thought* and *perceived*. The same holds *a fortiori* for the sexual organs. Localizations can absolutely not be taken for granted where the lived experience of the body is concerned: under the pressure of morality, it is even possible to achieve the strange result of a body without organs—a body chastised, as it were, to the point of being castrated.

The perceived–conceived–lived triad (in spatial terms: spatial practice, representations of space, representational spaces) loses all force if it is treated as an abstract 'model'. If it cannot grasp the concrete (as distinct from the 'immediate'), then its import is severely limited, amounting to no more than that of one ideological mediation among others.

That the lived, conceived and perceived realms should be interconnected, so that the 'subject', the individual member of a given social group, may move from one to another without confusion—so much is a logical necessity. Whether they constitute a coherent whole is another matter. They probably do so only in favourable circumstances, when a common language, a consensus and a code can be established.

XIX

If indeed every society produces a space, its own space, this will have other consequences in addition to those we have already considered. There is no doubt that medieval society—that is, the feudal mode of production, with its variants and local peculiarities—created its own space. Medieval space built upon the space constituted in the preceding period, and preserved that space as a substrate and prop for its symbols; it survives in an analogous fashion itself today. Manors, monasteries, cathedrals— these were the strong points anchoring the network of lanes and main roads to a landscape transformed by peasant communities. This space was the take-off point for Western European capital accumulation, the original source and cradle of which were the towns.

Capitalism and neocapitalism have produced abstract space, which includes the 'world of commodities', its 'logic' and its worldwide strategies, as the power of money and that of the political state. This space is founded on the vast network of banks, business centres and major productive entities, as also on motorways, airports and information lattices. Within this space the town—once the forcing-house of accumulation, fountainhead of wealth and centre of historical space—has disintegrated.

Abstract space works in a highly complex way. It has something of a dialogue about it, in that it implies a tacit agreement, a non-aggression pact, a contract, as it were, of non-violence. It imposes reciprocity, and a communality of use. In the street, each individual is supposed not to attack those he meets; anyone who transgresses this law is deemed guilty of a criminal act. A space of this kind presupposes the existence of a 'spatial economy' closely allied, though not identical, to the verbal economy. This economy valorizes certain relationships between people in particular places (shops, cafés, cinemas, etc.), and thus gives rise to connotative discourses concerning these places; these in turn generate 'consensuses' or conventions according to which, for example, such and such a place is supposed to be trouble-free, a quiet area where people go peacefully to have a good time, and so forth. As for denotative (i.e. descriptive) discourses in this context, they have a quasi-legal aspect which also works for consensus: there is to be no fighting over who should occupy a particular spot; spaces are to be left free, and wherever possible allowance is to be made for 'proxemics'—for the maintenance of 'respectful' distances. This attitude entails in its turn a logic and a strategy of property in space: 'places and things belonging to you do not belong to me'. The fact remains, however, that communal or shared spaces, the possession or consumption of which cannot be entirely privatized, continue to exist. Cafés, squares and monuments are cases in point. The spatial consensus I have just described in brief constitutes part of civilization much as do prohibitions against acts considered vulgar or offensive to children, women, old people or the public in general. Naturally enough, its response to class struggle, as to other forms of violence, amounts to a formal and categorical rejection. Every space is already in place before the appearance in it of actors; these actors are collective as well as individual subjects inasmuch as the individuals are always members of groups or classes seeking to appropriate the space in question. This pre-existence of space conditions the subject's presence, action and discourse, his competence and performance: yet the subject's presence, action and discourse, at the same time as they presuppose this space, also negate it. The subject experiences space as an obstacle, as a resistant 'objectality' at times as implacably hard as a concrete wall, being not only extremely difficult to modify in any way but also hedged about by Draconian rules prohibiting any attempt at such modification. Thus the *texture* of space affords opportunities not only to social acts with no particular place in it and no particular link with it, but also to a spatial practice that it does indeed determine, namely its collective and individual use: a sequence of acts which embody a signifying practice even if they cannot be reduced to such a practice. Life and death are not merely conceptualized, simulated or given expression by these acts; rather, it is in and through them that life and death actually have their being. It is within space that time consumes or devours living beings, thus giving reality to sacrifice, pleasure and pain. Abstract space, the space of the bourgeoisie and of capitalism, bound up as it is with exchange (of goods and commodities, as of written and spoken words, etc.) depends on consensus more than any space before it. It hardly seems necessary to add that within this space violence does not always remain latent or hidden. One of its contradictions is that between the appearance of security and the constant threat, and indeed the occasional eruption, of violence.

XX

'Change life!' 'Change society!' These precepts mean nothing without the production of an appropriate space. So long as everyday life

remains in thrall to abstract space, with its very concrete constraints; so long as the only improvements to occur are technical improvements of detail (for example, the frequency and speed of transportation, or relatively better amenities); so long, in short, as the only connection between work spaces, leisure spaces and living spaces is supplied by the agencies of political power and by their mechanisms of control—so long must the project of 'changing life' remain no more than a political rallying-cry to be taken up or abandoned according to the mood of the moment.

XVIII

From a less pessimistic standpoint, it can be shown that abstract space harbours specific contradictions. Such spatial contradictions derive in part from the old contradictions thrown up by historical time. These have undergone modifications, however: some are aggravated, others blunted. Amongst them, too, completely fresh contradictions have come into being which are liable eventually to precipitate the downfall of abstract space. The reproduction of the social relations of production within this space inevitably obeys two tendencies: the dissolution of old relations on the one hand and the generation of new relations on the other. Thus, despite—or rather because of—its negativity, abstract space carries within itself the seeds of a new kind of space. I shall call that new space 'differential space', because, inasmuch as abstract space tends towards homogeneity, towards the elimination of existing differences or peculiarities, a new space cannot be born (produced) unless it accentuates differences. It will also restore unity to what abstract space breaks up—to the functions, elements and moments of social practice. It will put an end to those localizations which shatter the integrity of the individual body, the social body, the corpus of human needs, and the corpus of knowledge.

48
Railroad Space and Railroad Time

(1978)

Wolfgang Schivelbusch

"Annihilation of space and time": this is how the early 19th century characterizes the effect of railroad travel. The concept is based on the speed that the new means of transport is able to achieve. A given spatial distance, to be covered, traditionally, in a fixed duration of travel or transport time, can suddenly be dealt with in a fraction of that time: to put it another way, the same duration now permits one to cover the old spatial distance many times over. In terms of transport economics, this means a shrinking of space: "Distances practically diminish in the exact ratio of the speed of personal locomotion," Lardner says in his *Railway Economy*.[1]

The nation's contraction into a metropolis, as described in the *Quarterly Review*, conversely appears as an expansion of the metropolis: by establishing transport lines to ever more outlying areas, it tends to incorporate the entire nation. The epoch of suburbs, of the amoebic proliferation of the formerly contained cities into the surrounding countryside, begins with the railroads. This is Lardner, 1851:

> It is not now unusual for persons whose place of business is in the centre of the capital, to reside with their families at a distance of from fifteen to twenty miles from that centre. Nevertheless, they are able to arrive at their respective shops, counting-houses, or offices, at an early hour of the morning, and to return without inconvenience to their residence at the usual time in the evening. Hence in all directions round the metropolis in which railways are extended, habitations are multiplied, and a considerable part of the

former population of London has been diffused in these quarters.[2]

The notion that the railroad annihilates space and time is not related to that expansion of space that results from the incorporation of ever new spaces into the transport network. What is experienced as annihilated is the traditional space-time continuum which was characterized by the old transport technology. Organically embedded in nature as it was, that technology, in its mimetic relationship with the space traversed, permitted the traveler to perceive that space as a living entity. Bergson speaks of the "durée," duration, of the road from one place to another: this is not an objective mathematical unit. It is dependent on transport technology, the way, according to Durkheim, a society's space-time perceptions are a function of its social rhythm and its territory.[3] "What is decisive," says Erwin Straus, discussing the psychology of distances, "is not the objectively measured distance, but the relation of such distance to potentiality."[4] The transport technology is the material substratum of potentiality, i.e., it is in equal measure the material substratum of the traveler's space-time perception. If an essential element of a given sociocultural space-time structure undergoes change, this will affect the entire structure. Our perception of space-time loses its accustomed orientation.

Thus, the idea that the railroad annihilates space and time has to be seen as that kind of reaction of the perceptive powers, which, formed by a certain transport technology, suddenly find it replaced by an entirely new one.

Compared to the eotechnical, the space-time relationship created by the railroad appears abstract and disorienting, because the railroad in realizing Newton's mechanics negates precisely all that characterized eotechnical traffic: it does not appear embedded in the space of the landscape the way coach and highway are; it seems to strike its way through it.[5]

We have clearly stated the two contradictory moments of the same motion: on the one hand, the railroad opens up new spaces that were not accessible before it; on the other, it does so by destroying space, viz., the space in-between. That in-between space, or travel space, which it was possible to 'savour' while using the slow and work-intensive eotechnical form of transport, disappears on the railroads. The railroad knows only points of departure and destination. "They (the railways—W.S.) only serve the points of departure, way stations, and terminal, which are mostly at great distances from each other," says a French author in 1840; "they are of no use whatsoever to the intervening spaces, which they traverse with disdain, providing them only with a useless spectacle."

As the space between the points that are served, the traditional traveling space, is destroyed, those points move into each other's immediate vicinity: one might say that they collide. They lose their old "here and now," which used to be determined by the spaces between. The isolation that spatial distance created between localities was the very essence of their here-and-now, their self-assured and complacent individuality. Heine's vision of the North Sea breaking on his doorstep in Paris is tinged with "tremendous foreboding" because both localities—Paris and the North Sea—are still presented in their mutually isolate, "worlds apart" here-and-now: thus their collision appears unfathomable. Thirty years later, as a fine-mesh network of railroad lines connects all the essential landscapes of France and the rest of Europe with each other, that kind of consciousness is no longer real. The landscapes appear, regardless of their geographical remoteness, as close and as easily accessible as the railroads have made them.

But if Normandy and Brittany are part of the Western Railway, being its destinations, then the point of departure of that same railway, the station in Paris, becomes the entrance hall to those regions. This is a common enough notion in the 19th century: it can be found in every one of Baedeker's travel guides that recommends a certain railroad station for each journey. In his journal, Mallarmé emphasizes it by printing, under the heading "Gazette et programme de la quinzaine," the following sub-headings representing equally important institutions for entertainment: *Les librairies, Les theatres, Les gares*. Thus a trip to some region served by the railroad appears no more or less important than a visit to the theater or the library: the purchase of a train ticket is equivalent to that of one to the theater. The landscape thus purchased becomes imaginary, being to the railroad as the stage is to the theater. The distance from the entrance hall of a Paris train station to the target landscape becomes more or less commensurate with the distance from the theater lobby to the box seat.

The fate wrought upon the landscape by their conquest by the railroads affects *goods* even sooner: as long as production and consumption are strictly regional—which they were until the beginning of modern transportation—, the goods remain part of the local here-and-now of their place of production. Their route of circulation can be perceived at a glance. Only when modern transportation creates a definite spatial distance between place of production and place of consumption do the commodities become homeless. In the *Grundrisse* Marx makes an observation about the relation between spatial distance and the nature of commodities; it tells us a good deal about how modern transportation has affected our perception of the world of goods: "This locational movement—the bringing of the product to market, which is a necessary condition of its circulation, except when the point of production is itself a market—could more precisely be regarded as the transformation of the product *into a commodity*."[6] (Italics original.)

With the spatial distance that the product covers on its way from its place of production to the market it also loses its local identity, its here-and-now. Its concretely sensual properties which are experienced at the place of production as a result of the labor process (or, in the case of the fruits of the land, as a result of natural growth) appear quite different in the distant marketplace. There, the product, now commodity, realizes its economic value, and simultaneously gains new qualities as an object of consumption. No longer is it seen in the original context of the original here-and-now of its place of production but in the new here-and-now of the marketplace: cherries offered for sale in the Paris market seem to be products of that market, just as Normandy seems to be a product of the railroad that takes you there.

The landscapes, joined to each other and to the metropolis by the railways, and the goods that are torn out of their local relation by modern transportation, share the fate of losing their hereditary place, their traditional here-and-now, or, as Walter Benjamin sums it up in one word, their aura.

The detaching of the landscape from its original isolation, its opening-up by the railroad, can well be defined as a loss of its aura, considering how Benjamin characterizes the aura and its loss in his essay "The Work of Art in the Age of Mechanical Reproduction." The notions of here-and-now and distance are integral parts of Benjamin's concept of aura. He defines the "aura of natural objects" as "the unique phenomenon of a distance, however close it may be."[7] The aura of a work of art is "its unique existence at the place where it happens to be."[8] This spatial-temporal singularity, its "happening-but-once-ness," the *genuineness* of the object, according to Benjamin, is destroyed by reproduction. "The situations into which the product of mechanical reproduction can be brought may not touch the actual work of art, yet the quality of its presence is always depreciated."[9] It is tempting to apply this statement to the landscapes that have been made accessible by the railroad: while being opened up to tourism they remain, initially at least, untouched in their physicality—but their easy, comfortable, and inexpensive accessibility robs them of their previous value as remote and hard-to-get-to places. The *devaluation* of land-scapes by their exploitation for mass tourism by means of the railroad in the 19th century and air traffic in the 20th century is a familiar occurrence. As soon as the railroad reaches the seaside towns of southern England that had been strongholds of the aristocracy long into the 19th century, the middle classes take them over. Then the upper crust retires to remote localities such as Scotland, Ireland, and the Lake District.[10] Contemporary airplane charter tourism is continuously engaged in further devaluation of formerly exclusive, very remote tourist regions.

The de-auralization of means of reproduction of which Benjamin speaks is an expression of the same trend that brought the masses "closer to" the landscapes in the 19th century: "The desire of contemporary masses to bring things 'closer' spatially and humanly, which is just as ardent as their bent toward overcoming the uniqueness of every reality by accepting its reproduction."[11] The landscapes are made available to the masses by means of tourism: this is merely a prelude, a preparation for making *any* singular thing available by means of reproduction. When spatial distance is no longer experienced, the differences between original and reproduction diminish.

The landscapes lose their Now in an entirely concrete sense: the railroads deprive them of their local time. As long as they remained isolated from each other, they had their individual times; London ran four minutes ahead of time in Reading, seven minutes and thirty seconds ahead of Cirencester time, fourteen minutes ahead of Bridgewater time.[12] This patchwork of time zones was no problem as long as traffic between the places was so slow that the temporal differences really did not matter; but the temporal foreshortening of the distances, effected by the trains, now confronts not only the places but also their differing local times with each other. Under traditional circumstances, a supraregional schedule would be impossible: times of departure and arrival are valid only for the place whose local time is being used. For the next station, with its own time, that previous time is no longer valid. Regular traffic needs standardized time, and this is quite analogous to the way in which the technical collective of rail and carriage undermined individual traffic and brought about the transportation monopoly.

In the 1840s, the individual English railway companies proceed to standardize time, while not coordinating their efforts with each other. Each company institutes a new time on its own line. The process is so novel that it is repeated daily, in the most cumbersome manner, as Bagwell describes, a propos of the Grand Junction Company's procedure:

Each morning an Admiralty messenger carried a watch bearing the correct time to the guard on the down Irish Mail leaving Euston for Holyhead. On arrival at Holyhead the time was passed on to officials on the Kingston boat who carried it over to Dublin. On the return mail to Euston the watch was carried back to the Admiralty messenger at Euston once more.[13]

When, after the establishment of the Railway Clearing House, the companies decide to cooperate and form a national railroad network, Greenwich Time is introduced as the standard time valid on all the lines.[14] Yet railroad time is not accepted as anything but schedule time until late in the century. As the rail network grows denser, incorporating even more regions into traffic, the retention of local times becomes untenable: in 1880, railroad time becomes general standard time in England. In Germany, official recognition comes in 1893; as early as 1884, an international conference on time standards, held in Washington, D.C., divided the world into time zones.

In the United States, the process is more complicated, as there is no cooperation whatsoever between the private railroad companies. Each company has its own time, in most cases, the local time of the company's headquarters. In stations used by several different lines there are clocks showing different times: three of these in Buffalo, six in Pittsburgh.[15] In 1889, the US is divided into four time zones, essentially unchanged to this day, officially, at first, only in terms of railroad time; in practice, these become regional standard times, although they are given legal recognition only in 1918.

The notion that communication, exchange, motion bring humanity enlightenment and progress, and that isolation and disconnection are the obstacles to be overcome on this course, is as old as the bourgeois modern age. The bourgeois cultural development of the last three centuries can be seen as closely connected with the actual development of traffic. In retrospect, it is easy to see what significance the experience of space and time had in bourgeois education when one considers the Grand Tour—which was an essential part of that education, before the industrialization of travel. The world was experiencing in its original here and now. The traveling subject experienced localities in their spatial individuality. One's *education* consisted in the assimilation of this spatial individuality of the places visited by means of an effort that was both physical and intellectual. The 18th century's travel novel becomes the *Bildungsroman* (novel of education) of the early 19th. The motion of travel, that physical and intellectual effort in space and time, dominates both.

The railroad, that destroyer of experiential space and time, thus also destroys the Grand Tour's educational experience. Henceforth, the localities are no longer spatially individual or autonomous: they are moments in the traffic that makes them possible. As we have seen, that traffic is the physical manifestation of the circulation of goods. From now on, the places visited by the traveler become ever more similar to the commodities that are part of the same circulatory system. For 20th-century tourism, the world has become one big department store of landscapes and cities.

NOTES

1 Dionysius Lardner, *Railway Economy* (London, 1850), p. 35.
2 Lardner, p. 36.
3 Emile Durkheim, *Les formes élémentaires de la vie religieuse* (Paris, 1912), pp. 14–15, 628–629.
4 Erwin Straus, *Von Sinn der Sinne* (Berlin, 1956), p. 409.
5 Pitirim A. Sorokin, *Sociocultural Casualty, Space, and Time* (Durham/N.C., 1943), p. 197.
6 Karl Marx, *Gundrisse: Foundations of the Critique of Political Economy (Rough Draft),* trans. Martin Nicololaus (London, 1973), p. 534.
7 Walter Benjamin, *Illuminations,* trans. Harry Zohn and ed. Hannah Arendt (New York, 1968), p. 224.
8 *Ibid.,* p. 222.
9 *Ibid.,* p. 223.
10 John A.R. Pimlott, *The Englishman's Holiday* (London, 1947), p. 118.
11 Benjamin, p. 225.
12 Philip S. Bagwell, *The Transport Revolution from 1770* (London, 1974), p. 124.
13 *Ibid.,* p. 125.
14 "The precise standardization of time measurement dates from the founding of the Royal Observatory in Greenwich in 1675." See Gerald J. Whitow, *The Nature of Time* (London, 1972). As was the case with the later standard time, the original Greenwich time emerged from the needs of an expanding traffic, the ship traffic of the 17th century.
15 John Stover, *American Railroads* (Chicago, 1961), p. 157.

49
A Time for Space and a Space for Time

The Social Production of the Vacation House (1980)

Anthony D. King

If one purpose of this volume is to ask what can be understood about society by examining its built environment, then studying the social production of the vacation house has an important contribution to make: it poses questions about the economic basis of society, about its forms of temporal organisation and about the ideas and beliefs which influence people's behaviour.

Strictly speaking, 'vacation house' is a contemporary American term for what earlier might have been called a summer cottage, cabin or seaside residence or today in different places, a country cottage, holiday chalet, bungalow, *Ferienhaus, Zomerhaus, maison de campagne* or any of the large variety of terms which describe what is broadly, if not exactly, the same thing. Though the term 'second home' masks important ideological and social properties expressed by 'country cottage' or 'cabin', the following definition of this phenomenon serves well enough for this chapter: 'the occasional residence of a household that usually lives elsewhere and which is primarily used for recreational purposes'.

Starting from current explanations of greater leisure, disposable income and improved transportation, therefore, this chapter suggests that the development of the mass vacation house can more adequately be understood by reference to four main factors: (1) the emergence of advanced industrial capitalism in the second half of the nineteenth century and the creation of an extensive economic surplus; (2) the increasing differentiation and specialisation of space and building form associated with this development; (3) changes in the social organi-

sation of time consequent upon industrialisation and developments in transport technology; and (4) the more widespread social diffusion of the cultural and ideological beliefs of an elite. These more general theoretical themes are discussed in the first half of the chapter. They are then illustrated by reference to a case study, the emergence of the holiday bungalow and weekend or country cottage in England between 1870 and 1914. Finally, some comments on the contemporary vacation house suggest the relationship between social beliefs, behaviour and the built environment.

DIFFERENTIATION AND SPECIALISATION AS CHARACTERISTICS OF INDUSTRIAL CAPITALISM

Central to capitalism, as an economic system, was the creation and selective appropriation of a surplus, an amount of wealth created by labour over and above what is necessary to satisfy society's basic wants.

Industrial capitalism, however, produced not only a surplus of wealth but also, for a sizeable minority, a surplus of time. While the development of factory production in the early nineteenth century meant, for the new working class, longer work hours and, in comparison with their agricultural forbears, a loss of traditional rural holidays, for the growing minority of capitalist employers and rentiers of industrial society it meant an increase of leisure. By the mid-nineteenth century there already existed a substantial class of the latter living on income from stocks and shares. As industrialisation and the size of the surplus increased, as markets expanded and workers gained more control over their conditions of labour from the 1860s, increased prosperity and leisure became available to a larger proportion of the population, at first, the middle class and then, towards the end of the century, some of the skilled working class.

The most obvious environmental expression of these developments—surplus capital and surplus time—was in the new purpose-built leisure environments of the nineteenth century, the seaside resorts. These, developing from the earlier socially elite practice of visiting inland spas, had grown especially from the mid-eighteenth century, and by the first decades of the nineteenth were a principal location for aristocratic and upper-class leisure. With the rapid expansion of bourgeois society and developments in rail transport between the 1840s and 1860s, the seaside resorts were to provide one of the safest sources in Britain for the investment and circulation of surplus capital. In a very real sense, therefore, the *functional* origin of the modern vacation home, if not its actual form or precise motivations, can be found in the terraces, squares or marine residences of the mid-nineteenth-century resort.

Two other features characteristic of capitalist industrial development are those of increasing specialisation and differentiation. In all societies, the creation of an economic surplus has led to greater social differentiation.

But the most immediate effects of industrialisation were on social stratification: the vast increase in the size of the surplus and its uneven distribution created greater inequalities; new industrial and scientific techniques generated a host of new occupations, each with its particular social status; and a vast growth in material culture (especially in housing and material consumption) allowed this stratification to be expressed in different ways. Thus, in comparison with the relatively simple modes of stratification in rural, agricultural economies of pre-industrial Europe, there emerged, in the late eighteenth and nineteenth centuries, a highly differentiated system of social stratification, not least manifest in the dwellings produced for different social class groups.

Differentiation and specialisation also characterised changes in the social organisation of time. The pre-industrial year of the rural peasant was divided according to nature's seasons and their associated activities, ploughing, sowing or harvesting; 'agricultural time' was task-oriented, not clock-oriented; holidays were literally 'holy days', religious fairs and festivals, often associated with slack periods in the agricultural year.

The pre-industrial day, like the year, was organised according to 'nature's time', the day's activities regulated by the advent of dawn and dusk or occasionally by tasks. For the peasant, time was not abstracted or rationalised, divided by watch and clock, but structured according to tasks, meals, events and places.

Time, however, is also a social and cultural commodity, a device, according to Bergson, invented by man to stop everything happening at once. Industrialisation brought a radical change in the social organisation of time and man's orientation to it.[1] It was, indeed, the differentiation and rationalisation of time which Weber saw as one of the fundamental characteristics of the spirit of capitalism. 'Industrial time' is clock time, oriented by time-measuring machinery rather than the completion of a given task: the day of the early nineteenth-century industrial worker became increasingly organised by the clock and factory whistle. With the diffusion of clocks and watches, urbanisation and the development of railways, there emerged a totally new orientation to, and organisation of, time, with 'local time' being suppressed in favour of 'London time'. Railways and factory production meant that time was 'tabled', the day and week increasingly differentiated into socially and economically meaningful units.

With the triumph of industrial capitalism in the later nineteenth century, the annual calendar of working life was steadily modified, the statutory 'bank holiday' established from 1871, the length of the working week reduced and, in different trades and regions over the following decades, an annual paid holiday introduced. Like material wealth, however, such 'free time' was obviously inequitably distributed, itself a dimension of social stratification.

For the industrial worker, not only was working time increasingly distinct from non-working time but, with rising living standards and greater free time, positive 'recreation' was distinguished from other non-work activity. As stated more fully elsewhere, this recreational time was increasingly accommodated, between

1850 and 1914, in the town, in the park, sports ground, music hall, pub, club house and, with the development in transport technology, in the specialised recreational resorts at the seaside, where again new building forms, catering solely for leisure—the pier, promenade, pavilion, winter gardens and boarding house—developed.

To summarise, then, the economic transformations of industrial capitalism gave rise to new social formations, changes in the social organisation of time and a highly differentiated, functionally specialised building and spatial environment. These environments were stratified not only according to social class but also according to the times and seasons when they were used.

It is within this framework, therefore, that the development of the modern, purpose-built vacation house can be understood. It is a specialised dwelling type designed for a particular function, location, social group, time and, if possible, with a distinctive form and appearance. In these terms, the development of a specialised vacation house, at anything like a popular as opposed to an elite level, occurred in England in the last quarter of the nineteenth century.

THE 'COUNTRY COTTAGE'

The idea of the rich and powerful having two or more dwellings, one in the city as the principal locus of social and political activity, the other in the country, for recreational use and as a symbol of power and status, common in many societies, had been well established in England since the fifteenth century and earlier. It was this traditional elite which provided the model for the new aristocracy of wealth created by the Industrial Revolution, and for most of the nineteenth century the country remained the private 'leisure environment' of an aristocratic and wealthy commercial and industrial class. Until the middle of that century, the majority of the population lived, worked and played in rural areas; for them 'the country', as a distinct and *preferred* location for leisure, had neither particular significance nor meaning. Only for an elite, moving between country and town, did it have a particular association with leisure, as well as a distinct social meaning.

For the growing urban bourgeoisie, the principal settings for leisure were the developing seaside resorts which, with the odd exception, catered almost entirely for a middle- and upper-middle-class clientele.

In the last two decades of the century, this situation was to change. For the expanding urban middle class, with the aristocracy as a model for social emulation, the country was to become, in modern terminology, a recreational resource. The reasons were many. By the 1890s, not only was England the most urbanised country in the world, but people were aware of the fact. By the late 1870s, the railway network practically covered the country: with the help of improved road surfaces and better carriages, access to previously remote rural areas was gained. Rising profits from industry and commerce had inflated the size of the urban bourgeoisie, especially in London. Developments in shipping, American agriculture, refrigeration and other factors in an increasingly global economy had brought agricultural decline and, with growing emigration from rural areas, the decay of rural cottages in the last years of the century. Not only the railway but, from the middle 1890s, the bicycle—or a combination of both—brought rural areas within travelling distance of the towns, far smaller in size than they are today. Where the country had previously been the semi-private leisure environment of the elite, it now became more available to the urban middle class and even, in the early twentieth century, to the lower middle class.

THE EMERGENCE OF THE 'WEEK-END'

In the social reorganisation of time consequent upon industrialisation, the weekend, as a socially differentiated unit of non-working free time, has emerged as one of the most important leisure institutions in modern society.

The concept of the weekend, of either one and a half or two days from Friday night or Saturday noon to Monday morning of free 'leisure time', is relatively recent, and is associated only with industrial societies.

Lexical recognition of this new temporal unit apparently occurs in the late 1870s: the first recorded use of 'week-end' is in 1879, and by 1900 the term had become commonplace. The geography of its use is clearly located in the new urban industrial regions of the Midlands and north-west England and the new leisure environment developed in response to them.

In a steady secularisation of time, the weekend was replacing the Sabbath as a period to punctuate the month: for an upper-class minority at least, 'weekending' had become 'part of the British constitution'.

In the majority of these examples, the new temporal concept of the weekend was defined in relation to place, a place different from the normal location of work and residence. The weekend was not simply a *duration* of time but also a spatial–temporal unit. The link was established by new modes of travel—the railway, bicycle and then the car. With the separation of work from residence, it had also a social dimension. The 'working week' was spent in town, in the company of office colleagues: the 'week-end', at home (or occasionally, at the 'cottage'), in the company of wife and children.

Thus, with middle-class holidays away from home in the 1860s, a week's paid holiday for some manual workers gradually being introduced from the 1880s and the weekend institutionalised by the end of the century, there were—within the context of surplus wealth— new 'social units' of time to be accommodated in the built environment.

THE BUNGALOW AND WEEKEND COUNTRY COTTAGE

The development of a purpose-built dwelling to meet these particular social, spatial, temporal and ideological needs of the expanding middle class took place in the last three decades of the century. The first bungalows built and named as such, speculatively built as a specialised seaside house for summer use, appeared on the north Kent coast, some two hours' journey by train from London, in 1869–70. Though bungalows and 'seaside cottages' were being designed in the late 1870s, the earliest reference to 'country cottage' in the modern sense so far identified is in 1887 and to a 'week-end cottage' in 1904, although 'the evolution of the popular week-end cottage' had come about 'in the twenty years previous to this' (i.e. 1884–1904).

Though the early bungalows and many small country houses built at this time had the function of second homes, many were mainly for summer use, though they were also being used for weekends by the 1890s and probably earlier. Thus, an estate of Sussex bungalows and small houses built in the late 1880s within easy rail distance of London were for 'people of moderate means in a city like ours where grime and smoke, bustle and hurry make us long for the country and its freshness where, at a small expense, we may pass a quiet week-end'. At the seaside, the bungalow had developed in response to subtle value changes among middle-class urban populations. Early nineteenth-century resorts had been essentially social places, providing—in the assembly rooms, promenades, theatres, crescents and squares—opportunity for group enjoyment, social rituals and personal display. The bungalow was an early symbol of the rejection of this behaviour. It represented a search for solitude, a quest for quiet, and isolation from the city crowd. In this, it was essentially an *urban* house-type, performing a social function conceivable only when the links with community life (and the apparatus for sustaining them) could be taken for granted.

From the late 1880s, the bungalow was to emerge as a specialised house type specifically developed for popular—as opposed to elite—use as a vacation house. It was, first and foremost, an *additional* or second dwelling, initially (1870–1900) for a wealthy urban middle and upper middle class; subsequently (1890–1914 and later) it was utilised by a far wider clientele. In this, as in its form, location and site, it embodied and symbolised two principal characteristics of modern industrial capitalism: surplus wealth and surplus time. And at a time when the size of this economic surplus was greater than ever before, it also symbolised the vast inequalities in the distribution of wealth.

The particular locations for which the early bungalows were designed, and the names by which they were known—seaside, countryside, riverside, hillside bungalows—demonstrate its use of location and site as a recreational resource. Its isolated setting, perched on a hillside or river bank, 'consumed' the space around; its overall design and layout determined by the requirements of leisure, relaxation and idleness. The essential element of the bungalow was its horizontality: early models were large, generally single-storey and often with a veranda all round. Here, as elsewhere, space was used for time-consuming, low-energy—generally horizontal—activities: billiards, boating, sleeping, sitting in the lounge, writing. It provided for the 'sedentary society', the veranda accommodating the deck-chair (an invention of the 1880s), for gazing at distant views, and balconies for 'the matitudinal cigarette'. Its internal spaces provided 'for comfort of the kind so needful in the bungalow after a pull on the river or a game or tennis'. It was, in short, a purpose-built building for the consumption of surplus free time.

THE CONTEMPORARY VACATION HOUSE

Whatever the varied motives for second homes, what is evident from the architectural literature are its many social functions. That the vacation house is essentially a mass phenomenon, generated by mass society, is manifest in the emphasis its owners place on originality and individualism.

The house becomes an instrument of self-expression: a 'symbol of self', yet also a symbol of status. Owning an inessential house is an important index of having arrived: people 'enjoy the distinction of having one'.

In a society increasingly spatially, temporally and socially fragmented by work, commuting and leisure, or by role and generation, the vacation house provides the setting for a reassertion of familial activities and values. In societies with high geographical mobility, such as in North America, the vacation house is thought to provide a relatively stable base to which far-flung kin return to renew familial bonds. For wealthy parents, it is an opportunity to keep adolescents in tow, yet independent of parental control. It is a place to share with visitors, entertain friends or simply use as hospitality.

This emphasis on family or friends' activity, particularly if business associates are involved, heightens the need for the original, the unique, even bizarre, reflecting on the owner's individuality and status. It has also spatial implications. Accommodation is flexible, catering for eight, ten or even more occupants, twice the size of the average nuclear family. Indoors, the emphasis is on 'togetherness', conviviality and family-strengthening activities. This requires that communal space for relaxation, dining and talking is, compared with the 'first home', relatively large. As in the early upper-class bungalows, time-consuming activities require additional space: a bar, hobby room, library, sauna, swimming pool, solarium

or patio. The presence of people throughout the day, and the temporary exchange of conventional sex roles, means that the preparation of food is integrated into eating–living areas, rather than isolated in a specific 'kitchen'. Yet 'the main difference between normal and holiday domesticity is the diminished importance of the bedroom … the living room becomes the sole *raison d'être* of the house when life is a series of fourteen-hour outdoor days.'

CONCLUSION

The shift in terminology apparent from the 1960s, from 'holiday' or 'vacation homes' to 'second homes', '*résidences secondaire*' or '*Zweitwohnungen*', is evidence of a subtle and also ambiguous change in the perception of the phenomenon. In one sense, for critics the parameters are those of social justice, a concern that, where thousands are without homes and millions just rent them, a privileged minority own two. In the other sense, however, the ideology of consumption is unquestioned. Where 'the last metaphysical right, the right of property ownership' is seen as fundamental, the acquisition of a second, vacation home becomes a positive goal: 'besides a second bathroom, second telephone and second car, many American families either own or are planning to acquire a second home.'

The vacation house as a special building, for use at a particular time and in a particular location, is a good illustration of the propensity for modern society to create organisational patterns and then for people to live within the strictures that such organisation imposes. Though apparently 'free agents', we none the less live in a society whose social, spatial and temporal organisation is intricately structured, even if subject to change. In societies where capital accumulation and property ownership is encouraged, the further growth in ownership of vacation houses, with a long-established cultural tradition behind it—not only within the owner's own society but, increasingly, in other societies as well—is, for the minority who can afford it, likely to continue, the need being met by new commercial developments. Because of the pressure to accumulate capital, the popularisation of vacation houses and their increasing acquisition, and use become a significant influence on the way in which people spend their surplus time and wealth.

NOTE

1 See especially E.P. Thompson, 'Time, work discipline and industrial capitalism', *Past and Present,* vol. 38, 1967, pp. 56–97.

50
A Room of One's Own
(1929)

Virginia Woolf

But, you may say, we asked you to speak about women and fiction—what has that got to do with a room of one's own? I will try to explain. When you asked me to speak about women and fiction I sat down on the banks of a river and began to wonder what the words meant. The title women and fiction might mean, and you may have meant it to mean, women and what they are like, or it might mean women and the fiction that they write; or it might mean women and the fiction that is written about them, or it might mean that somehow all three are inextricably mixed together and you want me to consider them in that light. But when I began to consider the subject in this last way, which seemed the most interesting, I soon saw that it had one fatal drawback. I should never be able to come to a conclusion. I should never be able to fulfil what is, I understand, the first duty of a lecturer to hand you after an hour's discourse a nugget of pure truth to wrap up between the pages of your notebooks and keep on the mantelpiece for ever. All I could do was to offer you an opinion upon one minor point—a woman must have money and a room of her own if she is to write fiction; and that, as you will see, leaves the great problem of the true nature of woman and the true nature of fiction unsolved. But in order to make some amends I am going to do what I can to show you how I arrived at this opinion about the room and the money.

What idea it had been that had sent me so audaciously trespassing I could not now remember. The spirit of peace descended like a cloud from heaven, for if the spirit of peace dwells anywhere, it is in the courts and quadrangles of Oxbridge on a fine October morning. Strolling through those colleges past those ancient halls the roughness of the present seemed smoothed away; the body seemed contained in a miraculous glass cabinet through which no sound could penetrate, and the mind, freed from any contact with facts (unless one trespassed on the turf again), was at liberty to settle down upon whatever meditation was in harmony with the moment. As chance would have it, some stray memory of some old essay about revisiting Oxbridge in the long vacation brought Charles Lamb to mind. Certainly he wrote an essay—the name escapes me—about the manuscript of one of Milton's poems which he saw here. It was LYCIDAS perhaps, and Lamb wrote how it shocked him to think it possible that any word in LYCIDAS could have been different from what it is. To think of Milton changing the words in that poem seemed to him a sort of sacrilege. This led me to remember what I could of LYCIDAS and to amuse myself with guessing which word it could have been that Milton had altered, and why. It then occurred to me that the very manuscript itself which Lamb had looked at was only a few hundred yards away, so that one could follow Lamb's footsteps across the quadrangle to that famous library where the treasure is kept. Moreover, I recollected, as I put this plan into execution, it is in this famous library that the manuscript of Thackeray's ESMOND is also preserved—but here I was actually at the door which leads into the library itself. I must have opened it, for instantly there issued, like a guardian angel barring the way with a flutter of black gown instead of white wings, a deprecating, silvery, kindly gentleman, who regretted in a low voice as he waved me back that ladies are only admitted to the library if accompanied by a Fellow of the College or furnished with a letter of introduction.

That a famous library has been cursed by a woman is a matter of complete indifference to a famous library. Venerable and calm, with all its treasures safe locked within its breast, it sleeps complacently and will, so far as I am concerned, so sleep for ever. Never will I wake those echoes, never will I ask for that hospitality again, I vowed as I descended the steps in anger. Still an hour remained before luncheon, and what was one to do? Stroll on the meadows? Sit by the river? Certainly it was a lovely autumn morning; the leaves were fluttering red to the ground; there was no great hardship in doing either. But the sound of music reached my ear. Some service or celebration was going forward. The organ complained magnificently as I passed the chapel door. Even the sorrow of Christianity sounded in that serene air more like the recollection of sorrow than sorrow itself; even the groanings of the ancient organ seemed lapped in peace. I had no wish to enter had I the right, and this time the verger might have stopped me, demanding perhaps my baptismal certificate, or a letter of introduction from the Dean. The outside of the chapel remained. As you know, its high domes and pinnacles can be seen, like a sailing-ship always voyaging never arriving, lit up at night and visible for miles, far away across the hills. Once, presumably, this quadrangle with its smooth lawns, its massive buildings and the chapel itself was marsh too, where the grasses waved and the swine rooted. Teams of horses and oxen, I thought, must have hauled the stone in wagons from far countries, and then with infinite labour the grey blocks in whose shade I was now standing were poised in order one on top of another. And then the painters brought their glass for the windows, and the masons were busy for centuries up on that roof with putty and cement, spade and trowel. Every Saturday somebody must have poured gold and silver out of a leathern purse into their ancient fists, for they had their beer and skittles presumably of an evening. An unending stream of gold and silver, I thought, must have flowed into this court perpetually to keep the stones coming and the masons working; to level, to ditch, to dig and to drain. But it was then the age of faith, and money was poured liberally to set these stones on a deep foundation, and when the stones were raised, still more money was poured in from the coffers of kings and queens and great nobles to ensure that hymns should be sung here and scholars taught. Lands were granted; tithes were paid. And when the age of faith was over and the age of reason had come, still the same flow of gold and silver went on; fellowships were founded; lectureships endowed; only the gold and silver flowed now, not from the coffers of the king. But from the chests of merchants and manufacturers, from the purses of men who had made, say, a fortune from industry, and returned, in their wills, a bounteous share of it to endow more chairs, more lectureships, more fellowships in the university where they had learnt their craft. Hence the libraries and laboratories; the observatories; the splendid equipment of costly and delicate instruments which now stands on glass shelves, where centuries ago the grasses waved and the swine rooted. Certainly, as I strolled round the court, the foundation of gold and silver seemed deep enough; the pavement laid solidly over the wild grasses. Men with trays on their heads went busily from staircase to staircase. Gaudy blossoms flowered in window-boxes. The strains of the gramophone blared out from the rooms within. It was impossible not to reflect—the reflection whatever it may have been was cut short. The clock struck. It was time to find one's way to luncheon.

The scene, if I may ask you to follow me, was now changed. The leaves were still falling, but in London now, not Oxbridge; and I must ask you to imagine a room, like many thousands, with a window looking across people's hats and vans and motor-cars to other windows, and on the table inside the room a blank sheet of paper on which was written in large letters WOMEN AND FICTION, but no more. The inevitable sequel to lunching and dining at Oxbridge seemed, unfortunately, to be a visit to the British Museum. One must strain off what was personal and accidental in all these impressions and so reach the pure fluid, the essential oil of truth. For that visit to Oxbridge and the luncheon and the dinner had started a swarm of questions. Why did men drink wine and women water? Why was one sex so prosperous and the other so poor? What effect has poverty on fiction? What conditions are necessary for the creation of works of art?—a thousand questions at once suggested themselves. But one needed answers, not questions; and an answer was only to be had by consulting the learned and the unprejudiced, who have removed themselves above the strife of tongue and the confusion of body and issued the result of their reasoning and research in books which are to be found in the British Museum. If truth is not to be found on the shelves of the British Museum, where, I asked myself, picking up a notebook and a pencil, is truth?

Have you any notion of how many books are written about women in the course of one year? Have you any notion how many are written by men? Are you aware that you are, perhaps, the most discussed animal in the universe? Here had I come with a notebook and a pencil proposing to spend a morning reading, supposing that at the end of the morning I should have transferred the truth to my notebook. But I should need to be a herd of elephants, I thought, and a wilderness of spiders, desperately referring to the animals that are reputed longest lived and most multitudinously eyed, to cope with all this. I should need claws of steel and beak of brass even to penetrate the husk. How shall I ever find the grains of truth embedded in all this mass of paper? I asked myself, and in despair began running my eye up and down the long list of titles. Even the names of the books gave me food for thought. Sex and its nature might well attract doctors and biologists; but what was surprising and difficult of explanation was the fact that sex—woman, that is to say—also attracts agreeable essayists, light-fingered novelists, young men who have taken the M.A. degree; men who have taken no degree; men who have no apparent qualification save that they are not women.

Every page in my notebook was scribbled over with notes. To show the state of mind I was in, I will read you a few of them, explaining that the page was headed quite simply, WOMEN AND POVERTY, in block letters; but what followed was something like this:

Condition in Middle Ages of,
Habits in the Fiji Islands of,
Worshipped as goddesses by,
Weaker in moral sense than,
Idealism of,
Greater conscientiousness of,
South Sea Islanders,
age of puberty among,
Attractiveness of,

Offered as sacrifice to,
Small size of brain of,
Profounder sub-consciousness of,
Less hair on the body of,
Mental, moral and physical inferiority of,
Love of children of,
Greater length of life of,
Weaker muscles of,
Strength of affections of,
Vanity of,
Higher education of,
Shakespeare's opinion of,
Lord Birkenhead's opinion of,
Dean Inge's opinion of,
La Bruyere's opinion of,
Dr Johnson's opinion of,
Mr Oscar Browning's opinion of, …

Here I drew breath and added, indeed, in the margin, Why does Samuel Butler say, 'Wise men never say what they think of women'? Wise men never say anything else apparently. But, I continued, leaning back in my chair and looking at the vast dome in which I was a single but by now somewhat harassed thought, what is so unfortunate is that wise men never think the same thing about women.

Whatever the reason, all these books, I thought, surveying the pile on the desk, are worthless for my purposes. They were worthless scientifically, that is to say, though humanly they were full of instruction, interest, boredom, and very queer facts about the habits of the Fiji Islanders. All that I had retrieved from that morning's work had been the one fact of anger. The professors—I lumped them together thus—were angry. But why, I asked myself, having returned the books, why, I repeated, standing under the colonnade among the pigeons and the prehistoric canoes, why are they angry? Possibly they were not 'angry' at all; often, indeed, they were admiring, devoted, exemplary in the relations of private life. Possibly when the professor insisted a little too emphatically upon the inferiority of women, he was concerned not with their inferiority, but with his own superiority. That was what he was protecting rather hot-headedly and with too much emphasis, because it was a jewel to him of the rarest price. Life for both sexes—and I looked at them, shouldering their way along the pavement—is arduous, difficult, a perpetual struggle. It calls for gigantic courage and strength. More than anything, perhaps, creatures of illusion as we are, it calls for confidence in oneself. Without self-confidence we are as babes in the cradle. And how can we generate this imponderable quality, which is yet so invaluable, most quickly? By thinking that other people are inferior to one self.

So thinking, so speculating I found my way back to my house by the river. Lamps were being lit and an indescribable change had come over London since the morning hour. It was as if the great machine after labouring all day had made with our help a few yards of something very exciting and beautiful—a fiery fabric flashing with red eyes, a tawny monster roaring with hot breath. Even the wind seemed flung like a flag as it lashed the houses and rattled the hoardings.

In my little street, however, domesticity prevailed. The house painter was descending his ladder; the nursemaid was wheeling the perambulator carefully in and out back to nursery tea; the coal-heaver was folding his empty sacks on top of each other; the woman who keeps the green grocer's shop was adding up the day's takings with her hands in red mittens. But so engrossed was I with the problem you have laid upon my shoulders that I could not see even these usual sights without referring them to one centre. I thought how much harder it is now than it must have been even a century ago to say which of these employments is the higher, the more necessary. Is it better to be a coal-heaver or a nursemaid; is the charwoman who has brought up eight children of less value to the world than the barrister who has made a hundred thousand pounds? It is useless to ask such questions; for nobody can answer them. Not only do the comparative values of charwomen and lawyers rise and fall from decade to decade, but we have no rods with which to measure them even as they are at the moment. I had been foolish to ask my professor to furnish me with 'indisputable proofs' of this or that in his argument about women. Even if one could state the value of any one gift at the moment, those values will change; in a century's time very possibly they will have changed completely. Anything may happen when womanhood has ceased to be a protected occupation, I thought, opening the door. But what bearing has all this upon the subject of my paper, Women and Fiction? I asked, going indoors.

For it is a perennial puzzle why no woman wrote a word of that extraordinary literature when every other man, it seemed, was capable of song or sonnet. What were the conditions in which women lived? I asked myself; for fiction, imaginative work that is, is not dropped like a pebble upon the ground, as science may be; fiction is like a spider's web, attached ever so lightly perhaps, but still attached to life at all four corners. Often the attachment is scarcely perceptible; Shakespeare's plays, for instance, seem to hang there complete by themselves. But when the web is pulled askew, hooked up at the edge, torn in the middle, one remembers that these webs are not spun in mid-air by incorporeal creatures, but are the work of suffering human beings, and are attached to grossly material things, like health and money and the houses we live in.

Here I opened the volume containing the Tragedies of Shakespeare. What was Shakespeare's state of mind, for instance, when he wrote LEAR and ANTONY AND CLEOPATRA? It was certainly the state of mind most favourable to poetry that there has ever existed. But Shakespeare himself said nothing about it. We only know casually and by chance that he 'never blotted a line'. Nothing indeed was ever said by the artist himself about his state of mind until the eighteenth century perhaps. Rousseau perhaps began it. At any rate, by the nineteenth century self-consciousness had developed so far that it was the habit for men of letters to describe their minds in confessions and autobiographies. Their lives also were written, and their letters were printed after their deaths. Thus, though we do not know what Shakespeare went through when he wrote LEAR, we do know what Carlyle went through when he wrote the FRENCH REVOLUTION; what Flaubert went through when he wrote MADAME BOVARY; what Keats was going through when he tried to write poetry against the coming death and the indifference of the world.

And one gathers from this enormous modern literature of confession and self-analysis that to write a work of genius is almost always a feat of prodigious difficulty. Everything is against the likelihood that it will come from the writer's mind whole and entire. Generally material circumstances are against it. Dogs will bark; people will interrupt; money must be made; health will break down. Further, accentuating all these difficulties and making them harder to bear is the world's notorious indifference. It does not ask people to write poems and novels and histories; it does not need them. It does not care whether Flaubert finds the right word or whether Carlyle scrupulously verifies this or that fact. Naturally, it will not pay for what it does not want. And so the writer, Keats, Flaubert, Carlyle, suffers, especially in the creative years of youth, every form of distraction and discouragement. A curse, a cry of agony, rises from those books of analysis and confession. 'Mighty poets in their misery dead'—that is the burden of their song. If anything comes through in spite of all this, it is a miracle, and probably no book is born entire and uncrippled as it was conceived.

But for women, I thought, looking at the empty shelves, these difficulties were infinitely more formidable. In the first place, to have a room of her own, let alone a quiet room or a sound-proof room, was out of the question, unless her parents were exceptionally rich or very noble, even up to the beginning of the nineteenth century. Since her pin money, which depended on the goodwill of her father, was only enough to keep her clothed, she was debarred from such alleviations as came even to Keats or Tennyson or Carlyle, all poor men, from a walking tour, a little journey to France, from the separate lodging which, even if it were miserable enough, sheltered them from the claims and tyrannies of their families. Such material difficulties were formidable; but much worse were the immaterial. The indifference of the world which Keats and Flaubert and other men of genius have found so hard to bear was in her case not indifference but

hostility. The world did not say to her as it said to them, Write if you choose; it makes no difference to me. The world said with a guffaw, Write? What's the good of your writing?

Next day the light of the October morning was falling in dusty shafts through the uncurtained windows, and the hum of traffic rose from the street. London then was winding itself up again; the factory was astir; the machines were beginning. It was tempting, after all this reading, to look out of the window and see what London was doing on the morning of the 26th of October 1928. And what was London doing? Nobody, it seemed, was reading ANTONY AND CLEOPATRA. London was wholly indifferent, it appeared, to Shakespeare's plays. Nobody cared a straw—and I do not blame them—for the future of fiction, the death of poetry or the development by the average woman of a prose style completely expressive of her mind.

For the reading of these books seems to perform a curious couching operation on the senses; one sees more intensely afterwards; the world seems bared of its covering and given an intenser life. Those are the enviable people who live at enmity with unreality; and those are the pitiable who are knocked on the head by the thing done without knowing or caring. So that when I ask you to earn money and have a room of your own, I am asking you to live in the presence of reality, an invigorating life, it would appear, whether one can impart it or not.

51
The Last Place They Thought Of

Black Women's Geographies (2006)

Katherine McKittrick

A small shed had been added to my grandmother's house years ago. Some boards were laid across the joists at the top, and between these boards and the roof was a very small garret, never occupied by any thing but rats and mice. It was a pent roof, covered with nothing but shingles, according to the southern custom for such buildings. The garret was only nine feet long and seven feet wide. The highest part was three feet high, and sloped down abruptly to the loose board floor. There was no admission for either light or air.

Harriet A. Jacobs

I begin this discussion of black women's geographies with the hiding place Harriet Jacobs [Linda Brent] describes in her slave narrative, *Incidents in the Life of a Slave Girl: Written by Herself*, her grandmother's garret. Learning from her slave owner, Dr. Flint, that her children would soon be "broken in" and that his abuses of her would escalate, Linda Brent devised a plan to flee his plantation in Edenton, North Carolina, with the purpose of saving herself and her children.[1] After concealing herself in neighbors' homes and a local swamp, Brent fled to the small 9′ × 7′ × 3′ attic above her grandmother's house. She describes the garret as her "loophole of retreat," a hideaway that set in motion her escape to the North and the emancipation of her children.

Linda Brent's experiences in her grandmother's garret exact, geographically, what she describes as the shape of mystery: Brent must suffer to avoid self and familial sufferings. The question of geographic freedom is wrapped up in the racial, sexual, and bodily constraints before and during her retreat to the attic. That which is outside the garret—human bondage and racial-sexual hierarchies, imminent and actual rape, the links between property, ownership, and racist-sexist punishments—are, for seven years, connected to the physically disabling perimeters of the 9′ × 7′ × 3′ cell.

Brent's spatial experiences and strategies illustrate how the geographic workings of slavery simultaneously produce spatial boundaries and subject-knowledges that can subvert the perimeters of bondage. That which is used to geographically displace and regulate black women during slavery, specifically patriarchal ways of seeing and white colonial desires for lands, free labor, and racial-sexual domination, rest on a tight hierarchy of racial power and knowledge that is spatially organized. This organization assumes white masculine knowledge and the logic of visualization, which both work to objectify Brent and her community and negate their unique sense of place. For a black woman such as Linda Brent, the logic of visualization and patriarchal knowledge means that her place and body are seen to be, and understood as, naturally subordinate to whiteness and masculinity; it also means that her seeable presence is crucial to Dr. Flint's sense of place. Race, sex, and gender—her seeable body-scale—inscribe Brent as worthy of captivity, violence, punishment, and objectification; her bodily codes produce her slave master's surroundings. If the geographies of slavery are primarily about racial captivities and boundaries, and the garret is both a site of self-captivity and a loophole of retreat, it becomes increasingly clear that it is Brent's different sense of place that allows her to explore the possibilities in the existing landscape.

Under slavery, geographic options such as escape, concealment, and racial-sexual safety can be, as Brent explains, bound up with troubling spatial strategies.

Disabling, oppressive, dark, and cramped surroundings are more liberatory than moving about under the gaze of Dr. Flint who threatens her "at every turn." Importantly, she claims that in the garret she is *not* enslaved and that her loophole of retreat is a retreat to emancipation. For Brent to declare that her emancipation begins in the garret—which she also repeatedly refers to as her dismal cell, her prison, and this dark hole—is evidence of how she uses the existing landscape and architecture to name the complicated geographies of black womanhood in/and slavery.

The garret makes available a place for Brent to articulate her lived experiences and emancipatory desires, without losing sight of the dehumanizing forces of slavery. She bores holes in the garret with a gimlet, in order to allow air in and observe her surroundings and her children's activities; this, along with her location within her grandmother's house, allows her to partially listen, see, and feel her immediate surroundings without formally participating in the daily activities of the town.

> Through my peeping-hole I could watch the children, and when they were near enough I could hear their talk. ... O, those long, gloomy [winter] days, with no object for my eye to rest upon, and no thoughts to occupy my mind, except the dreary past and the uncertain future! I was thankful when there came a day sufficiently mild for me to wrap myself up and sit at the loophole to watch passers by ... I heard many conversations not intended for my ears. I heard slave-hunters planning how to catch some poor fugitive. Several times I heard allusions to Dr. Flint, myself, and the history of my children. ... The opinion was expressed that I was in the Free States. Very rarely did any one suggest that I was in the vicinity ... [my grandmother's attic] was the last place they thought of. Yet there was no place, where slavery existed, that could have afforded me so good a place of concealment.

Brent's position in the garret—above ground level, unseen while being able to see within and across the plantation—quietly critiques and undoes traditional geographies. While she is in the garret, Brent undermines the patriarchal logic of visualization by erasing herself from the immediate landscape and *knowing* what she terms "a different story."

In the garret, in the last place they thought of, Linda Brent articulates the hidden spaces that are antagonistic to transparent space. The combination of perspective, disabling bodily pain, emancipation, and the racial-sexual violence outside the garret allow Brent to tell a different story, which is in the shape of mystery, a conundrum, a sense of place that explores alternative geographic options within and through racial-sexual oppressions. That black women's geographies are not easily resolvable for Brent is not surprising. The ways in which the paradoxical space of the garret and her individual spatial predicaments are presented in *Incidents in the Life of a Slave Girl* mark the tensions of geography rather than a simple solution to geographic domination. While Brent is concealed, looking outward into the landscape of terror and transparency, it is also very clear that her oppositional place in the garret remains punishable. What her geographies tell us—about the shape of mystery, spatial conundrums, a different sense of place, and racial-sexual particularities—are relevant, in part, because the question of geographic freedom is tied to the dismal perimeters of the garret and the threat of actions that would be taken by Flint *if* Brent were to be found and recaptured. Brent's desired place cannot be fully resolved on the existing geographic terms laid out for her; she rightly notes that, where slavery exists, there is no place that is wholly liberatory. Thus, while the geographic organization of blackness and black femininity are not dramatically shifted in Brent's narrative, her sense of place is useful in introducing the workings of racial-sexual displacement because her story is not only multifaceted, her geographic accounts from the garret illustrate what can and is manifested in "the last place they thought of," particularly when her oppositional geographies are caught up in violent geographic arrangements.

The last place they thought of hides Jacobs's/Brent's body, but the garret does not foreclose her geographic strategies and critiques. Indeed, this story presents a new kind of spatial positioning, through which her body is painfully protected deep within the crevices of power. A critical geographic reconfiguration is exposed—a terrain of struggle, which spans seven years and centralizes the terms under which Jacobs/Brent can bring her self into being across uneven geographies.

HOW BODILY GEOGRAPHY CAN BE

The history of the black diaspora converges with bodily schemas and racial codes. Most obviously, the geographies of transatlantic slavery were geographies of black dispossession and white supremacy, which assumed racial inferiority and justified enslavement. Geographies such as the slave ship, the slave auction block, slave coffles, and the plantation, are just some of the sites that spatialized domination under bondage. In particular, the ties between ownership and blackness rendered the black body a commodity, a site of embodied property, through ideological and economic exchanges. For black women, this legacy of captivity and ownership illustrates how bodily geography can be. Ownership of black women during transatlantic slavery was a spatialized, gendered, often public, violence; the black female body was viewed as a naturally submissive, sexually available, public, reproductive technology. The owned and captive body was thus most profitable if it was considered to be a healthy, working, licentious, reproductive body. These characteristics were considered measurable and quantifiable, seeable sites of wealth, sexuality, and punishment. Geographically, in the most crude sense, the body is territorialized—it is publicly and financially claimed, owned, and controlled by an outsider. Territorialization marks and names the scale of the body, turning ideas that justify bondage into corporeal evidence of racial difference.

Once the racial-sexual body is territorialized, it is marked as decipherable and knowable—as subordinate, inhuman, rape-able, deviant, procreative, placeless; or, to borrow from Dionne Brand, "the exposed, betrayed, valiant, and violated female self, the vulnerable and fearful, the woman waiting for the probable invasion" is made known through her bodily markings. Challenging these knowable bodily markers—asserting, for example that blackness does not warrant rape-ability—was/is punishable. Objectified black female sexualities represent the logical outcome of a spatial process that

is bound up in geographic discourses, such as territory, body/land possession, and public property. Geographic conquest and expansion is extended to the reproductive and sexually available body. Black women's own experiential and material geographies, consequently, indicate a very complex and difficult relationship with space, place, and dispossession.

I am interested in thinking about the "close ties" between black women and geography because the connection reveals, as mentioned, how bodily geography can be. While the geographies of black women are certainly not always about flesh, or embodiment, the legacy of racism and sexism demonstrates how social systems organize seeable or public bodily differences. The creative work of poet and theorist Marlene Nourbese Philip illustrates how black femininity, as a seeable body-scale, comes to be understood through uneven geographies and resistances.

Philip's figuring of black women's geographies moves between two important bodily processes: the social construction of "the space between the legs" and the racial-patriarchal uses of the space between the legs. Because female slave bodies are transformed into profitable sexual and reproductive technologies, they come to represent "New World" inventions and are consequently rendered axiomatic public objects. Black women are *the* mechanics of slavery:

> Between. The legs. The Black woman comes to the New World with only the body. And the space between. The European buys her not only for her strength, but also to service the Black man sexually—to keep him calm. And to produce new chattels—units of production—for the plantation machine. The Black woman. And the space between her legs. Is intended to help repopulate the outer space.[2]

By centralizing black women's reproductive organs, capacities, and sexualities—units of production—Philip locates where, and how, black women are situated in the creation of New World spaces. The spatialization of black femininity as "only the body" and "service" shows how black women's sense of place *and* those who see/consume the black body can be ensnared by the racial workings of sex and sexuality. She positions black women firmly in a body space that not only repeats Western

Enlightenment binaries of sexual difference (female = passive, all body) but also one that emphasizes the strong working body purchased for arduous physical and reproductive labor. Philip's analysis of the black body and the space between the legs shows how the logic of visualization, or the seeable black female body, naturalizes sexual difference and distinguishes black women from white women and men and black men. But the construction and uses of the space between the legs also disrupts normalized gender categories (male-aggressive, female-passive, male-public, female-private), which are predicated on whiteness. Specifically, the kind of black femininity Philip describes moves "between" white and nonwhite patriarchal gender categories. Not an innocent site of private passivity and respectability nor a wholly public and/or rational self, but rather a collection of ideological scripts that assert objecthood: useable, public, psychically empty, working-technology. This puts forth a complicated bodily geography, which troubles discussions outlined by some feminists and feminist geographers because it cannot easily reside within white gendered dichotomies. Importantly, Philip denaturalizes and subverts sites of white femininity and masculinity by outlining the complexities of naturalized and resistant black selves. She identifies the space between the legs as a real and an analytical geography, one which can name and/or alter body hierarchies. Philip places "displacement" and the "in between" by giving it flesh, violence, a history, and a voice.

The links Marlene Nourbese Philip makes between racist ideologies and embodiment, or social constructions and lived experiences, are also crucial. She emphasizes the different ways gender is lived via the experiential scale of the body in order to further denaturalize essentialist black places and spaces.

The "silence of the space between the legs" is not only written out and made available through Philip's poetic framework, it is also deeply connected to the physical landscape and the actual movement of bodies: real bodies are mutilated, bought, sold, trafficked; they also metropolize, industrialize, and create wealth. The enforced movement and placement of the space between the legs contributes to the built environment and colonization.

The space in between the legs symbolically, materially and physically goes several directions at once: it moves *out* of the body and reinscribes the invention of the black woman/woman-slave as knowable reproductive machine; it re-enters her body and shapes her captivity and other geographic material conditions; it subverts inner/outer and active/passive dichotomies by speaking through time/place/histories; it reproduces New World children; and, it signifies threat, reclamation and violation. So while the feminine black body is seemingly kept in place via "the space in between her legs" (inner space, oppressive definitions of the racial-sexual body), the space between the legs constructs contextual and subjective outsides. Gender position is rewritten and contested; the speaking body is unsilenced through the invention of S/Place:

> S/Place. Where the inner space is defined into passivity by, and harnessed to, the needs and functions of the outer space—the place of oppression. Run it down even further into Caribbean English: s/place mutates into "dis place." *"Dis place"*: the outer space—the plantation, the New World. *"Dis Place"*: the result of the linking of the inner space between the legs with the outer space leading to "dis placement." *"Dis Place"*—the space between. The legs. For the Black woman "dis placed" to and in the New World, the inner space between the legs would also mutate into *"dis place"*—the fulcrum of the New World.

S/Place, dis place, this place, is the body and mind coalescing to represent the places of black women in the New World. The geography of the body touches elsewhere—it moves between the local (the inner space between the legs), the outside (the place of oppression, the plantation), the New World, and circles back again to reinvent black (female/New World) diaspora histories. Philip negotiates her way out of transparent or knowable flesh by mobilizing bodily histories that demonstrate how identity and place are mutually constructed. While she notes the ways in which identity, space, and place are flexible and socially produced, geography remains a struggle for black women because racist-sexist schemas are also recyclable, lasting, and spatially rigorous.

Body disruptions, texts, histories, and inter/uptions demonstrate that the space between the legs is an analytically, historically, and socially produced category. Understood this way, terrains *outside* black women's bodies and produced by and through black femininity are also analytical, historical, socially produced— and therefore alterable.

GARRETING

In "Mama's Baby, Papa's Maybe: An American Grammar Book," Hortense Spillers writes that the life of Harriet Jacobs/Linda Brent is a story of "garreting." Spillers argues that Jacobs's slave narrative enables an exploration of black women's histories and lives, which are in "not-quite spaces."

The "not-quite" spaces of black femininity are unacknowledged spaces of sexual violence, stereotype, and sociospatial marginalization: erased, erasable, hidden, resistant geographies and women that are, due to persistent and public forms of objectification, not readily decipherable.

The process of garreting begins to get at the geographic projection of black femininity by locating what black women bring to bear on geographic negotiations: racist-sexist ideologies that mark black women as "not-quite" legitimate world citizens; practices of domination that regard black women's histories and lives as expendable; unacknowledged body-geographies that are integral to the production of white and nonwhite spaces; and oppositional paradoxical spaces. What is even more interesting to me about Spillers's essay are ways in which she signals how black women's geographies (post-Jacobs) are garretings—they are still unresolved because of the impact the black female body does and does not have upon traditional geographic arrangements. Black women's geographies still rest on those "not-quite" spaces and the "different stories" of displacement—but this is a workable and "insurgent" geography, which is produced in tandem with practices of domination. While "Mama's Baby, Papa's Maybe" is not a treatise on garreting per se, Spillers's grammatical decision—to transform the garret into a verb—within the context of her essay is important to address, in that it sets up the aforementioned tensions (the conundrums and antagonistic hidden geographies) as a genealogical geographic practice specific to black women. Ultimately, she identifies the meaningfulness of Jacobs's/

Brent's garret and opens up the question of symbolic, imaginative, and/or political geographic work the garret can do beyond the attic. Black women's knowable sense of place is often still found "in the last place they thought of," across the logic of white and patriarchal maps. But this different sense of place has been cast as a politicized location—peripheral standpoints, special vantage points, margins— through which the violence, the bodily histories, and the limitations of traditional geographic arrangements are mapped. I have recast it as "the last place they thought of"; geographies of black femininity that are not necessarily marginal, but are *central to* how we know and understand space and place: black women's geographies are workable and lived subaltern spatialities, which tell a different geographic story.

NOTES

1 Harriet A. Jacobs [Linda Brent], *Incidents in the Life of a Slave Girl: Written by Herself.* Linda Brent is the pseudonym Jacobs used to conceal her identity in *Incidents in the Life of a Slave Girl.* Born in slavery, Jacobs could read and write; the text was produced with the assistance of Lydia Marie Child.

2 Marlene Nourbese Philip, "Dis Place— The Space Between," *A Genealogy of Resistance and Other Essays,* 74.

REFERENCES

Jacobs, Harriet A. *Incidents in the Life of a Slave Girl: Written by Herself.* Jean Fagan Yellin, ed. Cambridge, MA, and London: Harvard University Press, [1861] 1987.

Philip, Marlene Nourbese. *A Genealogy of Resistance and Other Essays.* Toronto: The Mercury Press, 1997.

Spillers, Hortense. "Mama's Baby, Papa's Maybe: An American Grammar Book." In Angelyn Mitchell, ed., *Within the Circle: An Anthology of African American Criticism from the Harlem Renaissance to the Present,* pp. 454–481. Durham, NC, and London: Duke University Press, 1994.

52
Class Struggle on Avenue B
The Lower East Side as Wild Wild West (1996)

Neil Smith

On the evening of August 6, 1988, a riot erupted along the edges of Tompkins Square Park, a small green in New York City's Lower East Side. It raged through the night with police on one side and a diverse mix of anti-gentrification protestors, punks, housing activists, park inhabitants, artists, Saturday night revelers and Lower East Side residents on the other. The battle followed the city's attempt to enforce a 1:00 A.M. curfew in the park on the pretext of clearing out the growing numbers of homeless people living or sleeping there, kids playing boom boxes late into the night, buyers and sellers of drugs using it for business. But many local residents and park users saw the action differently. The city was seeking to tame and domesticate the park to facilitate the already rampant gentrification on the Lower East Side. "GENTRIFICATION IS CLASS WAR!" read the largest banner at the Saturday night demonstration aimed at keeping the park open. "Class war, class war, die yuppie scum!" went the chant. "Yuppies and real estate magnates have declared war on the people of Tompkins Square Park," announced one speaker. "Whose fucking park? It's our fucking park," became the recurrent slogan. Even the habitually restrained *New York Times* echoed the theme in its August 10 headline: "Class War Erupts along Avenue B."

Prior to the riot of August 1988, more than fifty homeless people, evictees from the private and public spaces of the official housing market, had begun to use the park regularly as a place to sleep. In the months following, the number of evictees settling in the park grew, as the loosely organized antigentrification and squatters' movements began to connect with other local

housing groups. And some of the evictees attracted to the newly "liberated space" of Tompkins Square Park also began to organize. But the city also slowly regrouped. City-wide park curfews (abandoned after the riot) were gradually reinstated; new regulations governing the use of Tompkins Square Park were slowly implemented; several Lower East Side buildings occupied by squatters were demolished in May 1989, and in July a police raid destroyed tents, shanties and the belongings of park residents. By now there were on average some 300 evictees in the park on any given night, at least three-quarters men, the majority African-American, many white, some Latino, Native Americans, Caribbean. On December 14, 1989, on the coldest day of the winter, the park's entire homeless population was evicted from the park, their belongings and fifty shanties hauled away into a queue of Sanitation Department garbage trucks.

It would be "irresponsible to allow the homeless to sleep outdoors" in such cold weather, explained a disingenuous parks commissioner, Henry J. Stern, who did not mention that the city shelter system had beds for only a quarter of the city's homeless people. In fact, the city's provision for the evicted ran only to a "help center" that, by one account, "proved to be little more than a dispensary for baloney sandwiches" (Weinberg 1990). Many evictees from the park were taken in by local squats, others set up encampments in the neighborhood, but quickly they filtered back to Tompkins Square. In January 1990 the administration of supposedly progressive mayor David Dinkins felt sufficiently confident of the park's eventual recapture that it announced a "reconstruction plan." In the next summer the basketball courts at the north end were dismantled and rebuilt with tighter control of access; wire fences closed off newly constructed children's playgrounds; and park regulations began to be more strictly enforced. In an effort to force evictions, city agencies also heightened their harassment of squatters who now spearheaded the anti-gentrification movement. As the next winter closed in, though, more and more of the city's evictees came back to the park and began again to construct semi-permanent structures.

In May 1991, the park hosted a Memorial Day concert organized under the slogan "Housing is a human right" and, in what was becoming an annual May ritual, a further clash with park users ensued. It was now nearly three years since protestors had taken the park, and, with almost a hundred shanties, tents and other structures now in Tompkins Square, the Dinkins administration decided to move. The authorities finally closed the park at 5:00 A.M. on June 3, 1991, evicting between 200 and 300 park dwellers. Alleging that Tompkins Square had been "stolen" from the community by "the homeless," Mayor Dinkins declared: "The park is a park. It is not a place to live" (quoted in Kifner 1991). An eight-foot-high chain-link fence was erected, a posse of more than fifty uniformed and plainclothes police was delegated to guard the park permanently—its numbers augmented to several hundred in the first days and during demonstrations—and a $2.3 million reconstruction was begun almost immediately. In fact, three park entrances were kept open and heavily guarded: two provided access to the playgrounds for children only (and accompanying adults); the other, opposite the Christodora condominium, provided access to the dog run. The closure of the park, commented *Village Voice* reporter Sarah Ferguson, marked the "death knell" of an occupation that "had come to symbolize the failure of the city to cope with its homeless population" (Ferguson 1991). No alternative housing was offered evictees from the park; people again moved into local squats, or filtered out into the city.

As the site of the most militant antigentrification struggle in the United States (but see Mitchell 1995), the ten acres of Tompkins Square Park quickly became a symbol of a new urbanism being etched on the urban "frontier." Largely abandoned to the working

class amid postwar suburban expansion, relinquished to the poor and unemployed as reservations for racial and ethnic minorities, the terrain of the inner city is suddenly valuable again, perversely profitable. This new urbanism embodies a widespread and drastic repolarization of the city along political, economic, cultural and geographical lines since the 1970s, and is integral with larger global shifts. Systematic gentrification since the 1960s and 1970s is simultaneously a response and contributor to a series of wider global transformations: global economic expansion in the 1980s; the restructuring of national and urban economies in advanced capitalist countries toward services, recreation and consumption; and the emergence of a global hierarchy of world, national and regional cities. These shifts have propelled gentrification from a comparatively marginal preoccupation in a certain niche of the real estate industry to the cutting edge of urban change.

Nowhere are these forces more evident than in the Lower East Side. Even the neighborhood's different names radiate the conflicts. Referred to as *Loisaida* in local Puerto Rican Spanish, the Lower East Side name is dropped altogether by real estate agents and art world gentrifiers who, anxious to distance themselves from the historical association with the poor immigrants who dominated this community at the turn of the century, prefer "East Village" as the name for the neighborhood above Houston Street. Squeezed between the Wall Street financial district and Chinatown to the south, the Village and SoHo to the west, Gramercy Park to the north and the East River to the east, the Lower East Side feels the pressure of this political polarization more acutely than anywhere else in the city.

Highly diverse but increasingly Latino since the 1950s, the neighborhood was routinely described in the 1980s as a "new frontier" (Levin 1983). It mixes spectacular opportunity for real estate investors with an edge of daily danger on the streets. In the words of local writers, the Lower East Side is variously a "frontier where the urban fabric is wearing thin and splitting open" (Rose and Texier 1988: xi) or else "Indian country, the land of murder and cocaine" (Charyn 1985: 7). Not just supporters but antagonists have found this frontier imagery irresistible. "As the neighborhood slowly, inexorably gentrifies," wrote one reporter, in the wake of the 1988 police riot, "the park is a holdout, the place for one last metaphorical stand" (Carr 1988: 17).

BUILDING THE FRONTIER MYTH

The social meaning of gentrification is increasingly constructed through the vocabulary of the frontier myth, and at first glance this appropriation of language and landscape might seem simply playful, innocent. Newspapers habitually extol the courage of urban "homesteaders," the adventurous spirit and rugged individualism of the new settlers, brave "urban pioneers," presumably going where, in the words of *Star Trek,* no (white) man has ever gone before.

As new frontier, the gentrifying city since the 1980s has been oozing with optimism. Hostile landscapes are regenerated, cleansed, reinfused with middle-class sensibility; real estate values soar; yuppies consume; elite gentility is democratized in mass-produced styles of distinction. So what's not to like? The contradictions of the actual frontier are not entirely eradicated in this imagery but they are smoothed into an acceptable groove. As with the Old West, the frontier is idyllic yet also dangerous, romantic but also ruthless.

The frontier imagery is neither merely decorative nor innocent, therefore, but carries considerable ideological weight. Insofar as gentrification infects working-class communities, displaces poor households, and converts whole neighborhoods into bourgeois enclaves, the frontier ideology rationalizes social differentiation and exclusion as natural, inevitable. The poor and working class are all too easily defined as "uncivil," on the wrong side of a heroic dividing line, as savages and communists. The substance and consequence of the frontier imagery is to tame the wild city, to socialize a wholly new and therefore challenging set of processes into safe ideological focus. As such, the frontier ideology justifies monstrous incivility in the heart of the city.

SELLING LOISAIDA

On the Lower East Side two industries defined the new urban frontier that emerged in the 1980s. Indispensable, of course, is the real estate industry which christened the northern part of the Lower East Side the "East Village" in order to capitalize on its geographical proximity to the respectability, security, culture and high rents of Greenwich Village. Then there is the culture industry—art dealers and patrons, gallery owners and artists, designers and critics, writers and performers—which has converted urban dilapidation into ultra chic. Together in the 1980s the culture and real estate industries invaded this rump of Manhattan from the west. Gentrification and art came hand in hand, "slouching toward Avenue D," as art critics Walter Robinson and Carlo McCormick (1984) put it. Block by block, building by building, the area was converted to a landscape of glamor and chic spiced with just a hint of danger.

The most insightful critique of this connection between art and real estate remains that by Rosalyn Deutsche and Cara Ryan in a classic article, "The fine art of gentrification" (Deutsche and Ryan 1984). The complicity of art with gentrification is no mere serendipity, they show, but "has been constructed with the aid of the entire apparatus of the art establishment." Linking the rise of the "East Village" with the triumph of neo-Expressionism in art, they argue that however countercultural its pose, the broad abstention from political self-reflection condemned Lower East Side art to reproducing the dominant culture. The unprecedented commodification of art in the 1980s engendered an equally ubiquitous aestheticization of culture and politics: graffiti came off the trains and into the galleries, while the most outrageous punk and new-wave styles moved rapidly from the streets to full-page advertisements in *The New York Times.* The press began sporting stories about the opulence of the new art scene—at least for some: Don't let the poverty of the Lower East Side fool you, was the message; this generation of young artists gets by with American Express Goldcards (Bernstein 1990).

The simultaneous disavowal of social and political context and dependence on the cultural establishment placed avant-garde artists in a sharply contradictory position. They came to function as "broker" between the culture industry and the majority of still-aspiring artists. Lower East Side galleries played the pivotal role: they provided the meeting place for grassroots ambition and talent and establishment money (Owens 1984: 162–163).[1] Representing and patronizing the neighborhood as a cultural mecca, the culture industry attracted tourists, consumers, gallery gazers, art patrons, potential immigrants—all fueling gentrification.

For the real estate industry, art tamed the neighborhood, refracting back a mock pretense of exotic but benign danger. It depicted the East Village as rising from low life to high brow. Art donates a salable neighborhood "personality," packaged the area as a real estate commodity and established demand. Indeed, "the story of the East Village's newest bohemian efflorescence," it has been suggested, "can also be read as an episode in New York's real estate history—that is, as the deployment of a force of gentrifying artists in lower Manhattan's last slum" (Robinson and McCormick 1984: 135).

PIONEERING FOR PROFIT

In his investigation of the workings of the Lower East Side real estate market, journalist Martin Gottlieb uncovered the results of the rent gap first hand. At 270 East Tenth Street, for example, while the combined sale price of building and land soared from $5,706 to $202,600 in five and a half years, the value of the building alone, according to city property tax assessors, actually fell from $26,000 to $18,000. And this is a typical result; even taking into account the structured undervaluation of buildings vis-à-vis the market, the land is much more valuable than the building. The perverse rationality of real estate capitalism means that building owners and developers garner a double reward for milking properties and destroying buildings. First, they pocket the money that should have gone to repairs and upkeep; second, having effectively destroyed the building and established a rent gap, they have produced for themselves the conditions and opportunity for a whole new round of capital reinvestment. Having produced a scarcity of capital in the name of profit they now flood the neighborhood for the same purpose, portraying themselves all along as civic-minded heroes, pioneers taking a risk where no one else would venture, builders of a new city for the worthy populace. In Gottlieb's words, this self-induced reversal in the market means that a "Lower East Side landlord can drink his milk and have it too" (Gottlieb 1982).

The economic geography of gentrification is not random; developers do not just plunge into the heart of slum opportunity, but tend to take it piece by piece. Rugged pioneersmanship is tempered by financial caution. Developers have a vivid block-by-block sense of where the frontier lies. They move in from the outskirts, building "a few strategically placed outposts of luxury," as Henwood (1988: 10) has put it. They "pioneer" first on the gold coast between safe neighborhoods on one side where property values are high and the disinvested slums on the other where opportunity is higher. Successive beachheads and defensible borders are established on the frontier. In this way economic geography charts the strategy of urban pioneering.

If the real estate cowboys invading the Lower East Side in the 1980s used art to paint their economic quest in romantic hues, they also enlisted the cavalry of city government for more prosaic tasks: reclaiming the land and quelling the natives. In its housing policy, drug crackdowns, and especially in its parks strategy, the city devoted its efforts not toward providing basic services and living opportunities for existing residents but toward routing many of the locals and subsidizing opportunities for real estate development. A 1982 consultants' report entitled *An Analysis of Investment Opportunities in the East Village* captured the city's strategy precisely: "The city has now given clear signals that it is prepared to aid the return of the middle class by auctioning city-owned properties and sponsoring projects in gentrifying areas to bolster its tax base and aid the revitalization process" (Oreo Construction Services 1982).

The city's major resource was its stock of "*in rem*" properties, mostly foreclosed from private landlords for nonpayment of property taxes. By the early 1980s the Department of Housing, Preservation and Development held over 200 such *in rem* buildings in the Lower East Side and a similar number of lots.

HPD would sell city-owned properties to developers, either by auction or at appraised value, in return for an agreement by developers that a vaguely specified 20 percent of rehabilitated or newly built units would be reserved for tenants unable to afford market rates. Developers would receive a tax subsidy in return. Initially some community groups gave the program tentative support; others sought to adjust the ratio of market rate to subsidized housing to 50:50, while others rejected the entire idea as a backdoor route to building minimal public housing.

"ANOTHER WAVE MORE SAVAGELY THAN THE FIRST": THE NEW (GLOBAL) INDIAN WARS?

Gentrification portends a class conquest of the city. The new urban pioneers seek to scrub the city clean of its working-class geography and history. By remaking the geography of the city they simultaneously rewrite its social history as a preemptive justification for a new urban future. Slum tenements become historic brownstones, and exterior facades are sandblasted to reveal a future past. Likewise with interior renovation. "Inner worldly asceticism becomes public display" as "bare brick walls and exposed timbers come to signify cultural discernment, not the poverty of slums without plaster" (Jager 1986: 79–80, 83, 85). Physical effacement of original structures effaces social history and geography; if the past is not entirely demolished it is at least reinvented—its class and race contours rubbed smooth—in the refurbishment of a palatable past.

The dramatic shifts affecting gentrifying neighborhoods are experienced as intensely local. The Lower East Side is a world away from the upper-crust *noblesse* of the Upper East Side three miles north; and within the neighborhood, Avenue C is still a very different place from First Avenue. Yet the processes and forces shaping the new urbanism are global as much as local. Gentrification and homelessness in the new city are a particular microcosm of a new global order etched first and foremost by the rapacity of capital. Not only are broadly similar processes remaking cities around the world, but the world itself impinges dramatically on these localities. The gentrification frontier is also an "imperial frontier," says Kristin Koptiuch (1991: 87–89). Not only does international capital flood the real estate markets that fuel the process, but international migration provides a workforce for many of the professional and managerial jobs associated with the new urban economy—a workforce that needs a place to stay. Even more does international migration provide the service workers for the new economy: in New York, greengrocers are now mainly Korean; the plumbers fitting gentrified buildings are often Italian, the carpenters Polish; the domestic workers and nannies looking after the houses and children of gentrifiers come from El Salvador, Barbados or elsewhere in the Caribbean.

Immigrants come to the city from every country where US capital has opened markets, disrupted local economies, extracted resources, removed people from the land, or sent the marines as a "peace-keeping force" (Sassen 1998). This global dislocation comes home to roost in the "Third-Worlding" of the US city (Franco 1985; Koptiuch 1991), which, combined with the threat of increasing crime and repressive policing of the streets, invites visions of a predacious assault on the very gentrification that it helped to stimulate.

"As if straight out of some sci-fi plot," writes Koptiuch (1991), "the wild frontiers dramatized in early travel accounts have been moved so far out and away that, to our unprepared astonishment, they have imploded right back in our midst."

As homes and communities are converted into a new frontier, there is an often clear perception of what is coming as the wagons are circled around. Frontier violence comes with cavalry charges down city streets, rising official crime rates, police racism and assaults on the "natives." And it comes with the periodic torching of homeless people as they sleep, presumably to get them "out of sight."

It is difficult to be optimistic that the next wave of gentrification will bring a new urban order more civilized than the first.

NOTE

1   Despite his critique, Owens (1984: 163) cops out at the end: "Artists are not, of course, responsible for 'gentrification'; they are often its victims." As Deutsche and Ryan comment: "To portray artists as the victims of gentrification is to mock the plight of the neighborhood's real victims" (1984: 104).

REFERENCES

Bernstein, Richard. 1990. "Why the cutting edge has lost its bite," *New York Times,* September 30.

Carr, Cynthia. 1988. "Night clubbing: reports from the Tompkins Square Police Riot," *Village Voice,* August 16.

Charyn, Jerome. 1985. *War Cries over Avenue C,* New York: Donald I. Fine, Inc.

Deutsche, Rosalyn. and Ryan, Cara G. 1984. "The fine art of gentrification," *October* 31: 91–111.

Ferguson, Sarah. 1991. "The park is gone," *Village Voice,* June 18.

Franco, Jean. 1985. "New York is a third world city," *Tabloid* 9:12–19.

Gottlieb, Martin. 1982. "Space invaders: land grab on the Lower East Side," *Village Voice,* December 14.

Henwood, Doug. 1988. "Subsidizing the rich," *Village Voice,* August 30.

Jager, M. 1986. "Class definition and the aesthetics of gentrification: Victoriana in Melbourne," in N.Smith and P.Williams (eds) *Gentrification of the City,* Boston, MA: Allen & Unwin.

Kifner, John. 1991. "New York closes park to homeless," *New York Times,* June 4.

Koptiuch, Kristin. 1991. "Third-worlding at home," *Social Text* 28:87–99.

Levin, Kim. 1983. "The neo-frontier," *Village Voice,* January 4.

Mitchell, Don. 1995. "The end of public space? People's Park, definitions of the public, and democracy," *Annals of the Association of American Geographers* 85(1):108–133.

Oreo Construction Services. 1982. "An analysis of investment opportunities in the East Village."

Owens, Craig. 1984. "Commentary: The problem with puerilism," *Art in America* 72(6): 162–163.

Robinson, Walter and McCormick, Carlo. 1984. "Slouching toward Avenue D," *Art in America* 72(6):135–161.

Rose, Joel. and Texier, Catherine. (eds) 1988. *Between C & D: New Writing from the Lower East Side Fiction Magazine,* New York: Penguin.

Sassen, Saskia. 1988. *The Mobility of Labour and Capital,* Cambridge: Cambridge University Press.

Weinberg, Bill. 1990. "Is gentrification genocide? Squatters build an alternative vision for the Lower East Side," *Downtown 181,* February 14.

SECTION 10

Shifting Perspectives

Optics for Revealing Change and Reworking Space

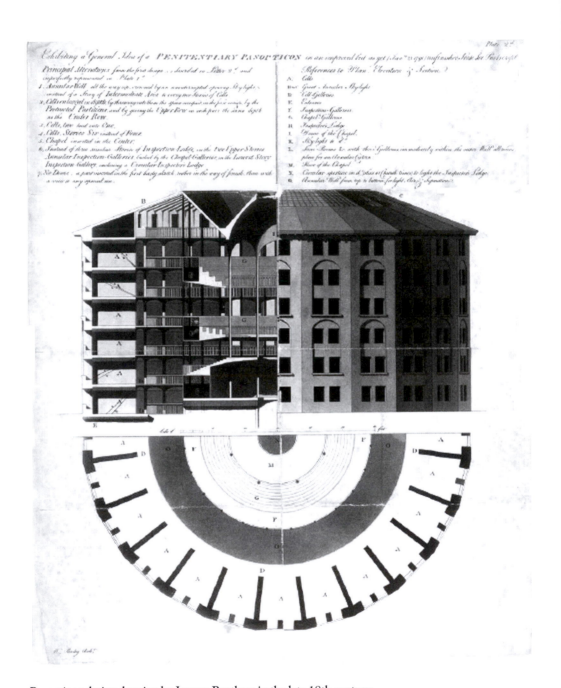

Panopticon design drawing by Jeremy Bentham in the late 18th century.
Source: Bentham Collection, University College London Library.
Reference to: Foucault, Michel. 1995 [1975]. "Panopticism," in *Discipline & Punish: The Birth of the Prison*. New York: Vintage, pp. 195–228.

SHIFTING PERSPECTIVES:
Optics for Revealing Change and Reworking Space

It is easy to overlook the patterns and spaces that shape our everyday activities and decisions. Likewise, it is often easier to grasp abuses of justice in faraway places, but fail to consider similar injustices closer to home. Probing such issues of (in)visibility can reveal the story of a place, expose what's there to be seen if only we pay attention. The pieces in this section do precisely that to revitalize old narratives; rethink traditional mores and norms; and think through the implications of shifting cultural, political, and economic values. Studies of space and place can alter our point of view or "optics" to unveil hidden ideologies that structure our everyday lives as the title for this section suggests. Such scholarship can enable what art critic John Berger (1990) calls new *ways of seeing*, and uncover what anthropologist James C. Scott (1992) refers to as *hidden transcripts*. The ability to reveal and rework the way in which we perceive and experience space raises consciousness, offers more hopeful narratives of inhabitance, and provides alternative ways to read, see, and live space and place. Spatial relationships can mask or reveal unjust situations, and looking closely at these conditions can allow people to see the world again and anew.

The work of the philosopher **Michel Foucault** offers often breathtaking reconceptualizations of the workings of power, knowledge, sexuality, and the spaces and social institutions of comportment. In this selection, Foucault describes the *panopticon*, a guard tower in the center of a circular prison with all cells facing inward, based on an 18th-century design by architect Jeremy Bentham (see figure at the beginning of Section 10). While never officially built as such, the panopticon presents the possibility of total surveillance, which Foucault uses as a jumping-off point for examining "modern disciplinary society." The panopticon is structured so that guards can observe any and all cells without being seen, and so all prisoners can see one another. While the prisoners are all effectively watching each other, at any time the guard may be watching them. The form—spatial and social—elicits self-discipline. Foucault argues that this pattern of self-regulation and surveillance is instrumental not only in architecture and planning, but also in social, economic, and political practices. He is less concerned with the panopticon as an actual space, focusing on it as a structure of surveillance and power that permeates society. He contends that disciplinary power frames social relations and shapes what people are able to know or do. Foucault refers to these disciplining material social practices as *technologies*, and shows how they are employed to reinforce hegemonic ideas and social norms.

In a related register, architect and critic **Juhani Pallasmaa** is concerned about the "hegemony of the marketable image." He argues that designers have privileged the sense of sight and emphasize two-dimensional renderings of buildings, at the expense of creating multi-sensory experiences of space. By attending more to the sale value of the image rather than the tactility and social value of an environment, architecture, he argues, gives up its role in crafting places of meaning. Taking architects and designers to task, Pallasmaa supplies a critique of contemporary image production and the commodification of built space. He argues instead for drawing upon the sense of touch, or *haptic experience*, and slowing down to engage all the senses (see also O'Neill 2001). Pallasmaa suggests that only by taking account of both our *ocular-centricity* and a fully embodied experience can architects and designers fulfill their social responsibilities and "strengthen the reliability and comprehensibility of the world."

The question of social responsibility is at the heart of many of the scholars' work in this section as their research to reveal injustice also invokes a call to action. Environmental degradation and environmental health hazards are often more pronounced among poor people and people of color. In 1987 a landmark study by the United Church of Christ looking at patterns of environmental hazards and dumping found that people of color bore these ills in significant disproportion to other groups. Decades later this trend continues even as writing and activism concerned with environmental justice has become more prominent. Geographer and American Studies scholar **Laura Pulido** here examines the persistence of environmental injustice in Los Angeles, California. Her findings expose the unequal harms of environmental racism. She argues compellingly that rather than using the concepts of race and racism to examine these patterns, the lens of white privilege offers a clearer spatial and structural approach to these vexing questions. Seeing the uneven landscape of environmental degradation through white privilege unmasks inequalities in the production of space more generally, and the ways in which these patterns benefit white people while people of color suffer higher rates of disease and illness in consequence.

Injustice is rarely confined to any one space. Scholarship on mobilities has revolutionized the way in which we understand movement through space and the flow of information, bodies, and commodities across space and time. In this selection, **Kevin Hannam, Mimi Sheller,** and **John Urry** address the space-time of movement through a sociological and geographical framework. Drawing upon the events of September 11, 2001, the authors outline an interdependent framework of *mobilities*, *immobilities*, and *moorings* that shape our everyday lives, including the ways in which privilege and position infuse the space-time of motion, pause, and fixity. Hannam, Sheller, and Urry describe how our expectations of fixed spaces such as a country's borders are erroneous, demonstrating how every thing and every being is at least partially on the move, from diseases to airplanes, bodies to territorial borders, database information to economic capital.

These selections advance arguments that span the local to the global and back again, but does a focus on injustice at one scale obscure what happens at another? Might attention to scalar questions reveal the connections among injustices and the responses to them? The geographical concept of *scale*, and particularly the production of scale, can illuminate such robust understandings of social, political, and economic power relations. While geographers originally conceptualized scale as essentially given—a nested hierarchy descending from the global, national, and urban scales—critical geographers challenged this simple categorization to argue that scale, like all aspects of space, is socially produced and constantly shifting (Smith 1992; Marston 2000). Critical feminist geographer **Geraldine Pratt** and literary theorist **Victoria Rosner** have reimagined scale in a more fused way to show how scales are permeated with one another. In this selection, the authors work from the feminist maxim that the "personal is political" to trouble the binary of global/local, most especially in the ways in which it parallels notions of masculine/feminine. Pratt and Rosner's compelling notion of *the global and the intimate* reveals the ways in which geographic scales infuse one another in the people's experience and action. In their framework, intimate relations are simultaneously global and local, just as the global is experienced in and through the intimate and all the scales in between.

If scale distinguishes a sort of verticality of spatial experience, geographers have also conceptualized lateral relationships among distinct places to recognize similarities of experience. Employing a theoretical method which she terms *countertopography*, critical geographer **Cindi Katz** traces the ways in which space and time unfold in disparate but interrelated political economies to expose processes that link everyday lives in seemingly distinct geographies. By examining how disinvestment and deskilling play out in a Sudanese village and the Harlem neighborhood of New York City, Katz stitches together the everyday difficulties of children traveling further and further afield to obtain the resources they need to sustain themselves and reproduce their communities. The contour lines of these counter-topographies connect places that seem quite different on the surface to reveal common analytical effects of capitalist globalization in distinct locales. These ideas suggest a corrective to Marxist geographer David Harvey's (1989) notion of *time-space compression,* which marks how the technological shifts of capitalist globalization have allowed for greater connection to more people and materials in faster ways than ever before. Katz's work makes clear that time-space compression is the experience of wealthy and powerful people and places as it reveals patterns of *time-space expansion*, whereby those with limited means under these conditions are often forced to travel further and work longer hours to simply maintain their way of life.

We, like the scholars in this section, find it useful to underscore the similarities of the obstacles and contradictions faced by people across space and place, and learn from the range of responses to these conditions. In her work along these lines Cindi Katz offers a framework that complicates resistance so that it encompasses *resilience, reworking,* as well as *resistance.* This framework suggests that change can take place in different ways, through small gestures and large. Environmental psychologist and geographer Caitlin Cahill's (2006) work takes up and questions the ways in which anyone can claim agency, self-determination, and power over their body and space. Working with young people of color in US cities, Cahill asks who possesses the agency to define which bodies and livelihoods are "at risk" and act upon those bodies and lives through policies and representations. Similarly, political scientist Richard Pithouse (2006) argues for a "politics of the poor" that identifies with the struggles of urban slum dwellers in Durban, South Africa, and refuses to script this population and their spaces as an "epidemic."

Other scholars draw upon critical theoretical frameworks to offer insights and challenges to specific material conditions. Environmental psychologist and IT designer Joan Greenbaum's (2004) scholarship builds on Foucault's critique of disciplinary power and dominant technologies by examining the use and reach of various workplace technologies. She looks at how corporations expand their oversight of workers by using such readily available things as smart phones, home computers, and so on to increase profits and control the workforce more intensely. In making a pointed critique of architectural practices in the context of contemporary capitalism, William Mangold (2014) draws upon both Harvey and Pallasmaa to elaborate on the spatial consequences when designers and inhabitants are subject to the bottom line of profit.

The scholars discussed here focus on ways in which spaces and places can be seen differently and presented anew, using these insights to create change and more just environments. As these readings make clear, particular configurations of space can foster or hide injustice, but space can also be made to reveal and reduce injustice and inequality. Exposing inequalities in and through space and spatial arrangements as well as commonalities of spatial experience, such as these pieces do, offers opportunities for contesting the status quo and organizing for change through new spatial and social practices.

SUGGESTIONS FOR FURTHER READING

Please see *peopleplacespace.org* for extended and additional lists of readings.

Berger, John. 1990. *Ways of Seeing: Based on the BBC Television Series.* New York: Penguin Books.

Boo, Katherine. 2012. *Behind the Beautiful Forevers: Life, Death, and Hope in a Mumbai Undercity*, 1st edn. New York: Random House.

Borden, Iain, Barbara Penner, and Jane Rendell (eds). 1999. *Gender Space Architecture: An Interdisciplinary Introduction.* New York: Routledge.

Browne, Kath. 2006. "Challenging Queer Geographies." *Antipode* 38(5): 885–893.

Cahill, Caitlin. 2006. "'At Risk'? The Fed Up Honeys Re-Present the Gentrification of the Lower East Side." *WSQ: Women's Studies Quarterly* 34(1/2): 334–363.

Caldeira, Teresa P.R. 2001. *City of Walls: Crime, Segregation, and Citizenship in São Paulo*. Berkeley: University of California Press.

Castells, Manuel. 1996. *The Rise of the Network Society*. New York: Blackwell.

Crang, Mike. 2000. "Public Space, Urban Space and Electronic Space: Would the Real City Please Stand Up?" *Urban Studies* 37(2): 301–317.

Fernandes, Sujatha. 2011. *Close to the Edge: In Search of the Global Hip Hop Generation*. New York: Verso.

Greenbaum, Joan M. 2004. *Windows on the Workplace: Technology, Jobs, and the Organization of Office Work*. New York: Monthly Review Press.

Harvey, David. 1989. "Time-space Compression and the Rise of Modernism as a Cultural Force." In *The Condition of Postmodernity: An Enquiry into the Origins of Cultural Change*, pp. 260–283. Malden: Wiley-Blackwell.

hooks, bell. 2003. "Choosing the Margin as a Space of Radical Openness." In *The Feminist Standpoint Theory Reader: Intellectual and Political Controversies*, edited by Sandra Harding, pp. 153–160. New York: Routledge.

Jameson, Fredric. 1990. *Postmodernism, Or, The Cultural Logic of Late Capitalism*. Raleigh, NC: Duke University Press Books.

Low, Setha. 2004. *Behind the Gates: Life, Security, and the Pursuit of Happiness in Fortress America*. New York: Routledge.

Mangold, William. 2014. "Architecture and the Vicissitudes of Capitalism." In *Architecture in the Age of Uncertainty*. London: Ashgate.

Marston, Sallie A. 2000. "The Social Construction of Scale." *Progress in Human Geography* 24(2): 219–242.

Marx, Karl, and Fredrick Engels. 1988. "Estranged Labor." In *The Economic and Philosophic Manuscripts of 1844 and the Communist Manifesto*, trans. Martin Milligan, 1st edn. New York: Prometheus Books.

O'Neill, Máire Eithne. 2001. "Corporeal Experience: A Haptic Way of Knowing." *Journal of Architectural Education* 55(1): 3–12.

Pithouse, Richard. 2006. "Thinking Resistance in the Shanty Town." *Mute* 2(3): 16–31.

Scott, James C. 1992 [1987]. *Domination and the Arts of Resistance: Hidden Transcripts*. New Haven, CT: Yale University Press.

Smith, Neil. 1992. "Geography, Difference and the Politics of Scale." In *Postmodernism and the Social Sciences*, edited by Joe Doherty, Elspeth Graham, and Mo Malek, pp. 57–78. New York: Palgrave Macmillan.

Venturi, Robert, Denise Scott Brown, and Steven Izenour. 1996. *Learning from Las Vegas. The Forgotten Symbolism of Architectural Form*. Cambridge, MA: MIT Press.

Ward, Anthony. 1996. "The Suppresion of the Social in Design." In *Reconstructing Architecture: Critical Discourses and Social Practices*. Dutton and Mann (eds). Minneopolis: University of Minnesota Press, pp. 27–58.

Wright, Melissa W. 2006. *Disposable Women and Other Myths of Global Capitalism*. New York: Routledge.

53
Panopticism

(1975)

Michel Foucault

Bentham's Panopticon is the architectural figure of this composition. We know the principle on which it was based: at the periphery, an annular building; at the centre, a tower; this tower is pierced with wide windows that open onto the inner side of the ring; the peripheric building is divided into cells, each of which extends the whole width of the building; they have two windows, one on the inside, corresponding to the windows of the tower; the other, on the outside, allows the light to cross the cell from one end to the other. All that is needed, then, is to place a supervisor in a central tower and to shut up in each cell a madman, a patient, a condemned man, a worker or a schoolboy. By the effect of backlighting, one can observe from the tower, standing out precisely against the light, the small captive shadows in the cells of the periphery. They are like so many cages, so many small theatres, in which each actor is alone, perfectly individualized and constantly visible. The panoptic mechanism arranges spatial unities that make it possible to see constantly and to recognize immediately. In short, it reverses the principle of the dungeon; or rather of its three functions—to enclose, to deprive of light and to hide—it preserves only the first and eliminates the other two. Full lighting and the eye of a supervisor capture better than darkness, which ultimately protected. Visibility is a trap.

To begin with, this made it possible—as a negative effect—to avoid those compact, swarming, howling masses that were to be found in places of confinement, those painted by Goya or described by Howard. Each individual, in his place, is securely confined to a cell from which he is seen from the front by the supervisor; but the side walls prevent him from coming into contact with his companions. He is seen, but he does not see; he is the object of information, never a subject in communication. The arrangement of his room, opposite the central tower, imposes on him an axial visibility; but the divisions of the ring, those separated cells, imply a lateral invisibility. And this invisibility is a guarantee of order. If the inmates are convicts, there is no danger of a plot, an attempt at collective escape, the planning of new crimes for the future, bad reciprocal influences; if they are patients, there is no danger of contagion; if they are madmen there is no risk of their committing violence upon one another; if they are schoolchildren, there is no copying, no noise, no chatter, no waste of time; if they are workers, there are no disorders, no theft, no coalitions, none of those distractions that slow down the rate of work, make it less perfect or cause accidents. The crowd, a compact mass, a locus of multiple exchanges, individualities merging together, a collective effect, is abolished and replaced by a collection of separated individualities. From the point of view of the guardian, it is replaced by a multiplicity that can be numbered and supervised; from the point of view of the inmates, by a sequestered and observed solitude (Bentham 1995, 60–64).

Hence the major effect of the Panopticon: to induce in the inmate a state of conscious and permanent visibility that assures the automatic functioning of power. So to arrange things that the surveillance is permanent in its effects, even if it is discontinuous in its action; that the perfection of power should tend to render its actual exercise unnecessary; that this architectural apparatus should be a machine for creating and sustaining a power relation independent of the person who exercises it; in short, that the inmates should be caught up in a power situation of which they are themselves the bearers. To achieve this, it is at once too much and too little that the prisoner should be constantly observed by an inspector: too little, for what matters is that he knows himself to be observed; too much, because he has no need in fact of being so. In view of this, Bentham laid down the principle that power should be visible and unverifiable. Visible: the inmate will constantly have before his eyes the tall outline of the central tower from which he is spied upon. Unverifiable: the inmate must never know whether he is being looked at at any one moment; but he must be sure that he may always be so. In order to make the presence or absence of the inspector unverifiable, so that the prisoners, in their cells, cannot even see a shadow, Bentham envisaged not only venetian blinds on the windows of the central observation hall, but, on the inside, partitions that intersected the hall at right angles and, in order to pass from one quarter to the other, not doors but zig-zag openings; for the slightest noise, a gleam of light, a brightness in a half-opened door would betray the presence of the guardian. The Panopticon is a machine for dissociating the see/being seen dyad: in the peripheric ring, one is totally seen, without ever seeing; in the central tower, one sees everything without ever being seen.

It is an important mechanism, for it automatizes and disindividualizes power. Power has its principle not so much in a person as in a certain concerted distribution of bodies, surfaces, lights, gazes; in an arrangement whose internal mechanisms produce the relation in which individuals are caught up. The ceremonies, the rituals, the marks by which the sovereign's surplus power was manifested are useless. There is a machinery that assures dissymmetry, disequilibrium, difference. Consequently, it does not matter who exercises power. Any individual, taken almost at random, can operate the machine: in the absence of the director, his family, his friends, his visitors, even his servants (Bentham 1995, 45). Similarly, it does not matter what motive animates him: the curiosity of the indiscreet, the malice of a child, the thirst for knowledge of a philosopher who

wishes to visit this museum of human nature, or the perversity of those who take pleasure in spying and punishing. The more numerous those anonymous and temporary observers are, the greater the risk for the inmate of being surprised and the greater his anxious awareness of being observed. The Panopticon is a marvellous machine which, whatever use one may wish to put it to, produces homogeneous effects of power.

A real subjection is born mechanically from a fictitious relation. So it is not necessary to use force to constrain the convict to good behaviour, the madman to calm, the worker to work, the schoolboy to application, the patient to the observation of the regulations. Bentham was surprised that panoptic institutions could be so light: there were no more bars, no more chains, no more heavy locks; all that was needed was that the separations should be clear and the openings well arranged. The heaviness of the old 'houses of security', with their fortress-like architecture, could be replaced by the simple, economic geometry of a 'house of certainty'. The efficiency of power, its constraining forces, have, in a sense, passed over to the other side— to the side of its surface of application. He who is subjected to a field of visibility, and who knows it, assumes responsibility for the constraints of power; he makes them play spontaneously upon himself; he inscribes in himself the power relation in which he simultaneously plays both roles; he becomes the principle of his own subjection. By this very fact, the external power may throw off its physical weight; it tends to the non-corporal; and, the more it approaches this limit, the more constant, profound and permanent are its effects: it is a perpetual victory that avoids any physical confrontation and which is always decided in advance.

Bentham does not say whether he was inspired, in his project, by Le Vaux's menagerie at Versailles: the first menagerie in which the different elements are not, as they traditionally were, distributed in a park (Loisel 1912, 104–107). At the centre was an octagonal pavilion which, on the first floor, consisted of only a single room, the king's salon; on every side large windows looked out onto seven cages (the eighth side was reserved for the entrance), containing different species of animals. By Bentham's time, this menagerie had disappeared. … the Panopticon also does the work of a naturalist. It makes it possible to draw up differences: among patients, to observe the symptoms of each individual, without the proximity of beds, the circulation of miasmas, the effects of contagion confusing the clinical tables; among schoolchildren, it makes it possible to observe performances (without there being any imitation or copying), to map aptitudes, to assess characters, to draw up rigorous classifications and, in relation to normal development, to distinguish 'laziness and stubbornness' from 'incurable imbecility'; among workers, it makes it possible to note the aptitudes of each worker, compare the time he takes to perform a task, and if they are paid by the day, to calculate their wages (Bentham 1995, 60–64).

So much for the question of observation. But the Panopticon was also a laboratory; it could be used as a machine to carry out experiments, to alter behaviour, to train or correct individuals. To experiment with medicines and monitor their effects. To try out different punishments on prisoners, according to their crimes and character, and to seek the most effective ones. To teach different techniques simultaneously to the workers, to decide which is the best. To try out pedagogical experiments—and in particular to take up once again the well-debated problem of secluded education, by using orphans. One would see what would happen when, in their sixteenth or eighteenth year, they were presented with other boys or girls; one could verify whether, as Helvetius thought, anyone could learn anything; one would follow 'the genealogy of every observable idea'; one could bring up different children according to different systems of thought, making certain children believe that two and two do not make four or that the moon is a cheese, then put them together when they are twenty or twenty-five years old; one would then have discussions that would be worth a great deal more than the sermons or lectures on which so much money is spent; one would have at least an opportunity of making discoveries in the domain of metaphysics. The Panopticon is a privileged place for experiments on men, and for analysing with complete certainty the transformations that may be obtained from them. The Panopticon may even provide an apparatus for supervising its own mechanisms. In this central tower, the director may spy on all the employees that he has under his orders: nurses, doctors, foremen, teachers, warders; he will be able to judge them continuously, alter their behaviour, impose upon them the methods he thinks best; and it will even be possible to observe the director himself. An inspector arriving unexpectedly at the centre of the Panopticon will be able to judge at a glance, without anything being concealed from him, how the entire establishment is functioning. And, in any case, enclosed as he is in the middle of this architectural mechanism, is not the director's own fate entirely bound up with it? The incompetent physician who has allowed contagion to spread, the incompetent prison governor or workshop manager will be the first victims of an epidemic or a revolt. "By every tie I could devise", said the master of the Panopticon, "my own fate had been bound up by me with theirs'" (Bentham 1995, 177). The Panopticon functions as a kind of laboratory of power. Thanks to its mechanisms of observation, it gains in efficiency and in the ability to penetrate into men's behaviour; knowledge follows the advances of power, discovering new objects of knowledge over all the surfaces on which power is exercised.

REFERENCES

Bentham, Jeremy. Panopticon. In Miran Bozovic (ed.), *The Panopticon Writings*, London: Verso, 1995.

Loisel, Gustave. *Historie des ménageries*, II, 1912.

54
Toward an Architecture of Humility
On the Value of Experience (1999)

Juhani Pallasmaa

Architectural culture, in its social context and core values, has undergone significant shifts over the past half century. When I began my studies in the late 1950s in Helsinki, the heroic Modernist mission still molded architects' collective ambitions. Architecture enjoyed high social status and positive symbolic connotations; architects were seen as the builders of our national identity. Then, beginning in the early 1960s, the postwar ideals of late-Corbusian plasticity and gravitas gave way to structural and modular clarity, prefabrication, transparency, and visual simplicity; Miesian structural classicism and traditional Japanese buildings were inspirations for an architecture of reduction and deliberate anonymity that sought to mirror industrialization.

During the decade following the Paris Spring of 1968, architecture shifted again, becoming politicized; the art of building was scorned as an elitist practice in the service of power; aesthetic yearnings were condemned. The 1980s saw a harsh questioning of Modernist ideology and a renewed interest in formalism. This decade witnessed efforts to reconstruct the identity of the architect, the self-esteem and social role of the discipline; nothing less than a new paradigm was sought.

Today, architects in Finland have largely succeeded in reestablishing a sense of professional identity and mission. And yet the tumultuous changes of recent decades continue to be felt, for the architectural profession has lost much of its prestige as well as its acknowledged position among the shapers of national culture. Indeed, the social significance of the art of architecture is now perilously tenuous. Competition over fees, new quasi-rational practices, the imperatives of cost and speed, and, perhaps most insidiously, the obsession with the image are eroding the soil of architecture.

This brief narrative of the changing values and fortunes of architects in a corner of the world where modern architecture has played an undisputed social role forms the background to my critical views of recent developments. The tendencies I describe, however, are hardly confined to Scandinavia; they appear to be universal, although they vary from place to place. Aware of the dangers of generalization, I believe we must still try to identify cultural undercurrents that inevitably influence architecture. I should acknowledge that many contemporary architects and critics, professional journals, and educational institutions are working to resist the negative influences of our time. Indubitably poetic works of architecture continue to be created in this age of obsessive materialism. And in some sense negative cultural phenomena actually strengthen architecture's humanist mission: resistance to the decay of spiritual and cultural values is now the shared task of architects and artists.

The widespread rejection of the Modernist doctrine, with its emphasis on social morality, has inspired impressive aesthetic diversity, but it has also produced a climate of arrogance, cultural incoherence, and narcissism. As the understanding of architecture as a *social* art has diminished, the idea of architecture as a form of studio art has intensified: contemporary "neo-avant-garde" works are presented today as products of individual genius. And yet

paradoxically, artistic authenticity and autonomy of architecture are today being undercut
by three cultural tendencies: the commodification of buildings, the self-defeating search
for newness, and the hegemony of the marketable image. These cultural tendencies are
supported by both commercialized architectural
journalism and the voracious global entertainment and tourism industries.

Is architecture relinquishing its potential to
embody high-minded cultural and collective
values? Is it working to support ideological and
commercial brainwashing and exploitation
rather than cultural and historical understanding? Is the emphasis on transient construction turning architecture into disposable
scenery?

Despite the current critical and media focus
on celebrity designer-artists, architecture
continues to be that art with the most irrefutable
and unavoidable grounding in social life. In
addition to merely evaluating the aesthetic
relevance of individual projects, architectural
theory, criticism, and education should survey
this now-neglected cultural ground—the
preconditions of the art of architecture. Both
education and practice would benefit from a
rigorous cultural analysis of the prevailing state
of architecture. What, for instance, is the
collective mental background that informs the
alarming conservatism—the nostalgic quasi-
classicism—of American collegiate and corporate architecture? Is it cultural insecurity? A
deeper suppression of the idea of (and hope for)
progress? And what kinds of mental defenses
work to create our sickeningly regressive
domestic architecture?

VISUAL IMAGES

Architectural publication, criticism, and even
education are now focused relentlessly on the
enticing visual image. The longing for singular,
memorable imagery subordinates other aspects
of buildings, isolating architecture in disembodied vision. As buildings are conceived and
confronted through the eye rather than the
entire body—as the camera becomes the
ultimate witness to and mediator of architecture—the actual experience of a building, of
its spaces and materials, is neglected. By
reinforcing visual manipulation and graphic
production, computer imaging further detaches

architecture from its multisensory essence; as
design tools, computers can encourage mere
visual manipulation and make us neglect our
powers of empathy and imagination. We
become voyeurs obsessed with visuality, blind
not only to architecture's social reality but also
to its functional, economic, and technological
realities, which inevitably determine the design
of buildings and cities. Our detachment from
experiential and sensory reality maroons us in
theoretical, intellectual, and conceptual realms.

HAPTIC EXPERIENCES

Recent dramatic changes in the temporal
quality of experience have themselves affected
architecture, which now must compete, for
immediacy of impact, with today's frenetic
forms of expression and communication—with
fashion, advertising, Web culture, and so on.
But while the visual image has an immediate
impact, other dimensions of architectural
experience require empathy and interpretation,
an understanding of cultural and social contexts,
and a capacity for envisioning the temporal
endurance of buildings beyond momentary
fashions. Appreciation of the sensory qualities
of architecture requires slowness and patience
(this is true for both the design process and the
experience and judgment of the finished
building). The impact of time, the effects of use
and wear, and the processes of aging are rarely
considered in contemporary design or criticism.
Alvar Aalto believed that the value of a building
is best judged fifty years after completion. The
prospect that few new buildings will even last
fifty years does not invalidate the significance of
time and duration in architectural appreciation.

Authentic architectural settings—fully realized microcosmic entities—strengthen our sense
of reality; thus, a desire for haptic architecture is
clearly emerging in reaction to ocular-centricity.
Haptic sensibility savors plasticity, materiality,
tactility, and intimacy. It offers nearness and
affection rather than distance and control.
While images of architecture can be rapidly
consumed, haptic architecture is appreciated
and comprehended gradually, detail by detail.
While the hectic eye of the camera captures a
momentary situation, a passing condition of
light or an isolated and carefully framed
fragment (photographic images are a kind of
focused gestalt), the experience of architectural

reality depends fundamentally on peripheral and anticipated vision. The perceptual realm that we sense beyond the sphere of focused vision—the event anticipated around a corner, behind a wall, or beneath a surface—is as important as the camera's frozen image. This suggests that one reason why contemporary places so often alienate us—compared with those historical and natural settings that elicit powerful emotional engagement—has to do with the poverty of our peripheral vision. Focused vision makes us mere observers; peripheral perception transforms retinal images into spatial and bodily experience, encouraging participation.

SOCIAL RESPONSIBILITIES

The ocular and hence hedonistic bias of contemporary architecture is exacerbated and in turn intensified by architects' loss of social empathy and mission. Issues of planning, social housing, mass production, and industriali-zation—all important to early Modernism—are now rarely touched on in publications or academic programs. Modernism sought to respond to the typical and ordinary conditions of life; contemporary elitist architecture favors the unique and the exceptional. This detach-ment of architectural language from the ground of common experience has produced a kind of architectural autism. Compare, for instance, the fantasy projects so often assigned in studios of the past decade with the socially oriented design problems of the 1950s and 1960s.

Architectural design, as well as writing and criticism, should acknowledge the need for civic responsibility. Architecture should strengthen the reliability and comprehensibility of the world. In this sense, architecture is fundamentally a conservative art; it materializes and preserves the mytho-poetic ground of constructing and inhabiting space, thus framing human existence and action. Through estab-lishing a horizon of existential understanding, architecture encourages us to turn our attention away from architecture itself: authentic architecture suggests images of ideal life.

The mastery of structure and material and the presence of skilled craftsmanship are essential to good architecture. The general weakening of our sense of tectonic reality—a weakening intimately related to the emphasis

on surface and appearance—is caused partly by the diminishing role of craft in construction but even more by the growing power of contractors and by the increasing importance of short-term economics at the expense of architectural value. Architecture is too often viewed as a short-lived speculative commodity rather than as a cultural and metaphysical manifestation that frames collective understanding and values. And although projects that question or ridicule this large social role are now celebrated—both avant-garde and corporate projects often emit the fetid air of architectural necrophilia—architecture cannot escape its foundations in real experience. In an age of simulation and virtual reality, we still long for a home.

CONTINUING VITALITY

Despite the general drift toward meaninglessness, some recent work offers glimpses of the continuous vitality of architecture. In so much current building, technology is used merely as a form of visual imagery. In contrast, Renzo Piano designs exemplary structures that combine technological ingenuity with contextual concern and ecological morality. Such work underscores the fact that truly ecological architecture derives from invention and refinement, not from technical or aesthetic regression. The delightful buildings of Glenn Murcutt are elegant blends of reason and modesty, common sense and poetry, techno-logical sophistication and ecological subtlety; they are unique buildings—responses to a particular landscape—with universal applic-ability. Alvaro Siza's architecture fuses a contemporary formal and spatial complexity with a reassuring sense of tradition and cultural continuity. Sverre Fehn explores the mythical and poetic ground of construction. Steven Holl resensualizes space, material, and light. Peter Zumthor's recent projects convincingly unite opposites: conceptual strength with sensual subtlety, thought with emotion, clarity with mystery, gravity with lightness.

Western industrial culture values power and domination. Referring to a way of philosophizing that does not try to bundle the multitude of human discourses into a single system, Gianni Vattimo has introduced ideas of "weak ontology" and "fragile thought."[1] We can, I would argue, identify a "weak" or "fragile" architecture, or, more precisely, an architecture of the "fragile image," as opposed to the prevalent architecture of strong images. Whereas the latter strives to impress and manipulate, the architecture of fragile image is contextual, multisensory, and responsive. It is concerned with experiential interaction and sensual accommodation. This architecture grows gradually, scene by scene, rather than quickly manifesting a simple, domineering concept.

We can distinguish between an architecture that offers less in its real material encounter than its images promise and an architecture that opens up new layers of experience and meaning when confronted in its built, contextual, and full reality. Visiting a building by Alvar Aalto, for instance, is a richer experience than viewing its image. His works are masterpieces of an episodic architecture that aims to achieve a specific ambiance rather than a formal authority. The paved pathways by Dimitris Pikionis that lead to the Acropolis in Athens, Lawrence Halprin's Ira's Fountain in Portland, Oregon, and Carlo Scarpa's meticulously crafted architectural settings are further examples of an architecture whose full power does not rely on imagery. The work of Pikionis is a dense conversation with time and history; Halprin's designs explore the threshold between architecture and nature; Scarpa's architecture creates a dialogue between concept and making, visuality and hapticity, artistic invention and tradition. Such architecture obscures the categories of foreground and background, object and context; it evokes a liberated sense of natural duration. An architecture of courtesy and attention, it asks us to be humble, receptive, and patient observers.

Focused on visual imagery, detached from social and contextual considerations, much of the architecture of our time—and the publicity that attempts to convince us of its genius—has an air of self-satisfaction and omnipotence. Buildings attempt to conquer the foreground rather than to create a supportive background for action and perception. Our age seems to have lost the virtue of architectural neutrality, restraint, and modesty. Many contemporary architectural projects seem impudent and arrogant. Authentic works of art, however, remain suspended between certainty and uncertainty, faith and doubt. Architectural culture on the threshold of the new millennium would do well to nurture productive tensions: cultural realism and artistic idealism, determination and discretion, ambition and humility.

NOTE

1 Gianni Vattimo, *The End of Modernity* (Baltimore, MD: Johns Hopkins University Press, 1991).

55
Rethinking Environmental Racism

White Privilege and Urban Development in
Southern California (2000)

Laura Pulido

The concept of environmental racism—the idea
that nonwhites are disproportionately exposed to
pollution—emerged with the United Church of
Christ's study, *Toxic Waste and Race in the United
States* (1987). Given the social, ecological, and
health implications of environmental hazards,
geographers have explored environmental racism
with the goal of contributing to better
policymaking. Studies have sought to determine
if inequalities exist and the reasons for such
disparities, and to make recommendations
(Cutter 1995). While these are obviously
important research contributions, studying
environmental racism is important for an additional reason: it helps us understand racism.

Although the study of racial inequality is not
new to geographers environmental racism offers
us new insights into the subject, particularly its
spatiality. Unfortunately, scholars of environmental racism have not seriously problematized
racism, opting instead for a de facto conception
based on malicious, individual acts. There are
several problems with this approach. First, by
reducing racism to a hostile, discriminatory act,
many researchers, with the notable exception of
Bullard (1990), miss the role of structural and
hegemonic forms of racism in contributing to
such inequalities. Indeed, structural racism has
been the dominant mode of analysis in other
substantive areas of social research, such as
residential segregation and employment
patterns.

A second and related concern is that racism
is not conceptualized as the dynamic sociospatial
process that it is. Because racism is understood
as a discrete act that *may* be spatially expressed,
it is not seen as a sociospatial relation both
constitutive of the city and produced by it. As a
result, the spatiality of racism is not understood,
particularly the relationship *between places*.

A final problem with a narrow understanding
of racism is that it limits claims, thereby
reproducing a racist social order. By defining
racism so narrowly, racial inequalities that
cannot be attributed directly to a hostile,
discriminatory act are not acknowledged as
such, but perhaps as evidence of individual
deficiencies or choices. Yet if we wish to create a
more just society, we must acknowledge the
breadth and depth of racism.

I investigate how racism is conceptualized in
the environmental-racism literature. Using Los
Angeles as a case study, I apply an alternative
concept of racism, white privilege, in addition
to more common understandings of discrimination, to explain disparate environmental
patterns. I identify three specific issues that
contribute to a narrow conception of racism:
first, an emphasis on individual facility siting;
second, the role of intentionality; and third, an
uncritical approach to scale. Typically, a study
may acknowledge environmental inequity if
nonwhites are disproportionately exposed to
pollution, but environmental *racism* is only
conceded if malicious intent on the part of
decision-makers can be proven. I argue that the
emphasis on siting, while obviously important,
must be located in larger urban processes, and
thus requires us to "jump scales" in our analysis
(N. Smith 1993). This is especially true given
recent findings that pollution concentrations
are closely associated with industrial land use.

This research recasts issues of intentionality
and scale, as it requires us to examine the

production of industrial zones, their relation to other parts of the metropolis, and the potentially racist nature of the processes by which these patterns evolved.

A focus on white privilege enables us to develop a more structural, less conscious, and more deeply historicized understanding of racism. It differs from a hostile, individual, discriminatory act, in that it refers to the privileges and benefits that accrue to white people by virtue of their whiteness. Because whiteness is rarely problematized by whites, white privilege is scarcely acknowledged. According to George Lipsitz, "As the unmarked category against which difference is constructed, whiteness never has to speak its name, never has to acknowledge its role as an organizing principle in social and cultural relations" (1995: 369). White privilege is thus an attempt to name a social system that works to the benefit of whites. White privilege, together with overt and institutionalized racism, reveals how racism shapes places. Hence, instead of asking if an incinerator was placed in a Latino community because the owner was prejudiced, I ask, why is it that whites are not comparably burdened with pollution? In the case of Los Angeles, industrialization, decentralization, and residential segregation are keys to this puzzle. Because industrial land use is highly correlated with pollution concentrations and people of color, the crucial question becomes, how did whites distance themselves from both industrial pollution and nonwhites?

ENVIRONMENTAL RACISM IN LOS ANGELES COUNTY

There have been six systematic studies of environmental racism in Los Angeles (five at the county level and one at the city), examining three environmental hazards: uncontrolled toxic waste sites treatment storage and/or disposal facility (TSDFs), and air toxins based on the Toxic Release Inventory (TRI)

All studies found that nonwhites were disproportionately exposed. Most vulnerable were working-class Latinos.

The results of these six studies suggest important racial and spatial patterns associated with these three forms of pollution. First, it appears that most industrial hazards in southern California are concentrated in the greater

central and southern part of Los Angeles County. This older core is inhabited by people of color, while whites live on the periphery. Within this large zone, one group of hazards follows a major transportation corridor, the Interstate-5 freeway and the railroad, stretching from east Los Angeles through downtown and into the eastern San Fernando Valley. A second major grouping forms a wide swath from downtown to the harbor. This distribution reflects both contemporary and historic industrial patterns. Second, as previously stated, all studies found evidence of environmental racism, even when accounting for income.

Third, it is working-class Latinos, and to a lesser extent, African Americans, who are disproportionately impacted. This reflects both patterns of residential segregation, as well as Latinos' historic and continuing role as the region's low-wage working class (Scott 1996; Morales and Ong 1993; Ong and Blumenberg 1993). What is significant is the degree to which almost no whites live in these areas and therefore are not exposed to the hazards under consideration. There is simply far less pollution in the outlying areas. I maintain that we can only understand these contemporary patterns by examining the historical development of urban space at the regional scale and that these processes are inherently racialized. While some forms of environmental racism are directly attributable to overt acts of discrimination, I will emphasize how white privilege contributed to this larger pattern.

THE HISTORICAL GEOGRAPHY OF WHITE PRIVILEGE AND ENVIRONMENTAL RACISM IN LOS ANGELES

The data suggest that people of color's disproportionate exposure to pollution in Los Angeles is not by chance. Although the geography of environmental racism is the result of millions of individual choices, those choices reflect a particular racial formation, and are a response to conditions deliberately created by the state and capital. My goal is to show the historical evolution of these patterns and how racism contributed to the spatial patterns associated with environmental racism.

Early suburbanization (1848–1920s) emanated partly from the refusal of middle-class whites to live near immigrants and people of color. Whites pursued suburbanization for many reasons, but regardless of their motives, their choice was predicated on white privilege.

As whites moved outward, Chicanos, African Americans, Japanese Americans, Chinese Americans and the remnant Indian population were relegated to San Pedro, Watts, and the central city (including downtown and the eastside).

Beginning in the 1920s, residential segregation was violently enforced. As a result, for thousands of "Mexicans, Japanese, and Negroes who lived amidst commerce and industry in the small ghettos of central Los Angeles and San Pedro[,] there were a million white Americans who resided in the suburbs sprawling north to Hollywood, east to Pasadena, south to Long Beach, and west to Santa Monica" (Fogelson 1993: 147). These early differences in environmental quality were codified by zoning laws in the 1920s, which resulted in a concentration of industrial activity in nonwhite and immigrant areas.

As suburbanization continued, what were once the near suburbs became the inner city, as white workers moved away, and people of color subsequently took their place, a process known as ethnic succession. Consequently, wealthy whites were never systematically burdened by pollution, while over time, the white working class was able to escape by taking advantage of new housing opportunities. Thus, regardless of class differences, all whites enjoyed white privilege, albeit to varying degrees.

The Depression and World War II greatly intensified the process of white suburbanization, but instead of it being a private project, the state actively subsidized suburbanization, to the detriment of people of color living in the central city.

Federal policies, such as Titles I and VI of the Federal Housing Act (FHA), sought to increase the housing supply in an overtly racist way. Perhaps of greatest significance was the institutionalization of redlining practices by the Home Owners Loan Corporation (HOLC) and the FHA. Although these measures were intended to protect small homeowners from foreclosure, they ranked neighborhoods in descending order from "A" to "D," with profound consequences for future urban development. "A" ratings were reserved for "newer, affluent suburbs that were strung out

along curvilinear streets well away from the problems of the city" (in Jackson 1980: 424). At the other extreme were nonwhite neighborhoods. Indeed, HOLC's survey of the Los Angeles area shows the suburban communities of Pasadena, Beverly Hills, Santa Monica, and Palos Verdes as all "A" areas. Working-class white communities were "B," and Black, Latino, and Asian neighborhoods, primarily in the eastside, central Los Angeles, and south of downtown, were "C" and "D" (US Division of Research and Statistics 1939).

Indeed, neighborhoods are not merely groupings of individuals, homes, and commerce, they are *constellations of opportunities* with powerful consequences, for both the recipient and nonrecipient populations. Although whites must go to ever greater lengths to achieve them, relatively homogeneous white spaces are necessary for the full exploitation of whiteness (Frankenberg 1993).

Due to 150 years of racism as well as recent social and economic shifts, southern California remains highly segregated, despite a reduction in overt forms of racism. Three interrelated factors help explain why the central city remains a nonwhite place, and whites continue to dominate the periphery: immigration, residential mobility, and economic restructuring. These factors also help explain why Latinos, in particular, are disproportionately exposed to industrial pollution.

Immigration has dramatically affected both the economy and residential patterns of the region. Immigrants have moved into these black and brown spaces because they are affordable and accessible.

Many of the industries and land uses associated with environmental hazards are concentrated in central Los Angeles, and, to a lesser extent, along industrial arteries. Both blacks and Latinos are disproportionately exposed, but for somewhat different reasons. As the most segregated population, black Angelenos were confined to south Los Angeles beginning in the 1920s.

Despite the fact that blacks were only intermittently hired in them, south Los Angeles housed many Fordist industries, the majority of which left in the 1970s and 1980s. This "rust belt" not only harbors various environmental hazards but, as a politically weak and industrially oriented area, attracts projects like incinerators and the proposed Pacific Pipeline. Thus, blacks' exposure to environmental hazards is largely a function of severe spatial containment and the historic practice of locating hazardous land uses in black areas.

In contrast, Latinos' exposure is more a function of their role as low-wage labor within the racialized division of labor and the historic relationship between the barrio and industry. Latinos have *always* lived close to industry, but unlike blacks, they have, at times, been hired in large numbers (Morales and Ong 1993; Ong and Blumenberg 1993). Latinos' contemporary exposure cannot be understood outside of industrial and immigration shifts. Over the last twenty years, the region has undergone a simultaneous industrial decline and expansion. While the finance and service sectors have grown dramatically, manufacturing declined in Los Angeles in the 1980s. In the 1990s, however, a selective reindustrialization was realized (Scott 1996) by high-technology industries and low-wage Latino labor. As a result, Latinos live near industry, since both are concentrated in central Los Angeles and industrial corridors, and they are exposed to hazards on the job (Ong and Blumenberg 1993). Thus, their exposure is a function of their class and immigrant status, as well as their racial position. As Latinos, they live where brown and black people have historically lived, or in spaces vacated by the white working class.

Environmental hazards are concentrated in central Los Angeles (including the inner suburbs) in several distinct ways. First, because a significant portion of these communities are industrially zoned, industry continues to locate there. Yet because of the poverty of central Los Angeles and its land fragmentation and poor services, few of the large, well-financed firms in growth sectors move there. Instead, small polluting activities and large-scale hazards, such as incinerators, are drawn to these areas, as "cleaner industries are dissuaded from locating in the area because of the toxic contamination" (LA Design Action Planning Team 1990: 12). According to one official from Paramount, an inner suburb, "we provide a place for industry that nobody wants" (Carbajal in Flanigan 1999).

Beyond the general unsightliness, such land uses pose a severe threat to residents. Because of the lack of buffers and the hazardous nature of industry, there have been mass evacuations, school contaminations, explosions, potential cancer clusters, and workers killed. Newer suburban communities do not have the same concentration of hazardous industrial activities, and enjoy more effective zoning and land-use regulations.

In short, looking at the region as a whole, it is clear that people of color are disproportionately exposed to a particular set of environmental hazards. Such patterns are not the result of any single decision or particular act. Instead, they are the result of urban development in a highly racialized society over the course of 150 years.

CONCLUSION

I have argued that restrictive conceptions of racism characterize the environmental racism literature. In particular, the emphasis on siting, intentionality, and scale have contributed to conceptualizing both racism and space as discrete objects, rather than as social relations. These dominant conceptions are problematic because they prevent us from understanding how racism shapes places and the relationships between places, and thereby limits our ability to detect environmental racism. I have sought to challenge this approach by employing the concept of white privilege, which offers a more structural and spatial understanding of racism. Such a shift requires acknowledging that multiple forms of racism exist, including less conscious forms not characterized by malicious intent and hostility. White privilege allows us to see how environmental racism has been produced—not only by consciously targeting people of color (as in the incinerator cases)—but by the larger processes of urban development, including white flight, in which whites have sought to fully exploit the benefits of their whiteness.

In urban areas, explanations of environmental inequality must include careful consideration of residential patterns, land use, and industrial development. The history of suburbanization reveals that although many forces contributed to decentralization, it has largely been an exclusionary undertaking. Moreover, the state has played a central role in crafting such opportunities, choices, and landscapes. Although, in Los Angeles, nonwhites have always lived adjacent to industry, people of color have recently begun moving into the suburbs, and have taken over what were once white industrial suburbs. Over time, these industrial suburbs have become part of the inner city, and are increasingly populated by people of color. As a result, central Los Angeles with its concentration of industrial hazards remains a nonwhite space. In contrast, whites continue to move to the periphery, which is relatively cleaner. These patterns developed over a century and continue to inform the present, illustrating how various forms of racism shape our landscapes.

This paper raises a host of policy, scholarly, and political issues. From a policy perspective, I have argued for the need to direct more attention to industrial zones and pollution clusters, rather than just the siting process and individual facilities. While the latter are clearly important, particularly in terms of future pollution, most industrial pollution does not involve new sitings, but is the product of already existing facilities, land uses, and zoning.

Scholarship on environmental racism can also be strengthened. It is essential that researchers begin to situate their work in terms of a larger sociospatial dialectic. Such a move would not only illuminate the geographic and historical context in which these patterns developed, but would also help us appreciate the extent to which places are shaped by various forms of racism. Relatedly, the fact that many geographers are hesitant to pursue these avenues of research underscores the need for greater breadth within our discipline and the limitations of specialization. As a discipline that is intimately associated with both human–environment relations and the study of space, we should be at the forefront of contributing new theoretical, empirical, and technical insights on the topic of environmental justice.

The issue of racism itself raises both scholarly and political concerns. I believe that as geographers, we need to diversify and deepen our approach to the study of racial inequality. Our traditional emphasis on mapping and counting needs to be complemented by research that seeks to understand what race means to people and how racism shapes lives and places. For instance, within the field of environmental racism, a key question that has not been seriously addressed is differential exposure. In other words, how might different experiences and histories of racism result in distinct geographies of exposure, say for instance, between the Shoshone nation, rural Blacks in the South, and an urban Asian

American community in the San Francisco Bay area? Not only are such questions important in and of themselves, but they would help geography build bridges to other disciplines, such as ethnic studies.

But the question of racism within the discipline goes beyond research. And, as I have shown, our approach to the subject, unfortunately, speaks volumes about the collective politics of our discipline. What are we to make of a body of literature that purports to address the question of racism but is estranged from mainstream scholarly understandings of racism? Why do so many scholars cling to such a narrow conception of racism? What are the consequences of such an approach in terms of our research, teaching, and political efficacy? Perhaps a serious interrogation on the subject of racism is in order. At the very least, I hope that this paper demonstrates how individual scholars contribute to the reproduction of larger discourses and conceptions of race—regardless of their motives. The point is not to lay blame, but to become aware of the larger political and moral consequences of our actions.

REFERENCES

Bullard, Robert D. 1990. *Dumping in Dixie*. Boulder, CO: Westview Press.

Cutter, Susan L. 1995. Race, Class and Environmental Justice. *Progress in Human Geography* 19: 107–118.

Flanigan, James. 1999. Downey Takes Lead to Revive Gateway Cities. *Los Angeles Times*, June 16: C1, C4.

Fogelson, Robert M. 1993. *The Fragmented Metropolis: Los Angeles, 1850–1930*. Berkeley: University of California Press.

Frankenberg, Ruth. 1993. *White Women, Race Matters*. Minneapolis: University of Minnesota Press.

Jackson, Kenneth T. 1980. Race, Ethnicity, and Real Estate Appraisal: The Home Owners Loan Corporation and the Federal Housing Administration. *Journal of Urban History* 4: 419–452.

LA Design Action Planning Team. 1990. Boyle Heights, Los Angeles. Planning Department, Box C1518, Los Angeles City Archive.

Lipsitz, G. 1995. The Possessive Investment in Whiteness: Racialized Social Democracy and the "White" Problem in American Studies. *American Quarterly* 47: 369–387.

Morales, Rebecca and Paul Ong. 1993. The Illusion of Progress: Latinos in Los Angeles. In *Latinos in a Changing Economy,* ed. R. Morales and F. Bonilla, pp. 55–84. Newbury Park, CA: Sage.

Ong, Paul and Evelyn Blumenberg. 1993. An Unnatural Trade-off: Latinos and Environmental Justice. In *Latinos in a Changing U.S. Economy,* ed. R. Morales and F. Bonilla, pp. 207–225. Newbury Park, CA: Sage.

Scott, Allen. 1996. The Manufacturing Economy: Ethnic and Gender Divisions of Labor. In *Ethnic Los Angeles,* ed. R. Waldinger and M. Bozorgmehr, pp. 215–244. New York: Sage.

Smith, Neil. 1993. Residential Segregation and the Politics of Racialization. In *Racism, the City, and the State*, ed. M. Cross and M. Keith, pp. 128–143. New York: Routledge.

United Church of Christ, Commission for Racial Justice. 1987. *Toxic Wastes and Race in the United States.* New York: United Church of Christ.

US Division of Research and Statistics. 1939. Federal Home Loan Bank Board. Residential Security Map. Sections 1–4. Record Group 95, Box 101. National Archives and Records Administration, College Park, MD.

56
Editorial: Mobilities, Immobilities and Moorings

(2006)

Kevin Hannam, Mimi Sheller, and John Urry

INTRODUCTION

Mobility has become an evocative keyword for the twenty-first century and a powerful discourse that creates its own effects and contexts. The concept of mobilities encompasses both the large-scale movements of people, objects, capital and information across the world, as well as the more local processes of daily transportation, movement through public space and the travel of material things within everyday life. Issues of movement, of too little movement or too much or of the wrong sort or at the wrong time, are central to many lives, organizations and governments. Dreams of "hyper-mobility" and "instantaneous communication" drive contemporary business strategy, advertising and government policy while also eliciting strong political critiques from those who feel marginalized or harmed by these new developments. Fears of illicit mobilities and their attendant security risks increasingly determine logics of governance and liability protection within both the public and private sectors. From SARS and avian influenza to train crashes, from airport expansion controversies to controlling global warming, from urban congestion charging to networked global terrorism, from emergency management in the onslaught of tsunamis and hurricanes to oil wars in the Middle East, issues of "mobility" are centre-stage. Many public, private and not-for-profit organizations are seeking to understand, monitor, manage and transform aspects of these multiple mobilities, and of the new "immobilities", social exclusions and security threats that may be associated with them.

MOBILITY SYSTEMS AND MOBILITY GOVERNANCE

Mobilities are centrally involved in reorganizing institutions, generating climate change, moving risks and illnesses across the globe, altering travel, tourism and migration patterns, producing a more distant family life, transforming the social and educational life of young people, connecting distant people through "weak ties" and so on. The human body and the home are transformed, as proximity and connectivity are imagined in new ways and often enhanced by communication devices and likely to be "on the move". Changes also transform the nature, scale and temporalities of families, "local" communities, public and private spaces, and the commitments people may feel to the "nation".

Crucially, the nation itself is being transformed by these mobilities, as is the city. New economic and political geographies of "state rescaling" and urban restructuring emphasize the historicity of social space, the polymorphism of geographies, the restructuring of scale and the remaking of state space. Drawing on Harvey's historical geography of capitalism and Lefebvre's theory of the production of space, Brenner for example argues that deterritorialization and reterritorialization, or what we also call mobilities and moorings, occur dialectically, and that the "contemporary round of global restructuring has entailed neither the absolute territorialization of societies, economies, or cultures onto a global scale, nor their complete deterritorialization into a supraterritorial, distanceless, placeless, or borderless space of flows" (Brenner, 2004, p. 64). Instead, "the image of political-economic space as a complex, tangled mosaic of superimposed and interpenetrating nodes, levels, scales, and morphologies has become more appropriate than the traditional Cartesian model of homogenous, self-enclosed and contiguous blocks of territory that has long been used to describe the modern interstate system" (Brenner, 2004, p. 66). This shift away from the "traditional, Westphalian model of statehood" based on national-territorial containers towards more "complex, polymorphic, and multiscalar regulatory geographies" (Brenner, 2004, p. 67) is, we would add, fundamentally related to the emergence of complex mobility systems and their restructuring of both space and time.

Mobilities cannot be described without attention to the necessary spatial, infrastructural and institutional moorings that configure and enable mobilities—creating what Harvey (1989) called the "spatial fix". Thus the forms of detachment or "deterritorialization" associated with "liquid modernity" (Bauman, 2000) are always accompanied by rhizomic attachments and reterritorializations of various kinds. There are interdependent systems of "immobile" material worlds and especially some exceptionally immobile platforms, transmitters, roads, garages, stations, aerials, airports, docks, factories through which mobilizations of locality are performed and re-arrangements of place and scale materialized. The *complex* character of such systems stems from the multiple fixities or moorings often on a substantial physical scale that enable the fluidities of liquid modernity, and especially of capital. Thus "mobile machines", mobile phones, cars, aircraft, trains and computer connections, all presume overlapping and varied time-space immobilities (Graham and Marvin, 2001; Urry, 2003). There is no linear increase in fluidity without extensive systems of immobility, yet there is a growing capacity for more flexible and dynamic scalar shifting, polymorphism of spatial forms and overlapping regulatory regimes. We can refer to these as affording different degrees of "motility" or potential for mobility (Kaufmann, 2002), with motility now being a crucial dimension of unequal power relations.

Even as the materiality of mobility systems becomes more complex, material changes simultaneously seem to be "de-materializing" connections, as people, machines, images, information, power, money, ideas and dangers are "on the move", making and remaking networks at an increasingly rapid speed across the world. Social networks are underpinned by technologies based upon time-frames transcending human consciousness. Computers make decisions in nanosecond time, producing instantaneous and simultaneous effects. Pervasive computing produces a switching and mobility between different self-reproducing systems, such as the Internet with its massive search engines, databases of information storage and retrieval, world money flows (Leyshon and Thrift, 1996), intelligent transport systems (Sheller, 2006), robotic vision machines under the oceans, and vision machines more generally (Thrift, 2001; Kaplan, 2006).

In sum, the emerging mobilities paradigm challenges the ways in which much social science research has been relatively "a-mobile" until recently. Accounting for mobilities in the fullest sense challenges social science to change both the objects of its inquiries and the methodologies for research. Our approach to mobilities problematizes both "sedentarist" approaches in the social science that treat place, stability and dwelling as a natural steady-state, and "deterritorialized" approaches that posit a new "grand narrative" of mobility, fluidity or liquidity as a pervasive condition of post-modernity or globalization (see Sheller and Urry, 2006; Cresswell, 2002). It is part of a broader theoretical project aimed at going beyond the imagery of "terrains" as spatially fixed geographical containers for social processes, and calling into question scalar logics such as local/global as descriptors of regional extent (see Brenner, 2004; Tsing, 2002 on tracking "rhetorics of scale" and what counts as relevant scales). If we use metaphors that imply moving beyond both geographical fixity and also beyond disciplinary boundaries, we also recognize the politically contested nature of such mobilities.

AIRPORTS, CITIES AND MOBILITY DISASTERS

To illustrate some elements of the emerging mobilities paradigm we turn briefly to two iconic examples of the significance of complex interlocking mobility and mooring systems in the world today: airports and urban disasters. Both are illustrative of some of the complex problems created for the re-scaled governance, regulation and control of the dynamic interfaces of transportation, communication, provisioning, software sorting and scheduling systems.

Contemporary airports have historically developed from military airports and the drive for "airpower", which afforded a huge military advantage to those who controlled the "cosmic view" from the air (Kaplan, 2006). This socio-technical system has been turned into a form of mass mobility that requires an exceptionally extensive and immobile place, the airport-city with tens of thousands of workers orchestrating the four million air journeys taking place each day. This airport space is a "space of transition" that facilitates the shrinkage of the globe and the transcendence of time and space (Gottdiener, 2001, pp. 10–11), especially by "seamlessly" connecting major "global" cities (Urry, 2000)—though mainly for the hypermobile elite. The *system* of airports links together places, forming networks that bring connected places closer together, while distancing those places that are not so connected. They are one of many "transfer points" (Kesselring, 2006), "places of in-between-ness" involved in being mobile but immobilized in lounges, waiting rooms, cafés, amusement arcades, parks, hotels, stations, motels, harbours—an immobile network so that others can be on the move.

Airports are also a place of "cybermobilities" (Adey and Bevan, 2006) in which software keeps the airport system functioning smoothly and transforms it into a kind of "code/space" (Dodge and Kitchin, 2004). Wood and Graham (2006) further suggest that automated software for sorting travellers as they pass through automated surveillance systems, such as iris-recognition systems, is increasingly producing a "kinetic elite" whose ease of mobility differentiates them from the low-speed, low-mobility majority. Software also enables the tight coupling of distinctive airport systems—from the baggage X-ray and passenger surveillance systems to air traffic control and mechanical systems, passenger ticketing and ground transportation, and human resource systems that manage flight crews, ground workers and security staff—such that breakdowns in one component of an airport system often have knock-on effects which can cause lengthy delays.

Increasingly air terminals are becoming like cities but also in what has been called the frisk society, cities are becoming like airports. The use of technologies such as detention centres, CCTV, Internet cafés, GPS systems, iris-recognition security, WiFi hotspots and intermodal traffic interchanges are first trialled within airports before moving out as mundane characteristics of cities, places of fear and highly contingent ordering within the new world disorder. And daily flows through airports contribute immensely to the production of contemporary urbanism, including diasporic cultural communities, "ethnic" restaurants and neighbourhoods, distant families and cosmo-politan identities, and exclusive zones and corridors of connectivity for the fast-tracked kinetic elite. Indeed as other analysts of global networks argue, the increase in cross-border transactions and of "capabilities for enormous geographical dispersal and mobility" go hand-in-hand with "pronounced territorial concen-trations of resources necessary for the management and servicing of that dispersal and mobility" (Sassen, 2002, p. 2).

More generally, the mobilities of money laundering, the drug trade, sewage and waste, infections, urban crime, asylum seeking, arms trading, people smuggling, slave trading and urban terrorism all make visible the already existing chaotic juxtaposition of different spaces and networks. Thus global diseases rapidly move and the "world has rapidly become much more vulnerable to the eruption and, more critically, to the widespread and even global spread of both new and old infectious diseases. … The jet plane itself, and its cargo, can carry insects and infectious agents into new ecologic settings" (Mann, cited in Buchanan, 2002, p. 172). Only a few long-range transport connections are necessary to generate pandemics, such as those threatened by SARS that spread across the very mobile Chinese diaspora in 2003, especially moving between south China, Hong Kong and Toronto, or the feared global spread of avian influenza from birds to humans and then from human to human in a repeat of the 1918 flu epidemic that killed 50 million people worldwide.

Urban disasters bring to the fore the astounding fragility of complex mobility systems. The attack on the World Trade Center towers and their fiery collapse horrifically seared into global consciousness not only massive loss of human life, but also a vision of simultaneous destruction of multiple mobility systems and a disruption of the global discourse of unfettered mobility as a way of life (see Little, 2006). A huge node in the global financial trading system was shut down. A major station in the metropolitan transportation system was obliterated. A significant hub in the telephonic and electronic communications systems fell silent, while the mobile phone network was overwhelmed. And the crucial channels of governmental emergency coordination of police and fireman faltered. Bridges and tunnels were closed to traffic, crowds had to flee Manhattan on foot unable to contact loved ones, and air traffic was placed on an emergency footing. The attacks were perceived as targeting not just the United States at a national scale, but also specifically New York City as a "global city" of transnational mobility of capital, information and people.

The impact of Hurricane Katrina on the US Gulf Coast in September 2005 brought another major American metropolitan area to the point of chaos and total systems failure. The dysfunctional evacuation of New Orleans left the poor and the infirm in harm's way, many without cars and without an adequate public transportation system to leave the city. Once the storm hit and flooded out bridges, roads and the power grid, government coordination and civil order collapsed along with the communications systems. After the storm, the inability of the Federal Emergency Management Agency, FEMA, to bring aid quickly into the region, along with the unavailability of the many National Guard troops deployed to Iraq, left the storm's victims largely cut off from the outside world and from would-be rescuers. The ensuing media mobilization of reporters, cameras and satellite-broadcast images revealed to the world thousands of people trapped in a submerged city and facing the collapse of all provisioning systems, power, food, water, baby formula, diapers and medical supplies. The crisis underlined the total dependence of the urban US on complex and tightly interlocking systems of mobility, transportation and communication to sustain contemporary urban life.

These disasters elicited a US-wide resurgence of debate over the oil-based economy and the war in Iraq, global warming and the culture of automobility, the failure to invest in public transport and poor land-use planning in both urban and coastal areas, and the "shame" of continuing urban poverty and racial segregation within major American cities. All of these are issues of mobility *and* moorings: how to move and how to settle, what is up for grabs and what is locked in, who is able to move and who is trapped.

Mobilities thus seem to involve the analysis of complex systems that are neither perfectly ordered nor anarchic. There is an "orderly disorder" present within dynamic or complex adaptive systems as analysed in recent formulations. Dynamic systems possess emergent properties. They develop over time so that national economies, corporations and households are locked into stable "path dependent" practices, such as the steel-and-petroleum car. Disaster is one trigger for systemic change. But systems can also change through the accumulation of small repetitions reaching a "tipping point" as with the explosive growth of mobile phone use or communications between offices using faxes (Gladwell, 2002), or the small causes that could conceivably tip the car system into a post-car system (Urry, 2004).

AN AGENDA FOR MOBILITIES RESEARCH

While certain critics argue that there is no analytical purchase in bringing together so broad a field—encompassing studies of corporeal movement, transportation and communications infrastructures, capitalist spatial restructuring, migration and immigration, citizenship and transnationalism, and tourism and travel—we argue that the project needs to be developed further. Recent critical approaches have still had little effect in terms of how mainstream social science constitutes its object of inquiry. The new mobilities paradigm must be brought to bear, not only on questions of globalization and the deterritorialization of nation-states, identities and belonging, but more fundamentally on questions of what are the appropriate subjects and objects of social inquiry.

REFERENCES

Adey, Peter and Paul Bevan. (2006) Between the physical and the virtual: connected mobilities, in: M. Sheller and J. Urry (eds), *Mobile Technologies of the City* (London: Routledge).

Bauman, Zygmunt. (2000) *Liquid Modernity* (Cambridge: Polity Press).

Brenner, Neil. (2004) *New State Spaces: Urban Governance and the Rescaling of Statehood* (Oxford: Oxford University Press).

Buchanan, Mark. (2002) *Small World. Uncovering Nature's Hidden Networks* (London: Weidenfeld & Nicolson).

Cresswell, Tim. (2002) Introduction: theorizing place, in: G. Verstraete and T. Cresswell (eds), *Mobilizing Place, Placing Mobility* (Amsterdam: Rodopi).

Dodge, Martin and Robert Kitchin. (2004) Flying through code/space: the real virtuality of air travel, *Environment and Planning A,* 36, pp. 195–211.

Gladwell, Malcolm. (2002) *The Tipping Point: How Little Things Can Make a Big Difference* (Boston, MA: Little, Brown & Co).

Gottdiener, Mark. (2001) *Life in the Air* (Oxford: Rowman and Littlefield).

Graham, Stephen and Simon Marvin. (2001) *Splintering Urbanism* (London: Routledge).

Harvey, David. (1989) *The Condition of Post-modernity* (Oxford: Blackwell).

Kaplan, Caren. (2006) Mobility and war: the cosmic view of US 'air power', *Environment and Planning A*, 38(2), pp. 395–407.

Kaufmann, V. (2002) *Re-thinking Mobility. Contemporary Sociology* (Aldershot: Ashgate).

Kesselring, Sven. (2006) Pioneering mobilities: new patterns of movement and motility in a mobile world, *Environment and Planning A*, 38(2), pp. 269–279.

Leyshon, Andrew and Nigel Thrift. (1996) *Money/Space: Geographies of Monetary Transformation* (London: Routledge).

Little, Stephen. (2006) Twin Towers and Amoy Gardens: mobilities, risks and choices, in: M. Sheller and J. Urry (eds), *Mobile Technologies of the City* (London: Routledge).

Sassen, Saskia. (2002) Locating cities on global circuits, in: S. Sassen (ed.), *Global Networks, Linked Cities* (London: Routledge).

Sheller, Mimi. (2004a) Demobilising and remobilising the Caribbean, in: M. Sheller and J. Urry (eds), *Tourism Mobilities: Places to Play, Places in Play* (London: Routledge).

Sheller, Mimi and John Urry. (2006) The new mobilities paradigm, *Environment and Planning A*, 38(2), pp. 207–226.

Thrift, Nigel. (2001) The machine in the ghost: software writing cities. Paper presented to Hegemonies Conference, Centre for Science Studies, Lancaster University.

Tsing, Anna. (2002) The global situation, in: J. Inda and R. Rosaldo (eds), *The Anthropology of Globalization: A Reader* (Oxford: Blackwell), pp. 453–485.

Urry, John. (2000) *Sociology Beyond Societies* (London: Routledge).

Urry, John. (2003) *Global Complexity* (Cambridge: Polity Press).

Urry, John. (2004) The 'system' of automobility, *Theory, Culture and Society,* 21(4/5), pp. 25–39.

Wood, David and Stephen Graham. (2006) Permeable boundaries in the software-sorted society: surveillance and the differentiation of mobility, in: M. Sheller and J. Urry (eds), *Mobile Technologies of the City* (London: Routledge).

57
Introduction: The Global and the Intimate

(2012)

Geraldine Pratt and Victoria Rosner

Familiar feminist slogans like "the personal is the political" work by juxtaposing apparently incommensurate registers of experience and showing how categories defined in opposition to one another can produce pernicious exclusions. To disrupt traditional organizations of space, to forge productive dislocations, to reconfigure conventions of scale: these are the goals that underwrite many feminist investigations. In our own historical moment of growing global consciousness, they have led us to examine more carefully the ways in which the global and the intimate, typically imagined as mutually exclusive spheres, are profoundly intertwined. But linking the global and intimate does more than extend a common feminist practice; it may allow feminists to steer a somewhat different course through processes of globalization and relations of intimacy. Feminists have already noted the ways in which rhetorics of intimacy are built into the familiar local/global binary in the academic literature on globalization. This binary has been thoroughly criticized by feminists such as Doreen Massey (2005), Inderpal Grewal and Caren Kaplan (1994), Sallie Marston et al. (2005), and J.K. Gibson-Graham (1996) because it imaginatively constructs the local as a defense against powerful global forces in a way that seems to confirm the force and inevitability of certain modes of global capitalist expansion. By the same token, the local is often conceived as a defense against the forces of global capitalism in ways that call up established gender hierarchies of feminine and masculine. Local/global is a straightforward binary opposition,

juxtaposing two terms that occupy polar positions on a single map. Intimate/global, we would like to suggest, both is and is not a binary; while irrefutably a pairing, it juxtaposes and resists the flattening effect of most binaries by bringing together terms that, we will argue, offer an implicit critique of one another.

In shifting from the idea of the local to that of the intimate, we are employing terms that are not defined *against* one another but rather draw their meaning from domains that are more elliptically related. We step out of hierarchical ontologies of scale or frameworks of micro-macro or the general and specific (see Marston et al. 2005; Gibson-Graham 1996). Intimacy is thus potentially and productively disruptive of the geographical binaries and hierarchies that often structure our thinking. By pairing the global and the intimate we aim to expose the patterns that recur when gender, sex, and the global imaginary combine.

Why is this exploration of the relationships between the global and the intimate a feminist project? Because we believe that the methodologies of feminism have proven particularly adept at exposing the universalist assumptions of international relations, social theory, and geographical models. Because feminism has a track record of success with slicing through the sometimes impersonal rhetorics of academic discourse. Because the sensitivities and suspicions that feminism has bred in us are part of what led us and our contributors to turn a skeptical eye on the sometimes uncritical affirmations of globalization. Because the same training has kept alive our collective belief that the analytical lens of gender relations can help to produce a more nuanced, complete, and just account of the world we share.

To invoke the global, we realize, risks reinscribing a set of pernicious assumptions that have come to infuse this term. The global repeats the claims of the universal male subject; unlocatable, a global outlook can seem to speak from everywhere, from a god's eye view. An implicit sexualization also runs through much of the literature of globalization. J.K. Gibson-Graham (1996) for instance, argues that the metaphorics of rape and victimization permeate descriptions of globalization. Economics appears to trump all other factors and to define the global as little more than a network of markets and producers. Capitalism is figured as one cohesive, over-powering economic system. Women in particular are too often represented as passive objects of impersonal and unstoppable economic forces, either coerced to migrate or confined within the local scale, mired in their bodies and familial relations.

If discourses of globalization often rely on the same old stereotypes of masculinity and femininity, if the so-called "global village," including global feminisms, often yields familiar categories of us and them, powerful and powerless, simply invoking the category of "the intimate" cannot unsettle these entrenched positions. Intimacy, after all, is equally caught up in relations of power, violence, and inequality and cannot stand as a fount of authenticity, caring, and egalitarianism. Svetlana Boym (1998) writes that intimacy, "may be protected, manipulated, or besieged by the state, framed by art, embellished by memory, or estranged by critique". Intimacy does not reside solely in the private sphere; it is infused with worldliness. Nor is it purely personal: intimacy takes on specific political, social and cultural meanings in different contexts. Feminists need to be skeptical of the ways in which the global and the intimate cross-pollinate in the new world order: from policymakers who deploy the language of idealized heterosexuality in the service of universalizing a single archetype of family; to the production of intimacy as a pageant for international media consumption; to the ways in which intimate tokens of gender identity, such as wearing "the veil", can rapidly metamorphose into potent symbols of cultural change and clash.

The pairing of the global and the intimate also asks us to consider how national visions of the global, particularly those located in the global north, tend to exclude anything that does not align with assumptions of northern hegemony and centrality. When you come down to the level of the intimate, the level of personal contact and exchange, individual differences and similarities become visible. This level of engagement forces the recognition of, for instance, the existence of cosmopolitan cities outside of the north; the presence of agency among so-called victims of globalization; the tendency to position middle-class Anglo women as modal subjects and to assume that all Anglo- and non-Anglo women share the same values and desires; and the uneven distribution of ethics and responsibilities world-wide.

THE INTIMATE

"Intimate," from the Latin "intimus," or innermost, is a word that invokes a cluster of related ideas: privacy, familiarity, love, sex, informality, and personal connection. Intimacy suggests something hidden away from the larger world, apparent only to the one or few on the inside. It refers to that which is walled off from the public sphere, from governance and regulation, from oversight. Intimacy has been traditionally associated with the feminine—and not coincidentally, has sometimes been sidelined in scholarly inquiries. Feminist approaches to the intimate have sought to redress this exclusion and have distinguished within the sphere of intimacy a number of rubrics, prominently including feeling and affect; attachments to friends, families, and lovers; and the personal. Looking more closely at the development of this work can help us to see the diverse ways in which the discourse of intimacy can be connected to that of the global.

Feminist work on feeling has sought to place emotional life on the agenda of scholars, to understand feelings as important not just for psychologists but for fields of study as widely ranging as geography, political science, literature, anthropology, and economics. Often understood as the shifty and loose cousin of reason, emotion has been valued by both feminist and queer theorists not in spite of its variability and irrationality but because of it. This area of feminist inquiry carefully walks a line between investigating a central and vital aspect of human life and avoiding the reductive historical association of women with emotion.

The study of feeling can bring a valuable dimension to the subject of study, but it can also redound in interesting ways through a consideration of the feelings of the one doing the studying.

For many feminists emotion can be a potent analytic tool for discerning social injustices. Feminist scholars have been particularly attentive to what Sianne Ngai (2005) terms "ugly feelings," negative emotions that can be seen as expressions of thwarted agency, structural conflicts between women, or, in the most optimistic expressions, conduits to the raising of consciousness. In this context, anger has been of special importance. Audre Lorde writes, "The angers of women can transform difference through insight into power. For anger between peers births change, not destruction, and the discomfort and sense of loss it often causes is not fatal, but a sign of growth" (Lorde 1984). Anger becomes not just a subject for study by psychologists and a destructive or ego-driven force, but an agent of positive transformation. Implicit in Lorde's statement is the idea that the researcher/activist/writer does not stand outside the interplay of feelings in human exchange but is a part of the scene that she is trying to understand and impact. Though researchers might prefer to see themselves as detached observers, everyone, to put it most plainly, has feelings.

In recent studies across the academy, discussion of intimate feelings has expanded from emotion into the realm of affect, that is, into the body (including various non-organic bodies and technologies that produce affective bodily capacities), as well as the mind. This shift is anchored in feminist thought. Michael Hardt (2007), for instance, locates the precursors of the widespread interest in affect in a feminist focus on the body and explorations of emotion within queer theory. His influential term "affective labor" describes embodied labor "that produces or manipulates affects such as a feeling of ease, well-being, satisfaction, excitement, or passion" (1999, 26). This is work that is most often done by women, or at least work that is most frequently associated with women's traditional capacities as caregivers, soothers, sex workers, or amanuenses. What Patricia Clough calls "the affective turn" in contemporary scholarship both grounds emotional life in the body and gestures towards something excessive in both emotions and the body: 'affect constitutes a nonlinear complexity out of which the narration of conscious states such as emotion are subtracted, but always with a "never-to-be-conscious autonomic remainder"' (Clough 2007). Affect theory challenges feminists to think beyond the body and emotions in a globalized frame; it speaks to the grounding and ungrounding of emotional life in relationships, both human and beyond, gesturing to and inculcating the experience of planet-wide interconnection.

The intimate forces our attention on a materialized understanding of the body when we theorize on a global scale. Is it possible to theorize global processes while remaining attentive to the pleasures and travails of individual embodiment? How might we find ways to hold on to emotion, attachment, the personal, and the body when we move into a more expansive engagement with the world? How, in other words, can we find the intimate in the global?

THE GLOBAL

"The global" typically evokes a historical conjuncture of economic, regulatory and cultural forces that are called globalization or global restructuring. Some identifying features are these: deregulation of markets, privatization of services, flexible production, structural adjustment, a proliferation of governmental bodies alongside and beyond the nation state, networked connectivity, increased spatial mobility, transnational organizing, complex and creative intermingling of cultural forms, and the deep burrowing of capital accumulation into the body and circuits of affect. Women and girls have been at the center of these many transformations and dislocations. As C. George Caffentzis wrote in 1993 of World Bank strategies to manage debt crisis: "The African body, especially the female body, has been attacked" (1993, 31). Similarly, Chandra Mohanty writes: "[i]t is especially on the bodies and lives of women and girls from the Third World/South— the Two-Thirds World—that global capitalism writes its script" (2002): 499–535, 514.

Feminist engagements with these processes are vast and diverse; in fact, a hallmark of feminist scholarship is a certain skepticism about large, simplifying narratives of globalization. As Kathleen Stewart (2007) explains, the terms globalization, neoliberalism and advanced capitalism cannot begin to describe the current situation and individuals' life circumstances. Feminist engagement with the global has been marked by persistent critique, not only of mainstream global processes and discourses of globalization but also critique of western feminists' fascination with and representations of women in the global south. We will review some of these criticisms and then consider the centrality of intimacy for the way that feminists have sought to think global processes and their place within them, including the potential for feminist solidarity around the globe.

Feminist theorists have long noted the absence of gender as an explicitly theorized category and object of empirical investigation in both mainstream and more critical approaches to globalization. As Mary Hawkesworth notes, "While … authoritative analyses of globalization disagree about many things … they converge on one point: the near total absence of any reference to women or to feminism" (2006, p. 173, n. 1). Gendered and sexualized metaphors of intimacy nonetheless undergird globalization discourses, both popular and scholarly, in unacknowledged and consequential ways. Charlotte Hooper (2001) has traced the implicit masculinities celebrated in popular discourse on globalization. Examining *The Economist* through the 1990s, she notes that, even though the "new man" of global restructuring may be less formal and more technocratic than his forebears, as an aggressive risk taker pursuing capitalist adventures across the globe, he remains a resolutely masculine figure. The economy appears to trump all other (feminized) factors and capitalism is figured as one cohesive globally-extensive system that can "have its way" with any local place it may seek to enter. By the same token, metaphors of the mismanaged body run through discourses of economic structural adjustment; Patricia Price (2000) describes how failing third world economies are typically subjected to regimes of "belt tightening" and "fat cutting". Unexamined, these metaphors of the slovenly or sexualized body nonetheless do considerable work, that of naturalizing and legitimating the seeming inevitability of global restructuring: the image of the fat, poorly managed body legitimates the massive privatization of state services; a victimized local economy appears to have no agency to stop her aggressor.

Feminists also express concern about the ways in which the intimate nuclear family, the protection of women and children and some of the triumphs of second-wave feminism have been redeployed to both restrict the reach of ethical obligation and lend moral authority to global economic restructuring, increased securitization of national borders, policing within and beyond the nation, and military aggression world-wide. On the one hand, the family model, in particular the relation between parent and child, dominates and restricts our thinking about care; we tend to associate care with proximity, and have few conceptual tools for imagining geographies of care beyond the national community. On the other, the model of the family is all too easily redeployed internationally; women and children are particularly effective vectors for sentimental politics, which can fuel both ethnic nationalisms and an abstracted, liberal human rights regime. Feminists have worried about the ways that their scholarship can be taken to support one of the most dangerous geographical imaginings of our time: the construction of a security state that justifies itself through its benevolent protection of women and children. Nancy Fraser (2009) troubles as well over the "elective affinities" between some of the powerful critiques made by second-wave feminists, in particular of state bureaucracies and the family wage, and neoliberalism and emergent forms of capitalism. The clawback of the welfare state, the attendant devolution of service provision to non-governmental organizations, and the expansion of women's waged employment in casualized, low paying jobs since the 1970s may bear only a perverse resemblance to the emancipatory ideals of second-wave feminism, but the latter nonetheless endow these trends with a higher moral—legitimating—significance.

THE GLOBAL AND THE INTIMATE: A GUIDE

By placing the global and the intimate into near relation, we hope to forge a distinctively feminist approach to pressing questions of transnational relations, economic development, global feminist mobilization and intercultural exchange.

Intimacy does not work within the same territorial or juridical logics as privacy, the local, or even the global. At the same time, the stain of what we call the global complicates and compromises intimacy in productive ways by opening it to histories of imperialism, national formation, global economic development, systematic humiliation and deprivation, and gender and sexual inequality. Joining the global and the intimate requires a constant attention to proportion, as well as to scale. It forces us to question what is big and what is small, what is important and what is inconsequential.

REFERENCES

Boym, Svetlana. "On Diasporic Intimacy: Ilya Kabakov's Installations and Immigrant Homes." *Critical Inquiry* 24, no. 2 (Winter 1998): 498–524.

Caffentzis, C. George. "The Fundamental Implications of the Debt Crisis for Social Reproduction in Africa." In Mariarosa Dalla Costa and Giovanna F. Dalla Costa (eds), *Paying the Price: Women and the Politics of International Economic Strategy*. London: Zed Books, 1993.

Clough, Patricia. "Introduction." In Patricia Ticineto Clough with Jean Halley (eds), *The Affective Turn: Theorizing the Social*, pp. 1–33. Durham, NC: Duke University Press, 2007.

Collins, Patricia Hill. "The Social Construction of Black Feminist Thought." *Signs* 14, no. 4 (1989): 745–773.

Fraser, Nancy. "Feminism, Capitalism and the Cunning of History." *New Left Review* 56 (March–April 2009): 97–117.

Gibson-Graham, J.K. *The End of Capitalism (as we knew it): A Feminist Critique of Political Economy*. Malden, MA: Blackwell, 1996.

Grewal, Inderpal, and Caren Kaplan. *Scattered Hegemonies: Postmodernity and Transnational Feminist Practices*. Minneapolis: University of Minnesota Press, 1994.

Hardt, Michael. "Affective Labor," *boundary 2*, 26, no. 2 (1999): 89–100.

Hardt, Michael. "Foreword: What Affects Are Good For." In Patricia Ticineto Clough with Jean Halley (eds), *The Affective Turn: Theorizing the Social*, pp. ix–xiii. Durham, NC: Duke University Press, 2007.

Hawkesworth, Mary. *Globalization and Feminist Action*. Lanham, MA: Rowman and Littlefield, 2006.

Hooper, Charlotte. *Manly States: Masculinities, International Relations and Gender Politics*. New York: Columbia University Press, 2001.

Lorde, Audre. "The Uses of Anger: Women Responding to Racism." In *Sister Outsider*, pp. 124–133. Berkeley, CA: Crossing Press, 1984.

Marston, Sallie A., John Paul Jones III, and Keith Woodward. "Human Geography Without Scale," *Transactions of the Institute of British Geographers* 30 (2005): 416–432.

Massey, Doreen B. *For Space*. London: Sage, 2005.

Mohanty, Chandra Talpade. "'Under Western Eyes' Revisited: Feminist Solidarity through Anticapitalist Struggles." *Signs* 28, no. 2 (2002): 499–535.

Ngai, Sianne. *Ugly Feelings*. Cambridge, MA, and London: Harvard University Press, 2005.

Price, Patricia. "No Pain, No Gain: Bordering the Hungry New World Order." *Environment and Planning D: Society and Space* 18 (2000): 91–110.

Stewart, Kathleen. *Ordinary Affects*. Durham, NC: Duke University Press, 2007.

58
On the Grounds of Globalization

A Topography for Feminist Political Engagement (2001)

Cindi Katz

Globalization is nothing new. Global trade has been going on for millennia—though what constitutes the "globe" has expanded dramatically in that time. And trade is nothing if not cultural exchange, the narrow distinctions between the economic and the cultural having long been rendered obsolete.

Globalization has been the signature dish of capitalism—a system of social relations of production and reproduction nourished by uneven development across a range of spatial scales, from the local or regional to the national or supranational, the ambitions of which have always been global—since its birth in Europe more than five centuries ago. European-born mercantile capitalism early on was driven by a real expansion for markets and the goods to trade across them. This was nothing new, particularly, until the agents of capital began to assemble an empire and deployed the physical and symbolic violence intended to redirect toward European interests the globe Europeans were "discovering."

Globalization, of course, is just another way of saying (and doing) imperialism, and since, worldwide, we are living in the shards of a Eurocentric but global capitalism, it behooves us to understand its work in the world, including the searing unevenness of capital's investments and disinvestments, the social costs of the privatization of public life, and the excruciating predations of all manner of state violence.

Part of that project might be to examine the intersecting effects and material consequences of so-called globalization in a particular place, to reveal a local that is constitutively global but whose engagements with various global imperatives are the material forms and practices of *situated knowledge*. Examining these effects and practices as such is a means to develop a politics that works the grounds of and between multiply situated social actors in a range of geographical locations who are at once bound and rent by the diverse forces of globalization. That is where topography comes in.

"Topography," according to the *Oxford English Dictionary* (1971), is "the accurate and detailed delineation and description of any locality." But there is an ambiguity there because topography is also "the features of a region or locality collectively." The thing itself as much as the description of it are produced, and unraveling the processes of how they came to be can reveal the powerful interests vested in topography and topographical knowledge. This work, which persists to this day within and outside of geography ... was purposive, partial, and, of course, interested, and it was usually conducted for political leaders or military commanders. Not much has changed. Topographical data are routinely fed to any number of global databases using geographical information systems (GIS) that facilitate resource extraction, surveillance, and rule and, if necessary, attack across geographic scale by various social actors.

What I offer here is a noninnocent topography of globalization and its entailments as a vehicle for developing a gendered oppositional politics that moves across scale and space. The place in question is in central eastern Sudan, a village that I call Howa, where I have worked, and sometimes lived, since 1980. In producing this topography, I have no intention of offering "the local" as a bulwark against "the global," or as an instance of something more true, real, or differentiated in a rapidly homogenizing world. Homogenization is not the script of globalization so much as differentiation and even fragmentation.

Thus, without romanticizing the local scale or any particular place, I want to get at the specific ways globalization works on particular grounds in order to work out a situated, but at the same time scale-jumping and geography-crossing, political response to it. Tracing the contour lines of such a "countertopography" to other sites might encourage and enable the formation of new political-economic alliances that transcend both place and identity and foster a more effective cultural politics to counter the imperial, patriarchal, and racist integument of globalization.

A TOPOGRAPHY OF GLOBALIZATION

I address moments of globalization that have produced distinct but connected arenas of transformation and trace some of the gendered political practices they call forth. The three moments, or traces, of globalization I examine are economic restructuring, "time-space expansion," and Sudan's enduring civil war. In Howa, these moments have prompted distinct, though limited, political responses that I have separated analytically as reworking, resilience, and resistance.

In Howa, the effects of restructuring were most directly experienced through the Suki Project, a massive state-sponsored and multilaterally funded agricultural development project. Its intent and effect were to transform an area of mixed land use, with minimal cash crop production, into a political ecology geared largely to cash cropping and full incorporation into the national and global economies. Much of the area around the village was cleared and leveled to support the irrigated cultivation of cotton and groundnuts for the world market, while animal husbandry and forestry were relegated to marginal off-project lands. These lands were therefore subjected to a much more intense use than before, straining local political ecologies.

I was particularly interested in what happened to children as subjects and "objects" of social reproduction under these conditions. Because of

the nature of cotton and groundnut cultivation in the irrigation project, more, not less, family labor was required after the project than before. Moreover, increased land use intensity around the project led to collateral environmental changes that increased the time required for the more distant procurement of wood and grazing of animals, both largely children's tasks. The pace of commodification and monetization of the economy had also intensified, in part because goods that were formerly held in common or free, such as wood or milk, were becoming more difficult to procure, and in part because a wealth of products from other parts of Sudan or further afield were being introduced into local markets, and a growing number of residents were seduced by them.

These shifts regrooved the particular gendered and otherwise differentiated relations of production and reproduction in Howa, increasing children's labor time and reducing possibilities for attending school.

Nevertheless, one of the most palpable changes I witnessed in the wake of these shifts in the local and broader political economy was a villagewide mobilization on behalf of schooling girls. In less than a generation, village leaders had deployed the resources of a series of self-help initiatives to build and staff a girls' elementary school, and by 1995 the finishing touches on a coeducational secondary school (with separate classes for girls and boys) were being put in place. The change in a period of less than fifteen years was astonishing; in 1981 only 4 percent of all girls between seven and twelve years old attended school, but by 1995 over 43 percent of girls that age were attending school.

These local efforts indicate a politics of *reworking* in the face of some of the devastating shifts associated with restructuring.

Built upon these iterations and effects of restructuring is a reformulation of the time-space of everyday life that reveals another path of globalization. I call this process *time-space expansion*. While David Harvey, drawing on Marx, notes that one of the signal effects of advanced capitalism is "the annihilation of space by time" (273), which creates one of the characteristic conditions of postmodernity, *time-space compression*, I found something quite different in rural Sudan. From the vantage point of capital, the world may be shrinking, but, on the marooned grounds of places such as Howa, it appeared to be getting bigger every day. After a grueling decade and a half of structural adjustments and political upheaval in Sudan, people in Howa survived by maintaining a semblance of the patterns and practices of production that long had sustained them: agriculture, animal husbandry, and forestry. But this was only viable now if carried out over an extended physical arena. The terrain of social production and reproduction had expanded from perhaps five kilometers in 1980 to two hundred kilometers by 1995, the distance men routinely traveled to participate in the charcoal trade. Time-space expansion also represented a transformation of the old constellation of activities that involved men's long absences from the village. People still farmed (but also worked as agricultural laborers up to a hundred kilometers away), kept animals (by sending them out with relatives to distant pastures), and cut wood (but now in areas of the South targeted for deforestation as part of the northern government's war effort) (see Katz 2000). The more things stayed the same, the more different they were. The old constellation inscribed a new geography and was bolstered by intensified labor migration among village men to various towns in Sudan and to the Gulf States, Libya, and Saudi Arabia, a wholly new source of work since the 1980s.

CONSTRUCTING COUNTERTOPOGRAPHIES

If topography is traditionally seen as embodying landscapes along with their description and delineation, I have chosen here to mobilize topography as a distinct research method. To do a topography is to carry out a detailed examination of some part of the material world, defined at any scale from the body to the global, in order to understand its salient features and their mutual and broader relationships. Because they routinely incorporate both "natural" and social features of a landscape, topographies embed a notion of process, of places made and nature produced. If "history is lifeless without topography," so, too, are topographies without history. Not only can a sense of sedimented process be read off the land itself, but producing topographies necessarily situates places in their broader context and in relation to other areas or geographic scales, offering a means of under-

standing structure and process. Indeed my project here is driven by the notion that producing a critical topography makes it possible to excavate the layers of process that produce particular places and see their intersections with material social practices at other scales of analysis. Revealing the embeddedness of these practices in place and space invites the vivid revelation of social and political difference and inequality.

Accomplishing such a move involves the construction of a *countertopography*. And here I want to draw on a more metaphorical sense of topography that refers to a central aspect of topographical maps—the contour line. Contour lines are lines of constant elevation, connecting places at precisely the same altitude to reveal a terrain's three-dimensional shape. I want to imagine a politics that maintains the distinctness of a place while recognizing that it is connected analytically to other places along contour lines that represent not elevation but particular relations to a process (e.g., globalizing capitalist relations of production). This offers a multi-faceted way of theorizing the connectedness of vastly different places made artifactually discrete by virtue of history and geography but which also reproduce themselves differently amidst the common political-economic and socio-cultural processes they experience. This notion of topography involves a precision and specificity that connects distant places and in so doing enables the inference of connection in uncharted places in between. As with contour lines, the measurements of elevation at select sites enable a line to be drawn without measuring every spot on earth. Such connections are precise analytic relationships, not homo-genizations. Not all places affected by capital's global ambition are affected the same way, and not all issues matter equally everywhere. By constructing precise topographies at a range of scales from the local to the regional and beyond, we can analyze a particular issue—say de-skilling—in and across place, mapping sites connected along this contour line.

The larger intent is to produce counter-topographies that link different places analytic-ally and thereby enhance struggles in the name of common interests. In many ways this builds an oppositional politics on the basis of situated knowledges. Doing topographies therefore builds upon feminist and Marxist insights concerning exploitation, oppression, and power (see Hartsock 1984; Haraway 1988; Mohanty

1988). If situated knowledges suggest local particularities of the relations of production and reproduction, their conscious apprehension in a globalized and multiply differentiated world offers fertile political connections across space and scale that have the fluidity to match and confront the deft global mobility of capitalist investment and disinvestment successfully. But the notion of situated knowledge itself only gets us partway there.

Situated knowledge assumes knowledge at a single point, the knowing subject, and the particularity of that subject's vision is both its strength and its downfall. If the brilliance of the idea was in making clear that all seeing, all knowing was from somewhere, and that that somewhere was socially constituted, allowing for and occluding particular insights, the implication of sites underlying knowledge has produced other problems. First, although situatedness may imply a locale, it is most often attributed to a mobile and multiply constituted subject, or subject-position (see Henriques et al. 1984). In any topographic mapping, however, a subject's position in the landscape is a point, and therefore a space of zero dimensions. Thus the language of site and situatedness has tended to facilitate a collapse of dimensionality rather than opposite.

Second, while "situated" alludes to some-where, it specifies no place in particular. Situatedness suggests location in abstract relation to others but not any specific geography, leading to a politics of "sites" and "spaces" from which materiality is largely evacuated.

Ignoring the difference that space makes diminishes political responses by avoiding the ways specific historical geographies embody and help reproduce particular social relations of power and production. Finally, situatedness is simultaneously universal—everything is situated—and specific—to the point of being zero dimensional. The politics of extension and translation, from the site to the global, is too easily assumed in the insistence on situatedness, when, of course, that is what has to be explained.

Doing topography, by contrast, already assumes the historical examination of social process in three-dimensional space. It takes for granted that space is both the bearer and reinforcer of social relations, and that if these relations are to be changed so too must their material grounds.

What politics might work the contours connecting carceral California, sweatshop New York, maquiladora Mexico, and structurally adjusted Howa, and back again?

In previous work (Katz 1998), I have traced one such line, from Howa to Harlem and back again. I wanted to understand the displacement and de-skilling of young people in the wake of the redlining and disinvestment in their communities. For example, by examining cuts in funds for public housing, public open space, health care, and social welfare benefits and the skewed distribution of funds for education in New York City, I have drawn comparisons between New York City and Howa in the means by which social reproduction was secured. I have compared disinvestments in social reproduction in working-class New York with the lack of public investment in social reproduction in Howa. The former were spurred by waves of economic restructuring that shifted many manufacturing jobs elsewhere, while the latter resulted from the "development" policies pursued by the Sudanese state (in conjunction with international financial institutions) that undermined the traditional means of production and of reproducing local relations in Howa. It seemed to me that in both places, large segments of the generation currently coming of age were being derailed to a marginalized zone in which there were few guarantees for sustained—let alone meaningful—work as adults. In sub-sequent years, large numbers of this "excessed" population appear to have been "warehoused" as a matter of state policy, as we see in prisons in the United States and in the army or people's militias in the case of Sudan. Nevertheless, in both settings I have found remarkable resilience at the community level and a tendency for people to organize to rework the conditions confronting them if not actually to resist them outright. I think of the remarkable increase in support for formal education for girls and boys in Howa in just a single generation and compare that with block-by-block efforts by neighbor-hood residents in New York to reject crack cocaine and hound its purveyors away. The numbers of children in primary school in Howa more than doubled in less than fifteen years, while recent reports in New York indicate equally dramatic reductions in crack use by young people over a similar period.

Whereas I originally understood the compa-rison between the two cases more sequentially as an examination of the kinds of displacements children can suffer in the transition from an agricultural to an industrial economy and from an industrial to a postindustrial economy the perspective offered by doing a topographical analysis affords a more productive and spatialized understanding of the problems. Not only does this kind of analysis reveal the simultaneity of different kinds of disruptions but, making good on John Berger's brilliant insight that it is now "space not time that hides consequences from us," it also reveals the intertwined consequences of globalizing capitalist production in ways that demand a different kind of politics (1974, 40; see Soja 1989). My argument is that if the disruption of social reproduction in Howa and Harlem are two effects of a common set of processes, and I think they are, then any effective politics challenging a capital-inspired globalization must have similar global sensitivities, even as its grounds are necessarily local. This is different from a "place-based" politics. It is not merely about one locale or another, nor is it a matter of building coalitions between such diverse places, vital as that is. Precisely because globalization is such an abstraction, albeit with varying forms, struggles against global capital have to mobilize equivalent, alternative abstractions. Built on the critical triangulation of local topographies, countertopographies provide exactly these kinds of abstractions interwoven with local specificities and the impulse for insurgent change.

REFERENCES

Berger, John. 1974. *The Look of Things*. New York: Viking.

Haraway, Donna J. 1988. "Situated Knowledges: The Science Question in Feminism as a Site of Discourse on the Privilege of Partial Perspective." *Feminist Studies* 14(3):575–599.

Hartsock, Nancy. 1984. *Money, Sex, and Power: Toward a Feminist Historical Materialism*. Boston, MA: Northeastern University Press.

Harvey, David. 1989. *The Condition of Postmodernity*. Oxford: Blackwell.

Henriques, Julian, Wendy Holloway, Cathy Urwin, Couze Venn, and Valerie Walkerdine. 1984. *Changing the Subject: Psychology, Social Regulation, and Subjectivity*. London and New York: Methuen.

Katz, Cindi. 1998. "Disintegrating Developments: Global Economic Restructuring and the Eroding Ecologies of Youth." In *Cool Places: Geographies of Youth Cultures*, ed. Tracy Skelton and Gill Valentine, pp. 130–144. London: Routledge.

Katz, Cindi. 2000. "Fueling War: A Political-Ecology of Poverty and Deforestation in Sudan." In *Producing Nature and Poverty in Africa*, ed. Vigdis Broch-Due and Richard A. Schroeder, pp. 321–339. Stockholm: Nordiska Africainstitutet and Transaction Press.

Mohanty, Chandra Talpade. 1988. "Feminist Encounters: Locating the Politics of Experience." *Copyright* 1 (Fall): 30–44.

Oxford English Dictionary. 1971. Oxford: Oxford University Press.

Soja, Edward W. 1989. *Postmodern Geographies: The Reassertion of Space in Critical Social Theory*. London; New York: Verso.

SECTION 11

The Spatial Imagination

Identity map drawn after 9/11 by Muhammad, Male, Arab-American, Age 14.
Referenced in: Fine, Michelle and Selçuk Sirin. 2008. "Negotiating the Muslim American Hyphen: Integrated, Parallel, and Conflictual Paths," in *Muslim American Youth: Understanding Hyphenated Identities through Multiple Methods*. New York: New York University Press, pp. 121–150.

THE SPATIAL IMAGINATION

As we move through our everyday routines, it is possible to imagine and enact alternative ways of living. Part of this remaking of the spaces and interactions of daily life involves new understandings and representations of our place in the world. We use the term *spatial imagination* to hint at these possibilities, and broaden earlier work on ways in which the imagination is instrumental in shaping our lives. Sociologist C. Wright Mills (1961) developed the idea of the *sociological imagination* as a conceptual tool to compare individuals' personal biographies to larger social situations and histories and connect "personal troubles to public issues." Geographer David Harvey (1973, 2005) coined the term *geographical imagination* in building upon Mills's concept by bringing geography into the mix of biography and history. The concept of the geographical imagination expresses the literal and metaphorical ways in which people conceptualize and render space (see Gregory 1994). As educational philosopher Maxine Greene (2000) writes,

> To call for imaginative capacity is to work for the ability to look at things as if they could be otherwise. To ask for intensified realization is to see that each person's reality must be understood to be interpreted experience—and that the mode of interpretation depends on his or her situation and location in the world. … To tap into the imagination is to become able to break with what is supposedly fixed and finished, objectively and independently real.

To imagine, then, is, in Greene's words, to "make empathy possible." The imagination is a tool for reaching greater understanding of self and other, while making plans to change the injustices of everyday life. Intimate and global, the *spatial imagination* can open up ways to take notice of being in the world and our implication in making, remaking, and being made by the geographies in which we live, work, and play.

Literary theorist **Edward Said** takes up the myths and histories of our environments as *imaginative geographies*: those ideas we have about a space or place's past that form the political, economic, and social experience of the present. In our selection from his piece "Invention, Memory, and Place," Said's focus is the contentious relationship between the State of Israel and Palestine. Retelling the story of Israel's rise through the demise of Palestine, Said shows how myths that assert an actual place in the world through claims to various locations and identities remain fixed to those places, such as the Abrahamic faiths' (Jewish, Christian, and Muslim) attachment to the City of Jerusalem. Said leaves the reader asking who has the right to land and on what basis. In his monumental *Orientalism*, Said (1979) likewise demonstrates how Western society posits an imaginary "Orient" through travelogues, art, literature, and scholarly work in order to justify and advance its colonial ambitions and practices.

The spatial imagination influences the way in which we perceive bodies and the place of identity and identification. Critical social psychologists **Selçuk R. Sirin** and **Michelle Fine** examine what they call the *hyphenated identities* of race, nation, ethnicity, gender, and sexuality of Muslim American youth in New York City in the aftermath of the violence, hatred, and distrust directed at this population following September 11, 2001. Questioning whether these young people would identify themselves as Muslim, American, or some combination, the authors drew on interviews and identity maps, and found three ways in which the youth embodied their multiple selves. One identity map, for example, shows a map of a young Muslim boy who lives such a hyphenated identity that he draws a line down the middle of his own face that splits his emotions and his sense of his national and personal identity (see figure at the beginning of Section 11). The spatial imaginations of these young people reflect their attempts to integrate or at least negotiate their multiple identifications, and call into question the imposed delimitations of place and identity.

The mapping of identities in place reaches far back into history. As South Asian historian **Thongchai Winichakul**'s careful examination of the historical geography of Siam/Thailand shows, spatial imaginations are at once more malleable than might be assumed and influential in producing material geographies. Winichakul's work reveals that the borders drawn on maps are far from fixed. Their histories stray from the static "official" boundary lines that delimit country from country at any single moment. French colonials in (then) Siam were infuriated to find border markers shifting almost daily in remote swamps and woods as tribal groups moved these markers as was convenient for their livelihoods. These sorts of contested and impermanent borders show how geographic distinctions are imagined and implemented from the perspective of those in power, and may not be sustainable on the ground or representative of material reality.

The way in which we imagine space also draws upon our actual experiences of space and place. For example, Americans increasingly navigate with the assistance of a GPS device, and often talk about distances in terms of the amount of time it takes to travel by car, because it is largely a driving culture. But not all cultures measure space in the same way. Thomas Gladwin's influential *East is a Big Bird: Navigation and Logic on Puluwat Atoll* (1995), for instance, demonstrated how the people of the Caroline atolls navigate long distances without a compass, imagining their oceanic world in ways that might confound conventional Western spatial imaginaries. Likewise, anthropologist **Richard Feinberg** and his colleagues' participatory work on symbolism, seafaring, navigation, and the oral traditions of the Anutan people in Polynesia examines their unique way of thinking about, experiencing, and moving through space. We include a selection of Feinberg's work in which he and his collaborators describe how the Anutans can navigate hundreds of miles between small islands using their own naming conventions and readings of coastal reefs, tidal movements, and constellations of stars in the night sky.

Questioning the totalizing power of capitalist interests through gendered representations of the body, critical geographer **J.K. Gibson-Graham**'s feminist critique of political economy offers a spatial imagination that moves beyond such oppressions. Drawing on political economic theory and activism, they illuminate how our imaginations are stifled not only by the economic systems we participate in but by the ways in which they are theorized as well. In more recent work, Gibson-Graham (2006) argues that one significant way of enacting alternate economies is by creating and sustaining alternate communities. They describe activist projects in the Philippines, India, and Massachusetts that elaborate on how blends of informal, wage, and alternate economies enact resistance to dominant capitalist modes of production and consumption.

The architect **Bernard Tschumi** concludes this section with a commentary on the fragmented urban conditions and oppressive spatial formations of late capitalism. Framed in terms of a series of negating prefixes (de, dis, ex), Tschumi argues that society has become deregulated and decentered. As such, he argues for a new set of spatial relationships and interactions that don't follow the Cartesian rules of space and time. His work asks: if the spaces of our lives were composed like a film script that one could cut and splice, what new social and spatial relationships might emerge? In this idea of *disjunction*, Tschumi offers a way to think about how space, in the form of buildings and cities, could be reconfigured to move beyond and alter the fixities of regulated life, both imagined and real.

Imagining alternative places and societies has a long history in design and literature, dating back to the publication of *Utopia* in 1516 by Thomas More, and well before that. Utopias— simultaneously "good place" and "no place"—are visions that try to convey the types of places and ways in which people would like to live or could live their ideals. Utopian visions have encompassed a wide range of living conditions and social relations, but what virtually all of them have in common is the ability to reveal the conflicts and desires of their particular milieu as a step toward imagining alternatives. These ideal visions can stimulate reflection and change, focusing beyond the present in order to help define the places and relations we hope for and might help to make (Eaton 2002). Artists such as Robert Irwin and Allan Wexler have also added valuable insights through the ways in which they have re-imagined existing places and social interactions (see Weschler 2009; Kester 2004).

While some authors explicitly recognize and articulate how our ways of imagining space affect our social and spatial realities, in many cases it takes effort on the part of the reader to recognize the gaps between what is thought or said and what actually exists. In a related text, political scientist Benedict Anderson's (1983) concept of *imagined communities* denotes communities formed in and through imagined connections rather than propinquity. It scales conceptually to notions of nation and nationalism, which presuppose common origin or unified values with others whom one may never know (see also Billig 1995). As the spatial imagination plays a role in producing notions of social and spatial reality, it also becomes a tool to address the disconnections between the lived or actual and the imagined, which are often indicative of social or spatial injustices. As the poet William Butler Yeats wrote, "In dreams begin responsibilities." The writings in this section suggest ways in which the spatial imagination is and can be a resource of that responsibility to redress the unequal spatialities of our everyday lives.

SUGGESTIONS FOR FURTHER READING

Please see *peopleplacespace.org* for extended and additional lists of readings.

Anderson, Benedict. 1983. *Imagined Communities: Reflections on the Origin and Spread of Nationalism*. New York: Verso.

Barkawi, Tarak and Keith Stanski (eds). 2012. *Orientalism and War*. New York: Columbia University Press.

Billig, Michael. 1995. *Banal Nationalism*. London; Thousand Oaks, CA: Sage.

Eaton, Ruth. 2002. *Ideal Cities: Utopianism and the (Un)built Environment*. New York: Thames & Hudson.

Fine, Michelle and Selçuk Sirin. 2008. "Negotiating the Muslim American Hyphen: Integrated, Parallel, and Conflictual Paths." In *Muslim American Youth: Understanding Hyphenated Identities through Multiple Methods*. New York: New York University Press, pp. 121–150.

Gibson-Graham, J.K. 2006. *A Postcapitalist Politics*. Minneapolis: University of Minnesota Press.

Gladwin, Thomas. 1995. *East Is a Big Bird: Navigation and Logic on Puluwat Atoll*. Cambridge, MA: Harvard University Press.

Greene, Maxine. 2000. *Releasing the Imagination: Essays on Education, the Arts, and Social Change*. San Francisco, CA: Jossey-Bass.

Gregory, Derek. 1994. *Geographical Imaginations*. Malden, MA: Wiley-Blackwell.

Harvey, David. 1973. *Social Justice and the City*. Baltimore, MD: The Johns Hopkins University Press.

Harvey, David. 2005. "The Sociological and Geographical Imaginations." *International Journal of Politics, Culture & Society* 18(3/4): 211–255.

Kester, Grant H. 2004. *Conversation Pieces: Community and Communication in Modern Art*. Berkeley: University of California Press.

Mills, C. Wright. 1961. *The Sociological Imagination*. New York: Grove Press.

More, Thomas. 2012. *Utopia*. London: Penguin Books.

Said, Edward W. 1979. *Orientalism*. Princeton, NJ: Vintage.

Sawalha, Aseel. 2011. *Reconstructing Beirut: Memory and Space in a Postwar Arab City*. Austin: University of Texas Press.

Scoates, Chris, and Debra Wilbur (eds). 1999. *Custom Built: A Twenty-year Survey of Work by Allan Wexler*. New York: Distributed Art Publishers.

Tsing, Anna Lowenhaupt. 2004. *Friction: An Ethnography of Global Connection*. Princeton, NJ: Princeton University Press.

Weschler, Lawrence. 2009. *Seeing is Forgetting the Name of the Thing One Sees: Expanded Edition*. Berkeley: University of California Press.

Wilson, Matthew W. 2009. "Cyborg Geographies: Towards Hybrid Epistemologies." *Gender, Place & Culture* 16(5): 499–516.

Yeats, William Butler. 2004. *Responsibilities*. Whitefish, MT: Kessinger Publishing.

59
Invention, Memory, and Place

(2000)

Edward W. Said

Over the past decade, there has been a burgeoning interest in two overlapping areas of the humanities and social sciences: memory and geography or, more specifically, the study of human space.

Memory and its representations touch very significantly upon questions of identity, of nationalism, of power and authority. Far from being a neutral exercise in facts and basic truths, the study of history, which of course is the underpinning of memory, both in school and university, is to some considerable extent a nationalist effort premised on the need to construct a desirable loyalty to and insider's understanding of one's country, tradition, and faith.

These remarks immediately transport us to the vexed issue of nationalism and national identity, of how memories of the past are shaped in accordance with a certain notion of what "we" or, for that matter, "they" really are. National identity always involves narratives—of the nation's past, its founding fathers and documents, seminal events, and so on. But these narratives are never undisputed or merely a matter of the neutral recital of facts. In the United States, for example, 1492 was celebrated very differently by people who saw themselves as victims of Columbus's advent—people of color, minorities, members of the working class, people, in a word, who claimed they had a different collective memory of what in most schools was celebrated as a triumph of advancement and the collective march forward of humanity. Because the world has shrunk—for example, communications have been speeded up fantastically—and people find themselves undergoing the most rapid social transformations in history, ours has become an era of a search for roots, of people trying to discover in the collective memory of their race, religion, community, and family a past that is entirely their own, secure from the ravages of history and a turbulent time. But this too has provoked very sharp debate and even bloodshed.

In other words, the invention of tradition was a practice very much used by authorities as an instrument of rule in mass societies when the bonds of small social units like village and family were dissolving and authorities needed to find other ways of connecting a large number of people to each other. The invention of tradition is a method for using collective memory selectively by manipulating certain bits of the national past, suppressing others, elevating still others in an entirely functional way. Thus memory is not necessarily authentic, but rather useful. The Israeli journalist Tom Segev shows in his book *The Seventh Million* that the Holocaust was consciously used by the Israeli government as a way of consolidating Israeli national identity after years of not paying much attention to it. Similarly, historian Peter Novick, in a recently published study of the image of the Holocaust amongst American Jews, shows that before the 1967 war and the Israeli victory against the Arab states, American Jews paid very little attention to that appallingly horrible episode (and in fact tried consciously to deemphasize it as a way of avoiding anti-Semitism).[1] It is a long way from those early attitudes to the construction of the Holocaust Museum in Washington. Similarly the controversy surrounding the memories of the Armenian genocide is fuelled by the Turkish government's denial of its role.

My point in citing all these cases is to underline the extent to which the art of memory for the modern world is both for historians as well as ordinary citizens and institutions very much something to be used, misused, and exploited, rather than something that sits inertly there for each person to possess and contain. Thus the study and concern with memory or a specifically desirable and recoverable past is a specially freighted late twentieth-century phenomenon that has arisen at a time of bewildering change, of unimaginably large and diffuse mass societies, competing nationalisms, and, most important perhaps, the decreasing efficacy of religious, familial, and dynastic bonds. People now look to this refashioned memory, especially in its collective forms, to give themselves a coherent identity, a national narrative, a place in the world, though, as I have indicated, the processes of memory are frequently, if not always, manipulated and intervened in for sometimes urgent purposes in the present.

As for geography, or geography as I want to use the word, as a socially constructed and maintained sense of place, a great deal of attention has been paid by modern scholars and critics to the extraordinary constitutive role of space in human affairs. Consider, as an easy instance, the word *globalization*, which is an indispensable concept for modern economics. It is a spatial, geographical designation signifying the global reach of a powerful economic system. Think of geographical designations like Auschwitz, think of what power and resonance they have, over and above a particularly specifiable moment in history or a geographical locale like Poland or France. The same applies to Jerusalem, a city, an idea, an entire history, and of course a specifiable geographical locale often typified by a photograph of the Dome of the Rock, the city walls, and the surrounding houses seen from the Mount of Olives; it too is overdetermined when it comes to memory, as well as all sorts of invented histories and traditions, all of them emanating from it, but most of them in conflict with each other. This conflict is intensified by Jerusalem's mytho-logical—as opposed to actual geographical—location, in which landscape, buildings, streets, and the like are overlain and, I would say, even covered entirely with symbolic associations totally obscuring the existential reality of what as a city and real place Jerusalem is. The same

can be said for Palestine, whose landscape functions in the memories of Jews, Muslims, and Christians entirely differently. One of the strangest things for me to grasp is the powerful hold the locale must have had on European crusaders despite their enormous distance from the country. Scenes of the crucifixion and nativity, for instance, appear in European Renaissance paintings as taking place in a sort of denatured Palestine, since none of the artists had ever seen the place. An idealized landscape gradually took shape that sustained the European imagination for hundreds of years. That Bernard of Clairvaux standing in a church in Vezelay, in the heart of Burgundy, could announce a crusade to reclaim Palestine and the holy places from the Muslims never fails to astound me, and that after hundreds of years of living in Europe Zionist Jews could still feel that Palestine had stood still in time and was theirs, again despite millennia of history and the presence of actual inhabitants. This too is also an indication of how geography can be manipulated, invented, characterized quite apart from a site's merely physical reality.

But what specially interests me is the hold of both memory and geography on the desire for conquest and domination. Two of my books, *Orientalism* and *Culture and Imperialism*, are based not only on the notion of what I call imaginative geography—the invention and construction of a geographical space called the Orient, for instance, with scant attention paid to the actuality of the geography and its inhabitants—but also on the mapping, con-quest, and annexation of territory both in what Conrad called the dark places of the earth and in its most densely inhabited and lived-in places, like India or Palestine.

We should never have left or given up India or Algeria, say some, using strange atavistic sentiments like the Raj revival—a spate of TV shows and films like *The Jewel in the Crown, A Passage to India, Gandhi*, and the fashion of wearing safari suits, helmets, desert boots—as a way of periodically provoking nostalgia for the good old days of British supremacy in Asia and Africa, whereas most Indians and Algerians would likely say that their liberation came as a result of being able after years of nationalist struggle to take hold of their own affairs, reestablish their identity, culture, and language, and, above all, reappropriate their territory from the colonial masters. Hence, to some extent, we witness the remarkable emergence of an Anglo-Indian literature by Anita Desai, Salman Rushdie, Arundhati Roy, and many others, re-excavating and re-charting the past from a postcolonial point of view, thereby erecting a new postimperial space.

All of what I have been discussing here—the interplay between geography, memory, and invention, in the sense that invention must occur if there is recollection—is particularly relevant to a twentieth-century example, that of Palestine, which instances an extraordinarily rich and intense conflict of at least two memories, two sorts of historical invention, two sorts of geographical imagination. I want to argue that we can go behind the headlines and the repetitively reductive media accounts of the Middle East conflict and discern there a much more interesting and subtle conflict than what is customarily talked about. Only by understanding that special mix of geography generally and landscape in particular with historical memory and, as I said, an arresting form of invention can we begin to grasp the persistence of conflict and the difficulty of resolving it, a difficulty that is far too complex and grand than the current peace process could possibly envisage, let alone resolve.

Let us juxtapose some relevant dates and events with each other. For Palestinians 1948 is remembered as the year of the *nakba*, or catastrophe, when 750,000 of us who were living there—two-thirds of the population—were driven out, our property taken, hundreds of villages destroyed, an entire society obliterated. For Israelis and many Jews throughout the world 1998 was the fiftieth anniversary of Israel's independence and establishment, a miraculous story of recovery after the Holocaust, of democracy, of making the desert bloom, and so on. Thus, two totally different characterizations of a recollected event have been constructed. What has long struck me about this radical irreconcilability at the origin of the Palestinian–Israeli conflict is that it is routinely excluded from considerations of related subjects concerning ethnic or collective memory, geographical analysis, and political reflection. This is most evident in studies of the German catastrophe as well as of ethnic conflicts in former Yugoslavia, Rwanda, Ireland, Sri Lanka, South Africa, and elsewhere.

Perhaps the greatest battle Palestinians have waged as a people has been over the right to a remembered presence and, with that presence, the right to possess and reclaim a collective historical reality, at least since the Zionist movement began its encroachments on the land. A similar battle has been fought by all colonized peoples whose past and present were dominated by outside powers who had first conquered the land and then rewrote history so as to appear in that history as the true owners of that land. Every independent state that emerged after the dismantling of the classical empires in the post-World War Two years felt it necessary to narrate its own history, as much as possible free of the biases and misrepresentations of that history by British, French, Portuguese, Dutch, or other colonial historians.

Yet the fate of Palestinian history has been a sad one, since not only was independence not gained, but there was little collective understanding of the importance of constructing a collective history as a part of trying to gain independence. To become a nation in the formal sense of the word, a people must make itself into something more than a collection of tribes, or political organizations of the kind that since the 1967 war Palestinians have created and supported. With a competitor as formidable as the Zionist movement, the effort to rewrite the history of Palestine so as to exclude the land's peoples had a disastrous effect on the quest for Palestinian self-determination. What we never understood was the power of a narrative history to mobilize people around a common goal. In the case of Israel, the narrative's main point was that Zionism's goal was to restore, reestablish, repatriate, and reconnect a people with its original homeland. It was the genius of Herzl and Weizmann to draft thinkers like Einstein and Buber, as well as financiers like Lord Rothschild and Moses Montefiore, into giving their time and effort in support of so important and historically justified a scheme. This narrative of reestablishment and recovery served its purpose not only amongst Jews but also throughout the Western (and even in some parts of the Eastern) world. Because of the power and appeal of the Zionist narrative and idea (which depended on a special reading of the Bible) and because of the collective Palestinian inability as a people to produce a convincing narrative story with a beginning, middle, and end (we were always too disorganized, our leaders were always interested in maintaining their power, most of our intellectuals refused to commit themselves as a group to a common goal, and we too often changed our goals) Palestinians have remained scattered and politically ineffective victims of Zionism, as it continues to take more and more land and history.

As I suggested above, collective memory is not an inert and passive thing, but a field of activity in which past events are selected, reconstructed, maintained, modified, and endowed with political meaning.

Along with the idea of Israel as liberation and independence couched in terms of a reestablishment of Jewish sovereignty went an equally basic motif, that of making the desert bloom, the inference being that Palestine was either empty (as in the Zionist slogan, "a land without people for a people without land") or neglected by the nomads and peasants who facelessly lived on it. The main idea was to not only deny the Palestinians a historical presence as a collectivity but also to imply that they were not a people who had a long-standing peoplehood.

With the rise of the PLO, first in Jordan, then after September 1970 in Beirut, a new Palestinian interest arose in the past, as embodied in such disparate activities as organized historical research and the production of poetry and fiction based upon a sense of recovered history, formerly blotted out but now reclaimed in the poetry of Zayyat, Darwish, Hussein, and al-Qassem, in the fiction of Kanafani and Jabra, as well as in painting, sculpture, and historical writing such as Abu-Lughod's collection *The Transformation of Palestine*. Later work such as the compilations of Walid Khalidi—*Before Their Diaspora* and *All That Remains*—Rashid Khalidi's study *Palestinian Identity*, Sabry Jiryis's *The Arabs in Israel*, Bayan al Hout's study of the Palestinian elites, Elia Zureik's *The Palestinians in Israel*, and many others, all by Palestinian scholars, gradually established a line of dynastic descent, between the events of 1948 and before and after the catastrophe, that gave substance to the national memory of a Palestinian collective life that persisted, despite the ravages of physical dispossession, military occupation, and Israeli official denials.[2] By the middle of the 1980s, a new direction had begun to appear in Israeli critical histories of the canonized official memories. In my opinion their genesis lay to some considerable extent in the aggravated, but close colonial encounter between Israelis and Palestinians in the occupied territories. Consider that with the accession to power of the right-wing Likud in 1977 these territories were renamed Judea and Samaria; they were onomastically transformed from "Palestinian" to "Jewish" territory, and settlements—whose object from the beginning had been nothing less than the transformation of the landscape by the forcible introduction of European-style mass housing with neither precedent nor basis in the local topography—gradually spread all over the Palestinian areas, starkly challenging the natural and human setting with rude Jewish-only segregations. In my opinion, these settlements, whose number included a huge ring of fortresslike housing projects around the city of Jerusalem, were intended visibly to illustrate Israeli power, additions to the gentle landscape that signified aggression, not accommodation and acculturation.

Let me note in a very brief conclusion what the interplay among memory, place, and invention can do if it is not to be used for the purposes of exclusion, that is, if it is to be used for liberation and coexistence between societies whose adjacency requires a tolerable form of sustained reconciliation. Again I want to use the Palestinian issue as my concrete example. Israelis and Palestinians are now so intertwined through history, geography, and political actuality that it seems to me absolute folly to try and plan the *future* of one without that of the other. The problem with the American-sponsored Oslo process was that it was premised on a notion of partition and separation, whereas everywhere one looks in the territory of historical Palestine, Jews and Palestinians live together. This notion of separation has also closed these two unequal communities of suffering to each other. Most Palestinians are indifferent to and often angered by stories of Jewish suffering since it seems to them that as subjects of Israeli military power anti-Semitism seems remote and irrelevant while their land is taken and homes are being bulldozed. Conversely most Israelis refuse to concede that Israel is built on the ruins of Palestinian society, and that for them the catastrophe of 1948 continues until the present. Yet there can be no possible reconciliation, no possible solution unless these two communities confront each's experience in the light of the other. It seems to me essential that there can be no hope of peace unless the stronger community, the Israeli Jews, acknowledges the most powerful memory for Palestinians, namely, the dispossession of an entire people. As the weaker party Palestinians must also face the fact that Israeli Jews see themselves as survivors of the Holocaust, even though that tragedy cannot be allowed to justify Palestinian dispossession. Perhaps in today's inflamed atmosphere of military occupation and injustice it is perhaps too much to expect these acknowledgements and recognitions to take place. But, as I have argued elsewhere, at some point they must.

NOTES

1   See Peter Novick, *The Holocaust in American Life* (New York, 1999), pp. 146–203.

2   See *The Transformation of Palestine: Essays on the Origin and Development of the Arab–Israeli Conflict,* ed. Abu Lughod (Evanston, Ill., 1971); Walid Khalidi, *Before Their Diaspora: A Photographic History of the Palestinians* (Washington, D.C., 1984); *All That Remains: The Palestinian Villages Occupied and Depopulated by Israel in 1948,* ed. Walid Khalidi (Washington, D.C., 1992); Rashid Khalidi, *Palestinian Identity: The Construction of Modern National Consciousness* (New York, 1997); Sabri Jiryis, *The Arabs in Israel,* trans. Inca Bushnag (New York, 1976); Bayan al Hout, *Political Leadership and Institutions in Palestine, 1917–48* [Arabic] (Beirut, 1984); and Elia Zureik, *The Palestinians in Israel: A Study in Internal Colonialism* (London, 1979).

60
Negotiating the Muslim American Hyphen

(2008)

Selçuk R. Sirin and Michelle Fine

Immigrant minority youth form their identity by becoming a member of a collective group based on racial, ethnic, or religious background and by negotiating among different cultural frameworks (Berry 1990; LaFramboise et al. 1993; Suárez-Orozco 2004). A study of immigrant Muslim youth in the United States provides many opportunities to understand how young people find their paths as Muslims and Americans. Beyond bicultural identifications, these youth craft their identity from multiple sources of social identification. Borrowing from Deaux (2006), we argue for the notion of *hyphenated selves* in order to understand how youths create and enact their identities when political or social conditions place them in tension. We use this idea to help us think about how youth negotiate, embody, and narrate their multiple selves, at the hyphen, in a fractured world, nation, community, home, or school.

We are most interested in understanding how young people experience the psychological and political jolt of "excluded citizenship" (Pinson 2008): how they think about, embody, and represent the pivot on which their identities join or split. We also seek to understand how historic and contemporary political conditions enable, complicate, or eviscerate the very delicate hyphens at which young people struggle to construct meaningful narratives of themselves. And we want to understand under what conditions these hyphenated selves move toward critical consciousness and activism. By theorizing about hyphenated selves, we are exploring what happens socially and psychologically when young people craft narratives of themselves from identities that hyphenate and

then perforate, when they are separated from the larger body politic, and when they become internal exiles in their own nation.

NEGOTIATING THE MUSLIM AMERICAN HYPHEN

Beyond measuring the degree to which youth identify with their multiple cultures, we also wanted to understand qualitatively how they negotiated, both psychologically and socially, these sometimes unrelated, sometimes parallel, and sometimes conflictual lives. Through the maps and focus groups, we tried to determine how young people create meaning at the hyphen. Overall, we found that young people devise very complex dynamics at the hyphen, mainly with their "American" and "Muslim" identities but sometimes also with their ethnic identities, political engagements, school, music, or fashion. That is, they engage across contexts in what Verkuyten and de Wolf called a "flexible expression" of identities as social practices, across a wide web of contexts, often having to "explain and justify their identity, not only in interactions with dominant group members but also in relation to their own group" (2002, 371). We relied on maps, surveys, and interviews to unearth these identity-negotiation processes with a focus on "change, hybridity and self-determination" (Verkuyten and de Wolf 2002, 375). As Sunil Bhatia has pointed out, immigrants engage in "ongoing negotiations between voices of assignation and assertion," reflecting a dialogical model of acculturation in the context of cultural difference, identity politics, and increasing globalization and transnational communication (Bhatia 2007, 186).

In our survey of the younger group, we grouped maps using the general framework found in the "bicultural identity" literature showing that although some perceive their dual cultural identities as "integrated," others perceive them as "oppositional," more challenging to integrate (Benet-Martinez et al. 2002; Phinney and Devich-Navarro 1997). For the older cohort, with data from 118 young adults, we were able to test these differences further using a more refined framework with three metacategories: integrated, parallel, and conflictual. Specifically, the maps were coded as (1) "integrated" if the Muslim and American identities were fully blended in a nonconflicting way, (2) "parallel identities" if both identities were depicted as separate worlds, or (3) "conflictual" if the maps represented tension, conflicting elements, hostility, or irreconcilability of the identities.[1] With this coding framework, we were able to better differentiate parallel and conflictual paths, emphasizing the important difference between living in multiple different worlds and struggling with tensions between worlds.

We also examined the maps...by gender. We found a pattern of interest: young Muslim women were more likely to display "integrated" identities than men were, similar to the trend we observed in the younger group. Together these findings show that in both groups, the girls and young women, compared with their male peers, were more likely to produce maps representing a dynamic tension between their identifications with Muslim and American selves. For the boys and young men, however, the modal path seemed to be a process of living in parallel worlds, sometimes with struggle. The young people chose each of these three commonly observed paths in order to make sense of their Muslim and American identities in a highly contentious moment in history and place. Next we explore these paths as integration, parallel lives, and conflict.

Integrated Paths

Several of the participants, mostly women, told us that their layered identities gave them wide "access to the rest of the world." Iman described an almost chemical transformation that came from the layering of her many selves: "You're like a new culture. It's like those new restaurants that mix ... you're like a *fusion* ... a new fusion. And it's just interesting to be you, you know, because you're fusing two cultures in one." Through focus groups and identity maps, we discovered the many different ways that young men and women combine creatively several different aspects of their personhood.

Such a journey is not uncommon among Muslims, as the United States is often not the first country to which Muslims immigrate after they leave their country of origin. Once these immigrants arrive in the United States, however, they find only a few substantial Muslim communities, such as Dearborn, Michigan; Bay Ridge, New York; or Paterson, New Jersey. Even those who move into these enclaves when they first arrive in this country often move out to other parts of the country once they begin raising their children. As a result, a large number of second-generation Muslim immigrants are living in places without a sizable Muslim community. Tariq, a nineteen-year-old Pakistani man attending college in New York City, told us how he negotiated his identity in one such town.

I grew up in the US my whole life but I never really adapted to my family's culture. I mean I did to a certain extent, but I never really spoke the language too much in my area. There weren't a lot of Muslims, so I had all American friends and did a lot of American things. You don't necessarily agree with the government or the policies. Maybe some of the cultural things that go on, but to me, America is like a melting pot of all these cultures. I'm one piece of that. I don't think when you say you are [an] American Jew, there's one thing you can identify with. I guess there is the government, the things you see on TV, and the front that we have, but to me there's so much more than that. There's so many more parts to our culture, the American culture. ... In my house there are some things like my parents don't let me watch at night, you know, like filthy movies or whatever, listening to bad music, but it's part of American culture here. And you know, I had those values of like Pakistan or Islam, but I also have the American customs and culture too 'cause I grew up here, I can't, I don't totally alienate myself from it 'cause if

I didn't like it, I wouldn't live here anymore. But I do like it, as much as we say we don't agree with it. Yes, there are some things that totally don't agree with Islam either, but I'm living here and I choose to live here, 'cause I do like some of the stuff, whether it is un-Islamic or not. … I don't see why I can't call myself American and Muslim.

Several of the young people feel it is "definitely an advantage" to be aware of and part of more than one ethnic or cultural group. When Marina, a fifteen-year-old Egyptian girl, presented her identity map, her beautiful face was framed by a pale blue flowered *ḥijāb*, she spoke excitedly about the thrilling challenge of the hyphen: "Islam gives me meaning and the US holds the promise of freedom to wear *ḥijāb*, practice religion like my brothers, to be educated and to educate others." In the hyphen, she can embrace what she loves about her religion and culture, but she can also separate from what she finds oppressive. Azarene agreed, showing an identity map that painted freedom and education as central to women's well-being across Islam and America.

While all the youths identified their Muslim selves in their identity maps, they varied greatly in the levels of their religiosity, ranging from cultural to spiritual to pious to questioning.

Living in Parallel Worlds

A smaller group of our interviewees told us that they live in, and commute between, two parallel, separate worlds. These youth experienced their Muslim and American selves in different compartments of life, with seemingly little tension. Our surveys revealed that those who live parallel lives were significantly more involved in social and cultural activities of their home culture than were those experiencing conflict or integration. With identities rooted firmly in two worlds, these young people engage substantially in the social (i.e., hanging out with people from their home culture) and cultural activities of their home countries (i.e., eating food, listening to music, and watching TV originating from one's home culture).

While commuting between worlds may sound effortless, a number of the young people described the burdens of living in parallel worlds as "suppressing." They selectively enact specific parts of their identity at home and in school with peers. Farid, an eighteen-year-old Afghan freshman, spoke through his identity map about how he negotiated his identity across contexts.

I didn't grow up around any Afghan people at all. I grew up in a completely white neighborhood, so the music that I listen to, the culture that I was brought up in, was completely white American. And at the same time I am clearly always going to be different [from] American people, because it is hard to ignore the difference, physical appearances and stuff like that. I do have a few Afghan friends, and I have cousins and when I hang out with them, I am like the white kid. But when I hang out with white kids, they treat me well, but I don't know I always feel I am different, and I don't think they notice that I am different … for instance, I don't necessarily like football, but I would go to football games and be bored there because I felt like that was what I was supposed to be doing. You know what I mean? There is just a lot of stupid stuff that I did that I didn't really want to do just because I thought that it would help me fit in.

While the youth elaborated on how Islam shapes their identities, they were explicit about what it means to be "American." Loyal to religion, ethnicity, community, family, and the United States, the young people spoke with both pride and concern about their nation, the United States. When discussing patriotism, they listed the "freedoms" and "liberties" available to them in the United States, and then they quietly listed the violations they had witnessed and experienced. Although they highlighted the differences between their home cultures and mainstream US culture, they had not yet learned how to live in both worlds with ease. The process of identity negotiation for youth who take a journey on this path involves learning how to switch on and off between two parallel worldviews, that is, jumping between the sides of the hyphen. There are developmental questions here that we cannot fully answer at this point. For example, we do not know whether those youths who choose to live in two parallel worlds have tried (and failed) in their efforts to develop hybrid identities, or whether they simply never attempted to do this.

CONFLICT AT THE HYPHEN

Reconciling and claiming both American and Islamic values in the United States at this moment in history is a struggle for some young Muslim men and women. Despite the popular imagination and scholarly claims about the incompatibility assumption, however, we found only a small number of young people who seemed to experience being Muslim in direct conflict with mainstream US values and traditions.

Conflict at the hyphen is sparked not only between religious (e.g., Muslim) and national (e.g., American) identities but also between ethnic (e.g., Palestinian) and national identities or between war (here) and peace (over there). Azhar, an eighteen-year-old Pakistani man, eloquently explained how he was negotiating across his Pakistani, American, and Muslim identities, sometimes encountering a great degree of conflict and struggle along the way:

> There has always been this struggle of sort of conflating or managing all these identities within me. The main conflict comes from Islam and America. I am American born. I have lived all my life in America. I love everything, that is, I love a lot of things about America. I love the civil rights movement. I love the fact that you have this sense of individuality. But at the same time, you look at what Islam has been in conflict in the West with. You look at Orientalism, you look at imperialism. These are the sorts of things that create a backlash within Muslim communities and countries in the twentieth century. Being the child of twentieth-century-born Pakistani parents, there is definitely some of that sentiment that is ingrained in me. If you look at Sayyid Mawdudi, he is one of the premier twentieth-century Islamic scholars, and he is a very anti-Western person. Those ideas get grouped in with family values sometimes, and then sometimes it brings upon this stereotype within you that everything that's with America is wrong. ... So you always see this struggle within me saying that Islam is the ideal. You know there is always this struggle to define Islam as the ideal way of life within me. There is always this constant struggle between defining my values as a Muslim or an American.

While many of the young men and women celebrate the advantages of their multicultural and religious identities, they also were keenly aware of the weight of living "between" and "within" multiple cultures or selves (Sarroub 2005; Wiley et al. 2006). When we began our work with the Muslim American youth, we thought we would find a large segment going through what Usman described here. To our surprise, however, only a small portion seem to report the kind of identity conflict that is so prevalent in both the scholarly literature and public discussions of youth who negotiate their identities across racial, ethnic, religious, and national boundaries. We certainly need more time and more data to determine the long-term developmental implications of the current historical context, but the early evidence suggests that young people are innovative, creatively reconciling the many challenges of living on the precarious hyphen of Muslim American.

A Flashpoint: Critiquing Muslims

As expected from any group under pressure, Muslims in general and particularly Muslims in the post-9/11 United States find it quite difficult to articulate their internal criticism of their religious backgrounds or the Muslim world in general. The difference between a "sellout" and an honest critique is not always clear in the minds of many. In the context of expansive surveillance, loyalty oaths loom large, and those who betray their own run the risk of being ostracized or exploited by the dominant group.

Because of these challenges, we did not hear much criticism of Islam. However, to our surprise (and we did not ask such questions in our surveys!) we noticed that those who were willing to criticize Islam or the Muslim world, as well as US government policies, tended to be the young people whose maps represented deep integration. As arbiters of many allegiances, they also show a willingness to take responsibility, that is, to note the points of tensions without feeling like a "sellout." Tariq, for example, explained the current relations between Muslims and the West by placing the blame on both sides: "You know it is not always like there is one right side or that there is one completely wrong side. Obviously both sides must be doing some wrong deeds. There must be something wrong on both sides that has led to a result of this." Another young man agreed, "I don't want to be the one to blame the West and say oh you guys initiated it first. Obviously Muslims have to do work within the communities to dispel these anti-Western feelings." Those who connect with both the Muslim and American communities also seemed to be able to be critical of not only American society but also the Muslim community in the United States and at large. Though without enough survey data to conduct a direct comparative assertion, we nonetheless suggest that those who develop integrated identities are probably more motivated to make such criticisms because they care about both their identities and the relationships between them.

CONCLUSION

We identified three important points about how young Muslim men and women form their identities. First, we found strong empirical evidence that Muslim American youth indeed develop strong commitments to both their Muslim identities and their American identities. This finding fundamentally challenges the dominant "incompatibility" hypothesis, which proposes that Muslim and "American" cultures are mutually exclusive. Second, we determined that two very different processes lead to an identification with the Muslim community and the mainstream US society. Third, we identified three forms of psychological work engaged by youth at the hyphen. Most young people have creatively *integrated* aspects of their Muslim and "American" selves. A smaller group—mostly male—describe *parallel* and relatively non-intersecting lives, between which they commute. Last, a quite small but important group embody and experience substantial *conflict at the hyphen*.

NOTE

1 In addition to surveys, we also gathered individual-level qualitative data using a novel technique we call "identity maps." Through these maps we tried to capture how young people creatively present their identities through drawings. The maps offered an additional opportunity to learn what goes on below the radar, that is, how identities are embedded in memory, fears, and emotions that might not be voiced in a focus group or survey.

Specifically, we gave the participants a blank sheet of paper and drawing materials (ink pens and colored markers), and the following instructions:

> Using the materials provided with this survey, please draw a map of your many ethnic, religious, and social identities. This should be an illustration of how you see yourself as a Muslim American person. You are free to design the map as you wish. You can use drawings, colors, symbols, words, whatever you need to reflect your multiple selves.

We gathered 137 maps, each matched to the survey data and, when possible, to the focus-group data. These maps are distributed throughout the book to illustrate key theoretical issues and to portray the ways in which youth embody their multiple identities.

REFERENCES

Benet-Martinez, Veronica, Janxin Leu, Fiona Lee, and Micheal Morris. (2002). Negotiating biculturalism: Cultural priming in blended and alternating Chinese-Americans. *Journal of Cross-cultural Psychology*, 33(5), 492–516.

Berry, John W. (1990). Psychology of acculturation: Understanding individuals moving between cultures. In R.W. Brislin (ed.), *Applied Cross-cultural Psychology*, pp. 232–253. Newbury Park, CA: Sage.

Bhatia, Sunil. (2007). *American Karma: Race, culture, and identity in the Indian diaspora*. New York: New York University Press.

Deaux, Kay. (2006). *To Be An Immigrant*. New York: Russell Sage.

LaFramboise, Teresa, H.L.K. Coleman, and Jardin Gerton. (1993). Psychological impact of biculturalism: Evidence and theory. *Psychological Bulletin*, 114(3), 395–412.

Phinney, Jean S., and Mona Devich-Navarro. (1997). Variations in bicultural identification among African American and Mexican American adolescents. *Journal of Research on Adolescence*, 7(1), 3–32.

Pinson, Hallel. (2008). The excluded citizenship identity: Palestinian/Arab Israeli young people negotiating their political identities. *British Journal of Sociology of Education*, 29(2), 201–212.

Sarroub, Loukia K. (2005). *All American Yemeni girls: Being Muslim in a public school.* Philadelphia: University of Pennsylvania Press.

Suárez-Orozco, Carola. (2004). Formulating identity in a globalized world. In M.M. Suárez-Orozco and D.B. Oin-Hilliard (eds), *Globalization: Culture and education in the new millennium*. Berkeley: University of California Press.

Verkuyten, Maykel, and Angela de Wolf. (2002). Being, feeling and doing: Discourses and ethnic self-definitions among minority group members. *Culture and Psychology*, 8(4), 371–399.

Wiley, Shaun, Krystal Perkins, and Kay Deaux. (2006). Through the looking glass: Ethnic and generational patterns of immigrant identity. Unpublished manuscript, City University of New York.

61
Maps and the Formation of the Geo-Body of Siam

(1996)

Thongchai Winichakul

Most studies on nationalism have suggested that the elements that define nationhood can be found in language, ethnicity, significant cultural traits, or a political unity. They are regarded as the essential common elements which constitute the identity of a nation. More recently, following the influential works by Anderson, Gellner, and Hobsbawm and Ranger,[1] the essentialism of the national identity is fundamentally denied. Many have turned to focus on how those elements were invented, and helped in creating the imagined nationhood. So far, none of them has paid attention to the most obvious constitutive element of a nation-state, namely its territory, as if it were merely a non-effective container of those essential elements. Supplemental to those attempts, therefore, this essay asks a similar question—how a nation is created as such an entity.[2] But it argues in a dissimilar way that nationhood was literally "formed" by the demarcation of its body, the territoriality of a nation. The case is Siam in the late nineteenth century.

THE GEO-BODY

Geographically speaking, the geo-body of a nation occupies a certain portion of the earth's surface which can be objectively identified. It seems to be concrete to the eyes and having a long history as if it were natural, and independent from technology or any cultural and social construction. Unfortunately, that is not the case. The study shows that the geo-body of a nation is merely the effect of modern geographical knowledge and its technology of representation, a map. The geo-body, the territoriality of a nation as well as its attributes such as sovereignty and boundary, are not only political but also cultural constructs. They were formulated on the soil where the indigenous spatial discourse had existed long before. The study emphasizes how the new geographical discourse displaced the existing indigenous concepts of space, through the innumerable meetings of the two kinds of knowledge, which generated conflicts, confrontations, miscommunication, serious and humorous misunderstandings.

It goes without saying that the empires and kingdoms in pre-modern Southeast Asia, probably not unlike others in the world, did not have the same kind of boundary as a modern state does. This was not due to lack of expertise or techniques, but to the fact that the concept of such a boundary did not exist. This does not mean, however, that there had been no knowledge of geography, no maps, or no limits of a country. Only that they were of other kinds.

The best known traditional maps from the region and from Siam in particular are the "Three-world" cosmographic maps. It is also well known how the architecture of a city and palace in the Hindu-Buddhist tradition is cosmographic in spirit.

"Siam" could also be expressed in a cosmographical sense rather than in political-geographical terms.

Modern geography from the West was a different kind of knowledge. It has a long history of shifts, turns and development from Ptolemy, the medieval T-O map, to Mercator and the modern mapping. Since the late eighteenth century, in Europe it has been indispensable to the modernist project of nationalism and nation-state. Undoubtedly it played a prominent role in colonialism. Not only was the political conquest by the West a new page of world history; also colonialism brought modern geography as it was in the nineteenth century and the nation-based political geography into contact with the indigenous knowledge of geography and political community. Dissemination and exchange of knowledge, confrontations and displacements ensued. Literally, colonialism created a new face of the globe.

THE NON-BOUNDED SIAM AND ITS MARGINS

Siam, like other kingdoms in Southeast Asia, was a hierarchical conglomeration of towns and cities whose supreme overlord acquired sacred power endowed in various places, objects and rituals, such as the throne, the palace, regalia, the white elephants, the coronation, and so on. But his (rarely her) control over the towns within the realm was uneven, usually waning with distance from the centre. Each town (*muang* in Thai) governed a certain area, mainly within its walls and the adjacent areas only, particularly the travelling paths and the passages through the jungles, mountains, and between towns. The limits of a town might be marked only sporadically at certain intervals, or there would be an agreement that the limit was at some specific point, or at the distance a guard could patrol. Above all, the markings might not be connected since not all areas needed to be marked. In other words, though a town had its territorial limits, its boundary was quite different from a modern boundary, and a town was usually not bounded. The limits might even be left vague or open between two friendly towns. Moreover, the limits of a town might or might not connect with those of another town. The areas beyond the authority of any town were virtually the "ungoverned", or "jungle" or "uncivilized" (*pa*, *thuan* in Thai). A pre-modern realm of a kingdom was a patchy territory full of hierarchically sovereign units. As its limits were marked by the frontier towns, the realm of a kingdom was usually not bounded either.

On the western frontier of Siam, the long ranges of mountainous jungles had been left unoccupied. Siam and Burma were arch-rivals of comparatively equal strength, and the mode of warfare at that time was basically to plunder and to depopulate the frontier towns of the enemy. This led both sides to abandon the area between their frontier towns as a natural buffer. For Siam a *khetdaen* (the term now used to translate boundary) was not necessarily connected or joined with the Burmese ones. It was the limit within which the authorities of a country could exercise their power.

In modern political geography, a state occupies a piece of the earth's surface determined by demarcated boundaries around it. Any doubts regarding a boundary must be resolved. Otherwise it could lead to serious conflicts between nations. But in a country which is not a tiny island, no one can see its geographical body. First, it is impossible simply because of the size. Second, even from a satellite view, the demarcation lines that go through mountains, jungles, seabeds and deserts are hardly identifiable. What is it then that makes the geo-body of a nation alive in our imagination and makes our discourse about it sensible? The answer: the map. Our conception of the nation with its finely demarcated body comes from nowhere else than the political map. A modern nation-state *must* be imaginable in mapped form; otherwise the geographical discourse of a nation would not work. Unfortunately, under the regime of modern geography, disconnected, disjoined or overlapping boundaries are unthinkable and unacceptable. They must be changed. The boundary of the modern kind must replace the indigenous geographical discourse and practices if a nation is to be conceivable in modern geographical terms.

"BOUNDARY CLASHES"

Modern geography was a powerful science in the hands of Europeans journeying to the East from the sixteenth century to nineteenth-century colonialism. Geographical inquiries, surveys and map-making were parts of the colonial advance and the main tasks of many diplomatic and exploratory missions. Key colonial officials were map-makers. Map-making was encouraged and rewarded with promotion. Unfortunately, in the case of Siam, map-makers had to rely on oral information from native people who might not be able to tell them where the limits of a country were. Even the native elite might have only a scant knowledge of the margins because such was not their concern.

When the British conquered southern Burma (Tenasserim) in 1826, they urged Siam to demarcate the boundary between the British-held and Siamese territories. For the Siamese court, a boundary demarcation was not a matter of concern. If the British really wanted to know their boundary, the court replied, they could ask the old inhabitants in the area. And that was it. Let the British do the demarcation if they feel the need.[3] Likewise, since the British wanted it, the king of Chiangmai, then a tributary north of Siam, allowed them to demarcate a border all by themselves in 1834, using information from local people. On the other hand, the ruler of Nakhonsithammarat, a Siamese city on the Malay peninsula looking after the Malay states on behalf of Bangkok, was once angry at the British for their repeated requests about the boundary between Siam and Kedah. The British were furious in their turn because Siam appeared to be uncooperative. Soon they learned that Siam had been annoyed by their repeated requests for boundary demarcation. But neither side quite understood the other's ideas.

Two decades later, the British were still urging that the boundary be demarcated. Siam finally agreed, for unknown reasons. It appears that in the period when their relations were amicable, from 1826 to the early 1840s, Siam was uncooperative. But when relations became strained, the Siamese court suddenly agreed to settle the boundary. The demarcation did not work smoothly, however. In most cases, disagreements were due to the simple fact that there had never been any boundary of the British kind before. In the traditional corridors, Siam now demanded a boundary/*khetdaen* which would keep both countries apart to prevent any collision. In other areas where trespassing between various realms had been allowed without hindrance, the British practice of border control, posting military guards along the "lines" and checking travellers, posed a grave concern to Siam.

In one incident in 1846, the British protested that a number of Siamese guards had entered into British territory, erecting a post to claim the area for Siam. They also charged the Siamese court with complicity in this action. The British took the matter seriously, analysing the reasons behind

Siam's aggressive move and concluding from their rationality in international politics that Siam no longer feared Burma so they no longer wanted the British to balance Burmese power. But actually, in that case, the Siamese court did not even know what their guards had done. The territorial claim *per se* was not yet a matter of the court's concern. An investigation finally found that the trouble-making guards had not in fact made any claim; they did not even discuss the matter with their boss or among themselves. The alleged boundary mark turned out to be "[a] heap of stones together with a small wooden house for religious purpose on top of them". It was likely that the guards did travel into British territory. But they did so as part of a customary spying mission, which was never meant to claim any territory. Candidly, the guards argued that they could not look after an area as far away as that since it was three days travel from their houses. Obviously, the British rationality in international politics was misplaced.

These are examples of what happened when different discourses of boundary confronted each other. But these were also moments when a new kind of boundary was presented and established in the field of signification in which the Siamese also participated. Semiotically speaking, the confrontations made the notions of "boundary" and "khetdaen" in Thai ambiguous. On the one hand it referred to the indigenous *khetdaen*. But on the other hand, the modern kind of boundary asserted itself as an alternative meaning of *khetdaen*. Ambiguity and possible shifts of meaning could happen at every moment the terms were translated, either in actual translation from Thai into English and vice versa, or in any communication in which the two notions were put forward in the same semantic field, such as boundary negotiation or map-making. The shifts occurred at various moments in favour of the more powerful discourse. We may say that incidents of the kind just cited, and in any forms of communication about boundary, were loci of modern geography and geo-body in the making.

THE EMERGENCE OF THE GEO-BODY

Alongside the conquest and later the defeat in the contest for the left bank of the Mekong, Siam introduced a new administrative system to integrate all those former tributaries which then became Siam's outlying provinces. The basic aim was to bring them under the direct control of the Bangkok government, thus establishing a new kind of territorial integrity. The new system based on territorial divisions was in fact named Monthon Thesaphiban, meaning the protection of space. It became a new mechanism to establish a new kind of sovereignty according to the new geographical vision of how Siam should be.

The new geographical desire was behind all the military expansionism, the administrative integration, and of course the mapping operations, from the very beginning to the final stages. It was a new discourse, a new language of space by which the kingdom of Siam would be conceived and represented. It became a mental frame for thinking and talking about the country geographically. But since the reality did not yet exist, the new geography provided the conceptual model of the geo-body of Siam. Modern geography and maps anticipated it. They created Siam. Drafts and sketches of the map of Siam were drawn before any survey finished, so the troops could have a desirable realm in mind and could use it to argue against the French who also had their version of the Siamese territory. Modern geographical discourse of mapping turned both the Europeans and the Siamese who submitted to its regime into its agency to establish all the requisites such as the modern kind of boundary, the unambiguous and exclusive sovereignty over a particular territory, and all the necessary practices for the reproduction of knowledge. In order to realize the desire to have the country mapped, the ambiguities necessary for the pre-modern hierarchical polity now faced extinction. Many had died for the establishment of the mapped space. The true losers of territories were those former tributary states, which were conquered and distributed among the regional powers.

From then on, the map of Siam and the discourse of the geo-body of Siam became powerful representations of nationhood. They provided a new, modernist way of knowing and speaking of Siam. The holy kingdom of the Siamese kingship, which used to be manifest as a cosmographie or religious space, now became the mapped Siam.

Perhaps it is most important that, through semiological conjunctures, the geo-body, the map and another constitutive element of nationhood—history—have become the discursive foundation, temporally and spatially, nationalism.

THE GEO-BODY AND HISTORY

In the conventional history, Siam had been a powerful but peaceful country in the region since its first kingdom at Sukhothai in the thirteenth century. Despite its fall to aggressive neighbours a few times, Siam was always able to restore its independence and move forward to civilization and prosperity. Evidence of its success was its vast empire up to the nineteenth century, with the realm covering most of Laos and Cambodia today, parts of today's Burma, Yunnan and the northern Malay states. Under the threats of the British and especially the French colonial powers in the late nineteenth century, Siam painfully ceded about one-third of its former territory in order to save its independence and its heartlands which became Thailand today. Apparently in this historiography, the historic moment I have described in this essay was merely the latest one in a series of struggles for national independence and glory. It was anything but the emergence of the geo-body and nationhood.

The narrative of the conventional history is different from my account because it is based on three strategic assumptions. First, it assumes that the geo-body and the Thai nationhood were primeval. Thai history is the story of the ups and downs of the Thai territorial nation, amidst threats from powerful outsiders, namely China, Burma and the Europeans. Therefore the entire history can be highlighted and captured in a well-known historical atlas which basically tells a story of the changing size of the Siamese realm.

Second, it assumes the context of modern international relations. Not only was the hierarchical relation between the overlords and the tributaries eliminated, but Siam in the nineteenth century also appeared as the victim of European colonialism, rather than a regional power in contest with the French, as suggested in my story.

Siam becomes the losing contestant in the context of regional expansionism. It is clear that the French and Siam's relative positions and relationship could be seen quite differently in the two political contexts.

Third, the conventional narrative always assumes Bangkok's point of view. This perspective is politically correct and acceptable only in the context set by the second assumption. One of the consequences of this assumption is the sanitization of the voices of the ultimate victims, those former tributaries and the indigenous political geography. In the Bangkok perspective, the annexation of former tributaries became the "reform of provincial administration" over its outlying provinces; the expansion became the "defence" of its territorial integrity; the resistance by some tributaries became the "internal" conflict, as opposed to the European "outsider" threat; and the successful "reform" became an emancipation of those tributaries from slavery and semi-vassalage to begin self-government. Indeed, if we merely change the point of view, the story of the administrative reform could be read very much like a history of colonization.

National identity has as its basis the binary opposition of We-Self and Others. It does not represent an intrinsically national quality. Any constitutive element of nationhood is merely a discursive field whose meanings may change, hence shifting its limits and altering the national identity. A late-coming nation-state like Siam usually realized its nationhood through the creative transculturation between the West and the indigenous. The confrontation and tension between the changing Western influence and the transforming indigenous culture never end. Consequently, national identity is always unfixed, contradictory and ambiguous. The modern Siamese nation emerged and has survived through this tension, not by anti-colonial heroism as conventional history usually suggests. Let us celebrate the history of this creative confrontation.

NOTES

1 Benedict Anderson, *Imagined Communities,* London: Verso, 1983; revised edition, 1991. Ernest Gellner, *Nations and Nationalism,* Ithaca, NY: Cornell University Press, 1983. Eric Hobsbawm and Terranee Ranger (eds), *The Invention of Tradition,* Cambridge: Cambridge University Press, 1983.

2 This article is an abridged version of Thongchai Winichakul, *Siam Mapped: A History of the Geo-body of a Nation,* Honolulu: University of Hawaii Press, 1994.

3 *The Burney Papers,* Bangkok: Vajiranana National Library, 1910–1914.

62
Drawing the Coral Heads

Mental Mapping and its Physical Representation
in a Polynesian Community (2003)

Richard Feinberg, Ute J. Dymon, Pu Paiaki, Pu Rangituteki, Pu Nukuriaki, and Matthew Rollins

Prior to the 1990s, cartographers devoted little attention to indigenous understandings of spatial organization. Anthropologists concerned with culture and cognition evince a longer history of interest in the subject. They have, for example, committed a good deal of energy to studying the wayfinding techniques employed by Pacific Island navigators. But even those researchers have often given short shrift to the detailed knowledge of local geography that non-Western and non-literate people frequently carry with them as they go about their daily business. This article depicts a mental map, shared by the Polynesians of Anuta in the eastern Solomons, of the ocean floor within a two- to three-mile radius of their island.

INDIGENOUS CARTOGRAPHY

We now recognize that many peoples outside of the Western tradition engaged in sophisticated cartographic activities well before European contact. Native Americans, for example, used their own equipment and such local materials as sealskin, hide, driftwood, bark and sand to create maps and charts. And the so-called Bushmen of the Kalahari Desert have shown remarkable ability to find their way around in what, to the Western observer, often seems to be an endless expanse of undifferentiated wilderness. Frequently, when compared with maps produced by surveyors using Western technology, the accuracy of indigenous maps is truly impressive (Thrower, 1972, 1996).

Historical cartographers have attempted to reconstruct the geographical thinking of non-Western peoples in order to gain insight into their beliefs and values. By the time they began to engage in this process, however, many communities with well-developed cartographic systems had vanished or changed to the point that little information was preserved about their earlier ways of thinking and living. Fortunately, durable artifacts, including maps, can sometimes elucidate the spatial knowledge and values of the people who made them. And there still exist a number of societies that have retained much of their traditional knowledge, often relying on visual observation and oral communication for transmission of skills and information.

The Star Compass

Pacific Islanders pass navigational information from one generation to the next through a variety of procedures. Master navigators on some islands teach their pupils a conceptual "star compass" by laying out shells and coral fragments into a circle to signify the rising and setting of the most important stars. A "sidereal compass" or "star compass" from the Caroline Islands of Micronesia typically has 32 "compass points". Those points, as described in most of the literature, are not evenly spaced since each stands for the actual rising or setting point of a particular star or constellation. Banana fibers might be strung across a kind of diagram to demonstrate the star courses. A small canoe of coconut leaves may be placed into the center, helping the student to visualize himself amid the various star paths. Coconut and pieces of coral may be used to represent as many as eight distinct swell directions. Frake (1995) noted similarities between the Oceanic star compass and those used by Persian, Arabian, Indian and even European navigators. The star compass provides an abstract structural model of the physical universe—the point is not absolute precision but to provide the navigator with tools that can enable him to reach his destination. Pacific island navigators memorize the rising and setting points of the stars and constellations and their positions relative to various islands. Sunrise and sunset are also important directional indicators.

Marshall Island "Stick Charts"

The star compass is primarily an abstract conceptual scheme. The only physical charts produced by local map makers in the insular Pacific prior to Western influence are the Marshall Islanders' so-called stick charts. The charts were constructed using fibers from a number of plants, including coconut, pandanus and banana, tied together to point in various directions. The arrangements of the sticks indicated wave patterns. Cowrie shells or pieces of coral represented islands, and sometimes major wave intersections. Some of the fibers indicated the distance at which a particular island comes into sight. This was important because, although distances between the various Marshallese islands are not great in comparison with many other parts of the Pacific, the only land consists of low coral islets which can just be seen from a few miles away by sailors aboard an outrigger canoe. To locate an island that the navigator is unable to see, he observes the relationship between the swells—driven by prevailing winds—and reflected or refracted waves resulting from the presence of an island, 75 miles (c. 120 km) from its nearest populated neighbor, Tikopia, and over 200 miles (c. 320 km) from the provincial capital. A national census in 2000 found Anuta's resident population to be 340 people. The island's small size, geographical isolation, and absence of significant commercially exploitable resources have limited contact with the outside world. As a result, even at the beginning of the 21st century, Anuta remains one of the most traditional communities in the Pacific.

A society so remote and so dependent on the sea must have an intimate relationship with its marine environment, and its members learn early in life to observe natural signs. One result of that close observation is the mental mapping of the seabed. This differs from "stick charts" in that Anutans make no attempt to represent submarine features by creating or manipulating physical objects. The map produced in collaboration with Feinberg, Dymon, Rollins and George is the first attempt to reproduce the Anutans' mental map using any kind of material representation. In that respect, it is more like the expert navigator's knowledge of the locations and trajectories of various stars and constellations, or their understanding of the locations of islands and archipelagoes in relation to the movements of celestial bodies. However, unlike those cognitive constructs—reproduced most famously by Tupaia and Cook—what we call the Anutans' "reef map" deals with features that are invisible from land and only can be seen when hovering directly overhead in a boat or canoe. Most of these features occur at depths of between 30 and 150 feet (c. 9–46 m) below the ocean surface.

Anutans have no indigenous name for the reef map per se. Rather, they speak simply of nga rau akau, "coral heads" and their locations (nga ngomea nga rau akau e turaki i ei). In speaking of the paper map that they constructed in collaboration with Feinberg, they might say te tuti o nga rau akau, "the writing [or drawing] of the coral heads"—hence, this article's title. Pu Paiaki, as indicated below, was regarded by Anutans as the island's most knowledgeable person with respect to the coral heads, their locations and their relationships to other submarine features. Other Anutan fishermen, however, are aware of the same kind of information, differing primarily in the extent and profundity of their knowledge.

THE MAPPING PROCESS

When Feinberg began the mapping process with Pu Tongotere, he drew a small outline of Anuta's contours and its most outstanding features in the center of a large notebook page. After working with Pu Nukuriaki, the page quickly became cluttered with information, and Feinberg's collaborator advised him to tape two sheets together to provide more space. When the double sheet became filled, Feinberg copied the information over onto a blank sheet approximately two feet by three feet. At that point, Pu Nukuriaki and Pu Rangituteki indicated dissatisfaction with the alignment of many features. They suggested that Feinberg tape two large sheets together, creating a blank sheet six feet long and four feet wide; that he draw an outline of the island in the center; and that he leave the rest untouched. They would then, with Pu Paiaki's assistance, fill in all the requisite information, starting over from the beginning.

With Pu Paiaki's guidance, Pu Rangituteki began by dividing the Anutan universe into four quadrants called *araavaka*, "canoe paths" to the north, east, south and west. The lines separating the quadrants more or less coincide with major Anutan directions: *tokerau maaro* to the northeast, *tonga maaro* to the southeast, *raki* to the west or southwest, and *pakatiu* to the northwest.

He then divided the sea into a series of concentric circles. The first beyond the surf line (*te pati o ngaru*) is *te akau penua*, "the land reef", that is, the portion of sea floor adjacent to the island. Beyond the *akau penua* is *te para penua*, "the land-related sandy floor". This area is marked by large stretches of sandy bottom, each encircled by coral ridges or coral heads. After the *para penua*, the bottom rises to form a relatively shallow ring known as *te unga o te akau*, "top of the reef", or simply *te akau*, "the reef", before it falls off to *te roto*, the deep sea.

Once Pu Rangituteki divided the ocean into quadrants, he began by noting reefs just outside the main passage in the area of *nga toka* and *te akau penua*. He then worked counterclockwise around the first concentric ring. At each point, he made sure to line up the marine feature with a visible geographical feature on the island or one of the two offshore boulders, Te Patu o Mangoo and Te Patu o Veu, confirming the correct location at each point with Pu Paiaki. When he had worked his way around the circle, he drew a line marking the *tapatapa*, the point at which one concentric ring gives way to the next, and repeated the same procedure with *te para* and *te punga o te akau*. In this manner, the team mapped approximately 300 coral heads within about a two-mile radius of Anuta plus two large coral banks, Te Aongo and Te Akau Motu, several miles beyond. Te Akau Motu, "The Separated Reef", is far enough away that it could not be drawn on the map, but the route to that coral bank is indicated in the northwestern corner.

INFORMATION GATHERED WITH THE MAPPING TEAM

Feinberg was struck by his Anutan friends' extensive knowledge of the seabed, especially that immediately surrounding the island and for a considerable distance to the south and west. Anutans have been traveling to other parts of the Solomon Islands for many decades and, as a result, have developed a good understanding of Solomons geography. By contrast, their knowledge of reefs, islands, and the ocean to the east seemed sketchy. This reflects the paucity of contact from the Polynesian heartland over a period of many generations. Oral traditions (see Feinberg 1998) cite visits from Samoa, Tonga, Rotuma and Tuvalu, but few of the visitors remained on Anuta, and the sporadic contact was evidently insufficient to preserve much detailed geographical knowledge of the major Polynesian archipelagos.

Unlike many Pacific Islanders, the Anutans do not have a system of marine tenure. Anyone on the island has access to any of Anuta's marine resources. However, particular people, past and present, are associated with particular reefs and fishing grounds. Typically, a reef is named for the first person to fish there: it is either given the name of the fisherman himself or of his canoe. For example, one group of coral heads (*rau akau*) is named *Nga Moumou* after Pu Raropuko Moumouipenua. Another was named after an Anutan with an extensive fungus infection; the spot was called *Kaipaariki*, the Anutan word for ringworm. Some Anutans have been particularly energetic in their search for new fishing grounds, and it may be that one person discovers several reefs. Or a particular canoe may be used by a series of fishermen searching for new spots to fish. As a result, several marine features may share the same name. Anutans avoid confusion by specifying, for example, Kapivaka behind Pu Aatapu as opposed to Kapivaka in the Tokerau Maaro.

In some cases, a name is descriptive of a feature's characteristics and location. The Anutans have different expressions for different kinds of coral head and different kinds of sandy patch. A *pupua* is a small patch of sand that is more or less oval in shape and surrounded by coral. An *ainaina* is a larger patch of sand surrounded by reef. A *kau aapua* is a patch of sand surrounded by reef and is similar to an *ainaina*. A *para* is a very large expanse of sandy bottom. *Tapatapa* refers to the boundary or end of a reef shelf.

Despite some discussion and occasional debate, by the time they were done, Pu Paiaki and Pu Rangituteki were confident of the locations of the reefs and other map features. After several long days of effort, the team produced a map that included approximately 300 items.

MAPPING AND MAP MAKING

Rundstrom (1990: 155) calls mapping "the fundamental process of lending order to the world". In saying this, he is referring especially to the making and development of mental maps. While mapping in Rundstrom's sense may be a pan-human activity, different peoples lend order to the world in different ways (L. Irwin, 1994). Anutan seafarers, for example, experience the world far differently from most Americans, and that experience is reflected in their perceptions—as inferred from both the reef map and their oral accounts.

In addition to direct experience, one's mental map is shaped by descriptions and information gathered by others, whether compiled in books or passed on through oral traditions. Through such processes of cultural transmission, places that otherwise might have remained little more than names are fleshed out and described in detail. This information enables people to identify distant phenomena, including new fishing grounds, material resources and even other communities. In many cases, such as that of the Anutans, precise and detailed mental images or mental maps are passed on both orally and through concrete demonstration—the expert takes the novice to the fishing grounds and *shows* him how to find them by lining up with the appropriate land and sea marks.

COMPARING INDIGENOUS MAPS TO WESTERN STANDARDS

Historically, European observers thought maps produced by indigenous people to be less accurate than Western ones because they did not adhere to the Western cartographer's Cartesian coordinates and scales (Sundstrom 1996). Belyea (1998) studied American Indian maps and pointed out that while they lack many of the characteristics Western cartographers assume maps must contain, they satisfied the cartographic needs of the people who made and used them, and they apparently did so for hundreds of years.

Wayfinding is an important skill in many societies; indeed, it can often be a matter of life or death. Finding one's way on the ocean poses special problems and requires special skills because one may be out of sight of land for lengthy periods. Under such conditions, it is difficult to maintain one's bearings. Weather can change quickly, and currents may carry voyagers off course without their knowledge. All of these factors can compromise the prospect of successful landfall. Consequently, many Pacific islanders developed sophisticated techniques for plotting their course on the ocean and created complex maps and charts that they carried in their minds when they set sail—whether for nearby fishing grounds or distant shores.

Unlike Western cartographers, Anutans through most of their history have successfully passed seafaring and navigational knowledge from generation to generation without the benefit of written communication. In that way, their geographical understandings and techniques for dealing with the world around them underscore the contrast between cartographic efforts of one non-Western community and modern academic cartographers. At the same time, they remind us of the remarkable systems of cartographic and navigational understanding that have been lost as a result of European contact and because it simply did not occur to so many of our predecessors to ask the local experts what they knew.

REFERENCES

Belyea, Barbara (1998). 'Inland journeys, native maps', in *Cartographic Encounters: Perspectives on Native American Map-making and Map Use*, ed. Lewis, G. Malcolm, University of Chicago Press, Chicago and London.

Feinberg, Richard (1998). *Oral Traditions of Anuta: A Polynesian Outlier in the Solomon Islands*, Oxford Studies in Anthropological Linguistics, Volume 15, Oxford University Press, New York and Oxford.

Frake, Charles O. (1995). 'A reinterpretation of the Micronesian "star compass"', *The Journal of the Polynesian Society*, 104, 147–159.

Irwin, Lee (1994). *The Dream Seekers: Native American Visionary Traditions of the Great Plains*, University of Oklahoma Press, Norman, OK.

Rundstrom, Robert A. (1990). 'A cultural interpretation of Inuit map accuracy', *Geographical Review*, 20, 155–168.

Skelton, R.A. (1954). 'Captain Cook as a hydrographer', *Mariner's Mirror*, 40, 92–119.

Sundstrom, Lenea (1996). 'Mirror of Heaven: cross-cultural transference of the sacred geography of the Black Hills', *World Archaeology*, 28, 177–189.

Thrower, Norman J.W. (1972). *Maps and Man*, Prentice Hall International, Inc., Englewood Cliffs, NJ.

Thrower, Norman J.W. (1996). *Maps and Civilization*, University of Chicago Press, Chicago, IL.

63
How Do We Get Out of This Capitalist Place?

(1996)

J.K. Gibson-Graham

The spatialization of theoretical discourse owes something to structuralist theories in which linguistic or social elements are seen as defined relationally, via a "synchronic" articulation. But it is usually attributed more directly to poststructuralists like Foucault (see, for example, 1980) and Deleuze and Guattari (1987) as well as to "pre-poststructuralists" like Althusser and Gramsci, and the Marxian tradition to which they belong. Indeed, the spatial metaphors associated with Marxian analysis—"colonization," "penetration," "core and periphery," "terrains of struggle"—are not dissimilar to those of poststructuralism. Both types of theory represent space constituted by or in relation to "Identity"[1] or Form. While poststructuralist theory is concerned with problematizing the fixing of Identity and tracing the performance space of multiple and fluid identities, Marxian theory has generally been focused upon the performance space of one type of Form—the mode of production or, more particularly, Capitalism.

After struggling for so long to erect and strengthen the ramparts of an academic identity in the shadow of more established disciplines, geographers now find all sorts of strange beings camped outside or scaling the battlements eager to assume the language of geography, if not to take up positions its defense.

Massey (1993: 66) is concerned that the proliferation of metaphorical uses of spatial terms has blurred important distinctions between different meanings of space. And Smith and Katz are alarmed at the use of spatial metaphors in contemporary social and cultural (not exclusively poststructuralist) theory that take as their unexamined grounding a seemingly unproblematic, commonsense notion of space as container or field, a simple emptiness in which subjects and objects are "situated" or "located." These metaphorical attempts to contextualize, relativize and de-universalize social sites and speaking positions inadvertently invoke a standpoint at a set of coordinates, a location in a naturalized and asocial "absolute" space. Yet the very conception of absolute space, they caution, is *itself* socially produced, and historically specific: the representation of space as an infinite, prior and neutral container or grid, in which discrete entities operate independently of one another and of space itself, gained ascendancy with the philosophers Newton, Descartes and Kant and was "thoroughly naturalized" with the rise of capitalism between the seventeenth and nineteenth centuries (Smith and Katz 1993: 75–76). By proliferating spatial metaphors without problematizing the representation of space, social theorists reproduce a view of space that is "politically charged in its contemporary implications as much as in its historical origins" (p. 76).[2] An understanding of space as a coordinate system in which locations are clearly defined and mutually exclusive has contributed, for example, to an "identity politics (that) too often *becomes* mosaic politics" (p. 77, emphasis theirs), that is, a politics of competition and fragmentation.

As battles between metaphor and materiality, discourse and reality rage in and around us, and "the enemy" infiltrates our disciplinary boundaries, what better time might there be for a jump into space? An engagement with space allows us to confront some of the political and epistemological concerns about the relationship between discursivity, materiality, and politics that have arisen in the clashes between modern and postmodern feminist and urban discourses. It opens up possibilities of thinking from the outside in, both from the poststructuralist encampments into the protected dwelling of geography, and from the space of formlessness into the space of Form: "The outside insinuates itself into thought, drawing knowledge outside of itself, outside what is expected, producing a hollow which it can then inhabit—an outside within or as the inside" (Grosz 1994: 9).

By examining the spatial images that have been employed in feminist analyses of the body and the city, we may trace the political effects of privileging the materiality of women's experience and capitalist social relations. At the same time, we may discover some of the political potential of an alternative conceptualization in which discourse and other materialities are effectively intertwined.

In an attempt to address women's oppression, feminists may celebrate shopping, birth, homemaking, the fecund emptiness of woman's body, the shopping mall, the suburban home, the caring and nurturing functions, the woman-space. But in doing so they accept the boundaries of difference and separation designated by the discourses of capitalism and binary gender. Another feminist strategy has been to attempt to ignore or even reverse the spatialized binary by claiming back men's economic and urban space as rightfully women's. Women (particularly white female-headed households) have begun to desert the suburbs and, as one of the main groups involved in gentrification, have re-asserted their right to a central location in the city (Rose 1989). Women have successfully fought for child-care centers, vacation programs for school-age children, better community care for the elderly and disabled so that they can temporarily free themselves from the role of carer and claim a rightful place in the capitalist paid workforce (Fincher 1988). Indeed, the fact that such services are better provided for in cities contributes to the feminization of households in central urban areas. Significant though all these changes have been for women in the city, these strategies rest upon the assumption that women remain the carers, the supplementary workers in a capitalist system, who, if they undertake labor in the "productive"

spheres of the economy must also provide the "reproductive" labor. The central city is one space that allows the (exhausted) middle-class superwoman to function—it has become the site of a new "problem that has no name."[3]

Similar strategies of reversal are represented in "Take back the night" rallies and other urban actions where women have claimed their right to the city streets, pressing for better lighting, better policing of public transport, guarded parking stations, and other mechanisms of public surveillance of men's behavior (Worpole 1992). As the geography of women's fear has been made visible, so has the "reality" of male sexuality and the "inevitability" of violence against women been accepted. While greater public surveillance is advocated, women are simultaneously warned not to trespass into public space where, on the streets at night or on public transport after work hours, they are most certainly "asking" to become players in a rape script.

Feminist strategies of celebration and reversal are all contributing to changes in the livability of urban space for women. But what might be the cost of these changes if they rest upon the acceptance of both the Phallus and Capital as the "Identities" which define women/space, if they force women/space into the victim role that the sexual rape script allocates and the subordinate role that the economic urban script confers? What potentialities are suppressed by such a figuring of women and space? Perhaps we can only answer these questions by looking to alternative notions of Identity to see how they might differently configure women/space, as well as other possibilities they might entail.

PREGNANT SPACE, POSTMODERN SPACE

How might we appreciate differently the spatiality of female sexuality and potential new ways for women to dwell in urban space?

How might this respatialization of the body contribute to new geographies for women in the city? It might lead us to identify the multiple urban spaces that women claim, but not solely in the name of consumer desire or reproductive/biological function. Here one could think of the heterotopias of lesbian space, prostitution space, bingo space, club space, health spa, body building and aerobics space, nursing home space, hobby space—all terrains of public life in which women's agency is enacted in an effective, if indeterminate manner. One could identify the ways in which such spaces are regulated and ordered by dominant discourses of heterosexuality, health, youth, beauty, and respectability and influenced by discourses of transgression. One could explore and map an urban performance space of women that is defined in terms of positivity, fullness, surface and power. But in order for such a reinscription not to fall back into simply celebrating woman-space in the city, theoretical work must continually and repeatedly displace (rather than only reverse) the binary hierarchy of gender.

One strategy of displacement might lead us to deconstruct and redefine those consumption and reproductive spaces/spheres that are the designated woman-space in the discourse of urban capitalism. Within geography, for example, the urban restructuring literature points to the massive involvement of women in the paid workforce where they are active in a variety of economic roles apart from that of final consumer or reproducer of the capitalist labor force. Feminist geographers and sociologists are researching women in office space (Pringle 1988), in finance space (McDowell 1994), in retail space (Dowling 1993), in ethnic small business (Alcorso 1993), in industrial space (Phizacklea 1990)—again all public arenas in which women's agency is enacted. In some texts we may even see glimmers of spaces beyond or outside capitalism, where women operate in noncapitalist spaces of production and contribute to the reproduction of noncapitalist economic forms.[4]

Despite these glimmers, what characterizes much of the restructuring literature is an overriding sense of "capitalocentrism" in that women's entry into the paid labor force is understood largely in terms of the procurement by capital of cheaper, more manipulable labor. Capital has positioned the superexploited female worker just as it has produced women's roles as reproducers (of the capitalist workforce) and consumers (of capitalist commodities). Any attempt to destabilize woman's position and spatiality within urban discourse must dispense with the Identity of Capitalism as the ultimate container[5] and constituter of women's social and economic life/space.

It would seem that the rethinking of female sexuality and the creation of alternate discourses of sexuality and bodily spatiality are well in advance of the rethinking of economic identity and social spatiality (Grosz 1994b). Indeed, even the most innovative cultural and poststructuralist theorists tend to leave this terrain untouched:

Individuals do not appear to appropriate capital but to be appropriated to it. People are caught in its circuits, moving in and out of its paths of mobility, seeking opportunistic moments (luck, fate, fame or crime) which will enable them, not to redistribute wealth, but to relocate themselves within the distributional networks of capital.

(Grossberg 1992: 328)

The capitalist relation consists of four dense points—commodity/consumer, worker/capitalist—which in neoconservative society are effectively superposed in every body in every spacetime coordinate. When capital comes out, it surfaces as a fractal attractor whose operational arena is immediately coextensive with the social field.

(Massumi 1993: 132)

Despite the postmodern interest in chora, in nomadology and smooth space, the identity of Capital confronts us wherever we turn. Do we only ever dwell in a capitalist space? Can we ever think outside the capitalist axiomatic?

The economy constitutes a worldwide axiomatic, a "universal cosmopolitan energy which overflows every restriction and bond," (Marx) a mobile and convertible substance "such as the total value of annual production." Today we can depict an enormous, so-called stateless, monetary mass that circulates through foreign exchange and across borders, eluding control by the States, forming a multinational ecumenical organization, constituting a supranational power untouched by government decisions.

(Deleuze and Guattari 1987: 453)

Here Deleuze and Guattari are difficult and elusive. Their capitalist axiomatic is all-pervasive and innovative, seemingly able to coopt and reterritorialize all lines of flight out of its territory into new opportunities for self-expansion, able to set and repel its own limits (1987: 472). Yet at the same time they reserve a space for the minority, for the becoming of everybody/everything outside the totalizing flow of capital:

> The undecidable is the germ and locus par excellence of revolutionary decisions. Some people invoke the high technology of the world system of enslavement: but even, and especially, this machinic enslavement abounds in undecidable propositions and movements that, far from belonging to a domain of knowledge reserved for sworn specialists, provides so many weapons for the becoming of everybody/everything, becoming-radio, becoming-electronic, becoming-molecular. … Every struggle is a function of all these undecidable propositions and constructs revolutionary connections in opposition to the conjugations of the axiomatic.
>
> (1987: 473)

In the footnote to this statement the authors mention the domain of "alternative practices" such as pirate radio stations, urban community networks, and alternatives to psychiatry (1987: 572). Here we catch a minimal glimpse of what might lie outside the flows of Capital. The capitalist axiomatic closes and defines—in the sense of fully inhabiting—social space (evoking the closure and definition of Cubism), yet it is also in motion, providing a space of becoming, of undecidability. This space is reminiscent of the constitutive (pregnant) space of the Impressionists. It is a space of mists and vapors, of movement and possibility, of background that might at any moment become foreground—a "space of excess" and indeterminacy within the modern space of fullness and closure.

If we are to take postmodern spatial becomings seriously then it would seem that we must claim chora, that space between the Being of present Capitalism and the Becoming of future capitalisms, as the place for the indeterminate potentiality of noncapitalisms.[6] In this space we might identify the range of economic practices that are not subsumed to capital flows. We might see the sphere of (capitalist) reproduction as the space of noncapitalist class processes that deterritorialize and divert capitalist flows of surplus value. We might see the sphere of (capitalist) consumption as the space of realization and consumption of commodities produced under a range of productive relations—cooperative, self-employed, enslaved, communal as well as capitalist. What violence do we do when we

interpret all these spaces as existing *in* Capitalism, as cohering within the coded flows of axiomatic capital? We risk relegating space/life to emptiness, to rape, to non-becoming, to victimhood.

NOTES

1 Here I refer to Identity (or the Idea) in the symbolic domain, implying the quest for ultimate definition or for the fixing of signifier to signified. In this chapter, I move between three "types" of identity in order to develop their overlaps, connections, and contradictions: *Identity* as defined above, the *identity* of "the social" as a complex totality (often referred to as society and sometimes divided into culture, economy and polity) and individual *identity*, that which constitutes subjectivity and agency. In this chapter I play with these three senses of identity, slipping between and among them with barely a warning. I hope that this little game will be more productive than confusing for the reader.

2 Smith and Katz see it, paraphrasing Lefebvre, as a "conception of space appropriate for a project of social domination," one that "expresses a very specific tyranny of power" (p. 76). In Rose's (1996) reading, Smith and Katz argue that "spatial metaphors which refer to absolute space are regressive because absolute space serves to freeze and thus to sanction the socio-spatial or theoretical status quo" (pp. 2–3).

3 See Friedan (1963).

4 See, for example, Katz and Monk (1993).

5 So that household labor and self-employment (which may be understood as outside capitalist relations of production) are seen as somehow taking place "within capitalism," as are noncapitalist forms of commodity production (e.g., independent or communal production).

6 Such a space also resembles Rose's (1993) "paradoxical space," a space that is productive of multiple and contradictory identities, or that of de Lauretis who discovers in the "elsewhere" or "space-offs" of hegemonic discourses the interstices in which the "subject of feminism" may emerge (quoted in Rose 1993: 139–140).

REFERENCES

Alcorso, Caroline. 1993 "And I'd like to thank my wife": gender dynamics and the ethnic "family business." *Australian Feminist Studies* 17: 93–108.

Deleuze, Gilles and Felix Guattari. 1987 *A Thousand Plateaus: Capitalism and Schizophrenia,* trans. B. Massumi. Minneapolis: University of Minnesota Press.

Dowling, Robyn. 1993 Femininity, place and commodities: a retail case study. *Antipode* 25(4): 295–319.

Fincher, Ruth. 1988 Class and gender relations in the local labour market and the local state. In J. Wolch and M. Dear (eds), *The Power of Geography*. London: Unwin Hyman, pp. 93–117.

Foucault, Michael. 1980 Questions in geography. In C. Gordon (ed.), *Power/Knowledge: Selected Interviews and Other Writings 1972–1977*. New York: Random House, pp. 63–77.

Friedan, Betty. 1963 *The Feminine Mystique*. New York: W.W. Norton & Co.

Grossberg, Lawrence. 1992 *We Gotta Get Out of this Place: Popular Conservatism and Postmodern Culture*. New York and London: Routledge.

Grosz, Elizabeth. 1994 *Volatile Bodies: Toward a Corporeal Feminism*. Bloomington, IN: Indiana University Press.

Katz, Cindi and Janice Monk. (eds) 1993 *Full Circles: Women over the life course*. New York and London: Routledge.

Massey, Dorreen. 1993 Industrial restructuring as class restructuring: production decentralization and local uniqueness. *Regional Studies* 17(2): 73–89.

Massumi, Brian. 1993 *A Reader's Guide to Capitalism and Schizophrenia: Deviations from Deleuze and Guattari*. Cambridge, MA: MIT Press.

McDowell, Linda. 1994 Working in the city: spaces of power. Paper presented at the annual meeting of the Association of American Geographers, San Francisco.

Phizacklea, Annie. 1990 *Unpacking the Fashion Industry*. London: Routledge.

Pringle, Rosemary. 1988 *Secretaries Talk: Sexuality, Power and Work*. Sydney: Allen & Unwin.

Rose, D. 1989 A feminist perspective on employment and gentrification: the case of Montreal. In J. Welch and M. Dear (eds), *The Power of Geography: How Territory Shapes Social Life*. Boston, MA: Unwin Hyman, pp. 118–138.

Rose, Gillian. 1993 *Feminism and Geography: The Limits of Geographical Knowledge*. Cambridge: Polity Press.

Rose, Gillian. 1996 As if the mirrors had bled: masculine dwelling, masculinist theory and feminist masquerade. In N. Duncan (ed.), *(Re)placings*. London: Routledge.

Smith, Neil and Cindi Katz. 1993 Grounding metaphor: towards a spatialized politics. In S. Pile and M. Keith (eds), *Place and the Politics of Identity*. London: Routledge, pp. 67–83.

Worpole, Ken. 1992 *Towns for People: Transforming Urban Life*. Buckingham: Open University Press.

64
De-, Dis-, Ex-

(1987)

Bernard Tschumi

Cities today have no visible limits. In America, they never had. In Europe, however, the concept of "city" once implied a closed and finite entity. The old city had walls and gates. But these have long ceased to function. Are there other types of gates, new gates to replace the gates of the past? Are the new gates those electronic warning systems installed in airports, screening passengers for weapons? Have electronics and, more generally, technology replaced the boundaries, the guarded borders of the past?

The walls surrounding the city have disappeared and, with them, the rules that made the distinction between inside and outside, despite politicians' and planners' guidelines, despite geographical and administrative boundaries. In *"L'Espace Critique"*, Paul Virilio develops a challenging argument for anyone concerned with the making of urban society: Cities have become *deregulated*. This deregulation is reinforced by the fact that much of the city does not belong to the realm of the visible anymore. What was once called urban design has been replaced by a composite of invisible systems. Why should architects still talk about monuments? Monuments are invisible now. They are *disproportionate*—so large (at the scale of the world) that they cannot be seen. Or so small (at the scale of computer chips) that they cannot be seen either.

Remember: architecture was first the art of measure, of proportions. It once allowed whole civilizations to measure time and space. But speed and the telecommunications of images have altered that old role of architecture. *Speed* expands time by contracting space; it negates the notion of physical dimension.

Of course, physical environment still exists. But, as Virilio suggests, the appearance of permanence (buildings as solid, made of steel, concrete, glass) is constantly challenged by the immaterial representation of abstract systems, from television to electronic surveillance, and so on. Architecture is constantly subject to reinterpretation. In no way can architecture today claim permanence of meaning. Churches are turned into movie houses, banks into yuppie restaurants, hat factories into artists' studios, subway tunnels into nightclubs, and sometimes nightclubs into churches. The supposed cause-and-effect relationship between function and form ("form follows function") is forever condemned the day function becomes almost as transient as those magazines and mass media images in which architecture now appears as such a fashionable object.

History, memory, and tradition, once called to the rescue by architectural ideologists, become nothing but modes of disguise, fake regulations, so as to avoid the question of transience and temporality.

When the philosopher Jean-François Lyotard speaks about the crisis of the grand narratives of modernity ("progress," the "liberation of humanity," etc.), it only prefigures the crisis of any narrative, any discourse, any mode of representation. The crisis of these grand narratives, their coherent totality, is also the crisis of limits. As with the contemporary city, there are no more boundaries delineating a coherent and homogeneous whole. On the contrary, we inhabit a fractured space, made of accidents, where figures are disintegrated, dis-integrated. From a sensibility developed during centuries around the "appearance of a stable image" ("balance," "equilibrium," "harmony"), today we favor a sensibility of the disappearance of unstable images: first movies (twenty-four images per second), then television, then computer-generated images, and recently (among a few architects) disjunctions, dislocations, deconstructions. Virilio argues that the abolition of permanence—through the collapse of the notion of distance as a time factor—confuses reality. First deregulation of airlines, then deregulation of Wall Street, finally deregulation of appearances: it all belongs to the same inexorable logic. Some unexpected consequences, some interesting distortions of long-celebrated icons are to be foreseen. The city and its architecture lose their symbols—no more monuments, no more axes, no more anthropomorphic symmetries, but instead fragmentation, parcellization, atomization, as well as the random superimposition of images that bear no relationship to one another, except through their collision. No wonder that some architectural projects sublimate the idea of *explosion*. A few architects do it in the form of drawings in which floor plans, beams, and walls seem to disintegrate in the darkness of outer space. Some even succeed in building those explosions and other accidents (by giving them the appearance of control—clients want control—but it's only a "simulation").

Hence the fascination for cinematic analogies: on the one hand, moving cranes and expressways and, on the other, montage techniques borrowed from film and video—frames and sequences, lap dissolves, fade-ins and fade-outs, jump cuts, and so forth.

One must remember that, initially, the sciences were about substance, about foundation: geology, physiology, physics, and gravity. And architecture was very much part of that concern, with its focus on solidity, firmness, structure, and hierarchy. Those foundations began to crumble in the twentieth century. Relativity, quantum theory, the uncertainty principle: this shakeup occurred not only in physics, as we know, but also in philosophy, the social sciences, and economics.

How then can architecture maintain some solidity, some degree of certainty? It seems impossible today—unless one decides that the accident or the explosion is to be called the rule, the new regulation, through a sort of philosophical inversion that considers the accident the norm and continuity the exception.

No more certainties, no more continuities. We hear that energy, as well as matter, is a discontinuous structure of points: punctum, quantum. Question: could the only certainty be the point?

The crises of determinism, or cause-and-effect relationships, and of continuity completely challenge recent architectural thought. Here, bear with me if I go through a rather tedious but quick recapitulation of "meaning" in architecture—without entering into a detailed discussion of Ferdinand de Saussure or Émile Benveniste. Ethnologists tell us that, in traditional symbolic relations, things have meanings. Quite often the symbolic value is separated from the utilitarian one. The Bauhaus tried to reconcile the two into a new functional duo of signifier and signified—a great synthesis. Moreover, the Bauhaus attempted to institute a "universal semanticization of the environment in which everything became the object of function and of signification" (Jean Baudrillard). This functionality, this synthesis of form and function, tried to turn the whole world into a homogeneous signifier, objectified as an element of signification: for every form, every signifier, there is an objective signified, a function. By focusing on denotation, it eliminated connotation.

Of course, this dominant discourse of rationality was bound to be attacked. At that time, it was by the surrealists, whose transgressions often relied on the ethics of functionalism, *a contrario*. In fact, some fixed, almost functionalist expectations were necessary to the surrealists, for they could only be unsettled through confrontation: the surreal set combining "the sewing machine and the umbrella on the dissecting table" only works because each of these objects represents a precise and unequivocal function.

The transgressed order of functionality that resulted reintroduced the order of the symbolic, now distorted and turned into a poetic phantasm. It liberated the object from its function, denounced the gap between subject and object, and encouraged free association. But such transgressions generally acted upon singular objects, while the world was becoming an environment of ever-increasing complex and abstract systems. The abstraction of the following years—whether expressionist or geometric—had its architectural equivalent. The endlessly repeated grids of skyscrapers were associated with a new zero-degree of meaning: perfect functionalism.

Fashion upset all that. It had always addressed issues of connotation: against fashion's unstable and ever-disappearing image, the stable and universal denotations of functionalism appeared particular and restrictive.

Partly fascinated by such connotations, partly longing for some long-lost traditional forms, architectural postmodernism in the seventies attempted to combine—to quote Charles Jencks—"modern techniques with traditional building, in order to communicate both with the public *and* with an elite" (hence "double-coding". It was above all concerned with *codes*, with communicating some *message*, some *signified* (perhaps characterized by irony, parody, eclecticism). Architectural post-modernism was totally in line with the mission of architecture according to dominant history, which has been to invest shelter with a given meaning.

Ten years later, the illusion was already vanishing. The Doric orders made of painted plywood had begun to warp and peel. The instability, the ephemerality of both signifier and signified, form and function, form and meaning could only stress the obvious, what Jacques Lacan had pointed to years before: that there is no cause-and-effect relationship between signifier and signified, between word and intended concept. The signifier does not have to answer for its existence in the name of some hypothetical signification. As in literature and psychoanalysis, the architectural signifier does not represent the signified. Doric columns and neon pediments suggest too many interpretations to justify any single one. Again, there is no cause-and-effect relationship between an architectural sign and its possible interpretation. Between signifier and signified stands a barrier: the barrier of actual use. Never mind if this very room was once a fire station, then a furniture storage room, then a ritualistic dance hall, and now a lecture hall (it has been all of these). Each time, these uses distorted both signifier and signified. Not only are linguistic signs arbitrary (as de Saussure showed us long ago), but interpretation is itself open to constant questioning. Every interpretation can be the object of interpretation, and that new interpretation can in turn be interpreted, until every interpretation erases the previous one. The dominant history of architecture, which is

a history of the signified, has to be revised, at a time when there is no longer a normative rule, a cause-and-effect relationship between a form and a function, between a signifier and its signified: only a deregulation of meaning.

The deregulation of architecture began long ago, at the end of the nineteenth century, with the world fairs of London and Paris, where light metallic structures radically changed the appearance of architectural solids. Suddenly, architecture was merely scaffolding supporting glass, and it was discrediting the "solid," symbolic character of masonry and stone. Human scale ceased to be an issue, as the logic of industrial construction took over. Human proportions from the ages of classicism and humanism were rapidly replaced by grids and modular systems, a superimposition of light and materials that were becoming increasingly immaterial—another form of deconstruction.

In the mid-seventies, nostalgic architects, longing for meaning and tradition, applied sheetrock and plywood cutouts to those scaffoldings, but the images they were trying to provide were weak in comparison to the new scaffoldings of our time: the mediatized images of ephemeral representations.

"To represent construction or to construct representation" (Virilio): this is the new question of our time. As Albert Einstein said, "There is no scientific truth, only temporary representations, ever-accelerating sequences of representation." In fact, we are forced to go through a complete reconsideration of all concepts of figuration and representation: the constant storm of images (whether drawings, graphs, photographs, films, television, or computer-generated images) increasingly negates any attempt to restore the Renaissance ideal of the unity of reality and its representation. The concept of double-coding was the last and futile attempt to keep some of that ideal intact by establishing a new relation between communication and tradition. It is the word "tradition" that misled much of the architectural scene in the late seventies and made some aspects of architectural post-modernism what I think will soon appear as a short-lived avatar of history: a form of contextual eclecticism that has been recurrent throughout architectural history, with and without irony, allegory, and other parodies.

In any case, the problem is not a problem of images: gables and classical orders, however silly, are free to be consumed by whoever wishes to do so. But to pretend that these images could suggest new rules and regulations in architecture and urbanism by transcending modernism is simply misplaced.

There are no more rules and regulations. The current metropolitan deregulation caused by the dis-industrialization of European and American cities, by the collapse of zoning strategies, contradicts any attempt to develop new sets of regulating forces, however desirable it may be for some. The 1987 Wall Street "crash" and its relation to the economic deregulation that immediately preceded it is another illustration that an important change has taken place. Let me go back again to Virilio's argument. In the Middle Ages, society was self-regulated, auto-regulated. Regulation took place at its center. The prince of the city was the ruler; there was a direct cause-and-effect relationship between rules and everyday life, between the weight of masonry and the way that buildings were built.

In the industrial era, societies became artificially regulated. The power of economic and industrial forces took over by establishing a coherent structure throughout the whole territory: control was defined at the limits, at the edges of society. The relation between rules and everyday life ceased to be clear, and so large bureaucracies and administrators took over. Regulation was not at the center anymore but at the periphery. Abstract architecture used grids on its sheds International-style, before it discovered that one could decorate the same shed Multinational-style, regardless of what happened in them. Function, form, and meaning ceased to have any relationship to one another.

Today we have entered the age of deregulation, where control takes place *outside* of society, as in those computer programs that feed on one another endlessly in a form of autonomy, recalling the autonomy of language described by Michel Foucault. We witness the separation of people and language, the decentering of the subject. Or, we might say, the complete decentering of society.

Ex-centric, dis-integrated, dis-located, dis-juncted, deconstructed, dismantled, dis-associated, discontinuous, deregulated … de-, dis-, ex-. These are the prefixes of today. Not post-, neo-, or pre-.

SECTION 12

Democratic Prospects and Possibilities

Occuprint poster designed in support of Occupy Wall Street.
Source: Lalo Alcaraz, 2011, New York, NY.

DEMOCRATIC PROSPECTS AND POSSIBILITIES

The readings in this volume have looked at many aspects of environmental experience, raising questions about how space and place are produced, and how this can be done in more just and equal ways. When scholars and activists speak, write, and take actions for *social and spatial justice*, they argue for processes, practices, and places that are more open, accessible, and democratic. Arriving at the end of this book, it is intriguing to think about the future of our social and spatial relationships. What alternatives might exist to the spaces and places we currently experience? What do we believe spaces and experiences should be like?

As the previous section highlighted ways in which we can imagine spatial alternatives, this final section gathers together writings that analyze or suggest ways in which spaces and places may become more democratic and open to transformation. These selections show how space and place are not innate but emerge through contingent ideas, structures, and practices. The process of making and remaking places confirms our agency and responsibility in producing spaces—both material and imagined—that emphasize equality, justice, and democracy. While each of these authors has a distinct point of view, two main threads that tie these readings together are their belief in democratic praxis, and an acceptance of life as an open and dynamic process.

Susan Saegert begins this section by arguing for a pragmatic approach to life grounded in first-hand experience and emotional engagement with the world. As an environmental psychologist and urban scholar, Saegert suggests that individual subjectivity is constructed relationally and serves as the basis for democratic openness. For her, *pragmatism*, as articulated by the psychologist and philosopher John Dewey, represents an approach to democracy that allows for continual reassessment based on the experiences and interactions of people. Pragmatism indicates a set of values that are not fixed, and a process of living that remains receptive to new information, experience, and knowledge. Tying together the work of Kurt Lewin and Pierre Bourdieu, Saegert looks at how individuals' *lifespace* (Lewin's term) or *habitus* (Bordieu's term) shape social situations and experiences of place. She argues that living in a pragmatic way would open up our structured selves to uncertainty, participation, and the cultivation of democratic communities and material worlds.

Similar to the open-endedness advocated by pragmatism, contingent and emergent relations form the crux of the theories of social theorist **Gilles Deleuze** and psychoanalyst **Félix Guattari**. Indeed, many scholars place them in a line of thought that extends back to Dewey. They go further to claim that producing true democracy and democratic space necessitates rethinking power relations, and challenge us to consider how society can be reworked without hierarchical relationships. They argue that our current social arrangement is like a tree, or a book, that is uni-directional and fails to account for the multiplicity of connections people make. Deleuze and Guattari's alternative develops the metaphor of the *rhizome*, an organism that grows horizontally and sends shoots out in many directions. The authors suggest that rhizomatic *assemblages* allow for *lines of flight*—radical leaps that allow escape from confining structures—and moments termed *plateaus* when and where multiple actors and paths converge to create intensified periods of experience or production. Deleuze and Guattari imagine that these possibilities emerge within the existing social system, and in doing so they disrupt and eventually kill off old systems of capitalist hegemony, allowing for the development of more equal social and spatial relationships.

The revolutions and uprisings of the Arab Spring are examples of what Deleuze and Guattari would call plateaus. **Lila Abu-Lughod** uses these moments of democratic protest and possibility to trace the implications and hopes in North Africa and the Middle East. Using an anthropological approach to examine the experiences of rural village life in Egypt, she shows how patterns there are tied to national issues being contested in urban areas. Abu-Lughod indicates how the use of social media like Facebook, which was successfully employed in national demonstrations, has other consequences in remote villages. Because people are known personally, they can become victims of brutality or, more positively, they can voice their ideas, establish practical agendas, and ameliorate the conditions of people with whom they are familiar. She cautions that what may seem indirect, anonymous, and philosophical is really personal, local, and lived, and should be taken into account during periods of political change. Abu-Lughod's analysis is useful in understanding how places and social relations are co-produced, as well as the patterns that may resist or propel social transformation.

Urban planner and designer **Michael Sorkin** is also interested in the patterns that structure social relations and how they may be undone. He argues that traffic is a good way to understand the landscape as well as social relations in the US under contemporary capitalism. The system of highways and the system of capitalism both benefit from the smooth flow of people, products, and information, and numerous institutions work hard to segregate people and reduce conflict for the benefit of speed. However, Sorkin argues, the human character of places begins with face-to-face interactions, which introduce what he terms *friction*. Friction, often experienced bodily through accidents and encounters, slows things down and can bring difference into these uniform systems. The friction of *difference*—extending the work of Iris Marion Young (Section 7)—allows for communities to develop through processes of interaction and engagement. Sorkin suggests that in the construction of cities and spaces, the role of the body in democracy be reconsidered to emphasize experiences that bring people into contact with each other.

To conclude this volume, geographer **Roger A. Hart** returns us to one of the most basic relationships between people and place: the spaces of childhood play. Hart raises important questions about why people play and argues that providing appropriate space and resources for play is necessary for children's physical and psychological development. More significantly, he suggests that childhood play is the basis of democratic society. Like John Dewey (1997), Hart contends that democracy develops through social and interactive processes, beginning in childhood. The ability to play freely, finding challenges and negotiating conflicts, is fundamental to a society that wants its citizens to be engaged, thoughtful, and creative participants in that society. Hart leaves us wondering how to support the creation of democracy in the making of spaces and places, and who today's children will grow up to be.

While spaces and social practices should support and embody democratic openness, there are many forms and directions this may take, and many ways of framing these arguments. In addition to the authors included in this section, and all of those in this volume, there are a variety of research and design projects to guide us toward thinking and living more democratically. Philosophers Suzanne Langer (1942) and Hannah Arendt (1998) have contributed to understanding democracy and meaning-making through processes of public engagement and spatial experience. David Harvey's work, including the seminal *Social Justice and the City*, is insightful and instructive for the way in which it spatializes ideas of justice through Marxist analysis. Developmental psychologist Donald Winnicott (2005) and psychologists Mihaly Csikszentmihalyi and Eugene Rochberg-Halton (1981) have looked at *play* and its physicality in the making of growing selves as well as the transactions with things and places we cultivate to become the selves we strive to be.

Many designers and artists have developed methods and examples that challenge the spatial status quo. Jeremy Till is an English architect who argues for more contingent spatial processes and relations, and has helped put together a very useful book and website of alternative design practices called *Spatial Agency* (see Awan et al. 2011). Samuel Mockbee was the founder of Rural Studio, an architecture program that advocates for citizen architects and emphasizes a participatory approach to community building (1998; also see Douglas 2010). Nato Thompson (2012) and the Creative Time gallery in New York City have put together exhibitions and publications that highlight socially engaged art projects. This list is by no means conclusive, but perhaps a useful starting point. The writers included here encourage you to look for ways to live and make our world a more open and equitable place, and to find support in the things you have read here.

SUGGESTIONS FOR FURTHER READING

Please see *peopleplacespace.org* for extended and additional lists of readings.

Arendt, Hannah. 1998. *The Human Condition*. Chicago, IL: University of Chicago Press.

Awan, Nishat, Tatjana Schneider, and Jeremy Till. 2011. *Spatial Agency: Other Ways of Doing Architecture*. New York: Routledge.

Bell, Bryan, Katie Wakeford, Steve Badanes, Roberta Feldman, Sergio Palleroni, Katie Swenson, and Thomas Fisher. 2008. *Expanding Architecture: Design as Activism*. New York: Metropolis Books.

Braidotti, Rosi. 2013. *The Posthuman*. Cambridge: Polity Press.

Bridge, Gary. 2005. *Reason in the City of Difference*. New York: Routledge.

Buchanan, Ian, and Gregg Lambert (eds). 2005. *Deleuze and Space*. Toronto, Ont: University of Toronto Press, Scholarly Publishing Division.

Csikszentmihalyi, Mihaly, and Eugene Rochberg-Halton. 1981. *The Meaning of Things: Domestic Symbols and the Self*. Cambridge; New York: Cambridge University Press.

DeFilippis, James, and Susan Saegert. 2012. *The Community Development Reader*. New York: Routledge.

Dewey, John. 1997. "The Individual and the World." In *Experience and Education, The Individual and the World*, pp. 291–305. New York: Free Press.

Douglas, Sam Wainwright. 2010. *Citizen Architect*. Carnivalesque Films/Big Beard Films.

Fine, Michelle. 2001. "Changing Minds: The Impact of College in a Maximum Security Prison." Available online at http://web.gc.cuny.edu/che/changingminds.html.

Fisher, Thomas R. 2006. *In The Scheme of Things: Alternative Thinking on the Practice of Architecture*. Minneapolis: University of Minnesota Press.

Ghannam, Farha. 2002. *Remaking the Modern: Space, Relocation, and the Politics of Identity in a Global Cairo*, 1st edn. Berkeley: University of California Press.

Giroux, Henry A. 2002. *Public Spaces, Private Lives: Democracy Beyond 9/11*. New York: Rowman & Littlefield.

Haraway, Donna J. 1990. "A Cyborg Manifesto: Science, Technology, and Socialist-Feminism in the Late Twentieth Century." In *Simians, Cyborgs, and Women: The Reinvention of Nature*, pp. 149–181. New York: Routledge.

Hertzberger, Herman, Loila Ghäit, Marielee von Ulijmen, and Ina Rike. 2005. *Lessons for Students in Architecture*. Rotterdam: 010 Publishers.

Hou, Jeffrey (ed.). 2010. *Insurgent Public Space: Guerrilla Urbanism and the Remaking of Contemporary Cities*. New York: Routledge.

James, William. 1907. "What Pragmatism Means." In *Pragmatism and Other Writings*, edited by Giles Gunn, pp. 24–40. Harmondsworth: Penguin Classics.

Jameson, Fredric. 2007. *Archaeologies of the Future: The Desire Called Utopia and Other Science Fictions*. London: Verso.

Langer, Susanne K. 1942. *Philosophy in a New Key; A Study in the Symbolism of Reason, Rite and Art*. Cambridge, MA: Harvard University Press.

Martín-Baró, Ignacio. 1996. *Writings for a Liberation Psychology*, edited by Adrianne Aron and Shawn Corne. Cambridge, MA: Harvard University Press.

Mockbee, Samuel. 1998. "The Rural Studio." In *The Everyday and Architecture*, edited by Sarah Wigglesworth and Jeremy Till, pp. 72–79. New York: Academy Press.

Shiffman, Ron, Rick Bell, Lance Jay Brown, and Lynne Elizabeth (eds). 2012. *Beyond Zuccotti Park: Freedom of Assembly and the Occupation of Public Space*. New York: New Village Press.

Soja, Edward W. 2010. *Seeking Spatial Justice*. Minneapolis: University Of Minnesota Press.

Thompson, Nato (ed.). 2012. *Living as Form: Socially Engaged Art from 1991–2011*. Cambridge, MA: The MIT Press.

Tocqueville, Alexis de. 2004. *Democracy in America*. Trans. Arthur Goldhammer. New York: Literary classics of the United States.

Winnicott, Donald W. 2005. *Playing and Reality*. New York: Routledge.

65
Restoring Meaningful Subjects and "Democratic Hope" to Pyschology

(2014)

Susan Saegert

As matter of fact every individual has grown up, and always must grow up, in a social medium. His responses grow intelligent, or gain meaning, simply because he lives and acts in a medium of accepted meanings and values. Through social intercourse, through sharing in the activities embodying beliefs, he gradually acquires a mind of his own. The conception of mind as a purely isolated possession of the self is at the very antipodes of the truth. The self achieves mind in the degree in which knowledge of things is incarnate in the life about him; the self is not a separate mind building up knowledge anew on its own account. ... True individualism is a product of the relaxation of the grip of authority of customs and traditions as standards of belief. ... Hence a democratic society must, in consistency with its ideal, allow for intellectual freedom and the play of divers gifts and interests.

(Dewey, 1916/1944)

The quotation above links the freedom of the subject and the truthfulness of our knowledge to an inclusive, tolerant democratic society understood broadly as including everyday practices, beliefs and values as well as democratic and inclusive institutions. Democratic practices and institutions are more hopes than assured realities because of the circular dependence of them on subjects capable of democratic engagement with others and the origins of such subjects in social practices and institutions. Democratic and tolerant communities of inquirers are key for the existence of subjects capable of democracy; an experimental,

inquiring, tolerant approach to living is the hallmark of a democratic subject.

This paper takes up and further develops neglected strands in psychological thought that embrace the contingency of subjectivity, understand it as applying to the psychologist as well as the subject of psychology, and that look to democratic and inclusionary forms of social inquiry as the most likely to advance both knowledge and freedom of the subject. It maps out relationships between conceptions of the subject and the potential for meaningful subjectivity and democratic hope. Meaningful subjectivity is understood as including the tension between ourselves as determined by discourse and condition but also capable of insights and taking part in creative action. As individuals we come into inherited fields of action and thought in which we are personally positioned. The world is not seen as a given nor as fully knowable. It is met with the awareness of limitations, errors (possibly even fatal ones), delusions, and potentially unique insights. Our particular selves and the collective selves we most embrace or seek to challenge are mutually defining. These conditions apply to ourselves as psychologists, researchers, and citizens at large. A subjectivity with democratic potential is simultaneously constructed historically, socially, materially and discursively (overlapping categories) and through the accident, effort, weaknesses and successes of being and will. For democracy to be necessary and possible, there must be a world beyond the self that discursively, materially, socially and in everyday life nurtures, challenges, shapes, hurts, rewards, disappoints and fulfills us. Democratic subjects have the capacity to engage with that world so as to contribute to the shape of individual and collective projects that have lesser and greater promise for individual and collective flourishing. Obviously this is a big and ambitious terrain, and one that I can only begin to address in this essay.

This paper outlines briefly the limitations of current psychological conceptions of subjectivity. I then examine the work of Lewin as a more robust conceptualization of subjective life but one hampered by a weak analysis of embeddedness in material/social context and discourse. Classical American Pragmatism, as developed by writers such as William James and John Dewey, is introduced for its firmer situating of the self materially and socially, placing knowledge of the world within context and discourse. Pragmatism offers numerous ideas that are especially important for democratic hope. Pragmatists argue that because of our individually limited and uncertain situatedness vis à vis discourse and experience, a broad inclusive community of inquirers is the best warrant for true and useful knowledge. By pragmatist accounts, we are very much creatures of the world we are born into and subject to its institutions, exclusions, power relations, physical properties, and ways of thinking. Yet we remake ourselves individually and collectively (though not fully by intention) through modes of engagement with others that promote tolerant inclusive discourse, decision making and action. In this view, thought and feeling work together as intelligence. Thus democratic processes make room for emotional engagements that can interrupt existing patterns, challenge received representations, produce new sympathies and desires, and promote democratic processes. Over time, the hope is that these will leave their residue in history, practice, habits, discourse, institutions and power arrangements.

THE WORK OF KURT LEWIN

Kurt Lewin and his research group are characterized by Kurt Danziger as the "lost continent" of Berlin. Lewin and his group worked in Weimar Germany under conditions of "unrelieved instability and intense social conflict" that influenced the conception of human experience and personality and in the main bolstered an alliance between psychologists

and the increasingly militaristic state (Danziger, 1990). Lewin's research group was predominantly Jewish, often female, and Eastern European making an alliance with the state unlikely and alerting them to the "embeddedness of the personality in social situations" (Danziger, 1990). That awareness translated into an understanding of psychological inquiry as intersubjective engagement (Danziger, 1990). … Lewin's psychology was for Danziger a lost continent because it represented uncertainty as inherent in psychological reality and social processes, and reality as emergent, thus going against the grain of psychology's focus on control and prediction.

Lewin's idea of how the human mind worked and how it resided in the larger fields of interpersonal relationships, group dynamics, culture and anti- or pro-democratic processes applied to both the researcher and the researched in a way that culminated logically in action research. … The core of Lewin's theory concerns the nature of the "lifespace". The lifespace is a completely psychological construct though its content and dynamics rest within a foreign hull, a psychological ecology that influences the lifespace but is not part of it. The lifespace is topologically organized through force fields into regions which are self-bounding as a result of dynamic tensions arising from, on the one hand, desires and repulsions (valences), and, on the other, beliefs and perceptions concerning the conditions of attaining goals and avoiding negative objects. A person is contained within a region until the tensions of the particular force field encompassing the person at the moment are resolved or changed through either a rearrangement of psychological dynamics or changes in the environment. Psychological experience then is determined by our internal (and not necessarily conscious) desires, intents, fears, and ignorances, and also by the structure of particular situations, tasks, spaces, forms of interaction, etc. Goals change as we pursue our interests, achieve or fail to achieve our goals, and move into circumstances in which we perceive and feel new conditions and possibilities.

Lewin's discussion of group dynamics employs the same notions of force fields and regions of inclusion and exclusion. When he writes of the differences between the personality structure of Americans and Germans, Lewin seems to imply a sort of historical genealogy of character shaped by culturally distinct social practices not dissimilar to Bourdieu's account of the ways that "habitus" shapes tastes and behavioral repertoires (Bourdieu, 1977/1972; Lewin, 1997). Both are field theorists but Bourdieu's field encompasses both sociological and psychological fields simultaneously, with sociological fields constraining psychological fields. Both Bourdieu and Lewin see differences among cultures and for Bourdieu, social classes, as self-reproductive. However, Lewin offers two routes out of this reproductivity, both related to his hopes for democracy. On the one hand he believes that leaders have the capacity to organize group relations in democratic, laissez faire, or authoritarian channels. In Lewin and his research group's development of participatory action research, the process of democratic social inquiry is both a paradigm for democratic society and means of pursuing that end.

PRAGMATIC "TRUTH" AND DEMOCRATIC HOPE

Pragmatism presents a particular view of human experience that is inseparable from social inquiry, a position characterized as "a conception of human experience as motivated inquiry, organized and guided by an examination of the consequences of action" (MacGilvray, 2000). Pragmatists share many of Lewin's core conceptions: the task and context dependence of what we know and do; the unity of thought, feeling and action as we move through time, space, our lives and our thoughts; the instability of particular goals and identities as contexts change yet the anchoredness of both in social and personal histories as well as current rigidities of the environment; and a sense that the outcome of activities and inquiries are determined not by prior conditions but by the dynamics of a changing terrain both internal and external to the individual.

A pragmatic approach to knowledge, value, and action in the post-modern context involves building on Dewey's embrace of the inherent uncertainty of knowledge, the capacity of human beings for growth through experience, and the necessity of the cultivation of democratic communities and institutions for such growth to occur.

For pragmatists, ideas needed to be endlessly tested against experience even as experience is inevitably a partial product of ideas. Experience unfolds as particular people pursue their interests and find out whether or not their efforts work. Since there are many individual actions and experiences, there are many truths at any particular moment. As James stated, "The truth is not a stagnant property inherent in it. Truth *happens* to an idea. It *becomes* true, is *made* true by events" (James, 1995/1906–1907). Dewey in virtually all of his work and after him Westbrook (2005) infer from this that the pragmatist notion of truth rests on endless and inclusive inquiry that is best encouraged by an open and democratic society.

Westbrook's linkage of the pragmatist concept of truth to democratic processes is crucial to the concept of inquiry set forth in this paper:

pragmatism—by virtue of its methodological commitment to experimental inquiry—is not neutral between democrats and fascists but rather has a powerful elective affinity with democracy. That is, democracy too is (in part, at least) a set of methods, and at their best the methods of democracy and pragmatic inquiry intersect. Pragmatic inquiry shares a "discourse ethics" with democracy. Pragmatists who embrace Dewey's conviction that politics should be a mode of "organized intelligence" believe that the intelligence of political communities, like that of all effective communities of inquiry, should be organized democratically. "Democracy is a requirement for experimental inquiry in any area", Putman says. "To reject democracy is to reject the idea of being experimental."

(Westbrook, 2005)

This argument brings into confluence the several aspects of pragmatism that I believe have important implications for psychological inquiry (as well as for other disciplines): an experimental understanding of truth in which its shared linguistic root with the word experience is important and the linking of truth as pragmatically conceived to the goals of an inclusive and democratic community. As Peirce put it, "men and words reciprocally educate each other" (*Essential Peirce*, Vol. I). In this view, both truth and the extent to which social processes are in fact inclusive and democratic are made true by events, and by the particular people involved.

But not everything can be made to be true even if the belief that it is true is widely held. Views may be widely held because the punishments for departing from them are severe, the rewards for agreeing great, or the voices of those who disagree too far out of the conversation to be heard. Democratic inclusiveness is an elusive goal. At any point in time, both truth and democracy are hopes.

FEELING AS THE CRUCIBLE OF WISDOM

Feelings are the medium through which our experience of the world tests the adequacy of our knowledge and of received wisdom. On the one hand, emotions are error prone but on the other hand they also alert us to perhaps undiscovered potential truths that arise from our particular position in the world as well as our ability to reflexively deploy signs.

"Feeling" genuinely has at all times two meanings: feeling in the sense of an internal state as in "I feel sad" and feeling in the sense of seeking information through sensory experience of something or someone outside ourselves, as in "If you run your hand over the surface, you can feel its unevenness". … Feelings effectively make particular phenomena or actions more salient than others, provide direction, and keep the actor engaged with a particular project.

Pragmatists see in the cultivation of feeling a way to expand human solidarity and also to have larger more satisfying experiences as a result. Dewey develops the connection of social history and norms to mundane feelings in his argument about the relationship of values and aesthetic tastes to the everyday impulses, attractions and repulsions of normal life in virtually all of his major works. Some passages from *Art as Experience* (1934) provide an example of the fundamental significance that Dewey accords feeling in all its manifestations. Early in the book, he anchors aesthetic experience in rudimentary feelings:

Impulsions are the beginning of complete experience because they proceed from need: from a hunger and demand that belongs to the organism as a whole and that can be supplied only by instituting definite relations (active relations, interactions) with the environment.
(Dewey, 1934)

However, feelings in practice are as often hostile, angry, hurt, ashamed, vengeful, etc. as they are sympathetic, loving, trusting, and cooperative. Social history places individuals in opposition to each other's interests in situations in which some have more power than others. Emotions are not only the location of expanded social identity, sympathy and cooperation, they are also the arena for hurt, subjugation, conflict, and resistance.

POWER, DISCORD, DOMINATION AND RESISTANCE AS REFLEXIVE MOMENTS

The individual and society are held together in experience through discourse and through cohabitation in a world that conditions the possibility of action and the satisfactions and distresses of life. Dewey and Peirce would agree with Bourdieu (2005) in stating the case against the distinction of the social and the individual:

In so far as he or she is endowed with a habitus, the social agent is a collective individual or a collective individuated by the fact of embodying objective structures. The individual, the subjective, is social and collective. The habitus is socialized subjectivity, a historic transcendental, whose schemes of perception and appreciation … are the product of collective and individual history.

Unlike Dewey, Bourdieu has clearly articulated how this understanding of the production of individuals and society, as well as knowledge, perpetuates oppositional interests anchored in inequality of power and resources. The concept of habitus can simplistically be defined as the physical and social world historically constructed and transmitted by particular social groups within particular institutional, political and cultural histories of development. Through engagement with a habitus, a person becomes him/herself in a way that socially reproduces the culture and society and especially its unequal distribution of power and resources while also finding a unique space of being afforded by the possibilities of the habitus.

Foucault and Bourdieu both socialize felt life. In their accounts, suffering brought about by the production of knowledge in service to power naturalizes the conditions of those feelings and delegitimizes proscribed desires.

Both Foucault's challenge and Bourdieu's realism point to the gaps in pragmatist theory surrounding the exercise of power through discourse and practice, and sometimes in the name of democratic social processes. Dewey in *The Public and its Problems* showed himself aware of these issues, but perhaps idealistically (and perhaps hegemonically) hopeful of their resolution through inquiry made public rather than through struggle.

> The essential need … is the improvement of the methods and conditions of debate, discussion and persuasion. That is *the* problem of the public. We have asserted that this improvement depends essentially upon freeing and perfecting the processes of inquiry and of dissemination of their conclusions. Inquiry, indeed, is the work which devolves upon experts. But their expertness is not shown in framing and executing policies, but in discovering and making known the facts upon which the former depend. … It is not necessary that the many should have the knowledge and skill to carry on the needed investigations; what is required is that they have the ability to judge of the bearing of the knowledge supplied by others upon common concerns.
>
> (Dewey, 1927)

CONCLUSIONS

The implications of this argument for psychology turn on repositioning subjectivity both as an intellectual topic and a lived experience. This involves reformulating our conceptions of the self, understanding our selves as composed and situated in the same limited ways as the selves we study, understanding our relations with the selves we study as part of social and interest saturated projects, and understanding the methods and contexts of our inquiries as part of the making of democratic or anti-democratic communities.

The alignment of social inquiry with concerns for social inclusion and more just social policies and practices has made much progress in the last decades as feminists, critical race theorists, queer theorists, critical theorists and a host of other inquirers have entered the arena of social inquiry.

In the pragmatic tradition, a next move would involve a more deliberate democratic positioning of inquiry. To transform modes of inquiry as well as social practices it is important to remember Bourdieu's point (and the practices of feminist, black, queer, disabled, and other marginalized or silenced populations) that there is no substitute for organizing oppositional interests to contest these relationships and to develop more democratic institutional forms. Within the pragmatist framework, the engagement of oppositional interests promotes the growth of knowledge and of selves as capable of engaging successfully with the world.

The democratization of inquiry and the development of social practices that promote and sustain more democratic and inclusive institutions rest on the cultivation of whole ways of being and modes of association. Unequal capacities to mobilize power produced through fields of social positionality, experienced emotionally and reproduced through the bodily enactment of feeling and the routinized habits of practice are resilient. To change them involves "not only a transformation of habitus themselves through a perhaps arduous retraining, but also transformation of the very conditions, emotional and otherwise, of the production and reproduction of habits" (Emirbayer and Goldberg, 2005).

Thus the project of democratic social inquiry needs to occur in actually shared spaces and everyday practices with an aim to transforming consciousness in places and in bodies that support this change.

REFERENCES

Bourdieu, Pierre. 1977. *Outline of a Theory of Practice*. Cambridge: Cambridge University Press.

Bourdieu, Pierre. 2005. *The Social Structures of the Economy*. Cambridge, UK; Malden, MA: Polity.

Danziger, Kurt. 1990. *Constructing the Subject: Historical Origins of Psychological Research*. Cambridge; New York: Cambridge University Press.

Dewey, John. 1916. "The individual and the world" In *Democracy and Education*. New York: Free Press.

Dewey, John. 1927. *The Public and Its Problems*. Chicago: Swallow Press.

Dewey, John. 1934. *Art as Experience*. New York: Capricorn Books.

Emirbayer, Mustafa and Chad Alan Goldberg. 2005. "Pragmatism, Bourdieu, and collective emotions in contentious politics." *Theory and Society*, Vol. 34, Issue 5–6, pp. 469–518.

Foucault, Michel. 1984. *The Foucault Reader*. New York: Pantheon.

James, William. 1995 [1906]. *Pragmatism*. New York: Dover Publications.

Lewin, Kurt. 1948. *Resolving Social Conflict*. New York: Harper & Brothers.

Lewin, Kurt, Ronald Lippitt and Ralph White. 1939. "Patterns of aggressive behavior in experimentally included social climates." *Journal of Social Psychology*. 10(2): 269–99.

MacGilvray, Eric. 2000. "Five Myths about Pragmatism, Or, Against a Second Pragmatic Acquiescence" *Political Theory* Vol. 28, No. 4, pp. 480–508

Peirce, Charles S, Nathan Houser, Christian J. W. Kloesel, and Peirce Edition Project. 1992. *The Essential Peirce. Selected Philosophical Writings Volume 1, (1867–1893) Volume 1, (1867–1893)*. Bloomington: Indiana University Press.

Westbrook, R.B. 2005. *Democratic Hope: Pragmatism and the Politics of Truth*. Ithaca NY: Cornell University Press.

66
Rhizome

(1987)

Gilles Deleuze and Félix Guattari

INTRODUCTION: RHIZOME

In a book, as in all things, there are lines of articulation or segmentarity, strata and territories; but also lines of flight, movements of deterritorialization and destratification. Comparative rates of flow on these lines produce phenomena of relative slowness and viscosity, or, on the contrary, of acceleration and rupture. All this, lines and measurable speeds, constitutes an *assemblage*. A book is an assemblage of this kind.

A first type of book is the root-book. The tree is already the image of the world, or the root the image of the world-tree. This is the classical book, as noble, signifying, and subjective organic interiority (the strata of the book).

The radicle-system, or fascicular root, is the second figure of the book, to which our modernity pays willing allegiance. This time, the principal root has aborted, or its tip has been destroyed; an immediate, indefinite multiplicity of secondary roots grafts onto it and undergoes a flourishing development.

The multiple *must be made*, not by always adding a higher dimension, but rather in the simplest of ways, by dint of sobriety, with the number of dimensions one already has available—always $n - 1$ (the only way the one belongs to the multiple: always subtracted). Subtract the unique from the multiplicity to be constituted; write at $n - i$ dimensions. A system of this kind could be called a rhizome. A rhizome as subterranean stem is absolutely different from roots and radicles. Bulbs and tubers are rhizomes. Plants with roots or radicles may be rhizomorphic in other respects altogether: the question is whether plant life in its specificity is not entirely rhizomatic. Even some animals are, in their pack form. Rats are rhizomes. Burrows are too, in all of their functions of shelter, supply, movement, evasion, and breakout. The rhizome itself assumes very diverse forms, from ramified surface extension in all directions to concretion into bulbs and tubers. When rats swarm over each other. The rhizome includes the best and the worst: potato and couchgrass, or the weed. Animal and plant, couchgrass is crabgrass. We get the distinct feeling that we will convince no one unless we enumerate certain approximate characteristics of the rhizome.

1 and 2. Principles of connection and heterogeneity: any point of a rhizome can be connected to anything other, and must be. This is very different from the tree or root, which plots a point, fixes an order.

A rhizome ceaselessly establishes connections between semiotic chains, organizations of power, and circumstances relative to the arts, sciences, and social struggles. A semiotic chain is like a tuber agglomerating very diverse acts, not only linguistic, but also perceptive, mimetic, gestural, and cognitive: there is no language in itself, nor are there any linguistic universals, only a throng of dialects, patois, slangs, and specialized languages. There is no ideal speaker-listener, any more than there is a homogeneous linguistic community. Language is, in Weinreich's words, "an essentially heterogeneous reality." There is no mother tongue, only a power takeover by a dominant language within a political multiplicity. Language stabilizes around a parish, a bishopric, a capital. It forms a bulb. It evolves by subterranean stems and flows, along river valleys or train tracks; it spreads like a patch of oil.

3. Principle of multiplicity: it is only when the multiple is effectively treated as a substantive, "multiplicity," that it ceases to have any relation to the One as subject or object, natural or spiritual reality, image and world. Multiplicities are rhizomatic, and expose arborescent pseudomultiplicities for what they are. There is no unity to serve as a pivot in the object, or to divide in the subject. There is not even the unity to abort in the object or "return" in the subject. A multiplicity has neither subject nor object, only determinations, magnitudes, and dimensions that cannot increase in number without the multiplicity changing in nature.

An assemblage is precisely this increase in the dimensions of a multiplicity that necessarily changes in nature as it expands its connections. There are no points or positions in a rhizome, such as those found in a structure, tree, or root. There are only lines.

All multiplicities are flat, in the sense that they fill or occupy all of their dimensions: we will therefore speak of a *plane of consistency* of multiplicities, even though the dimensions of this "plane" increase with the number of connections that are made on it. Multiplicities are defined by the outside: by the abstract line, the line of flight or deterritorialization according to which they change in nature and connect with other multiplicities. The plane of consistency (grid) is the outside of all multiplicities. The line of flight marks: the reality of a finite number of dimensions that the multiplicity effectively fills; the impossibility of a supplementary dimension, unless the multiplicity is transformed by the line of flight; the possibility and necessity of flattening all of the multiplicities on a single plane of consistency or exteriority, regardless of their number of dimensions. The ideal for a book would be to lay everything out on a plane of exteriority of this kind, on a single page, the same sheet: lived events, historical determinations, concepts, individuals, groups, social formations.

4. Principle of asignifying rupture: against the oversignifying breaks separating structures or cutting across a single structure. A rhizome may be broken, shattered at a given spot, but it will start up again on one of its old lines, or on new lines. You can never get rid of ants because they form an animal rhizome that can rebound time and again after most of it has been destroyed. Every rhizome contains lines of segmentarity according to which it is stratified, territorialized, organized, signified, attributed, etc., as well as lines of deterritorialization down which it constantly flees. There is a rupture in the rhizome whenever segmentary lines explode into a line of flight, but the line of flight is part of the rhizome. These lines always tie back to one another. That is why one can never posit a dualism or a dichotomy, even in the rudimentary form of the good and the bad. You may make a rupture, draw a line of flight, yet there is still a danger that you will reencounter organizations that restratify everything, formations that restore power to a signifier, attributions that reconstitute a subject—anything you like, from Oedipal resurgences to fascist concretions. Groups and individuals contain microfascisms just waiting to crystallize. Yes, couchgrass is also a rhizome. Good and bad are only the products of an active and temporary selection, which must be renewed.

How could movements of deterritorialization and processes of reterritorialization not be relative, always connected, caught up in one another? The orchid deterritorializes by forming an image, a tracing of a wasp; but the wasp reterritorializes on that image. The wasp is nevertheless deterritorialized, becoming a piece in the orchid's reproductive apparatus. But it reterritorializes the orchid by transporting its pollen. Wasp and orchid, as heterogeneous elements, form a rhizome.

5 and 6. Principle of cartography and decalcomania: a rhizome is not amenable to any structural or generative model. It is a stranger to any idea of genetic axis or deep structure. It is our view that genetic axis and profound structure are above all infinitely reproducible principles of *tracing*. All of tree logic is a logic of tracing and reproduction.

The rhizome is altogether different: a *map and not a tracing*. Make a map, not a tracing. The orchid does not reproduce the tracing of the wasp; it forms a map with the wasp, in a rhizome. What distinguishes the map from the tracing is that it is entirely oriented toward an experimentation in contact with the real.

The map is open and connectable in all of its dimensions; it is detachable, reversible, susceptible to constant modification. It can be torn, reversed, adapted to any kind of mounting, reworked by an individual, group, or social formation. It can be drawn on a wall, conceived of as a work of art, constructed as a political action or as a meditation. Perhaps one of the most important characteristics of the rhizome is that it always has multiple entryways; in this sense, the burrow is an animal rhizome, and sometimes maintains a clear distinction between the line of flight as passageway and storage or living strata (cf. the muskrat). A map has multiple entryways, as opposed to the tracing, which always comes back "to the same."

Have we not, however, reverted to a simple dualism by contrasting maps to tracings, as good and bad sides? Is it not of the essence of the map to be traceable? Is it not of the essence of the rhizome to intersect roots and sometimes merge with them? Does not a map contain phenomena of redundancy that are already like tracings of its own? Does not a multiplicity have strata upon which unifications and totalizations, massifications, mimetic mechanisms, signifying power takeovers, and subjective attributions take root? Do not even lines of flight, due to their eventual divergence, reproduce the very formations their function it was to dismantle or outflank? But the opposite is also true. It is a question of method: *the tracing should always be put back on the map*.

There are very diverse map-tracing, rhizome-root assemblages, with variable coefficients of deterritorialization. There exist tree or root structures in rhizomes; conversely, a tree branch or root division may begin to burgeon into a rhizome. The coordinates are determined not by theoretical analyses implying universals but by a pragmatics composing multiplicities or aggregates of intensities. A new rhizome may form in the heart of a tree, the hollow of a root, the crook of a branch. Or else it is a microscopic element of the root-tree, a radicle, that gets rhizome production going. Accounting and bureaucracy proceed by tracings: they can begin to burgeon nonetheless, throwing out rhizome stems, as in a Kafka novel. An intensive trait starts working for itself, a hallucinatory perception, synesthesia, perverse mutation, or play of images shakes loose, challenging the hegemony of the signifier. In the case of the child, gestural, mimetic, ludic, and other semiotic systems regain their freedom and extricate themselves from the "tracing," that is, from the dominant competence of the teacher's language—a microscopic event upsets the local balance of power.

To be rhizomorphous is to produce stems and filaments that seem to be roots, or better yet connect with them by penetrating the trunk, but put them to strange new uses. We're tired of trees. We should stop believing in trees, roots, and radicles. They've made us suffer too much. All of arborescent culture is founded on them, from biology to linguistics. Nothing is beautiful or loving or political aside from underground stems and aerial roots, adventitious growths and rhizomes.

Thought is not arborescent, and the brain is not a rooted or ramified matter. What are wrongly called "dendrites" do not assure the connection of neurons in a continuous fabric. The discontinuity between cells, the role of the axons, the functioning of the synapses, the existence of synaptic microfissures, the leap each message makes across these fissures, make the brain a multiplicity immersed in its plane of consistency or neuroglia, a whole uncertain, probabilistic system ("the uncertain nervous system"). Many people have a tree growing in their heads, but the brain itself is much more a grass than a tree.

Arborescent systems are hierarchical systems with centers of significance and subjectification, central automata like organized memories. In the corresponding models, an element only receives information from a higher unit, and only receives a subjective affection along preestablished paths.

Such is indeed the principle of roots-trees, or their outcome: the radicle solution, the structure of Power.

To these centered systems, the authors contrast acentered systems, finite networks of automata in which communication runs from any neighbor to any other, the stems or channels do not preexist, and all individuals are interchangeable, defined only by their *state* at a given moment—such that the local operations are coordinated and the final, global result synchronized without a central agency.

Let us summarize the principal characteristics of a rhizome: unlike trees or their roots, the rhizome connects any point to any other point, and its traits are not necessarily linked to traits of the same nature; it brings into play very different regimes of signs, and even nonsign states. The rhizome is reducible neither to the One nor the multiple. It is not the One that becomes Two or even directly three, four, five, etc. It is not a multiple derived from the One, or to which One is added ($n + 1$). It is composed not of units but of dimensions, or rather directions in motion. It has neither beginning nor end, but always a middle (*milieu*) from which it grows and which it overspills. It constitutes linear multiplicities with n dimensions having neither subject nor object, which can be laid out on a plane of consistency, and from which the One is always subtracted ($n - 1$). When a multiplicity of this kind changes dimension, it necessarily changes in nature as well, undergoes a metamorphosis. Unlike a structure, which is defined by a set of points and positions, with binary relations between the points and biunivocal relationships between the positions, the rhizome is made only of lines: lines of segmentarity and stratification as its dimensions," and the line of flight or deterritorialization as the maximum dimension after which the multiplicity undergoes metamorphosis, changes in nature. These lines, or lineaments, should not be confused with lineages of the arborescent type, which are merely localizable linkages between points and positions. Unlike the tree, the rhizome is not the object of reproduction: neither external reproduction as image-tree nor internal reproduction as tree-structure. The rhizome is an antigenealogy. It is a short-term memory, or antimemory. The rhizome operates by variation, expansion, conquest, capture, offshoots. Unlike the graphic arts, drawing, or photography, unlike tracings, the rhizome pertains to a map that must be produced, constructed, a map that is always detachable, connectable, reversible, modifiable, and has multiple entryways and exits and its own lines of flight. It is tracings that must be put on the map, not the opposite. In contrast to centered (even polycentric) systems with hierarchical modes of communication and preestablished paths, the rhizome is an acentered, nonhierarchical, nonsignifying system without a General and without an organizing memory or central automaton, defined solely by a circulation of states. What is at question in the rhizome is a relation to sexuality—but also to the animal, the vegetal, the world, politics, the book, things natural and artificial—that is totally different from the arborescent relation: all manner of "becomings."

A plateau is always in the middle, not at the beginning or the end. A rhizome is made of plateaus. Gregory Bateson uses the word "plateau" to designate something very special: a continuous, self-vibrating region of intensities whose development avoids any orientation toward a culmination point or external end.

We call a "plateau" any multiplicity connected to other multiplicities by superficial underground stems in such a way as to form or extend a rhizome. We are writing this book as a rhizome. It is composed of plateaus. We have given it a circular form, but only for laughs. Each morning we would wake up, and each of us would ask himself what plateau he was going to tackle, writing five lines here, ten there. We had hallucinatory experiences, we watched lines leave one plateau and proceed to another like columns of tiny ants. We made circles of convergence. Each plateau can be read starting anywhere and can be related to any other plateau. To attain the multiple, one must have a method that effectively constructs it.

We ourselves were unable to do it. We just used words that in turn function for us as plateaus. RHIZOMATICS = SCHIZOANALYSIS = STRATOANALYSIS = PRAGMATICS = MICROPOLITICS.

The book as assemblage with the outside, against the book as image of the world. A rhizome-book, not a dichotomous, pivotal, or fascicular book. Never send down roots, or plant them, however difficult it may be to avoid reverting to the old procedures.

Write to the nth power, the $n - 1$ power, write with slogans: Make rhizomes, not roots, never plant! Don't sow, grow offshoots! Don't be one or multiple, be multiplicities! Run lines, never plot a point! Speed turns the point into a line! Be quick, even when standing still! Line of chance, line of hips, line of flight. Don't bring out the General in you! Don't have just ideas, just have an idea (Godard). Have short-term ideas. Make maps, not photos or drawings. Be the Pink Panther and your loves will be like the wasp and the orchid, the cat and the baboon. As they say about old man river:

He don't plant 'tatos
Don't plant cotton
them that plants them is soon forgotten
But old man river he just keeps rollin' along.

A rhizome has no beginning or end; it is always in the middle, between things, interbeing, *intermezzo*. The tree is filiation, but the rhizome is alliance, uniquely alliance. The tree imposes the verb "to be," but the fabric of the rhizome is the conjunction, "and ... and ... and ...".

67
Living the "Revolution" in an Egyptian Village
Moral Action in a National Space (2012)

Lila Abu-Lughod

I missed the revolution by ten days. Cairo had seemed normal when I passed through on January 14, 2011. I had been to Damascus and Beirut and was heading to Jerusalem after three weeks in Egypt. I had long since stopped spending much time in Cairo, too attached to the friends my family had made through fieldwork in a village in Upper Egypt to take precious time away from them on visits to the country.

Like most of the rest of the world, I had to watch the uprising on television—Al-Jazeera, the BBC, and, sometimes, French television. I was struck by the networks' consistent vantage point: a reporter speaking from a balcony or rooftop overlooking the masses below in Tahrir Square. Occasionally, there were interviews with individuals down in the crowd. Sporadic reports appeared from the streets of Alexandria, Suez, or Port Said, where people were also demonstrating.

I was by turns thrilled, frightened, exhilarated, worried. I got e-mails from friends and colleagues saying they were heading off to Tahrir on the first day. They did not report back. When Mubarak's long-awaited speech came, I was as flabbergasted by his refusal to relinquish power as all those in Tahrir who held up shoes in protest. When he finally gave up, I sent messages of congratulations to my colleagues and friends in Cairo. They were proud and a little stunned at what they had helped bring about.

But I was missing something. What was happening elsewhere in the country?

CAIRO, THE STATE, AND THE VILLAGE

As an anthropologist who had spent most of my time in Egypt living in the countryside, I knew that Tahrir was the symbolic center of Cairo and Cairo the dominant center of Egypt, but a significant proportion of the 80 million or so Egyptians neither lived in nor identified with Cairo. From the late 1970s through the 1980s, I had worked with Awlad 'Ali Bedouins on Egypt's northwest coast, people who prided themselves on their distinction and distance from the "people of the Nile Valley." From the early 1990s on, I had been spending my time in rural Upper Egypt, a region historically on the margins of power and wealth. The distance my friends in the Upper Egyptian village felt from Cairo took a different form than it had on the coast. They were farther away from the capital in kilometers but had more regular traffic with it than my Bedouin friends. Many of the village men who had been conscripted into the army had spent time in Cairo. Long a destination for migrants seeking solutions to regional poverty, landlessness, and unemployment, Cairo had also been temporary home to many villagers' family members—grandfathers, fathers, uncles, husbands, sons, nephews. Some migrants returned to the village when they retired. Others came back with cancer, to die. Still others never came back, making new lives for themselves even if they sent money home or returned for the occasional funeral.

More and more women and children are now making the trip. The most talented and studious children in local Qur'anic schools go to compete in annual recitation competitions, bringing back certificates, prize money, and memories of Cairo's sights and sounds, including the Citadel and the zoo. Most of the women who go to Cairo stay in the building the village bought on the city's outskirts to use as a base. It is always full of people seeking specialist medical treatment.

Cairo also came to their village. It came directly in the form of the people who pulled up in fancy cars or air-conditioned buses to visit the pharaonic sites that were their "heritage." Confidently striding around in their sunglasses, jeans, and tight tops or their suits and ties, they chatted loudly on their cell phones in the distinctive dialect of the capital. They were oblivious to those who looked to them like shabby Upper Egyptian peasants trying to invite them to their makeshift stands to purchase potato chips and chocolate bars melting in the sun. They picked their way through the dust, debris, and donkey dung. My friends in the village watched them with some moral disdain. The city women were showy and loud; the men were smug. Yet it stung villagers to know that these others were richer than they, were more powerful, and looked down on them; the locals were convinced that their own schools, the goods available to them in their markets, their opportunities for jobs and futures, and even their medical care were all inferior to the goods, services, and prospects enjoyed by these urban visitors.

In the more indirect form of government policy, Cairo had long come to the village in devastating ways. If, under Nasser, policy had arrived as land reform that benefited many, in the Mubarak era it had come in the form of structural adjustment, demanded by international financial organizations and enforced by the government. My family's arrival in the village in the early 1990s had coincided with a new round of implementation that involved removing subsidies for wheat. People were panicking. They were starting to grow wheat on their small plots of land for fear that they would not be able to afford their staple food: bread.

Cairo came to them too in the heavy price they paid for privatization and other neoliberal economic reforms. The removal of public funds for education and health care had made the local government clinics eerily empty. Broken equipment could not be replaced; there were no longer free medicines; doctors rarely showed up. Public hospitals had become places of last resort. Medicines, blood, and even food had to be provided to patients by family members. Schools were also hit hard by neoliberal reforms. Mass public education had been instituted in the 1960s and had produced a huge educated middle class. Now the school system had been stripped. Village schools were overcrowded, teachers underpaid, and the standard of learning and teaching abysmal.

Some of the ways Cairo had come to this village and region were distinctive. Because it is located at a key site for tourism in an area rich in antiquities—second only to the Pyramids of Giza in interest for tourists—it had been subject to government control, not to mention suspicion and harassment of its residents, for a very long time. Dire restrictions on building and expansion subjected people to crowding and continual run-ins with the authorities.

In recent years, as those in Egypt's tourism ministry joined hands with the antiquities service and with consultants from the World Bank, USAID, and many others advising them on how to maximize the tourist industry, the villagers again had paid a price. Nearby, after years of threats, the government had finally succeeded in removing a whole community from the Theban Hills, bulldozing residents' houses after they left to ensure that they would not return—families that had lived on these hills overlooking ancient tombs for 200 years. They were offered substitute housing in a distant area of desert, far from their fields, markets, transport, relatives, and social worlds. Last year, the talk was about removing the inhabitants of the neighboring hamlet.

Although the villagers had experienced the security apparatus in these unique ways since the late 1990s, they shared with subalterns across Egypt the direct experience of repressive and arbitrary power at the hands of the security forces, the police, state officials, and even army officers (during military service). If the youth who filled Tahrir Square were galvanized by the publicity on Facebook about police brutality against one young man in Alexandria named Khalid Sa'id—yanked out of a cybercafé and beaten to death—many more could connect this "martyrdom" to personal experience. As Mahmud, a young man I had known since he was six years old, eloquently explained to me, "I came into this world 23 years ago and have never known anything but Hosni Mubarak as president of Egypt and the specter of the police who strike fear in people because of their power and the way they fabricate charges against innocent people."

LIVING THE REVOLUTION LOCALLY

As Mahmud would explain, "This was a revolution of all Egyptians and it had to happen." Would the uprising put the police and the army on notice? If the security police in the village are just a little more circumspect after what happened in Tahrir Square, I thought, this will have been a gift from Cairo to people in this Upper Egyptian village.

The bigger gift, I was to discover when I exchanged e-mails (for the first time) with some of the young men in the village whom I knew well, is that the events in Cairo had emboldened the village youth to take new responsibility for their local situation. It began, they explained, with the "day of lawlessness" on January 28, when, as Al-Tayeb explained, "all the police stations and prisons in the country collapsed." That was the day the security forces attacked the demonstrators in Cairo and released (or are accused of releasing) prison inmates to attack the crowds. In the village too, fear was struck by the escape of prisoners from the jail in nearby Armant. The young men immediately formed popular committees to protect their village, though they had few arms and the prisoners were rumored to have taken many from the police stations. The young men guarded all entrances and exits to their village, questioning any strangers seeking to enter. Thank God, they said, everyone was kept safe and there was little damage from these "thugs and thieves." This success gave them confidence.

These popular committees then began to meet to figure out how to solve the problems of the village. They started a Facebook page for their group, which now has over 350 members, young men and a few young women, who discuss the issues and try to decide how best to serve their community's needs. Although they use Facebook, they are not cosmopolitan youth writing in English and demanding "democracy," like the bloggers who became instantly famous after Tahrir. Internet access is still not widely available in this village. The young village

activists write in colloquial Arabic and they called themselves the "Good Youth in Village x" [*shabab al-khayr fi* x]. A translation that captures the spirit better might be the "Youth of Good Works." Their priority is the well-being of their village, and their goal is to undertake local improvements. They determine the community's most urgent needs and volunteer their energy to address them. Their first initiative was to solve the crisis of the distribution of bread, then the shortage of bottled cooking gas, then the high price of meat, and then garbage collection in the neglected public areas of the village. They even managed to start a new weekly market. Four months later, they had turned their attention to the needs of a set of families newly displaced from the Theban Hills by the antiquities and tourist authorities. They are helping them get the compensation they were promised and have set up cooperatives to collect donations to help them buy land elsewhere in Egypt. Some have begun building homes for needy villagers.

One of the most controversial issues in the discussions, flagged by my friends and reflected on the Good Youth's Facebook page, was what to do about the official village council. Most were adamant that they should not work through or with the council. They considered the council members corrupt, aligned with the old regime. In explaining why a revolution had been necessary, Mahmud had told me, "It had become clear as day that corruption flowed through its [the regime's] blood." The Good Youth accused the "elected" council members of trying to block or undermine their work. They understood the reason for their obstructionism to be that the members would not benefit personally from the work. Self-interest was the evil.

If the political players among the elite in Cairo have been shuffled a bit, the army somehow has come out unscathed (despite the close ties of the generals with the regime and the enormous wealth they have garnered), and some of the more activist and organized groups, like textile workers, the intelligentsia, and the Islamic Brotherhood, imagine they will have more say in what happens to Egypt next, it is still hard to think how the villagers I know will have any more political say at the national level than they had before. In the first days, they felt intimately connected to Tahrir. The older generation watched on television but the young people who had had friends there were especially traumatized because they had access to the Internet and watched the violence on YouTube.

Yet, because the nation-state is experienced everywhere that local councils, security police, and government economic policy are at work, the young people's activism must be considered national. Their efforts were directed at those forces of the nation-state that operated locally. They stood up to some and tried to ameliorate the negative impact of others on their neighbors and kin. People in this village face a special dilemma that may not be shared with others in the country, though the economic impact of the disruptions is not negligible anywhere. They had no jobs to return to at the end of the demonstrations. As foreigners were evacuated from Egypt and many cancelled their trips, there were no tourists. An immediate and difficult consequence of the uprising in Cairo, then, was economic crisis for people already at the margins who depended on tourism directly and indirectly—for customers, jobs in hotels, markets for their vegetables, and, at the smallest scale, people to buy postcards, scarves, and the occasional fake antiquity furtively unwrapped from its newspaper covering. It is this situation that they are struggling most with now.

One of the young men turned around the first question I had posed to him: "What was your reaction to what happened in Tahrir Square?" Al-Tayeb wrote, "I cannot describe my joy. ... We were waiting for some change to happen but never expected that it would be a revolution of this sort. It surprised us as much as it surprised the world. And it was not just what happened in Tahrir Square; in every village and every hamlet of every village was another square like Tahrir." Yet what happened in his village shows that each local "Tahrir Square" was unique. Affected by the same national policies and state institutions, each region and location experienced them through the specific problems they created for people locally. And each group that felt itself to be part of what these young men described as this "glorious revolution" has taken up a different set of projects. People across Egypt seem to be using different languages for their activism as well. In Al-Tayeb's village, the youth speak the moral language of responsibility, selflessness and community welfare, the struggle against corruption and self-interest. It is a strong language of social morality, not of rights. They do not speak of democracy, but in tackling problems directly and personally, they are living it. Will what happens in Cairo in the future support them? Or will the new arrangement continue in the path of the old? I was not optimistic. According to Al-Tayeb, the regime had "ruined people's lives politically and materially, morally and socially." In June, as I was writing this, though, Al-Tayeb was ending his e-mails with optimistic slogans. His first message to me closed with "Revolution until Victory/The Army and the People United." A few weeks later, it was "Revolution until Victory/Revolution until Lawfulness and Justice."

68
Introduction: Traffic in Democracy

(1999)

Michael Sorkin

A few months ago, Mayor Giuliani closed the 50th Street crosswalks at Fifth and Madison Avenues. The reason was to combat 'congestion' in midtown Manhattan (of course, what he meant was automotive congestion). Forcing walkers to cross the street in order to cross the street enabled cars to turn right or left onto the opposing one-way avenues without having to worry about negotiating with pedestrians.

In the mayor's scheme, pedestrians are inconvenienced to convenience cars. As a result, 50th Street has become a contested zone in the fight over the right to move: crossing the street is now an act of civil disobedience. Reflecting this proscription, a policeman has been installed on each corner to assure compliance. Although this breaches the historic understanding between New York pedestrians and police that jaywalking laws are ridiculous and will therefore be ignored, it is consonant with the mayor's (the ex-prosecutor's, the urban disciplinarian's) penal comprehension of time and space. A prison, after all, is built on the abstraction of every dimension of time but length and on the devolution of spatial choice to a clockwise or counter route around the exercise yard.

The mayor's strictures against crossing derive from a desire to enhance the 'flow' of traffic. Flow seeks to increase speed (and save time) by prioritizing the faster means of movement. Safety is often foregrounded as the reason for this system of preferences; the potential for danger, confusion and slow-down resulting from the undisciplined mix gives rise to elaborate structures for vetting what traffic engineers call 'conflict' between modes. Typically, this means slower vehicles yield to faster ones and pedestrians to all, walkers deferring to cars, cars to trains, trains to planes, and so on.

Modern city planning is structured around an armature of such conflict avoidance. Elevated highways, pedestrian skyways, subway systems and other movement technologies clarify relations between classes of vehicles for the sake of efficient flow. This traffic strategy is mirrored in (and derived from) the idea of zoning by use, another gambit based on the idea of separating 'incompatible' activities and persons. For both, the segregating clarity of the movement hierarchy is presented as evidence of the 'rationality' of the system.

Traffic codes and historic laws of rights of way codify urban styles of deference in motion. These rules of accessibility form criteria for determining who may go where and when. As such, these rights of way—which grant temporary permission to use private or public property for passage—structure a primal rite of *giving ground* and can thus serve us here as a concrete, that is, physical, exemplum of the deference to one's neighbor that urban existence daily demands. The homey concreteness of this instance should not, however, trivialize it or turn it into some plodding metaphor for more 'abstract' instances of giving way. For, though speed—and indeed almost instantaneous 'movement'—is now conceived as the determining factor of our new global economic and political order, the slower, physical flow of vehicular and human traffic remains a neglected issue. Not only is it true that it is primarily information and capital that travels at lightning speed and crosses all territorial barriers while the diaspora of despised peoples moves at a much slower pace and while strictures against movement—set up by inhospitable nations and opportunistic corporations—increase, it is also the case that urban density and movement through it has to be thought through politically, in these terms, rather than approached as merely a set of technical problems.

Growth complicates matters by introducing a vector of continuous transformation into the general pattern of urban distances. Under the contemporary regime of growth, this relationship has escaped rational management. The typical American—and increasingly global—result has been sprawl without end, the rapid outward movement of the urban periphery. As stable adjacencies and proximities are disrupted by the growth of the edge and the resultant transformation of the center, the system has produced its characteristic form: the 'edge city' in which uses are continuously relocated to re-establish proximity both by introducing new lateral relations oblivious to the center and by creating a physical texture in which hierarchies are highly repetitive and places increasingly indistinguishable.

There is a potentially ethical relation between speed and purpose, a system of rights that awards access to speed (and space) differentially. This demands a nuanced—and contested—ethics of privilege in a complex system that must weigh the rights of ambulances and strollers against more general rights of way and place. Such an ethics can derive from a very large number of criteria which—taken alto-gether—describe the politics of urban circu-lation. Indeed, the negotiated character of any urban spatial encounter begs an ethical reading of all of its components.

Energy, for example, is needed to produce motion. The ethics of energy expenditure—which is today articulated largely on the side of conservation—could arguably be invoked in defense of either side of the pedestrian/automotive question. On behalf of cars, the argument would come from their greater momentum (derived from both greater mass and greater speed), from the idea that their efficiency derives from smooth and speedy operation. The economy of stop and start opposes—in its inefficiency—the conservation of automotive energy.

The counter-argument is that cars are *intrinsically* wasteful of energy. This is a large

claim, based on a global paradigm of conservation, not just a local one. Here, pedestrians become the alpha-means of low-energy travel, the ideal movers. This hierarchy puts walkers at the top, followed by human-powered transport—such as bikes, and so on down the line—the criterion being that the more energetic always yields to the least, reversing orthodox priorities. Propinquity—neighborliness—is the ground and problem of democracy,

City politics is deeply inscribed in questions of propinquity and access, in the legibility and tractability of routines of circulation and contact: the *currency* of propinquity is exchange, the most vital measure of the city's intensity.

The public spaces of the city are pre-eminently the spaces of circulation and exchange, overwhelmingly streets and sidewalks. We judge the good city by the quality of its public life and hence of its public space, yet the very idea of public space is now under siege. Formerly, attempts to *limit* it hid behind expressions of fear of its decline, but this disguise is now unnecessary. The notion of public space is attacked outright as itself a mask. The forces arrayed against public space come from a number of different and even opposed directions: from economic and social drives toward privatization; identity politics; communi-tarianism; from sprawl and the resulting growth of cyburbia, that pale blue zone of connectivity without place. As the idea of a universal public is supplanted by a desire for and embrace of multiple publics, traditional formulations of physical consent are becoming strained.

While the notion of public space was never meant to refer exclusively to a geographically delimited space that was open to all, it seems indisputable that the broader notion cannot dispense with such spaces. It is most likely because public space is so often and so readily conceived as dependent on a decorporealization of its citizenry—a demotion and even denigration of the particular and the physical—that the notion of public space has become so *abstract*, so divorced from any theorization of physical locations. This is also why notions such as the 'electronic town hall' have been so easy to sell, as though its very incorporeality guaranteed its publicity. Public space never comes down to a social abstraction from the individual body (in a famous quip, Marx mocked the naivety of such formulations: 'I have never encountered an abstract man, only concrete men'), it is, rather, a matter of reconfiguring the individual citizen's relation to his or her body and to those of other citizens.

What must be acknowledged and understood is the enormous anxiety that marks the decline of space as the primary medium of urban exchange. This need not take place on the terrain of nostalgia, as a simple mourning of the loss of once-familiar, now disappearing forms of human contact. It is a matter of grasping the consequences of—and often altering—the ways in which contemporary strategies of the virtual compete with historic ideas of location as the basis of propinquity. We've got to watch out: the fundamental epistemology of the city—the way it constructs its meanings—is being transformed as physical presence ceases to be the privileged means of participation and enjoyment of urban life.

The human character of cities begins with face to face interactions. From the city's styles of intensifying such intercourse descends any description of the urban economy and its politics. Traffic is one medium of this commerce, the sum of those instrumentalities of motion by which propinquity is engineered, the means by which we are enabled physically to encounter different circumstances within the city. While no mode of movement will make a difference if the character and variety of places between which we travel fail to reflect a sufficient range of differences, the dialogue of intersection between public and private is mediated and—in part—invented by the available means of circulating between them.

The relationship between propinquity and publicity begins with this statistical necessity: democratic deliberation is only possible in an environment that conduces both consensus and accident. This continual potential for conflict is vital to deliberation and marks the vigor of difference within culture. The design of urban systems demands a beautifully negotiated balance between the predictable and the unexpected, in order to produce the largest number of accidental discursive events.

Of course, this idea of constant encounter inevitably produces friction, the simple result of rubbing subjects together. (It's no accident that *frottage* is the 'classic' urban perversion.) Urban friction is the signal of boundary and a symptomatic constituent of urban social gradients. Such friction—by signaling difference—

locates the internal edges of the city as well as potential sources of conflict. Yet, the very idea of accommodation is produced by such conflict, heightened by the physical character of urban life. It is no tautology to suggest that the only training for living together is living together. Racial tolerance is never concretized in the absence of the other, which is why anti-Semitism, and racism of all forms, thrives where there are no Jews, no racial others, in sight.

The city thus produces citizenship through the repetitive confrontation of citizens with an environment that organizes its prejudices and privileges physically, which is to say measurably. Unfortunately, traffic today is never thought about against the background of these concerns; it is approached as merely a technological problem and thus is saddled with the myths of technology, pinioned between visions of tractability and autonomy. Traffic engineers seek utopian solutions and fear 'Frankensteinian' rebellions, see-sawing on the only two possibilities offered by technology and its discontents.

The foregrounding of the means of motion in city planning has proved disastrous. Cities have historically been obliged to play catch-up with existing transportation technologies, successively refitting themselves with systems that do not love them; urban space has been rent and scarred by railways and freeways, clogged and scored by pollution and metal. Yet the appeal of motion-based urbanism is rendered 'obvious' by discourses that effectively substitute the freedom to move unobstructed and in isolation for freedom of association. To the list of freedoms we have added the freedom of speedy dissociation.

Modern movement culture is increasingly serviced by capsules of intermediacy, by trains, planes, automobiles and elevators. These instrumentalities now make time for sitting in front of the video and computer screens with which they are being fitted. Just as the view from the railway car window forever altered not simply the landscape but our fundamental perceptions of time and space, so the window of the monitor represents a shift in our perceptual and psychical relationship to exteriority. Virtual travel embodies a remarkable economy of energy as the experience of motion is efficiently stripped from actual mobility.

Traffic—at whatever scale—is defined by the relationship between speed and flow, a quality that has by now obtained a quasi-metaphysical status. Like the circulation of capital, the circulation of traffic is most perfectly efficient when it attains the status of a constant— perpetual motion. But, while stasis is the enemy of a flowing system of perfect efficiency, it is also indispensable to its functioning: flow needs nodes.

The node is the corollary of flow, implying not simply centrality (and therefore direct-ionality) but cease, the place where motion stops, enabling transfer (to foot, to another means, to another purpose). Flow imposes its own idea of efficiency, always calibrated to keeping going, not stopping, overcoming impedance and resisting inertia. The consequences are dramatic: nodal architecture subsumed by strategies of flow is predominant in the American landscape: the strip, the shopping mall, the suburbs, the edge city.

In America, the car is the main means for activating this landscape. Because the car seeks to optimize both speed and flow it looks for a conflict-free environment. In a mixed system, this means that either traffic must be separated strictly or a hierarchy must arise. Stop signs and traffic lights (as well as pedestrian barricades and cops on the corner) are means for sorting out this conflict. Traffic lights, which are meant to increase the efficient utility of the street, are, however, designed from the position of the car, directed primarily at resolving potential conflicts among vehicles. By any measure, pedestrians are disadvantaged: the space of the car, which predominates, is always a danger to them. Although the ideal for traffic is an easy mingling, we only produce technologies predicated on separation. The automobile system seeks invariably to exclude other modes that might come into conflict with it.

Los Angeles is the omega of the spatial city and the prototype of the city of the edge. Los Angeles—and cities like it—seek to create a consistent culture of the particle, in which an ostensibly egalitarian set of property relations is matched to a similarly conceived strategy of circulation. The experiment conducted with the use of cars in Los Angeles succinctly recapitulates Thomas Jefferson's Cartesian fantasy of the organization of American space. The grid—the instrument of an equality achieved by the surrender of difference in space or rather by the reduction of the arena of difference to a rigidly circumscribed territory— functions only if there is an even distribution of use, or if it runs like 'clockwork,' no caesura, no surcease, *and* if there are no intersections. This was Jefferson's fundamental error: he saw the grid as constituted purely of the aggregated surfaces of infinite squares, their boundaries immaterial, pure edge.

The Jeffersonian grid, however, generates both territories *and* interstices. Each square contains not simply its own surface but also four extra-territorial intersections which must be shared through negotiation. The conundrum is that an intersection is both a deterrent to flow and a necessity for contact. As a practical matter, the grid system only works at very low loadings, where the possibilities of conflict are greatly reduced. As anyone who has driven the LA grid late at night knows, this kind of geometrical freedom—in which one encounters public space as almost purely private—can be exhilarating. At higher rates of utilization, though, contact becomes impediment.

In cities like Los Angeles, the loadings on the grid are thrown into disequilibrium by the inequalities of use that culture imposes on the system. Zoning by class and by function, as well as the extremely uneven distribution of energy and motion over the diurnal cycle, distort the stable, static relationships that are at the core of the Cartesian fantasy: Thomas Jefferson never imagined the rush hour. Planning in Los Angeles is a history of successively failed panaceas for this problem. Coordinated traffic signals (traffic timing being the bedrock of the fantasy of flow) is one strategy for introducing hierarchy, great blocks of traffic shifted around the gridded zones, like trains of space in a synchronicity of flow. Urban expansion is another, but such growth—that old frontiers-person's hankering after infinity—reaches its limits in LA, the edge of the continent. Thus, the classic LA solution was to introduce the next order of physical gridding: the freeway.

Freeways are a symptom of both the spatial and temporal disequilibrium of real life, a mismatch of a technological fix with a conceptual difficulty. Freeways understand the city from the position of the car. Like other concentrating styles of motion, they try to reconcile the actual nodality of the system (the exits, if not the communities, are discreet) with the fantasy of a continuous fabric of equalized relationships. Los Angeles traffic effectively models the condition of American democracy with its inherent conflicts between an egalitarian model of social relations and a rapidly expanding system of privileges increasingly at odds with it.

The huge, warped, point-grid of freeway nodes raises the grid a notch, finding its curves at topographic scale. But again, like the city itself, the system feels intermediate. There is a dialectic of distortion produced by the relationship of the efficient placement of freeway exits and the prior claims of the existing condition—farms, forests, houses, towns, and so on. Unlike the Jeffersonian grid which seeks to organize nothingness into a map of potential, the freeway grid is predicated on the prior existence of places of value and therefore lacks the geometric rigor of its Jeffersonian counterpart, reversing its priority of dispersal by searching out the already existing intersection, seeking concentrations or their potential.

To begin again will mean reconsidering the place of the body in democracy. Accident demands the retention of urban difference, not its reduction to a series of empty, abstracted, visual distinctions. But if not by abstraction, how should the city be divided?

It is time to reinstate a notion of neighborhood that is simultaneously bounded and open. To achieve appropriate legibility, and to engender productive rates of and settings for accidental encounter, neighborhoods must be secured to the body, to both its scale and constraints. Thus, a neighborhood must be meaningfully physical, configuring the blend of the social and the dimensional.

No modern neighborhood—inasmuch as it is home to computers, televisions, phones, faxes, and so on—will ever be as small as the agora of antiquity; it is thus impossible to return to this scale in some real sense. Nor is it possible voluntaristically to return to the older metaphor of incorporation, since our bodies and our conditions are *materially* different. But it is possible—and indeed necessary—to think about and construct our cities in a way that binds them to the body and what it can do. For the modern body has, it turns out, redoubled and contradictory functions: it serves not only as tool but as that which incarnates the accident as such. That is, whereas in antiquity accidents had a place and thus a body could expect to *meet* with them, in modernity accidents are not given a place and thus a body could only *be* one. The body now bears the burden of being the only place where the accident resides. In other terms, only the body—through work—can introduce difference into an otherwise uniform system.

69
Containing Children

Some Lessons on Planning for Play from
New York City (2002)

Roger A. Hart

INTRODUCTION

The opportunity to play is a basic right,
fundamental to children's development. It is an
irony of urban development that children in
many of the world's poorest neighbourhoods
have more freedom to play outdoors close to
their homes than children in middle-class areas
of the same cities or in the high-income nations.
It is true that they often play in unsafe and
unsanitary conditions, but the irony remains
that opportunities for play do not necessarily
improve with what we commonly call
"development". As cities develop, there is a
tendency for children to be increasingly
contained. This paper is written in the belief
that local government policies can significantly
affect this trend. New York serves as a valuable
case study in this regard. Play and recreation
have not been a priority here in recent years,
but there have been periods when it was taken
extremely seriously, especially during the
massive waves of immigration. Although New
York is a wealthy city, it has always had large
numbers of poor families. Today, many children
in New York City have no regular safe access to
outdoor play places and there are critical
inequities in the quality of provision.

This paper focuses primarily on the play and
informal games of younger children rather than
on the formally organized sports and games of
older children and teenagers. No particular age
marks this transition; the only principle we need
recognize is that children themselves should
have choice. The core quality that distinguishes
play and makes it valuable to a child's
development is that it is voluntary. A child must

be free to play. Much of what adults prescribe or
schedule for children is not truly play. Free play
has been separated here from the broader category
of recreation and sports to emphasize its
importance; there is a tendency for city planners
and policy makers to think of play as frivolous in
comparison to sports and organized games.

WHY CITY GOVERNMENTS SHOULD CARE ABOUT CHILDREN'S PLAY

Although politicians can gain considerable
political capital from opening playgrounds, play
is often trivialized and placed low on the funding
agenda of cities. Municipal governments usually
think of children's play needs as being satisfied
through the provision of playgrounds and
recreational programmes. New York has been
no exception. But ever since playgrounds were
first constructed here at the turn of the century,
children in this city, as in others, have shown far
less interest in them than planners anticipated.
There are two major reasons why play should be
a priority for city governments: first, play is
important to children's development and,
second, free play in public space is important for
the development of civil society and, hence, for
democracy.

Play is fundamental to all domains of
childhood and adolescent development—
physical, intellectual, social and emotional.
People tend to value it most for healthy exercise
and the growth and development of physical
skills. Less obvious is its value for the
development of children's understanding and
thinking. Children have an urge to explore,

touch, manipulate and experiment with their world in order to understand it. This has had important influence on the design of many pre-schools and kindergartens but not much on public playgrounds. The value of play for creativity is also little recognized by those who plan and design public settings. But when adults in New York City recall their own play experiences, they recall creatively adapting the environment to suit their needs—inventing their world. When children have the freedom in space and time to play with one another, they find ways to pass on their culture to peers through games, song and dance, but also to transform it. Creativity, resourcefulness, invent-iveness and flexibility are important to all children. Play with peers is extremely important to social, moral and emotional development. In free play, children learn to understand others and to develop skills of cooperation, sharing and caring. Finally, it has long been established that play can offer children a way to establish a sense of control in difficult circumstances. The important principle is that a setting should allow this kind of play to take place, not that it be planned or scheduled. For this reason, cities in conflict sometimes establish safe play zones for children. Belfast, for instance, has a large full-time staff that helps communities to establish play opportunities for children.

The second major reason that cities should recognize the importance of public play is its relationship to the building of civil society. As will be described in this paper, much of the motivation for establishing playgrounds in New York, as elsewhere, has involved the control of children through their spatial segregation. But this is not an adequate solution for the development of civil society in a democracy. It proceeds from a model of socialization in which civil society is entirely passed down to children, rather than one in which children participate in building that society. Children need opportunities to interact with people of different social classes, cultures and ages and to learn how to cooperate with them. When they play together and form groups to engage in different activities, they are shaping culture and building communities. We know from research that friendships are not formed in the cooperative setting of classrooms, but in play. This issue of play must be added to the other important arguments for why public space is so fundamental to civil society in a democracy.

SEGREGATING CHILDREN: THE BATTLE FOR SIDEWALKS AND STREETS

Children wish to explore and experience a wider range of settings than public playgrounds can offer. Rather than assuming they need specific places and specific activities designed for them, the goal should be to establish the conditions within which they can find and create their own play. Children should be able to expand their competence gradually by exploring, playing and experimenting within a diverse physical world. They should be able to extend their social world too, knowing that at any time they can return to the safety of a home base. It is important for city agencies to create the physical environments that enable families and other care givers to offer children opportunities to explore and play freely.

ORGANIZING PLAY

By emphasizing free play, this paper might appear to argue from some romantic position that all we need to do in planning for young children's play is to leave them alone. Children certainly need the chance to invent their own activities and to carry them out without constant intervention from adults. But there is a need for adults to adopt a supportive role. They should be available nearby as good role models, supplying modest resources for play and responding to any emergencies. Parents, family members or trusted neighbours are not always available to play this role. According to the Playground Association of America, the original purpose of play leaders was to help communities develop recreation programmes where they live. But the playground movement quickly became over-professionalized and lost this collaborative community spirit. A number of social commentators have concluded that the reformers who worked on the early playgrounds in New York City were controlling agents who might best be called "play organizers". In contrast, those adults today who recall the "parkies" of the 1940s and 1950s do so with great affection. These were friendly officials who lent out equipment, kept a watchful eye for crime or bullying and were sometimes available with a word of advice. They have now all disappeared in New York, with the budget cuts beginning in the 1970s, which particularly affected the parks and recreation department.

Today, with a very limited budget, the city relies on summer youth employment programmes to provide a small number of playworkers. This is a good idea in that young adults are greatly admired by young children. But they work for short terms, have little training and often move around so much that they cannot easily establish the necessary trusted relationships. The problem is also not just the amount of funding available, but its source. The city relies increasingly upon public/private partnerships, and those who have the money determine much of what is funded. Even in well-funded Central Park, private donors want to see their money spent in visible form—on play equipment and benches, not on salaries for people who could support a truly rich play environment.

CHILDREN AS CONSUMERS AND THE PRIVATIZATION OF PLAY SPACES

The growing belief that privatization can replace government investment threatens children's use of public space, which should be inclusive and democratic. It cannot be, if some can afford it and others cannot. In New York City, better-off families send their children to a wide range of after-school programmes and "pay-for-play" places, whereas children of the poor are commonly left with little option but to be isolated inside their homes, watching television. There used to be thousands of play and recreation workers in New York City; now, there is barely a recreation department at all. The absence of caring adults in parks is a major reason why children are not allowed to play in public spaces anymore. Private funders do invest in some public parks, but usually very selectively. For example, the Central Park Conservancy has used considerable private funds to restore this flagship park. It is no accident that it is surrounded by the city's richest homes. Fortunately, Central Park is also a model of broad-based use by people from different groups and classes, but it has not been possible to obtain similar private funding for the play spaces that are so needed in low-income neighbourhoods. If local governments continue to rely on private solutions, they need, simultaneously, to redefine their role. They need to monitor equity in provision and to establish greater support for communities that cannot afford to create the settings their children need.

REMOVING CHALLENGE FROM PLAY ENVIRONMENTS

Ever since the Playground Association of America was formed in 1907, virtually all public play equipment has been designed to encourage active play. Swings, slides and climbing equipment have often been installed over hard surfaces and there have been many accidents, but not until the early 1970s was playground safety of sufficient concern for the US Consumer Product Safety Commission to create guidelines. Since then, there has been growing public concern about the dangers of play equipment. Approximately 200,000 children are injured in playgrounds throughout the United States every year, about 60 per cent of the injuries caused by falls.

Playground safety should be a concern but not at the expense of the design of interesting and challenging play equipment. What began as a concern for safety has become a paranoid attempt to create no-risk environments. Individuals are no longer responsible for their own actions and lawyers commonly sue for damages from playground injuries; some awards have gone as high as US$33 million. Whilst accident levels are high, the level of concern is out of proportion; accident rates for children in their homes are far higher. Physical challenge is fundamental to children's enjoyment of play; it will not be possible to remove this by design. Some children, if not challenged, will find dangerous ways to use playgrounds. Others are less likely to develop the physical competencies that can protect them from injury in some other place or time. Because of children's restricted freedom, playgrounds have become the sole place for many to find opportunities to develop and test their competencies. Obvious hazards should certainly be removed, but the redesign of playgrounds should not lead to the removal of challenge. It is also naïve to think that good play environments can be achieved only through design. Responsible adults also need to be available. They should intervene, however, only when truly dangerous activities occur.

Children must learn to manage their own safety by engaging in appropriate risk taking.

The other solution is to think of public play areas more broadly. Play environments could afford opportunities for a much larger repertoire of activities, many of them not at all dangerous: playing in sand, water and other materials; social dramatic play; constructing things with different kinds of "loose parts".

DESIGNING FOR ADULT CONVENIENCE RATHER THAN CHILDREN'S INTERESTS

When asked to recall their favourite place to play, adults do not generally describe playgrounds but, rather, the places forgotten by planners. Children's playground design has seldom been based on observing or listening to children. Adult theories of what children need for their development have been influential, however. Before the large-scale movement to build public playgrounds, many local efforts were influenced by the newly emerging theories of child development. The playgrounds that resulted were not always as sterile as those we know today. For example, in 1889, two playgrounds built in poor districts by the New York Society for Parks and Playgrounds included not only swings and seesaws but also "… small wagons, wheelbarrows, shovels, footballs, flags, drums, banners and a sand pile."

But the beliefs underlying large-scale playground development in New York had to do with encouraging healthy physical, social and moral development through activity, teamwork and personal discipline. The emphasis on physical play has continued in public playground design to this day. The few applications of child development theories in the design of playgrounds have been very superficial. For example, in the 1950s, fantasy themes were introduced with such features as rocket ship towers because it was believed this would encourage dramatic play. During the 1960s and 1970s, when creativity was being promoted by toy manufacturers and adopted by middle-class parents, the designers of some public playgrounds built abstract forms to replace the earlier themed shapes, believing that this would do more to foster imagination and creativity. Unfortunately, the inventiveness lay only with the designer— there were no opportunities for children to

modify or move equipment in any way. The adventure playgrounds that appeared briefly in the late 1960s were a significant contrast, but their demise has been described above. Public playgrounds continue to be relatively sterile environments that allow only for running, jumping, climbing and swinging. To support a wider repertoire of play, children need diversity and manipulability in their environment. But it is difficult to create playgrounds with "loose parts" when there is no staff to maintain the environment. Playgrounds of fixed manufactured equipment are designed for ease of maintenance, and in response to fears of liability.

Sometimes "protecting children" is an excuse for laziness or for the unwillingness of adults to provide a good play setting for children. Sand boxes are a good example. They have always been popular with young children since the beginning of the play movement. But sand play has disappeared from almost all public playgrounds in New York City—a clear indication of the lack of importance given to children's preferences. The reason given is the possible presence of animal faeces in the sand. But protecting sand boxes from animals by covering them at night and by periodic cleaning with chlorine and water is not difficult if modest staffing is available.

Children need conditions within which they can direct their own activities as much as possible. Given their limited range, a safe diverse setting close to home is necessary. The natural environment is more diverse than any expensive play equipment. For young children, contact with the natural world is also beneficial for many other reasons. Instead of single playgrounds within a housing complex, it is possible to create throughout the outdoors a diverse topography, with hills, a diversity of vegetation and different surface materials for children to play with. This fine-grained landscape could be created right outside the doors of children's homes. Further away, older children would be able to find the open spaces they need to be able to create games.

CONCLUSIONS

It has been argued that public play provision has changed in New York according to a changing series of concerns for children and, sometimes, fears of children. Provision has been achieved largely through segregating children into special places called playgrounds, rather than trying to find ways of meeting children's needs close to where they live, in collaboration with their family and community. The perspectives of children and parents have rarely been considered.

Any city wishing to improve its planning of public spaces with children in mind needs to develop and present to the public a clear vision of why children's play is important to its citizens. This paper has suggested that public play opportunities are very important for two major reasons: first, because all children need play opportunities for their full development; and second, because play in public space is important for the building of civil society. At a time of increasing commercialization in play provision all over the world, local governments need to take on the role of monitoring equity in the provision of public space for all children, particularly for families that cannot afford to purchase play opportunities and others who are denied access due to their special needs. NGOs wishing to influence and encourage governments can usefully connect with the newly emerging Child Friendly City Movement and its focus on the creation of housing areas that enable safe play. They can also use the UN Convention on the Rights of the Child[1] as a tool in their advocacy, for it carries clear statements of the rights of children to play and for them to have a say in all such matters that directly concern them.

NOTE

1 The UN Convention on the Rights of the Child recognizes play as a universal right in art 31: "States Parties recognize the right of the child to rest and leisure, to engage in play and recreational activities appropriate to the age of the child, and to participate freely in cultural life and the arts."

Copyright information

SECTION 1: DIVERSE CONCEPTIONS BETWEEN PEOPLE, PLACE, AND SPACE

Harvey, David. 2005. "Spacetime and the World," in *Cosmopolitanism & Geographies of Freedom*. New York: Columbia University Press, pp. 135–165.

Koolhaas, Rem. 2002. "Junkspace." *October*, Vol. 100. Cambridge, MA: MIT Press, pp. 175–190.

Kwon, Miwon. 1997. "One Place after Another: Notes on Site Specificity." *October*, Vol. 80. Cambridge, MA: MIT Press, pp. 85–110.

Lewin, Kurt. 1997 [1943]. "Psychological Ecology," in *Resolving Social Conflicts and Field Theory in the Social Sciences*. New York: Harper & Row, pp 298–300.

Low, Setha. 2014. *Spatializing Culture: An Engaged Anthropological Approach to Space and Places*. New York: Routledge.

Ruddick, Susan. 1996. "Constructing Differences in Public Spaces: Race, Class, and Gender as Interlocking Systems." *Urban Geography*, 17(2): 132–151.

SECTION 2: HUMAN PERCEPTION AND ENVIRONMENTAL EXPERIENCE

Debord, Guy. 2006 [1958]. "Theory of the Derive," "Definitions," and "Preliminary Problems in Constructing a Situation," in *Situationist International Anthology*, ed. and trans. Ken Knabb. Oakland, CA: Bureau of Public Secrets/AK Press.

Gibson, James J. 1979. *Ecological Approaches to Visual Perception*. Boston, MA: Houghton Mifflin.

Lynch, Kevin. 1960. "The City Image and Its Elements," in *The Image of the City*. Cambridge, MA: MIT Press.

Milgram, Stanley and Denise Jodelet. 1970. "Psychological Maps of Paris," in H.M. Proshansky et al. (eds), *Environmental Psychology: People and their Physical Setting*. New York: Holt, Rinehart & Winston.

Sommer, Robert. 2008 [1969]. "Spatial Invasion," in *Personal Space: The Behavioral Basis for Design*. Engelwood Cliffs, NJ: Prentice Hall, pp. 26–38.

SECTION 3: PLACE AND IDENTITY

Anderson, Kay J. 1987. "The Idea of Chinatown: The Power of Place and Institutional Practice in the Making of a Racial Category." *Annals of the Association of American Geographers*, 77(4): 580–598.

Halberstam, Judith J. 2005. "The Brandon Archive," in *In a Queer Time and Place: Transgender Bodies, Subcultural Lives*. New York: New York University Press, pp. 22–46.

Hayden, Dolores. 1995. "Urban Landscape History: The Sense of Place and the Politics of Space," in *The Power of Place*. Cambridge, MA: MIT Press, pp. 14–43.

Loos, Adolf. 1983 [1900]. "The Poor Little Rich Man," in *Spoken into the Void*. Cambridge, MA: MIT Press.

Miller, Daniel. 2008. "Migration, Material Culture and Tragedy: Four Moments in Caribbean Migration." *Mobilities*, 3(3): 397–413.

Proshansky, Harold M. et al. 1983. "Place-Identity: Physical World Socialization of the Self." *Journal of Environmental Psychology*, 3: 57–83.

SECTION 4: POWER, SUBJECTIVITY, AND SPACE

Bourdieu, Pierre. 2007 [1984]. "The Habitus and the Space of Life-styles," in *Distinction: A Social Critique of the Judgement of Taste*. Cambridge, MA: Harvard University Press.

Dovey, Kim. 2008. "Tall Storeys," in *Framing Places: Mediating Power in Built Form*. New York: Routledge.

Gilmore, Ruth Wilson. 2007. "Mothers Reclaiming Our Children," in *Golden Gulag: Prisons, Surplus, Crisis, and Opposition in Globalizing California*. Berkeley: University of California Press, pp. 181–240.

Graham, Stephen D.N. 2005. "Software-sorted Geographies." *Progress in Human Geography*, 29(5): 562–580.

Pred, Allan. 1985. "The Social Becomes the Spatial, the Spatial Becomes the Social: Enclosures, Social Change and the Becoming of Places in the Swedish Province of Skåne," in *Social Relations and Spatial Structures*, edited by Derek Gregory and John Urry. New York: Palgrave Macmillan, pp. 337–365.

Wright, Melissa W. 2001. "Desire and the Prosthetics of Supervision: A Case of Maquiladora Flexibility." *Cultural Anthropology*, 16(3): 354–373.

SECTION 5: MEANINGS OF HOME

Blokland, Talja. 2008. 'You Got to Remember You Live in Public Housing': Place-Making in an American Housing Project." *Housing, Theory and Society*, 25(1): 31–46.

Cooper, Claire. 1974. "The House as Symbol of the Self," in *Designing for Human Behavior*, ed. J. Lang et al. Stroudsberg, PA: Dowden, Hutchinson and Ross, pp. 130–146. (Reprinted in H.M. Proshansky, W.H. Ittelson, and L.G. Rivlin (eds) *Environmental Psychology: People and their Physical Settings*: 2nd edn). New York: Holt, Rinehart & Winston, 1976. pp. 435–448.)

Imrie, Rob. 2004. "Disability, Embodiment and the Meaning of the Home." *Housing Studies*, 19(5): 745–763.

Rybczynski, Witold. 1986. "Domesticity," in *Home: A Short History of an Idea*. New York: Viking Press, pp. 51–75.

Wise, J. MacGregor. 2000. "Home: Territory and Identity." *Cultural Studies*, 14(2): 295–310.

Wood, Denis, and Robert J. Beck. 1994. *Home Rules*. Baltimore, MD: Johns Hopkins University Press.

SECTION 6: "PUBLIC" AND "PRIVATE"

Chauncey, George. 1995. " 'Privacy Could Only Be Had in Public': Gay Uses of the Streets," in *Stud: Architectures of Masculinity*. Princeton, NJ: Princeton Architectural Press, pp. 224–267.

Friedman, Alice T. 1998. "People Who Live in Glass Houses: Edith Farnsworth, Ludwig Mies van der Rohe, and Phillip Johnson," in *Women and the Making of the Modern House: A Social and Architectural History*. New York: Harry N. Abrams, pp. 128–159.

Iveson, Kurt. 1998. "Putting the Public Back into Public Space." *Urban Policy and Research*, 16(1): 21–33.

Kingwell, Mark. 2008. "The Prison of 'Public Space.'" *Literary Review of Canada*.

Mitchell, Don. 2003. Excerpt from "To Go Again to Hyde Park: Public Space, Rights, and Social Justice," in *The Right to the City: Social Justice and the Fight for Public Space*. New York: Guilford Press, pp.13–42.

Zhang, Li. 2001. "Contesting Crime, Order, and Migrant Spaces in Beijing," in *China Urban: Ethnographies of Contemporary Culture*, ed. Nancy Chen et al. Durham, NC: Duke University Press, pp. 201–222.

SECTION 7: THE URBAN EXPERIENCE

Benjamin, Walter. 1939 [1935]. "Paris—Capital of the Nineteenth Century," in *The Arcades Project*. Cambridge, MA: Harvard University Press, 1999. (1935 version: pp. 3–13; 1939 version: pp. 14–26.)

Certeau, Michel de. 1984. "Walking in the City," in *The Practice of Everyday Life*. Berkeley: University of California Press, pp. 91–110.

Jacobs, Jane. 1961. "The Uses of Sidewalks: Contact," in *The Death and Life of Great American Cities*. New York: Vintage, pp. 53–74 (sidewalk ballet).

Simmel, Georg. 1971. "The Metropolis and Mental Life," in *Georg Simmel on Individuality and Social Forms*, ed. Donald N. Levine. Chicago, IL: University of Chicago Press, pp. 324–340.

Simone, AbdouMaliq. 2004. "People as Infrastructure: Intersecting Fragments in Johannesburg." *Public Culture*, 16(3): 407–429.

Young, Iris Marion. 1990. "City Life and Difference," in *Justice and the Politics of Difference*. Princeton, NJ: Princeton University Press.

SECTION 8: LANDSCAPE: NATURE AND CULTURE

Carney, Judith. 2000. "The African Origins of Carolina Rice Culture." *Cultural Geographies*, 7(125): 125–149.

Chawla, Louise. 1990. "Ecstatic Places." *Children's Environments Quarterly*, 7(4): 18–23.

Jackson, J.B. 1984. "A Pair of Ideal Landscapes," in *Discovering the Vernacular Landscape*. New Haven, CT: Yale University Press, pp. 9–55.

Pollan, Michael. 1998. "Beyond Wilderness and Lawn." *Harvard Design Magazine*. Reprinted in *Nature, Landscape and Building for Sustainability*, 2008.

Wolford, Wendy. 2004. "This Land Is Ours Now: Spatial Imaginaries and the Struggle for Land in Brazil." *Annals of the Association of American Geographers*, 94(2): 409–424.

SECTION 12: DEMOCRATIC PROSPECTS AND POSSIBILITIES

Abu-Lughod, Lila. 2012. "Living the 'Revolution' in an Egyptian Village: Moral Action in a National Space." *American Ethnologist*, 39: 21–25.

Deleuze, Gilles, and Félix Guattari. 1987. "Rhizome," in *A Thousand Plateaus: Capitalism and Schizophrenia*. Minneapolis: University of Minnesota Press, pp. 3-25.

Hart, Roger A. 2002. "Containing Children: Some Lessons on Planning for Play from New York City." *Environment and Urbanization*, 14(2): 135–148.

Saegert, Susan. 2014. *Restoring Meaningful Subjects and "Democratic Hope" to Psychology*. New York: Routledge.

Sorkin, Michael. 1999. "Introduction: Traffic in Democracy," in *Giving Ground: The Politics of Propinquity*. New York: Verso, pp. 1–15.

Further recommended reading lists: *peopleplacespace.org*

In addition to the selected excerpts and introductory texts, we have also included a brief list of suggested readings for each section to guide readers to additional resources in their area(s) of concern.

At *peopleplacespace.org*, the editors and a series of expert invited guests whose research develops from an environmental social science perspective are continually updating lists for recommended readings on the twelve sections of this book as well as a series of additional topics. Drawing from experts' work on mapping and resistance to the production of digital place and space, from international perspectives on housing to young people and ecology, a catalog of Further Recommended Reading Lists may be found at the end of this volume with summaries and selected citations on our online site. Other recommendations will continue to be developed and shared via the website, and these lists and citations are easily downloadable. We hope these lists may be of help to the student, instructor, and interested reader as they expand their own understanding of environmental social science. Readers are welcome to add their contributions to these lists as well by commenting on each list and being in dialog with our group of experts.

Our hope is that a new generation of scholarship and activism will recognize the important spatial and temporal aspects of this scholarship, and be able to draw fruitfully upon the contributions of thinkers that have come before. We call special attention to the critical work needed to help confront inequalities and injustices. What in this book can best inform you to help you deal with these issues? What will you read in this book today to help you understand what lies ahead for us and the rest of the world?

Archives, Exhibitions, Art, and the Urban Public
Gabrielle Bendiner-Viani

Participatory Action Research
Caitlin Cahill

Critical Inquiry and Social Reproduction
Hillary Caldwell

Food, Psychology, and the Environment
Christine C. Caruso

International Perspectives on Planning and Social Housing
Isabel Cuervo

People, Place, and Digital Media
Gregory T. Donovan

Discursive and Material Productions of Nature
Jason Douglas

Environmental Factors in Drug Use and Abuse
Martin J. Downing, Jr.

Human-Coastal Environment Relations
Bryce DuBois

Education and Environmental Meaning
Valkiria Duran-Narucki

Financialization at Home, in the City
Desiree Fields

Gender, Sexuality, and Space
Jen Jack Gieseking

Waste and Sustainability
Tsai-Shiou Hsieh

Representations of Children of War
Aida Izadpanah

Humans, Animals, and Conservation Environments
Hannah Jaicks

Young People and Ecology
Bijan Kimiagar

Sustainability in Life, Place, and Justice
Do Lee

Production, Governance, and Lived Experience in Suburbia
Pengfei Li

Design and Social Responsibility
William Mangold

Destabilizing the Map through Critical Cartography and Resistance
Einat Manoff

Children in Urban Environments
Anupama Nallari

Neighborhoods and Mental Health
Nicole Schaefer-McDaniel

Wayfinding, Movement, and Mobility
Aga Skorupka

Health and Social Media
Collette Sosnowy

Children's and Young People's Participation in Political Spaces
Jennifer Tang

Places and Spaces of Psychiatry
Lauren Tenney

Health and Environment
Meredith L. Theeman

Index